THE FRAGILITY OF CONSCIOUSNESS

The Fragility of Consciousness

Faith, Reason, and the Human Good

FREDERICK G. LAWRENCE

Edited by Randall S. Rosenberg and
Kevin M. Vander Schel

UNIVERSITY OF TORONTO PRESS
Toronto Buffalo London

ISBN 978-1-4875-0132-7

(Lonergan Studies)

Library and Archives Canada Cataloguing in Publication

Lawrence, Frederick G., author
The fragility of consciousness : faith, reason, and the human good /
Frederick G. Lawrence ; edited by Randall S. Rosenberg and Kevin
M. Vander Schel.

(Lonergan studies)
Includes bibliographical references and index.
ISBN 978-1-4875-0132-7 (cloth)

1. Hermeneutics – Religious aspects – Christianity.   2. Theology.
3. Faith and reason.   4. Christianity and culture.   5. Christian ethics.
I. Rosenberg, Randall S., editor   II. Vander Schel, Kevin, editor
III. Title.   IV. Series: Lonergan studies

BR118.L39 2017   230.01   C2016-905653-8

University of Toronto Press acknowledges the financial assistance to its
publishing program of the Canada Council for the Arts and the Ontario
Arts Council, an agency of the Government of Ontario.

Contents

Author's Preface   vii

Editors' Introduction   xvii

Part One: The Hermeneutic Revolution and the Crisis of Culture

1 Martin Heidegger and the Hermeneutic Revolution   5
2 Hans-Georg Gadamer and the Hermeneutic Revolution   24
3 Gadamer and Lonergan on Augustine's *Verbum Cordis* – the Heart of Postmodern Hermeneutics   45
4 A Jewish and a Christian Approach to the Problematic of Jerusalem and Athens: Leo Strauss and Bernard Lonergan   72
5 Voegelin and Gadamer: Continental Philosophers Inspired by Plato and Aristotle   160
6 "Transcendence from Within": Benedict XVI and Jürgen Habermas on the Dialogue between Secular Reason and Religious Faith   193

Part Two: Theology and the Human Good

7 The Fragility of Consciousness: Lonergan and the Postmodern Concern for the Other   229
8 The Recovery of Theology in a Political Mode: The Example of Ernest L. Fortin, AA   278
9 The Economic Good of Order and Culture in Relation to Solidarity, Subsidiarity, and Responsibility   296
10 The Human Good and Christian Conversation   326

vi   Contents

11 Grace and Friendship: Postmodern Political Theology and
    God as Conversational   353
12 Growing in Faith as the Eyes of Being-in-Love with God   384

The Writings of Frederick G. Lawrence   405

Index   415

Author's Preface

This selection of my writings has been a "labor of love" on the part of many. Initially, Glenn "Chip" Hughes had the idea for such a collection and assembled many articles, before he realized that his other obligations would prevent him from pursuing the project in a timely manner. After several years, Randy Rosenberg and Kevin Vander Schel committed themselves to the project, and constructed and developed this present volume. These writings manifest an ad hoc quality, most of them having been contingent upon invitations to contribute to one or another conference or volume. Regretful that I did not manage to gather and organize these essays in the way that the team of editors has so generously and insightfully done here, I cannot adequately express how grateful I am to each and every one of them for all the work they have put into bringing these hitherto difficult-to-access essays to light in this volume.

The editors have correctly understood that in these articles I have chiefly performed what Bernard Lonergan in *Method in Theology* explained as the functional specialty of "dialectics." I have tried to do this in the classical mode of "friendly conversation," and there was no way (or desire) to bring all that I had learned from Lonergan to bear in the mode of "always knowing better" while trying correctly to understand the work of the philosophers and theologians discussed here. For one thing, Lonergan has helped me to "reach up to their minds," and studying them has helped me to comprehend what he "was up to" more deeply. For another, I have been providentially blessed to have personal contact with such teachers (and sometimes colleagues) as Bernard Lonergan, Karl Barth, Hans-Georg Gadamer, Eric Voegelin, Johann Baptist Metz, René Girard, and Ernest Fortin (with whose great teacher, Leo Strauss, I have become familiar through his writings). In interpreting the writings of these thinkers as well as those of others whose works I have studied over the years I hope that I have followed what Lonergan, Barth, and Gadamer each repeatedly encouraged their students to do, namely, to "make the best of them."

Perhaps these examples of how and what I have learned from authors I deemed worth reading carefully provides a "proximate model" for my students and readers. When I became convinced that the church has to respond to the questions that arise in each generation, I discerned that, as one who had experienced what I still believe was the best of both pre- and post-Vatican II Catholic Christianity, my calling to what used to be spoken of as the "intellectual apostolate" was to contribute as well as I could to the examination of these questions, while helping students to join me in this.

In my efforts during my first years of philosophy to understand neoscholastic handbooks by Grenier and Gredt, I had the good fortune to come across Bernard Lonergan's articles of the late 1940s in *Theological Studies* on "The Concept of the *Verbum* in the Thought of St Thomas Aquinas." Lonergan later described these studies as an attempt "to effect an advance in depth that is proportionate to the broadening influence of historical research. It is to grasp questions as once they were grasped. It is to take the *opera omnia* of such a writer as St Thomas Aquinas and to follow through successive works the variations and developments of his views."[1] Then, as I was working one summer in a parish in south-central Los Angeles,[2] I chanced upon *Insight* at Horan's Catholic Bookstore. *Insight* is an elaborate transposition of the generalized empirical method that Lonergan in *Verbum* had discovered Aquinas *performed* to understand intelligible emanations as the analogy for relations of origin or processions in his trinitarian theology. The focus of the analogy is on the two basic internal experiences we all have of "insight into images" grounding the processions in which we express what we've understood, and of reflective understanding's grasp of the "virtually unconditioned" that grounds our affirmations or negations of matters

---

1 Bernard Lonergan, *Insight: A Study of Human Understanding*, Collected Works of Bernard Lonergan 3, ed. Frederick E. Crowe and Robert M. Doran (Toronto: University of Toronto Press, 1992), 769.

2 Here I must record what a debt of gratitude I owe to my two wonderful priest-mentors, whose dedication as pastors in the Archdiocese of Los Angeles was ever engaged with the spirit of wonder and inquiry, John Coffield and Francis Roughan.

of fact. These fundamental operations are not only applicable to both natural science and scholarship, but also indispensable for epistemology and critically grounded metaphysics. Because such metaphysics is a general heuristic structure of being – i.e., everything that can be correctly understood and judged (but here below, never completely) – it in no way falls under the strictures of the post-Heideggerian criticisms of *Onto-theologie*; and at the same time I believe it takes care of the all the legitimate concerns of the present-day turn to a "God without being."

During the college years leading up to philosophy, I was greatly taken with the works of St Augustine, John Henry Newman, and Christopher Dawson. Then while studying philosophy, along with Lonergan's work on the retrieval of Aquinas on *gratia operans*, the *Verbum* articles, and *Insight*, I was able to read most of the first two volumes of Karl Rahner's *Theological Investigations* and to use his prayer books (one of which was done with his Jesuit brother, Hugo); and I started to read the second edition of *Geist in Welt* with a German dictionary. I was also deeply moved by the book *Prayer* and the article "God Has Spoken in Human Words,"[3] by Hans Urs von Balthasar.

Then I was sent to study theology at the Gregorian University in Rome when the second session of Vatican II was to begin. During the discussion of the schema on the mystery of the church, I was astonished to hear rumors of a consensus growing among theological experts working with bishops to the effect that, although they were not satisfied with understanding the reality of the church in terms of the prevailing centuries – long use of legal categories drawn from the most mature of the human sciences – they did not consider themselves as having an adequate alternative for explaining the nature of the church, so that *Lumen Gentium* became a prime example of the crucial role played in the authoritative conciliar documents of Vatican II by *ressourcement*. During these Roman years, I was befriended and encouraged by New Yorkers Joseph Komonchak and David Tracy, and (as Phillip Berryman had done earlier and has continued to do) by Frank Colborn from Los Angeles, to keep pursuing my interest in Lonergan. Friends who were classmates, especially Emile Piscitelli and Arthur Kennedy, shared their attempts to understand Lonergan's philosophy and theology. With Matthew Lamb, a Trappist who was sent to the Gregorian for his licentiate in theology, I spent many happy hours in David Tracy's room in the Casa Santa Maria

---

3 In *The Liturgy and the Word of God* (Collegeville, MN: The Liturgical Press, 1959), 33–52.

on the Via dell'Umiltà listening to tapes of Lonergan's Toronto lectures on method and trying to understand him, after Tracy had returned to Rome and was doing his doctorate on the development of Lonergan's thought. All these friends gave me a real apprehension of what Paul meant about "iron sharpening iron."

Listening to discussions within and surrounding the Council in Rome raised questions about theology as reason illumined by faith, to be sure, but also as itself a human science. My courses, and especially my conversations with Fr Lonergan, made it plain that theology is also an undertaking which requires both non-reductionist historical scholarship and a critical appropriation of the other human sciences. These were precisely the topics being taken seriously in the way Lonergan taught all his courses, especially *De methodo theologiae*, his graduate *exercitatio* course.

Almost every time I went to Fr Lonergan's room to ask questions, he'd ask me if I knew German to refer me to something I should read in German. Eventually it dawned on me that if I wanted to be serious about theology, I should get to know the German context – not only its great theologians and philosophers, but also their groundbreaking explorations of the implications that follow from the fact that the data of the human sciences include meaning. In his *exercitatio* course, Lonergan brought up the New Frontiers in Theology series that centered on hermeneutics and history; and one could not help but notice his frequent mentioning of the significance for his work of Gadamer's *Wahrheit und Methode*. And so when I left Rome to get my doctorate in theology, taking the kindly advice of Lukas Vischer, I matriculated at the University of Basel, the last academic home of Karl Barth, where his successor Heinrich Ott and historian of theology Max Geiger took me under their wings.

It was an extremely rich time to be doing graduate studies in theology in the German-speaking world. Ott and Geiger were deeply engaged with the problematic of integrating hermeneutics and history into theology, as was the Jaspers-inspired liberal theologian Fritz Buri. Basel's New Testament scholars, Oscar Cullmann and Bo Reicke, were in constant conversation with scholars of the old Marburg School led by Rudolf Bultmann and his students. The so-called New Hermeneutics, featuring Gerhard Ebeling at Zurich and other post-Bultmannians such as Günther Bornkamm were also involved. Basel was also the home of Balthasar, and I first heard him at a conference with Kurt Stalder. There I met those preparing to be pastors who would be my confrères at the Theological Seminar and library, where many of our seminars met

– most memorably, Karl Barth's last three and a half semesters in which he alternated between Vatican II documents and Calvin and Schleiermacher. I was soon ensconced in Balthasar's Barth book, a marvelous orientation to my theological studies in Basel's Theologische Fakultät. Afterwords I struggled through *Herrlichkeit*'s massive volumes "Im Raum der Metaphysik" – my true introduction to German philosophy – and *Glaubhaft ist nur Liebe* has remained dear to me over the years.

To advance the cause of Marx's Eleventh Thesis on Feuerbach about not only interpreting history but also making it, European political theology was on the rise. Johann Baptist Metz (with whom Matthew Lamb did his doctorate), to enter into solidarity with German Jewish thinkers related to the Frankfurt School (especially Walter Benjamin), turned from theology in a Rahnerian vein. Like others, Eric Voegelin, for instance, Metz was determined to take seriously the conditions that had made the Shoah possible in Germany. In the Lutheran tradition, Jürgen Moltmann said his political turn was in continuity with Karl Barth's *Römerbrief* that had started a hermeneutic revolution in theology contemporaneously with Heidegger's in philosophy. In his *Theology of Hope*, Moltmann intended to answer the challenge of Marx's Eleventh Thesis, but in the vein of Ernst Bloch's philosophy of hope.

After a long period wondering about doing a dissertation related to the thought of Karl Rahner, I decided to learn all I could about the Kantian, Hegelian, and Heideggerian background that would be required to do my dissertation on the hermeneutic circle in Hans-Georg Gadamer. I frequently attended seminars at the relatively nearby Freiburg University with the likes of Bernhard Welte, Bernard Casper, and Klaus Hemmerle; and each Thursday my wife and newborn son drove in our VW to Heidelberg for Gadamer's *Doktorandenseminar* in the morning, afternoon lecture, and office hours.

When I finished my thesis proposal and gave it to Prof. Geiger, at our meeting to discuss it, Prof. Geiger put the fateful question, "Aber, Herr Lawrence, ist es Theologie?" And that is how I got into doing the dissertation "Believing to Understand: The Hermeneutic Circle in Gadamer and Lonergan," basically an exposition of Gadamer's philosophical hermeneutics on the general dynamics of human anticipation of the future in light of the past, followed by a presentation of Lonergan's development as a parade example that included: (1) his appropriation of the horizon of explanatory theory in retrieving the genesis of St Thomas on grace and freedom; (2) his appropriation of the horizon of cognitional interiority in his retrieval of Aquinas on the processions both of the *verbum incomplexum* (i.e., of concept, definition) from the act of direct understanding and of the *verbum complexum* (i.e., of judgment, affirmation, or assent) from the act of reflective understanding, and then, pivoting toward the future, his methodical transposition of Aquinas's analysis of intelligent and rational interiority into the context of modern natural and human science in *Insight*; and finally (3) his appropriation in *Method in Theology* of interiority as existential with the breakthrough to the ontological structure of the hermeneutic circle thematized in the functional specialization pertinent not only to theology but to all human sciences. The recognition of the primacy of being in love and its implications for the concrete and performative hermeneutic circle "from above downwards" (the way of healing and heritage) and "from below upwards" (the way of creativity) offers an explanatory account of Gadamer's more descriptive notion of the medial structure of *wirkungsgeschichtliches Bewusstsein*.

While I was doing the dissertation, Matt Lamb kept me informed about Metz's political theology; and Jürgen Habermas (the Frankfurt philosopher who was already well known for his engagement with the students involved in the uprisings then rampant in Germany) published his critical review of Gadamer's *Truth and Method* in a full issue of *Philosophische Rundschau* (edited by Gadamer and Helmut Kuhn) dedicated to Habermas's outstanding literature survey covering every relevant contemporary approach to the social sciences from the perspective of the need for a critical social theory oriented toward *praxis*. These developments led me to realize that immersion in Gadamer's thought also required my engagement with social and political theory. It also happened that Lonergan had often encouraged his students to read the works of Eric Voegelin:[4] *The New Science of Politics* and the three volumes of *Order and History*. As a professor of law in Vienna, Voegelin, from his background in the thought of Ottmar Spann and Hans Kelsen, like Gadamer (after Heidegger caused him to study Greek classics under Paul Friedländer), went back to school with Plato and Aristotle. In my estimation, each of their very practically and politically oriented interpretations of the Greek philosophers complemented each other. Unlike Gadamer in Heidelberg, who was in close proximity with

---

4 As I recall, in Habermas's survey (mentioned above) Voegelin's work only received brief mention in a footnote, perhaps because, although critical of Max Weber, it does not fit into a more sociologically oriented interest.

such scripture scholars as the great Old Testament scholar Gerhard von Rad, Voegelin, having emigrated to the US and teaching at Alabama University, took time to learn Hebrew with a local rabbi to read the Hebrew Bible before writing *Israel and Revelation*. In short, Metz and Habermas also helped me to appreciate Voegelin, and Voegelin helped me to understand them; and each of them helped me in my work on Gadamer and Lonergan.

Before I finished the dissertation, Boston College Jesuits Joseph Flanagan (chair of philosophy), William Leonard, and his successor Thomas O'Malley (chairs of theology), invited me to come to the Theology Department in 1971 to teach undergraduate core courses and a graduate course each semester. I was eager to make use of what I had learned from Lonergan's Latin theological texts to teach "bread and butter" theology courses in those early years on Trinity, Grace, and Christology at the graduate level, as well as to share what I'd been learning by developing courses on Theology as Hermeneutical and Theology as Political. Fr Flanagan asked me to help him to create a center for Lonergan studies at BC, and so in 1973 he urged me to hold a Lonergan Workshop at Boston College, which I took to be a way both to continue collaboration with fellow Lonergan students in Rome, who by then were teaching in the States, and to be faithful to my friends from the days of preparation for the priesthood in California and at the North American College. The Workshop now approaches its 45th year.[5]

While I was teaching and still working on my dissertation (defended at Basel in 1975), Joseph Flanagan conceived the idea of bringing members of the Philosophy and Theology Departments together to work out an alternative to the core – a four-year set of interdisciplinary great books courses, Perspectives in Western Civilization.[6] A crucial turning-point

---

5 Through the years, the Workshop has been supplemented by many weekend workshops, featuring speakers such as Gadamer, Voegelin, Metz, Komonchak, Tracy, Robert Doran, Michael McCarthy, N.T. Wright, Bernard McGinn, J. Patout Burns, et al. International Lonergan Workshops took place in Rome, Toronto, Mainz, and Jerusalem. In celebration of the Workshop's 30th anniversary, the nine Lonergan Workshop speakers, including Jon Levenson, Hermann Pottmeyer, and Timothy Radcliffe, OP, collaborated with BC's Church in the 21st Century in its inaugural year.

6 The Perspectives Program expanded beyond philosophy and theology (I) to include a course on literature, music, plastic arts, and architecture, Modernism and the Arts (II); politics, law, economics, and sociology, Horizons in the New Social Sciences (III); and the development of mathematics and the natural sciences, New Scientific Visions (IV).

in the early stages of planning for the course occurred when I encouraged Flanagan to invite an experienced professor who had come from Assumption College to BC's Theology Department in the same year I started at BC, Ernest Fortin. While doing his doctoral studies at the Sorbonne in France, he struck up a lasting friendship with Allan Bloom, and later studied with Leo Strauss at the University of Chicago. Fortin and I became friends partly because of our respective connections with Gadamer and Strauss, who were students together with Karl Löwith and Gerhard Krüger at Marburg. Each of them had been profoundly affected by Heidegger's hermeneutic "revolution in reading," which led them to undergo "the Socratic turn" in their careful reading of the ancient philosophers. Fortin came to the Theology Department as a joint appointment with Political Science, where David Lowenthal, Robert Faulkner, and Christopher Bruell – all former students of Strauss – were already teaching. Before Fortin joined in planning the entry-year course (of what would become the four-year Perspectives Program), a consensus had been forming in favor of juxtaposing biblical and theological texts with philosophical texts almost entirely focused on epistemological issues. Fortin convinced the group to reorient the readings toward the question about the best or right way to live. Under the theme "Athens and Jerusalem," it would devote a semester to reading texts from premodern philosophy and theology; and in the second semester, turning to "Modernity," it would concentrate on texts beginning with the re-orientation of philosophy by Machiavelli and the upheaval in theology by the Reformers and later on by thinkers, such as Kierkegaard and Nietzsche, who in their philosophical and theological concern with a more integral way of being human formed the chief sources of existentialism.

In the mid-1970s Fortin encouraged me to invite Gadamer (by then *emeritus* at Heidelberg) to come to BC. Fr Flanagan enabled him to teach a course for a semester each academic year (which he did for eight years into the mid-1980s).[7] Coincidentally, not too much later (after holding

---

Each summer all the different teachers with their different specialized expertise gather for a week to discuss the texts and subject matters used in all of these courses under the direction of Brian Braman.

7 In the initial year, this became a Jesuit collaboration, inasmuch as the late Fr Tom O'Malley contributed his pay for the semester to Gadamer, and recently deceased biologist Fr Don Plocke let Gadamer use his room in the Jesuit residence, Roberts House, where he ended up living each time he came to BC and was said to be a marvelously discreet guest.

the Stillman Chair for a year at Harvard Divinity School), Bernard Lonergan asked his Jesuit superiors if he could to come to Boston College from Regis College in Toronto. Robert Daly (then theology chair) quickly organized a Distinguished Lectureship for Lonergan, and he taught until illness caused him to be called back home to Canada where he died in 1984. Later on, David Tracy joked that he had "never before heard of the subjects of someone's dissertation coming to be with him!"

It was wonderful for me that, besides my helping him with his classes, Gadamer invited my wife, Sue, and me to lunch and conversation each Tuesday in the Faculty Dining Room throughout the years of his Boston College Visiting Lectureship. On such occasions, Gadamer often mentioned Heidegger's disappointment with him that he'd used the term consciousness (*Bewusstsein*) in *Truth and Method* – a term which has always tended to be *verboten* in Heideggerian circles. He was a bit taken aback, yet happy to hear how (with Lonergan's help) I'd grasped that he did not mean consciousness in either the idealist or the empiricist senses that presuppose the phenomenologically untenable subject/object split characteristic of the *Horizont der Vorhandenheit* so opposed by Heidegger.

It was also fortunate for all that Lonergan, having been provoked by Gustavo Gutierrez's comment that the problem with Latin American liberation theologians was that none of them knew enough about economics, decided to dedicate his last productive years to revising the 1944 version of his series of economics manuscripts composed during the fourteen years after the 1929 economic crash when he spent his spare time studying economics to understand the causes of the Depression. So for the course he taught each semester, he alternated between courses on topics from *Insight* and *Method in Theology* and courses in which he taught a text by a contemporary economist together with continuous revisions of his 1944 manuscript. Those years were also marked by the presence for a year at BC of Johann Baptist Metz at the same time as Jürgen Habermas (whose texts I translated each week for his lecture) was also a guest lecturer, as well as other wonderful theologians such as Nicholas Lash.

I mention all these names to convey to those who may be unfamiliar with it, the background of friendships without which the essays published here could never have been written. This background should also include the remarkable fact that these years at BC have been marked by BC President J. Donald Monan's gifts to Fr Lonergan of postgraduate fellowships, postdoctoral fellowships, and of the beautiful Lonergan

Center in Bapst Library; and also by his successor BC President William Leahy's gift of the house for Lonergan Fellows, now named after the late Joseph Flanagan. I was fortunate that through the years Patrick H. Byrne (Philosophy), and Charles C. Hefling, Matthew Lamb, Sebastian Moore, OSB, and Louis Roy, OP (Theology) joined Joe Flanagan and me on BC's faculty. Each of them studied, discussed, and helped me in too many ways to mention here, except to register my deep gratitude.

I also want to thank my older and newer friends, colleagues, and students through the years in the Theology, Philosophy, Political Science, and Economics Departments, who have supported and helped me to learn whatever is of value in these essays.

Editors' Introduction

The essays of Frederick G. Lawrence presented in this volume are the product of a long and interdisciplinary engagement with theology and hermeneutic philosophy. Lawrence's writings span a wide array of topics and concerns, and range from close interpretative studies of individual philosophers and theologians to careful systematic treatments of political theology, historical consciousness, trinitarian doctrine, and economic systems. Yet his work has exercised an especially notable impact in two specific areas.

First of all, his writings have played a prominent role in fostering the study of the thought of Bernard Lonergan, his former teacher and later colleague at Boston College. Lawrence has gained a national and international reputation as one of the most insightful and authoritative interpreters of Lonergan's philosophical and theological writings, and his own scholarly work has helped to cement Lonergan's legacy in twentieth-century Catholic thought.[1] Beyond his immense scholarly contributions, Lawrence has engaged in ongoing collaborative efforts throughout his career to help understand and develop Lonergan's thought, through the organization of annual workshops, regular conferences, edited volumes, and teaching initiatives.[2]

---

1 In 2007, 6–8 September, a conference on "Hermeneutics, Postmodernism, Relativism" was held in his honor at Divyadaan: Salesian Institute of Philosophy in Nashik, India.

2 Since 1974, Lawrence has served as director of the annual Lonergan Workshop and editor of the *Lonergan Workshop* journal. Since 1980, he has also been a member of the board of directors at Boston College's Lonergan Institute, and beginning in 1983 he was a member of the editorial board for *Method: Journal of Lonergan Studies*.

Yet Lawrence is also well regarded beyond the circles of Lonergan studies as an incisive and discerning reader of twentieth-century continental philosophy and hermeneutics. His essays on Martin Heidegger, Hans-Georg Gadamer, Jürgen Habermas, and Paul Ricoeur have appeared in numerous journals and anthologies.[3] He also has written articles on central continental thinkers too often neglected in wider discussions of philosophical hermeneutics, such as Leo Strauss, Eric Voegelin, and René Girard, and has furthermore provided standard translations of several significant works by Gadamer, Habermas, and others.[4]

In the background of these distinctive scholarly contributions is the interrelation of three academic contexts: Rome, Basel, and Boston. Lawrence studied with Lonergan at the Pontifical Gregorian University in Rome from 1963 to 1966, after the publication of Lonergan's *Insight* (1957) and during the time he was developing many of the ideas that would find mature expression in *Method in Theology* (1972). Together with several peers who have likewise enjoyed distinguished careers in theology and philosophy, Lawrence recognized the promise of

---

3 See, for example, "Gadamer and Lonergan: A Dialectical Comparison," *International Philosophical Quarterly* 20, no. 1 (1980): 25–47; "Gadamer, the Hermeneutic Revolution and Theology," in *The Cambridge Companion to Gadamer*, ed. Robert J. Dostal (Cambridge: Cambridge University Press, 2002), 167–200; "Paul Ricoeur's Practical Wisdom: Reflections on the Social Philosophy of Oneself as Another," in *Between Suspicion and Sympathy: Paul Ricoeur's Unstable Equilibrium*, ed. Andrzej Wiercinski (Toronto: The Hermeneutic Press, 2003), 502–17; and "Heidegger and Voegelin on Augustine," in *Hermeneutic Rationality. La rationalité herméneutique*, ed. Maria Luísa Portocarrero, Luis António Umbelino, and Andrzej Wiercinski, Reihe: International Studies in Hermeneutics and Phenomenology 3 (Berlin: LIT Verlag, 2011), 241–56.

4 See Frederick G. Lawrence, "Philosophy, History, and Apocalypse in Voegelin, Strauss, and Girard," in *Politics and Apocalypse*, ed. Robert Hamerton-Kelly, Studies in Violence, Mimesis, and Culture (East Lansing, MI: Michigan State University Press, 2007), 95–137. See also Hans-Georg Gadamer, *Reason in the Age of Science*, trans. Frederick G. Lawrence (Cambridge, MA: MIT Press, 1981); Jürgen Habermas, *The Philosophical Discourse of Modernity*, trans. Frederick G. Lawrence (Cambridge, MA: MIT Press, 1987); and Jürgen Habermas, *Philosophical-Political Profiles*, trans. Frederick G. Lawrence (Cambridge, MA: MIT Press, 1983). Additionally, Lawrence has translated several theological works. See, for instance, *The von Balthasar Reader*, ed. Medard Kehl and Werner Löser, trans. Robert J. Daly and Frederick G. Lawrence (Edinburgh: T &T Clark, 1982); and Lawrence's translations of Karl Rahner's homilies in *The Great Church Year: The Best of Karl Rahner's Homilies, Sermons* (New York: Crossroads Publishing, 1994).

Lonergan's thinking for re-evaluating the Catholic Church's complex relationship to modernity and for meeting the challenge of the emerging historical consciousness within Catholic theology. In the wake of these studies, Lawrence turned his attention to early twentieth-century continental philosophy and especially to Gadamer's landmark work in philosophical hermeneutics, which would become the focus of his subsequent doctoral studies at the University of Basel, culminating in a dissertation examining the hermeneutic circle in Lonergan and Gadamer.[5]

Since arriving at Boston College in 1971, Lawrence has worked consistently to bring these two influences together. Indeed, for a time, Gadamer and Lonergan worked as colleagues at Boston College. Lonergan taught in Boston College's theology department from 1975 to 1983. Following his retirement from the University of Heidelberg in 1968, and partly through Lawrence's invitation, Gadamer developed a close association with Boston College and served as a regular visiting faculty from 1974 to 1986.

In his own teaching and scholarship, Lawrence has been both a mainstay of Lonergan studies and an influential voice in Boston College's Departments of Theology and Philosophy. In 1974, he founded and coordinated the annual Lonergan Workshop, now in its 44th year. Since this time, he has also served as editor of the *Lonergan Workshop* journal, as well as of several supplemental volumes of essays treating the works of Gadamer, Voegelin, and Johann Baptist Metz.[6] In addition, he has directed dozens of dissertations in systematic and philosophical theology, and has played a principal role in shaping the curriculum of Boston College's Perspectives Program, an interdisciplinary honors program that introduces undergraduate students to central theological, philosophical, and political writings in the Great Books tradition.

This unique background is evident in his ongoing scholarly work. Lawrence's writings stand out for their patient and incisive analysis,

---

5 Lawrence's dissertation, "Believing to Understand: The Hermeneutic Circle in Gadamer and Lonergan," was completed in 1975 under the direction of Heinrich Ott. A copy is available in Boston College's Lonergan Institute.

6 Through 2015, the *Lonergan Workshop* journal includes nineteen volumes. Anthologies for special conferences include *Beginning and the Beyond: Papers from the Gadamer and Voegelin Conferences*, Supplemental Issue of the Lonergan Workshop Journal 4, ed. Frederick G. Lawrence (Atlanta, GA: Scholars Press, 1984); and *Communicating a Dangerous Memory: Soundings in Political Theology*, Supplementary Issue of the Lonergan Workshop Journal 6, ed. Frederick G. Lawrence (Atlanta, GA: Scholars Press, 1987).

bringing remarkable clarity to elusive themes and notoriously complex thinkers. This feature alone would make them valuable reading for students, teachers, or intellectuals interested in the course of twentieth-century philosophy and theology. Yet what sets these essays apart is their further capacity to illumine the rich co-inherence and the fruitful interrelation of Catholic theology and hermeneutic philosophy. Beyond advancing the fields of Lonergan studies, systematic theology, and hermeneutic philosophy individually, Lawrence's writings provide a commanding witness to the possibility and promise of bringing these disciplines into a productive interrelation.

Central Themes of the Volume

The present volume is the product of a persistent call to make the writings of Frederick Lawrence available to a broader audience, and it intends to illustrate his ongoing contributions to this dialogue between modern Catholic theology and hermeneutic philosophy. The twelve essays included here cover distinct topics and diverse thinkers yet also converge on several recurrent themes. In what follows, we highlight three such points of emphasis: (1) the practice of conversation, (2) the interplay of faith and reason, and (3) the crisis of culture.

Conversation as Praxis

The theme of conversation is a repeated point of focus in the twelve essays that comprise this volume, and it is a frequent emphasis among the various thinkers treated in these papers. Gadamer adopts the central metaphor of conversation to highlight the performative dimension of human understanding. Integrating insights from Heidegger's hermeneutics of facticity with his own close study of Socratic and Platonic dialectic, he describes conversation as the basic hermeneutic condition. This signals, on the one hand, the fundamental ubiquity of language – language is the air we breathe rather than an instrument we deploy at will.[7] Yet, on the other, it points to the heightened awareness that emerges through entering into "the logic of question and answer" and underscores the historically constituted character of human inquiry and interpretation.[8]

---

7 See below, "Hans-Georg Gadamer and the Hermeneutic Revolution," 33.
8 See below, "Hans-Georg Gadamer and the Hermeneutic Revolution," 36.

As Lawrence notes, Gadamer recognized that human beings "exist conversationally in relation to everything that is," and it is this participation in broader historical traditions and shared horizons of meaning that makes up the unending "conversation that we are."[9] Voegelin's method of meditative exegesis likewise carries a clear dialogical structure, as the search for understanding the order of being leads to the discovery of one's "specific humanity as that of a questioner," interrogating the various symbolizations and distortions that span human history.[10] Lonergan too accentuates the crucial priority of questions in the operations of human knowing. Through questioning we not only understand and judge in matters of fact but inquire into values and meaning of the human good, asking, "Who shall I become?" and "What's the right way to live?" Furthermore, Lonergan's conception of theology as a collaborative and interdisciplinary enterprise mediating between the Christian tradition and its cultural contexts has an unmistakably conversational cast, coordinating the various tasks of theological inquiry into an ongoing engagement with historical development.[11]

In addition to functioning as an explicit topic of philosophical reflection, the theme of conversation also underscores a characteristic feature of Lawrence's own scholarship. This emphasis is already evident in his overall approach, as many of his essays unfold as progressively deepening dialogues between these diverse thinkers, highlighting surprising points of continuity, as well as isolating areas of enduring conflict and disagreement. Lawrence's writings present conversation as the fundamental form of hermeneutic and theological praxis. His essays not only underscore the dialogical character of the operations of understanding and judgment, but also develop key themes of Lonergan's theology to cast the dimensions in explicitly conversational terms.

The operations of conscious human living find their ultimate fulfillment, for Lawrence, in religious conversion. Through conversion we enter into the conversation and "redemptive tension" between the inner word of the Holy Spirit – the love of God poured out into our hearts (Rom. 5:5) – and the outer word that is the incarnate meaning

---

9 See below, "Voegelin and Gadamer," 173. The theme of the "conversation that we are," as limned by Hölderlin in the poem "Friedensfeier," finds frequent mention in the writings of both Gadamer and Lawrence.

10 See below, "Voegelin and Gadamer," 179.

11 See Bernard Lonergan, *Method in Theology* (New York: Herder & Herder, 1972), on "Functional Specialties," 124–45.

given in Christ and his church.[12] This dynamic state of being in love with God is a real participation in the conversational life of the Father, Son, and Spirit. God's self-communication of grace marks "the catching up of our human being as conversationally stunted or deformed self-meaning into the self-meaning constitutive of the Trinity," opening up a new horizon of meaning and new possibilities for development.[13] In this imperfect sharing in the intrapersonal divine relations, "Christian community can appropriate for its foundations the intrinsically conversational character of its God."[14]

Faith and Reason

The larger conversation that guides Lawrence's work is both the historical problematic and contemporary shape of the relationship between faith and reason. Lawrence's navigation of this theme permeates this whole volume, but perhaps in its most concentrated form in the essays on Strauss and Lonergan, and on Benedict XVI and Jürgen Habermas. Eschewing the reductive options of fideism and rationalism, Lawrence operates within an integrative horizon where "faith and reason are like two wings on which the human spirit rises to the contemplation of the truth."[15]

Though he clearly avoids a fall into a fideism-rationalism dichotomy, Lawrence also resists the temptation to attribute an oversimplified harmony to these two kinds of knowledge – a brand of thinking evident in many of the impoverished texts of the neoscholastic manual tradition of the early to mid-twentieth century.[16] In Lonergan's frame, the "closed conceptualism" and "static essentialism" of the manual tradition tended to divide philosophy as the necessary truths derived from reason and theology as the contingent truths of revelation in such a way "that each limits its concern to its own allotted portion."[17] The

---

12 See below, "The Human Good and Christian Conversation," 344.

13 See below, "The Human Good and Christian Conversation," 351.

14 See below, "The Human Good and Christian Conversation," 352.

15 John Paul II, *Fides et Ratio* (Boston: Pauline Books and Media, 1998), 7.

16 For a brief overview of some of the key features of seminary formation and the manual tradition, see chapter 1 of Fergus Kerr, *Twentieth-Century Catholic Theologians: From Neoscholasticism to Nuptial Mysticisim* (Malden, MA: Blackwell, 2007).

17 J. Michael Stebbins, *The Divine Initiative: Grace, World-Order, and Human Freedom in the Early Writings of Bernard Lonergan* (Toronto: University of Toronto Press, 1995), 172.

relationship between these two disciplines within this methodological horizon amounts to mere non-contradiction, on the one hand, and a shared logical technique, on the other.[18]

Lawrence exhibits in this volume – in the manner of the later Lonergan – a more dynamic interplay between faith and reason, where theology is relegated neither to an isolated sphere cut off from human affairs nor to a set of propositions to be memorized. Rather, theology is a theoretical reflection on "concrete religion as it has been lived, as it is being lived, and as it is to be lived."[19] Perhaps the relationship between theology and philosophy is best understood as a circle, to borrow an image from John Paul II's encyclical, *Fides et Ratio*. Reason is stirred, writes John Paul II, "to explore paths which of itself it would not even have suspected it could take. This circular relationship with the word of God leaves philosophy enriched, because reason discovers new and unsuspected horizons."[20] Instead of restricting philosophy to necessary, self-evident truths, Lawrence leads us head on into the world of modernity and postmodernity – from Bacon, Descartes, Hobbes, Locke, Machiavelli, Hume, Kant, Rousseau to Nietzsche, Heidegger, Gadamer, Habermas, Derrida, and Foucault. He helps us navigate these thinkers with a position informed especially by Lonergan, but also Aristotle, Augustine, Aquinas, Voegelin, just to name a few, and does so with a spirit of friendship, a mood of generosity, and depth of understanding often absent in the academy today. One finds disclosed in Lawrence's work a heuristic eye to the integration of faith and the whole of human reality – friendship, politics, economics, culture, and the like.

Crisis of Culture

If the larger problematic of faith and reason permeates this volume, it is surely complicated by a contemporary crisis of culture. As John Paul II notes in the same encyclical, the role of the philosopher has changed in modern culture. The philosopher as lover of wisdom has been marginalized by "other forms of rationality" disconnected from

---

18 Stebbins, *The Divine Initiative*, 172.
19 Bernard Lonergan, "Lecture 3: The Relationship between Philosophy of God and the Functional Specialty 'Systematics,'" *Philosophical and Theological Papers 1965–1980*, Collected Works of Bernard Lonergan 17, eds. Robert C. Croken and Robert M. Doran (Toronto: University of Toronto Press, 2004), 209.
20 John Paul II, *Fides et Ratio*, 73, 92.

"the contemplation of truth and the search for the ultimate goal and meaning of life." Prioritizing instrumental reason, these forms of rationality "are directed – actually or potentially – towards the promotion of utilitarian ends, towards enjoyment or power."[21] Lawrence is attentive of course to the superstructural elements (positivism, scientism, postmodernism, etc.) that prioritize other forms of rationality. But he is also mindful of the "everyday, familiar domain of feeling, insight, judgment, and decision"[22] that is shaped by an unbridled consumerism with "persons understanding themselves," in the words of Lawrence, "as consumers or anonymous, identity-less generators of a never-ending series of new wishes demanding instantaneous satisfaction."[23]

Though Lawrence is certainly critical of these modern developments, his primary *modus operandi* is not widespread dismissal, but first, understanding, and then serious engagement. If the rise of modern science and the rise of historical studies created the conditions for a crisis in Catholic philosophy and theology in the twentieth century, as Lonergan himself suggested, then philosophy's contemporary role is one of "foundational methodology."[24] With Lonergan, Lawrence understands why contemporary believers are often unsympathetic to these modern developments, but their vision is blocked by a predominating classicism. The contemporary problem is "not a new religion, nor a new faith, but a belated social and cultural transition," namely, "the transition from classicist to modern culture." As Lonergan notes, "If we are not just to throw out what is good in classicism and replace it with contemporary trash, then we have to take the trouble, and it is enormous, to grasp the strength and the weakness, the power and the limitations, the good points and the shortcomings of both classicism and modernity."[25] Classicist culture, in Lonergan's account, refers to the assumption that there is "one culture" that is "both universal and permanent."[26] Lonergan recommends proceeding instead with an empirical understanding

---

21 John Paul II, *Fides et Ratio*, 47, 63.
22 Bernard Lonergan, "The Absence of God in Modern Culture," *A Second Collection*, ed. William F.J. Ryan, SJ and Bernard J. Tyrrell, SJ (Toronto: University of Toronto Press, 1976; repr. 1996), 111.
23 See below, "The Economic Good of Order and Culture in Relation to Solidarity, Subsidiarity, and Responsibility," 324.
24 See below, "Transcendence from Within," 208.
25 See below, "Transcendence from Within," 209.
26 Lonergan, *Method in Theology*, xi.

of culture: a culture is the set of meanings and values that inform a way of life, and there are as many cultures as there are different ways of life.[27] An empirical understanding of culture recognizes the dynamism of human cultures – that cultures may be "in process of slow development or rapid dissolution."[28] In this light, what is normative is not culture itself, but the transcultural core of human nature that is the source and measure of every culture. In other words, "culture" is not the normative measure of human beings, but human beings in their authenticity are the normative measure of cultures.

Finding his methodological roots in self-appropriation and authentic hermeneutic subjectivity, Lawrence engages many of the philosophical underpinnings that shape both the cultural superstructure and the everyday domain of meanings and values. This is evident, for example, in his penetrating conversation with postmodernism. Though he acknowledges the danger of its "relativistic and nihilistic manifestations," Lawrence regards the "understandable reaction of wholesale rejection" as "unwise" and "too undialectical."[29] He asks, "Don't we have to find a basis upon which postmodern concerns can be addressed without adopting postmodernism's destructive conclusions?" Lawrence appropriates Lonergan as a "Christian and Catholic thinker who actually shares many of the deepest concerns of postmodernism," but in a way "that takes relativity seriously without being relativistic – and that takes the absurdity and apparently random and chaotic dimensions of our world experience fully seriously without capitulating to nihilism in any form."[30]

Structure of the Volume

We have structured the volume in two parts. The first, "The Hermeneutic Revolution and the Crisis of Culture," concerns Lawrence's more specific philosophical treatments of particular thinkers in regards to the tradition of philosophical hermeneutics and postmodernity. Principally,

---

27 Lonergan, "The Absence of God in Modern Culture," 101.
28 Lonergan, *Method in Theology*, xi.
29 See below, "The Fragility of Consciousness," 230.
30 See below, "The Fragility of Consciousness," 230.

these writings offer incisive analyses of the thought of Heidegger, Gadamer, Strauss, and Voegelin, but throughout Lawrence also relates these thinkers to one another, to Lonergan's thought, and to broader themes in the Catholic intellectual tradition.

The second part, "Theology and the Human Good," continues Lawrence's reflection on the tradition of philosophical hermeneutics and postmodernity found in Part 1, but does so in a way that integrates more explicitly the theological framework that Lonergan introduced in *Method in Theology*. These more constructive pieces address the growing political and contextual emphases in theology and also offer helpful contributions in interpreting Lonergan's rich, but often neglected, trinitarian thought and discussions of genuine community.

Selection of Essays

Among the more difficult decisions in compiling a volume of this kind is choosing which essays to exclude. The collection of essays presented here was compiled according to several considerations. First, we have included several essays that both stand alone as full reflections on a given thinker or topic and also express the rich interconnections of Lawrence's work overall. We have also selected essays with more limited availability,[31] and have included more recent essays that illustrate the ongoing vitality of Lawrence's engagement with hermeneutic philosophy and the Catholic intellectual tradition.

Four of the selections offered here are influential and well-known pieces reprinted from earlier collections. The essays "The Fragility of Consciousness: Lonergan and the Postmodern Concern for the Other" and "The Human Good and Christian Conversation" were published in the volume *Communication and Lonergan: Common Ground for Forging the New Age*, ed. Thomas J. Farrell and Paul A. Soukup (Kansas City, MO: Sheed and Ward, 1993), 173–211 and 248–68. "Voegelin and Gadamer: Continental Philosophers Inspired by Plato and Aristotle" was included in the volume *Eric Voegelin and the Continental Tradition: Explorations in Modern Thought*, Eric Voegelin Institute Series, ed. Lee Trepanier and Steven F. McGuire (Columbia, MO: University of Missouri Press,

---

31 While many of Lawrence's essays in the *Lonergan Workshop* journal certainly merit inclusion, for example, these are easily accessible online.

2011), 192–218.[32] "Transcendence from Within: Benedict XVI and Jürgen Habermas on the Dialogue between Secular Reason and Religious Faith" appeared in *Christianity and Secular Reason Classical Themes and Modern Developments*, ed. Jeffrey Bloechl (South Bend, IN: University of Notre Dame Press 2012).

Several other selections were originally published as journal articles. The essays "Martin Heidegger and the Hermeneutic Revolution," "Hans-Georg Gadamer and the Hermeneutic Revolution," "Gadamer and Lonergan on Augustine's *Verbum Cordis* – the Heart of Postmodern Hermeneutics," and "A Jewish and a Christian Approach to the Problematic of Jerusalem and Athens: Leo Strauss and Bernard Lonergan" appeared in *Divyadaan: Journal of Philosophy and Education* 19, nos. 1–2 (2008): 7–30, 31–54, 55–86, and 217–318.[33] "Grace and Friendship: Postmodern Political Theology and God as Conversational" appeared in *Gregorianum* 85, no. 4 (2004): 795–820.

The remaining essays are more recent unpublished pieces. The essay "The Recovery of Theology in a Political Mode: The Example of Ernest L. Fortin, AA" was written for the 2010 roundtable discussion "Immortal Longings: Reason, Faith, and Politics in the Work of Father Ernest Fortin," held at Boston College. "Growing in Faith as the Eyes of Being-in-Love with God" was a 2010 talk delivered at Boston College's The Church in the 21st Century Center. "The Economic Good of Order and Culture in Relation to Solidarity, Subsidiarity, and Responsibility" presents an extended version of a talk given at the Sixth Annual Conference on Economics and Catholic Social Thought, held in Chicago, Illinois on 3–4 April 2014.

It seems fitting to offer a brief note on the formatting of the essays. Our aim was to format for consistency whenever possible, while at the same preserving the distinctive style and context of each essay. Hence, we maintained the diversity of heading styles that appear in various essays. To change the headings and subheadings in chapters 7 and 10, for example, would have compromised, in our judgment, the clarity of presentation. We also replaced, wherever appropriate,

---

32 Reprinted by permission of the University of Missouri Press, Columbia, Missouri, 65201. Copyright © 2011 by the Curators of the University of Missouri.

33 The original title of the latter essay is "The Hermeneutic Revolution and Bernard Lonergan: Gadamer and Lonergan on Augustine's Verbum Cordis – the Heart of Postmodern Hermeneutics."

numerous references to earlier versions of Lonergan's works with the most updated rendering in the *Collected Works of Bernard Lonergan*. Also, in general, where Lawrence quotes from a German source in English, and another translation is not indicated, the translation is his own.

It is our hope that the selection of essays offered here will spur further interest in Lawrence's work. Toward this end, we have included an illustrative bibliography of Lawrence's writings at the end of this volume.

We would like to express our gratitude to the peer reviewers for their helpful suggestions and critical feedback. This publication came to fruition through the great professionalism of the University of Toronto Press. In particular, we thank the humanities editor, Richard Ratzlaff, for his editorial wisdom and keen guidance throughout this process. We are grateful as well for the generous support of The Lonergan Institute at Boston College, especially to Dr. Kerry Cronin and Dr. Patrick Byrne. Finally, the appearance of this volume would not have been possible without the many decades of hospitality, love, and dedication offered by Fred and Sue Lawrence.

THE FRAGILITY OF CONSCIOUSNESS

PART ONE

The Hermeneutic Revolution
and the Crisis of Culture

1 Martin Heidegger and the Hermeneutic Revolution

Homo timens Deum, voluntatem eius in Scripturis sanctis diligenter inquirit.

Augustine, *De doctrina christiana* III.1.1

Die Selbstgewissheit und das Sich-selbst-haben im Sinne Augustins is etwas ganz anderes als die cartesische Evidenz des *cogito*.

Heidegger, "Augustinus und der Neoplatonismus," 298[1]

I. The Postmodern Hermeneutic Revolution

The word "postmodern" is emblematic of the hermeneutic revolution that has taken place during the twentieth century. Here the controversial notion of postmodernity in philosophy and theology will be understood in terms of three watersheds in the history of hermeneutics: ancient or premodern, modern, and postmodern.

A. The Ancient Hermeneutics of Augustine

In the Christian tradition, Augustine of Hippo's *De doctrina christiana* marked the ancient or premodern watershed of hermeneutics.[2] It left its

---

1 Martin Heidegger, "Augustinus und der Neuplatonismus" (*Sommersemester* 1921), *Phänomenologie des religiösen Lebens*, Gesamtausgabe 60, ed. Claudius Strube (Frankfurt: Vittorio Klostermann, 1995), 298.

2 The classic treatments are Henri I. Marrou, *Saint Augustin et la fin de la culture antique* (Paris: E. de Boccard, 1958); Charles N. Cochrane, *Christianity and Classical Culture* (Oxford: Clarendon Press, 1940).

imprint on Christian learning and on medieval and early Reformation theology. Preceded by the establishment of the canon of sacred scripture and the rise of the dogmatic creeds of the great ecumenical councils, it was a theory of education as centered on the study of the Bible, and it took creeds and a dogmatic theological context for granted. Augustine understood education as the activity of the mind "by which faith is engendered, nourished, defended, and strengthened."[3] He rooted his hermeneutics in liturgical practice, especially baptism and Eucharist, and in the Christian praxis of love. It was a "hermeneutics of love"[4] and a "hermeneutics of consent."[5]

B. The Modern Hermeneutics of Spinoza

The modern revolt against the "Great Tradition" and the radicalization of the "hermeneutics of suspicion"[6] by Marx, Nietzsche, and Freud (Ricoeur) characterizes the second great watershed in Western hermeneutics. Its classic expression is Baruch Spinoza's *Theologico-Political Treatise*.[7] Gotthold Lessing's "gaping abyss," which historical-critical method tries to bridge, was created by the presuppositions of Enlightenment epistemology. The relationship between the contingencies of

---

3 Augustine, *De trinitate* XIV.1.3.

4 See Ernest Fortin, "Augustine and the Hermeneutics of Love: Some Preliminary Considerations," *The Birth of Philosophic Christianity: Studies in Early Christian and Medieval Thought*, Ernest L. Fortin: Collected Essays 1, ed. Brian Benestad (Lanham, MD: Rowman and Littlefield, 1996), 1–19.

5 The expression comes from Ben F. Meyer, "Conversion and the Hermeneutics of Consent," *Critical Realism and the New Testament* (Allison Park, PA: Pickwick Publications, 1989), 57–75.

6 This term comes from Paul Ricoeur, *Freud and Philosophy: An Essay on Interpretation*, trans. D. Savage (New Haven and London: Yale University Press, 1970). See Hans-Georg Gadamer, "The Hermeneutics of Suspicion," *Hermeneutics: Questions and Prospects*, ed. Gary Shapiro and Alan Sica (Amherst: University of Massachusetts Press, 1984).

7 On Spinoza see Hans-Georg Gadamer, *Wahrheit und Methode. Grundzüge einer philosophischen Hermeneutik* (Tübingen: Mohr Siebeck, 1962), 169–72. English translation: *Truth and Method*, second, revised edition, trans. and revised by Joel Weinsheimer and Donald Marshall (New York: Crossroad, 1991), 181–4. In the text, I have usually used my own translations, not because I judge them to be more adequate, but just for reasons of time. See also Leo Strauss, *Spinoza's Critique of Religion* (New York: Schocken Books, 1975); *Persecution and the Art of Writing* (Glencoe, IL: Free Press, 1951); Nicholas Boyle, "Lessing, Biblical Criticism and the Origins of German Classical Culture," *German Life and Letters*, New Series 34 (1981): 196–213.

history and the truths of faith reflected the subject-object split and the "problem of the bridge" in the epistemologies of Descartes, Locke, and others. Since the eighteenth century, the historical-critical method removed the retrieval of ancient sources, church history, and the history of dogma from the hands of ecclesiastical authorities.

Kant sought the limits of reason to *"make room for* faith." Kant's modern philosophy, which limited philosophy to the limits of immanentist or truncated reason, coordinated well with the classic Protestant doctrines of *sola fide, sola gratia,* and *sola scriptura.* His position eventually led to the basic tendencies of liberal Protestantism. These include: (1) the relativism associated with Troeltsch's "Christ without absolutes";[8] (2) the historicism manifest in the so-called quest for the historical Jesus from Strauss through Harnack and Schweitzer to Bultmann and the present;[9] and (3) the subjectivism evident in Albrecht Ritschl's and Wilhelm Hermann's grounding of theology in "religion within the limits of reason alone," which reduces religion to imagination and subordinates it to morality.[10]

C. Figures in the Postmodern Hermeneutics Revolution

1. Karl Barth

Liberal Protestant theology – *Kulturprotestantismus* as it was called in German-speaking countries – was symptomatic of the breakdown of the traditional hermeneutics of consent. It closed the gap between the modern world and the ancient classics by accommodating Christianity to the present. Karl Barth's teachers, Wilhelm Hermann and Adolf Harnack, were among the nineteenth-century theologians who gave a religious endorsement to the modern secular belief that human beings can take their destiny into their own hands *etsi Deus non daretur.* The liberal Protestant signatories in support of the German war effort in World War I

---

8 See Sarah Coakley, *Christ Without Absolutes: A Study of the Christology of Ernst Troeltsch* (Oxford: Clarendon Press, 1988).

9 See Stephen Neill and Tom Wright, *The Interpretation of the New Testament 1861 to 1986* (Oxford: Oxford University Press, 1988); and Meyer, *Critical Realism and the New Testament.*

10 See Roger A. Johnson, *The Origin of Demythologizing in the Theology of Rudolf Bultmann: Philosophy and Historiography* (Leiden: Brill, 1974), especially on Bultmann's teacher, Wilhelm Hermann.

convinced the young Swiss pastor Karl Barth that the liberal approach to Christianity was a dead end.[11]

Against the background of Kierkegaard, Dostoevsky, Nietzsche, and Overbeck, Barth rediscovered the Bible, especially Paul's letter to the Romans.[12] In his *The Epistle to the Romans*, Barth so wrestled with and rethought Paul's *Sache* (subject matter) as to break down the walls separating the twentieth century from evangelical origins.[13] According to Hans-Georg Gadamer, his explosive act of rebellion initiated the third watershed, the postmodern "hermeneutic revolution."[14]

2. Young Heidegger

Martin Heidegger's "hermeneutic breakthrough" from neo-Kantian transcendental philosophy and from *Weltanschauung*-philosophies (worked out between 1919 and the publication of *Sein und Zeit* in 1927) is generally acknowledged to be the postmodern hermeneutic revolution's "ground-zero."[15]

Methodological remarks on his analysis of Paul's letters to the Thessalonians and the Galatians in his "Einleitung in die Phänomenologie der Religion (1920/21)" reveal that Heidegger agreed with Barth about

---

11 See Eberhard Busch, *Karl Barth: His Life from Letters and Autobiographical Texts*, trans. John Bowden (Philadelphia: Fortress Press, 1976); also the review of this work by Hans W. Frei, in *Types of Christian Theology* (New Haven: Yale University, 1992), 147–63.

12 See Busch, *Karl Barth: His Life from Letters and Autobiographical Texts*, 60–125.

13 Karl Barth, *Römerbrief* (Zurich: Zollikon, 1984 [1922]).

14 See Hans-Georg Gadamer, "Existentialism and the Philosophy of Existence," *Heidegegger's Ways*, trans. J.W. Stanley (Albany: SUNY Press, 1994), 1–13 at 2.

15 Based on his life experience and personal knowledge of Heidegger, it was Gadamer I believe who pioneered this opinion, "Die religiöse Dimension," *Neuere Philosophie I. Hegel, Husserl, Heidegger*, Gesammelte Werke 3 (Tübingen: Mohr Siebeck, 1987), 308–19 at 309. English translation: "The Religious Dimension (1981)," *Heidegger's Ways*, 167–80 at 171. Other key researchers follow, especially: Theodore Kisiel, "Theological Beginnings: Toward a Phenomenology of Christianity," *The Genesis of Heidegger's Being and Time* (Berkeley and Los Angeles: University of California, 1993), 69–115; on the years 1915–19, "Heidegger (1920–21) on Becoming a Christian: A Conceptual Picture-Show," 175–91. Also see John Van Buren, *The Young Heidegger: Rumor of the Hidden King* (Bloomington, IN: Indiana University, 1994), 133–56; and "Martin Heidegger, Martin Luther," *Reading Heidegger from the Start: Essays in His Earliest Thought* (Albany: SUNY Press, 1994), 159–74. See Walter Strolz, "Herkunft und Zukunft: Martin Heideggers frühe Auslegung urchristlicher Lebenserfahrung," *Herder Korrespondenz* 4 (1996): 203–7. Most recently, see Jean Greisch, *L'Arbre de vie et l'Arbre du savoir. Les racines phénoménologiques de l'herméneutique Heideggerienne (1919–1923)* (Paris: du Cerf, 2000).

the inadequacies of Troeltsch's version of liberal Protestantism.[16] Heidegger's demolition of putative scholarly neutrality was part and parcel of his hermeneutic phenomenology of factical life. Heidegger found a paradigm for the finitude-*cum*-fallenness so central for the analysis of facticity in Augustine's account of the roots of sin. Commenting at length on Book X of the *Confessions*, he uncovered the typical structures of *Dasein* thereafter transposed into completely secular terms in *Sein und Zeit*.[17]

3. Hans-Georg Gadamer

As we see now in Heidegger's famous "Natorp Report (1922)"[18] and the *Phänomenologische Interpretationen zu Aristoteles: Einführung in die phänomenologische Forschung*,[19] Aristotle played a key role in the secularizing of Augustine's framework. Heidegger's recognition of the priority of the truth of existence over the propositional truth dominant in the sciences of nature and mathematics had a life-changing effect on Hans-Georg Gadamer, who had just finished his doctorate at Marburg in 1922 when Paul Natorp asked Gadamer to evaluate the report for him. This spurred Gadamer to attend Heidegger's Aristotle lectures, and eventually to write his *Habilitationsschrift* under him.

Heidegger's hermeneutic breakthrough blossomed fully in Gadamer's *Wahrheit und Methode* (1960), more than thirty years after *Being and Time*. The hermeneutics of facticity resonated deeply with Gadamer's humanistic and philological formation. *Truth and Method* starts with a

---

16 See Martin Heidegger, 1. "Einleitung in die Phänomenologie der Religion" (*Wintersemester* 1920–1); 2. "Augustinus und der Neuplatonismus"; 3. "Die philosophischen Grundlagen der mittelalterlichen Mystik," Gesamtausgabe 60, 19–30.

17 Heidegger, "Augustinus und der Neuplatonismus," 157–299. See James K.A. Smith, "*Confessions* of an Existentialist: Reading Augustine after Heidegger," Part I: *New Blackfriars* 82 (2001): 273–82; Part II: *New Blackfriars* 82 (2001): 335–47.

18 Martin Heidegger, "Phenomenological Interpretations with Respect to Aristotle: Indications of the Hermeneutical Situation," trans. Michael Baur, *Man and World* 25 (1992): 355–93; English translation of "Phänomenologische Interpretationen zu Aristoteles [Anzeige der hermeneutischen Situation]," ed. Hans-Ulrich Lessing, *Dilthey Jahrbuch* 6 (1989): 236–69.

19 Martin Heidegger, *Phänomenologische Interpretationen zu Aristoteles. Einführung in die phänomenologische Forschung* (*Wintersemester* 1921–2), Gesamtausgabe 61, ed. Walter Bröcker and Käte Bröcker-Oltmanns (Frankfurt: Vittorio Klostermann, 1994). English translation: Richard Rojcewicz, *Phenomenological Interpretations of Aristotle: Initiation into Phenomenological Research* (Bloomington: Indiana University Press, 2001).

recovery of truth in art, humane letters, and legal, ethical, theological, and philosophical disciplines. It goes on to elaborate an ontological transposition of Plato's dialectic – an ethical ontology. In his debate with Jürgen Habermas about the universality of hermeneutics,[20] Gadamer finally made fully explicit how hermeneutic philosophy as an embodiment of Aristotle's *phronesis* reenacts practical philosophy. Hermeneutic ontology as postmodern is practical philosophy in Aristotle's sense.

4. Bernard Lonergan

A less well-known aspect of the postmodern hermeneutic revolution was motivated by the crisis in Roman Catholic theology's mediation between religion and culture engendered by the church's reaction to modernity.[21] This attempted damage-control established what Heidegger, in his 1919 letter to Fr. Engelbert Krebs, called "the Catholic system"[22] – that is, a Romanized control of meaning through ahistorical orthodoxy. According to philosopher and theologian Bernard Lonergan, the crisis was in large part due to what he called the church's "classicist mentality." It was a wholesale failure to come to terms either with modern science or with historical mindedness.

Lonergan's response was hermeneutical. It involved a critical acceptance of modern history and modern science. He transposed his radical interpretation of Thomas Aquinas's concept of *verbum*[23] in his book, *Insight: A Study of Human Understanding* (1957).[24] Coming critically to

---

20 See Jürgen Habermas, *On the Logic of the Social Sciences,* trans. Shierry Weber Nicholson and Jerry A. Stark (Cambridge: MIT Press, 1988); Gadamer's first response, originally in *Philosophische Rundschau* 9 (1961): 241–76, now appears as Supplement I in *Truth and Method,* 460–91.

21 See Bernard Lonergan, "Theology in its New Context," and "Belief: Today's Issue," *A Second Collection,* ed. W. Ryan and B. Tyrrell (London: Darton, Longman & Todd, 1974), 55–67, 87–99.

22 Hugo Ott, "The Struggle with the Faith of My Birth," *Martin Heidegger: A Political Life,* trans. Allan Blunden (London: Harper Collins/Basic Books, 1993), 41–121 at 106–7.

23 See Bernard Lonergan, *Verbum: Word and Idea in Aquinas,* Collected Works of Bernard Lonergan 2, ed. Frederick E. Crowe and Robert M. Doran (Toronto: University of Toronto Press, 1997), which originally appeared as articles in *Theological Studies* 7 (1946): 349–92; 8 (1947): 35–79; 8 (1947): 404–44; 10 (1949): 3–40; and 10 (1949): 359–93.

24 Bernard Lonergan, *Insight: A Study of Human Understanding* (New York: Philosophical Library, 1957).

terms with human facticity and historicity, he transposed his earlier groundbreaking interpretation of Aquinas's thought on grace and freedom[25] in his 1972 work, *Method in Theology*.[26] For Lonergan the integrity of method as hermeneutical demonstrates that in the postmodern (or any) era, science, scholarship, philosophy, and theology can only be genuine in the measure that they "head one into being authentically human."[27]

II. The Phenomenological Context of the Hermeneutic Revolution

The postmodern hermeneutic revolution is based on the realization that the interpretation of the originative classics of Western culture intimately affects and is affected by human beings' concrete solution to the problem of living together. It confronts head-on the fact that historical efforts to make sense of our lives entail a primordial self-interpretation that settles the issue of "the one thing most needful" (Lk 10: 42). Thinkers as different as Barth, Heidegger, Gadamer, and Lonergan (and a host of others) share in bringing about the postmodern revolution in hermeneutics. Each of them underlines the intimate link in philosophy, theology, and ordinary living between careful reading and the way human beings personally and communally ask practical questions about the right way to live. Each of them realizes that the key to interpreting any classic work lies in the concrete manner in which people make sense of their lives or the way a culture makes sense of the way people living together make sense of their lives. There is an existential, practical, and even political link between interpretation and self-understanding.

---

25 See Bernard Lonergan, *Grace and Freedom: Operative Grace in the Thought of St Thomas Aquinas*, Collected Works of Bernard Lonergan 1, ed. Fredrick E. Crowe and Robert M. Doran (Toronto: University of Toronto Press, 2000), originally published in *Theological Studies* 2 (1941): 289–324; 3 (1942): 69–88, 375–402, and 533–78.

26 Bernard Lonergan, *Method in Theology* (New York: Herder & Herder, 1972).

27 Bernard Lonergan, "Method: Trend and Variations," *A Third Collection: Papers by Bernard J.F. Lonergan, SJ*, ed. Frederick E. Crowe (Mahwah, NJ: Paulist, 1985), 13–22 at 21: "Being a scientist is just an aspect of being human, nor has any method been found that makes one authentically scientific without heading one into being authentically human."

Postmodern hermeneutics demands a revised understanding of the received teaching that hermeneutics is a "graft" on phenomenology.[28] Years ago Don Ihde spoke helpfully of two different orientations within phenomenology.[29] The first type of phenomenology takes its bearings from sense perception, and is oriented toward some "pure" perception. It is typified by Husserl (to whom Heidegger was grateful for giving him "new eyes"[30]) and by the early Merleau-Ponty. The second takes its bearings from language, and is oriented toward language-in-use and dialogue. Heidegger, Gadamer, the later Merleau-Ponty, and Paul Ricoeur are key representatives of this type, which is actually hermeneutic philosophy.

The problem with the "graft" metaphor is that it covers over the discontinuity between the two kinds of phenomenology. Rather than being a continuation of the phenomenology of perception in another medium, linguistic or hermeneutic philosophy is a critique of the model of and validity of pure perception. Let us examine this critique briefly.

The most obvious aspect of the critique regards the epistemic role of pure sense intuition and the aim (set forth in Husserl's "Philosophy as a Rigorous Science" [1910–11]) of establishing philosophy as an apodictically rigorous science. Husserl declared in the *Krisis-Abhandlung* of 1935 (regarding what others were saying about this goal) that "der Traum ist ausgeträumt."[31] Are neither the putative pure perception nor the transcendental reduction capable of guaranteeing objective validity? Or does it mean that the posing of the epistemological problem of cognitional objectivity is itself incorrect? The hermeneutic critique is unambiguous about these issues. It rejects the wrongheaded presuppositions of the modern epistemological question; it discards the

---

28 Paul Ricoeur introduced this metaphor to characterize the relationship between hermeneutics and phenomenology in *Le conflit des interprétations* (Paris: du Seuil, 1969), 7, and developed the implications of "graft" in *Du texte à l'action. Essais d' herméneutique II* (Paris: du Seuil, 1986), 39–73.

29 See Don Ihde, "Language and Two Phenomenologies," *Southern Journal of Philosophy* (Winter, 1970): 399–408.

30 Martin Heidegger, *Ontologie. Hermeneutik der Faktizität*, Gesamtausgabe 63 (Frankfurt: Vittorio Klostermann, 1988), 5.

31 See Gadamer's commentary in "Die phänomenologische Bewegung," *Neuere Philosophie I. Hegel, Husserl, Heidegger*, Gesammelte Werke 3 (Tübingen: Mohr Siebeck, 1987), 128–36 on the passage in *Husserliana* VI, Beilage XXVIII to §73.

epistemic ultimacy of perception; and it demolishes both the "myth of pure perception" and the validity of transcendental grounding in the Fichtean mode.

Less obviously perhaps, the hermeneutic critique of the phenomenology of perception raises questions about the exclusive attention paid to intentionality, even when supplemented by the later Husserl's notions of *Lebenswelt* and constitution. In executing his analysis of human facticity, Heidegger evoked hermeneutics precisely because the phenomenology of perception's exploration of the noetic and noematic poles of human horizon cannot do justice to non-intentional or performative consciousness. As Gadamer wrote:

> Heidegger's own contribution already presupposes this phenomenological overcoming of the rigid opposition between the consciousness and object. When he once – I think it was in the year 1924 in Marburg – invoked the scholastic distinction between *actus signatus* and *actus exercitus* that struck us as a new saying. That beyond the objectifyng conduct of consciousness and its perfection in science there exists in human conduct and in human world-experience a much more profound stratum, with which philosophy has to do, corresponded with our dissatisfactions regarding neo-Kantianism.[32]

In short, as will be explained later on, the luminosity of consciousness is primordially interpretative.

The hermeneutic critique of the phenomenology of perception, therefore, displaces any "intuitionism" or "perceptualism" from primacy. Because human being (*Dasein*) is primordially interpretative, first philosophy is hermeneutic; both perception and its phenomenology are derivative. No longer truncated by the preoccupation with sense intuition, hermeneutic phenomenology relegates sense perception's world of immediacy to a subordinate status within the far larger and richer world mediated by meaning.

In Heidegger and Gadamer, the hermeneutic turn of phenomenology arose in reaction to the Cartesian or Kantian or Fichtean cognitional biases that are characteristic of the varieties of then dominant neo-Kantianism. To borrow Jean Greisch's expression, hermeneutic

---

32 Gadamer, "Die phänomenologische Bewegung," 127.

phenomenology chose the tree of life instead of the tree of knowledge.[33] This means a refusal to accept Kant's account of the theoretical sciences of mathematics and of the subhuman natural sciences as the exclusive normative framework for philosophical inquiry. Does the postmodern hermeneutic revolution thereby turn to the irrational, as did some versions of *Lebensphilosophie* or existentialism? Not necessarily. The hermeneutic breakthrough rejected the exclusive claim to normativity by science and by the epistemologically oriented problematic of modern philosophy. If it opened philosophy to what had been considered irrational moods and feelings or decisionism, it did not necessarily intend the wholesale repudiation of science and the truth of reason. Hermeneutic analysis seeks instead the intelligibility of spheres of performative consciousness that previous science or epistemologically oriented philosophies mistakenly judged irrational and irrelevant to issues of truth. Hermeneutic philosophy fully recognizes that moods, feelings, decisions, and practical actions occur within history, and so are primordially meaning-laden. Primordial self-meaning, then, is fraught with interpretation of the self, the world, and God.

More importantly, hermeneutic philosophy's option in favor of the tree of life recognized that the quest for direction in the stream of life means that, implicitly and performatively, all our thoughts, words, and deeds are either discovering or missing insight into the right way to live. Ethical, practical, or political questions have a priority in the genesis of philosophic and theological discourse. Hence, any philosophical departure preoccupied with the scientific or epistemological validity of knowledge misses the way these issues are rooted in that primordial and integrally interpretive quest. The truth of fact is crucial, but its crucialness is a function of the more basic truth of existence.

As Heidegger pointed out about Marx's tenth thesis on Feuerbach, we need to acknowledge that in interpreting history we are already making history. Along with ethics, practical/political philosophy, and theology, hermeneutic philosophy acknowledges in their proper cognitive status all the arts and humane disciplines relegated by Marxists to the sphere of the epiphenomenal. So, too, as the enterprise of comprehensive reflection on the conditions of human living, it recognizes the architectonic significance of painting, sculpture, architecture, myth,

---

33 See Jean Greisch, "L'arbre de vie et la terre promise de la raison," *L'Arbre de vie et l'Arbre du savoir*, 33–50.

ritual and worship, literature, and all the disciplines whose subject matters are constituted by meaning and value.

Taking seriously all these more obviously hermeneutic experiences and disciplines plunges philosophic and theological investigation into the Nietzschean zone of issues that cannot fit into, and so apparently relativize, any ready-made or conventional meanings and values. Not only are there changes in historical horizon relative to any given standpoint, but there are also pivotal shifts of standpoint that radically transform all one's meanings and values: one experiences a switch from one horizon to another, or even a replacement of one horizon by another. Therefore, the perspectival character of all finite human knowing, evaluating, and deciding cannot be adequately accounted for in terms of intentionality analysis. Unlike ordinary phenomenology, the postmodern hermeneutic revolution requires philosophy and theology to bring those displacements, reversals, or conversions that crucially condition the way human beings move interpretatively from one horizon of living to another into the bright light of day.

III. The Pivotal Role of Heidegger on Augustine and the Truth of Existence

Heidegger's meditative exegesis on Book X of Augustine's *Confessions* – a book dedicated to memory – constituted an important phase in his reaction to the modern notion of the self.[34] Descartes's eternal truths are a technical attempt of truncated reason to gain what Nicholas Lash has rightly called a "privileged point from which to timelessly survey the world."[35] Heidegger realized that the ideal of universal clarity and precision for the sake of prediction and control cannot account for the ineluctable contingency of the terrestrial events and the human freedom so central to his hermeneutics of facticity.

The self as participant narrator in Augustine's *Confessions* becomes a model for Heidegger in his quest to relinquish modern philosophy's ahistorical, atemporal decontextualizing of the self. Against that tactic of fragmentation and isolation, he returns with Augustine to the wholesomeness of re-membering, re-collecting *memoria*. In Augustine's *Confessions*, the project of *memoria* is to recover the self *coram Deo*. It is

---

34 Heidegger, "Augustinus und der Neuplatonismus," 157–299.
35 See Nicholas Lash, "Remembering the Future" (Unpublished paper presented at Boston College, 2002).

significant to Heidegger that the truth at stake in the *Confessions* is the truth of existence. As Augustine says at the outset of Book X.1.1: "Truth it is that I want to do, in my heart by confession in your presence, and with my pen before many witnesses."[36] According to Robert Dodaro:

> The pretense of the *Confessions* is that God does not need to know Augustine; Augustine needs to know himself. And he can only know himself by coming to know concretely how, in what manner, God knows him and loves him. Confession is thus Augustine's tried-and-true mode of self-discovery because it involves a minute and attentive recollection of his history; a recollection in which he is revealed to himself within the providential love of God which he gratefully and painfully recalls to have been present at each significant juncture of his past and present life.[37]

And so Heidegger follows Augustine's analysis of the obstacles to self-knowledge within human interiority along the path of memory *coram Deo* from *ipse mihi occurro* through *quaestio mihi sum* to *molestia (oneri) mihi sum*.

The truth of existence at stake in this quest aids Heidegger in elucidating the "dependence of the possibility of explication on the level of and anticipatory grasp of interpretation in terms of history, history of the spirit or ideas, and performative history."[38] In theologian Rowan Williams's words, one stops conceiving "interiority in terms of space – outer and inner, husk and kernel," and asks, "What if our 'inner life' were better spoken of in terms of extension in time? the time it takes to understand?"[39] In terms of Augustine's truth of existence (and quoting Williams again), "the self is not a substance one unearths by peeling away layers until one gets to the core, but an integrity one struggles to bring into existence."[40] For Augustine as for Heidegger, self-knowledge is always provisional and contingent.

---

36 Augustine, *The Confessions*, trans. M. Boulding, OSB, ed. J. Rotelle, OSA (Hyde Park, NY: New City Press, 1997), 181.

37 Robert Dodaro, "Loose Canons: Augustine and Derrida on Their Selves," *God, the Gift, and Postmodernism,* ed. J.D. Caputo and M.J. Scanlon (Bloomington: Indiana University, 1999), 79–111 at 83.

38 Heidegger, "Augustinus und der Neuplatonismus," 231.

39 Rowan Williams, "Interiority and Epiphany: A Reading in New Testament Ethics," *On Christian Theology* (London: Blackwell, 2000), 239–64 at 240.

40 Williams, "Interiority and Epiphany: A Reading in New Testament Ethics," 240.

Heidegger interprets the light (of truth) as possessing a "totally determinate, existential, performative meaning" not to be understood in terms of "the metaphysics of things."[41] Augustine's notion of care is specified phenomenologically as *cura* (*Bekümmerung*) for oneself that unfolds in *uti* as utilitarian expeditiousness and *frui* or enjoyment that orients the utility appropriate to finite goods toward the *frui* of the highest good. Heidegger focuses on the performative self-meaning in fundamental human caring (*curare, Bekümmertsein*) for one's own facticity and existence.

To begin with, then, one is a burden to oneself, and is scattered among a multitude of possibly meaningful directions in life instead of being focused on the "one thing needful": "When at last I cling to you with my whole being there will be no more anguish or labor for me, and my life will be alive indeed, because filled with you... [B]ut I am not full of you, and so I am a burden to myself."[42] Under the weight of *molestia*, care grounds a horizon of expectation that is actuated either as fear of adversities or desire for prosperity. Alternating periods of prosperity and adversity penetrate each other over time. In view of the incessant oscillation between griefs and joys, Augustine says, one "does not know which will win the day." Care, then, is an historical process, experienced as a tension between fear and delight. One ceaselessly shifts back and forth between them without pause. All of life is a *tentatio*, a trial.

Human beings do not come to know themselves except through *tentatio*. Heidegger stresses that to acknowledge both the *quaestio mihi factus sum* and to respond to the query, *Quid amo?*, one has to engage in an existential exploration or quest in which our primordial *esse, nosse,* and *amare* are performatively oriented to God as the Truth, the *beata vita*.[43] Heidegger presents the inextricable threesome of *esse, nosse,* and *amare* as operative in our consciousness (= conscience in Augustine), but not yet known objectively. Prior to being expressly known and without necessarily ever having been objectified, these facets of the structure of facticity's (1) occurrence, (2) preconceptual awareness, and (3) love are performed in relation to others, the world, oneself, and God. When they are actuated in a lifetime's actions and sufferings, they constitute human *Existenz*. Heidegger recognizes that for Augustine, performative

---

41 Heidegger, "Augustinus und der Neuplatonismus," 199.
42 Augustine, *Confessions* X.28.39; 203.
43 Heidegger, "Augustinus und der Neuplatonismus," 298.

human living can only be rightly evaluated in relation to God as norm or standard. Like the self, God cannot be conceived of regionally as an object alongside the rest of the spatio-temporal objects in the universe. The coming-to-light, through confession, of human *Existenz* is correlative with the coming-to-light of God. By using the technique of the formal indication of the structures of this preconceptual reality of performance, Heidegger tried to extricate Augustine's quest from what he considered the taint of Neoplatonism or of metaphysics to discover the constitutive foundational hermeneutics of facticity or *Existenz*. But he also fails to come fully to terms with the central issues for Augustine: sin and grace.

A. Sin and Grace

Augustine did not work out a speculative theory on the distinction between divine grace and human freedom because it was not until the year 1230 that Christian theologians, during the gradual reception of Aristotle by the Latin West, distinguished systematically between natural and supernatural orders.[44] When Heidegger interpreted Augustine by thematizing performance rather than content (the *how* versus the *what*), his chief concern was the formal indication of the structures of facticity and of performative/constitutive meaning.[45] In the interpretation of Book X and in the appendices to that interpretation, Heidegger was not challenged by Augustine to clarify unambiguously the relationship between human sinfulness and *molestia* (with its concomitant forms of concupiscence). Heidegger's notation *"Molestia = Faktizität"* means that the difficulties attendant upon concupiscience constitute the range of possible meanings that make up the factical starting point of human living.[46] Are they, then, built into the original constitution of the human being's fallibility? Or are they a denaturing of *Existenz*, and caused by sin?

Because Augustine (in contrast to Thomas Aquinas) did not have a rounded theory of human nature, he suggested both that human beings are a question to themselves because of their fallenness, and

---

44 J. Michael Stebbins, "The Thirteenth Century Breakthrough," *The Divine Initiative* (Toronto: University of Toronto Press, 1995), 67–92; Bernard Lonergan, *Grace and Freedom*, 3–20.

45 Heidegger, "Augustinus und der Neuplatonismus," 9–14.

46 Heidegger, "Augustinus und der Neuplatonismus," 241–6.

that justification by grace does not so eliminate fallenness as to remove *tentatio*. Thomas Aquinas reinterpreted Augustine's uncreated light by which we consult the eternal reasons to judge the truth in terms of Aristotle's idea of a *nous poietikos* (agent intellect).[47] Lonergan aphoristically summed up the implication of this reinterpretation for the two thinkers: "For Augustine our hearts are restless until they rest in God; for Aquinas, not our hearts, but first and most our minds are restless until they rest in seeing Him."[48]

Hence, for Aquinas human beings are questions to themselves, or they possess their beings as a question about being, not because of the fallennness due to sin, but because the human intelligence is an infinite potency. But such a conclusion is the specialized product of abstract reflection. Augustine's penetrating understanding stands at the start of Christian speculation on grace and freedom. For him the restless heart has rightly to exercise *frui* and *uti* in relation to the created order and to the creator, respectively.[49] Properly, one can only enjoy the infinite; one makes use of the finite. If one seeks enjoyment from the finite, which ought only to be used for the sake of infinite enjoyment of the creator, one's loving becomes disordered.

Heidegger does not clearly distinguish the "restless heart" as a potentiality to be actuated in utility and enjoyment from the heart as disoriented by cupidity and concupiscence. Why not? To suggest an answer, one need only recall Jesuit theologian Gustave Weigel's frequent observation, "All things human, given enough time, go badly." I suppose that Heidegger's existential analysis locates the panorama of human evil daily apparent to us in relation to the four states of human liberty that permeated Augustine's thinking – first, the state of innocence in paradise; second, the postlapsarian state in which, as the tradition put it, *posse peccare et non posse non peccare*; third, the redeemed state in which human beings can either avoid or commit mortal sin; and fourth, the state of impeccability in heaven. It seems that the condition in which humans are virtually unable to keep from sinning is the dominant state in which human beings exist. No wonder that Heidegger conflated fallenness with finitude!

Recent investigation of the period between 1919 and 1927 reveals that Heidegger did conflate fallenness with human finitude, remaining

---

47 Lonergan, *Verbum*, 78–99.
48 Lonergan, *Verbum*, 100.
49 Heidegger, "Augustinus und der Neuplatonismus," 271–3.

faithful to the methodological atheism he demanded of philosophy.[50] From the time of the Aristotle interpretations done soon after his lectures on Augustine, Heidegger left aside any discussion of grace and sin. Whereas for the author of the *Confessions* fallenness contingently affects facticity because of sin (as original and personal, actual and habitual), in Heidegger fallenness becomes virtually synonymous with the ease and frequency with which human actions miss by too much or too little the mean of virtue in Aristotle's *Nicomachean Ethics*.[51] Moreover, sinful human structures tacitly ground Heidegger's dramatic account of the inevitable *Ruinanz* to which human existence is subject.[52]

Once Heidegger departed Augustine's orbit to concentrate on Aristotle, he interpreted *moles* (*molestia*) and *tentatio* as simply challenges to human seriousness and authenticity. He thus radicalized the teaching of the early modern state of nature theorists (Hobbes, Locke, and Rousseau), who, as part of their strategy to separate religious opinion from political power, wanted to replace the biblical accounts of the Fall with their versions of the state of nature, in which they reinterpret sin as natural. But Christian theology distinguishes fallibility (as a property of human nature's finitude) from fallenness, which is a result of sin. Dropping the concept of "nature" as metaphysical and essentialist, Heidegger located human existence in the state of fallen man, prescinding from the reality of redemption.

B. The Truth of Existence and Propositional Truth

Heidegger cannot help mentioning, yet he does not highlight, that when Augustine links remembrance, vulnerability, and remorse, he relates the performative truth of existence to ordinary (non-theoretical)

---

50 Heidegger, "Phänomenologische Interpretationen zu Aristoteles," 236–69 at 241: "'Atheistic' not in the sense of a materialism or any similar theory. Any philosophy that is what it is and understands itself, has to know, as the factical How of its life-interpretation (and precisely when in doing so it still has a presentiment of God) that, in religious terms, the wresting back of its life being enacted is a raising the hand against God. Only in this way does it maintain its honor, i.e. in accord with the possibility before God available to it as such; here atheistic conveys: holding oneself free from the misguided state of concernedness that merely discusses religiosity."

51 Heidegger, "Phänomenologische Interpretationen zu Aristoteles," 109, in relation to the passage in *Nicomachean Ethics* II.5 (1006b, 28–34).

52 Heidegger, "Phänomenologische Interpretationen zu Aristoteles," 131–55.

propositional truth: "I have met plenty of people who would gladly deceive others, but no one who wants to be deceived."[53] Augustine dramatizes the truth issue:

> People love truth in such a way that those who love something else wish to regard what they love as truth and, since they would not want to be deceived, are unwilling to be convinced that they are wrong. They are thus led into hatred of the truth for the sake of that very thing which they love under the guise of truth. They love the truth when it enlightens them, but hate it when it accuses them.[54]

In these sentences, since the issue is existential self-knowledge, "truth" here refers to the truth of existence; but this cannot be meaningful if propositional truth does not also play a significant role in the unfolding of the truth of Augustine's existence. We recall how important this ordinary meaning of truth is for him, for example, in the questions he posed to the Manichees about astrology. The evidence adduced in Book VII (6.8–10) regarding the fate of twins born under the same constellation at the same time was conclusive for him. Later on in his story (VII.17.23), his contact with the *Platonici* convinced him that the real is not the same as a body and that the true Logos is the guide for existence. He was distraught because his already habituated will did not allow him to live in the light of the true Logos. In other words, he could not align the truth of his existence with the truth his mind affirmed as true.

Book X meditates on the hindrances to self-knowledge in his life, while showing that these hindrances can only be overcome to the extent that God, who is Truth, reveals Augustine to himself. Augustine's "doing of the truth," therefore, makes finding out the truth in the ordinary sense of correct judgments an integral part of the process of ongoing conversion, and of transcending illusory selves. As Augustine prayed toward the end of Book X:

> You are the Truth, sovereign over all. I did not want to lose you, but in my greed I thought to possess falsehood along with you, just as no one wants to tell lies in such a way that he loses his own sense of what is true. That

---

53 Augustine, *Confessions* X.23.33; 200.
54 Augustine, *Confessions* X.23.34; 201.

was why I lost you, for you did not want to be possessed in consort with a lie.[55]

C. Heidegger's Provocative Ambiguities

Heidegger's notorious insouciance about the significance of truth in the ordinary sense of discovering and affirming truly what is actually so contributes to the view that he, like the deconstructionists and genealogists who follow in his wake, is a relative perspectivist, or a relativist. The concern here is not to settle definitively whether this is so, but only to say that Heidegger is sufficiently equivocal on the issue of propositional truth to spawn a followership that, in the name both of a caricature of propositional truth and of arguments based upon Kant and/or Nietzsche, unambiguously rejects truth in the sense of a verifiable possibility.

The rejection of truth in the ordinary sense – often considered synonymous with "postmodernism" – can be read positively as a thoroughgoing critique of all notions of the truth based on fallaciously extrinsic criteria. It is true that there are no extrinsic criteria for the truth grounded on the "in here" versus "out there" metaphors of a container. Once extrinsicism is abolished, then the profound manner in which the human attainment of propositional truth is conditioned by the more intricate criteria of the truth of existence must be recognized. I would say that this recognition is the hallmark of postmodern hermeneutics.

In his interpretation of Augustine, Heidegger came close to acknowledging the way the acceptance of grace and rejection of sin concretely condition the historical unfolding of human facticity. Perhaps because of the residues of what he believed to be Neoplatonism in Augustine's thinking, especially what he called the untenable "axiologizing" involved in Augustine's thematization of the highest good,[56] Heidegger could not agree with the bishop of Hippo's Christian solution to the problem of existence. Whether his rejection of Christianity is based on a good- or bad-faith opposition to what he later called "ontotheology," it is impossible not to admit that he did turn away from thinking about

---

55 Augustine, *Confessions* X.41.66; 220.
56 Heidegger, "Augustinus und der Neuplatonismus," 286–7.

the ultimate structures of human facticity in terms of sin and grace. At the end of the day, Heidegger conflated finitude and fallenness.

The question, then, is whether this conflation of human finitude and fallenness does not lie at the root of the division between the benign Nietzscheans, such as Gianni Vattimo, and "gloatingly negative" nihilists, such as certain followers of Jacques Derrida and Michel Foucault. Classically, four different senses of negativity can be distinguished: (1) the negation of actuality referred to by the statement "is not" – the nothingness of non-existence, non-occurrence; (2) the negativity of potency, prime matter, or undifferentiated energy; (3) the negativity of finite natures that distinguishes creaturely species from God and from each other; (4) and the negativity related to the objective falsity of sin. When the ambiguity about negativity that unavoidably follows from the confusion of finitude and fallenness is combined with the failure to acknowledge the correct understanding of true judgments, a perverse and often masked openness is abetted by a cunning willingness to confuse all of these distinct meanings of negativity with each other.

IV. Conclusion

Jürgen Habermas referred to the achievement of Hans-Georg Gadamer as the "urbanization of Heidegger."[57] It is true that Gadamer's hermeneutics is more moderate and more philologically astute than Heidegger's. But is it enough to suggest that Gadamer's philosophy is just a taming or domestication of the wilder, more rustic thought of Heidegger? My response to this question is the topic of my second lecture on Hans-Georg Gadamer's contribution to the "hermeneutic revolution."

---

57 See Jürgen Habermas, "Urbanisierung der Heideggerschen Provinz: *Laudatio auf Hans-Georg Gadamer*," in Hans-Georg Gadamer and Jürgen Habermas, *Das Erbe Hegels. Zwei Reden aus Anlaß des Hegel-Preises* (Frankfurt am Main: Suhrkamp Taschenbuch, 1979), 9–31.

2 Hans-Georg Gadamer and the Hermeneutic Revolution

Ich bin … der Überzeugung, Denken und Schulung von anderen im Denken, freie Urteilskraft zu üben und im anderen zu wecken, ist als solches ein eminent politisches Tun. In diesem Sinne glaube ich, daß auch meine eigene Urteilsfähigkeit immer an der Urteil des Anderen und seiner Urteilsfähigkeit ihre Grenze findet und von ihm bereichert wird. Das ist die Seele der Hermeneutik.

Hans-Georg Gadamer,
"Von Lehrenden und Lernenden," 158[1]

I. The Influence on Gadamer of Heidegger's Aristotle Interpretation

Hans-Georg Gadamer always stressed the integral connection between Heidegger's reappropriation of the Aristotelian notion of *praxis* with his own retrieval of Aristotle's critique of Plato's Idea of the Good.[2] That Idea epitomizes the inauthentic *Vorhandenheit* to be resisted and overcome by the hermeneutics of facticity. It becomes Heidegger's model for mistaking the meaning of Being insofar as it projects the answer to the Platonic question about the good into the beyond so that it reflects the contours of a this-worldly already-out-there-now object. Aristotle's analysis of *phronesis* as an *allo genos gnoseos* (i.e., in contradistinction to

---

1 Hans-Georg Gadamer, "Von Lehrenden und Lernenden," *Das Erbe Europas. Beiträge* (Frankfurt: Suhrkamp, 1989), 158.
2 See Hans-Georg Gadamer, "Selbstdarstellung Hans-Georg Gadamer (1975)," *Hermeneutik II. Wahrheit und Methode. Ergänzungen, Register*, Gesammelte Werke 2 (Tübingen: Mohr Siebeck, 1986), 477–508 at 484–7.

techne on the one hand, and to the threesome of *nous*, *sophia*, and *episteme* on the other)[3] becomes the model for the hermeneutics of facticity, serving Heidegger's critique of the forgetfulness of Being in favor of *Vorhandenheit* throughout the history of philosophy. As Gadamer put the issue:

> The elucidation of the modes of being true in Book VI of "Nicomachean Ethics" had for Heidegger this significance above all, that the primacy of judgment, of logic, and of "science" for the understanding of the facticity of human living reached a decisive delimitation in this text. An *allo genos gnoseos* came into its own right, which does not know objects and does not wish to be objective knowledge, but rather intends the clarity proper to factically lived *Dasein*. So besides Aristotle's Ethics the Rhetoric was important for Heidegger, because it knows about pragmata and pathemata – and not about objects.[4]

Phronesis is a habitual sense for the doable, a care for what is practically good here and now, in Isaiah Berlin's words, an "acquaintance with relevant facts of such a kind that it enables those who have it to tell what fits with what; what can be done in given circumstances and what cannot, what means will work in what situations and how far, without necessarily being able to explain how they know this or even what they know." This mode of "trueing" (*aletheuein*), according to Heidegger, cannot be adequately represented either in terms of looking at the already-out-there-now or in terms of producing. The standpoint of producing locates the overall form of Being-in-the-world in the will that proleptically projects the "world" in willing itself. The standpoint of *phronesis* notes that we make preferential choices in light of the *hou heneka* – the "that-for-the-sake-of-which" everything and anything is chosen and done.[5] This contrast between our habitual prudential sense for the doable and the kind of abstract explicitness proper to the logical

---

3 See Aristotle, *Nicomachean Ethics* VI.5 1140a 24ff; VI.9 1141b 33ff.

4 See Hans-Georg Gadamer, "Die religiöse Dimension," *Neuere Philosophie I. Hegel, Husserl, Heidegger*, Gesammelte Werke 3 (Tübingen: Mohr Siebeck, 1987), 308–19 at 312.

5 See Manfred Riedel, "Hermeneutik und Gesprächsdialektik," *Hören auf die Sprache. Der hermeneutische Weg zur praktischen Philosophie* (Frankfurt: Suhrkamp, 1990), 127–8; *Being and Time*'s transposition of this is: "resoluteness" toward oneself, the proleptical projecting of "wanting to have a conscience" that first provides one's ability to be a whole (in the anticipation of death) its full "transparency" (128).

idea of *episteme* signals the radical nature of how starting from Aristotle in the first Freiburg and early Marburg periods helped Heidegger to realize a comprehensive reflection on Being. According to Heidegger, we have to make an *Urentscheidung,* a fundamental option for the "one thing needful," to find our bearings in accord with the mean in the realm of passions and of practical ends. Thus the point of departure for the hermeneutics of facticity as directly inspired by Aristotle is the ethical virtue that both establishes and enables us to be faithful to a decisive orientation. This fixes our basic disposition in relation to the striving and desiring that moves us to action according to the right *logos.*[6]

Being and Time's reappropriation of *phronesis,* however, was ambiguous inasmuch as the anticipation of death replaced the notion of the good implicit in Aristotle and explicit in Plato. It is not altogether clear whether the standpoint of producing holds sway over *Entschlossenheit* (resoluteness). Manfred Riedel thinks that Heidegger grounds

> the roots of the transcendence in practice from the viewpoint of *poiesis* – as if the idea of the good is determined out of the horizon of producing. That motivates the emphasis on the project-character of understanding, the orientation of action by the projecting and ultimately in terms of the self-project of the that-for-the-sake-of-which. The good is displaced back into *Dasein.*[7]

There is a similarity between the resolute facing of death and the *phronimos*'s insight into the good here and now, inasmuch as both the good as the comprehensive end of human living and death can only be known provisionally and *en typo* (sketchily at best). This parallel obscures the differences between *techne* and *phronesis*; the resulting ambiguity perhaps fits into Heidegger's Nietzsche-like atheism. We may interpret Heidegger's exploitation of the open texture of our implicit, tacit, anticipatory knowledge of the good either in Kantian terms as an asymptotic goal; or in the more Nietzschean terms of radical historicism. To the extent that Heidegger follows Nietzsche, we can figure that resoluteness enacts the primacy of self-will. And so Karl

---

6 See Aristotle, *Nicomachean Ethics* II.2 1103b 32, 34; 1106a 1–4; and Riedel, "Seinsverständnis und Sinn für das Tunliche," *Hören auf die Sprache*, 143–5.

7 Riedel, "Hermeneutik und Gesprächsdialektik," *Hören auf die Sprache*, 127.

Löwith connects Heidegger's existential ontology with the "decision-ist" political theory of Carl Schmitt:

> … a decisionism that shifts the "capacity-for-Being-a-whole" of the Dasein that is always one's own to the "totality" of the state that is always one's own. To the self-assertion of one's own Dasein corresponds the self-assertion of political existence, and to "freedom toward death" corresponds the "sacrifice of life" in the political exigency of war. In both cases the principle is the same, namely "facticity," what remains of life when one does away with all life-*content*.[8]

II. Gadamer's Integral Hermeneutics

Hans-Georg Gadamer's reputation became worldwide with the publication in 1960 of his fundamental work, *Wahrheit und Methode* (*Truth and Method*),[9] appearing when he was sixty. Gadamer said he finally forced himself to write that book after so many years because whenever his students had spoken proudly of having been formed by him, they were invariably met with the puzzled question, "Who?" For years they begged him to let the wider world know the teacher they had experienced in those seminars first in Marburg, then in Leipzig (where he had also been Rector under the Communist regime), briefly in Frankfurt, and finally at Heidelberg.[10] So Gadamer spent the vacations of the better part of a decade pulling together notes going back to 1933 to

---

8 Karl Löwith, "The Occasional Decisionism of Carl Schmitt"; "Postscript: The Political Decisionism of Martin Heidegger and Friedrich Gogarten's Theological Decisionism"; and "European Nihilism: Reflections on the Spiritual and Historical background of the European War," *Martin Heidegger and European Nihilism*, ed. Richard Wolin, trans. Gary Steiner (New York: Columbia University, 1995), 137–69, 173–234 at 215.

9 Hans-Georg Gadamer, *Wahrheit und Methode. Grundzüge einer philosophischen Hermeneutik* (Tübingen: Mohr Siebeck, 1960); English translation: *Truth and Method*, 2nd revised ed., trans. and revised by Joel Weinsheimer and Donald G. Marshall (New York: Crossroad, 1991). Throughout, I have used my own translations, not because I judge them to be more adequate, but just for reasons of time.

10 For information on Gadamer's life, see his "Selbstdarstellung Hans-Georg Gadamer" in *Hermeneutik II*, 479–508; and *Philosophische Lehrjahre. Eine Rueckschau* (Frankfurt: Vittorio Klostermann, 1977); English translation: *Philosophical Apprenticeships*, trans. R. Sullivan (Cambridge, MA: MIT Press, 1985), in which the first article mentioned appears under the title "On the Origins of Philosophical Hermeneutics," 178–93.

write a book based upon his experience as an interpreter of what in America have come to be called "Great Books." Heidegger had stunned the world of continental philosophy in his confrontation with the then more famous neo-Kantian philosopher, Ernst Cassirer.[11] It is not surprising then that Gadamer refrained from writing his theory of interpretation in the abstract *de jure* style of Emilio Betti, the contemporary post-Kantian philosopher of the Cassirer school.[12] Gadamer grounded his theory instead on his factual and phenomenologically ostensible practice of interpreting texts, doing history, and appreciating works of art. His own Heidegger-inspired meditation on Aristotle's teaching on *phronesis* became the absolute heart of this project of philosophical hermeneutics.

To be sure, Gadamer took Heidegger's insight into the relevance of the problematic of *phronesis* for human historicity in a less ambiguous direction than did his master. Heidegger's early interpretation of Aristotle's passage, which was about finding the mean in the preferential choice of the good instead of the bad, commented on Aristotle's observation about missing the mark in right action either by excess (*hyperbole*) or defect (*ellipsis*) to the effect that to fall prey to carelessness is to

become hyperbolic and to strengthen a more facile fulfillment and overweening concern, i.e., to maintain and preserve one's *Dasein*. Hyperbolic *Dasein* manifests itself at once as elliptical: it heads away from the difficult, from that which is *monachos*, simple, (without short-cuts), it does not set any end for itself, it will not commit itself to a primal decision, and (be repeatedly) committed to it.[13]

Heidegger later interpreted this issue in the light of *Dasein*'s "capacity-for-Being-a-whole" and in the direction of its eventual resolute choice of itself. Löwith called this move "decisionist," because the ethical context had completely become a background matter.

---

11 See Ernst Cassirer and Martin Heidegger, *Disputa sull'eredità Kantiana. Due documenti (1928 e 1931)*, ed. Riccardo Lazzari (Milan: Edizione Unicopli, 1990).

12 See Emilio Betti, *Die Hermeneutik als allgemeine Methodik der Geisteswissenschaften* (Tübingen: Mohr Siebeck, 1962).

13 Martin Heidegger, *Phänomenologische Interpretationen zu Aristoteles. Einführung in die phänomenologische Forschung* (*Wintersemester* 1921–2), Gesamtausgabe 61, ed. Walter Bröcker and Käte Bröcker-Oltmanns (Frankfurt: Vittorio Klostermann, 1994), 109; cited in Riedel, "Seinsverstänis und Sinn für das Tunliche," *Hören auf die Sprache*, 143–4.

Gadamer did not abandon the ethical context, and stressed instead that there is a *logos* immanent in the *prakton* as apprehended by *phronesis*; and there is enacted a mode of *aletheuein* – a disclosure of the truth in action – that cannot be adequately conceived on the model of theory (i.e., science or theoretical wisdom). Because contingent intelligibility and truth are at stake, in Gadamer's reappropriation of practical wisdom there is no decisionism as ultimately grounded in the arbitrariness of resolute choice. Thus, when Gadamer recalls Heidegger's explication of the five modes of being true (as he calls the dianoetic virtues) in *Nicomachean Ethics* VI, he stresses "an *allo genos gnoseos* which does not know objects and that does not want to be knowledge, but intends the clarity possible to factically lived *Dasein*."[14] Gadamer joins Heidegger in being inspired by the Greek closeness to concrete, factual human life to oppose the pretentions of scientism and the abstractness of neo-Kantian epistemology. But while Heidegger used *praxis* and *phronesis* to interrupt the dominance of propositional truth and apodictic foundationalism (an interruption that became the centerpiece of so-called postmodern philosophers), Gadamer used practical reason to explain the cogency of hermeneutic reason.

How differently Gadamer approached Aristotle's practical philosophy is clear in a 1930 essay entitled "Praktisches Wissen." Gadamer is concerned to show how Aristotle is united with Plato and Socrates in opposition to the Sophists. After reinterpreting the "intellectualist" character of Platonic ethics in reference to several dialogues by explaining Plato's teaching on true usefulness, the transition to Gadamer's treatment of Aristotle begins by saying, "Only friends can give counsel. This is why *synesis* ... is one form of practical-dianoetic virtue in Aristotle."[15] Note that he first mentions the explicitly communicative and other-oriented dimensions of deliberative excellence never elaborated in Heidegger's treatments of Aristotle's analysis of *phronesis*.

For Heidegger Plato's Idea of the Good epitomizes the forgetfulness of Being. For Gadamer, the Platonic "Idea" is neither an intelligible content nor a prefiguring of a law of nature in modern physics, as it was for the neo-Kantians. The hypothesis of ideas is "not so much a 'doctrine'

---

14 Hans-Georg Gadamer, "Heidegger und die Griechen," *Neuere Philosophie I. Hegel, Husserl, Heidegger*, 286.

15 See Hans-Georg Gadamer, "Praktisches Wissen," *Griechische Philosophie I*, Gesammelte Werke 5 (Tübingen: Mohr Siebeck, 1985), 230–48 at 239.

but indicates a direction of inquiry, the development and discussions of whose implications was the task of philosophy, that means, of Platonic dialectic."[16]

> Plato does not pursue politics in accord with the principles of a theory of ideas – just as little did he give lessons in a doctrine of ideas. The path on the heights toward the vision of a place beyond the heavens is one and the same as the path in the depths proper to a care left to oneself about one's own Being. Philosophy is not politics for the reason that Plato believed naïvely in an abstract synthesis of the cosmic and the human good, but because the philosopher and the true statesman live in the same care. In both there must be true knowledge, and that means: they must know the good. But one cannot know the good from a distance and for everybody, but originally for oneself. Only out of this concern for one's own self (the "soul") does there grow true knowledge, whose truths are fruitful, and this persistent concern is philosophy.[17]

Here Gadamer and fellow Platonist and political philosopher, Leo Strauss, seem to agree in opposing Heidegger's exaggeration and caricature of theory in Plato. As Gadamer put it: for Plato, "practical knowledge is not reinterpreted in the theory of ideas; on the contrary, even still in the Socratic mode of practical knowledge, the theory of ideas, the knowledge of everlasting being, is immersed in the concrete knowledge of man."[18] But Gadamer stresses *phronesis* as "the reasonable ability to reflect on what is useful for oneself – namely, for one's own *Existieren* (*EN* 1140a 25, *eu zen*)" in a way that Strauss does not. "Ability to reflect is the only relevant ability, for there is no knowledge of what is good for one's own existing available in advance."[19] Like Strauss, Gadamer is explicit about how practical wisdom as "the sense for oneself and one's own best" is political, embracing the sense for economics, for the politically advisable, for justice, for organization or lawmaking.[20] The practically wise person discovers what is best for himself in what is common to the polis, and insofar as this is true, it is what the polis needs.

---

16 Gadamer, "Selbstdarstellung Hans-Georg Gadamer," 502.
17 Gadamer, "Praktisches Wissen," 239.
18 Gadamer, "Praktisches Wissen," 240.
19 Gadamer, "Praktisches Wissen," 241.
20 Gadamer, "Praktisches Wissen," 243.

Gadamer differs from Heidegger in specifying the role of *nous* or intelligence in the exercise of practical wisdom as a "seeking and deliberating resolution" of the issue: what is to be done? It has to will the end, the ultimate good as goal of action which is grasped without demonstration; and it has to let the proximate means for fulfilling the goal occur to it in the particular situation here and now. The intelligibility grasped by it is not something given, but something to be done that enables the achievement of the good.

Whereas Heidegger equated practical wisdom with (a later notion of) conscience and then isolated it, Gadamer brings out that precisely because sound judgment involves a performative deliberation with oneself about one's own affairs, it implies the ability to take counsel or deliberate with others and understand their practical judgments. *Synesis* is the ability to understand by which we follow others as they tell us about their deliberations about what is best for them by applying our own knowledge in the practical sphere to the situation of the other. "Only when one puts oneself in the position of the other and inquires into what is best for oneself does one have the understanding and judgment for the other that is required."[21] This communicative dimension of practical wisdom makes it the hermeneutical virtue *par excellence*.

Thus, for Gadamer, if the paradigm of the hermeneutics of facticity as the key to the analysis of *Dasein* is sound judgment, it realizes itself discursively in existential dialectic. A central passage in Plato's *Republic* (521c 5–8) puts what is at stake in dialectic: "This ought not to be so easy and trivial as the spinning of a shard, but it is the conversion of the soul [*psyches periagoge*] from the day that is like night to the real day – the way out toward being as such, what we call genuine philosophy." For Gadamer the model role of *phronesis* in discovering the one thing needful time after time is similar to the primacy of the question in true dialectic: in understanding every formulated and affirmed answer, we are drawn into a further question. When dialectic as the human capacity to hold a conversation and give a reasonable account moves to the center of the hermeneutics of facticity, then fidelity to the idea of the good means being faithful to one's questions all along the line. *Dasein*'s self-understanding in terms of the highest possibility of Being becomes,

---

21 Gadamer, "Praktisches Wissen," 245–6.

as Gadamer put it in his Heidegger-inspired reconstruction of Plato's dialectic, the being-in-the-truth of human *Dasein*.[22]

III. Gadamer and the Hermeneutics of Facticity

Barth and Heidegger had started a revolution in reading the originative classics of Western culture by making us realize that the interpretation of any classic text is dependent upon our concrete solution to the problem of living, that is, on our asking and answering the question about the right way to live, and thereby of settling personally what is of concern to us. It fell to Gadamer's *Truth and Method* to explain the philosophical basis and implications of this revolution. This explanation embraces: (1) a critique of aesthetic consciousness in the light of an ontology of the work of art;[23] (2) a critique of historical consciousness in the light of an ontology of *Verstehen* and of effective-historical consciousness;[24] and (3) an ontology of language.[25]

Although Gadamer used Heidegger's hermeneutics of facticity to overcome aesthetic, Romantic, and historical consciousness,[26] he nevertheless stands in an odd relationship to Heidegger. For example, in *Unterwegs zur Sprache* (1959) Heidegger explained that after the *Kehre* the entire vocabulary in *Being and Time*'s analysis of facticity had had to be abandoned, because the whole enterprise of the hermeneutics of facticity was still too imbued with the Husserlian and Idealist starting point of transcendental subjectivity, explicit self-consciousness (reflective self-awareness), and self-possession. After his "turning" (in the early 1930s), Heidegger reached the conclusion that all conventional philosophical conceptualities had been tainted by the biases of one or another "language of metaphysics," which he strove to overcome.[27] He felt he was in what Gadamer calls a "linguistic emergency" (*Sprachnot*).[28]

---

22 See Hans-Georg Gadamer, *Platos dialektische Ethik* (Hamburg: Meiner, 1984), 60–2.

23 Gadamer, *Wahrheit und Methode*, 1–161; *Truth and Method*, 1–169.

24 Gadamer, *Wahrheit und Methode*, 162–360; *Truth and Method*, 171–379.

25 Gadamer, *Wahrheit und Methode*, 361–465; *Truth and Method*, 381–491.

26 Gadamer, *Wahrheit und Methode*, 250–61; *Truth and Method*, 265–71.

27 For an intellectual biography of Heidegger, see Otto Pöggeler, *Der Denkweg Martin Heideggers*, 1st ed. (Pfullingen: Neske, 1963; 2nd ed. 1983 includes the important *Nachwort*), 319–55.

28 Hans-Georg Gadamer, "Die Sprache der Metaphysik," in the *Heideggers Wege* section of *Neuere Philosophie I. Hegel, Husserl, Heidegger*, 229–37.

Gadamer disagreed with him. He did not think there is such a "language of metaphysics" whose vocabulary is automatically "used up" or necessarily caught in the strictures of its past usages, because at root any language is dialogical. This means that even the so-called language of metaphysics only makes sense in the actual past usages of it, and so in light of the questions being asked and answered in it. For Gadamer, recovering those questions liberates language by de-rigidifying and de-scholasticizing it; re-asking the questions to which linguistic statements are intended to be answers helps us realize that language plays the role of a horizon that frames our asking and answering of questions. In genuine philosophy, such inquiry cannot dry up or freeze. Language's true point of access is the interplay of questions and answers.[29]

This means that Gadamer could take up Heidegger's hermeneutics of facticity and, in the context of his own motivating questions about art and the historical and humane sciences (the *Geisteswissenschaften*, *lettres*, humanities), use it even to convey the chief point of the "turning" in a way that would be accessible to phenomenological verification. In generalizing Heidegger's hermeneutical breakthrough, Gadamer's emphasis was this: "Man is what he is in constantly affecting the world and in constantly experiencing the effect of the world upon himself. Not in the isolated freedom of being-over-against, but in daily relation-to-world, in letting oneself in for the conditionings of the world does man win his own self. So, too, does he gain the right position of knowing."[30] This utterly harmonizes with the "post-turning" Heidegger, who spoke about *Ereignis* and *Lichtung*, of *Es gibt* ..., of language as the house of Being and the human being as the shepherd of Being.

Gadamer was convinced that the hermeneutics of facticity was correct to situate interpretation within a horizon of caring. Heidegger's insight regarding the ubiquity of language, namely, that human beings live within language rather as the air they breathe than as an instrument they deploy at will, was also absolutely right: people are human in existing conversationally in relation to everything that is.[31] In getting to the bottom of the relationship between truth as "dependent upon

---

29 Hans-Georg Gadamer, "Zwischen Phänomenologie und Dialektik," *Hermeneutik II*, 3–23 at 10–12.

30 Hans-Georg Gadamer, "Goethe und Philosophie," *Kleine Schriften II. Interpretationen* (Tübingen: Mohr Siebeck, 1967), 82–96 at 94.

31 Gadamer, *Wahrheit und Methode*, 340–60; *Truth and Method*, 358–79.

the temporal-historical movement proper to *Dasein*" and reason as "the self-empowered capacity to perceive truth and make it binding," Gadamer confirmed that reason is "made possible by what it is not."[32] But he did not want us to draw the implication from the experience of reason's and truth's dependency or conditionedness that they are mere "tools in the service of a higher, unconscious, and irresponsible power ..."[33] For Gadamer "it is the essence of our reason and our spirit to be capable of thinking against what is to our own advantage, to be able to detach ourselves from our needs and interests and to bind ourselves to the law of reality."[34] Reason is the capacity to acknowledge reality even against our own self-interest: "To be taught, even against our own subjectively certain convictions – that is the way of mediation of authentically historical truth."[35]

In describing his strategy in *Truth and Method*, Gadamer has written: "It made sense to bring the game-play of language into closer connection with the game-play of art in which I had contemplated the parade example of the hermeneutical. Now to consider the universal linguistic constitution of our experience of the world in terms of the model of game-play certainly does suggest itself."[36] Indeed, when people first learn to speak, it is not so much a learning process as a "game of imitation and exchange." As Gadamer tells us, "In the receptive child's drive to imitate the forming of sounds, the enjoyment in such forming of sounds is paired with the illumination of meaning. No one can really answer in a reasonable manner the question when their first understanding of meaning occurred." Theologian Austin Farrer put this beautifully when he wrote:

Our humanity is itself a cultural heritage; the talking animal is talked into talk by those who talk at him ... His mind is not at first his own, but the echo of his elders. The echo turns into a voice, the painted portrait steps

---

32 Hans-Georg Gadamer, "Über die Ursprünglichkeit der Philosophie: 1. Die Bedeutung der Philosophie für die neue Erziehung, 2. Das Verhältnis der Philosophie zu Kunst und Wissenschaft," *Kleine Schriften I. Hermeneutik* (Tübingen: Mohr Siebeck, 1967), 11–38 at 17 and 19.
33 Gadamer, "Über die Ursprünglichkeit der Philosophie," 18.
34 Gadamer, "Über die Ursprünglichkeit der Philosophie," 20.
35 Gadamer, "Über die Ursprünglichkeit der Philosophie," 21.
36 Gadamer, "Zwischen Phänomenologie und Dialektik," 5.

down from the frame, and each of us becomes himself. Yet by the time we are aware of our independence, we are what others have made us. We can never unweave the web to the very bottom ... Nor is it only parental impresses of which we are the helpless victims. How many persons, how many conditions have made us what we are; and, in making us so, may have undone us.[37]

Gadamer's claim that we learn everything in language games has nothing to do with the subjective attitude of "just playing" or not being serious. In fact, game-play in general only gets going when players get serious, in the sense of not holding themselves back as "just playing" and not really serious.[38] Language for Gadamer is not a set of tools such as vocabulary, grammar, syntax, and so on, but language-in-use. Language is used in conversation. Because conversation has the structure of game-play, language exists concretely as language games.[39] As Gadamer tells us: "The life of language consists ... in the constant further playing out of the game we started when we learned to speak ... It is this continuously played game in which the mutual life together of people is played out."[40]

Conversation is structured as game-play, and so has the spirit of game-play with its characteristic "lightness, freedom, and the luck of success – of being fulfilling, and of fulfilling those who are playing."[41] This is evident when we achieve mutual understanding or agreement:

Mutual understanding happens by the fact that talk stands up against talk, but does not remain static. Instead, in talking to each other we pass over into the imaginative world of the other, we as it were open ourselves up to them, and they do so to us. So we play into each other until the game

---

37 Austin Farrer, *Love Almighty and Ills Unlimited* (London: Collins/Fontana, 1967/1966), 114.

38 Hans-Georg Gadamer, "Mensch und Sprache," *Hermeneutik II*, 146–54 at 152; English translation: "Man and Language (1966)," *Philosophical Hermeneutics*, trans. and ed. David E. Linge (Berkeley: University of California Press, 1976), 59–68 at 66.

39 So Gadamer finds himself in agreement with Wittgenstein, who hit upon the same insight completely independently. See Hans-Georg Gadamer, "Die phänomenologische Bewegung," *Kleine Schriften III. Idee und Sprache* (Tübingen: J.C.B. Mohr, 1972), 150–89, esp. 185–9; "The Phenomenological Movement (1963)," *Philosophical Hermeneutics*, 130–81, esp. 173–7.

40 Gadamer, "Mensch und Sprache," 152; "Man and Language," 66.

41 Gadamer, "Mensch und Sprache," 152; "Man and Language," 66.

of giving and taking, the conversation proper, begins. No one can deny that in such real conversation there is something of chance, the favor of surprise, finally also of lightness, yes, even of elevation, which pertains to the nature of game-play. And truly the elevation of conversation is experienced not as a loss of self-possession, but, even without our actually attending to it, as an enrichment of ourselves.[42]

As we come together in conversation, and are now ... led on further by the conversation, then what is determinative is no longer people as holding themselves in reserve or as willing to be open, but the law of the subject matter about which the conversation is going on, which releases speech and response and finally plays everyone into itself. So wherever a conversation has been successful, afterwards everyone is, as we say, filled with it. The play of speech and response gets played out further in the inner conversation of the soul with itself, as Plato so beautifully named thinking.[43]

Focusing on the role of conversation in human life and thought keeps philosophy from being narrowed down to either the phenomenology of perception or logical preoccupations with concepts, propositions, and inferences. The conversational point of departure lets one get back to the roots of all answers in questions. Gadamer celebrates the great British historian and philosopher R.G. Collingwood for having first articulated "the logic of question and answer."[44] Gadamer went beyond Collingwood to show how, when that "logic" is retrieved concretely in dialectic or friendly conversation, it is structured as a game, not just because understanding itself occurs and grows in the to and fro of question and answer; but, as he rather unconventionally observes, this "happens from the side of the things themselves. The subject matter 'yields' questions."[45]

What we are doing when we are truly conversing is understanding and interpreting. Both words in English can be used to correctly translate Gadamer's key term *Verstehen*, which in German covers both the act of insight but also the act of articulation or *Auslegung*, by which we talk to ourselves, laying out in language what we actually understand.

---

42 Hans-Georg Gadamer, "Zur Problematik des Selbstverständnisses," *Hermeneutik II*, 131; "On the Problem of Self-Understanding (1962)," *Philosophical Hermeneutics*, 56–7.
43 Gadamer, "Mensch und Sprache," 152; "Man and Language," 66.
44 Gadamer, *Wahrheit und Methode*, 351–60; *Truth and Method*, 369–79.
45 Gadamer, "Zwischen Phänomenologie und Dialektik," 6.

"Interpretation belongs to the essential unity of understanding. Whatever is said to us must be so received by us that it speaks and finds a response in our own words and in our own language."[46]

That understanding for Gadamer always involves interpretation is preeminently true in understanding texts:

> Whoever wants to understand a text always performs a projection. We project a meaning of the whole, as soon as a first meaning is manifest in the text. Such a meaning in turn only becomes manifest because one is already reading the text with certain expectations of a determinate meaning. Understanding what is there to be understood consists in working out such a projection which of course gets constantly revised by what emerges in penetrating its meaning further ... Any revision of the projection exists in virtue of the possibility of casting up a new projection; ... rival projections toward the elaboration can be generated one after the other, until the unity of sense is fixed unequivocally; ... the interpretation is initiated with anticipatory notions that get replaced by more adequate ones: precisely this ongoing newly-projecting that constitutes the movement of meaning proper to understanding and interpreting is the process that Heidegger describes.[47]

Whenever we read a text, "there is no author present at the discussion as an answering partner, and no subject matter present which can be so or otherwise. The text as a work stands on its own." Does this mean that there is no dialogue? Not at all.

> It seems that here the dialectic of question and answer, insofar as it has any place at all, is only available in one direction, which means from the side of the one seeking to understand the work of art, who questions it and who is called into question by it, and who tries to listen for the answer of the work. As the person one is, one may, just like anyone thinking, be the inquirer and responder at once, in the same manner as happens in a real conversation between two people. But this dialogue of the understanding reader with oneself surely does not seem to be a dialogue with the text, which is fixed and to that extent is finished. Or is this really how it is? Or is there an already finished text given at all?

---

46 Gadamer, "Zur Problematik des Selbstverständnisses," 131; "On the Problem of Self-Understanding," 57.

47 Hans-Georg Gadamer, "Vom Zirkel des Verstehens," *Hermeneutik II*, 57–65 at 59–60.

In this case the dialectic of question and answer does not come to a standstill ... The reception of a poetic work, whether it be by our outer ear or by that inner ear that listens attentively when we are reading, presents itself as a circular movement in which answers rebound into further questions and provoke new answers. This motivates our abiding with the work of art, of whatever kind it may be. Abiding is obviously the authentic characteristic in the experience of art. A work of art never gets exhausted.[48]

This is where Gadamer locates the processes of translation in the sense of construing the meaning of something in one language into the terms of another language. We might say that translation is just an exaggerated case of what happens as we make our way through life in general. "Human living as conversational" means that we are constantly making sense of what presents itself in the foreground of our experience in terms of our linguistic horizon. We do this by trying to find the right word with which to articulate and communicate our experience (both to ourselves and to others), by a process of trial and error, and we rarely if ever achieve a stage of definitiveness beyond all provisionality. As Gadamer tells us:

If any model can really illustrate the tensions residing in understanding and interpretation, it is that of translation. In it the strange or alien is made our own as strange or alien, and that means neither that it is just permitted to stay alien, nor that it is constructed in one's language by a sheer imitation of its very strangeness; but in [translation] the horizons of past and present are merged in an ongoing movement as it constitutes the very nature of understanding and interpretation [*Verstehen*].[49]

IV. Gadamer and Integral Christian Hermeneutics

Rowan Williams suggests that both Ludwig Wittgenstein and Dietrich Bonhoeffer converged in differing ways on Gadamer's view of human living described above:

Wittgenstein and Bonhoeffer more clearly presuppose that to interpret the symbolic, linguistic, and behavioral complex that "addresses" us in

---

48 Gadamer, "Zwischen Phänomenologie und Dialektik," 9.
49 Hans-Georg Gadamer, "Hermeneutik," *Hermeneutik II*, 425–36 at 436.

the human world is to have one's own pattern of speech and action conditioned (not determined) by it, to be provoked (called forward) by the ways in which it touches, confirms, resonates, or questions what we have done and said. To interpret means interweaving a text (words and actions, words *and* actions) with our human project, acquiring a partner, a pole of difference that refuses to allow our "project" to return endlessly on itself, as if it were indeed generated from a well of unsullied interiority, "self-consciousness."[50]

Like Williams, Gadamer recognizes that life proceeds by interpretation in a process in which the subject is displaced from the center, so that human beings become themselves by playing into a direction of meaning and value that is moving in and through the interplay of subjects with the world. The game-play structure of life comes into its own perhaps more strikingly in the Christian experience of grace and faith than in the experience of art (though there is no need necessarily to separate the two kinds of experience). As Williams phrases the issue of achieving human wholeness "in ... belonging to God, a wholeness achieved in trust or hope rather than analysis":

My own identity's "ungraspable" quality thus becomes not an elusive level of interiority, but the unknowable presence of the creator's absolute affirmation, the mysteriousness of grace, past, present, and future, not of the "true self" as a hidden thing. My unity as a person is always out of my field of vision (I can't see my own fact), just as the divine condition for there being fields of vision at all, for there being a world or worlds, is out of my field of vision (I can't see my own origin).[51]

In parallel fashion Gadamer states:

All understanding in the end is self-understanding, but not in the mode of a prior or finally achieved self-possession. For this self-understanding is always realized only in the understanding of a subject matter, and does not have the character of a free self-realization. The self that we are does

---

50 Rowan Williams, "Suspicion of Suspicion: Wittgenstein and Bonhoeffer," *The Grammar of the Heart: New Essays in Moral Philosophy and Theology*, ed. Richard H. Bell (San Francisco: Harper & Row, 1988), 36–53 at 48.
51 Williams, "Suspicion of Suspicion: Wittgenstein and Bonhoeffer," 43.

not possess itself. One could better put it that instead it happens. And that
is what theology really says, that faith is just such an event, in which a
new man is founded. And it says further that it is the Word that needs to
be believed and understood and by which we overcome the abysmal lack
of self-knowledge in which we live.[52]

Gadamer has transposed Bultmann's ideas about self-understanding
(as possibly still too tainted by an idealistic subjectivism and existentialism) into the framework of the game-play structure of human life, and
from this perspective considered the relationship of Christian faith to
understanding and interpretation in human life.

Whatever is said to us we must receive into ourselves so that it speaks to
us and finds a response in our own words in our own language. This holds
utterly true for the text of proclamation that cannot really be understood if
it does not appear as being said to our very own selves. Here it is the sermon in which the understanding and interpretation of the text attains its
full reality. Neither the explicating commentary nor the exegetical labors
of the theologians, but the sermon stands in the immediate service of the
proclamation inasmuch as it not only mediates the understanding of what
the Holy Scripture tells us, but witnesses to it at the same time. However,
the proper fullness of understanding lies not in the sermon as such, but
in the manner in which it is accepted as a call that impinges on each one
of us.[53]

Gadamer has also criticized Bultmann's overemphasis upon the historical-critical mediation of New Testament texts. Once he half-jokingly
told me, "Bultmann forgets that the books of the New Testament are not
books in the ordinary sense of the term." He was agreeing with Franz
Overbeck and his friend and colleague Helmut Kuhn that these texts
belong to the genre of *Urliteratur*. This implies that "if we understand
under the meaning of the text, the *mens auctoris*, i.e., the 'verifiable' horizon of understanding of any given Christian writer, then we accord the

---

52 Gadamer, "Zur Problematik des Selbstverständnisses," 130; "On the Problem of Self-
   Understanding," 55.
53 Gadamer, "Zur Problematik des Selbstverständnisses," 131–2; "On the Problem
   of Self-Understanding," 57–8. This is a point also made powerfully by Bernard
   Lonergan in his essay, "Pope John's Intention," *A Third Collection: Papers by Bernard
   Lonergan, SJ*, ed. Frederick E. Crowe (Mahwah, NJ: Paulist Press, 1985), 224–38.

authors of the New Testament a false honor. Their proper honor ought to lie in the fact that they announce the tidings about something that surpasses the horizon of their own understanding – even if they happen to be named John or Paul."[54] Gadamer appeals to a similar aspect of "hearing the Word" in elucidating how language works in terms of the concrete experience of word:

> When I say "word" [*das Wort*], I do not mean the word whose plural are the words [*die Woerter*] as they stand in the dictionary. Nor do I mean the word whose plural are the words [*die Worte*] which with other words go to make up the context of a statement. Rather I mean the word that is a *singularetantum*. That means the word that strikes one, the word one allows to be said to oneself, the word that enters into a determinate and unique life-situation; and it is good to be reminded that behind this *singularetantum* stands ultimately the linguistic usage of the New Testament.[55]

I would like to point out three aspects of what Gadamer has written about the Christian message in the New Testament as an instance of *Urliteratur*. First, the authors of the holy scriptures "present themselves as faithful witnesses of an authentic tradition which begins with the first community and with the immediate witnesses"; and so they are less authors, strictly speaking, than intermediate witnesses. For Gadamer, not every religious message counts as witness, but witness is the distinguishing mark of the Christian message or gospel. It witnesses to the passion of Jesus and the resurrection promise of salvation. "It is an authentic witness because it refers to a particular event: the death of Jesus on the cross. It is a human being who suffers the death of a criminal and who, in full awareness of being the Son of God and of being God, insists on the title 'Son of Man' and accepts the fate of creatures."[56]

Second, Gadamer brings out that the New Testament has the special status of "eminent text." There are three categories of such texts: (1) *announcements* of the kind common in law, such as promulgated

---

54 Hans-Georg Gadamer, "Die Marburger Theologie," *Neuere Philosophie I. Hegel, Husserl, Heidegger*, 197–208 at 207; English translation: "Martin Heidegger and Marburg Theology (1964)," *Philosophical Hermeneutics*, 198–212 at 210.

55 Hans-Georg Gadamer, "Sprache und Verstehen," *Hermeneutik II*, 184–98 at 192. See also ch. 5, 260–1.

56 Hans-Georg Gadamer, "Témoignage et Affirmation," *La testimonianza*, ed. E. Castelli (Rome: Istituto di studi filosofici, 1972), 161–5 at 164.

verdicts or statutes; (2) *affirmations* as are made in poetry (works of art "made out of" language) on the one hand, and philosophy on the other; (3) *addresses* as in religious texts, and especially the scriptures and the preaching/hearing by which they are applied down the ages. For Gadamer an "eminent text" is one which "capture(s) a purely linguistic action and so possesses an eminent relationship to writing and writtenness. In it language is present in such a way that its cognitive relationship to the merely given outside the text disappears just as much as is its communicative relation in the sense of the one being addressed."[57] As an eminent text, according to Gadamer, the Christian scripture has a normativity that is virtually equivalent to what is justified by the idea of inspiration:

> The primordial question to which the text has to be understood as an answer has here ... by reason of its origin an inherent supremacy and freedom ... The classical text is "telling" only when it speaks "primordially," i.e., "as if it were spoken just to me alone." That does not at all imply that what speaks in this way is measured against an extra-historical concept of norm. Just the contrary: what speaks in this way thereby posits a standard. Herein lies the problem. The primordial question to which the text is to be understood as an answer in such a case *lays claim to an identity of meaning which always has already mediated the distance between presence and past.*[58]

The "eminent text" therefore entails "an exceptional mode of historical being, the historical enactment of preservation which – in ever renewed corroboration – allows something to be true."[59] It is proper to such a work to have "an identifiability, a repeatability, and a worthiness to be repeated" that only can be predicated of something that once functioned in the past and continues to function in any succeeding temporal context in an originative way. This means that it is normative; but it also becomes constitutive of ourselves. Luther saw this when he said that the gospel has a *pro me* character. So when we come into contact with the gospel as an eminent text, we realize our "immediate and binding affinity" to a reality which "as past is at once unattainable and presently

---

57 Hans-Georg Gadamer, "Nachwort zur 3. Auflage (1972)," *Hermeneutik II*, 449–78 at 475; *Truth and Method*, 551–79 at 576.
58 Gadamer, "Nachwort zur 3. Auflage (1972)," 476, 577–8.
59 Gadamer, *Wahrheit und Methode*, 271; *Truth and Method*, 287.

relevant."[60] The gospel, "far from being evidence documenting something bygone that we may not care to interpret and make our own, is already speaking to us and to every person in history in a way that is uniquely appropriate to that particular place and time."[61] This means that as an eminent text the gospel has an autonomous meaning that is self-interpreting and self-authenticating.[62]

Third, Gadamer stresses about the Christian message that the proclamation of the good news and the messianic promise do not have the status of a symbolic form of recognition, common to all religious traditions. Instead, in the context of the incarnation and Easter message, the meaning of the Christian message's "This is you" has the status of *sign*. "A sign is something only given to one who is ready to accept it as such."[63] According to Gadamer, "the uniqueness of the gospel message lies in the fact that it must be accepted against all expectation and hope," because "the claim of the Christian message – and this is what gives it its exclusivity – is that it alone has really overcome death through the proclamation of the representative suffering and death of Jesus as a redemptive act."[64] As Gadamer radically put it:

It is not the infinite wealth of life possibilities that is encountered in [the Christian] "this is you," but rather the extreme poverty of the *Ecce homo*. The expression must be given a quite different emphasis here: "this is you" – a man helplessly exposed to suffering and death. It is precisely in the face of this infinite withholding of happiness that the Easter message is to become Good News.[65]

As a sign, Gadamer tells us, this "is not something that takes the place of seeing, for what distinguishes it precisely from all reports or from its

---

60 Gadamer, *Wahrheit und Methode*, 273; *Truth and Method*, 289.

61 Gadamer, *Wahrheit und Methode*, 274; *Truth and Method*, 289.

62 As Gadamer effectively put it in *Wahrheit und Methode*: "The classical ... is as Hegel says, 'that which signifies itself and so also interprets itself'. – Ultimately this means: the classical is what preserves itself, *because* it signifies itself and interprets itself ..." (273–4; *Truth and Method*, 289).

63 Hans-Georg Gadamer, "Aesthetic and Religious Experience," *The Relevance of the Beautiful and Other Essays*, ed. Robert Bernasconi, trans. Nicholas Walker (Cambridge: Cambridge University Press, 1986), 140–53 at 152.

64 Gadamer, "Aesthetic and Religious Experience," 153, 151.

65 Gadamer, "Aesthetic and Religious Experience," 151.

opposite, silence, is the fact that what is shown is only accessible to the one who looks for himself and actually sees something there."[66]

V. Conclusion

We have seen how Gadamer's thought used basic insights of Heidegger to fashion not merely a tamed version of Heidegger's thought, but to work out an integral hermeneutics. This hermeneutics decisively surpasses the subjectivism and Kantianism of theologian and exegete Rudolf Bultmann's subjectivist appropriation of Heidegger's thought, and it also overcomes all rationalism in philosophy, all rationalist separations of reason and faith. For Gadamer, philosophy is always a kind of *fides ex auditu*, where faith refers both to the beliefs of one's culture, society, and religion in the sense of the understandings and judgments of fact and value embodied in our concrete traditions, and to the illumination of reason by love, in the sense of Augustine's *pondus meum amor meus, eo feror quocumque feror* (my weight is my love; by it I move wherever I move).[67] And so Gadamer cannot be reduced to an "epigone of Heidegger." He is a master in his own right.

The one, however, who developed the second, Augustinian or even Pascalian sense of faith more than it was given to Gadamer to accomplish was the Canadian philosopher and theologian, Bernard Lonergan. Our next talk(s) turn to his still largely unknown contribution to the "hermeneutic revolution."

---

66 Gadamer, "Aesthetic and Religious Experience," 152.
67 Augustine, *Confessions* XIII.9.10.

3 Gadamer and Lonergan on Augustine's *Verbum Cordis* – The Heart of Postmodern Hermeneutics

Daß nicht Sätze, nicht die unwiderleglich Behauptung und nicht das siegreiche Gegenargument Wahrheit verbürgen, sondern daß es auf eine andere Art der Bewährung ankommt die dem Einzelnen nicht möglich ist, wies mir meine Aufgabe zu, am Anderen die eigenen Grenzen nicht so sehr zu erkennen, als ein paar Schritte weit zu überwinden.

H.-G. Gadamer, "Die Aufgabe der Philosophie," 167[1]

If you wish to be of service, it is necessary (1) that you "exist" yourself, so that it is not a matter of the blind leading the blind, and (2) that you try to effect a conversion in others rather than to prove them wrong.

B. Lonergan, *The Ontological and Psychological Constitution of Christ*, 23[2]

I. The Hermeneutic Notion of Consciousness

Central to Heidegger's breakthrough to hermeneutic philosophy is the dismantling of phenomenology as propped on egology. The hermeneutic analysis of the "I am" in Augustine's *Confessions* acknowledges that the act of existence proper to the human being as a unity, an identity, and a whole is neither primordially accessible, nor imaginable, nor

---

1 H.-G. Gadamer, "Die Aufgabe der Philosophie," *Das Erbe Europas. Beiträge* (Frankfurt: Suhrkamp, 1989), 167.
2 Bernard Lonergan, *The Ontological and Psychological Constitution of Christ*, Collected Works of Bernard Lonergan 7, ed. Michael G. Shields and Frederick E. Crowe (Toronto: University of Toronto Press, 2002), 23.

correctly conceivable in the mode of a perceptual object.[3] In Augustine's terms as recovered by Heidegger, the human ego's *esse* (act of existing) is enacted by a preconceptual, pre-reflective *nosse* (the performative self-awareness concomitant with human agency) and *amare* (the primary orientation or connaturality of the will's desire for the good).[4]

Many years after *Being and Time* and after the reception of *Wahrheit und Methode*, Hans-Georg Gadamer frequently mentioned Heidegger's dissatisfaction with his continued use of the term *Bewußtsein* as in the term *wirkungsgeschichtliches Bewußtsein*:[5] it was still too neo-Kantian, too Cartesian, too weighed down by the "subjective objectivism of modernity." Gadamer ran the risk of using "consciousness" to express just what the early Heidegger had taught him, because it was faithful to Heidegger who, on the way to *Sein und Zeit*, applied the scholastic expressions, *actus exercitus* and *actus signatus*, to retrieve the innate, performative reflexivity proper to human presence-to-self-in-the-world that endows human beings with *conscientia*.[6] After the *Kehre*, Heidegger dropped all such references, while Gadamer continued to use them creatively.

Consciousness in Gadamer's usage, therefore, refers to the same reality Augustine spoke of in terms of *nosse*. This usage has been further confirmed in Salvino Biolo's exhaustive research into the meaning of the cognates of *nosci/noscor* in the *opera omnia*.[7] One chapter is entitled, "The conscious psychological subject is the 'ego-mens' as 'memoria-sui.'"[8] Without any dependence on Heidegger, Biolo makes explicit what remained implicit in Heidegger's pioneering 1921 Augustine interpretation.

---

3   Bernard Lonergan, *Verbum: Word and Idea in Aquinas*, Collected Works of Bernard Lonergan 2, ed. Frederick E. Crowe and Robert M. Doran (Toronto: University of Toronto Press, 1997), 187–8, 212–14; originally, the articles in this volume appeared in *Theological Studies* 7 (1946): 349–92; 8 (1947): 35–79; 8 (1947): 404–44; 10 (1949): 3–40; and 10 (1949): 359–93.

4   See Martin Heidegger, "Anhang II, 8. Das Sein der Selbst [Schlußstück der Vorlesung]," *Phänomenologie des religiösen Lebens*, Gesamtausgabe 60 (Frankfurt: Vittorio Klostermann, 1995), 298–9.

5   See also Rod Coltman, *The Language of Hermeneutics: Gadamer and Heidegger in Dialogue* (Albany: SUNY Press, 1998), 2 and the anecdotes repeated at note 4, 127.

6   See Gadamer's commentary in "Die phänomenologische Bewegung," *Neuere Philosophie I. Hegel, Husserl, Heidegger*, Gesammelte Werke 3 (Tübingen: Mohr Siebeck, 1987), 127.

7   Salvino Biolo, SJ, *L'autocoscienza in S. Agostino*. Analecta Gregoriana (Rome: Editrice Pontificia Università Gregoriana, 2000).

8   Biolo, *L'autocoscienza in S. Agostino*, 80–107.

Gadamer's willingness to use the word "consciousness" in a non-Kantian way and to place it at the center of the hermeneutic problematic constitutes a remarkable confluence with the thought of Bernard Lonergan. Recently French thinkers Michel Henry,[9] Jean-Luc Marion,[10] Marc Richir,[11] and Jean Greisch have also acknowledged this performative dimension of consciousness or awareness.

Hermeneutic consciousness reveals philosophical hermeneutics as a phenomenology of language rather than a phenomenology of perception. Jean Greisch's explication of Heidegger's turn from Husserlian phenomenology contrasts Heidegger's and Jacques Derrida's manners of deconstruction. He cites Jean Grondin, who has laid great emphasis on Gadamer's retrieval of Augustine's theory of the *verbum cordis* in the *De trinitate*.[12] Augustine, in seeking a created analogy for divine processions, discovered an internal procession within the *mens* as consciousness when human beings move from sense perception to human speech or writing. For Derrida, in his deconstruction of Saussure and Husserl, this discovery is logocentric. According to Greisch, Gadamer on the *verbum internum*, as opposed to Derrida's attack on interiority in *Speech and Phenomena* and in *Grammatology*, is consistent with Heidegger's hermeneutic breakthrough.

II. The Soul's Dialogue with Itself

In Part III of *Wahrheit und Methode* Gadamer unfolds a history of the idea of language.[13] The section "Language and Logos" registers Gadamer's reservations about the "logocentric" forgetfulness of human language because of its preoccupation with the world of theory (where

---

9 Michel Henry, *Phénoménologie matérielle* (Paris: PUF, 1990) and *Généalogie de la psychanalyse* (Paris: PUF, 1985).

10 Jean-Luc Marion, "Does the *Cogito* Affect Itself? Generosity and Phenomenology: Remarks on Michel Henry's Interpretation of the Cartesian *Cogito*," *Cartesian Questions: Method and Metaphysics* (Chicago: University of Chicago, 1999), 96–117.

11 Marc Richir, *L'expérience du penser. Phénoménologie, philosophie, mythologie* (Grenoble: Jérôme Millon, 1996).

12 See Jean Greisch, citing Jean Grondin, *L'universalité de l'herméneutique*, ix–xi, in *L'Arbre de vie et l'Arbre du savoir. Les racines phénoménologiques de l'herméneutique Heideggerienne (1919–1923)* (Paris: du Cerf, 2000), at 94 and 131.

13 Hans-Georg Gadamer, "Prägung des Begriffs 'Sprache' durch die Denkgeschichte des Abendlandes," *Wahrheit und Methode. Grundzüge einer philosophischen Hermeneutik*, 2nd ed. (Tübingen: Mohr Siebeck, 1965), 383–414.

terminology and the logical control of meaning reign).[14] The section "Language and Verbum" then turns to consider the hitherto unexploited richness of Christian reflection on the mysteries of the Incarnate Word and the Trinity.[15]

Jesus says in John 8:42: "If God were your Father you would love me, for *ego ... ek tou Theou exelthon*: I have come forth from the Father." Gadamer recalls the patristic adoption of the Stoic distinction between *verbum insitum* (*logos endiáthetos*) and *verbum prolatum* (*logos prophorikos*) to illuminate this mystery. However, "that the Word is with God from all eternity is the victorious doctrine of the church in its defense against subordinationism, and it situates the problem of language, too, entirely within inner thought."[16] And so the Stoic duality of inner thought and its secondary and diminished externalization in spoken language had to be abandoned, because the assertion of Jesus as the divine Word made man implies no diminishment of Christ's divinity whatsoever. As Gadamer recognized, both Augustine's *De trinitate* (Books VIII–XV) and Thomas Aquinas's trinitarian theology imply that "the greater miracle of language lies not in the fact that the Word becomes flesh and emerges in external being, but that which emerges and externalizes itself in utterance is always already a word."[17]

Gadamer does not make the mistake Jean Grondin[18] and Günther Figal[19] seem to make when they suggest that Augustine simply adopted the Stoic pair, *verbum prolatum* and *verbum insitum*. Gadamer and Lonergan also point out that in his commentary on the prologue to John's gospel Augustine went beyond the Stoic distinction to avoid Arianism.[20] As Lonergan said, "He cut between these Stoic terms to discover a third

---

14 Gadamer, *Wahrheit und Methode*, 383–95.

15 Gadamer, *Wahrheit und Methode*, 395–404.

16 Gadamer, *Wahrheit und Methode*, 397; *Truth and Method*, 420.

17 Gadamer, *Wahrheit und Methode*, 397; *Truth and Method*, 420.

18 Jean Grondin, "Gadamer and Augustine: On the Origins of the Hermeneutical Claim to Universality," *Sources of Hermeneutics* (Albany, NY: State University of New York Press, 1995), 99–110; "Unterwegs zur Rhetorik. Gadamers Schritt von Platon zu Augustin in 'Wahrheit und Methode,'" *Hermeneutische Wege. Hans-Georg Gadamer zum Hundertsten*, ed. G. Figal, J. Grondin, and D. Schmitt (Tübingen: Mohr Siebeck, 2000), 207–18.

19 Günther Figal, "The Doing of the Thing Itself: Gadamer's Hermeneutic Ontology of Language," *The Cambridge Companion to Gadamer*, ed. Robert Dostal (Cambridge: Cambridge University Press, 2002), 102–25 at 114ff.

20 Gadamer, *Wahrheit und Methode*, 397; *Truth and Method*, 460.

verbum that was neither the *verbum prolatum* of human speech nor the *verbum insitum* of man's native rationality but an intermediate *verbum intus prolatum.*"[21]

Gadamer agrees with Lonergan's statement that "as Augustine's discovery was part and parcel of his own mind's knowledge of itself, so he begged his readers to look within themselves and there to discover the speech of spirit within spirit, an inner *verbum* prior to any use of language, yet distinct both from the mind itself and from its memory or its present apprehension of objects."[22] Understanding the process in ourselves by which understanding and conceiving occur, we uncover the finite analogue for the *emanatio intelligibilis* in God.

Gadamer explains that theology could not understand the Incarnation correctly without first finding an adequate analogy for the eternal procession of the Word as uttered from the Father as uttering. According to Augustine, especially in XV.10–15, the true word or *verbum cordis* is completely independent of its external utterance in one or another conventional language. "When Augustine and the Scholastics consider the problem of the *verbum* in order to attain the conceptual means to elucidate the mystery of the Trinity, they are concerned exclusively with the inner word, the word of the heart, and its relation to the '*intelligentia.*'"[23] Only in this way could they do justice to the complete divinity and consubstantiality of the Son with God, and cast light on the relations of origin or processions that ground the existence of the Three Persons in God.

Human speech mirrors the Trinity inasmuch as the "word, which is true, because it states what is in reality so is not something for the sake of itself, nor does it want to be: *nihil de suo habens, sed totum de illa scientia de qua nascitur*. It has its being in revealing."[24] Only so can the inner word be "the mirror and image of the divine Word."[25] Lonergan, commenting on a passage in *De trinitate* XV.xii.22 (also cited by Gadamer), lays out the elements of Augustine's argument:

> In this passage, then, the Augustinian *verbum* is a nonlinguistic utterance of truth. It differs from expression in any language, for it is *linguae nullius*.

---

21 Bernard Lonergan, "Introduction," *Verbum*, 3–11 at 6.

22 Lonergan, *Verbum*, 6.

23 Gadamer, *Wahrheit und Methode*, 397; *Truth and Method*, 420.

24 Gadamer, *Wahrheit und Methode*, 398; *Truth and Method*, 421.

25 Gadamer, *Wahrheit und Methode*, 397; *Truth and Method*, 420.

It is not primitive but derived: *gignitur, exoritur, nascitur*. This total dependence is, not blind or automatic, but conscious and cognitive: *quod scimus loquimur; de visione scientiae visio cogitationis exoritur; qui quod loquitur*. Finally, this total dependence as conscious and known is the essential point. It makes no difference whether the *verbum* has its ground in memory or in recently acquired knowledge. What counts is its truth, its correspondence with things as known: *verbum simillimum rei notae; imago eius; verbum verum de re vera, nihil de suo habens, sed totum de illa scientia de qua nascitur; dum tamen verbum sit verum, id est, de notis rebus exortum.*[26]

Aquinas distinguished (1) the movement from potency into act, when understanding interrupts questioning with the insight that apprehends the answer, and (2) the procession of act from act when understanding is perfected in the utterance of the inner word. Gadamer says that in human beings, "one word originates *totaliter* from another – i.e., has its origin in the mind – like the deduction of a conclusion from the premises (*ut conclusio ex principiis*)."[27] This kind of causality is unique to the spiritual order: the word proceeds *because* of understanding, where (in Gadamer's words) "the emergence of thought is not a process of change (*motus*), not a transition from potentiality into act, but an emergence *ut actus ex actu*."[28]

By consulting a much wider range of Aquinas's texts, Lonergan elucidates what Gadamer is saying here more clearly in terms of Thomas's distinction between apprehensive and formative abstraction:

The principal efficient cause of *apprehensive abstraction* is agent intellect; the instrumental efficient cause is the illuminated phantasm; hence not only is the impression of the species *qua* a *passio* but also the consequent second act, *intelligere* is a *pati*; again the procession of species *qua* and *intelligere* from agent intellect and phantasm is a *processio operati*; but ... the procession of *intelligere* [within the actuated possible intellect] from species *qua* is *processio operationis*. Now *formative abstraction* proceeds from apprehensive abstraction just as apprehensive abstraction proceeds from agent intellect and phantasm; hence its procession is *processio operati*; and, as the ground of this procession, *intelligere* is named *dicere*. However, the procession of

---

26 Lonergan, *Verbum*, 7–8.
27 Gadamer, *Wahrheit und Methode*, 400; *Truth and Method*, 423–4.
28 Gadamer, *Wahrheit und Methode*, 400–1; *Truth And Method*, 424.

the formative abstraction has a special property; it is an *emanatio intelligibilis*, an activity of rational consciousness, the production of a product because and inasmuch as the sufficiency of the sufficient grounds for the product are known. Just as we affirm existence because and inasmuch as we know the sufficiency of the sufficient grounds for affirming it, so also we mean and define essences because and inasmuch as we understand them.[29]

Like Lonergan, Gadamer has recourse to Thomas Aquinas as Augustine's faithful interpreter on this issue. He understands that Christian theology alone has uncovered how "the mental emergence that takes place in the process of thought, speaking to oneself" constitutes a specific kind of production, which "is at the same time a total remaining within oneself." Lonergan quotes Aquinas's principle: "quanto perfectius procedit, tantum magis est unum eo a quo procedit" (The more perfectly a thing proceeds, the more it is one with that from which it proceeds).[30] In all other kinds of production, the product is external to the act of production. In the intelligible emanation of the word as understood from understanding as uttering it, "the word originates not partially but wholly (*totaliter*) in the intellect."[31] What differentiates this kind of production is that it consists not only in a *processio operati* but in a *processio intelligibilis*. Since there is no production or efficient causality in God, only the latter is an appropriate analogy for the divine procession.

Although Gadamer holds generally that we cannot come to true understanding without using language both in the genesis of understanding and in formulating our understanding, here he is insisting that the *verbum cordis* or inner word at the heart of this process is not reducible either to the previous use of language by which we come to understand any *Sache*, or to the conventional language in which we fully appropriate and express what we have newly understood.

The inner word ... is the subject matter thought through to the end (*forma excogitata*). Since a process of thinking through is involved, we have to acknowledge a processual element in it. It proceeds *per modum egredientis*.

---

29 Lonergan, *Verbum*, 188.

30 Lonergan, *Verbum*, 206, citing Thomas Aquinas, *Summa contra Gentiles* IV.11, §§1–7.

31 Gadamer, *Wahrheit und Methode*, 420; *Truth and Method*, 423.

> It is not utterance but thought; however, what is achieved in this speaking to oneself is the perfection of thought. So the inner word, by expressing thought, images the finiteness of our discursive understanding ... All thought is speaking to oneself.[32]

How is this seemingly un-hermeneutical point relevant for hermeneutic philosophy, since in the literature of hermeneutic philosophy, it is generally regarded as a mortal sin to distinguish among the outer word, the thing meant, and the inner word? Gadamer is not afraid to make such distinctions. The necessity of an inner word in our coming to know supports Gadamer's teaching that an intrinsic linguisticality, a naturally dialogical component, is essential to human beings as human. When Gadamer says in the quotation above that the inner word is not an utterance, by "utterance" he means a *verbum prolatum*, an outer word in the sense of an oral or written expression. When he says it is "thought," he means that it is the *verbum intus prolatum*, the inner word, concept, or definition. The inner word emerges because understanding apprehends itself in its own act; and this inner word is the condition of the possibility of the meaning we give the thing meant.

Now Gadamer and Lonergan both disagree with the decadent scholastic idea that knowledge is primarily intuition and that the intuition produces a perfect, if impoverished, replica of a universal *a parte rei* in the intellect. Yet this disagreement does not imply a sheer subjectivism on their part; nor does their position entail the dominance of putative acts of reflection and production, making human beings the lord and master of reality. Gadamer explains why.

> The inner unity of thinking and speaking to oneself ... implies that the inner mental word *is not formed by a reflective act*. A person who thinks something – i.e., says it to himself – means by it the thing that he thinks. His mind is not directed back toward his own thinking when he forms the word. The word is, of course, the product of the work of the mind. It forms the word in itself by thinking the thought through ... It remains entirely within the mental sphere. This gives the impression that what is involved is a relationship to itself and that speaking to oneself is a reflective act ... In fact there is no reflection when the word is formed, *for the word is not expressing the mind but the thing intended*. The starting point for

---

32 Gadamer, *Wahrheit und Methode*, 399; *Truth And Method*, 422.

the formation of the word is the substantive content (the *species*) that fills the mind. The thought seeking expression refers not to the mind but to the thing. Thus the word is not the expression of the mind but is concerned with the *similitudo rei*. The subject matter that is thought (the *species*) and the word belong as closely together as possible. Their unity is so close that the word does not occupy a second place in the mind beside the "*species*"; rather, the word is that in which knowledge is consummated – i.e., that in which the *species* is fully thought. Thomas points out that in this respect the word resembles light, which is what makes color visible.[33]

Gadamer underlines the *Vollzugs*-character of the inner word. Its generation does not involve an explicit act of reflection; nor does its nature involve any representation or picture, but "resembles light" instead.

III. Practical Wisdom: Prudential Judgment and Judgment

1. Phronesis

Gadamer is famous for rehabilitating *phronesis* in the philosophy of ethics and philosophy generally.[34] Inspired by Heidegger's 1922 and 1923 interpretations of Aristotle, which (Kisiel argues) provided the philosophical framework for *Sein und Zeit*,[35] Gadamer made Aristotle's teaching on practical wisdom and judgment the center of his hermeneutic philosophy. The move has been much discussed in the scholarship. Gadamer often tells how Heidegger startled his young students by exclaiming of *phronesis*, "Das ist das Gewissen!" Gadamer's own comment on conscience in the course of a discussion of Kant is suggestive in this context:

However conscience is not a lasting habit, but it is something that strikes one, what awakens one. Isn't there something like conscience "broadly

---

33 Gadamer, *Wahrheit und Methode*, 405; *Truth and Method*, 426.

34 Rod Coltman gives a serviceable summary with references to the American reception of Gadamer on *phronesis* in "Heidegger and Gadamer on Aristotle: The Facticity of *Phronésis* and the Phenomenon of Application," *The Language of Hermeneutics*, 11–24.

35 See Theodore Kisiel, "Theological Beginnings: Toward a Phenomenology of Christianity," *The Genesis of Heidegger's Being and Time* (Berkeley and Los Angeles: University of California, 1993), 69–115.

understood"? Surely one cannot deny that the wakefulness of conscience depends on the substantive orders within which one stands. Thus the autonomy of ethical reason has the character of intelligible self-determination. But that does not exclude the fact that all human actions and decisions are empirically conditioned. At least in judging others ... one cannot turn one's gaze from this conditioning.[36]

Gadamer does not equate the *phronesis* of Book VI of the *Nicomachean Ethics* with conscience, yet many connotations of this dianoetic virtue are similar to things mentioned above about conscience. Besides being an actual exercise of moral judgment, conscience also embraces the concrete education, socialization, and acculturation of *nous* that condition the exercise of conscience. So besides being the habitual presence within moral subjects of the ethos in which their *nous* is developed, *phronesis* also acts in two senses, involving knowledge and choice. In judgments they apply "the underpinning substantiality of laws and mores" to the concrete and particular situations of action.[37] They also make preferential choices of the better courses of action.

The habitual dimension of *phronesis* is a prime instance of *wirkungsgeschichtliches Bewußtein*: "The possibility of knowledge depends on the way one is, but again, however, this being of any given person bears the previous imprint of his or her education and way of life."[38] The ambiguity in Gadamer's treatment of the operative aspect of *phronesis* reflects Aristotle's account in *Nicomachean Ethics* III, in which *prohairesis* or preferential choice means both a judgment about and a choice of or commitment to the best course of action. Not surprisingly Aquinas distinguished more clearly between the cognitive and effective/affective dimensions of prudence, namely, *judicare* (practical knowing) and *praecipere* (an act of the will).[39]

---

36 Hans-Georg Gadamer, "Über die Möglichkeit einer philosophischen Ethik (1963)," *Neuere Philosophie II: Probleme, Gestalten*, Gesammelte Werke 4 (Tübingen: Mohr Siebeck, 1987), 175–88 at 180; English translation: "On the Possibility of Philosophical Ethics (1963)," *Hermeneutics, Religion, and Ethics*, trans. J. Weinsheimer (New Haven: Yale University Press, 1999) 18–36. In a footnote Gadamer reminds us that Thomas Aquinas held that conscience refers primarily to an act, and, only in a loose sense, to habit.

37 Gadamer, "Über die Möglichkeit einer philosophischen Ethik (1963)," 183.

38 Gadamer, "Über die Möglichkeit einer philosophischen Ethik (1963)," 183.

39 See Frederick E. Crowe, "Universal Norms and the Concrete *Operabile* in St Thomas Aquinas," *Three Thomist Studies*, ed. Michael Vertin (Boston: Supplementary Issue of *Lonergan Workshop* 16, 2000), 38–52.

As a mode of what Aristotle called *aletheuein* (living in the truth), *phronesis* enacts a mutual mediation of *logos* and *ethos*. Gadamer speaks of the transaction in *phronesis* as follows:

> Ethical knowing discerns the doable, that which a situation demands, and it knows this doable thing on the basis of a deliberation that refers the concrete situation to what is generally considered just and right.[40]
>
> ...
>
> What is considered right, in that which we affirm or deny in the judgment about ourselves or about others, follows our general notions of what is good and right; still, it only attains its proper determinacy in the concrete reality of the case. This is not just a case of applying a universal rule. Instead it is a matter of the authentic deed that is relevant, and for which the typical figures of the virtues and of the structure of the "mean," which, Aristotle demonstrates, offer no more than a vague scheme. Hence the precise virtue of *phronesis* – by which we hit the mean directly and attain the concretization that generally proves to be something like the doable (*praktòn agathón*), is by no means a special distinction of one who philosophizes.
>
> ...
>
> It is thus surely not as if ... *phronesis* had only to do with finding the correct means to pregiven ends. By means of the concretion, ethical deliberation only settles the "end" itself in its concretion, that is, as "what is to be done" (as *praktòn agathón*).[41]

Precisely because prudence or practical wisdom "encompasses in itself both the means and the ends in a unique manner,"[42] Gadamer reminds us, the opposite of true judgment in prudential matters is "neither error nor deception, but blindness" or scotosis. Anyone with disordered passions or loves cannot discern the good rightly, "because whether a person can carry out such a reflection depends on the being of the person. For one overwhelmed by disordered affections precisely this kind of reflection, which means the ability to take one's bearings or to orient oneself in relation to the basis of one's ethical deliberation, is a lost cause."

---

40 Gadamer, "Über die Möglichkeit einer philosophischen Ethik (1963)," 183.
41 Gadamer, "Über die Möglichkeit einer philosophischen Ethik (1963)," 184.
42 Gadamer, "Über die Möglichkeit einer philosophischen Ethik (1963)," 183–4.

Gadamer considers this relationship between one's ethos, one's being or character, and one's capacity to deliberate and judge well in ethical matters paradigmatic for the hermeneutic experience of human beings. In other words, in every field of human knowing and doing, something like the structures elucidated in the analysis of *phronesis* are at work. This is related to what Lonergan says about judgment.

2. Judgment: Differentiating and Generalizing Phronesis

Recall that in the discussion of the inner word above, Lonergan distinguished two different grounds for the *processio intelligibilis* of two distinct inner words. The first is the proportion of the act of understanding or insight to the procession of the word, the concept, the definition: "We mean and define essences because and inasmuch as we understand them." The second had to do with "affirming existence because and inasmuch as we know the sufficiency of the ... grounds for affirming it." This procession occurs "because and inasmuch as the sufficiency of the sufficient grounds for the product are known."[43]

Gadamer's discussion of the *verbum cordis* is confined to the first procession, that of the *verbum incomplexum*. Lonergan's study of word and idea in the thought of Thomas Aquinas revealed how, to account for Augustine's emphasis on *veritas*, Aquinas complemented Aristotle's account of *noesis* as insight or understanding with a further account of reflective insight and judgment. Because Lonergan investigated the entirety of Aquinas's thought on *verbum*, he also elaborated the procession of the *verbum complexum* of judgment (*compositio vel divisio*).

Lonergan was enabled to grasp Aquinas's achievement on reflection and judgment because of his prior familiarity with John Henry Newman's appropriation of Aristotle's *phronesis* in working out the "illative sense" in *An Essay in Aid of a Grammar of Assent*.[44] There is a direct kinship between Newman's elucidation of "arguments too various for direct enumeration, too personal and deep for words, too powerful and concurrent for refutation," and Gadamer's rehabilitation of prejudice.[45]

---

43   Lonergan, *Verbum*, 188.

44   Bernard Lonergan, "*Insight* Revisited," *A Second Collection: Papers by Bernard J.F. Lonergan, SJ*, ed. William Ryan and Bernard Tyrrell (London: Darton, Longman & Todd, 1974), 263.

45   Joseph Dunne has developed the parallel more broadly in *Back to the Rough Ground: Practical Judgment and the Lure of Technique* (Notre Dame, IN: University of Notre Dame, 1993).

Newman's proposal that Aristotle's analysis of *phronesis* as a concrete mode of human knowing is appropriate not just in the realm of moral judgment but in all fields of human knowing anticipated Heidegger, Gadamer, and Lonergan. Because Gadamer espoused Heidegger's disclosure-model of truth as *a-letheia*, the difference between insight and interpretation and reflective understanding and judgment was not a central issue for him. (He told me more than once that he might just as well have called *Truth and Method* "*Insight* and Method.")

For Lonergan, as for Heidegger and Gadamer, the hermeneutic revolution implies that the epistemological question is no longer the first relevant question about human knowledge. As Lonergan agreed, the genuine issue is not the *quaestio juris* but the *quaestio facti*: not *whether* we know but *what* do we do when we know?

Quite early on, Lonergan learned both from Augustine's early dialogues at Cassiciacum and especially from Newman's *Grammar of Assent* that questions about the nature of human knowledge can only be answered by reflecting on one's own experience of coming to know. Newman thus preceded Heidegger and Gadamer in carrying out the hermeneutic explication of performative acts of consciousness. From the time of his early unpublished Blandyke Papers, Lonergan was convinced that Newman's discoveries about apprehension and assent were congruent with his own experience of knowing.

Odd then that Newman depended on Aristotle's description of *phronesis* to develop his insights into the illative sense, and that the illative sense helped Lonergan understand reflective understanding and judgment. Yet this roundabout set of influences did enable Lonergan to thematize Aquinas's account of the cognitional acts of reflective understanding and judgment (*noesis*) and the correlative known content (*noema*) of the *actus essendi* or act of existence (no more than implicit in Aristotle's metaphysics) – a parade example of *Wirkungsgeschichte* in action. Thomas Aquinas goes beyond Aristotle on the issue of truth.[46] In

---

46 See Lonergan, *Verbum*, 84–5 on the incompleteness of Aristotle's account of knowledge from Thomas Aquinas's point of view: "The problem of knowledge, once it is granted that knowledge is by identity, is knowledge of the other." Aquinas learned from Aristotle that "knowledge is by identity; the act of the thing as sensible is the act of sensation; the act of the thing as intelligible is the act of understanding." Aquinas went beyond Aristotle to ascertain that "the act of the thing as real is the *esse naturale* of the thing and, except in divine self-knowledge, that *esse* is not identical with knowing it."

Lonergan's summary, "Truth is the medium in which being is known; truth formally is found only in judgment; and existence is the act of being."[47]

So Newman helped Lonergan discover that Thomas Aquinas did not think of judgment as an intuition of concrete, actual existence added to a previous intellectual synthesis. According to this basically Scotist and Ockhamist view – instantiating what Gadamer called the nominalist prejudgment or the horizon of *Vorhandenheit*[48] (against which the radical deconstructionists and genealogists inveigh) – we reach judgment through a prior, intuitive knowledge of existence. Instead, Thomas taught that we only know the actuality of being through the actuality of truth. In Lonergan's words, first we "reach the unconditioned, secondly we make a true judgment of existence, and only thirdly in and through the true judgment do we come to know actual and concrete existence."[49]

Lonergan thematizes true judgment as hermeneutical and *phronesis*-like in its recognition that we do not know being or the concrete by *apodeixis*. Newman pointed the way:

It is by the strength, variety, or multiplicity of premises, which are only probable, not by invincible syllogisms, – by objections overcome by adverse theories neutralized, by difficulties gradually clearing up, by exceptions proving the rule, by unlooked-for correlations found with received truths, by suspense and delay in the process issuing in triumphant reactions, – by all these ways, and many others, it is that the practised and experienced mind is able to make a sure divination that a conclusion is inevitable, *of which his lines of reasoning do not actually put him in possession*. This is what is meant by a proposition being "as good as proved," a conclusion as undeniable "as if it were proved," and the reasons for it "amounting to a proof," for a proof is *the limit of converging probabilities*.[50]

...

---

47 Bernard Lonergan, "*Insight*: Preface to a Discussion," *Collection: Papers by Bernard Lonergan, SJ*, ed. Frederick E. Crowe (New York: Herder & Herder, 1967), 152–63 at 160.

48 On Gadamer's dismantling of the horizon of *Vorhandenheit*, picture thinking, and Scotist and Ockhamist presuppositions generally, see Frederick G. Lawrence, "Ontology *of* and *as* Horizon: Gadamer's Rehabilitation of the Metaphysics of Light," *Revista Portuguesa de Filosofia* 56, 3/4 (2000): 389–420.

49 Lonergan, "*Insight*: Preface to a Discussion," 163.

50 John Henry Newman, *An Essay in Aid of a Grammar of Assent*, ed. I.T. Ker (Oxford: Clarendon Press, 1985), 208.

> The processes of reasoning which legitimately lead to assent, to action,
> to certitude, are in fact too multiform, subtle, omnigenous, too implicit,
> to allow of being measured by rule, ... they are after all personal, – verbal
> argumentation being useful only in subordination to a higher logic.[51]

Besides the what-is question, on which Gadamer is most eloquent, there is the is-it question. When we ask, "Is it so? Does it exist?," we must already have realized that our prospective judgment is conditioned. We answer the question when reflective understanding grasps both the conditions and that the conditions *happen to be fulfilled*. The unconditioned attainable by human beings is the *virtually* unconditioned, not the formally unconditioned that has no conditions whatsoever. The key to knowing the truth for Lonergan, then, is that reflective understanding is not a matter of attaining some almost tangible sense of "already-out-there-now" or "already-in-here-now" presence, or of comparing the guess or hypothesis to some logical or empirical standard; it is the far more delicate issue of discerning whether there are any further relevant questions regarding the sufficiency of evidence relevant to the prospective judgment.

Thus for Lonergan "fact" means neither data nor absolute necessity, but just the verified possibility proper to the virtually unconditioned. *If this grasp of the unconditioned is authentic*, the knower achieves independence of merely subjective viewpoints, attitudes, and orientation; and from the knower's grasp of the matter-of-fact fulfillment of conditions the judgment proceeds rationally – the second kind of *verbum cordis*.

As a rational act judgment posits or rejects a synthesis: Yes, it exists; or No, it does not exist. As Lonergan tells us, "Every human judgment in this life rests, in the last analysis, upon contingent matters of fact," and "no synthesis of concepts, of itself, constitutes a judgment ... [And] there can be no human knowledge of real possibility or of real necessity without matter-of-fact judgments."[52] If Lonergan is closer to Gadamer, who elucidated the human experience of truth as hermeneutical by highlighting both the role of questioning and the *phronesis*-character of judgment, he is also clearer than Gadamer about rejecting the positivist or Kantian conception of knowledge as a combination of concepts and empirical intuitions within the horizon of *Vorhandenheit*.

---

51 Newman, *An Essay in Aid of a Grammar of Assent*, 303.
52 Lonergan, "*Insight*: Preface to a Discussion," 159–60.

3. Judgment and Authenticity

Lonergan opposes a "forgetfulness of being" based on "picture think-ing." Picture thinking does not acknowledge that "the original rela-tionship of cognitional activity to the universe of being must lie in the intention of being" exercised in human questions for understanding and reflection.

> Each of us lives in a real world of his own. Its contents are determined by his *Sorge*, by his interests and concerns, by the orientation of his living, by the unconscious horizon that blocks from his view the rest of reality. To each of us his own private real world is very real indeed. Spontaneously it lays claim to being the one real world, the standard, the criterion, the absolute, by which everything is judged, measured, evaluated. That claim ... is not to be admitted. There is one standard, one criterion, one absolute, and that is true judgment. In so far as one's private real world does not meet that standard, it is some dubious product of animal faith and human error. On the other hand, in so far as one's private real world is submitted constantly and sedulously to the corrections made by true judgment, ... it is brought into conformity with the universe of being.[53]

For Lonergan, human living is a self-correcting process of learning. Once inquiry and gradually developing understanding yield to the question, Is it so? the process of reflection, doubting, marshalling and weighing the evidence, and judging "is not as verification is imagined by the naive to be a matter of looking, peering, intuiting, but as verifica-tion in fact is found to be, namely, *a cumulative convergence of direct and indirect confirmations any one of which by itself settles just nothing.*"[54] Lonergan emphasizes the self-correcting character of human know-ing. His phrase, "virtually unconditioned," acknowledges the contin-gency and fallibility of human knowledge central for the hermeneutic notion of truth. It stresses the proximate criterion of truth – the reflec-tive grasp of the virtually unconditioned. The fact that such a criterion exists puts Heidegger's *Gegenwendigkeit der Wahrheit* – that facticity's experience of the truth cannot help but be mixed with error because true judgments depend on the authenticity of human knowers – into

---

53 Lonergan, "*Insight*: Preface to a Discussion," 158.
54 See Bernard Lonergan, "The Dehellenization of Dogma," *Second Collection*, 31.

a different context. Lonergan regards this existential aspect of true judgments in terms of what he calls the "remote criterion of truth," which is altogether congruent with Gadamer's statement above on the concrete possibility of *phronesis*. For Lonergan, "The remote criterion is the proper unfolding of the detached and disinterested desire to know. In negative terms this proper unfolding is the absence of interference from other desires that inhibit or reinforce and in either case distort the guidance given by the pure desire."[55] The remote criterion of truth calls subjects themselves into question, because "all [their] efforts to remove the doubt will proceed from the same suspected source."[56] The issue is the "habitual and actual disinterestedness and detachment of the subject[s] in [their] cognitional activities." Certitude would reach the absolute of infallibility only if the obscure region of the remote criterion of truth "were to become completely clarified, either in fact, or more radically, as a matter of principle."[57] Heidegger is certain that such complete clarity will never be forthcoming in this life; Lonergan agrees. However, he does not suppose that certitude or indubitability is the criterion of true judgment, as Heidegger seems to hold with Descartes. Lonergan's agreement with Heidegger therefore regards not individual judgments, taken singly, then, but rather the possibility of "constant and sedulous" correction of "one's world" by true judgment in a world in which human beings are alienated from themselves.

IV. Socratic Reversal/Conversion

Until the early 1960s, Lonergan conceived the appropriation of the truth in terms of three components. The first two components Lonergan shares with Gadamer. First there is "the problem of *learning*, of gradually acquiring the accumulation of habitual insights that constitute a viewpoint, and eventually of moving from lower to higher viewpoints."[58] This involves adapting our sensibilities to the requirements of the knowledge of the truth and the willingness to make the decisions

---

55 Bernard Lonergan, *Insight: A Study of Human Understanding*, Collected Works of Bernard Lonergan 3, ed. Frederick E. Crowe and Robert M. Doran (Toronto: Toronto University Press, 1992), 573.
56 Lonergan, *Insight*, 574.
57 Lonergan, *Insight*, 575.
58 Lonergan, *Insight*, 582.

needed to live consistently with the truths we know. The second component, *identification*, is provided by insight and formulation. Insight grasps the intelligible correlations that clarify the data under inquiry, so that we can distinguish and relate the various elements of the problem and pose the appropriate questions.

The third component is *orientation* – the characteristic concern of Heidegger, who from 1919 onwards was overwhelmingly preoccupied with bringing about a radical change in orientation in philosophy. In *Insight* Lonergan thought orientation centered chiefly around rational consciousness's reflection and judgment: we have to make the virtually unconditioned and true judgment the guide of our life. He knew that this would also encompass a "volitional appropriation of the truth that consists in our willingness to live up to it," but by the time he finished writing *Insight* in 1953 he had not fully understood that the radical change needed in orientation for self-appropriation remained implicit in that work.

In 1958, however, he acknowledged that the habitual – "constant and sedulous" – exercise of correct judgment does not occur without a conversion. He spoke of a specifically philosophical conversion from the *homo sensibilibus immersus* to *homo maxime est mens hominis* (*Sum. theol.*, 1–2, q. 29, a. 4 c.)";[59] or of an "intellectual conversion *ex umbris et imaginibus in veritatem.*"[60]

To fully explicate conversion as a radical change in orientation that demands a revolution in one's living, Lonergan correlated Newman's basic theorem in *The Idea of a University* about human knowing as "a whole whose parts are organically related" with the "contemporary phenomenological notion of horizon."[61] He also had to break through to the intention of value that is only implicit in the notion of being, and to clarify that "the fourth level of intentional consciousness – the level of deliberation, evaluation, decision, action – sublates the prior levels of experiencing, understanding, judging." In this context it became clear to him that "the speculative intellect or pure reason is just an abstraction,"[62] and that "a life of pure intellect or pure reason without the

---

59 Lonergan, "*Insight*: Preface to a Discussion," 158, note 10.
60 Bernard Lonergan, "Cognitional Structure," *Collection*, 236.
61 Bernard Lonergan, "Theology and Man's Future," *Second Collection*, 141–2.
62 Bernard Lonergan, *Method in Theology* (New York: Herder & Herder, 1972), 340.

control of deliberation, evaluation, responsible choice is something less than the life of a psychopath."[63]

Heidegger, Gadamer, and Lonergan shared philosophy's characteristic resistance to the disorder of the age. Each saw scholastic or academic philosophy and theology in a state of flaccid sterility and in need of serious reform. Just as philosophy originally challenged the higher education of the Sophists to undergo a Socratic reversal, so Heidegger, Gadamer, and Lonergan in their differing ways make *Umkehr/Kehre* or conversion a theme not to be shirked.

Heidegger's tremendous impact on German philosophy in the early 1920s was inseparable from his concern with *conversio vitae*. He stressed the twilight character of human facticity during the critical period between the World Wars. At that time it made a certain sense to insist that because of human fallibility, all human understanding and interpretation are provisional, and every truth apprehended no more than a half-truth. And so Jean Grondin, in his Gadamer biography, evokes Heidegger's farewell speech to his students upon departing from Freiburg for Marburg: "It began with the words: 'To be awake to the fire in the night ...' Heidegger spoke further 'of fire and light, of brightness and darkness,' and the 'mission of man to take a stand between the disclosure of Being and its withdrawal.'"[64] In Grondin's description Heidegger's philosophic undertaking is suspended between the two poles of wakefulness and of night.[65] This description was confirmed by Gadamer soon after he read those lectures on Aristotle (then recently published in the *Gesamtausgabe*) that had made such an impression upon him when he first heard them as a young man. He expressed his astonishment that such a young man could have had so deep a sense of *Ruinanz* – that all things human, given enough time, go badly. Grondin encapsulates Heidegger's angle of vision as follows: "Understanding and interpreting [*Verstehen*] is, so to speak, a flickering wakefulness in the night, which is more encompassing than any light."[66] Heidegger's hermeneutically transformed phenomenological heightening of awareness (*Besinnung*) was to be in the service of a wakeful alertness to the fire in the night. In *Sein und Zeit*, though, the only counter to the forgetfulness of Being is resoluteness in the face of one's death, of one's nothingness, of the night of the world.

---

63 Lonergan, *Method in Theology*, 122.
64 Jean Grondin, *Hans-Georg Gadamer. Eine Biographie* (Tübingen: Mohr Siebeck, 1999), 125.
65 Grondin, *Hans-Georg Gadamer. Eine Biographie*, 124.
66 Grondin, *Hans-Georg Gadamer. Eine Biographie*, 123.

After *Sein und Zeit* Heidegger said that the underlying condition of truth is freedom; but the dispensations of destiny or Being hardly permit people to be free. Inevitably, human authenticity can never come unambiguously into the clear; the best we can do is face the fact that any authenticity we achieve is always beset by inauthenticity due both to uncontrollable factors within us and to economic, social, political, and cultural conditions outside us. After technology has become the ontology of the world, the oblivion of being requires a massive reversal of human orientation toward a poetic dwelling that attends to the "Fragwürdigkeit des Seins." George, Trakl, Rilke, and especially Hölderlin were the proximate models. As Gianni Vattimo (sharing Gadamer's opinion about Heidegger) puts it, we cannot overcome nihilism; all we can do is try for recovery (*Verwindung*), and "make do" with its trauma.

Lonergan was concerned with the crisis of culture as it threatens Catholic faith and theology. Of the inauthenticity in Catholic tradition he said in the early 1960s, "The theology is still scholastic, but the scholasticism is decadent ... The sacred name of science is still invoked, but one can ask with Edmund Husserl whether any significant scientific ideal remains, whether it has not been replaced by the conventions of a clique."[67] He was aware that these are symptomatic of general human inauthenticity and of what in *Insight* he called "moral impotence."[68] Lonergan was convinced that philosophic or intellectual conversion was not something that human beings simply could make up their minds to execute because "we do not know ourselves very well; we cannot chart the future; we cannot control our environment completely or the influences that work on us; we cannot explore our unconscious and preconscious mechanisms. Our course is in the night; our control is only rough and approximate; we have to believe and trust, to risk and dare."[69]

V. The Priority of Religious Conversion: Falling-in-Love and Friendship

During his post–World War II days in Freiburg, Heidegger pursued the radical openness linked to *Fragwürdigkeit*; in the famous *Spiegel* interview from late in his life, Heidegger gestured toward an indeterminate

---

67 Bernard Lonergan, "*Existenz* and Aggiornamento," *Collection*, 246–7.
68 Lonergan, *Insight*, 650.
69 Lonergan, "*Existenz* and Aggiornamento," *Collection*, 242.

eschatology when he said, "Only a god can save us!" Until the mid-1960s, Lonergan was rather like Gadamer whose conventionally successful life as a decent and promising young man was jolted by Heidegger into realizing the centrality for philosophic inquiry of Socratic nescience (*Nichtwissen*). Gadamer's hermeneutics as a clarification of the *phronesis*-structure of human life and of the human sciences is always closely associated with Platonic dialectic, the kind of friendly conversation that tries to free those sharing in the conversation from the perennial threat of domination by sophistry and inauthenticity. Early contact with Newman and Thomas Aquinas convinced Lonergan that Christian belief goes hand-in-hand with the creative nescience of the pure, detached, and disinterested desire to know for which true judgment lights the way and requires us to keep our doing consistent with our knowing.

Before 1965 Lonergan thought that philosophical and theological culture lacked widespread self-appropriation of people's rational self-consciousness. After losing a lung to cancer and going through a lengthy recovery period, Lonergan realized more clearly, first, that a prior moral conversion is needed to heighten the probabilities of such philosophic or intellectual conversion; and, second, that the probabilities for such a moral conversion require a prior religious conversion, in which the key component is the gift of God's love.[70]

Until 1965 Lonergan's priorities were similar to those of Aquinas, but in the context of modern science and history. Understandably perhaps, he took the theological virtue of faith (especially as belief in divinely revealed truths) for granted, and was preoccupied above all with self-appropriation as intellectual conversion. After 1965 Lonergan started sounding more like Heidegger. In something like a *Kehre*, Lonergan underwent a reversal from the perspective of Thomas Aquinas to that of Augustine as these are presented in that statement already quoted from *Verbum* – "For Augustine our hearts are restless until they rest in God, for Aquinas, not our hearts, but first and most our minds are restless until they rest in seeing Him." He began to grasp even more deeply the implications of the move from "the abstract and static context dictated by logical clarity, coherence, and rigor and into the concrete, open, and ongoing context dictated by attention, inquiry, reflection, and deliberation."[71]

---

70 Lonergan, *Method in Theology*, 122, 243.
71 Bernard Lonergan, "The Response of the Jesuit as Priest and Apostle in the Modern World," *Second Collection*, 170.

Although in *Verbum* and *Insight* Lonergan had broken through to the hermeneutic notion of consciousness, he still operated in an intellectualist frame of mind, expressed in terms of faculty psychology. In the late 1960s, he realized that intentionality analysis resituates the problem of human authenticity so that it cannot be handled in terms of "faculty psychology with its consequent alternatives of voluntarism, intellectualism, sentimentalism, and sensism." He saw that philosophic conversion depends on the free decision of existential subjects to devote themselves "to the pursuit of understanding and truth, and on the success with which they remain faithful to that commitment." Such commitment and such fidelity are not to be taken for granted. As Newman wrote in *The Idea of a University*, "Quarry granite rock with razors, or moor the vessel with a thread of silk; then you may hope with such keen and delicate instruments as human knowledge and human reason to contend against those giants, the passion and pride of man."[72] As Lonergan wrote in 1969:

> To live intelligently, reasonably, responsibly, an adult has to form some view of the universe, of man's place in the universe, of his role along with other men. He may do so by appealing to myth, or to science, or to philosophy, or to religion. He may do so explicitly, consciously, deliberately, or he may do so implicitly, inadvertently, without deliberation. He may confront what he beholds, or try to escape in debauchery and drugs, or rage fanatically against it, or collapse in existential despair. Such is the human condition and such the human problem. A mythic solution will do only for the immature. A scientific solution is out-of-date, for philosophy has become existential; it is concerned with man in his concrete existing; and there the issue is authenticity. I have argued that man exists authentically in the measure that he succeeds in self-transcendence, and I have found that self-transcendence has both its fulfillment and its enduring ground in holiness, in God's gift of his love to us.[73]

After 1965, therefore, Lonergan found himself in the perspective of the tenth book of the *Confessions* commented on so long ago by a Heidegger on his trajectory away from conventional Christianity. In 1921

---

72 John Henry Newman, *The Idea of a University*, ed. I.T. Ker (Oxford: The Clarendon Press, 1976), 177.

73 Bernard Lonergan, "The Future of Christianity," *Second Collection*, 155.

Heidegger mentioned and quoted, but neither emphasized nor kept on mentioning, Augustine's conviction that intellectual and moral conversion are only made possible by the gift of God's love. Unlike Heidegger, Lonergan brought to light how the liberation of the existential subject occurs in religious conversion; and that falling in love with God is not a human achievement but a divine gift. As he wrote:

> Now there is a profound difference between particular acts of loving and the dynamic state to which we refer when we speak of falling in love and of being in love. That dynamic state, while it has its causes, conditions, occasions, none the less once it occurs and as long as it lasts, is a first principle in one's living. It is the origin and source that prompts and colors all one's thoughts and feelings, all one's hopes and fears, all one's joys and sorrows. Moreover, such being-in-love is of three kinds. There is being-in-love with the domestic community, with one's mate and one's children. There is being-in-love with the civil community, eagerly making one's contribution to its needs and promoting its betterment. There is being-in-love with God. Of this love St Paul spoke when he wrote to the Romans: "The love of God is poured forth in our hearts by the Holy Spirit who has been given us" (Rom. 5: 5).[74]

For Lonergan the gift of God's love is a "type of consciousness at its root, as brought to its fulfillment, as having undergone conversion, as possessing a basis that may be broadened and deepened and heightened and enriched but never superseded, as ever more ready to deliberate and evaluate and decide and act with the easy freedom of those who do all good because they are in love."[75] Nevertheless, he stressed that any attainment of human authenticity is always dialectical, because it "never is some pure, serene, secure possession" but is "always precarious."[76] And so we come full circle, since for Lonergan authentic postmodern hermeneutics is a critically and methodically mediated hermeneutics of love.

For Gadamer's hermeneutics of living in the truth, the recovery of *phronesis* is also an existential issue. Philosophic reflection on ethics is

---

74 Lonergan, "Theology and Man's Future," *Second Collection*, 145.
75 Lonergan, "The Response of the Jesuit as Priest and Apostle in the Modern World," *Second Collection*, 173.
76 Lonergan, "The Response of the Jesuit as Priest and Apostle in the Modern World," *Second Collection*, 165–6.

mainly a matter of heightening and sharpening our awareness of operations we perform more or less well because we are human beings and not gods. For him, the sociocultural background of laws and customs ultimately provides those who have been brought up well the concrete guidance for prudential judgments and preferential choices. Habermas famously objected that oppressive and distorting social and cultural conditions dramatically lower the probability of the practically wise persons, which Gadamer seems to take for granted.[77] When we recall Aristotle's teaching that *phronesis* is an acquired dianoetic virtue that presupposes the attainment of the other moral virtues, we realize that becoming a *phronimos* or *spoudaios* would indeed require a prior moral conversion from satisfactions to true values.[78]

Surely, Gadamer's Aristotle-inspired reflections on friendship[79] furnish the indispensable complement to his *phronesis*-centered philosophical hermeneutics and ethics. We recall Aristotle's teaching that friendship properly is based on a sharing of virtues or excellences; and that these excellences emerge from self-knowledge and rightly ordered self-love, which enable friends to want what is best for their friends – virtue and wisdom. Knowing this full well, Gadamer takes up the genesis of the excellences that make friendship possible. Characteristically in this respect, he says friendship has to be understood analogously. From this perspective he notes how the choice of models for living plays an important role in the initiating and living out of friendships. We thus understand how friendship leads to the realization of people's highest

---

77 The beginning of the so-called *Ideologiekritik* debate was Jürgen Habermas's review of *Wahrheit und Methode*, "Der hermeneutische Ansatz," in *Zur Logik der Sozialwissenschaften*, published as a *Sonderheft* of the journal edited then by Hans-Georg Gadamer and Helmut Huhn, *Philosophische Rundschau* 5 (Februar 1967; Tübingen: J.C.B. Mohr Siebeck): 149–76.

78 Gadamer's response to Habermas is basically that to have any worthwhile liberation you need a critical mass of practically wise persons. We are left, as it were, to choose between a virtuous circle and a vicious circle. A sufficiently virtuous world, according to Gadamer, is either already present, or all is lost. Such a world cannot be assumed, according to Habermas, and so the world that exists needs liberation by Habermas's procedural constraints and symmetries in norm-formation. Christians claim the need for divine redemption on account of Jesus Christ's salvific death and resurrection, which is already effective, but only perfected eschatologically.

79 Hans-Georg Gadamer, "Friendship and Self-knowledge: Reflections on the Role of Friendship in Greek Ethics (1985)," *Hermeneutics, Religion, and Ethics*, 128–41.

aspirations.[80] For Gadamer solidarity achieved in developing friendships is what makes the existence of practically wise people possible.

In Lonergan's trinitarian theology, grace is conceived of as a created participation in the intra-trinitarian relations among Father, Son, and Holy Spirit. One aspect of this fourfold sharing is the grace of charity, which Thomas Aquinas understood by analogy with Aristotle's account of friendship in the *Nicomachean Ethics*. Lonergan gave us a glimpse of how all that Gadamer has retrieved from Aristotle may be subsumed into a theology of grace in his essay, "Finality, Love, Marriage," upon which I have also reflected.[81]

VI. Reprise

Postmodern hermeneutics is defined here in contrast to ancient and modern hermeneutics. It is then argued that phenomenology has been sublated by hermeneutics. Heidegger's study of Augustine's *Confessions* was shown to be emblematic of this hermeneutic primacy. His destructive, existential analysis of Augustine on the self and interiority demonstrates the efficacy of the 1919 breakthrough to the postmodern notion of hermeneutic consciousness. This retrieval of consciousness as hermeneutic and the recognition of the primacy of the truth of existence become central for both Gadamer and Lonergan.

Heidegger's account was criticized on two points. First, his conflation of facticity and fallenness becomes a serious problem in postmodern philosophy in its attempt to free itself from premodern metaphysics and modern epistemology, science, and technology.

Second, Heidegger neglected, even disregarded propositional truth and correct judgment, relegating them to a relatively insignificant role. While granting primacy to the truth of existence, Heidegger's caricature of truth as rigid correctness is remedied in Gadamer's analysis of *phronesis*. In his teaching about reflective understanding and judgment, Lonergan brought together Augustine's concern for *veritas*, Newman's "illative sense," and Aquinas's *compositio vel divisio*. He was thus

---

80 See too Hans-Georg Gadamer, "Freundschaft und Solidarität," *Hermeneutische Entwurfe. Vorträge und Aufsätze* (Tübingen: Mohr Siebeck, 2000), 56–65.

81 See Bernard Lonergan, "Finality, Love, Marriage," *Collection*, 16–53; and see Frederick G. Lawrence, "Grace and Friendship: Postmodern Political Theology and God as Conversational," ch. 11, below.

able to differentiate and generalize *phronesis* for all fields of knowing and acting. Clearly, the postmodern alternative to delusion and ideology is neither foundationalism nor naive absolutism but the virtually unconditioned.

Gadamer's and Lonergan's legitimate, non-exorbitant account of truth involved the retrieval of the hermeneutics of interiority in Augustine and Thomas Aquinas. The "inner words" of interpretation and judgment, and the preconceptual and pre-propositional questions and acts of understanding, reflection, and deliberation from which they proceed, provide the key for hermeneutic philosophy. The correct account of interpreting and judging dismantles the picture-thinking of the horizon of *Vorhandenheit* – the justifiable core of deconstruction. Only an adequate retrieval of the hermeneutics of interiority can take seriously Aristotle's observation about the *pollachôs legetai* notion of being.

Because of conflating fallenness and facticity, Heidegger gave a Nietzschean twist to his radically Augustinian probing of the truth of existence. He took a stand on the issue of the end of innocence in philosophy, arguing that if any humanly attainable authenticity is always partially inauthentic, the opacities in the area of human historicity (i.e., Lonergan's "remote criterion of truth") call propositional truth into question – at least regarding the most important matters. Some postmodern thinkers like Paul Ricoeur moderate Heidegger by drawing upon motifs from the Kantian *Critiques*, while Jacques Derrida (before his reconciliation with his teacher Emmanuel Lévinas) pushes further than Heidegger did in the direction of Nietzsche's "magic of the extreme" (to use Eric Voegelin's term), and Richard Rorty treats Nietzsche's relative perspectivism as gospel.[82] The significant point, however, is that Heidegger made authenticity a central issue for postmodern hermeneutics.

This concern with authenticity pushes hermeneutic philosophy to the threshold of theology. Why? Because the question of truth cannot be fully answered without raising the issue of conversion. Lonergan distinguishes three conversions – intellectual, moral, and religious. In the measure that it becomes existential, philosophy has explicitly to come to terms both with human moral impotence and sin and with divine grace through the traditions, myths, symbols, rituals, and institutions

---

82 See Eric Voegelin, "Wisdom and the Magic of the Extreme: A Meditation," *Published Essays 1966–1985*, Collected Works 12, ed. Ellis Sandoz (Baton Rouge: Louisiana State University Press, 1990), 315–75.

available in the given culture. Gadamer believes that philosophy proper should not cross the limits specified by Kant's transcendental dialectic, so, although his philosophical hermeneutics peaks in the treatment of *phronesis* and of friendship, as we saw in the preceding lecture, he cannot help crossing that line to speak of the hermeneutics of proclaiming the gospel. Gadamer's hermeneutic reflection embraces the entirety of the Western tradition, even Christian theology.[83]

In Lonergan's work integral hermeneutics embraces theology as a collaborative and interdisciplinary enterprise that mediates between Christian tradition and the cultures in which it is imbedded.[84] He conceives theology as a transposition of Thomas Aquinas's *lectio, disputatio,* and *praedicatio* into a functionally specialized project in which different tasks are distinguished, disciplinary triumphalism is reduced, and people work together to appropriate and communicate the mystery of love and awe. Such theology engages in multiple acts of understanding, judgment, and decision as it applies past traditions to the present. In this enterprise it is likely that religious, moral, and intellectual conversions either are not present or are imperfect. Therefore, the performance of theologians will be dialectical. And so ultimately Lonergan's postmodern hermeneutics is integral because it integrates the critical dimension inspired by suspicion into a retrieval and creativity based on trust.

---

83 See ch. 2 above, "Hans-Georg Gadamer and the Hermeneutic Revolution," and my articles, "The Seriousness of Play: Gadamer's Hermeneutics as a Resource for Christian Mission," *From One Medium to Another: Communicating the Bible through Multimedia,* ed. R. Hodgson and P. Soukup (Kansas City: Sheed & Ward, 1997), 109–31; and "Gadamer, the Hermeneutic Revolution, and Theology," *The Cambridge Companion to Gadamer,* 167–200.

84 See Lonergan, *Method in Theology.*

4 A Jewish and a Christian Approach to the Problematic of Jerusalem and Athens: Leo Strauss and Bernard Lonergan

In the wake of the *Tractatus Theologico-Politicus*, the *Ethics*, the *Histoire des variations des églises protestantes*, the *Dictionnaire historique*, and the *Réponse aux questions d'un provincial* ... what men craved to know was what they were to believe, and what they were not to believe. Was tradition still to command their allegiance, or was it to go by the board? Were they to continue plodding along the same old road, trusting the same old guides, or were they to obey new leaders who bade them to turn their backs on all those outworn things, and follow them to other lands of promise? The champions of Reason (*rationaux*) and the champions of Religion (*religionnaires*) were, in the words of Pierre Bayle, fighting desperately for the possession of men's souls, confronting each other in a contest at which the whole of thoughtful Europe was looking on.

Paul Hazard, *The European Mind 1680–1715*, 8–9[1]

With these words, Paul Hazard, Flemish historian of ideas at the Sorbonne, dramatically conveyed the transition the Enlightenment brought about in relation to the age-old problematic of Jerusalem and Athens because of not only the confrontation of faith (in the sense of belief) with modern science but also the acute contentiousness between naturalistic and religious humanism. Hazard wove the rise of world travel and the impact of the Lisbon earthquake, with a narrative focused on the implications generated by the modern scientific "myth of rigor and proof," together with the rise of historical consciousness. He described in detail how what Paul

---

1 Paul Hazard, *The European Mind 1680–1715*, trans. J. Lewis May (London: Penguin Books, 1964), 8–9; originally published as *La crise de la conscience européenne* (Paris, 1935).

Ricoeur has termed the "hermeneutics of suspicion" eroded the traditional or premodern "hermeneutics of consent" or "of love." Although the quotation above shows that Hazard's story of the modern version of the perennial tension between Jerusalem and Athens highlights the impact of events upon what was considered to be a Christian culture, modernity has raised issues that beset Jewish and Christians believers alike.

I. Faith

"Jerusalem" refers to the faith that Jews and Christians believe originated with God's calling of Abraham, the common father of the Jewish, Christian, and Islamic religions, from Ur of the Chaldeans.[2] That faith is fundamentally the remembrance of God's saving acts in history: leading Moses and the Hebrews out of Egypt into their formal constitution as God's people of the covenantal promise on Sinai; the rise and downfall of the Davidic kingdoms of Israel and Judah; and the exile in Babylon and return to Jerusalem. After the founding of the second Temple, Israel's beliefs crystalized in the symbols of Torah, Temple, Land, and Jewish ethnicity.[3] In the course of Hebrew prophecy, of the wisdom teachings, and the rise of apocalyptic prophecy, that faith began to suggest that the universalist implications of Israel's election involved an expansion of the ideas of salvation and messiah.[4] Yahweh, the liberator

---

2 On the biblical background of the idea of faith, see the summary by Avery Dulles, SJ, *The Assurance of Things Hoped For: A Theology of Christian Faith* (New York: Oxford University Press, 1994), 7–19. On the complications attending the three different appropriations of Abraham by Judaism, Christianity, and Islam that divide the three faiths as much as (if not more than) they unite them, see Jon D. Levenson, *Inheriting Abraham: The Legacy of the Patriarch in Judaism, Christianity, and Islam*, Library of Jewish Ideas (Princeton, NJ and Oxford: Princeton University Press, 2012).

3 See N.T. Wright, *The New Testament and the People of God* (Minneapolis: Fortress Press, 1992), especially, "Story, Symbol, Praxis: Elements of Israel's Worldview," 215–44.

4 See Wright, "The Beliefs of Israel," and "The Hope of Israel," *The New Testament and the People of God*, 244–338; but this should not be interpreted in a supercessionist sense, since Israel will always be Gentile Christians' "older brothers in the faith," as John Paul II phrased it on his historic visit to the Jewish Synagogue in Rome. Also see Wright's interpretation of this relationship in "Christ, the Law and the People of God: Romans 9–11," *The Climax of the Covenant: Christ and the Law in Pauline Theology* (Minneapolis: Fortress Press, 1993), 231–56. Christians now, and unfortunately too belatedly, understand that Jesus Christ as savior of the world and not only the Jews is a deeply *Jewish* belief about the expected messiah. However, see the devastating narrative by David Nirenberg in his *Anti-Judaism: The Western Tradition* (New York: W.W. Norton, 2013).

of Israel, is also the creator of the universe and Lord over all nations, who are destined both to receive the commandments but also to share in redemption. In fulfillment of this, according to Christian belief, the redemptive love mediated into history by the eschatological Jewish messiah named Jesus is universal.[5]

Jewish political theologian Jacob Taubes writes in his book *The Political Theology of Paul*:

But the word of God cannot just go awry! The word of God is after all true and firm, as the prayer of the Jews emphasizes daily. No, it didn't go awry. Because not all who descend from Israel *are* Israel. That is the key sentence. This means "all" according to the flesh is not identical to the "all" according to the promise. Not everyone. The apostle takes the election of Israel seriously. This is embarrassing for modern Christianity, but that's the way it is … Because he understands himself to be an apostle of the Jews to the Gentiles and understands this as a calling. In Galatians there is nothing about a conversion in the sense of being overwhelmed. Rather there is a calling. From the womb I have selected you, that's what it means in Jeremiah to be a prophet, and here is what it means to be an apostle. Naturally, this means: an apostle *from the Jews* to the nations.[6]

A long trail of errors[7] throughout the Common Era generated a long-standing oblivion within the Christian community about Paul's teaching as here interpreted by Jacob Taubes and the authentic general Christian teaching stated here in a sermon by Swiss theologian Karl Barth:

It is not a matter of course that we belong to Jesus Christ and he to us. "Christ hath become a servant of the Circumcision for the sake of the truth

---

5 On the relationship between Christianity and the Jewish faith, see Francesco Rossi de Gasperis, *Cominciando da Gerusalemme. La sorgente della fede e dell' esistenza cristiana* (Rome: Edizione Piemme, 1997). The author kindly sent me this book, and I wholly agree with its anti-supercessionist thesis, and about the continued relevance for serious Christians of Jerusalem in the primordial sense.

6 Jacob Taubes, *The Political Theology of Paul*, trans. Dana Hollander (Stanford: Stanford University Press, 2004), 47–8 (italics original).

7 Malcolm Hay, *Europe and the Jews: The Pressure of Christendom on the People of Israel for 1900 Years* (Boston: Beacon Press, 1961) provides a helpful tracing of the "trail of errors" in the history of Christian tradition also documented more amply and from a distinct point of view by David Nirenberg's *Anti-Judaism: The Western Tradition*.

of God, to confirm the promises which came unto the Fathers" (Romans 15:8). That is: Christ belonged to the people of Israel. This people's blood was in his veins, the blood of the Son of God. He took on the nature of this people when he took on humanity, not for the sake of this people, nor because of the advantage of its blood and race, but for the sake of the truth, viz., for the sake of demonstrating the truthfulness and faithfulness of God. Because God had made a covenant with, and given his presence and the promise of an unparalleled redemption to, this and only this people: a stiff-necked and evil people (Exodus 32:9), but precisely this people – not to reward and lift up the Jews, but to confirm and fulfill this free, gracious promise of God "made to the Fathers," Jesus Christ became a Jew. He said once of himself that to the lost sheep of the house of Israel and only to them was he sent (Matthew 15:24; cf. 10:5–6). That means for us, who are not Israel, a locked door. If it is nevertheless open, if Christ nevertheless belongs to us too as we to him, then it must once again be true in a special sense that "Christ hath received us unto the praise of God." That this is so, we are reminded by the existence of the Jewish people to this very day.[8]

Christians hold that the decisive liberation of history from sin was accomplished on the cross of Jesus and in his resurrection. The consensus among many Christian theologians is that although Jesus understood his mission to be exclusively to "the lost sheep of the house of Israel," it was only general refusal of his message by the Jews that made possible the insight on the part of his followers – St Paul above all – into the universal scope and efficacy of Jesus's redemptive act in the sending of the Holy Spirit to everyone.[9] This led eventually to a transformation of the central symbols of Jewish identity: God's election of Jewish ethnicity is revealed decisively to have been for the sake of the salvation of all people (which is, of course, also a Jewish teaching); Jesus becomes

---

8 Karl Barth, "Die Kirche Jesu Christi," *Theologische Existenz Heute* 5 (Munich: C. Kaiser, 1933): 11–19; republished in *Predigten, 1921–1935*, ed. Holger Finze, *Karl Barth Gesamtausgabe*, Abt. 1. *Predigten* (Zürich: Theologische Verlag, 1998). Here cited in the English translation by Charles Dickenson by Horst-Heinz Deichmann, "Appendix One: Opening Remarks to the First Deichmann Lecture Series," in Larry W. Hurtado, *How on Earth Did Jesus Become a God? Historical Questions about Earliest Devotion to Jesus* (Grand Rapids, MI: Eerdmans Publishing Co., 2005), 208.

9 See Erik Peterson, "The Church from Jews and Gentiles," *Theological Tractates*, ed., trans., and with an introduction by Michael J. Hollerich (Stanford: Stanford University Press, 2011), 40–67.

for Christians what Torah is for the Jews; and, according to N.T. Wright, "Jesus and the church together are the new Temple; the world ... is the new Land."[10]

In a very broad sense, therefore, faith is integral to the central process by which God forms humanity into what in Rowan Williams's words is "an unrestricted fellowship of holiness."[11]

II. Reason

In "Athens" Socrates and Plato originated the traditional meaning of reason – philosophers asking about the right way to live in such a manner that their queries could not be satisfied by conventional wisdom articulated practically in the laws of the polis (*nomoi*) and in traditional opinions (*doxai*) expressed in a commonsense way. These shared meanings of a politically organized people bring to light a concrete solution to the problem of living together in relation to the divine. For the Greeks, myth is poetic discourse, a form of conversing among "people as members immersed in their indigenous communities" who "narrate what appears to be necessary to them" in terms of global and compact consciousness.[12] Shared opinions and divine law (*theios nomos*) grow out of stories (*mythoi*) for the most part handed down and believed in poetic terms rather than those of philosophic knowledge (*logos, epistēme*), which is based on true and certain knowledge of the first causes or principles of things.

Socratic reason has to do with the examination of opinions in the speech and response of dialectic. As a form of conversing that strives for a theoretical account of things, philosophic reasoning becomes increasingly independent of the city and all that it takes for granted,[13] because science or *epistēme* in the strict sense is the logically

---

10 Wright, *The New Testament and the People of God*, 366, note 31.
11 Rowan Williams, "Theological Integrity," *New Blackfriars* 72, no. 847 (March 1991): 140–51 at 144.
12 Gerhard Krüger, *Abendländische Humanität* (Stuttgart: W. Kohlhammer, 1953), 15–16; see also G. Krüger, *Einsicht und Leidenschaft. Das Wesen des platonischen Denkens* (Frankfurt: Klostermann, 1939); and H.-G. Gadamer, *Platos dialektische Ethik und andere Studien zur platonischen Philosophie* (Hamburg: F. Meiner, 1968).
13 Krüger, *Abendländische Humanität*, 15–16. See also Leo Strauss, *The City and Man* (Chicago: Rand McNally, 1963).

consistent account which Socrates typically sought, but knew he had not attained. It was Aristotle who explicitly elaborated the requirements of the logical ideal of science or *apodeixis* in his *Posterior Analytics*.[14] *Pistis* or "belief," on the other hand, regards what is held as true or assented to on the basis of someone else's knowledge, rather than one's own firsthand knowing. From the standpoint of philosophy's goal of replacing authoritative opinions about what is highest and best with universal, necessary, and certain knowledge, belief (*pistis*) may take on a pejorative connotation through its association with opinion, myth, and law.

However, according to Aristotle, the *pepaideumenos* or well-educated person would never attempt to subject every field of inquiry to the rigor (*akribeia*) of the logical ideal, since not all fields are susceptible of it.[15] Consequently, philosophy as embodied in Aristotle is not rationalist in the mode of Descartes's or Spinoza's *more geometrico*. Paradoxically, Aristotle's most basic investigations in metaphysics and in practical and political philosophy have a structure not unlike the classic one of faith seeking understanding: the philosopher starts his dialectical ascent to knowledge from the best available opinions, using the light of *nous* to take them more seriously than they take themselves.[16] As a matter of fact, in one of his letters Aristotle stated that as he became more

---

14 That is, true and certain knowledge of things by their universal, certain, and necessary causes. On the way Aristotle conceived this, see Patrick H. Byrne, *Analysis and Science in Aristotle* (Albany: State University of New York Press, 1977).

15 Aristotle, *Nicomachean Ethics* I.3 1094b12ff. See Ernest L. Fortin, "The Paradoxes of Aristotle's Theory of Education in the Light of Recent Controversies," in *The Birth of Philosophic Christianity: Studies in Early Christian and Medieval Thought*, Ernest L. Fortin: Collected Essays 1, ed. Brian Benestad (Lanham, MD: Rowman and Littlefield, 1996), 209–22.

16 Patrick H. Byrne pointed out to me the point made in a typescript by C.D.C. Reeve, "Aristotle's Philosophical Method," in the following at pages 30–1: "Since *euphuia* is what enables people 'to discern (*krinousi*) correctly what is best by a correct love or hatred of what is set before them' (*Top.* VIII 14, 163ᵇ 15–16), it seems to be the power philosophy has and dialectic lacks. Since it aims to achieve 'what is best,' it seems to be the sort of *euphuia* referred to in the following passage: 'A person doesn't aim at the end [the good] through his own choice; rather, he must by nature have a sort of natural eye to make him discern (*krinei*) well and choose what is really good. And the person who by nature has this eye in good condition is *euphuês*. For it is the greatest and finest thing ... and when it is naturally good and fine, it is true and complete *euphuia* (*NE* III 5 1114ᵇ 5–12)."

isolated and withdrawn, he was becoming ever more a lover of myth (*philomythoteros*).[17]

Hence, the traditional way of formulating the issue as between Jerusalem and Athens has been in terms of "faith" (meaning *belief* defined as assent to truths that are not immanently generated by one's own acts of understanding and conceiving, reflecting and judging) and "reason" (meaning the range of reason when it functions without the aid of revealed teachings or *theologoumena*). There has always been a tension between faith in this sense and reason in this sense.[18] Eric Voegelin has suggested that a "dogmatomachy" waged against each other by partisans of both faith and reason arose chiefly since the time of the European Renaissance, and helped to transform this tension into a disjunction in an unprecedented way. The ground of the premodern tension was a *distinction* that depended upon the reflective differentiation of reason vis-à-vis faith instead of a *separation* between belief and reason. In contrast, the ground of the modern disjunction has been a *separation* between the two that has dominated the climate of opinion from the seventeenth century until our own day.

---

17 Cited in Eric Voegelin, "Was ist politische Realität?" *Anamnesis* (Munich: Piper, 1968), 283–354 at 299: "Je einsamer und zurückgezogener ich bin, um so mehr werde ich zum Liebhaber des Mythos (*philomythoteros*)."

18 This tension was first expressed by Tertullian (d. 197), in terms of inquiring what Jerusalem and Athens could possibly have to do with each other, and by St Jerome's Letters 21 and 22, describing the nightmares caused him by the threat posed to Christian faith by philosophy. With the recovery of Plato and Aristotle by Alfarabi, the tension became, if anything, exacerbated, as can be seen in the plea to read the Qu'ran in the light of reason by Averroës, in the *Decisive Treatise and Epistle Dedicatory*, trans. Charles E. Butterworth (Chicago: distributed by the University of Chicago Press for Brigham Young University Press-Islamic translation Series, 2002); also "The Decisive Treatise: Determining What the Connection Is between Religion and Philosophy," trans. George F. Hourani, in *Medieval Political Philosophy*, ed. Ralph Lerner and Muhsin Mahdi (Ithaca, NY: Cornell University Press, 1963), 163–85. This tradition of Alfarabi that insisted on reading revealed texts in the light of reason (in its Platonic *sive* Aristotelian versions) also influenced Maimonides and the so-called Latin Averroists, Siger of Brabant and Boethius of Dacia, and Dante later on. Alain de Libera's *Raison et Foi. Archéologie d'une crise d'Albert le Grand à Jean Paul II* documents this issue especially in the work of Albert the Great in the Middle Ages. Clearly, too, Thomas Aquinas's *Summa contra Gentiles*, based on his appropriation of Aristotle's thought as manifest in his *Commentaries*, was evidence of the seriousness of the tension. In this regard see, too, Ernest L. Fortin, *Dissent and Philosophy in the Middle Ages: Dante and His Precursors*, trans. Marc A. LePain (Lanham, MD: Rowman & Littlefield, 2002).

Such philosophical histories of human intellect as d'Alembert's preface to the *Encyclopédie* and Lessing's "The Education of the Human Race," portrayed a massive cultural transition from the faith (or beliefs) of the naive and immature stage of humankind to the critically reflective and the mature "reason," which coincided with the rise of modern science and of modern critical history[19] in tandem with enormous social and economic changes, which brought with them novel forms of literature, arts and sciences, human sciences, and non-Western religions. Now thoughtful people could initiate the project of emancipating humankind from all non-human bonds.

Kant, having asked, "What is Enlightenment?" in his famous essay with that same title, answered, "Man's release from his self-incurred tutelage." Modern "reason," then, is driven by the desire to gain its own autonomy in all domains and in every mode of thought and conduct. If henceforth fidelity to "reason" meant engaging in a quest for human fulfillment freed from every constraint, this entailed operating outside of and often opposing the beliefs that until then had set standards for the personal and collective goals in the culture. Both "faith" and a "supernatural order" regularly began to be regarded as *dépassé*.

In discussions about reason's compatibility with religious belief, it began to be taken for granted that living in the light of "reason" alone is synonymous with practicing one or another form of *rationalism*. Rationalism here means a conception of the range of reason that excludes (either implicitly or explicitly) the possibility of true knowledge of anything that it is not intrinsically or extrinsically conditioned by space and time. This includes revelation, faith, belief, grace, and beatitude after death – in short, anything "supernatural." The claim of reason's sufficiency, together with the claim of humankind's ability to attain sustained moral behavior without God's intervention, inevitably follows from this.

---

19 Such figures as Niccolò Machiavelli (1469–1527), Thomas Hobbes (1588–1679), René Descartes (1596–1650), Benedict Spinoza (1632–77), John Locke (1632–1704), Pierre Bayle (1647–1706), Montesquieu (1689–1755), Voltaire (François-Marie Arouet, 1694–1778), Jean le Rond d'Alembert (1717–83), David Hume (1711–76), Denis Diderot (1713–84), Immanuel Kant (1724–1804), and figures such as Gotthold Ephraim Lessing (1729–81) and J.A.H. Reimarus (1729–1814) forged the prevailing modern image or concept of reason discussed in this paper.

III. Athens and Jerusalem: Leo Strauss on Premodern vs. Modern Rationalism

As a Roman Catholic seminarian taking census in the early 1960s in various Southern California parishes, I first encountered the specifically modern problematic of Jerusalem and Athens in relation to repercussions of post-Enlightenment rationalism among educated members of mainstream churches in the course of interviews with Christians who had fallen away. In part it was because my seminary training had not prepared me to confront these issues intelligently that I read Paul Hazard after being sent to Rome to study theology in 1963. After college and then after leaving the seminary, I did a doctoral dissertation at the University of Basel on the hermeneutic circle in Hans-Georg Gadamer and Bernard Lonergan. Upon coming to Boston College as an instructor in 1971, my colleague Ernest Fortin encouraged me to begin studying the works of the Jew and political philosopher Leo Strauss. Strauss's personal discovery of esoteric writing as a clue to the nature of premodern philosophy made it possible for him to distinguish it from modern rationalism, and so to reframe the problematic of Jerusalem and Athens as a revival of the *querelle des anciens et des modernes.*

Lonergan's courses on method in theology at the Gregorian University had already introduced me to Strauss's colleague at Marburg University, Hans-Georg Gadamer, who claimed that Martin Heidegger and Karl Barth were the pioneers of a hermeneutic revolution in search of new foundations for scholarly reading and research in response to the discontinuity in Western tradition wrought by the Enlightenment's "prejudice against prejudice." Each in his own way initiated a post-critical reading of classic texts and criticized the arrogance so often linked to practitioners of historical-critical method. They undertook a phenomenological exploration of human historicity to acknowledge the relativity of contingent perspectives while avoiding out-and-out relativism. Gadamer regarded the philosopher and the theologian both to be elucidating and enacting the humanly inevitable circle of believing to understand and understanding to believe.

Strauss was, like Gadamer and fellow students at Marburg University (Karl Löwith, Gerhard Krüger, and later, Hans Jonas) also devoted to Martin Heidegger. He was greatly affected by his encounter with the thought of Heidegger. In hindsight, we realize that Heidegger had unceasingly attempted to meet the challenge of Nietzsche adequately. He thus helped careful readers of his works to realize that Nietzsche was the *fons et origo* of "postmodernism," which was an immoderate or extreme reaction to Enlightenment rationalism, which came to be embodied in the varieties of deconstructionist or genealogical historicism.

Heidegger's own project of *Destruktion* was a strategy for recovering the question about Being, in a way that – although Heidegger may have envisaged something like a Platonic reform of German education[20] – was completely lacking in political prudence, as is sadly documented by the episode of his rectorate under the Hitler regime. In contrast, the young Strauss as a Jew in Germany found himself in a "theologico-political predicament." This was an outgrowth both of Strauss's youthful increasing disenchantment with the political, cultural, and religious forms of Zionism as his successive critiques of each form of Zionism widened and deepened. While authoring introductions to key selections in the *Jubiläumsausgabe* from Moses Mendelsohn's writings for the Jewish Academy of Sciences in Berlin, he immersed himself in a study of the notorious *Pantheismusstreit* to explore the intellectual, moral, and political intricacies of the respective relationships to Lessing on the part of Friedrich H. Jacobi (1743–1819) and Mendelsohn, which surrounded the reception of Spinoza's thought. This eventually led to his recovery of *les anciens*, in which he followed a Heidegger-inspired disengagement of classic texts and their authors from the distorting and trivializing effects of tradition (as in the – to Strauss's mind – notorious case of the Christian reduction of Aristotelian philosophy to an *ancilla* or servant of theology). From his studies on Spinoza, Strauss's further questions led in two directions: first, as regards the originality of Hobbes that he considered more radical than Spinoza's; and second, in relation to the insufficiency of Spinoza's criticisms of Maimonides. He discovered that much more significant than the conventionally accepted influence of Aristotelian science upon Maimonides was the fact that he was much more profoundly a Platonic philosopher, a conclusion Strauss came to on the basis of his examination of Maimonides's chief sources, Alfarabi and Avicenna.[21]

---

20 See Christian Sommer, "Métapolitique de l'université. Le programme platonicien de Heidegger," *Les études philosophiques* 93 (2010/2): 255–75.

21 See Leo Strauss, *Philosophy and Law: Contributions to the Understanding of Maimonides and His Predecessors*, trans. Eve Adler (Albany, NY: SUNY Press, 1995), especially, "The Philosophical Foundation of the Law: Maimonides's Doctrine of Prophecy and Its Sources," 101–33.

After Strauss's turn to Maimonides, Alfarabi, Averroës, and Avicenna, he radically transformed the understanding of the relationship between ancient or premodern rationalism and modern rationalism. Like Gadamer, he learned from Heidegger to become ever more expressly aware of his prejudices to understand the classic texts, whether modern or ancient, on their own terms; but he then relinquished a certain academic style of *Geistesgeschichte* for what would have to be called a more philosophical and post-critical (i.e., post-historicist) approach. This was closely bound up with the fact that conventional scholarly approaches were incapable of handling the theological-political problem, which was ever at the forefront of what he conceived of as "first philosophy" in its proper depth.

When the Arab and Jewish thinkers helped him to realize the bearing of the political on their writing, and to register more clearly the absolute centrality of law for both Judaism and Islam in contrast to Christianity, he made a fundamental differentiation between the respective appropriations of philosophy by thinkers in these faith traditions. It became manifest to him that many of the leading and most highly esteemed thinkers during the so-called Age of Faith included atheists who were highly critical of their religions in private, while they were simultaneously reputed to be great public champions of their respective religious traditions. So he relentlessly questioned whether ideas of the compatibility between Jerusalem and Athens – ideas which became commonplace in Catholic Christian circles after the medieval reception of Aristotle into the Latin West – could be any longer taken for granted. Similarly, Strauss found ever more highly dubious the accommodations made by orthodox Jewish believers such as Martin Buber and Franz Rosenzweig (as Jewish examples) and representatives of what Karl Barth labeled *Kulturprotestantismus* (among Christians) with the modern foundations of philosophy.

A central clue came from Avicenna's indication of the significance of Plato's *Laws* on the topic of divinely revealed law,[22] and also on the

---

22 Leo Strauss, *Persecution and the Art of Writing* (Chicago: University of Chicago Press, 1953), at 10: "Philosopher-kings, and communities governed by philosopher-kings, were however the theme not of Aristotelian but of Platonic politics. And divine laws, which prescribe not merely actions but opinions about the divine things as well were the theme of Plato's *Laws* in particular. It is therefore not surprising that, according to Avicenna, the philosophic discipline which deals with prophecy is

importance of prophecy as an interaction within human beings between the imagination and what Aristotle termed the active or agent intellect (*nous poietikos*). After Strauss's death, Ernest Fortin took up the issue of the theme of prophetology so important to Alfarabi, Avicenna, and Maimonides in his treatment of the contrast between Siger of Brabant and Boethius of Dacia, and Dante Alighieri, on the one hand, and Thomas Aquinas on the other; he noted that neither Siger nor Boethius possessed the political skills they might have learned from Alfarabi in prosecuting their opinions, and which Dante Alighieri clearly demonstrated that he had learned. Indeed, Fortin was convinced that Dante is the parade example of what Strauss had uncovered about the possibility of philosophy's subverting faith and theology inasmuch as the person reputed to be the greatest Christian poet of the Middle Ages was in reality (as Fortin argued at length) a hidden atheist consummately skilled in the art of esoteric writing.[23]

The second direction of inquiry following upon Strauss's concentration on Spinoza was his discovery of how basic was Hobbes's critique of religion to the founding of modern political philosophy.[24] Strauss understood that Plato had achieved the basic criticism of religion vis-à-vis the divine law (*theios nomos*) at the roots of Greek polity. Plato, unlike Hobbes, was not writing in a world dominated by an organized religion such as Christianity, with its canon of scripture and a highly developed dogma or like rabbinic Judaism's commentary tradition, each of which

---

political philosophy or political science, and the standard work on prophecy is Plato's *Laws*. For the specific function of the prophet, as Averroës says, or of the greatest of all prophets, as Maimonides suggests, is the legislation of the highest type." For more information on this, see Joel L. Kraemer, "The Medieval Arabic Enlightenment," in *The Cambridge Companion to Leo Strauss*, ed. Steven B. Smith (Cambridge: Cambridge University Press, 2009), 137–70, and for scholarly notes regarding the passage in Avicenna's *On the Division of the Rational Sciences* to which Strauss is referring, see page 153 for the full quotation and notes 37 and 38 on the same page.

23 See Fortin, *Dissent and Philosophy in the Middle Ages: Dante and His Precursors*.

24 See Strauss's posthumously published *Hobbes's Critique of Religion and Related Writings*, trans. and ed. Gabriel Bartlett and Svetozar Minkov (Chicago: University of Chicago Press, 2011), and the instructive introduction by Heinrich Meier, 1–19. See, too, Heinrich Meier, *Leo Strauss and the Theologico-Political Problem*, trans. Marcus Brainard (Cambridge: Cambridge University Press, 2006); and *The Lesson of Carl Schmitt: Four Chapters on the Distinction between Political Theology and Political Philosophy*, trans. Marcus Brainard (Cambridge: Cambridge University Press, 1998).

provide an authoritative answer to the question of the best way to live as human.

*Jacob Klein's Contrast between "Natural" Ancients
and "Artificial" Moderns*

As we shall see, in *Hobbes's Critique of Religion and Related Writings*, Strauss gives a detailed account of Hobbes's teaching regarding the intelligible as the object and result of human making. This account may have been made possible by or at least harmonizes with a discovery made by his friend Jacob Klein in his 1914 publication, "Die griechische Logistik und die Entstehung der Algebra."[25] Klein insisted that the modern science (of Galileo, Kepler, and Descartes) is grounded in a new mathematics pioneered especially by François Viète (known as Vieta), Simon Stevin, and Descartes. He realized that understanding this point of departure correctly would enable him to recover the ancient Greek understanding of mathematics against which it profiled itself.[26] In lectures entitled "On a Sixteenth-Century Algebraist" and "Modern Rationalism" Klein explained how the distinction between "concepts which apply to objects" and concepts "which apply to concepts themselves" set the conditions for the modern generalizing of the Greek understanding of numbers because this capacity to generalize beyond what is immediately intelligible in sensible phenomena went hand-in-hand with the ability to express such second order generalizations by means of the symbolization using the terms of modern algebra. Such techniques enabled Stevins, for instance, to "identify ciphers, the signs meaning the various numbers, with the numbers themselves," which in turn made it possible for him to grasp that "the Zero and not the Unit is the principle of the Number and that Zero is the equivalent of a

---

25 Appearing originally in Jacob Klein, *Quellen und Studien zur Geschichte der Mathematik, Astronomie und Physik*, Abt. B: *Studien* 3, fasc. 1 (Berlin, 1931), 18–103 (Part I); fasc. 2 (1936), 122–235 (Part II); and in English as *Greek Mathematical Thought and the Origin of Algebra*, trans. Eva Brann (Cambridge, MA: MIT Press, 1968).

26 See Klein, the first chapter of Part II, "On the difference between ancient and modern conceptualization," *Greek Mathematical Thought and the Origin of Algebra*, 117–25, which describes a shift from the intelligibility of number as of a multitude of definite units via a second order generalization expressed in symbols as related to a system of other symbols resulting in the number of an indefinite multitude.

geometric point by comparing directly the succession of ciphers with a line."[27] And so Klein could say:

> Our [meaning of] rationalism is a symbolic one … It is the true expression of the paradox … that the mind, which is supposed to be sufficient to understand the world, is preconceived as a mind alienated from the same world. We approach the world not directly but by means of concepts, which are abstractions of abstractions and which at the same time we interpret as being in direct contact with the world.[28]

Thus, Klein's study of Vieta's interpretation of Diaphantus's secret breakthroughs in reconceiving geometry in terms of the language and techniques of algebra (along with further developments introduced by Stevin and Descartes) allowed Klein to clarify by contrast the "unnatural" and "abstract" character of modern mathematics with the "natural" way the Greeks thought about number.

In the course of explaining why Hobbes could not accept Descartes's refutation of the *Deus deceptor* argument in the *Meditations*, Strauss's study of Hobbes's philosophic critique of religion (of revelation, of scripture, of miracles, of the comprehensibility of God and of the world) showed how Hobbes set the stage for modern science's role in the modern project. What made it possible for Strauss to confirm his hypothesis of the contrast between the ancients and the moderns, was Hobbes's grasp of something akin to Galileo's *mente concipio* when joined to the phenomenalist conviction that we can know with certainty only what appears to the senses.[29] This as it were completed the break with a natural orientation to nature by means of the natural scientific "mathematization" of nature, as evinced by the significant role of the *res extensa* that is susceptible of being mapped onto a number field in Descartes's thought. In this way, Hobbes parted ways with the ancient and "natural" idea of art, in accord with which art fits into an already intelligibly

---

27 See Jacob Klein, *Lectures and Essays*, ed. Robert B. Williamson and Elliott Zuckerman (Annapolis, MD: St John's College Press, 1983), 35–42 and 53–65.

28 Klein, "Modern Rationalism," *Greek Mathematical Thought and the Origin of Algebra*, 63. Incidentally, this corresponds at least roughly to the scholastic doctrine of the degrees of abstraction, in which mathematics is the result of the second degree of abstraction that leaves aside sensible or common matter.

29 Strauss, *Hobbes's Critique of Religion*, 98–9.

ordered cosmos. This becomes the heart of Strauss's contrast between the *artificial* starting point of modern political philosophy and the *natural* starting point of the premodern authors – Maimonides, the Arabs, and Plato – to which he returned.

Strauss on Hobbes's Role in Rejecting the Premodern Tradition

In describing the role of historical scholarship in changing "the old order," Paul Hazard made no bones about the fact that, however important to the Enlightenment project attacking the Catholic Church might have been, undermining the authority of the Bible was of incomparably greater significance.[30] Be that as it may, Strauss understood that for Hobbes the blend of philosophy and dogma in Catholic and Christian theology, which justified "powers invisible" and "the Kingdom of Darknesse" in people's minds, presented an ultimate threat to his rational theory of government based on the "mortal god" or Leviathan, with its monopoly on "powers visible" over life and death. To dismantle the very possibility of revelation, therefore, was not only constitutive for Hobbes's political theory; but, according to Strauss, such a critique also laid the foundations for modern science as opposed to science as understood by classical philosophy.

> But the philosophic politics that rested on the foundations conceived by Socrates had not only refused an association with theology; it had also not *been able* to refuse this; in any case it had provided theological politics with some of its most dangerous weapons. Hence, a *new* politics was required

---

30 See Hazard, *The European Mind 1680–1715*, 59–60: "In some dim recess, at the far end of their libraries, poring over their books, cogitating, comparing, and collating, specialists, investigators, experts, auditing the account-books of History, pursue their thankless and seemingly innocuous task. If they like it, and they say they love it, then by all means let them get on with it. Pinpointing a date here, and another one there, totting up the tale of years, how they squabble among themselves! When ordinary folk heard the din of their wrangles, they just laughed. A lot of dryasdusts at their futile games again, they said. But when these learned gentlemen finish their task, or rather their installment of it (for they began it long ago, as far back as the Renaissance, and finish it they never will), they will have sown more seeds of unrest in quiet minds, and done more to undermine faith in history, than all your open scoffers and anti-religious fanatics ever succeeded in doing." See, too, Hazard's two chapters, "Richard Simon and Biblical Exegesis," and "Bossuet at Bay," 213–31 and 232–52.

that would not merely be independent of theology, but that would also make any relapse into theological politics impossible for all future time. In other words, what was required was a politics that did not, like classical politics, *precede* revelation and hence, as it seemed, had not risen to meet the claim from the outset, and therefore *succeeded* revelation. Hence, the critique of revelation is not merely a subsequent, though necessary, *supplement* to Hobbesian politics, but its *presupposition*, indeed the presupposition of Hobbes's philosophy in general.[31]

Hobbes, Strauss saw, was "killing two birds with one stone": "revelation, or the polemic against revelation is what makes the acceptance of classical politics impossible for Hobbes."[32] Premodern science stressed the intelligibility both of the cosmos as the superhuman whole, and of the first mover in terms of an emphasis on teleology (or final causality) as the answer to the question about the ground of the mysterious whole (as in the case of Aristotle's divine *nous* as prime mover of all things). Hobbes, however, was determined to show that the first cause like the caused universe as a whole is unintelligible, as well as to eliminate teleology altogether from the realm of science as a product of "vain imaginings" and to replace it with an exclusive focus on efficient causality. Hobbes's cause is accounted for and represented or imagined as *power* on the model of human beings' exercise of musculature in acts of pushing or pulling.[33]

---

31 Strauss, *Hobbes's Critique of Religion*, 28.

32 Strauss, *Hobbes's Critique of Religion*, 26.

33 In the introduction to Strauss, *Hobbes's Critique of Religion*, 14, note 37 (which quotes from the 1964 preface to *Hobbes politische Wissenschaft in ihrer Genesis*), Heinrich Meier cites a note in which Leo Strauss states that only in his review of Raymond Polin's book on Hobbes, which appeared in *What Is Political Philosophy? And Other Studies* (Glencoe, IL: Free Press, 1959), 170–96, did he say that he had solved a problem regarding the Hobbesian authorship of a work entitled *Horae Subsecivae*. The note on page 8 of that 1964 preface reads: "According to Hobbes, the only peculiarity of man's mind which precedes the invention of speech, i.e., the only natural peculiarity of man's mind, is the faculty of considering phenomena as causes of possible effects, as distinguished from the faculty of seeking the causes or means that produce 'an effect imagined,' the latter faculty being 'common to man and beast': not 'teleological' but 'causal' thinking is peculiar to man. The reason why Hobbes transformed the traditional definition of man as the rational animal into the definition of man as the animal which can 'inquire consequences' and hence which is capable of science, i.e., 'knowledge of consequences,' is that the traditional definition implies that man is by nature a social animal, and Hobbes must reject this implication (*De cive*, I, 2). As

In *Natural Right and History* Strauss says that Hobbes joined Epicurean materialism with Platonic mathematicism to develop "an island of intelligibility" that supersedes the support from the cosmic whole as traditionally conceived[34] and so envisaged civilization as a conquest of nature by technical expertise – what Bacon called "the relief of man's estate," or again what Descartes predicted would make man "the master and possessor of nature." Moreover, by simultaneously overcoming classical politics and refuting the claim of revelation to be rationally tenable, Hobbes thereby surmounts with one stroke the two great causes of civil war – classical republicanism and ecclesiastical political power.[35]

---

a consequence, the relation between man's natural peculiarity and speech becomes obscure. On the other hand, Hobbes is able to deduce from his definition of man his characteristic doctrine of man: man alone can consider himself as a cause of possible effects, i.e., man can be aware of his power; he can be concerned with power; he can desire to possess power; he can seek confirmation for his wish to be powerful by having his power recognized by others; he can be vain or proud; he can be hungry with future hunger, he can anticipate future dangers, he can be haunted by long-range fear. Cf. *Leviathan*, chs. 3 (15), 5 (27, 29), 6, (33–6), 11 (64), and *De homine* X.3."

34 Leo Strauss, *Natural Right and History* (Chicago: University of Chicago Press, 1953), 169–77 at 174. See also Richard R. Velkley's discussion of Strauss's volume *Hobbes's Critique of Religion* in *Heidegger, Strauss, and the Premises of Philosophy: On Original Forgetting* (Chicago: University of Chicago Press, 2011), 145: "Hobbes's aim of constructing an 'island of intelligibility' exempt from chance and superseding the question of the cosmic support of the human entails this liberation from teleology."

35 See Pierre Manent, *An Intellectual History of Liberalism*, New French Thought, trans. Rebecca Balinski (Princeton, NJ: Princeton University Press, 1994), 21–2:

> Thus at the origin of Hobbes's construction lay the two great doctrines of protest against the Church's political power: classical republicanism (Aristotle and Cicero) and Protestantism. These led to a political and social catastrophe. Now, notice that these two great movements consisted of appealing to a prestigious past (antiquity) or a pure one (primitive Christianity) against a corrupted present. Or, put differently, the Catholic confusion between nature and grace, expressed in Aristotelian scholasticism, naturally led to appeals to pure nature (antiquity) or to grace alone (Protestantism). Why did these two appeals lead to an unprecedented disorder?
>
> The problem was that, whatever the intrinsic merits of classical antiquity and primitive Christianity, these two great doctrines existed in England only as *opinions*. They were available to all, providing a ready-made argument or pretext whenever anyone's vanity inclined him to disobedience. What had in ancient times been experience, now became an opinion that proved to be ruinous for civic life. Consequently – and this is the polemical heart of the Hobbesian vision – the deplorable political effects of these opinions refuted their claim to reflect an experience authoritatively.

Nevertheless, Strauss understands precisely what is at stake in Hobbes's option: "Since man must understand himself in the light of the whole or of the origin of the whole which is not human, or since man is the being that must try to transcend humanity, he must transcend humanity in the direction of the subhuman if he does not transcend it in the direction of the superhuman."[36]

Hobbes considered nature as given to be incomprehensible, and therefore God is also incomprehensible. The incomprehensibility seems to be due to the randomness or chanciness or contingency that affects all terrestrial realities – something Aristotle also noted. However, premodern nominalists held fast to – Strauss says they "had faith in"[37] – the idea of a natural correspondence between human knowledge and the world to be known (i.e., in the words of Strauss, "the natural origins of the universals"). However, because they held that only knowledge obtained with regard to sensible knowing could be certain, any correspondence between sensed particulars and universals exists only in the mind and not in reality. Nevertheless, for the premodern nominalists, *natura occulte operatur in universalibus*. In contrast Hobbes saw no reason to agree with these opinions, and, applying Occam's razor rigorously, he held that we only understand what we make.[38]

Strauss writes: "It is not the fact of nature as a comprehensible order that lies, for Hobbes, at the basis of every possible orientation in the world, but the fact of *art*: while the works of nature are incomprehensible,

---

36 See Leo Strauss, *Thoughts on Machiavelli* (Glencoe, IL: Free Press, 1958), 78.

37 Strauss, *Natural Right and History*, 168–79 at 174–5.

38 See Strauss, *Natural Right and History*, especially 172: Hobbes "was forced to wonder whether the universe did not leave room for an artificial island, for an island to be created by science." And at 173: "Generally stated, we have absolutely certain or scientific knowledge only of those subjects of which we are the causes, or whose construction is in our own power or depends on our arbitrary will. The construction would not be fully in our power if there were a single step of the construction that is not fully exposed to our supervision. The construction must be conscious construction; it is impossible to know a scientific truth without knowing at the same time that we have made it. The construction would not be fully in our power if it made any use of any matter, i.e., of anything that is not itself our construct. The world of your constructs is wholly unenigmatic because we are its sole cause and hence we have perfect knowledge of its cause. The causes of the world of our constructs does not have a further cause, a cause that is not, or not fully, within our powers; the world of our constructs is therefore the desired island that is exempt from the flux of blind and aimless causation."

in principle, the works of art are comprehensible in principle."[39] Hobbes saw that human art was capable of overcoming the dimension of chance in terrestrial events, and because of the certainty regarding the methodical steps enacted in making, he was sure that art could render nature manipulable, manageable, and controllable.

Plato's Socrates acknowledged that the know-how of the artisans or craftsmen who possess habitual and valid knowledge (*techne* or technical expertise) regarding parts of being could be used as a model to be transcended in wisdom's quest for knowledge of the whole. As we see in the *Gorgias*, the open-ended quest to understand the whole is what differentiated philosophy or the "good" rhetoric from the Sophists' misuse of *techne* as depicted in the "bad" rhetoric of Polus and Callicles. Again, the premodern understanding of art involved imitating or perfecting the intelligibility of nature as an ordered whole, whereas "Hobbes's conception of 'art' differs from the traditional conception" insofar as it is "nothing but the human capacity to bring about useful effects on the basis of reflection." Strauss goes on to say,

> The philosophical tradition rejected by Hobbes understands art as imitation, or improvement, of nature (cf. Aristotle, Physics 2.8, paragraph 5 and Leviathan, chap. 7); it presupposes thereby that nature is an (intelligible) order. Now, if one claims the historical incomprehensibility of nature, as Hobbes does, art can no longer be the imitation of nature; art loses its natural model; it turns into a model-less sovereign invention. But even if, or rather, all the more because art remains the decisive fact for the philosophical orientation, art now has significance for a different reason than hitherto: art is the criterion of evidence for Hobbes for a different reason from that of the tradition. The evidence of art is generally grounded in the fact that the artisan *knows* what he does excellently. But this knowledge can be understood in an entirely different way. For the originator of the tradition, Socrates-Plato, the knowledge that is decisive for the artisan is turning-one's-gaze-away-toward-something, namely, toward an *order*, which he wants to reproduce. And the knowledge of the artisan is therefore excellent because knowledge of the form or order through which and for the sake of which each thing is what it is, is genuine knowledge (cf. Gorgias 503e–504a with Phaedo, Republic).[40]

---

39 Strauss, *Hobbes's Critique of Religion*, 111.
40 See Strauss, *Hobbes's Critique of Religion*, 113–14.

Art, then, is the centerpiece of what Strauss calls Hobbes's "philosophy of civilization"; and the key to Hobbes's conception of art is his constructivist transformation of nominalist gnoseology. Hobbes's transformation of political philosophy into a technical affair was based on the truth of the dictum, *verum et factum convertuntur*, upon which the doctrines both of "knowledge as power" and the "conquest of nature for the relief of man's estate" are founded. Moreover, for Strauss this presupposition is the seed of the modern historicist idea of culture.

Strauss on Christianity's Role in the Decline of Modern Reason

Strauss was convinced that the Christian manner of elevating the goal of human transcendence, far from enhancing the philosophic way of life, had a corrupting effect instead. Strauss preferred Maimonides's rabbinical and Jewish focus on the law as what made it possible for belief to be integrated into Platonic political philosophy. The medieval Islamic and Jewish philosophers were the ones who had demonstrated how to do this. As Shlomo Pines wrote in a tribute to his collaborator in the English translation of *The Guide of the Perplexed*,[41]

> The philosophy (from Machiavelli and Hobbes to Nietzsche) was mainly engaged in undermining foundations and revealing the nakedness of the world and man, and it was true and destructive. In contradistinction, the medieval philosophers, whom Strauss learned to read, were true but not destructive, at least in Strauss's view. They knew of the position of man in a world in which there was neither providence nor immortality. They were aware of the dangers, which they as philosophers had to face, and they recognized the fact that the majority of mankind is unable to withstand philosophic truths. As a consequence, out of fear for their own safety, but also caring for the society to which they belonged, the philosophers found a way to harmonize religion and philosophy without any concession on their part. They did it by using a style which reveals as it conceals. Strauss learned and taught how to decipher it …[42]

Thus, Maimonides could use his pagan theoretical wisdom to make the rational best of the two tables of commandments by showing how

---

41 Moses Maimonides, *The Guide of the Perplexed*, vols. 1 and 2, trans. and with an introduction by Shlomo Pines, introductory essay by Leo Strauss (Chicago: University of Chicago Press, 1963).

42 Shlomo Pines, "On Leo Strauss," *Independent Journal of Philosophy* 5, no. 6 (1988): 169–71.

the first table taught people a sane, non-fanatical, and practical knowledge of God, and the second table set forth the basic conditions for living together harmoniously and free of strife. From the perspective of his return to Socrates and Plato, the outcome of Strauss's assessment of Hobbes's achievement is that revealed religion, and above all, Christianity set up an unnatural standard for human living. This view is intimately connected with Strauss's discovery that Maimonides, by reputation the Jewish Aristotelian counterpart of Thomas Aquinas, actually appropriated Aristotle's philosophy in the Platonist mode of the great Islamic philosophers, Alfarabi and Avicenna. In *The City and Man* Strauss made the point that although Aristotle's philosophy was continuous in many ways with that of Plato, it no longer possessed the quality of ascent, which was characteristic of Plato. As a result, as Strauss pointed out in *Natural Right and History*, Aristotle virtually eliminated the typical Socratic-Platonic tension between the philosopher and the *polis*, because for him "there is no fundamental discrepancy between natural right and the requirements of political society."[43] For Aristotle natural right was independent of the law, which was always the paramount preoccupation of Jewish and Islamic philosophers.

Strauss argued that Aristotelian natural right was shorn of its Socratic-Platonic edge when appropriated by Thomas Aquinas's natural law theory:

> No doubt is left, not only regarding the basic harmony between natural right and civil society, but likewise regarding the immutable character of the fundamental propositions of natural law; the principles of the moral law, especially as formulated in the Second Table of the Decalogue, suffer no exception, unless possibly by divine intervention; the doctrine of *synderesis* or of the conscience explains why the natural law can always be duly promulgated to all men and hence to be universally obligatory.[44]

And if one wonders why Aquinas could be so certain about this transformation of Aristotle on natural right, Strauss explains that:

> It is reasonable to assume that these profound changes are due to the influence of the belief in divine revelation. If this assumption should prove to be

---

43 Strauss, *Natural Right and History*, 156.
44 Strauss, *Natural Right and History*, 163.

correct, one would be forced to wonder, however, whether the natural law as Thomas Aquinas understands it is natural law strictly speaking, i.e., a law knowable to the unassisted human mind, to the human mind which is not illuminated by divine revelation … The ultimate consequence … is that natural law is practically inseparable from natural theology.[45]

Strauss's contention that "modern law was partly a reaction to this absorption of natural law by theology" becomes even more plausible when one considers that in Thomas Aquinas's *Treatise on Law* the New Law of grace overshadowed both the natural law and the Old Law.[46] Indeed, as a Christian theologian, Aquinas did sublate ancient philosophy's view of the whole into what he himself conceded was an indemonstrable interpretation of the origin and the end of the mysterious whole with a doctrine of creation and a reinterpretation of beatitude. Christian theologians also transformed Aristotle's "good life," which was already superior to mere "life," into "eternal life" – a life attainable only by God's grace, which enables persons to live not just a virtuous but a "holy" life. In this way Christian theology systematically subordinated philosophic concern for "the one thing necessary" to the requirements of dogmatic beliefs that rationalists of any stripe would judge to be beyond reason or irrational.

Strauss regarded such developments as a blight upon Western thought, because revealed religion, especially Christianity, rendered what he considered the more "natural" ways of asking and answering questions about how people should live (as exhibited in the writings of Plato and Xenophon) implausible or even virtually inaccessible. This amounted to the creation of what Strauss called "a second cave" that would have to be demolished to return to the "first cave" – or the more natural way of knowing depicted in Plato's *Republic* or his *Laws*. We have seen how Klein radicalized the meaning of *Destruktion* taken from Heidegger in his movement from modern to ancient mathematics. Similarly, Strauss thought that penetrating "the second cave" caused by the perennial influence of revealed religion together with the modern reaction against it in Machiavelli, Hobbes, and Descartes enabled him to recover the "natural" sources of knowledge revealed in the radical questioning into the right or the best way to live as performed by the Socrates of Plato and Xenophon.

---

45 Strauss, *Natural Right and History*, 163–4.
46 Strauss, *Natural Right and History*, 164.

Ancient vs. Modern Rationalism

From Strauss's perspective, then, the great contemporary need is to recover the Socratic-Platonic rationalism that differs radically from the modern rationalism of Hobbes, Descartes, Spinoza, and their successors. In a reply to Alexandre Kojève connected with the publication of Strauss's commentary on Xenophon's *On Tyranny*, Strauss articulated the overall difference in orientation between ancient and modern as follows:

> On the basis of Kojève's presupposition, unqualified attachment to human concerns becomes the source of philosophic understanding: man must be absolutely at home on the earth, if not a citizen of a part of the habitable earth. On the basis of the classical presupposition, philosophy requires a radical detachment from human concerns: man must not be absolutely at home on earth, he must be a citizen of the whole.[47]

To be sure, premodern rationalists shared with believers the idea of a *trans-political* solution to the problem of human living in a fallen, derailed, or alien world. Even though (according to Strauss) they were nonbelievers, the medieval Islamic and Jewish philosophers in their prudence and moderation understood the role of religion in the morality of ordinary orthodox believers who generally were neither concerned with nor capable of grounding their moral conduct theoretically. The philosophers' questions about the right way to live demanded answers that could undergo the test of comprehending the human condition in relation to the whole of the cosmos. They thus transcended "the cave." The majority of people in the world of religious common sense dwell in "the cave" by believing the authoritative and symbolically expressed teachings. The medieval philosophical theologians were able to live a freely contemplative life and understood that the solution was only accessible to them "in speech"; they nevertheless cared about the moral integrity of society and attempted to provide believers with improved interpretations of authoritative teachings. As Strauss shows in *Persecution and the Art of Writing*, by making use of "a forgotten type of writing,"

---

47 See Leo Strauss, *On Tyranny: Revised and Expanded Edition, Including the Strauss-Kojève Correspondence*, ed. Victor Gourevitch and Michael S. Roth (New York: Free Press, 1991), 212.

they went beyond merely allegorizing biblical and traditional teachings that contradicted knowledge that unaided reason could attain. They did this both to exploit their theoretical grasp of reality as a whole and their powers to persuade people to observe the moral teachings commonly taught and followed by their religious communities, as well as to hide their private opinions.

The Islamic and Jewish philosophers disclosed for Strauss their premodern approach to "the essential limitation of the political" problem due to the "difficulty created by the misery of the just and the prosperity of the wicked"; this approach was provided by the Socratic view that the true dignity of the political actually depends on the trans-political, contemplative quest for wisdom of the philosophic way of life to which only the very few have access. Alfarabi, Avicenna, and Maimonides were quite aware of the insufficiency of morality understood as obedience to law under divine sanctions; they made it abundantly clear to their careful readers that they also knew about the human capacity to be virtuous from Aristotle's teaching in the *Nicomachean Ethics* regarding the magnanimous man, which was based on that person's noble pride, and did not depend on any intervention of divine grace.[48] Alternatively, revelation teaches that the insufficiency of morality is ultimately resolved only by divine and supernatural redemption, which alone can supply enough support for pious and loving obedience to the divine law. Strauss saw that the final authority for premodern rationalism is nature, "an impersonal necessity that replaces the personal gods." Modern rationalism, according to Strauss, uses biblical motifs to promote a solution to the problem of evil through the human capacity of science, technology, education, and "laws with teeth in them," instead of the trans-political resources of philosophy and revelation counted upon by believers in a supernatural solution.

Strauss's Interpretation of the Hebrew Scriptures

According to Rémi Brague, a French scholar of Judaism and Islam (who has studied the writings of Leo Strauss): "After the failure of a large-scale Jewish revolt against Rome, and beginning with the formation of the Academy at Javneh (ca. 70 CE), the rabbis worked to re-center

---

48 Leo Strauss, "Progress or Return?" in *Introduction to Political Philosophy: Ten Essays by Leo Strauss*, ed. Hilail Gildin (Detroit: Wayne State University Press, 1975), 277–8.

the whole experience of Israel on the Torah. The Torah had to be transmitted, and in order to protect it from possible distortions, it required the construction of a 'fence' of rules for the determination of its precise application." A few lines further on in the chapter, "The Law as an End: Judaism," Brague went on to say, "It is on the basis of the law that Judaism reinterpreted the series of events that made up the history of Israel and of the biblical texts that captured the memory of those events. The Covenant with God was brought down to the Law: 'There is no covenant outside of the Torah' [*Mekhilta de-R. Ishmael*, ed. H.S. Horowitz and I.A. Rabin (Frankfurt 1931), 32 on Exod. 12:6]."[49]

This confirms Strauss's claim that Judaism (like Islam) treats religion chiefly as a matter of the Law. In general, according to Brague, the Jewish approach to the Torah characteristically interpreted it in the light of reason.[50] It is often said that, having been introduced to philosophic texts by Christians in what is now Lebanon and in Alexandria, the tendency to read either the Bible or the Qur'an in the light of reason prevailed among both Jews and Muslims for centuries.[51] But countervailing tendencies were such that Averroës felt the need to write *The Decisive Treatise*, which urgently called upon Muslims to continue to read their sacred writings in the light of reason, and in the measure that fundamentalism has prevailed within Islam, in that measure, Averroës's call has been rejected.

In his two commentaries, "Jerusalem and Athens" and "On Genesis," Strauss's interpretation of the book of Genesis gives us a concrete example of the practice of reading the Bible in the light of reason. Strauss uses reason to scrutinize the book as having been carefully composed by a single author as that author's original audience would have been likely to understand it. It is incumbent upon the interpreter as much as

---

49 Rémi Brague, *The Law of God: The Philosophical History of an Idea*, trans. Lydia G. Cochrane (Chicago: University of Chicago Press, 2007), 187, 188. In his "Preface to *Spinoza's Critique Religion*," in *Jewish Philosophy and the Crisis of Modernity: Essays and Lectures in Modern Jewish Thought*, ed. with an introduction by Kenneth Hart Green (Albany, NY: State University of New York Press, 1997), 172, Strauss reminds us that "Jewish orthodoxy based its claim to superiority to other religions from the beginning on its superior rationality (Deut. 4:6)."

50 See Brague, the entire chapter in *The Law of God*, 187–208, as well as the chapter, "The State and Law: Ancient Israel," 41–60.

51 See Brague, "Islam: Law Rules," *The Law of God*, 146–56, and "The Aims of the Law: Islam, 150–86.

possible to understand precisely as the author understood himself to be communicating his message to that first audience, so that one tries to read the text in isolation from any and all traditions. Another example, to which Strauss often refers and defers, are the commentaries on the books of Genesis and Exodus by the Florentine Jewish scripture scholar, Umberto Cassuto.[52] In opposition to the fragmentation of the surface of the Hebrew scriptures stemming from Julius Wellhausen's documentary hypothesis, Cassuto used his reason to give a coherent account of differences that, while they seem to point to different oral traditions – say, "Yahwists," "Elohists" – that underlie the written text's surface, instead help to make good sense of the surface of the text by supposing that the book was the composition of a single author in which each part is carefully related to the whole.

These two approaches to interpretation of the Bible in the light of reason make clear that so-called rationalists who take pains to attend to the surface of the text do not necessarily end up singing in unison. In general, Strauss uses reason to open up ambiguities in the surface of the text in large part due to residual dependencies on tradition, while Cassuto uses reason to show how the textual evidence is ultimately compatible with traditional orthodox interpretations.

The work of Harvard scholar, Jon D. Levenson, contrasts with that of both Strauss and Cassuto. First, he values historical-critical scholarship more positively than either of them, even though, second, like Cassuto and unlike Strauss, in his desire to do justice to the authoritative texts, he does not think it necessary to prescind from the life of texts within succeeding faith-communities; third, again unlike Strauss, he performs what Gadamer meant by *hermeneutisches Bewusstsein*[53] inasmuch as he

---

52 See Umberto Cassuto, *A Commentary on the Book of Genesis: Part One, From Adam to Noah*, trans. Israel Abrahams (Jerusalem: Magnes Press, 1978); *A Commentary on the Book of Genesis: Part Two, From Noah to Abraham*, trans. Israel Abrahams (Jerusalem: Magnes Press, 1984); and *A Commentary on the Book of Exodus*, trans. Israel Abrahams (Jerusalem: Magnes Press, 1983).

53 "Hermeneutical consciousness" involves exposing oneself to the complications of the "history of effects" (effectual history, *Wirkungsgeschichte*) of the ongoing reception and interpretation of the texts. In his essay "Teaching the Texts in Contexts," *Harvard Divinity Bulletin* 35, no. 4 (Autumn 2007): 19–21, Jon D. Levenson described the value of historical-critical Bible study as follows: "The goal was to place the Hebrew Bible in its historical context, and we could do that only if we could reconstruct the cultural world in which its many documents were written – an arduous task but one that bore, and continues to bear, much good fruit." But that goal was

focuses on the role played by exegesis of the Hebrew Bible in Jewish and Christian communities in late antiquity and appreciates the way communal interpretations change the self-understandings of the communities involved. Strauss's hypothesis of the build-up of the "second cave" is evidence that he was aware of these diverse traditional exegetical streams; but his interest in these pales before his concentration on the distinction between the two radically different ways of life – the life of faithful obedience *or* the philosopher's life of free insight or unbounded inquiry. Whether reading the Bible or reading philosophical writings, his sole concern is expressed in the question, What truth is the text teaching us? For Levenson, the historical-critical approach is limited because

> there are dimensions of the text that it cannot help us understand very much, because a text can say more than any individual author meant; the whole is larger than the sum of the parts. When I say this, I am not talking as a mystic or even as a believer. I am talking as a student of literature (I majored in English in college). But I think what I am saying ought to be of great interest to all who see in scripture something more than what was on the mind of the human authors who wrote it, with all their human limitations.[54]

not enough for him, as he went on to say in the following passage: "As a practicing Jew, I found this very problematic. To me, it was clear that the Hebrew Bible has more than one context, and the meaning of a textual unit changes with the other textual units with which it comes into relationship – not just other biblical texts written by authors in other cultural contexts, but also postbiblical documents that the tradition has given us – in the Jewish case, the vast amount of rabbinic literature known as the *torah shebbe'al peh*, 'the Oral Torah.' My problem was not the standard problem Jewish traditionalists have with the proposition that the Torah, the Pentateuch, has a complicated compositional history and is not a unitary composition of Moses. That I readily accepted. I had never been a fundamentalist. My problem, rather, was that by assigning meaning only to the intention of the original authors, the whole into which the antecedent texts had come to be woven became meaningless, and the interaction of the parts with that whole became at best a matter of secondary importance. The closest we could come to giving a holistic reading was through what is called 'redaction criticism,' which studies the way the compositions came to be combined. The problem, though, is that when the whole text currently in our hands says something larger than what any author or redactor, in any period, intended, we can no longer say who the author is. With that, we have reached the limits of the author-centered method of interpretation to which all this research is devoted."

54 Jon D. Levenson, presentation upon receiving an honorary doctorate in divinity from St Mary's Seminary and University in Baltimore, May 10, 2007.

What Levenson says about the constraints on understanding the mind of the author, *mutatis mutandis*, would also hold true for the minds of the original audience to which the text was addressed.[55] It would be unfair to suppose that Levenson is not utterly interested in understanding the truth the text is communicating. So, once again, Strauss and Levenson offer two different ways of reading the Bible in the light of reason – but with contradictory views on what is entailed in receiving the truth of the scripture.

For all their differences vis-à-vis hermeneutical methods, Leo Strauss and Jon Levenson agree that scripture should not be interpreted through the lens of any metaphysics. For Strauss, biblical teaching and philosophy are utterly incompatible not only in principle, but also because Genesis explicitly excludes philosophy and metaphysics *tout court* and so operates on a different plane. Levenson simply rejects "the residue of the static Aristotelian conception of deity as perfect, unchanging being; the uncritical tendency to affirm the constancy of divine action, and the conversion of biblical creation theology into an affirmation of the goodness of whatever is."[56] In "On the Interpretation of Genesis" Strauss says about the opening verses of the first creation narrative, "It would appear, if we take this literally, that the earth in its primordial form, without form and void, was not created. Creation was formation rather than out of nothing."[57] The strict differentiation between biblical thought

---

55 In *Jesus of Nazareth: From the Baptism in the Jordan to the Transfiguration*, trans. Adrian J. Walker (New York: Bloomsbury, 2007), xix–xx, Joseph Ratzinger (Pope Emeritus Benedict XVI) states something like the same teaching as Levenson, but a bit more explicitly: "It is necessary to keep in mind that any human utterance of a certain weight contains more than the author may have been immediately aware of at the time. When a word transcends the moment in which it is spoken it carries within itself a 'deeper value.' This 'deeper value' pertains most of all to words that have matured in the course of faith history. For in this case the author is not simply speaking for himself on his own authority. He is speaking from the perspective of a common history that sustains him and that already implicitly contains the possibilities of its future, of the further stages of its journey … The author does not speak as a private, self-contained subject. He speaks in a living community, that is to say, in a living historical movement not created by him, nor even given by the collective, but which is led forward by a greater power that is at work."

56 Jon D. Levenson, *Creation and the Persistence of Evil: The Jewish Drama of Divine Omnipotence* (Princeton, NJ: Princeton University Press, 1988), xx, in a preface added to the 1994 edition to defend himself against critics by explaining his position more fully.

57 Strauss, "On the Interpretation of Genesis," *Jewish Philosophy and the Crisis of Modernity*, 357–76 at 362.

and Greek is still maintained when Strauss in "Progress or Return?" treats of the way Maimonides in the *Guide* regards the biblical text as having a secret teaching that is at most implicit in the literal sense.[58] In any case Strauss understands that the God of the Bible is incomprehensible, and this comes to sight in the unpredictability of God's changing ways of acting in relation to human beings and creation, for instance, in causing the Flood to bring about a fresh start especially for human creatures and then in making a covenantal promise never to do this again. Strauss says that this changeable character of God is shown even more dramatically when God says in connection with Abraham, Isaac, and Jacob, "I shall be gracious to whom I shall be gracious and I shall show mercy to whom I shall show mercy" (Ex. 33:19). Strauss links this to his translation of *Ehyeh-Asher-Ehyeh*, the name revealed to Moses: "I shall be what I shall be" (Ex. 3:13). Strauss and Levenson both agree that according to the plain sense of the creation and Fall narratives in Genesis as supported by other passages in the prophets and the writings, God created not only "heaven and earth," but he created evil, too.

If for Strauss God's incomprehensibility is a function of God's arbitrariness, for Levenson God is a reality divided within from the beginning. Like human beings, he too is caught up in a struggle in which the good part of God's self is in an incessant battle to overcome evil, including the evil pole within himself. For Strauss,

> Only after the creation of man did God "see all that He had made, and behold, it was very good." What then is the origin of evil or the bad? The biblical answer seems to be that since everything of divine origin is good, evil is of human origin. Yet if God's creation as a whole is very good, it does not follow that that all its parts are good or that creation as a whole contains no evil whatever: God did not finally will all parts of His creation to be good. Perhaps creation as a whole cannot be "very good" if it does not contain some evils. There cannot be light if there is not darkness, and

---

58 Strauss, "Progress or Return?" *Introduction to Political Philosophy*, 281: "The issue as [Maimonides] stated it was as follows: philosophy teaches the eternity of the world, and the Bible teaches creation out of nothing. This conflict must be rightly understood, because Maimonides is primarily thinking of Aristotle, who taught the eternity of the visible universe. But if you enlarge that and apply it not only to this cosmos, to this visible universe in which we live now, but to any cosmos or chaos which might ever exist, certainly Greek philosophy teaches the eternity of cosmos or chaos; whereas the Bible teaches creation, implying creation out of nothing."

the darkness is as much created as is light: God creates evil as well as He makes peace (referring to Is. 45: 7). However this may be, the evils whose origin the Bible lays bare after it has spoken of creation are a particular kind of evils: the evils that beset man.[59]

Strauss emphasizes the simplicity and naïveté of the primordial man and woman in the garden in which they encountered neither harshness nor need, and so were not overwhelmingly tempted toward the lack of charity or justice that might be required for the sake of sheer survival. The Fall or the disobedience that involved eating from the tree of knowledge of good and evil represents, according to Strauss's construal, "a first step in the education" of humankind by which they might advance in civilization, but one in which the decision to eat of the tree of knowledge of good and evil is almost accidental inasmuch as, while there was knowledge of disobedience, the fault was a matter of minimal responsibility. According to "On the Interpretation of Genesis," "We have no reason to suppose on the basis of the biblical account, as distinguished from later explanations, that man was guided by desire for knowledge of good and evil, for he would have had to have some knowledge of good and evil in order to have such desire. It is even hard to say that man desired to transgress the divine command. It comes out rather accidentally."[60] Again, "The Bible says nothing to the effect that our first parents fell because they were prompted by the desire to be like God; they did not rebel high-handedly against God; they rather forgot to obey God; they drifted into disobedience."[61] But the disobedience has as its principle "autonomous knowledge of good and evil, and knowledge which man possesses as himself, the implication being that the true knowledge is not autonomous …"[62] For Strauss philosophy alone is the paradigm of autonomous knowledge of the sort that would truly guide human beings in living their lives.

---

59 Strauss, "Jerusalem and Athens: Some Preliminary Reflections," *Jewish Philosophy and the Crisis of Modernity*, 377–405 at 384.

60 Strauss, "On the Interpretation of Genesis," *Jewish Philosophy and the Crisis of Modernity*, 372.

61 Strauss, "Jerusalem and Athens," *Jewish Philosophy and the Crisis of Modernity*, 387.

62 Strauss, "On the Interpretation of Genesis," *Jewish Philosophy and the Crisis of Modernity*, 372.

Biblical Revelation as Opposed to Philosophy

Therefore, for Strauss the biblical story of the order of creation and of the Fall is also an admonition against philosophy as a way of life.[63] In teaching that the sin of disobedience is reducible to the acquisition of the knowledge of good and evil and the flight from the life of simplicity, the Bible is rejecting any philosophic ascent from what is "first-for-us" (*proton pros hemas*) in faithful obedience to God's commands to knowledge of what is "first-in-itself" (*proton pros physin*) in cosmology, which discovers the kind of guidance for human life that is only attainable by the disinterested contemplation of the intelligibility of what is unchanging in the heavens. Moreover, for Strauss, Cain, the tiller of the soil, has the distinction of being the one who committed the first sin in the Bible that is not "accidental" but occurs with full knowledge of God's prohibition as well as full consent; he thereby becomes both the first founder of the city, and the first to introduce the human mastery afforded by the arts, and thus the first to enter the realm of the political.[64] So the Bible's concern for morality and justice in effect rules out not only the political philosophical asking and answering of the question of human justice (as the introduction to philosophy or "first philosophy") but also rejects theoretical cosmology. All of these strictures, according to Strauss, are epitomized by the fact that biblical Hebrew as well as the Hebrew scriptures as a whole have no word corresponding

---

63 Strauss, "On a Forgotten Kind of Writing," *What Is Political Philosophy?*, 221–2:
"Philosophy or science, the highest activity of man, is the attempt to replace opinion about 'all things' by knowledge of 'all things'; but opinion is the element of society; philosophy or science is therefore the attempt to dissolve the element in which society breathes, and thus it endangers society. Hence philosophy or science must remain the preserve of a small minority, and philosopher or scientists must respect opinions on which society rests. To respect opinions is entirely different from accepting them as true."

64 Strauss, "Jerusalem and Athens," *Jewish Philosophy and the Crisis of Modernity*, 387–8. See also Strauss, "Progress or Return?" *Introduction to Political Philosophy*, 279–80:
"That asocial perfection which is contemplation normally presupposes a political community, the city, which accordingly is considered by philosophers as fundamentally good, and the same is true of the arts, without whose services, and even model, political life and philosophic life are not possible. According to the Bible, however, the first founder of a city was the first murderer, and his descendants were the first inventors of the arts. Not the city, not civilization, but the desert, is the place in which the biblical God reveals Himself."

to the Greek "nature" or *physis*, and nature is the pivot upon which turns the fateful alternative of the Socratic (or Platonic and Aristotelian) critique of *nomos*, which is the humanly posited or conventional solution to the problem of living together in harmony that is based ultimately on a *theios nomos* or divine law.

In contrast, Levenson, who unlike Strauss does not really have philosophic or political fish to fry, interprets the creation and Fall rationally in the wake of the massive evil of Shoah. But perhaps more in accord with the Bible's descriptive and dramatic thrust, rather than saying that human beings are not responsible for evil, Levenson claims that the Bible teaches more radically and ultimately that it is the evil in God which is to blame for the evil of fault (*malum culpae*). It seems that both Levenson and Strauss follow what I have been told is the more traditional Talmudic-Midrashic approach to the Fall that avoids the overwhelming emphasis (characteristic of Christian interpretations) on human moral responsibility for sin.

Nevertheless, it seems that to deny or attenuate the claim that moral evil is due to the responsible decisions of human beings alone also presupposes that the truth of God's creating *ex nihilo sui et subjecti* is impossible; emphasizing this impossibility goes together with accenting the fact that the primordial waters (*tehom*) against which God acts formatively is a chaos, which is to say, radical, godless disorder and moral evil. So according to Levenson, (not unlike the teaching of modern Christian process theologies) we have a finite God who is dynamically caught up with the faithful in the struggle against evil. It seems that Lessing's basic argument in this regard – namely, that on the face of the biblical witness itself, God is either unable or unwilling to create a world without evil – seems to be the upshot of the interpretations of both Levenson and Strauss.

Levenson therefore conceives of God as involved in an unfinished struggle with evil both outside of himself and within himself. "Though the persistence of evil seems to undermine the magisterial claims of the creator-God, it is through submission to precisely those claims that the good order that is creation comes into being."[65] Hence, the faithfully observant Jew participates in God's ongoing forming and bringing

---

65 Levenson, *Creation and the Persistence of Evil*, 156.

order out of chaos. For Strauss, it is the philosophers who know how to put evil in the right perspective:

> It reproduces, and raises to perfection, the magnanimous flexibility of the true statesman, who crushes the insolent and spares the vanquished. It is free from all fanaticism because it knows that evil cannot be eradicated and therefore that one's expectations from politics must be moderate. The spirit which animates it may be described as serenity or sublime sobriety.[66]

Philosophy According to Strauss

Leo Strauss held that because of the multiplicity of conflicting myths or stories handed down by ancestral custom as legitimating (as well as legitimated by) the *theios nomos* or divine law, classical philosophy did not rely on conventional opinions alone for the answer to the question of how to live. Instead philosophers initiated rational inquiry about grounding law in the light of *nature* instead of mere custom. As political, philosophy lives in tension with the city because while the human being is open toward the political whole, the philosopher's consideration of divine law in the light of nature is based on a natural human openness to the natural whole as such. Hence, says Strauss, Socrates showed that contemplation of the superhuman cosmos as regards both the intelligibility and ground of the whole constituted the classical philosophic paradigm for attaining the *proton pros physin* or what is "first by nature," which alone is capable of providing a normative account of the whole. Strauss claimed that "to articulate the problem of cosmology means to answer the question of what philosophy is or what a philosopher is,"[67] because, as he writes elsewhere: "The Greek philosophic view has as its primary basis the simple notion that contemplation of heaven, an understanding of heaven, is the ground by which we are led to the right conduct. True knowledge, the Greek philosophers said, is knowledge of what is always. Knowledge of things which are not always, and especially knowledge of what happened in the past is knowledge of an entirely inferior character."[68] On its face, one cannot help asking

---

66 Strauss, "What Is Political Philosophy?" *Introduction to Political Philosophy*, 28.
67 Strauss, "What Is Political Philosophy?" *Introduction to Political Philosophy*, 38.
68 Strauss, "On the Interpretation of Genesis," *Jewish Philosophy and the Crisis of Modernity*, 373–4.

whether this last claim regarding knowledge of what "always is" (*aei on*) is not an overreaction to historicism. And doesn't that demand fail adequately to acknowledge first, that all human judgments regarding this-worldly realities are as conditioned as are the things known thereby; and, second, that this by no means entails the rejection of the human ability to attain absolute truth?

Traditionally, cosmology is considered one part of metaphysics. Since any appeal to cosmology that is not critically grounded may be dismissed out of hand as *gratis asseritur*, it is not surprising that Strauss says:

> Socrates was so far from being committed to a specific cosmology that his knowledge was knowledge of ignorance. Knowledge of ignorance is not ignorance. It is knowledge of the elusive character of the truth, of the whole. Socrates, then, viewed man in the light of the mysterious character of the whole. He held therefore that we are more familiar with the situation of man as man than with the ultimate causes of that situation. We may also say he viewed man in light of unchangeable ideas, i.e., of the fundamental and permanent problems.[69]

Strauss's intellectual probity moves him carefully to attenuate his claims regarding cosmological knowledge. The Platonic Socrates whom he esteems most highly did manage to transcend the cave of common opinion by having recourse to cosmology; but more importantly he evoked "the unchangeable ideas" that Strauss interprets to be "the fundamental and permanent problems."[70] Like Socrates, Strauss is far from being apodictic about propositional truth regarding what is highest and best. He repeatedly underscores the fact that Socratic wisdom and knowledge is knowledge of ignorance and so really a "love of knowledge" that makes him strive to know the whole in a manner that ever eludes his grasp. In other words, philosophic inquiry into the intelligibility of the cosmos is actually a never-ending task, so that the classic philosophers are identifiable precisely because they recognize

---

69 Strauss, "What Is Political Philosophy?" *Introduction to Political Philosophy*, 38–9.

70 From the standpoint of "foundational method" these may be understood as heuristic structures, which insofar as they are *foundational* or fundamental (or Strauss also calls them "eternal," implying an invariance over space and time) would involve metaphysics, although Strauss would have in all likelihood denied such an implication.

the limitations of philosophy, and are poignantly aware that philosophy is incapable of providing sufficient grounds for the laws of political society and of ethics. This explains Strauss's insistence that "at any rate, philosophy is meant, and that is the decisive point, not as a set of propositions, a teaching, or even a system, but as a way of life, a life animated by a peculiar passion, the philosophic desire or *eros*, not as an instrument or a department of human self-realization."[71] Strauss goes on to say:

> I must explain … why philosophy cannot possibly lead up to the insight that another way of life apart from the philosophic one is the right one. Philosophy is the quest for knowledge regarding the whole. Being essentially quest and being not able ever to become wisdom, as distinguished from philosophy, the problems are always more evident than the solutions. All solutions are questionable. Now the right way of life cannot be fully established except by an understanding of the nature of man, and the nature of man cannot be fully clarified except by an understanding of the nature of the whole. Therefore the right way of life cannot be established except by a completed metaphysics, and therefore the right way of life remains questionable.[72]

Strauss says that the originating philosophers transcended the dimension of religiously or culturally varying divine codes "by embarking on a free quest for the beginnings, for the first things, for the principles" to "determine what is by nature good, as distinguished from what is good merely by convention."[73] Strauss's doctoral dissertation under Ernst Cassirer was entitled "The Problem of Knowledge in the Philosophical Teachings of F.H. Jacobi." Jacobi opposed "der Alleszermalmender" Kant (Mendelsohn's epithet for Kant) by stressing man's primordial receptivity through a faith conceived as utterly more primordial than Kant's critical project (articulated in the *Vorrede* of the *Critique of Pure Reason*) of "discovering the limits of knowledge in order to make room for faith."[74] Soon after completing his doctoral work, in *Spinoza's Critique of Religion*

---

71 Strauss, "Progress or Return?" *Introduction to Political Philosophy*, 297.
72 Strauss, "Progress or Return?" *Introduction to Political Philosophy*, 297–8.
73 Strauss, "Progress or Return?" *Introduction to Political Philosophy*, 292.
74 An English translation of the extract of the doctoral dissertation published by Strauss himself has been published as "The Dissertation (1921)" in *Leo Strauss: The Early Writings (1921–1932)*, trans. and ed. Michael Zank (New York: SUNY Press, 2002), 53–61.

Strauss undertook a meta-critique of Spinoza's criticism of Maimonides's account of the faculties of sensation and imagination in relationship to intellect (the faculty of understanding). Strauss entered the realm of what might be termed premodern gnoseology, which was based on faculty psychology. He showed that Spinoza misinterpreted Maimonides on prophecy because, motivated by a desire to deprecate the prophets for being overly strong on fantasy, and weak as regards understanding, he followed Descartes's conflation of sense perception with imagination. Strauss realized that, as a matter of fact, Maimonides followed Aristotle's metaphysical psychology, which was far different from that of Descartes. In Maimonides's version of Aristotle, according to Strauss, sense perception and imagination are distinct, and while the imagination may be more prone than either the senses or the intellect to be mistaken as regards the truth (as is evident in dreams), sense perception combined with intelligence can hold imagination in check; and more positively, because of its natural plasticity the imagination, beyond serving the intellect for the sake of understanding corporeal reality correctly, can also aid in apprehending supersensible or incorporeal reality provided that the intellect removes the imagination's tendency to picture incorporeal reality in corporeal terms. Maimonides, following Alfarabi and Avicenna, thought this rationally demonstrated the possibility of prophecy.[75]

As we have already discussed, when Strauss turned to the thorough study of Thomas Hobbes, and especially Hobbes's reflections on Descartes's *Meditations*, he discovered that Hobbes joined Platonic mathematicism with Epicurean empiricism to invent a constructivism that represented an even more radical departure from the Aristotelian account (adopted by Maimonides) of sense perception, imagination, and reason, and which Strauss presumably took up again on his own. On the one hand, Hobbes confined sense perception to the apprehension of the concrete and particular, and in accord with his brand of nominalism, on the other hand, he emphasized the ability of intellect (as an instrument of desire and will) to deploy mathematics to emancipate the arts from any harmony with or constraint by nature precisely as understood by classical philosophy. Classically, the arts presupposed

---

75 Leo Strauss, *Spinoza's Critique of Religion*, trans. Elsa Sinclair (Chicago: University of Chicago Press, 1997), 183–5, translation of *Die Religionskritik Spinozas als Grundlage seiner Bibelwissenschaft. Untersuchungen zu Spinozas Politisch-Theologischen Traktat* (Berlin: Akademie-Verlag, 1930).

the contemplative attainment of objective and universal knowledge of the intelligibility of the world. As Strauss wrote: "The abandonment of the primacy of contemplation or theory in favor of the primacy of practice is the necessary consequence of the abandonment of the plane on which Platonism and Epicureanism have carried on their struggle. For the synthesis of Platonism and Epicureanism stands or falls with the view that to understand is to make."[76]

To my knowledge, Strauss's own position regarding human knowing maintains a rather more Aristotelian thrust:

This quest for the beginnings proceeds through sense perception, reasoning, and what [the Greeks] called *noesis*, which is literally translated by "understanding" or "intellect," and which we can perhaps translate a little bit more cautiously by "awareness" with the mind's eye as distinguished from sensible awareness. But while this awareness has certainly its biblical equivalent and even its mystical equivalent, this equivalent in the philosophic context is never divorced from sense perception and reasoning based on sense perception.[77]

We can glean something more of what Strauss thinks understanding involves from two other places. The first is a passage on Aristotle in "Jerusalem and Athens":

The Aristotelian god like the biblical God is a thinking being, but in opposition to the biblical God he is only a thinking being, pure thought: pure thought that thinks itself and only itself. Only by thinking himself and nothing but himself does he rule the world. He surely does not rule by giving orders and laws. Hence he is not a creator-god: the world is as eternal as god. Man is not his image: man is much lower in rank than other parts of the world. For Aristotle it is almost a blasphemy to ascribe justice to his god; he is above justice as well as injustice.[78]

Strauss here joins many others in translating *noesis noeseos* as "thought thinking thought," which must be construed as presupposing

---

76 Strauss, *Natural Right and History*, 177.

77 Strauss, "Jerusalem and Athens," *Jewish Philosophy and the Crisis of Modernity*, 118–19.

78 Strauss, "Jerusalem and Athens," *Jewish Philosophy and the Crisis of Modernity*, 396, with the following references to Aristotle, *Metaphysics* 1072b14–30; 1074b15–1075a11; *De anima* 429a19–20; *Eth. Nic.* 1141a33–b2, 1178b1–12; *Eth. Eud.* 1249a14–15.

that the act of understanding is essentially thinking or having either one thought or many thoughts. This is a conceptualist interpretation of Aristotle, with which I will take issue later on in this essay.

For now, I wish only to draw attention to Strauss's penchant for distinguishing between the sufficiency and the necessity of possible accounts of things into which he inquires. So, like both Aristotle and Kant, he required necessity, universality, and certainty when it came to determining whether statements are true. In his preoccupation with the logical control of meaning he speaks of philosophers as seeking "truth or clarity," where the force of the "or" seems to be not *vel* but *sive*. In many of his more forthright explanations Strauss's way of constantly ferreting out presuppositions, assumptions, and premises appears to be symptomatic of abstract deductivism, even though he tends to refrain from that sort of narrowness in his overall *performance* of interpreting historical meanings. Strauss frequently lays great stress upon possibility: the possibility of philosophy, of revelation, of prophecy, of miracles, and so forth.

In relation to Strauss's approach, I observe that whenever we try to understand the nature of a reality, first, in answering the *What is it?* question, or in responding to the *Why?* question, human intelligence concentrates on necessity (it has to be this way) and impossibility (it cannot be that way) in sorting through possibly relevant answers to those questions that insight comes up with. However, once one's act of understanding or insight has specified an abstract possibility or a possibly relevant intelligibility, there spontaneously arises the further *Is it so?* question, which reflects on warrants for affirming or denying the existence or truth when making a judgment on the possibly relevant intelligibility formulated as the answer to the *What?* or *Why?* questions. Such are the correlatives on the cognitional side to the distinct semantic referents, namely, (1) the abstract necessity of either form or essence (*eidos*) on the one hand, and (2) the concrete and contingent existence or occurrence of such abstract possibilities (*actus essendi* in Aquinas, whose account is more differentiated on this issue than Aristotle's), on the other.

In contrast, the conceptualist's exclusive concentration on universality, necessity, and certitude tends to conflate the difference between the articulation or formulation of a possibly relevant answer – i.e., an abstract possibility – with the judgment regarding its actual existence or occurrence. Again, the concentration upon universality, necessity, and certainty is closely associated with the desire to ascertain the *totality of the conditions* to correctly affirm any particular hypothesis or guess. However, the first approach can establish only possibility, and not fact; and the second demand exorbitantly flies in the face of ascertainable matter of fact. In order for human judgments to be reliable, they require no more than the fulfillment of not *all* but only the *pertinent* conditions to grasp the unconditioned character of evidence sufficient to affirm that a limited prospective judgment *happens to be* correct or true. This is, of course, just what Strauss, unlike so many historians of medieval philosophy, had done with respect to ascertaining, for instance, the Platonism of Alfarabi, Avicenna, Averroës, and Maimonides. The demand to know the totality of conditions is unreasonable, and only leads to skepticism, whereas the fulfillment of the conditions required for the grasp of sufficient evidence yields no more than a verified possibility, which is all we need, as long as the ones verifying the given hypothesis realize in all honesty that no further relevant questions occur to them.

Therefore, Strauss's insistence upon the "always is" (*aie on*) as the touchstone of normativity and absoluteness in the quest for a cosmological ground of meaning and existence excludes the relevance of contingent fact (Aristotle's "hypothetical necessity"). Does not Strauss require more than humanly attainable verified possibilities as the standard of truth even in relation to the most important questions for man as man? If this is the meaning of the Socratic-Platonic clarity about limitation of philosophy, how does it really differ from the position of Kant's dialectic in the *Kritik der reinen Vernunft*?

Moreover, recalling that in his treatment of Hobbes's critique of religion Strauss distinguishes between Hobbes's nominalism and traditional nominalism by stressing that the latter "had faith" in the correspondence between universals and the particular-individual-concrete realities known by sense perception, is Strauss himself a nominalist of the old school?

In a further statement from his essay "What Is Liberal Education?" one finds a discrepancy regarding his construal in "Jerusalem and Athens" of Aristotle's phrase, *noesis noeseos*. In the "Progress or Return?" lectures Strauss nuances the meaning of "understanding" by both affirming the superiority of understanding and distinguishing but not separating it from "awareness":

Philosophy ... must be on its guard against the wish to be edifying – philosophy can only be intrinsically edifying. We cannot exert our understanding without from time to time understanding something of importance; and this act of understanding may be accompanied by the awareness of our understanding, by the understanding of understanding, by *noesis noeseos*, and this is so high, so pure, so noble an experience that Aristotle could attribute it to his God ... By becoming aware of the dignity of the human mind, we realize the true ground of the dignity of man and therewith the goodness of the world, whether we understand it as created or as uncreated, which is the home of man because it is the home of the human mind.[79]

Here a dynamic "understanding of understanding" replaces the static "thought thinking thought" implied by Strauss's statement above from the "Jerusalem and Athens" essay. Similarly, to make sense of this statement (in contrast to the above-quoted statement from "Jerusalem and Athens" which seems to conflate understanding with awareness), it seems that here awareness is distinct enough from understanding to be capable of accompanying the act of understanding, and thus also able to understand understanding in an act of reflection on one's conscious acts of understanding when they occur "from time to time."

However, at another place in "Progress or Return?" Strauss seems implicitly to be using the scholastic distinction (revived by Gadamer and other phenomenologists) between *actus exercitus* and *actus signatus* to distinguish between conscious operations as performative but not explicitly reflected upon from conscious operations as thematized by explicit reflection. Here again Strauss mentions in very significant context the nexus between "understanding" and "awareness" in noting that philosophers "assume that on the basis of the knowledge of first principles, of the first principle, of the beginnings, it will be possible to determine what is by nature good, as distinguished from what is good merely by convention." He then goes on to say: "The quest for the beginning proceeds through sense perception, reasoning, and what they called *noesis*, which is literally translated by 'understanding' or 'intellect,' and which we can perhaps translate a little bit more cautiously by 'awareness,'" which he then suggests (by way of apposition) means "an awareness with the mind's eye as distinguished from sense perception."[80] (One thinks of the synoptic vision of the whole vouchsafed to

79 Leo Strauss, "What Is Liberal Education?" *Liberalism Ancient and Modern* (New York: Basic Books, 1968), 8.
80 Strauss, "Progress or Return?" *Introduction to Political Philosophy*, 292.

the one dragged out of the cave in Plato's myth in *The Republic*.) A few pages later, Strauss makes clear that this "awareness with the mind's eye" does not refer to understanding, but rather to something more akin to wonder (*thaumazein*) that Aristotle identified with the beginning of all philosophy:

> Classical philosophy is said to be based on the unwarranted belief that the whole is intelligible. Now this is a very long question. Permit me here to limit myself to say that the prototype of the philosopher in the classical sense was Socrates, who knew that he knew nothing, who therewith admitted that the whole is not intelligible, who merely wondered whether by saying that the whole is not intelligible we do not admit to having some understanding of the whole. For of something of which we know absolutely nothing, we of course could not say anything, and that is the meaning, it seems to me, of what is so erroneously translated by the intelligible, that man as man necessarily has an *awareness* of the whole.[81]

So, at the very least we say that it is not altogether clear what Strauss's own answer is to the question regarding what we actually do when we think we are knowing the truth, especially in relation to the terms, understanding, awareness, and intelligible/intelligibility.

Even so, an outstanding feature of Strauss's way of treating the question of knowledge is the remarkable and salutary emphasis he places on the role of asking questions. In comparison to Heidegger, who seems to have shifted from speaking of questioning as "the piety of thinking" (*die Frömmigkeit des Denkens*) to regarding questioning as a form of mastery and control in accord with the Baconian and Cartesian rhetoric of science in the relief of man's estate, the role questioning plays in Strauss's idea of philosophy as a way of life seems to be the key to his resolution of what he regarded as the incompatibility between the horizons of Jerusalem and of Athens. You will recall the passage from Strauss quoted above:

> Philosophy is the quest for knowledge regarding the whole. Being essentially quest and being not able ever to become wisdom, as distinguished from philosophy, the problems are always more evident than the solutions. All solutions are questionable. Now the right way of life cannot be

---

81 Strauss, "Progress or Return?" *Introduction to Political Philosophy*, 300.

fully established except by an understanding of the nature of man, and the nature of man cannot be fully clarified except by an understanding of the nature of the whole. Therefore the right way of life cannot be established except by a completed metaphysics, and *therefore the right way of life remains questionable.*[82]

Strauss on the God Question

We have to take seriously Strauss's next sentence: "But the very uncertainty of all solutions, the very ignorance regarding the most important thing, makes the quest for knowledge the most important thing, and therefore a life devoted to it, the right way of life."[83] That this statement seems to be inspired by what Lonergan named the pure, detached, unrestricted, and disinterested desire to know seems to be supported by the evidence presented by Heinrich Meier's relatively recent books on Strauss (based on what is perhaps an unsurpassed acquaintance with the data left behind by Strauss). Meier stresses the centrality of the theological-political problematic for Strauss as a philosopher. He quotes from a Strauss letter of 11 August 1946 to his friend from Marburg days, Karl Löwith. The correspondence includes a string of letters concerned with the central debate between philosophy and revelation dated earlier that same August, followed by one on 20 August.[84] In private notes Strauss explains that he "has once again suffered shipwreck." Strauss went on to write:

/Hereby, I cross out everything I have done until now – I must *really* start *entirely* from the beginning. / I have to clarify once again for myself what then is the authentic question – and I must alter my work plans accordingly (insofar as I am not bound by promise – to give lectures). / Until now I have assumed that the exhibition of the origin[al] concept of philosophy (along with a sketchy critique of the modern concept of philos[ophy] might have been able to suffice, because the right and the necessity of philos[ophy] is established for me. Under the influence of Kierkegaard and in remembrance

---

82 Strauss, "Progress or Return?" *Introduction to Political Philosophy*, 297.

83 Strauss, "Progress or Return?" *Introduction to Political Philosophy*, 297–8.

84 See also Leo Strauss, "'Correspondence Concerning Modernity,' Exchange of letters with Karl Löwith beginning October 1, 1946," *Independent Journal of Philosophy* 4 (1983): 105–19.

of my earlier doubt, I have to pose the question again, and as acutely as possible, whether indeed that is the case, becomes much more important than the theme "Socrates" and "Introduction to pol[itical] philosophy."[85]

Meier introduces such quotations to frame his account of Strauss's notes for a talk he was invited by Löwith to give at Hartford Theological Seminary.[86] Meier traces Strauss's concern with the confrontation between philosophy and revelation from the time of his early German books in the 1930s, *Die Religionskritik Spinozas*[87] and *Philosophie und Gesetz*[88] through the autobiographical preface (1962) to the late works on Xenophon and Aristophanes; and he has shown that Strauss was influenced by, yet differs from Nietzsche on "intellectual probity," as evidenced by the following remarkable quotation:

A new kind of fortitude which forbids itself every flight from the horror of life into comforting delusion, which accepts the eloquent descriptions of "the misery of man without God" as an additional proof of the goodness

---

85 For the quotation from Strauss's private note from the period of the 1946 correspondence with Karl Löwith, see Heinrich Meier, *Das theologische-politische Problem. Zum Thema von Leo Strauss* (Stuttgart: J.B. Metzler Verlag, 2003) at page 51, note 1 (The above translation of the following German passage is mine): / *Ich streiche alles, was ich bisher getan habe, hiermit durch – ich muss wirklich ganz von vorn anfangen. / Ich muss mir noch einmal klarmachen, was denn die eigentliche Frage ist – und ich muss meine Arbeitspläne entsprechend ändern (soweit ich nicht durch versprechen – Vorlesungen – gebunden bin). / Bisher habe ich angenommen, dass die Darstellung des ursprung[lichen] Philosophie-Begriffs (mit skizzierter Kritik des modernen Philos[ophie]-Begriffs) genügen könnte, da das Recht und die Notwendigkeit der Philos[ophie] für mich feststand. Unter dem Eindruck Kierkegaard's und in Erinnerung an meine früheren Zweifel, muss ich die Frage nochmals und so scharf wie möglich stellen, ob denn das der Fall ist, wird viel wichtiger als das Thema "Socrates" und "Introduction to pol[itical] philosophy."*

86 See Meier's references, *passim*, in *Das theologische-politische Problem* to a *scriptum* used as the basis for Strauss's January 1948 lecture at Hartford Theological Seminary, Hartford Connecticut, entitled "Reason and Revelation (1947–1948)" in the Leo Strauss Papers, Box 11, Folder 13. See page 16, and note 3. Let me note here the reservations (with which I have some sympathy) of my Boston College colleague, Professor Christopher Bruell, regarding the legitimacy or scholarly appropriateness of using private correspondence in a publically argued construction of a thinker's position.

87 Leo Strauss, *Die Religionskritik Spinozas als Grundlage seiner Bibelwissenschaft. Untersuchungen zu Spinozas Theologisch-politischen Traktat* (Berlin: Akademie-Verlag, 1930).

88 Leo Strauss, *Philosophie und Gesetz. Beiträge zum Verständnis Maimunis und seiner Vorläufer* (Berlin: Schocken Verlag, 1935).

of its cause, reveals itself eventually as the ultimate and purest ground for the rebellion against revelation. ... This final atheism with a good conscience, or with a bad conscience, is distinguished from the atheism at which the past shuddered by its conscientiousness. Compared not only with Epicureanism but with the unbelief of the age of Spinoza, it reveals itself as a descendant of biblical morality.[89]

Although Meier concedes that in his published writings Strauss left the impression that the confrontation between philosophy and revelation is a virtual toss-up, he argues *ex aliunde* and *a contrario* that such a conclusion on our part would be precipitous. Citing a letter from Strauss to his student, Seth Benardete, Meier underlines the importance for Strauss of a statement from Calvin's *Institutes*, which Strauss had discussed in a chapter on Calvin in his Spinoza book and used later on as a motto for his Aristophanes book.[90] The gravamen of the statement – paralleling the notorious tendencies of Martin Luther – is the authoritative prohibition of Christians from asking the question of God.[91] By inference, Meier arrives at the question: "Lenkt das Nein Calvins oder Luthers zum *quid sit deus?* die Aufmerksamkeit nicht auf die zentrale Frage?"[92] In the name of opposing idle curiosity as endangering the obedience of faith (not to mention a critique of the political and religious insouciance such inquiry might unleash), Calvin lays bare the central issue of the philosopher who stakes his life on free inquiry and uncoerced insight.

For Meier, Strauss the philosopher could not but investigate the underlying roots of the God-question in terms of the genuine and respectable human need for an ordered polity with laws that reinforce morality. In the end, Strauss's notes set forth the step-by-step process by which people concerned with political order generated the revelation of the monotheistic Christian God as omnipotent creator and legislator,

---

89 Strauss, "Preface to Spinoza's Critique of Religion," *Liberalism Ancient and Modern*, 224–59 at 256.

90 For the quotation of the 17 May 1961 letter to Benardete, see Meier, *Das theologische-politische Problem*, 47, note 42.

91 Meier notes in *Das theologische-politische Problem*, 46, that the motto Strauss chose for his *Socrates and Aristophanes* is taken from John Calvin's *Institutio christianae religionis*, whose interdict on asking *quid sit deus?* he had referred to more than three decades before in his *Die Religionskritik Spinozas*. At 47 Meier also refers to Luther's similar interdict.

92 See Meier, *Das theologische-politische Problem*, 47.

whose Incarnate Son dies for us, thereby using love to motivate obedient faith. Meier, who seems not to be able to overemphasize Strauss's Rousseau interpretation, interprets these preparatory notes for Strauss's lecture as an exposé of how the strategy Rousseau named "honoring the gods with their own wisdom" was realized.

Of course, for me as a Catholic theologian, Strauss's focus on Calvin (*sive* Luther) is one-sided, inasmuch as the Catholic tradition has rarely favored the *sacrificium intellectus* or the formula of Tertullian (who first asked what Jerusalem and Athens have to do with each other), *credo quia absurdum*.[93] Moreover, Strauss mentions the influence upon him of Kierkegaard,[94] who is another Protestant figure whose conception and affirmation of God has a fideist and voluntarist basis. Indeed, Robert Sokolowski has already pointed out Strauss's voluntarist conception of God.[95] Did Strauss regard the obscurantism of Calvin/Luther as typical or normative for Christianity? Did he suppose that the so-called Catholic intellectual tradition is no more than a disguise for an irrational and arbitrary choice to believe? If so, this is unsettling.[96] In any case, the evidence for Strauss's approach to the God question drawn from the notes for the lecture at Hartford Theological Seminary seems incontrovertible. What is still in question is whether Strauss intended his genealogy ironically or provocatively.

---

93 Meier refers to Tertullian, *De carne Christi* V, *Opera omnia*, ed. J.-P. Migne, Patrologia Latina 2 (Paris, 1866), 805B–807B in *Das theologische-politische Problem*, 36.

94 S.A. Kierkegaard, *Abschliessende unwissenschaftliche Nachschrift zu den Philosophischen Brocken. Gesammelte Werke*, Abt. 16, Bd. 1 (Düsseldorf/Köln, 1957), 202: "Denn gerade das Absurde is der Gegenstand des Glaubens und das einzige, was sich glauben läßt"; quoted in Meier, *Das theologische-politische Problem*, 36.

95 See Robert Sokolowski, "Appendix to Chapter 11," *The God of Faith and Reason: Foundations of Christian Theology* (Notre Dame: University of Notre Dame, 1982), 157–64.

96 This may have more to do with Meier than with Strauss, because in *The Lesson of Carl Schmitt: Four Chapters on the Distinction between Political Theology and Political Theology*, trans. Marcus Brainerd (Chicago: University of Chicago, 1998), Meier's rendition of Carl Schmitt's political theology as grounded in primordial mythic religiosity fails to draw the reader's attention to the distinction between biblical revelation and myth about which, in *Das theologische-politische Problem* (p. 54) Meier stresses in citing him that Strauss was always clear ("the philosopher would admit the essential difference between the Bible and myth"). So even if Meier is correct in finding that Schmitt *did* conflate myth and biblical faith, a responsible account should note the objective difference.

This section on Strauss and the Bible concludes with a quotation from "The Mutual Influence of Theology and Philosophy,"[97] published by Hilail Gilden as Part III of "Progress or Return?":[98]

> When we attempt to return to the roots of Western civilization, we observe that Western civilization has roots which are in conflict with each other, the biblical and the Greek philosophic, and this is to begin with a very disconcerting observation. Yet this realization has also something reassuring and comforting. The very life of Western civilization is the life between two codes, a fundamental tension. There is therefore no reason inherent in the Western civilization itself, in its fundamental constitution, why it should give up life. But this comforting thought is justified only if we live that life, if we live that conflict, that is. No one can be both a philosopher and a theologian or, for that matter a third which is beyond the conflict between philosophy and theology, or a synthesis of both. But every one of us can be and ought to be either the one or the other, the philosopher open to the challenge of theology or the theologian open to the challenge to philosophy.[99]

Leo Strauss was a philosopher open to the challenge of Jewish theology, perhaps because he considered doing so with Christian theology presumptuous. Bernard Lonergan was certainly a theologian who was open to the challenge of philosophy. But, as we shall see, while his analysis of modernity's involvement in "the longer cycle of decline" shares much with Strauss's analysis of modernity in terms of the "three waves of modernity," Lonergan's understanding of the nature of philosophy differs in significant ways from Strauss's. It is also one way that, even apart from revelation, he disagrees with Strauss.

IV. Bernard Lonergan's Christian Alternative

On Progress and Decline

If we compare Strauss's hypothesis of the "three waves of modernity"[100] with Lonergan's diagnosis in *Insight* of "the general bias" and "the

---

97 Leo Strauss, "The Mutual Influence of Theology and Philosophy," *Independent Journal of Philosophy* 3 (1979): 111–18.

98 Strauss, "Progress or Return?" *Introduction to Political Philosophy*, 249–310.

99 Strauss, "Progress or Return?" *Introduction to Political Philosophy*, 289–90.

100 Strauss, "The Three Waves of Modernity," *Introduction to Political Philosophy*, 81–98.

longer cycle of decline," we may note a certain complementarity. The key point both thinkers hold in common regarding the modern break with the "Great Tradition" has to do with the modern approach Niccolò Machiavelli proposed for confronting what Lonergan called "the familiar opposition between the idealism of human aspiration and the sorry facts of human performance,"[101] namely, the abandonment of the high ground of the truth about man. Space limitations prohibit a resumé of the way Strauss's frames the *Wirkungsgeschichte* of Machiavelli's solution. Here is one of Lonergan's summaries:

> For while it may happen that after each failure to carry out ideal aspiration man repents and reasserts the primacy of the ideal over the real, of what ought to be over what is, it may also happen that after repeated failure man begins to rationalize, to deform knowledge into harmony with disorderly loves. Such rationalization may involve any degree of culpability, from the maximum of a sin against the light, which rejects known truth, to the minimum of precluding such futurible advance in knowledge and virtue as without even unconscious rationalization would have been achieved. Moreover, this rationalization takes place not only in the individual but also and much more convincingly in the social conscience. For to the common mind of the community the facts of life are the poor performance of men in open contradiction with the idealism of human aspiration; and this antithesis between brutal fact and spiritual orientation leaves the will a choice in which truth seems burdened with the unreal and unpractical air of falsity. Thus it is that a succession of bold spirits have only to affirm publicly a dialectical series of rationalizations gradually to undermine and eventually to destroy the spiritual capital of a community; thus also a culture or a civilization changes its color to the objectively organized lie of ideology in a trans-Marxian sense and sin ascends its regal throne (Romans 5:21) in the Augustinian *civitas terrena*.[102]

Note that although both thinkers are concerned about individual and collective morality, rather than offering moralistic grounds for their respective analyses, they focus on the question, *quid sit homo*? for which the root issue is true rather than false understanding.

---

101 Bernard Lonergan, "Finality, Love, Marriage," *Collection*, Collected Works of Bernard Lonergan 4, ed. Frederick E. Crowe and Robert M. Doran (Toronto: University of Toronto Press, 1988), 26.
102 Lonergan, "Finality, Love, Marriage," *Collection*, 26–7.

Strauss's "wave hypothesis" in relation to modernity lays bare how the attacks on earlier waves by later ones were based on genuine recoveries of nature that, because of their incoherent or incomplete character, only succeeded in radicalizing the modern revolution. Lonergan's account of general bias has its basis in the fact that "if everyone has some acquaintance with the spirit of inquiry and reflection, few think of making it the effective center of their lives; and of that few, still fewer make sufficient progress to be able to withstand other attractions and persevere in their high purpose."[103] The commonsense use of human intelligence that specializes in dealing with the particular and the concrete is especially prone to general bias, "for common sense is incapable of analyzing itself, incapable of making the discovery that it too is a specialized development of human knowledge, incapable of coming to grasp that its peculiar danger is to extend its legitimate concern for the concrete and the immediately practical into disregard of larger issues and indifference to long-term results."[104] Accordingly, Lonergan distinguishes the shorter cycle of decline, due to individual and group biases from "the longer cycle, originated by the general bias of common sense."[105] The longer cycle entails the combination of the minor surrender of detached and disinterested intelligence on the level of common sense and the major surrender on the speculative level that renders human intelligence uncritical and incapable of discriminating social achievement from the social surd.[106] We conclude this section with Lonergan's sketch of the course of the longer cycle of decline in which we have been involved:

The medieval synthesis through the conflict of Church and State shattered into the several religions of the reformation. The wars of religion provided the evidence that man has to live not by revelation but by reason. The disagreement of reason's representatives made it clear that, while each must follow the dictates of reason as he sees them, he also must practice the virtue of tolerance to the equally reasonable views and actions of others. The helplessness of tolerance to provide coherent solutions to social

---

103 Lonergan, *Insight: A Study of Human Understanding*, Collected Works of Bernard Lonergan 3, ed. Frederick E. Crowe and Robert M. Doran (Toronto: Toronto University Press, 1992), 251.
104 Lonergan, *Insight*, 251.
105 Lonergan, *Insight*, 252.
106 Lonergan, *Insight*, 255.

problems called forth the totalitarian who takes the narrow and complacent practicality of common sense and elevates it to the role of a complete and exclusive viewpoint. On the totalitarian view, every type of intellectual independence whether personal, cultural, scientific, philosophic, or religious, has no better basis than non-conscious myth. The time has come for the conscious myth that will secure man's total subordination to the requirements of reality. Reality is the economic development, the military equipment, and the political dominance of the all-inclusive State. Its ends justify all means. Its means include not merely every technique of indoctrination and propaganda, every tactic of economic and diplomatic pressure, every device for breaking down the moral conscience and exploiting the secret affects of civilized man, but also the terrorism of a political police, of prisons and torture, of concentration camps, of transported or extirpated minorities, and of total war. The succession of less comprehensive viewpoints has been a succession of adaptations of theory to practice. In the limit, practice becomes a theoretically unified whole, and theory is reduced to the status of a myth that lingers on to represent the frustrated aspirations of detached and disinterested intelligence.[107]

Lonergan on the Status of Reason

Philosophy for Lonergan begins with but cannot be adequately identified with that of Socrates or Plato. Lonergan insists from the outset that concepts have dates, and that the acts of understanding from which they proceed occur in time and history – "from time to time." This is implicit in Strauss's hermeneutical stress upon understanding authors as they understood themselves in the context in which they wrote their books. Like Strauss, therefore, while Lonergan accepts historical-critical method, he, too, does not do so on historicist or relativist grounds. Lonergan implied near the beginning of his chief philosophical work, *Insight: A Study of Human Understanding*, that he would never shirk questions about the right way to live, but he also insisted that to do justice to or to take seriously the interesting questions in a world in which modern science and historicist versions of modern critical history predominate, the question about knowing – How do we know we know? – replaces the question about being *qua* being as first philosophy. For him,

---

107 Lonergan, *Insight*, 256–7.

it is more primordial than political philosophy and even more crucially related to assessing concrete solutions to the problem of how to live.

In a way this parallels Strauss's account of classic philosophy: the political question is of driving interest, but to answer it one has to involve oneself in the not primarily interesting question of the whole in the form of cosmology or metaphysics. According to Lonergan, before one can start metaphysical inquiry (i.e., natural theology, cosmology, or rational psychology), one must arrive at adequate answers to the questions of cognitional theory and epistemology. Moreover, to do this requires grasping the issue that Lonergan called "generalized empirical method," which goes beyond attentiveness to sense data to give an account of the data of internal experience, namely, the activities of sensing, imagining, inquiring, understanding, reflecting, weighing the sufficiency of evidence, and judging. In carrying out this challenge we do not begin with the typical so-called epistemological question about *whether* we know. One pursues instead the phenomenologically verifiable question regarding *what we in fact do* when we think we know. This means asking the question of "cognitional theory."[108] Only after one reaches a verifiable answer to this question does it make sense to ask, Why is doing *that* knowing, because only in light of the answer does the word *that* in that question refer to facts ascertained when we answer the cognitional theoretic question by paying attention to, understanding, and affirming our actual empirical experience of coming to know X. The latter question Lonergan refers to as "epistemology."[109] The metaphysical question comes last, because metaphysics requires critically grounded answers to the question, What do we know when we make true judgments about anything?

Today it is commonly assumed that after Kant, Nietzsche, and Heidegger "metaphysics" is *verboten*. Kant held that we cannot know (*Erkennen, Wissen*) anything objectively if it does not register on our

---

108 It is all-important not to confuse "cognitional theory" with what German philosophy tends to call *Erkenntnistheorie*, which is more properly (and quite commonly) translated as "epistemology," which traditionally inquires into the conditions of the possibility of something that purports to be knowledge, and responds by positing faculties or capacities such as, e.g., sensibility or, say, *Verstand* as the faculty of judgment as synthesizing subjects and predicates.

109 Epistemology in this sense is based not on putative human faculties or capacities that cannot be directly verified in experience, but in experientially verified and so factual operations that we are aware of performing when we ask and answer questions.

senses (*Empfindung*). Nietzsche said that all putative interpretation or knowledge is relative to one's perspective. And Heidegger skewered traditional metaphysics from Plato onwards as simply a forgetfulness of Being that habitually attends only to beings rather than Being (*Sein*, which might be better translated as "to be") and ultimately commits the intellectual sin of *Onto-theologie*. For Lonergan, however, metaphysics is a rather homely affair, which is implicated whenever anyone affirms a true proposition or asserts a real distinction. The point of metaphysics is simply to assign the most general equivalents in reality that specify and provide the grounds for, or conditions that must be fulfilled, if the affirmation or statement is to be true.[110] From this standpoint, anyone (whether Kant, Nietzsche, Heidegger, Levenson, or Strauss), who either affirms or denies correctly the existence of any reality engages implicitly or latently in metaphysics, whether they realize this or not.

For Lonergan reflectively to make explicit the metaphysics latent in human knowing is to articulate an integral heuristic structure of all that human beings can possibly know.[111] That is what Lonergan means by metaphysics, and he believed he worked out a metaphysics that is methodically grounded. This has nothing to do with relinquishing philosophy as ongoing *zetesis*, but neither does it identify philosophy with the knowledge of ignorance as in Strauss's interpretation of Socrates.[112] As *heuristic*, metaphysics is the integral structure of what is to be known by correct understanding and judgment. Metaphysics does not mean an exhaustive knowledge of the whole of Being; Lonergan is clear that only the infinite intelligence of God possesses knowledge of everything about everything. Metaphysical knowledge is anticipatory, and so it only integrates explanatory knowledge already attained, and names

---

110 In *Insight*, ch. 15, Lonergan specifies these metaphysical elements as the conjugate (or accidental) and central (or substantial) potency, form, and act that articulate the conditions that either do or do not provide the basis in reality for the truthfulness (or, if they do not, the falsehood) of any statements or distinctions. He also calls this general heuristic structure "a general semantics" of all that exists.

111 On metaphysics defined in terms of the conception, affirmation, and implementation of the integral heuristic structure of proportionate being, see *Insight*, 415–21.

112 In *Verbum* Lonergan referred to Thomas Aquinas's Commentary on Aristotle's mention in the *Metaphysics* that "only the pretensions of the Sophists led the wise to name their pursuit not wisdom itself but love of wisdom" (*In I Metaphys.*, lect. 3, § 56). See Bernard Lonergan, *Verbum: Word and Idea in Aquinas*, Collected Works of Bernard Lonergan 2, ed. Frederick E. Crowe and Robert M. Doran (Toronto: University of Toronto Press, 1997), 80.

what is still unknown; and in this way metaphysics can direct further inquiry rather than provide all the answers.

Lonergan's approach to both metaphysics and to the conception and affirmation of God is made possible by his painstaking investigation of the "uninteresting question" of cognitional theory. And the key to answering that question correctly centers on understanding direct and reflective acts or operations of understanding. "Thoroughly understand what it is to understand, and not only will you understand the broad lines of all there is to be understood but also you will possess a fixed base, an invariant pattern, opening upon all further developments of understanding."[113] Let's now consider what made it possible for Lonergan to make his discoveries about understanding, which is central to both his philosophy and his theology.

What Strauss and Klein learned from Heidegger about liberating the original thought of the genius from the sometimes choking, sometimes concealing tendrils of tradition, Lonergan learned on his own in the course of doing two studies on Thomas Aquinas's thought on operative grace published as *Grace and Freedom*[114] and on Aquinas's thought on the procession of the word published as *Verbum*. The combination of these two works enabled Lonergan's own thought to be guided by Aquinas's idea of wisdom, namely, the habit that enables one "to order and judge all things."[115] The precise meaning of this idea was established in *Verbum*, that second detailed study of the writings of St Thomas.[116] Thus, *scientia* is the speculative habit that makes one capable of deducing

---

113 Lonergan, "Introduction" and "Epilogue," *Insight*, 22, 769–70.

114 Lonergan's doctoral dissertation, completed in 1940 for the Gregorian University, was entitled, *Gratia Operans: A Study of the Speculative Development in the Writings of St Thomas of Aquinas*. In 1941 and 1942 Lonergan published what he called a "condensed and abbreviated version" in four articles in *Theological Studies*. These articles were collected and published in book form with the title *Grace and Freedom: Operative Grace in the Thought of St Thomas Aquinas*, ed. J. Patout Burns (London: Darton, Longman & Todd; and New York: Herder & Herder, 1971); and in 2000 both the dissertation and the book were published together under the same title as *Grace and Freedom: Operative Grace in the Thought of St Thomas Aquinas*, Collected Works of Bernard Lonergan 1, ed. Frederick E. Crowe and Robert M. Doran (Toronto: University of Toronto, 2000).

115 Thomas Aquinas, *Summa theologiae*, 1–2, q. 66, a. 5, ad 4m.

116 See Lonergan, *Verbum*, 78–87. This work was originally published as "The Concept of *Verbum* in the Writings of St Thomas Aquinas," *Theological Studies* 7 (1946): 349–92; 8 (1947): 35–79; 404–44; 10 (1949): 3–40, 359–93.

correct conclusions from the principles of any science; *intellectus* is the speculative habit that allows one to understand the *terms* of the first principles; *sapientia* is the habit of good judgment which enables one to select the correct meaning of the terms, which, linked together, yield the first principles to guide *scientia* and *intellectus*. For Aquinas, then, the habit of wisdom involves a generalization of judgment, whose property is to reduce any particular affirmation to its ultimate foundations or principles. "And what are the principles?" Lonergan asks. "The principles are not propositions. The principles are real causes, namely, sense and the light of intellect,"[117] in the realm of finite being. We shall return to a more precise discussion of this later on.

Lonergan and the Understanding of Understanding

None of the great contemporary non-Catholic thinkers such as Strauss, Heidegger (once he "lost his faith"), and Gadamer ever considered scholastic philosophy worth taking seriously.[118] Lonergan's experience with scholasticism as a young man was similar. However, in 1933 after undertaking a heavy regimen of reading in addition to his coursework in theology, he found that "Augustine [in *De beata vita*, *Contra academicos*, *De ordine*, and *Soliloquiae*] was so concerned with understanding, so unmindful of universal concepts, …" that [Lonergan then] "began a long period of trying to write an intelligible account of [his own] convictions [on knowing]."[119]

In Rome (1933–6), Lonergan, having committed himself to a serious study of "the Summa at first hand," "began to suspect that St Thomas was not nearly as bad as he is painted."[120] In the 1940s, he noted again

---

117 Bernard Lonergan, "Part One: Lectures on Mathematical Logic," *Phenomenology and Logic: The Boston College Lectures on Mathematical Logic and Existentialism*, Collected Works of Bernard Lonergan 18, ed. Philip J. McShane (Toronto: University of Toronto Press, 2001), 118–21.

118 Eric Voegelin did read such "Augustinian Thomists" as Henri de Lubac and Hans Urs von Balthasar, but they were not really scholastics in the sense intended here; he also read Étienne Gilson, who, as a philosopher was a careful historian of philosophy, unlike the typical scholastic philosopher.

119 See Lonergan, "Editor's Preface [by Frederick Crowe]," *Verbum*, note 28, xii–xiii, and xiv.

120 Cited from Lonergan's January 1935 letter to Henry Keane in Frederick E. Crowe, SJ, *Lonergan*, Outstanding Christian Thinkers Series, ed. Brian Davies, OP (Collegeville, MN: The Liturgical Press, 1992), 22.

"that Augustine talked a lot about *intelligere* and that Thomas didn't talk about universals – though knowledge of universals was supposed [by then dominant Thomistic interpreters] to be the be-all and end-all of science."[121] When Lonergan recovered Aquinas's understanding of understanding, he rejected the conceptualism[122] that prevailed within medieval, baroque, and modern scholasticism from Henry of Ghent and Duns Scotus through John of St Thomas and Francisco Suarez to the later Thomistic schools that emerged in the wake of Pope Leo XIII's *Aeterni Patris* in 1879. By giving a thorough account "of the psychological, metaphysical, and Trinitarian aspects of Thomist thought," Lonergan showed that "Aquinas attributed the key role in cognitional theory not to inner words, concepts, but to acts of understanding."[123] In contrast to the highly touted universal concepts (which are abstractions), acts of understanding (or insights) *pivot between* sense data and the conceptual formulations of terms and relations in definitions and formulae *because* they grasp *the intelligibility in the sensible*; without insight into data as imagined there can be no abstraction of the universal from the particular. We express and verify our understandings in language *because* and *in the measure* that we understand.

Besides recovering Aquinas's idea of direct understanding in response to what/why (*quid sit*) questions, Lonergan went on to give a proper account of Aquinas's grasp of the critical act of understanding that grounds the act of judgment in response to is-it-so (*an sit*) questions. Newman's *Essay in Aid of a Grammar of Assent* – the book Lonergan considered "*the* classic in epistemology"[124] – helped him to understand how Aquinas transformed Aristotle's account in the *De anima* III of the agent intellect (*nous poietikos*) by means of Augustine's (perhaps metaphorical) account of knowing the truth. "Augustine had advanced that our knowledge of truth originated not from without but from within us, yet not simply from within us but in some illumination in which we consulted the eternal grounds and norms of things. Aquinas explained that we consult the eternal ground and norms, not by taking a look at them

---

121 Lonergan, "Editor's Preface [by Frederick Crowe]," *Verbum*, note 28, xiii.
122 Conceptualism is related to the Husserlian issue of "sedimentation": roughly, answers without the prior questions to which they purport to be solutions.
123 See Bernard Lonergan, "*Insight* Revisited," *A Second Collection: Papers by Bernard J.F. Lonergan, SJ*, ed. William Ryan and Bernard Tyrrell (London: Darton, Longman & Todd, 1974), 263–78 at 267.
124 Frederick Crowe said Lonergan told him this.

but by having within us a light of intelligence that is a created participation of the eternal and uncreated light."[125] Having studied Aquinas at first hand in 1935, Lonergan had already realized he could "work out a luminous and unmistakable meaning to *intellectus agens et possibilis*."[126] His 1946–9 articles on word and idea in the thought of Aquinas reported Thomas's statement "that the Uncreated Light grounds the truth of our judgments, not because we see the Light, but because our intellects are created participations of it."[127] Clearly, Strauss could hardly countenance language referring to Uncreated Light, inasmuch as it unquestionably transcends the sensible limits of the *kosmos* congruent with ancient cosmology that he correlated with Platonic-Socratic political philosophy,[128] despite the fact that, as we will see below, it may be inferred legitimately from *noesis noeseos*, even if not as understood by Aristotle's medieval Arabic and Jewish interpreters Strauss so admired.[129] In a 1964 domestic exhortation to the Jesuit community of

---

125 Lonergan, *Insight*, 394.

126 Lonergan's January 1935 letter to Henry Keane cited by Crowe in *Lonergan*, 22.

127 Lonergan, *Insight*, 437. He spoke about human intelligence as a created participation in uncreated light in his 1962 course *De methodo theologiae*, now published as "The Method of Theology" in Bernard Lonergan, *Early Works on Theological Method* 2, Collected Works of Bernard Lonergan 23, trans. Michael G. Shields, ed. Robert M. Doran and H. Daniel Monsour (Toronto: University of Toronto Press, 2013), 489–91, in the following terms: "The human manner of knowing is, so to speak, transparent; that is, it is such that the conditions of knowledge are the very conditions of transcendence. Radically there are two conditions of human knowledge: a proximate condition, that judgment proceed from a grasp of the unconditioned; and a remote condition, that the whole cognitional process be governed by an unrestricted capacity and exigence, that is, by an intellect that is in potency to make and become all things, by a soul that is in a way all things through its natural desire to know that asks about everything, even about an infinite God, What is it?, and wonders about every quiddity, Is it really so? Now these conditions of knowledge are also conditions of transcendence, for both this unrestricted desire and exigence itself and the determination of this capacity to one thing through an unconditioned are proportioned to absolute transcendence."

128 See the final claim in Strauss's 1940 lecture, "Living Issues of German Postwar Philosophy," where he said that Nietzsche "reasserted hypothetically the doctrine of eternal return: to drive home that the elementary, the natural subject of philosophy still is, and always will be, as it had been for the Greeks, the Κόσμος, the world." Quoted in Meier, *Leo Strauss and the Theologico-Political Problem*, 138.

129 As Lonergan stated in *Verbum*, 90–1: "For Aquinas the term 'intellectual light' is not simply a synonym for the Aristotelian term 'agent intellect.' He debated with Avicennists whether agent intellect was immanent or transcendent. But he never

Regis College in Toronto, Lonergan drew alternative and definite implications of understanding the human mind as an immanent source of transcendence:

> That prior opaque and luminous being [of the human subject] is not static, fixed, determinate, once for all; it is precarious; and its being precarious is the possibility not only of a fall but also of fuller development. That development is open; the dynamism constitutive of our consciousness may be expressed in the imperatives, Be intelligent, Be reasonable, Be responsible; and the imperatives are unrestricted – they regard every inquiry, every judgment, every decision and choice. Nor is the relevance of the imperatives restricted to the world of human experience, to the *mundus aspectibilis*; we are open to God. Implicit in human inquiry is a natural desire to know God by his essence; implicit in human judgment about contingent things there is the formally unconditioned that is God; implicit in the human choice of values is the absolute good that is God.[130]

The transparency and transcendence built into the human act of judgment includes both a content (what is true or false) and "an act of a subject, personally committing the subject" in the assent, which is

---

thought of debating whether intellectual light is immanent or transcendent. Indeed, when he argued that agent intellect was immanent, he was arguing for an identification of agent intellect with the ground of intellectual light. Hence he could frame his conclusion in this significant fashion: 'Unde nihil prohibit ipsi lumini animae nostrae attribuere actionem intellectus agentis; et praecipue cum Aristoteles comparet lumini' ['And so nothing prevents our attributing the action of agent intellect to the light itself of the soul; and especially since Aristotle compares agent intellect to a light,' *Summa contra Gentiles*, 2, c. 77 ad fin]. Both the nature of the agent intellect and, in particular, Aristotle's comparison of agent intellect with light, lead one to identify agent intellect with the immanent cause of what we call the flash of understanding, the light of reason."

130 See Lonergan, "*Existenz* and *Aggiornamento*," *Collection*, 229–30. As Lonergan noted in *Verbum*, 75, referring to Thomas Aquinas, *In III De anima*, lect. 11, §§ 749–51 and *In Metaphys.*, lect 11,§§ 1899–1900: "Knowledge of the *quod quid est* [intelligible form] takes us outside time and space; but the act of *compositio vel divisio* [Aquinas's way of speaking about judgment] involves a return to the concrete, in particular, whatever may be hymned about eternal truths, human judgments always involve a specification of time." And then, at *Verbum*, 75–6, referring to Thomas Aquinas, *Super I Sententiarum*, d. 19, q. 5, a. 3 and *Summa theologiae*, I, q. 16, a. 7: "Since truth exists only in a mind, and since only the mind of God is eternal, there can be but one eternal truth."

divisible into "scientific certitude, opinion, belief." Aquinas's demand for a *resolutio in principia* in judgment meant going back "to concrete sensible data" and to the insights into that data as imagined; it does not refer only to abstract *principia per se nota*. But the norms of judgment in the case of the positive sciences require precisely a "reduction to sensible data." Lonergan inferred that Aquinas implicitly acknowledged that "the act of judgment is preceded by a marshaling of all the relevant evidence." To make a careful judgment, one's prior critical act of understanding has to grasp that the evidence necessitates the proposed judgment.

As I mentioned earlier, Lonergan linked the role of intellectual light in the act of judgment with Aquinas's characterization of wisdom: namely, "to order and judge all things."[131] "This ordering of all things," Lonergan pointed out, "does not proceed from some higher principle immanent within us, … but expresses that principle itself, namely our intellectual light, and not that bare light by itself but rather as it extends to and is applied to all things."[132] As for the nexus between wisdom's functions of ordering and of judgment, Lonergan explained that

> every judgment occurs within the context of other judgments by which the sense of that judgment is clarified and explained, its truth proven and defended, and its antecedents and consequences adduced in order to clarify it further. Corresponding to this network of judgments is the interconnection, the interdependence, and the multiple similarities and dissimilarities in things themselves. Therefore, because of the mutual connections among judgments, the mutual connections among things, and the correspondence between true judgments and things themselves, all judgment presupposes an ordering of all things.[133]

Once he had reached an understanding (verified in the writings of St Thomas) of what Aquinas meant by understanding and concept-formation, of what he meant by grasping the sufficiency of the evidence and judging, and then of what he meant by wisdom, Lonergan wrote the

---

131 For one of his clearest explanations of what this means, see Lonergan, "Part One: Lectures on Mathematical Logic," *Phenomenology and Logic*, 118–21.

132 Lonergan, "The Method of Theology," *Early Works on Theological Method* 2, 457.

133 Lonergan, "The Method of Theology," *Early Works on Theological Method* 2, 457.

book *Insight*. It is, I venture to say, an instance of recovering genuinely premodern rationality to shed light on the crisis of our times.

> After spending years reaching up to the mind of Aquinas, I came to a twofold conclusion. On the one hand, that reaching had changed me profoundly. On the other hand, that change was the essential benefit. For not only did it make me capable of grasping what, in the light of my conclusions, the *vetera* really were, but also it opened challenging vistas on what the *nova* could be.
>
> So it is that my detailed investigations of the thought of Aquinas on *gratia operans* and *verbum* have been followed by the present essay in aid of a personal appropriation of one's own rational self-consciousness … In the introduction I stated a program. Thoroughly understand what it is to understand, and not only will you understand the broad lines of all there is to be understood but also you will possess a fixed base, an invariant pattern, opening upon all further developments of understanding … I would say that it is only through a personal appropriation of one's own rational self-consciousness that one can hope to reach the mind of Aquinas, and once that mind is reached, then it is difficult not to import his compelling genius to the problems of this later day.[134]

Lonergan's essay in aid of the appropriation of rational self-consciousness involves a generalization of empirical method, based on adverting to the data of our consciousnesses in addition to the data of our senses. Just as we can attend to the fact that we are about to sneeze, so we can tell the differences among the activities of our various senses – seeing, hearing, tasting, smelling, and touching. Similarly, we can discern the difference between observing something and inquiring about it; between the insight that answers our inquiry and still being puzzled; between formulations based on understanding versus rote or memorized answers; between guesses or hypotheses and verified statements; and between affirmations that are measured and balanced and those that are rash or precipitous. In differentiating among any of these kinds of experience, we are adverting to the data of our consciousness. Such discernment doesn't have to be a recondite affair even though it happens to occur rarely.

---

134 Lonergan, *Insight*, 769–70.

I cannot here reprise Lonergan's transposition of Aquinas's gnoseology into a contemporary phenomenology of human knowing in mathematics and the natural sciences,[135] in the human sciences and ordinary living.[136] Nor can I convey the way Lonergan grounds epistemology in a verifiable cognitional theory, and moves from the latent metaphysics at work in all human knowing to an explicit metaphysics – in short, the overall achievement of *Insight*. Suffice it to say that *Insight* did demonstrate the isomorphism between the cognitional structure he uncovered in Aquinas and the structure people enact today, whether in the usual commonsense mode or in using the classical, statistical, genetic, and dialectical methods of legitimate science.[137]

Contrast with Strauss I: On Knowing

For this clarification-by-contrast with Strauss it is important to underline that although Lonergan learned about the operations of insight and judgment from the chiefly theological writings of Thomas Aquinas, the book *Insight* is written from a "moving viewpoint,"[138] which begins from what Lonergan called a "sufficiently cultured consciousness" that stipulates no religious stance whatsoever, so that after they have been carefully prepared for by what readers have already read as they proceed through the book, new presuppositions are gradually introduced. Without logically presupposing any premises derived from revealed dogmas or *theologoumena*, Lonergan establishes the nature of the structure of conscious intentionality, of objectivity, and of metaphysics. Step-by-step the reader's horizon becomes enlarged into a conscious quest in which understanding seeks faith, and it is not until chapter 20 that the argument reaches the threshold at which the reader may (but does not necessarily) feel interiorly compelled to pivot into the traditional theological mode of faith seeking understanding. Thus, by respecting the limits of unaided reason insofar as it avoids presuppositions that expressly involve revealed truth, Lonergan's rational procedure nevertheless undermines rationalism's grounds for excluding a priori any and all supernatural realities.

---

135 Lonergan, *Insight*, ch. 1–5 and 7.
136 Lonergan, *Insight*, ch. 6 and 7.
137 See Lonergan, "Isomorphism of Thomist and Scientific Thought," *Collection*, 133–42.
138 On the "moving viewpoint," which represents an application of Gödel's theorem, see Lonergan, *Insight*, 17–20.

For Strauss faith – i.e., belief – seeking understanding necessarily entails a *sacrificium intellectus*, precisely because it involves a decision to assent to (i.e., to affirm as true) contents that one has not verified firsthand. He seems to agree with Nietzsche that in many, perhaps most, cases these decisions are motivated by a failure of spiritedness (*thumos*) or courage in the face of the miseries besetting human existence. In any case, he seems to think any and all inquiry into what one already believes to be true necesarily entails the exercise of undue coercion upon the inquiring mind and the abandonment of unrestricted inquiry – not to mention love of this world. Strauss often seems to suppose that belief as the condition for the social communication of knowledge is a necessity only for the many, whereas the philosopher (like the "man from Missouri") wants *ad oculos* proof or at least logically rigorous rational demonstration for what would thereby no longer require the act of belief. Especially in his discussion of Spinoza and in *Philosophy and Law* Strauss states with regard to the most important questions both that even philosophers do not attain apodictic proof and that they never cease to be aware that putative solutions to problems fall short of certainty and so remain questionable. Consequently, the philosopher's calling vis-à-vis religious belief is to mount a dialectical defense of philosophy and the life of uncoerced inquiry, while understanding that the senses or reason can never demonstrate the impossibility of religious beliefs. It is not that easy to see why it would have to be the case that when thoughtful believers wonder how the tenets of their beliefs can make sense, and so seek some (even limited) understanding of them, they are so lacking in integrity when held to Strauss's standard of philosophy.

Further, Strauss's frequent stress on necessity, universality, and certainty of theoretical knowledge in accord with the Aristotelian logical ideal of science does seem exclusively to focus on the classical intelligibility that regards the *natures* that determine the lawful regularities governing finite beings. To be sure, classical intelligibility is expressed in abstract laws that are under the *ceteris paribus* (other things being equal) proviso that governs all the contingent realities under investigation. Although Strauss does refer to the discoveries of the natural sciences as being no more than hypothetical,[139] perhaps his orientation toward "eternal truths" obscures how we only know how often

---

139 Strauss, "Progress or Return?" *Introduction to Political Philosophy*, 266–7.

conditions actually enable abstract intelligibilities discovered by classical methods to occur through the frequencies verified by statistical method. Does Strauss regard the probabilities known to be intelligible by statistical method as mere chance (in accord with the view that probability is merely a cloak for ignorance)? As already mentioned above, classical laws in the realm of finite being are only verifiable if contingent conditions happen to be fulfilled *as a matter of fact*. How Strauss accounts for this dimension of intelligibility is not altogether clear.

Contrast with Strauss II: History,
Historicism, and Culture

This ambiguous stance toward any phenomena that do not meet the standard of the *aei on* (eternal truth or angelic *aevum*, which, although outside space and time, has a beginning and no end) has important implications for history in political philosophy. As we have seen, Strauss (like Klein) sought to use reason to transform Heidegger's project of wholesale *Destruktion*. The fruit of Heidegger's project was a *Verfallsgeschichte* that involves an unrelenting oblivion of Being (*Seinsvergessenheit*). In contrast, Strauss, in his determination to break out of the "second cave" more completely separated from nature than Plato's "cave" in the *Republic*, recovered the ancient art of reading to compose a history of the *querelle des anciens et modernes* uncompromised by historicist relativism or myths of progress.

In his complex renewal of classical political philosophy Strauss set nature in opposition to history. A rejection of the modern empirical notion of culture on the grounds that it ineluctably implies relativism and historicism was central to his renewal. As Strauss argued in *Natural Right and History*, relativism considers judgments, whether of fact or value, to be merely relative to their historical perspective. Strauss realized that a position that eliminates the unconditional or absolute character of truth renders values incapable of adjudication by reason; and this in turn leads inexorably to the nihilism of the Last Man. That is why Strauss wrote half-jokingly that Max Weber's ethical principle – "'Thou shalt have preferences'" – is "an Ought whose fulfillment is fully guaranteed by the Is" because any Ought's dependence on "what happens to be" eliminates the possibility of any intellectual or moral standard whatsoever. Hence Weber's observation comes as no surprise: "Then, of course, the saying about the 'Last Men' proper to this cultural development becomes truth: 'Experts without spirit or vision, voluptuaries without heart ...'"[140]

For Lonergan modern Catholic theology's ahistorical orthodoxy amounted to a wholesale repudiation of the modern empirical notion of culture. This incapacitated it for coming to terms with and so critically confronting "the historical knowledge of civilizations, cultures, religions, ideas, philosophies, sciences, and the arts." On Lonergan's analysis this position presupposes "classical conceptualism" inasmuch as it "conceives man as always essentially the same, a 'rational animal,'" and therefore "conceives human laws as universal, in accordance with some ideal construct about what ought to be; it considers the rest as *per accidens*, positive, less important." It remains however that Romanticism focused on "the particular, the singular, the positive, the subject, etc.," and modern philology was concerned "to reconstruct from an accurate knowledge of their language the whole culture of any people in all its aspects; hence, historical studies regarding law, state, religion, morality, art, literature, economy, etc.," though also flawed by counterpositions, were not entirely wrongheaded. It is not wrong to insist that "man is understood according to the particularity of time, culture, nation, and occupation," because "man is concrete, not some abstract ideal (rational animal), but evolving in a concrete context in freedom."[141] This is what the empirical notion of culture takes into account.

Of course, for Strauss, Max Weber provides a crucial test case by performatively and often explicitly demonstrating what is most seriously problematic about taking the empirical notion of culture seriously.[142] However, to analyze Weber's horizon from the standpoint of Lonergan's account of human rational self-consciousness, we may begin by noting that Max Weber agreed with Kant's denial of objective knowledge either of the truth of reality (i.e., the famous *Ding an sich*) or of true value (i.e., the truly vs. the apparently good). Kant's restriction of the possibility of objective knowledge to the phenomenal sphere relegated

---

140 Strauss, *Natural Right and History*, 47; see also Max Weber, *Die protestantische Ethik und der Geist des Kapitalismus* (München: C.H. Beck, 2004), 201: "Dann allerdings könnte für die 'letzten Menschen' dieser Kulturentwicklung das Wort zur Wahrheit werden: 'Fachmenschen ohne Geist, Genussmenschen ohne Herz ...'"

141 See Lonergan, "Appendix 2: Items Related to 'De Methodo Theologiae,'" *Early Works on Theological Method* 2, 661.

142 On this topic, see the monograph by Nasser Behnegar, *Leo Strauss, Max Weber and the Scientific Study of Politics* (Chicago: University of Chicago Press, 2003).

the truth both of any dimension of reality that cannot be directly apprehended by the senses (*Empfindung, Wahrnehmung*) and of morality to the noumenal realm. In that realm one can at most *think* (*denken*) rationally but not attain objective knowledge (*erkennen/wissen*). Kant argued that any such knowledge is always conditioned, and to attain the unconditioned one would have to ascertain the totality of conditions for any contingent fact – something that only the putative *intuitus originarius* proper to God achieves. Moreover, as Strauss understood in depth, Weber inserted Kantian presuppositions about the limits of reason into the radical perspectivism set forth so powerfully by Nietzsche in *The Genealogy of Morals*, which purports to demonstrate that not only is each and every moral position situated in and relative to its historical perspective, but so too is the perspective from which Nietzsche himself performed his genealogy. Hence, what Strauss called Nietzsche's hypothesis of the eternal return of the same.

In contrast, Lonergan could take the empirical notion of culture seriously because of having achieved the self-appropriation of his *naturally given* rational self-consciousness. Hence, although Strauss's fear that many or most proponents of the empirical notion of culture end up sacrificing all normativity in their investigations, Lonergan held that built into the dynamism of conscious intentionality are what he termed "natural and inevitable spontaneities" that demand empirical, normative, and absolute objectivity in the process of being attentive to the data, posing relevant questions, understanding and formulating possibly relevant answers to those questions, and then carefully verifying one's possibly relevant interpretations by reflecting on all the pertinent evidence. Having determined that classical conceptualism is at the root of the normative notion of culture and that classical conceptualism holds "that human nature is always the same, … that any change is only an incidental modification introduced to meet a merely accidental difference in circumstances," Lonergan deemed that bringing historical integrity into Christian theology meant jettisoning the normative notion of culture in favor of the empirical notion.

Classical conceptualism, according to Lonergan, tends to think of objectivity as something that can "get along without minds"; in doing historical interpretation it tends to advocate what he called "the principle of the empty head": to wit, (1) that one must empty one's head of all prior knowledge, education, interests, and prejudgments to avoid *eisegesis* in interpreting any and all historical data, and (2) that in the measure that one succeeds in doing this, one would be able to apprehend only what was in the text rather than the products of one's attentive, intelligent, reasonable, and responsible reading. Surely, as Strauss has demonstrated so clearly, the more one knows beforehand and the more truth one intends to learn from a text, the more likely one is to be aware of possibly alternative interpretations, and the more capable one will be of checking to see which is the most probable. Hence, not so differently from Strauss, Lonergan always insisted that as long as interpreters and historians formulate limited prospective historical judgments with the utmost care,[143] they can check their prospective judgments against the evidence afforded by the surface of the texts, and make historically correct judgments, even though such judgments, except when negative, are not certain but only probable.[144] Lonergan insisted that such a capacity was directly affected by the genuineness of the person doing the interpreting and judging.

Classical conceptualism's rejection as irrelevant of human historicity, Lonergan saw, tended also to go hand-in-hand with neglect of the corollary of the empirical notion of culture, namely, "the awareness that men individually are responsible for their lives and collectively are responsible for the world in which they live them."[145] No one could accuse

---

143 See Lonergan, "1962–9 Hermeneutics," *Early Works on Theological Method* 1, Collected Works of Bernard Lonergan 22, ed. Robert M. Doran and Robert C. Croken (Toronto: University of Toronto Press, 2010), 222:

> The criterion on the correctness of an insight is always the same: … Does it meet all the relevant questions? The trick to the question is: relevant to what? The simplest way of determining the meaning of that word "relevant" is "relevant to a determinate prospective judgment, a well-defined prospective judgment." And from that it immediately follows that judgment on one's interpretation of the text, on the correctness of one's understanding of the text, is going to be a piecemeal affair. It will not take in globally all the acts of understanding one has on reading the text. It will tend to be of the type: "At least the author means this; and at least he does not mean that."

144 About establishing "exact and positive information about what a thinker meant" by historical study, Lonergan wrote in "On God and Secondary Causes," *Collection*, 60: "Logically, the interpretation of a writer is a matter of formulating a hypothesis, working out its presuppositions and its implications, and verifying in the text the presuppositions, the hypothesis, and the implications. Deductions of what a writer must have meant are just so much fancy; in reality they are deductions from the hypothesis assumed by the interpreter; and whether the hypothesis is correct can be determined only with probability, a probability that increases only with the extent and the variety of the verification."

145 Lonergan, "*Existenz* and *Aggiornamento*," *Collection*, 229.

Strauss of that neglect! Moreover, it would be hard to justify calling Strauss a classical conceptualist. Strauss seems to advocate a kind of classicism by arguing that political philosophy's devotion to the permanently relevant problems (in accord with his interpretation of Plato's ideas) reintroduces normativity into political science. In rejecting classicism, Lonergan's basic approach was based on a position not altogether dissimilar to Strauss's, namely:

> The concrete being of man, then, is being in process. His existence lies in developing. His unrestricted desire to know leads him ever towards a known unknown. His sensitivity matches the operator of his intellectual advance with a capacity and a need to respond to a further reality than meets the eye and to grope his way towards it.[146]

Hence, his acceptance of the modern empirical notion of culture in the measure that it is critically grounded in the unrestricted desire to know, made it possible for him to write that "over and above mere living and operating, men have to find a meaning and value in their living and operating," and that "it is the function of culture to discover, express, validate, criticize, correct, develop, improve such meaning and value."[147] To perform that function of culture without sacrificing empirical, normative, and absolute objectivity depends on the existence of a critical mass of people who have undergone intellectual conversion as regards knowing, objectivity, and being. This comes down to making the cognitional structure immanent and operative in consciousness one's own, and doing that requires conversion. Lonergan's basic statement occurs in *Method in Theology*:

> Again, the issue is one's notion of objectivity. If one considers logical proof to be basic, one wants an objectivity that is independent of the concrete existing subject. But while objectivity reaches what is independent of the concrete existing subject, objectivity is itself not reached by what is independent of the concrete existing subject. On the contrary, objectivity is reached through the self-transcendence of the concrete existing subject, and the fundamental forms of self-transcendence are intellectual, moral

---

146 Lonergan, *Insight*, 649.
147 Bernard Lonergan, *Method in Theology* (New York: Herder & Herder, 1972), 31–2.

and religious conversion. To attempt to ensure objectivity apart from self-transcendence only generates illusion.[148]

Cognitional Structure

We have already seen how Lonergan supported Descartes's belief about people often being lost when it comes to asking important questions such as the question of God because they have never adequately asked and answered prior, uninteresting questions.[149] Asking the question about knowing – What are we doing when we think we are knowing?[150] – and engaging in introspective investigation of what actually occurs when we move from ignorance to knowledge may reveal a three-phased process.[151] The *first phase* is most obvious, that of the sensations and sense perceptions that make up our external experience of the seen, heard, smelled, tasted, and touched – the vast field of sense data. The *second phase* arises the moment we ask what and why about anything in our external experience. Inquiry wants to understand intelligible patterns that either describe or explain what we wonder about. If an act of understanding or insight occurs to us, we apprehend the intelligibility in the data as sensed or imagined; then we take possession of our insights by formulating what we have grasped in the terms and relations (concepts, definitions, sometimes, algorithms) of our guesses or hypotheses – interpretations that "make sense" of the data. The *third phase* of knowledge starts when we wonder whether our interpretative guess or hypothesis is correct; and so we check out our guesses or hypotheses by comparing the content of experience and the interpretation of the data in our definition or concept (Have we neglected any pertinent data? Are we sure we have asked every pertinent question?). What such questions want (or better demand) is a grasp of an absolute

---

148 Lonergan, *Method in Theology*, 338.

149 Lonergan, *Insight*, 27.

150 Lonergan, "Part One: Insight as Activity," *Insight*, 1–340; see also, "Cognitional Structure," *Collection*, 205–21.

151 Lonergan speaks of a *four*-phased process, starting with experience, questions for understanding, questions for reflection, followed by questions for deliberation that head toward judgments of value, decisions, and actions. Without prejudice to Lonergan's argument about God in *Insight*, it is complicated enough to concentrate on the first three phases for the purposes of this paper.

element or sufficient evidence, which is constituted as soon as we understand that all the data required by the interpretation are actually given, and that there are no data given that could call our interpretation into question. Once we have ascertained that evidence is sufficient we can posit absolutely about the object that up to that point has been only thought, conceived, or interpreted: "It is so!"

For Lonergan, then, knowledge in the full sense of the word is composed of several acts that occur on the three levels of experience, insight, and judgment. Many, perhaps most, people spontaneously suppose that the external experience of sensation is all there is to knowledge. For Lonergan, this is only the first phase of knowledge, which he calls the *empirical* phase of knowledge. Questions for understanding initiate the second phase of knowledge; called the *intelligent* phase, it seeks the intelligibility of the object of one's inquiry. The critical question, *Is it so?* wants to verify whether what we think *may* be so actually *is* so in reality; this *rational* phase of knowing demands sufficient evidence to affirm that a possibly relevant intelligibility is indeed so. Reality is only known in judgments brought about by indirect insight into the sufficiency of the relevant evidence, causing the knower to posit the reality absolutely, which means that it is the case independently of the subject's acts of knowing.

The Range of Knowing

Whenever we sense and ask and answer questions, we are activating our conscious intentionality, so that, starting from the *empirical* apprehension of data, the rest of the cognitional process actuates the *intelligent* and *rational* striving or quest for knowledge of reality. Lonergan says that we discover that, if we inquire or wonder whether anything transcends our questioning, this conscious striving has an unrestricted range. Such questioning itself demonstrates an unrestricted reach. Nothing lies outside our questioning about being.[152] The objectivity of our knowing is constituted by the fact that it is capable of knowing what simply is, and so that before we make a correct judgment about something this reality or that aspect of reality known transcends us as cognitional subjects.

---

152 See Lonergan, "Theories of Inquiry: Responses to a Symposium," *Second Collection*, 33–47; and "The Notion of Being," *Insight*, 372–98.

Once we truly know what knowledge is, and what objectivity is,[153] then we are prepared to ask what is meant by reality. If we conceive of reality as being, in the sense of everything that is the goal of our pure desire to know, we understand that reality is correlative to the intentional range of human wonder: being is everything about which we can ask questions. Further, it follows from the correlation between being and conscious intentionality as intelligent and rational that being includes all that can be known by intelligent grasp and reasonable affirmation.[154] In other words, we reject every irrational conception of reality, such as, for example, the common conception that reality is the object of some extraversion before any asking of questions. This includes either the extraversion of the senses (as in Hume's, or Locke's, or Kant's accounts)[155] or some sort of intellectual intuition (in the manner of, say, a Fichte or a Schelling),[156] which cannot be found or identified or introspectively verified by our acts of internal experiencing, understanding, and reflective reasoning.

The dynamism of conscious intentionality is unlimited, but the realm of human experience (which is an indispensable component of our judgments of existence or occurrence)[157] is limited. Within the horizon of being or reality as correlative to the range of conscious intentionality's wonder, therefore, Lonergan distinguishes between what we can have adequate or proper knowledge of (i.e., proportionate being) and

---

153 See "The Notion of Objectivity," *Insight*, 399–409.

154 Lonergan, "The Notion of Being," *Insight*, 372–98, where being is defined heuristically, in contradistinction to the common notion that being is a concept that denotes what is greatest in extension and least in intention: an utterly empty concept.

155 For a powerful contrast of Lonergan's position with that of perceptualism, whether of naive realism or of Kant, see Lonergan, "Metaphysics as Horizon," *Collection*, 188–204.

156 As Lonergan notes regarding so-called intellectual intuition (or *intellektuelle Anschauung*) in *Insight*, 294: "The uncritical realist would dispute our account of explanatory genera and species; on his view the empirical scientist understands not reality but phenomena; beyond the unities and relations, grasped by the scientist, there is a deeper reality, a metaphysical essence, apprehended by philosophic intuition. But what is the philosophic intuition? I have looked for it and failed to find it. I know no reason for affirming its occurrence."

157 See the distinction between analytic propositions (essentially tautologies: only a matter of definition) and analytic principles "of which the partial terms of an analytic proposition are existential if they occur in their defined sense in judgments of fact, such as the concrete judgment of fact or the definitively established empirical generalization," Lonergan, *Insight*, 331–8.

what we can have only improper or analogical knowledge of (i.e., transcendent being):[158] "Being is whatever can be grasped intelligently and affirmed reasonably. Being is proportionate or transcendent according as it lies within or without the range of man's outer and inner experience."[159] Because the criterion of reality is judgment, and not inner or outer experience, we can *know* what lies beyond our experience.

Perhaps the distinction between *proper* and *analogical* knowledge marks another crucial point of divergence between Lonergan and Strauss in relation to what lies beyond the range of possible experience. Does Strauss deny that analogical knowledge of transcendent being can be true? It is far from clear whether Strauss disregards the difference between metaphor or symbol on the one hand and analogy on the other, for the reason that, if they all lack univocal reference to the reality intended, they must also lack the clarity and precision required for knowledge in the strict sense. For Lonergan metaphors and symbols refer in an undifferentiated manner to realities (whether transcendent or not) in a global and compact way; in contrast, analogies are differentiated relational proportions engendered by reflective noetic control as grounded in correct understanding and judgment. When analogies refer to transcendent realities that are not conditioned by space and time they attain only an *imperfect* understanding of those transcendent realities; but, he insists, inasmuch as they provide a measure of precisely relevant intelligibility in relation to what remains intrinsically mysterious, their meaning is distinct from the global and compact manner of the metaphor or symbol. For example, a reality (e.g. "he came down from heaven") affirmed by belief in terms of symbol or metaphor can be more adequately and more fruitfully explicated in terms of an analogy based on the theorem of contingent predication, which is explicated in the natural theologies of both Lonergan and Thomas Aquinas.[160] Such analogical usage in no way denies either the fact that to understand God as God is in Godself, one would have to *be* God; nor does it fail to

---

158 For a clear account of this distinction, see Lonergan, "The Natural Desire to See God," *Collection*, 81–91.

159 Lonergan, *Insight*, 663.

160 On contingent predications of God and extrinsic denomination, see Lonergan, *Insight*, 684–87; and also, Bernard Lonergan, "The Divine Missions," in *The Triune God: Systematics*, Collected Works of Bernard Lonergan 12, translated from *De Deo Trino: Pars Systematica* (1964) by Michael G. Shields, ed. Robert M. Doran and H. Daniel Monsour (Toronto: University of Toronto Press, 2007), 439–69.

realize that no matter how great the similarity between the finite proportional relations formulated analogically and what is being affirmed about God, the dissimilarity is much greater than the similarity.[161] Isn't it properly philosophical to recognize how the analogous structure of the totality of being accords with Aristotle's teaching that each distinct kind of reality requires both its own method of thought and discourse and its own distinct criteria of judgment?

Lonergan argues that being or reality as *proportionate* to our capacity to understand encompasses all that can be experienced internally or externally as well as grasped by intelligent insight, and affirmed by rational judgment. While it is true that one normally understands and affirms what is only a part of the totality of being, Lonergan insists that the question of transcendent being cannot be reasonably shirked.[162] Even if one cannot attain exhaustive knowledge in that realm, if one seriously engages that question, one will be capable of arriving at an understanding and judgment regarding transcendent being that is correct, even though it is analogous.

Understanding and Affirming Divine Transcendence[163]

Within this differentiated framework, the primary question of God becomes a question regarding a reality that transcends the limits of our possible experience.[164] We know that there is no simple answer to this

---

161 See the classic authoritative definition of the Fourth Lateran Council (1215): "Inter creatorem et creaturam non potest tanta similitudo notari, quin inter eos maior dissimilitudo sit notanda" (Between creator and creature there may not be noted such a great similarity unless there be noted between them a greater dissimilarity). In an even more modest formulation, Lonergan, paraphrases Thomas Aquinas, *Summa theologiae*, 1, q. 16, a. 5, ad 2m: "The very truth or objectivity of divine knowledge of God is not a similarity between the knowing and the known but the absence of dissimilarity." See Lonergan, *The Triune God: Systematics*, 303 and note 34.

162 The topic of chapter 19 of *Insight* is "General Transcendent Knowledge," 657–708.

163 The following account of Lonergan's argument on God is greatly indebted to the late Giovanni Sala, SJ, "Der Gott der Philosophen – eine Alternative zum Gott der Christlichen Offenbarung?" *Mein Vater – Euer Vater*, Theologische Sommerakadamie 1999, ed. Anton Ziegenhaus (Buttenwiesen: Stella Maris Verlag, 2000), 33–57.

164 The phrase "possible experience" means, first, sensation or sense perception; second, our internal experience of conscious acts. God is not a datum in either sense, for the first is intrinsically conditioned by space and time, and the second is extrinsically conditioned by space and time, while God is absolutely unconditioned.

question, because we do not have any data on God that can become an adequate object for our knowledge of God. Here Strauss and Lonergan seem to be in full agreement. In *Insight* Lonergan insists that even were one to suspect that being is not completely intelligible because the existence of the universe is no more than a mere *matter of fact*, once one has the question whether and in what sense the world points beyond itself, the intelligent and reasonable person really has no recourse but to infer the correlation between reality as a whole and one's intelligent and reasonable striving. Why? Because if we acknowledge that the immanent, operative, and normative dynamism of conscious intentionality is intelligent and reasonable, we encounter the core of Lonergan's position on the question of God in *Insight*, namely, what he calls *the intrinsic intelligibility of being*.[165]

The issue of the intrinsic intelligibility of being is decisive when it comes to answering the question about God. It appears also to be the point at which the Straussian Socrates and Strauss himself part ways with Lonergan. Strauss held that Socrates's attestation that he knew nothing necessarily implied an awareness of the whole, and that it is a mistake to have translated *noesis noeseos* as an "understanding" of the whole. But according to Lonergan, the appropriation of the way our awareness as human beings who are awake operates leads to the discovery that awareness is the structured dynamism of conscious intentionality, which is almost certainly what is meant by Aristotle's phrase defining the *nous poietikos* in the *De anima* – "able to make and to become everything." For Aquinas this is the infinite potency of the *active* or *agent intellect*; and for Lonergan it is the pure, detached, unrestricted, and disinterested desire to know.

If, therefore, we pay attention to the correlation between reality and our intelligent and reasonable striving, it is only intelligent and reasonable to conclude that we cannot but identify reality with being. To know being, we need to ask questions and answer them correctly. If we are serious about seeking to know the truth about reality, we habitually resist speaking about mere matters of fact for which there is no intelligible explanation, because that is tantamount to speaking about nothing.[166] If being is correlative to intelligent and reasonable striving,

---

165 Lonergan, *Insight*, 696–8.
166 On mere matters of fact without explanation as nothing, see Lonergan, *Insight*, 528, 541, 613, 675–6.

then whatever being is known is so known only through answers to questions; it would be a contradiction to assert that any being is just a matter of fact, for which there is no explanation. (Clearly, this can only make sense if one has definitively excluded irrational accounts of knowledge of existence or occurrence by experience alone, as is the case with sensualism, materialism, perceptualism, etc.)

By now it must be obvious that significant implications follow from the inability to intelligently and reasonably avoid the affirmation that being means that which is to be known by intelligent grasp and rational affirmation. Once we realize that being is constituted in this manner, then we know that being is intelligible; and if being is completely constituted in this way and only constituted in this way, then being is completely intelligible.[167] It might help us to think of this in heuristic terms: we know about the complete intelligibility of being because we know that being is fully known when every intelligent question is answered.

Lonergan insists that once a person is committed to his or her reality as an intelligent and reasonable questioner, he or she must either admit the question of transcendence or give in to obscurantism by arbitrarily brushing questions aside.[168] Note the important convergence between Strauss and Lonergan, in that before being an issue of morality or moralism, intellectual probity on the highest plane is decisive: In Strauss's view, if Socratic cosmology constantly and necessarily ends with the honest admission of ignorance, then the universe is *not* completely intelligible. According to Lonergan the grasp of the notion of being defined as the totality that can be known by correct understanding and

---

167 Lonergan, *Insight*, 697.

168 See Lonergan, *Insight*, 569, where Lonergan uses one of Strauss's favorite quotes from Horace, *Epistolae*, I, 10, 24: "Besides myth there is mystery. Man's unanswered questions confront him with the 'known unknown,' and that confrontation may not be dodged. The detached and disinterested desire to know is unrestricted; it flings at us the name of obscurantists if we restrict it by allowing other desire to interfere with its proper unfolding; and while that unfolding can establish our naturally possible knowledge is restricted, this restriction on possible attainment is not a restriction on the desire itself; on the contrary, the question whether attainment is in all cases possible presupposes the fact that in all cases attainment is desired. Moreover, this unrestricted openness of our intelligence and reasonableness not only is the concrete operator of our intellectual development but also is accompanied by a corresponding operator that deeply and powerfully holds our sensitive integrations open to transforming change. Man by nature is oriented to mystery, and *naturam expellas furca, tamen usque recurret*." See also *Insight*, 661, 697, 706.

judgment grounds in all honesty the affirmation of the *complete intelligibility of being*. The core of this affirmation is an exigency within us not only for ever renewed investigations of the world, in which each and every answer compels ever further questions, but also an exigency within us to transcend this world, to go beyond the limits of every possible inner or outer experience. Lonergan's understanding here corresponds to Strauss's assertion of man's natural openness to the whole. For Lonergan the vivid sense of this exigency arises from one's natural and inevitable pure, disinterested, and unrestricted desire to know upon which the cogency of Lonergan's argument depends. The indispensable ground of this realization is correctly understanding self-transcendent understanding's role when it comes to the fulfillment of the human desire to know everything about everything.

If you do not feel compelled by this exigency, you may still ask why intellectual probity pushes us beyond the limits of every possible experience. You will come up against the fact that if we confine our questions to this world of being proportionate to our inner or outer experience, the world as a whole cannot be explained. Why not? The key here is the meaning of the term, "exists," which, as Strauss (in his letter to Löwith) learned from Kierkegaard, is a question not only about the actuality or occurrence of reality, but of one's existential stand on "the one thing needful." If your life is oriented in accord with the intelligent and reasonable *anangke* within you, you cannot but hold that if the world exists, it must be intelligible; it cannot exist as a mere matter of fact, for which no explanation has either to be inquired about or anticipated. Why? Because in the measure that one is intelligent and reasonable, one is convinced that whatever is not intelligible lies outside being.[169] That is the price of being consistently intelligent and reasonable.

If you agree with this, then the following argument will make sense. If the existence of the world as reality or being were ultimately an unintelligible fact, then it would be utterly alien to our intelligent and rational striving and so it would be outside being. From the perspective of the intelligent and reasonable account of knowing and being, which would include anyone who genuinely takes their stand on a scientific

---

169 Whatever exists must do so for a sufficient reason that provides the ground for our judging it to exist. The lack of intelligibility and reasonableness of an immoral act (or a basic sin) results in objective falsehood or the objective surd. Only in this improper sense do we speak of evil (which, according to Augustine and Aquinas, is always a privation of being) as existing.

approach to reality, an unintelligible matter of fact reduces to nothing. Intelligent and reasonable people are upset when they are told, "It just is that way, and that's all there is to it!" Most will agree that science is not in the business of affirming realities for which there is no explanation.[170] In Straussian terms, philosophers who know that the criterion of the real lies in rationally grounded judgment have to ask about what transcends space and time. Once they do so, the only satisfactory explanation that answers Leibniz's famous formulation of the question – Why is there something and not nothing? – has to be an unrestricted or infinite act of understanding.

At this point Lonergan reflects on the nature of "idea."[171] In accord with a verifiable account of knowledge as a compound of experience, understanding, and judgment, an idea is the intelligible content of an act of understanding. If we affirm that the only satisfactory explanation for the existence of the universe is an unrestricted act of understanding, then the content of such an unrestricted act of understanding is *the* complete intelligibility, and this would be identical with the idea of being as the ultimate explanation of everything else that exists. Because if the unrestricted act of understanding were identical with the idea of being, then it would not need any conditions outside itself to be true. It would be true unconditionally. In other words, if the idea of being is true, then it has to exist.

Note here that Lonergan has actually transposed the basic argument in which Aquinas claimed that we know that God exists inasmuch as we know that our judgment, "God is," is rationally grounded, and therefore true. The rational ground for the judgment is known from God's effects in the world.[172] According to the classic structure of the proof for God's existence, we first affirm the existence of a finite being, and then through an analysis based on a correct understanding of efficient, final, and exemplary causality, which demonstrates the intelligibility

---

170 An empirical scientist, who inquires into proportionate being that is intrinsically conditioned by space and time, must reject questions for which there are no relevant data to settle the issue.

171 Lonergan, *Insight*, 666–7, 664–701.

172 Thomas Aquinas, *Summa theologiae* I, q. 3, a. 4, ad 2; compare *Summa contra Gentiles* I, 12, no. 78. Lonergan relates his approach to the wider tradition in the brief paper, "The General Character of the Natural Theology of *Insight*," *Philosophical and Theological Papers 1965–1980*, Collected Works of Bernard Lonergan 17, ed. Robert C. Croken and Robert M. Doran (Toronto: University of Toronto Press, 2004), 3–9.

of contingent being, we affirm the intelligible link between this being and God as an ultimate intelligent cause. Lonergan's argument enucleates the various traditional proofs for God's existence insofar as they depart from the conditioned intelligibility of the world: "If reality is completely intelligible, God exists. But the world is completely intelligible. Therefore God exists."[173]

At this point it is possible to grasp the significance of the disagreement between Strauss's interpretation of Aristotle's expression for divine being, *noesis noeseos,* and Lonergan's. It is based, as Lonergan stresses in *Verbum,* on the way Thomas Aquinas took seriously Aristotle's theorem concerning knowledge by identity: in the human being the sense in act *is* the sensible in act, and the intellect in act *is* the intelligible in act. As regards God, we can reasonably say:

> The separate substance is at once a pure form and a pure act of understanding. When we understand we understand with respect to sensible data. But the separate substances understand yet have no senses. As their understanding is not of this or that sensible presentation, so it is not potency but act, and not by confrontation with the other but by and in identity with the self. "In his quae sunt sine materia, idem est intelligens et intellectum."[174] … If you object that modern interpreters translate *noêsis noêseôs* as 'thinking thought,' I readily grant what this implies, namely, that modern interpreters suppose Aristotle to have been a conceptualist. But also I retort that medieval translators did not write 'cogitatio cogitationis' but 'intelligentia intelligentiae.' It seems to follow that medieval translators did not regard Aristotle as a conceptualist.[175]

Again, the difficulty with the conceptualist approach to God becomes evident here as well. Prescinding from (or forgetful of) the role of understanding, the conceptualist image of knowledge often falls into three errors: first, by failing to account for the intentionality of consciousness, it imagines that the consciousness of the knower is cut off or isolated from the reality of the world referred to or intended by abstract conceptual representations; second, it thinks of the reality intended as

---

173 Lonergan, *Insight,* 695.

174 "In those things that are without matter, understanding is the same as the understood."

175 See Lonergan, *Verbum,* 196, where, at note 15, Lonergan refers to Thomas Aquinas, *In XII Metaphys.,* lect. 11; *Summa theologiae,* I, q. 79, art. 10; *De substantiis separatis,* c. 12 (Mandonnet ed., I, 117).

an "already-out-there-now" entity that through an impoverished (i.e., as compared to the contents of sense perception) conceptual replica can be managed or controlled; and third, it regards the knower's consciousness in itself to be unknowable. (We have seen that according to Strauss, Hobbes fell into all of these errors, and so revised or redefined the meanings of art and of nominalism.) The intellectualist approach, which explicitly acknowledges the role of understanding as pivoting between the concrete and the abstract, and emphasizes the role of questions within the structure of conscious intentionality, dismantles each of these presuppositions when it affirms that conscious intentionality's wonder is nothing but an openness to the totality of the reality of what *is*.

It almost cannot be stressed enough, however, that the reflective act of understanding apprehends the sufficiency of the evidence for an insight formulated as a guess or a hypothesis to assent to an affirmation or judgment as correct or true.[176] It is here that the issue of responsibility[177] as regards the presence or absence of dramatic, individual, group, or general bias becomes heightened even as the role of freedom – as in Strauss's phrases "free insight" and "uncoerced reason" – comes decisively into play. On this issue, then, Lonergan's crucial distinction between the proximate and remote contexts of judgment has an important bearing.[178] Because of the *proximate context* for making a limited judgment (say, the date of the beginning of the construction of the city of Tiberias in Northern Palestine, or the precise amount of global warming caused by human technology), the gathering and weighing of evidence for the judgment must be undertaken with the greatest care. But awareness of the *remote context* in which judgments are made pertains to the effect of the historicity and authenticity of the individual or the group upon the ability to make reasonable judgments. For example, in *Russian Studies* the legal historian Leonard Shapiro documented how the show of scrupulous legalism characteristic of Nazi judges functioned as a cover story for their unjust decisions.

Lonergan was never oblivious of the finitude of knowing subjects, and yet he insisted that the consciousnesses of embodied human subjects are always already caught up in an activity that is uniquely their own in virtue of a profound intention that is open to being in a comprehensive

---

176 Lonergan, "Reflective Understanding," *Insight*, 304–40.
177 On responsibility in judgment, see Lonergan, *Insight*, 297, 299.
178 Lonergan, "The Notion of Truth: *The Criterion of Truth*," *Insight*, 573–5.

manner. This supervening intentionality bestows meaning upon each of their cognitional operations, even when it cannot give an adequate and definitive account of itself while it is being actuated by cognitional and voluntary operations. He maintained that in spite of all the ways this profound intention or notion of being (which he affirms is coeval with being human) is situated and so admits of a perspectival character, people under the right conditions can still appropriate the dynamic structures by which it unfolds over time so long as they attentively, intelligently, and critically perform what Lonergan came to call the "turn toward interiority" in the manner of Augustine, Aquinas, and Newman.

The approach to the conception and affirmation of God grounded upon the self-appropriation of human rational self-consciousness leads to the further conclusion that "the notion at which we have arrived is the notion of a personal being." Lonergan goes on to say:

> As man, so God is a rational self-consciousness, for man was made in the image and likeness of God. But what man is through unrestricted desire and limited attainment, God is as an unrestricted act. But an unrestricted act of rational self-consciousness, however objectively and impersonally it has been conceived, clearly satisfies all that is meant by the subject, the person, the other with an intelligence and a reasonableness and a willing that is [one's] own.
>
> Moreover, as the idea of being is the notion of a personal God, so too it implies a personalist view of the order of the universe. For that order is not a blueprint such as might be drawn up by an architect for a building, nor is it a plan such as might be imposed by a government given to social engineering, but it is an intelligibility that is to be grasped only by compounding classical, statistical, genetic and dialectical methods, that includes the commands and prohibitions that express the willing of one about the willing of others, that has room for the forbearance with which even omnipotent will refuses to interfere with the will of other persons.[179]

Lonergan's Shift from Cognitional to Existential Interiority

The composition of *Insight* was obviously based on the assumption that people who had made that judgment of self-affirmation regarding themselves as knowers would follow through in the way they would

---

179 Lonergan, *Insight*, 691–2.

thenceforth make choices and take action. Years later, however, Joseph de Finance helped Lonergan to distinguish between horizontal and vertical exercises of liberty.[180] With this distinction he realized that self-affirmation, to be authentic, also involves the kind of decision or commitment that engages one in a vertical exercise of liberty. A horizontal exercise of liberty chooses among alternative courses of action *within an already fixed horizon*; but a vertical exercise of liberty places one in an entirely new horizon: one becomes a new self. Such reflections gave rise to Lonergan's post-*Insight* notions of "horizon" and "conversion" as a change in one's overall orientation, or one's entry into a new horizon. This development signaled a return to topics of *Grace and Freedom* he had treated earlier within a framework of metaphysical terms and relations. Henceforth he handled them in existential terms.

As Lonergan himself noted later on, *Insight* did not make as clear as it should have that even though, in investigating our personal interiority, we may have correctly affirmed the dynamic structures of our conscious intentionality, we would still have to commit ourselves to reorienting our lives in accord with the demands built into that dynamic structure; and this would be tantamount to undergoing an "intellectual conversion."

However, while expounding the metaphysics of proportionate being coordinate with cognitional structure in *Insight*, Lonergan already hinted at this requirement by stating that, first, the appropriation of the truth demands an orientation consistent with one's being as a knower; and, that second, such an orientation requires one to make a decisive commitment.[181] Only then did he set forth the ethics grounded in the imperious need to have our decisions and actions be consistent with what we know truly. In this way he established a natural basis (in the sense of a basis not dependent on revealed truths) for his treatment of divine transcendence (or natural theology): namely, that if the reality proportionate to our capacity to know adequately is to be completely intelligible, then this has also to hold true of whatever exists beyond our power to know properly or adequately (as explained above).

In accord with *Insight*'s moving viewpoint, then, Lonergan led readers to reflect explicitly on how the concrete pursuit of their personal commitment to attentive, intelligent, reasonable, and responsible living

---

180 Lonergan, *Method in Theology*, 40, 122, 237–8, 240, 269.
181 Lonergan, "The Appropriation of the Truth," *Insight*, 581–5.

inevitably comes up against what he named "moral impotence."[182] This entails the recognition that, because of moral evil our natural and inevitable human spontaneities operative in knowing, deciding, and acting do not suffice for living genuinely integrated human lives.[183] And if life in accord with intelligence, reason, and responsible morality is beyond our unaided human capacity to achieve, *Insight*'s moving viewpoint confronts readers with the question whether there exists a superhuman or divine solution to the problem of evil.

For readers trying to take the project of authentic existence seriously in the throes of moral impotence, chapter 20 of *Insight* provides a heuristic structure of a divine solution to the problem of evil. Many readers have had the sense as regards this chapter that the abstract character of the so-called proof for the existence of God in chapter 19 does no more than help one to achieve what Newman called a "notional" apprehension and assent to that way of conceiving and affirming God's existence.[184] Would not a person's "real" assent to God's existence based on the affirmation of the complete intelligibility of the real not also involve a response to an invitation to adoration by a personal God, who initiates us into a religious life in which God is acknowledged as presence and life, and to which one as a human being can respond with the confidence, surrender, and love that would result from God's gift?[185]

Strauss on the Fundamental Alternative

In *Natural Right and History* Strauss stated the fundamental alternatives:

> The fundamental question, therefore, is whether men can acquire that
> knowledge of the good without which they cannot guide their lives

---

182 On moral impotence, see Lonergan, *Insight*, 650–3.

183 Lonergan, "The Problem of Liberation," *Insight*, 653–6.

184 On Newman's distinction between "notional" and "real" apprehension and assent, see Lonergan, "Pope John's Intention," *A Third Collection*, ed. Frederick E. Crowe (New York: Paulist Press, 1985), 236.

185 Lonergan himself suggested as much in his famous footnote 1 in the epilogue to *Insight*, 754: "Since I believe personal relations can be studied adequately in the larger and more concrete context, the skimpy treatment accorded them in the present work is not to be taken as a denial of their singular importance in human living." Later on, in three lectures entitled "Philosophy of God and Theology," each followed by question periods (at St Michael's Institute, Gonzaga University, Spokane, WA in 1972), Lonergan elaborated his own criticisms of chapter 19 in *Insight*. See now Lonergan, "Philosophy of God and Theology," *Philosophical and Theological Papers 1965–1980*, 159–218.

individually or collectively by the unaided effort of their natural powers, or whether they are dependent for that knowledge on Divine Revelation. No alternative is more fundamental than this: human guidance or divine guidance.[186]

The ninth chapter of Lawrence Lampert's *The Enduring Importance of Leo Strauss* argues the thesis succinctly stated in the title: "Advancing the Enlightenment: Strauss's Recovery of Nietzsche's Theological-Political Program."[187] According to this argument (as far as I have understood it), Strauss ultimately thought that Nietzsche did recover the standpoint of nature at the end of the "waves of modernity." In principle, Strauss traces the recovery of the fundamental alternatives back through Halevi to Alfarabi's teaching that philosophy should rule religion. Nietzsche's retrieval of nature, therefore, is a postmodern retrieval of Alfarabi's teaching, so that, as Lampert tells us, Strauss's late student and expert on Islamic philosophy Muhsin Mahdi could quote "at length Nietzsche's statements in *Beyond Good and Evil* on the necessity that philosophy should rule religion," and could comment, "If these statements of the relation between philosophy and religion are somewhat bold, they are not, I suggest, revolutionary. Nor do they represent an innovation, but only a renovation, restoration, or revival of a strain in the philosophical tradition." Paraphrasing and citing Muhsin Mahdi, *Alfarabi and the Foundation of Islamic Political Philosophy*, Lampert continues:

Alfarabi traced the view that philosophy is responsible for ruling religion back to Plato and Aristotle, while tracing to Christianity the effort to wipe out memory of philosophic rule. He taught that "human religion ... should come after philosophy *in time* and teach the multitude the theoretical and practical matters that had been discovered in philosophy by means of persuasion and/or image making." For Alfarabi the philosopher's responsibility for religion is "the natural, internal development" of wisdom: "the instrument of preserving such wisdom is the philosopher-lawgiver who establishes the human religion, so that the theoretical and practical things discovered by demonstration and prudence are taught to the multitude

---

186 Strauss, *Natural Right and History*, 74.

187 Lawrence Lampert, *The Enduring Importance of Leo Strauss* (Chicago: University of Chicago Press, 2013), 268–310.

through rhetorical and poetic methods, and everyone is persuaded to accept correct opinions and perform salutary practices."[188]

According to Lampert, Strauss himself opted for a natural solution to the problem of evil; he goes on to argue that Strauss's option – which it is admittedly difficult to disagree that he made – owed a great deal to his growing understanding of Nietzsche the philosopher (as traced by Lampert himself in this book and in his earlier books, Leo *Strauss and Nietzsche* and *Nietzsche and Modern Times: A Study of Bacon, Descartes, and Nietzsche*).[189] But I do not think that to admit that Strauss could not and did not avoid the fundamental option for a natural solution grounded on the foundations he laid in his published works for education into the theological-political problematic, one has to agree with Lampert's Nietzschean predilections.

Lonergan on the Fundamental Alternative

Be that as it may, on the basis of his own recovery of nature Lonergan disagreed with all the positions stated in the preceding paragraph. Lonergan was fully aware that "even in those in whom the [divine] solution is realized, there are endless gradations in the measure in which it is realized and, by a necessary consequence, there are endless degrees in which those that profess to know and embrace the solution can fail to bring forth the fruits it promises in their individual lives and in the human situations of which those lives are part."[190] Lonergan was also aware of the disadvantages of a divine or supernatural solution in comparison to a simply natural one:

> Natural solutions would not exceed the bounds of humanism. Their faith would be not only believing to understand (*crede ut intelligas*) but also believing what only man in this life eventually could understand. The hope would reinforce the pure desire without introducing a displacement away from human concerns. Their charity would be a self-sacrificing love of God that bore no appearance of a contempt for human values. In contrast, the supernatural solution involves a transcendence of human-

---

188 Lampert, *The Enduring Importance of Leo Strauss*, 271–2.
189 Both published by University of Chicago Press in 1966 and 2001, respectively.
190 Lonergan, *Insight*, 748.

ism, and the imperfect realization of the supernatural solution is apt to oscillate between an emphasis on the supernatural and an emphasis on the solution. Imperfect faith can insist on believing to the neglect of the understanding that makes faith an effective factor in human living and history; and an even less perfect faith can endanger the general collaboration in its hurry to show forth its social and cultural fruits. Imperfect hope can so expect the New Jerusalem as to oppose any foretaste of intellectual bliss and union in this life; and an even less perfect hope can forget that a supernatural solution involves a real displacement of the center of human concerns. Imperfect charity lacks the resources needed to combine both true loving and the true transformation of loving. It can be absorbed in the union of the family, in the intersubjectivity of comrades in work and in adventure, in the common aspiration of associates in scientific, cultural, and humanitarian pursuits. On the other hand, it can withdraw from home and country, from human cares and human ambitions, from the clamor of the senses and the entanglement of the social surd, to fix its gaze upon the unseen ultimate, to respond to an impalpable presence, to grow inwardly to the stature of eternity. But imperfect charity, inasmuch as it is imperfect, will not realize at once the opposed facets of its perfection; if it is in the world, it ever risks being of the world; and if it withdraws from the world, the human basis of its ascent to God risks a contraction and an atrophy.[191]

When Lonergan states that a supernatural or divine solution renders "human perfection itself" a "limit to be transcended," the actual presence of a supernatural solution shifts the fundamental alternatives set forth by Strauss, insofar as Lonergan discounts neither the possibility nor the reality of "a humanism in revolt against the proffered supernatural solution." With all its noble intentions, in the end, such a rebellion "rests," according to Lonergan, "on man's proud content to be just a man, and its tragedy," he goes on to say, "is that, on the … supposition of a supernatural solution, to be just a man is what man cannot be."[192] Here Lonergan draws his own conclusions in the light of intellectual probity:

If he would be truly a man, he would submit to the unrestricted desire and discover the problem of evil and affirm the existence of a solution and accept the solution that exists. But if he would be only a man he has to be

---

191 Lonergan, *Insight*, 748–9.
192 Lonergan, *Insight*, 749–50.

less. He has to forsake the openness of the pure desire; he has to take refuge in the counterpositions; he has to develop what counter-philosophies he can to save his dwindling humanism from further losses; and there will not be lacking men clear-sighted enough to grasp that the issue is between God and man, logical enough to grant that intelligence and reason are oriented towards God, ruthless enough to summon to their aid the dark forces of passion and of violence.[193]

Summary Review

As is by now evident, this relatively brief account of Lonergan's stance on Jerusalem and Athens has traced the basic steps in a procedure grounded in a verifiable analysis of conscious intentionality's processes of understanding, judging, and deciding, together with the rational conception of reality that flows from it. Strauss would have probably disagreed with each of Lonergan's steps toward the affirmation of God's existence: first, the identification of reality with being; second, the identification of being with complete intelligibility; and third, the identification of complete intelligibility with the unrestricted act of understanding. Nevertheless, to restate Lonergan's procedure in rather more descriptive terms: If one thinks things through, it is difficult to be coherent in affirming the intelligibility of a part of the universe without also implicitly affirming the intelligibility of the whole; and in so doing of affirming, at least implicitly, a completely intelligible principle of the whole, which is God. In addition, Lonergan's analysis of the unrestricted act of understanding, which extrapolates from our limited insights and judgments regarding terrestrial data, works out at some length how the unrestricted act of understanding, insofar as it explains everything else, is endowed with an array of divine attributes.[194]

This comparison has suggested a contrast between, on the one hand, Strauss's tendencies as perhaps affected by conceptualism, and on the other, Lonergan's intellectualism. If correct, the suggestion has radical and systematic consequences in relation to the many disagreements that arose throughout the essay. Whatever the nature of those disagreements, none is more significant than the difference between their respective conceptions of divine transcendence. I suppose that a follower of

---

193 Lonergan, *Insight*, 750.
194 Lonergan, *Insight*, 680–92.

Strauss would probably argue that the roots of this difference are traceable to the tacit or express role played throughout Lonergan's work by Christian faith and theology. Then the implications drawn by Strauss in relation to Thomas Aquinas's approach to natural law would apply equally to Lonergan. Furthermore, that Lonergan's natural theology of God as an infinite act of understanding transcends not only space and time but also goes beyond necessity and impossibility only exacerbates this suspicion. Such an understanding would entail an understanding of God as able to create a universe by his understanding alone, as well as to create human beings in God's image and likeness, to issue commands, and to exercise providential care for terrestrial affairs, and yet it would eliminate the irrational unpredictability Strauss ascribes to the God of the Bible, and locate it in human beings.

Such a natural theology sets Lonergan apart not only from Strauss's conception, but also from that of all the Jewish interpreters of scripture discussed earlier. In appropriating what he interprets as the Socratic conviction that cosmology would provide the only way of unconditionally legitimating philosophic inquiry as the best way of life, Strauss denies the possibility of natural theology. In the foregoing account, however, the opposition between these two contradictory conceptions of divine mystery is rooted in the differences between their respective understandings of understanding, which would also explain their profound discrepancies about (1) the human transgression in the Fall, (2) the mysterious and humanly intractable character of the objective surd of sin, and (3) God's role in collaborating with humanity in redemption from sin.

Despite his apparent affirmation of the nobility and moral decency of premodern rationalism's adherence to both the Socratic justice of harming no one even in little things and the plausibility of Aristotle's account of the completely human morality of the magnanimous man, Strauss's conceptualism leads to a kind of "catch-22." It may be going too far to claim that Strauss combined a no-nonsense "Show me!" attitude with a demand for logically probative argumentation in a manner that entails an apodictic denial of what Catholic theology calls the "supernatural light of faith."[195] Still, his claim that accounting both theoretically and politically for the factual depredations that are justifiably attributable to Christians does confront Christian believers with obvious difficulties

---

195 For Strauss as a rationalist the supernatural dimension of creation is really no more than a figment of the human imagination motivated by a need for consolation in

surrounding their beliefs regarding the divine solution to the question of the right way to live; and these difficulties may lead dialectically to the same negation of a supernatural, divine-human solution to the problem of evil. It strikes me as ironic that Strauss's consistently stated conclusion that the options for either the life of reason or the life based on religious belief and obedience to a revealing God rest ultimately on an ungrounded decision[196] ends up in a kind of "fideism" – a stance which both overemphasizes the limits of reason and harbors the conviction that the tenets of *any* faith are irrational.

As suggested above, I think Strauss made the commitment to a natural solution to the problem of evil in good faith. I also suppose that a partial motive for Strauss (as a political philosopher) to reject the option of divine revelation – especially in its Christian dispensation – as the ultimate guide for human life is linked to the fact that the so-called natural solution can accommodate, in a way that the Christian solution cannot, the "realistic" protection of liberal democracy to safeguard the freedom to philosophize, which in the sphere of politics involves the willingness to make "hard" – i.e., cruel or immoral – choices. Even if it is true that Strauss entertains the political reasonableness of such choices, it is not altogether clear to me whether he actually approved of such measures.

Whatever may be true on that score, I want to emphasize that Strauss's apparent oscillation between a truncated reduction of human knowing to sense observation and/or logical argumentation and an acknowledgment of human beings' passionate desire to know everything about

---

the face of life's miseries and of death, whereas in *Grace and Freedom: Operative Grace in the Thought of St Thomas Aquinas*, Collected Works of Bernard Lonergan 1, 15–16, Lonergan speaks of: "grasping that the idea of the supernatural is a theorem, that it no more adds to the data of the problem than the Lorentz transformation theorem puts a new constellation in the heavens. What Philip the Chancellor systematically posited was not the supernatural character of grace, for that was already known and acknowledged, but the validity of a line of reference termed nature. In the long term and in the concrete the real alternatives remain charity and cupidity, the elect and the *massa damnata*. But the whole problem lies in the abstract, in human thinking: the fallacy in the early thought had been an unconscious confusion of the metaphysical abstraction, nature, with the concrete data which do not quite correspond; Philip's achievement was the creation of a mental perspective, the introduction of a set of coordinates, that eliminated the basic fallacy and its attendant host of anomalies."

196 See Strauss, "The Mutual Influence of Philosophy and Theology," 111–18; and "Preface to Spinoza's Critique of Religion," *Liberalism Ancient and Modern*, 224–59.

everything (or about the whole) makes the two alternatives of Jerusalem and Athens irreconcilable. I believe the process Lonergan earlier called "the self-appropriation of rational self-consciousness" and later on spoke of as "intellectual conversion" resolved that oscillation and led to implications that Strauss could not have coherently entertained. This brings us to my final comments regarding this comparison of Lonergan with Strauss.

Final Comments on Lonergan and Strauss on God

An adequate comparison between Lonergan and Strauss would demand a rather thick book, and I have only scraped the surface of the most important issues. Nevertheless, allow me to conclude this study.

After the completion of *Insight* in 1954 there began a period when Lonergan was composing *Method in Theology*, which was marked by article after article as it became clearer to Lonergan that *Insight*'s treatment of the question of God was too exclusively focused on the objective truthfulness of the *de jure* argument for God's existence and nature.[197] There were two aspects to his second thoughts on the matter, but I want to focus here on only one:

> *Insight* insists a great deal on the authenticity of the subject, on his need to reverse his counterpositions and develop his positions, on the importance, in brief, of intellectual conversion ... The direction in which *Insight* was moving ... implies not only intellectual but also moral and religious conversion. One might claim that *Insight* leaves room for moral and religious conversion, but one is not very likely to assert that the room is very well furnished.
>
> ... The trouble with ... *Insight* was that it ... treated God's existence and attributes in a purely objective fashion. It made no effort to deal with the subject's religious horizon. It failed to acknowledge that the traditional viewpoint made sense only if one accepted first principles on the ground that they were intrinsically necessary, and if one added the assumption that there is one right culture so that differences in subjectivity are irrelevant.[198]

---

197 Lonergan, "The Natural Knowledge of God," *Second Collection*, 117–33.
198 Lonergan, *Philosophical and Theological Papers 1965–1980*, 171–2.

Although Lonergan denied that there are first principles that are intrinsically necessary (or self-evident), he clearly agreed with Strauss that in modern times philosophy should no longer simply *begin* with metaphysics. In the last period of his life, Lonergan worked out a foundational methodology to account for the *de facto* subjective conditions for correctly conceiving and affirming God. He accepted the validity of metaphysics provided that it be methodically grounded in an intellectual conversion that bears fruit in a correct cognitional theory and a correct epistemology. From his later viewpoint, instead of simply rejecting the validity of *Insight*'s argument for the existence of God in a wholesale manner, he added an objective account of the subjective conditions for such an intellectual attainment and clarified how the objectivity of our knowledge is the achievement of *authentic* subjectivity: "Objectivity is attained by the self-transcendence of the concrete subject; and indeed the basic forms of self-transcendence are intellectual, moral, and religious conversion."[199] This holds true especially for knowledge of God, which amounts to the affirmation of an absolute meaning and value that concerns us unconditionally if we are authentically engaged in the quest for "the one thing needful." For Lonergan, to raise the question of God is to ask about the intelligibility, meaningfulness, and value of the universe.[200] Such questions, like all others, are conditioned (not determined) by their cultural horizons discussed above under the heading of the remote context of our judgments.

Strauss separated the way of life based on free questioning, uncoerced insight, and evident reasons from the life of belief or faith understood as obedience to authoritative claims based ultimately on arbitrary power. This puts even genuine believers on the defensive insofar as it follows that they are intellectually impotent and so need to depend on "vain imaginings" and external authority for support or consolation; at best, they are suspected of sacrificing whatever intellectual probity they may have possessed for the sake of socially indispensable moral underpinnings. In the name of a way of life devoted to free philosophic inquiry,

---

199 Lonergan, *Method in Theology*, 338.
200 The suspicion will not down: Do the vast majority of agnostics or atheists who refuse to raise *the* what-question regarding God do so because they have a premonition that successfully asking and answering it would require them to make decisions and changes in their way of life, which they are unwilling to undertake – namely, to undergo a radical conversion of life?

does not Strauss reduce biblical "purity of heart" to a fear-motivated obedience to God or religious authority, whether in respectable good faith or in contemptible bad faith?

In *Insight* Lonergan made the case that "if the humanist is to stand by the exigencies of his own unrestricted desire, if he is to yield to the demands for openness set by every further question, then he will acknowledge and consent to the one solution that exists, and if that solution is supernatural, his very humanism will lead beyond itself"[201] and become an *intellectus quaerens fidem*.[202] However, in the years after finishing *Insight* he realized that, taking into account the terrestrial sphere's dramatic, individual, group, and commonsense biases and the overwhelming prevalence of moral renunciation, the occurrence of such a coherent pursuit depends with the highest statistical probability (*ut in pluribus*) on the moral life (that Strauss regarded as secondary in relation to the theoretical or contemplative life), as a result of which reflection it becomes highly probable that the factor of morality is far from secondary in the measure that a moral conversion from disordered self-love to ordered (because rightly oriented) self-love is a prerequisite for intellectual conversion. Moreover – what is perhaps even more questionable from Strauss's viewpoint – Lonergan held that the probability of a person's being morally converted is usually based on a supernatural gift that is in no way the product of one's own knowing and choosing, but rather the gift of God's love that effects a religious conversion from oneself as the center of the universe to God, who is the center of the universe.

---

201 Lonergan, *Insight*, 749.
202 See the first section of the "Epilogue," *Insight*, 753–64.

5 Voegelin and Gadamer: Continental Philosophers Inspired by Plato and Aristotle

I. Introduction

Eric Voegelin (1901–85) and Hans-Georg Gadamer (1900–2002) are two significant figures in German-speaking or continental philosophy. They have a great deal in common. They each had long and fruitful academic careers and neither of them compromised with Hitler and National Socialism.

In 1938 Voegelin fled the Nazis from Austria into exile in the United States where he launched an extraordinary career while working in relatively obscure positions at the University of Alabama and Louisiana State University. Under the auspices of conservative American publishers William F. Buckley and Henry R. Luce, he entered the wider public sphere for a time in the 1950s and 1960s following the publication of *The New Science of Politics*.[1] Yet he remained something of an outsider even though the conservative branch of American political science considered him one of its leaders. Voegelin's auspicious return to Munich University to establish its Institute for Political Science in 1966 was not altogether happy. He was pleased to finish his career as the Henry Salvatore resident scholar at the Hoover Institute at Stanford University. In the United States, Germany, Austria, and eastern Europe there are political theorists and scholars in many other disciplines deeply indebted to his thought.

---

1 Eric Voegelin, *The New Science of Politics: An Introduction*, Charles R. Wallgreen Foundation Lecture, Winter Quarter, 1951 (Chicago: University of Chicago, 1952).

Gadamer remained in Germany until rather late in his life when, after being *emeritiert* as Ordinarius in Philosophy at Heidelberg, for over a decade he spent semesters as a distinguished visiting lecturer at the Catholic University of America, McMaster University in Canada, and Boston College. His academic career began in Breslau, and he held posts in Marburg, Leipzig, Frankfurt, and Heidelberg, where, partly due to his exceptional talent for friendship, he influenced West German universities and German philosophy after he succeeded Karl Jaspers to the chair in philosophy at Heidelberg. Gadamer shaped generations of students who have been active mainly in Germany, Italy, and North America.

Like Leo Strauss – a fellow student with Gadamer in his early Marburg days and a fellow leader with Voegelin in the field of political theory in America later on – both Voegelin and Gadamer confronted the crisis of modernity. Extremely sensitive to the extraordinary processes of Western deculturation during the last four centuries, they tried to recover what Strauss called the "Great Tradition," especially the classics of ancient Greek philosophy. In this project, the young Martin Heidegger of the lectures leading up to the publication of *Sein und Zeit* in 1927 convinced Gadamer and Strauss that the only retrieval worth attempting is one that recovers the ancient meanings and values of the classic texts as much as possible on their own terms – Greek, Latin, Arabic, or Hebrew, as the case might be. Independently of Heidegger, but very much in the same vein, Voegelin's return to the ancients was integrally connected with his reaction to the conventional "history of ideas" approaches to political thought and his decision to write a history of order.[2]

Neither Voegelin nor Gadamer, however, revived the *querelle des anciennes et modernes*. If Strauss considered Voegelin and Gadamer too imbued with historical mindedness, they, in turn, were under no illusion that Strauss was less historical in his approach than they were in theirs. However much must be learned from the ancients, we cannot completely transcend the social and political conditionings of our own time. We have to face the crisis of *our* time.

---

2 See Eric Voegelin, "From Political Ideas to Symbols of Experience," in *Autobiographical Reflections*, ed. Ellis Sandoz (Baton Rouge: Lousiana State University Press, 1989), 62–9.

II. Educational Backgrounds

Both thinkers were extremely fortunate in their education. Voegelin was educated in Vienna[3] at a time when, as he often emphasized, Jewish scholars contributed enormously to the city's educational and cultural institutions. The heritage of the classic experience of reason was everywhere in evidence – in museums and in institutions dedicated to ancient and medieval history and artistic culture, and in a rich diversity of circles or study groups, of which he enthusiastically availed himself as a precocious youngster. These "circles" for study and discussion kept his education from being dustily academic and enhanced his polymathic brilliance.

His early mentor at the University of Vienna, the social philosopher, Othmar Spann, introduced him to the "classic philosophers," Plato and Aristotle, and the German Idealists. Attending the seminars of neo-Kantian legal theorist, Hans Kelsen, brought him into contact with Adolf Merkl and Alfred von Verdross; and in the seminars of Ludwig von Mises, he became acquainted with leaders of the Austrian school of political economy such as Hayek, Morgenstern, Machlup, and Haberler. He formed life-long friendships at this time with peers Alfred Schütz, Felix Kaufmann, Emanuel Winternitz, and Friedrich Engel-Janosi, among many others. Thus, as testified to by his critical engagement with Max Weber[4] (who belonged to the Southwest German neo-Kantian school of Windelband and Rickert), Voegelin maintained a life-long preoccupation with the dynamics of public order and administration and with comparative sociology and history. At the age of thirty he realized his calling was to be a political scientist in the classic sense of the term, which required the careful study of all the ancient texts, so he learned Greek and Hebrew. Clearly, these interests were always cultivated in the context of philosophy as a comprehensive reflection on the human condition.

Neither Voegelin nor Gadamer were "specialists without spirit or vision" (*Fachmänner ohne Geist*, to paraphrase part of Weber's description of those who prevail in "the iron cage" of modernity: "voluptuaries without heart and specialists without spirit or vision"). Emblematic of the quality of both thinkers is their emphatic openness to the widespread

---

3 Voegelin, "University of Vienna," *Autobiographical Reflections*, 1–7.
4 Voegelin, "Max Weber," *Autobiographical Reflections*, 11–13.

influence in the German-speaking world of the circle surrounding the poet, educator, and spiritual leader, Stefan George.[5] They read Friedrich Gundolf on Goethe, Ernst Bertram on Nietzsche, and Max Kommerell on Jean Paul. They both avowed their indebtedness to Plato scholars in the circle, Heinrich Friedemann, Paul Friedländer,[6] and Kurt Hildebrandt, without whom their retrieval of Plato would have been impossible. Just as the elderly Gadamer, sitting in our car waiting to pick up our children from school, in a kind of reverie recited by heart Paul Valery's "Cimetière Marin," so in late autobiographical accounts, Voegelin spoke of how affected he was by that poem ever since he spent a year in France as a Rockefeller Fellow; he also recalled having difficulties at that time reading the works of Flaubert on account of the author's large vocabulary. Voegelin's writings are suffused with the deep literary interests manifested as well in his correspondence with American literary scholar Robert Heilman. Like Gadamer, who early on was expressly drawn to literature, Voegelin was sensitive to the corruption of a culture's language, having been schooled by the great Austrian journalist and editor of *Der Fackel*, Karl Kraus, and Austrian authors Heimito von Doderer and Robert Musil, as well as Thomas Mann from Germany.

As a young man Gadamer was shaped by German universities in Breslau (where he studied with Richard Hönigswald) and Marburg (where his father taught as a professor of pharmaceutical chemistry), and Freiburg where he went to study with Heidegger and Husserl in 1923. He remarks in his memoirs[7] how the relatively small faculty and habitually interdisciplinary character animating the University of Marburg in

---

5 See Voegelin, "Stefan George and Karl Kraus," *Autobiographical Reflections*, 16–19; "Autobiographical Statement at Age Eighty-two," in *The Beginning and the Beyond: Papers from the Gadamer and Voegelin Conferences*, Supplementary Issue of *Lonergan Workshop* 4, ed. Frederick G. Lawrence (Chico, CA: Scholars Press, 1984), 112; see also section VI in "Nietzsche, the Crisis, and the War," in *Published Essays, 1940–1952*, Collected Works of Eric Voegelin 10, ed. Ellis Sandoz (Columbia, MO: University of Missouri, 2000), 46–149. Gadamer has much to say about George in his memoir, *Philosophische Lehrjahre. Eine Rückschau* (Frankfurt am Main: Vittorio Klostermann, 1977), *passim*; see also, "Die Wirkung Stefan Georges auf die Wissenschaft (1983)," "Der Dichter Stefan George (1968)," and "Hölderlin und George," *Äesthetik und Poetik II. Hermeneutik im Vollzug*, Gesammelte Werke 9 (Tübingen: Mohr Siebeck, 1993), 258–60, 211–28, 229–44.
6 See Hans-Georg Gadamer, "Paul Friedländer," *Hermeneutik im Rückblick*, Gesammelte Werke 10 (Tübingen: Mohr Siebeck, 1999), 403–5.
7 See Gadamer, *Philosophische Lehrjahre.*

those days came close to realizing the ancient ideal of liberal arts and liberal education. Thus, initially inclined toward German literature, art, and history, the pressure exerted upon him by the bewilderment and disorientation brought about by the breakdown of the liberal myth of progress based on science and the devastation of bourgeois German assumptions during the First World War quite naturally turned him toward philosophy.

Of immense significance for the study of philosophy in Marburg were the networks of personal relationships. Gadamer's connection with the then leading figure of the "Marburg School" of neo-Kantianism and the supervisor of his doctoral dissertation, Paul Natorp,[8] widened to include loyalties to Nicolai Hartmann, at a time when Hartmann was freeing himself from the neo-Kantian system, and then to young Martin Heidegger. In the ranks of Gadamer's closest friends were scholars from the *Stefan-George-Kreis*, including Oskar Schürer[9] and Max Kommerell.[10] During his student days Karl Löwith,[11] Gerhard Krüger,[12] Walter Bröcker, Leo Strauss, and Jacob Klein were also peers and friends. When Natorp asked the 22-year-old Gadamer (who had just completed his dissertation) to read Martin Heidegger's so-called "Natorp Report" (composed on the occasion of a possible call to Karl Wundt's position at Marburg),[13] he was drawn to the radical young philosopher, who taught him to read the works of Luther, Augustine, Plato, and Aristotle in a way that transcended both the scholastic tradition (in which Heidegger had first been trained) and post-Enlightenment prejudices.

Gadamer sensed that Heidegger's return to Plato and Aristotle would aid him in his state of bewilderment in a way that neither the

---

8 See Gadamer, "Paul Natorp," *Hermeneutik im Rückblick*, 375–80.

9 See Gadamer, "Oskar Schürer," *Philosophische Lehjahre*, 80–92.

10 See Gadamer, "Max Kommerell," *Philosophische Lehrjahre*, 93–110.

11 See Gadamer, "Karl Löwith," *Hermeneutik im Rückblick*, 418–23.

12 See Gadamer, "Gerhard Krüger," *Hermeneutik im Rückblick*, 412–17.

13 Günther Neumann, editor of Martin Heidegger's Gesamtausgabe 62, says that the "Natorp Report" is an elaboration for the philosophical faculties at Marburg and Göttingen, who were considering whether to call Heidegger. See Martin Heidegger, "Anhang III: Phänomenologische Interpretationen zu Aristoteles (Anzeige der Hermeneutichen Situation)" in *Phänomenologische Interpretationen Ausgewählter Abhandlungen des Aristoteles zur Ontologie und Logik. Gesamtausgabe 62, II. Abteilung. Vorlesungen 1919–1944*, ed. Günther Neumann (Frankfurt am Main: Vittorio Klostermann, 2005), 341–575. English translation: Michael Bauer, trans., "Phenomenological Interpretations with Respect to Aristotle: Indication of the Hermeneutical Situation by Martin Heidegger," *Man and World* 25 (1992): 355–93.

reigning neo-Kantianism nor the alternative *Weltanschauungsphilosophie* (spawned by Friedrich Nietzsche) had been capable of doing. However, when, with Heidegger's help, he realized how ill-equipped he was philologically to undertake a genuine encounter with Plato and Aristotle and how discouraged he was about chances of becoming a genuine philosopher, Gadamer placed himself under the tutelage of classical philologist Paul Friedländer to gain sufficient competence in Greek philology to habilitate himself in that field. This enabled him to participate in the *Graeca* evenings at Rudolf Bultmann's home in Marburg, and eventually to advise Heidegger about Plato and Aristotle, and write his *Habilitation* on Plato's *Philebus* under Heidegger's direction.

For all Voegelin's grounding in history and in social and legal theory, Plato had so convinced him that authentic philosophy emerges in resistance to the disorder of the age that (side-by-side with and independently of Strauss) he pioneered the twentieth-century revival of political philosophy, with its primary focus on the classic correlation between the individual human soul and the governance of society as a whole, as the architectonic human science.

Gadamer always said that "Plato remained in the center of my studies."[14] His "mimetic reading" of the Platonic dialogues became crucial for his integration of the influences of the phenomenological tradition of Husserl and Heidegger, and of the hermeneutic tradition of Schleiermacher and Dilthey vis-à-vis the problematic of history (from Dilthey's *Jugendgeschichte Hegels* to Droysen) into hermeneutic philosophy, which he ultimately considered to be a renewal of Aristotle's *philosophia practica*. Unlike Voegelin, he did not have important things to say about Aristotle's *Politics*; and, unlike Leo Strauss, he denied that he was ever a *political* philosopher.

Among other factors, Schelling's *Philosophie der Offenbarung 1841/42* played a crucial role in Voegelin's transformation from masterful historian of political ideas into the author of the five volumes of *Order and History* (1956–1987). Voegelin was always more expressly open to religious experience and mysticism and to the religious dimensions of symbolism than Gadamer, perhaps due to the latter's rather strict adherence to the strictures of Kant's transcendental dialectic. Indeed,

---

14 See Hans-Georg Gadamer, "Selbstdarstellung Hans-Georg Gadamer," *Hermeneutik II. Wahrheit und Methode. Ergänzungen, Register*, Gesammelte Werke 2 (Tübingen: Mohr Siebeck, 1986), 487.

Gadamer often contrasted his interests with the way Heidegger was haunted throughout his life by theological preoccupations with divine mystery. Even so, the effects of having been a colleague and friend of Lutheran theologian and biblical scholar, Rudolf Bultmann (and members of the so-called Marburg School of theology, such as Heinrich Schlier), are evident in Gadamer's sensitive interpretations of religious texts. We will return below to discuss the issue of the relative significance of religious experience for the two thinkers.

III. Parallels in Procedure

Voegelin claimed that during his early sojourn in America[15] encounters with American thinkers George Santayana and John R. Commons (among others) immunized him against Heidegger's dangerous idiosyncrasies (as set forth in his Munich *Antrittsvorlesung*).[16] He realized the inadequacies of then current theories of consciousness "mired in neo-Kantian theories of knowledge, value-relating methods, historicism, descriptive institutionalism, and ideological speculations on history,"[17] so he worked out his own. Gadamer had no contact with the intelligent pragmatism or the down-to-earth institutional economics Voegelin encountered in the US. Rather ironically, then, his experience of Heidegger in the act of interpreting Aristotle was what brought about his discovery of the superficiality of the neo-Kantian approach that "started with the roof instead of the foundations" (in Strauss's phrase).[18]

---

15 See Eric Voegelin, "On George Santayana," and "On John R. Commons," in *On the Form of the American Mind*, Collected Works of Eric Voegelin 1, trans. Ruth Heim, ed. Jürgen Gebhardt and Barry Cooper (Baton Rouge: Louisiana University Press, 1995), 64–125 and 205–82. Originally Voegelin's first publication, following an American sojourn supported by a grant from the Rockefeller Foundation: *Über die Form des amerikanischen Geistes* (Tübingen: J.C.B. Mohr, 1928).

16 See Eric Voegelin, "Die deutsche Universität und die Ordnung der deutschen Gesellschaft," *Wort und Wahrheit* 8, no. 9 (1966): 497–518. English translation: "The German University and the Order of German Society: A Reconsideration of the Nazi Era," *The Intercollegiate Review* 20, no. 3 (Spring/Summer 1985): 7–27, especially the section devoted to Heidegger, 10–12.

17 See Eric Voegelin, *Anamnesis. Zur Theorie der Geschichte und Politik* (Munich: Piper Verlag, 1966), 7.

18 See Gadamer's own account of the impact upon him of reading the "Natorp Report" in his essay, "Erinnerungen an Heideggers Anfänge," in *Hermeneutik im Rückblick*, esp. 3–13.

To underline that meaning is to human beings as water is to fish, Voegelin (in *The New Science of Politics*) employed the metaphor of the "cosmion of meaning"[19] human beings inhabit. Voegelin and Gadamer each based their philosophies on the constitution of human living by performative meanings not susceptible of total transparency and control. Voegelin's anthropology conceived of human living as a search for direction in the flow of existence. Gadamer's hermeneutic philosophy wanted to make sense of the way human beings make sense of their lives in a world constituted and mediated by meaning.

Voegelin carried out what he called a "*zetema* ... in the classical sense ... a search for the truth both cognitive and existential"[20] as "a search for truth concerning the order of being."[21] For this purpose he employed a general theory of equivalences among compact or differentiated experiences and symbolizations.[22] On its face, this theory might seem similar to Ernst Cassirer's theory of symbolic forms. While this understanding of his theory is plausible, it is mistaken. Voegelin's position is more akin to Heidegger's radical concern with the truth of existence in stark contrast to Cassirer's program of expanding Kant's critique of pure reason into the highly sophisticated critique of culture shown in the famous 1929 confrontation between Heidegger and Cassirer at Davos. Cassirer's project was based on extrapolating from finite human reason in its unconditional and autonomous liberty to an infinite process of objectifying the spirit's formative spontaneity. In this way, the range of human symbolisms is conceived apart "from experience as it has actually arisen under specific historical, and therefore, contingent, conditions."[23] Cassirer's transcendental grounding depends on "the metabasis that leads [the human being] from the immediacy of his experience into the region of pure form. And only

---

19 Voegelin, *The New Science of Politics*, 27.

20 Eric Voegelin, "Toynbee's *History* as a Search for Truth," *The Intent of Toynbee's History*, ed. Edward T. Gargan (Chicago: Loyola University, 1961), 183.

21 Eric Voegelin, *Israel and Revelation: Order and History I* (Baton Rouge: Louisiana State University, 1956), xiv.

22 See Eric Voegelin, "Equivalences of Experience and Symbolization in History, *Published Essays 1966–1985*, Collected Works of Eric Voegelin 12, ed. Ellis Sandoz (Baton Rouge: Louisiana State University, 1989), 115–33.

23 Stephen Crowell and Jeff Malpass, "Introduction: Transcendental Heidegger," *Transcendental Heidegger* (Stanford, CA: Stanford University Press, 2007), 6.

in this form does he possess his infinity."[24] Like the early Heidegger, Voegelin eschewed foundations in the putative autonomy of the transcendental subject. His exploration was a matter of moving from symbolisms to the experiences that engendered them within concretely unfolding historical and contingent relationships. This correlation between experience and symbolization is completely concrete, while being completely open, because it makes room for differentiations of experience as they emerge from prior, global and compact stages of meaning. What calls forth more differentiated experience is the rise of new questions. Nevertheless, the exigency for the philosopher to account for every differentiation that arises over time does not necessarily mean that the more global and compact symbolizations possess less of the truth of existence. Voegelin, like Aristotle before him, and from whom he learned, never ceased to be a *philomythos*.[25]

The methodology at the heart of Voegelin's quest is "meditative exegesis." This is almost identical with what Gadamer speaks of as "hermeneutic reflection."[26] My hypothesis about the affinity of the two approaches is strengthened by the fact that each thinker seems to have learned the core of his method from Plato's Socratic dialectic. As Gadamer put it, "The task is to want to know that which one knows without knowing it. This is a precise definition of what philosophy is, and a good description of what Plato first recognized, namely, that the relevant knowledge here, *anamnesis*, is a salvaging from within and raising it up into explicit consciousness."[27] Socratic-Platonic dialectic,

---

24 Ernst Cassirer, "Davoser Disputation zwischen Ernst Cassirer und Martin Heidegger," in *Kant und das Problem der Metaphysik*, ed. Friedrich Wilhelm von Herrmann, Gesamtausgabe 3 (Frankfurt am Main: Klostermann, 1976), 286; cited by Riccardo Lazzari, "Introduzione: 'Critica della cultura' e 'Analytica dell'esserci' nel confronto fra E. Cassirer e M. Heidegger," in Ernst Cassirer and Martin Heidegger, *Disputa sull'eredità Kantiana. Due documenti (1928 e 1931)*, ed. Riccardo Lazzari (Milano: Edizione Unicopli, 1990), 67.

25 See Voegelin, "Was ist politische Realität?" *Anamnesis. Zur Theorie der Geschichte und Politik*, 289.

26 The title of one of Voegelin's essays pithily formulates the issue: "The Meditative Origin of the Philosophical Knowledge of Order"; originally, "Der meditative Ursprung philosophischen Ordnungswissens," *Zeitschrift für Politik* 28 (1981): 130–7. See Eric Voegelin, *The Drama of Humanity and Other Miscellaneous Papers 1939–1985*, Collected Works of Eric Voegelin 33, ed. William Petropulos and Gilbert Weiss (Columbia, MO: University of Missouri Press, 2004), 384–95.

27 See Hans-Georg Gadamer, "Der Tod als Frage," *Neuere Philosophie II. Probleme, Gestalten*, Gesammelte Werke 4 (Tübingen: Mohr Siebeck, 1987), 163–4.

like reading the Platonic dialogues itself, is an exercise in *anamnesis* in this sense. Entering into the questions and responses of dialectic brings about the de-sedimentation of one's language, so that *anamnesis* thematizes the concrete historical a priori of philosophical thinking.[28] Voegelin's account of *anamnesis* makes this even clearer:

> Remembering is the activity of consciousness by which what has been forgotten, i.e., the knowledge latent within consciousness, is raised up out of unconsciousness into a specific presence. In the *Enneads* (IV.3.20), Plotinus described this activity as the transition from non-articulated to articulate, self-perceiving thought. The non-articulated knowledge (*noema*) becomes conscious knowledge by an act of perceptive attending (*antilepsis*); and this antileptic knowledge is fixed again by language (*logos*). Remembering, then, is the process in which non-articulated (*ameres*) knowledge is elevated into the realm of linguistic imaginability [*Bildlichkeit*] (*to phantasmikon*) and through expression, in the pregnant sense of taking external shape (*eis to exo*), attains to linguistically articulated presence of consciousness.[29]

To my knowledge, Cassirer never emphasized the truth of existence the way Voegelin and Gadamer did. Gadamer was struck by the intense moral seriousness of Heidegger's reading of Aristotle; and Voegelin always highlighted the seriousness of the *spoudaios aner*, or of the *phronimos*. The issue is not propositional truth but truth in the sense of Aristotle's term, *aletheuein* (disclosure of what is true). As Heidegger said, "The two highest modes of *aletheuein* [in Aristotle] are *phronesis* and *sophia*."[30]

---

28 As Eric Voegelin explains in "Vorwort," *Anamnesis. Zur Theorie der Geschichte und Politik*, 12–13: "When remembrance reaches articulation in the linguistic expression of knowledge it falls to the conditions of the world; in the external world the symbol can separate from remembering consciousness, it can become opaque for the experience expressed; and the remembering knowledge can again sink from the presence of consciousness into the latency of oblivion. In times of social disorder, like our present time, we are surrounded by the detritus of symbols expressing past remembrance, as well as by the symbols of revolt against the state of oblivion; hence the work of remembrance must be started again."

29 Eric Voegelin, *Anamnesis. Zur Theorie der Geschichte und Politik*, 11.

30 See Martin Heidegger, *Plato's* Sophist, trans. Richard Rojcewicz and André Schuwer (Bloomington, IN: Indiana University Press, 1997), 19.

A. *The Dynamics and Scope of Meditative Exegesis in Voegelin*

In accord with Voegelin's model of experience and symbolization, meditative exegesis is the process by which the reader reenacts the experience that was brought to expression in the symbol, because unless one has the experience that engenders the symbol, one does not know what the symbol means. All the author (individually or collectively) can do is offer the symbol that would best evoke the appropriate experience. As Voegelin tells us in the Preface to *Israel and Revelation*,

> The order of history emerges from the history of order. Every society is burdened with the task, under its concrete conditions, of creating an order that will endow the fact of its existence with meaning in terms of ends divine and human. And the attempts to find the symbolic forms that will adequately express the meaning, while imperfect, do not form a senseless series of failures.[31]

In the introduction, Voegelin goes on to tell us,

> God and man, world and society form a primordial community of being. The community with its quaternion structure is, and is not, a datum of human experience. It is a datum of human experience insofar as it is known to man by virtue of his participation in the mystery of its being. It is not a datum of experience insofar as it is not given in the manner of an object of the external world but is knowable from the perspective of participation in it.[32]

The human being is not just partially involved in this participation, but "engaged with the whole of his existence, for participation is existence itself." Human participation in being is "illuminated by consciousness." However, "at the center of his existence man is unknown to himself and must remain so, for the part of being that calls itself man could be known fully only if the community of being and its drama in

---

31 See Eric Voegelin, "Preface," *Order and History I: Israel and Revelation*, Collected Works of Eric Voegelin 14, ed. Maurice Nolan (Columbia, MO: Missouri University Press, 2001), 19.

32 See Voegelin, "Introduction: *The Symbolization of Order*," *Order and History I: Israel and Revelation*, 39.

time were known as a whole ... Knowledge of the whole, however, is precluded ... and ignorance of the whole precludes essential knowledge of the part."[33] This ignorance about "the ultimate core of existence" gives rise to the anxiety of existence insofar as the little people know drops off into the vast penumbra of the "known unknown." This motivates them to create symbols to "render intelligible the relations and tensions between the distinguishable terms" in the field of the mystery of being. These symbols "interpret the unknown by analogy with the really, or supposedly, known."

Getting the correspondence of experience and symbolization right is not automatic but a matter of attunement. Because the processes of experience and symbolization are subject to external conditionings that either limit or enable adequate differentiatedness, they are also are liable to disorientations and distortions of human experience and a derailment of correlative symbolizations. Then attunement will imply the experience of "a turning around, the Platonic *periagoge*, an inversion or conversion toward the true source of order" that changes the structure of the participation in being into an emphatic "partnership with God."[34] This conversion is not something human beings achieve for themselves, but something they suffer.

In this way, Voegelin's ongoing practice of meditative exegesis is also a process of elaborating an ever-unfinished ontology of finitude within "the social field constituted by the philosopher's language" that he tells us "is not limited to communication through the spoken and written word among contemporaries, but extends historically from a distant past, through the present, into the future."[35] Philosophy means "the search for truth concerning the order of being,"[36] and it is enacted by "the creation of an order of symbols through which man's position in the world is understood."[37] The philosopher does this by participating in the horizon of his own time and in resistance to the forces of disorder that deform human existence.

---

33 Voegelin, "Introduction: *The Symbolization of Order*," *Order and History I: Israel and Revelation*, 40.

34 Voegelin, "Introduction: *The Symbolization of Order*," *Order and History I: Israel and Revelation*, 48.

35 See Eric Voegelin, "The Beginning of the Beginning," *Order and History V: In Search of Order* (Baton Rouge: Louisiana State University, 1987), 14.

36 Voegelin, *Order and History I: Israel and Revelation*, 24.

37 Voegelin, *Anamnesis. Zur Theorie der Geschichte und Politik*, 59.

If we think of Michael Oakeshott's metaphor of the great conversation of humankind, then we have to understand that Voegelin committed himself to entering into this conversation on the grand scale. His astonishing erudition ranges from ancient paleography to the ancient Chinese dynasties to the great modern Western philosophers. Moreover, he fundamentally changed his project twice: first, from the history of ideas to an anamnetic experiment that encompasses the transcultural history of equivalent symbolisms and engendering experiences; and second, from a linear and Euro-centric history to a transcultural one stretching back to pre-historical paleography.

B. The Dynamics and Scope of Hermeneutic
Experience in Gadamer

Gadamer's great work has a more adventitious, less intentional character than either Voegelin's *History of Political Ideas* or the more mature *Order and History*. From the outset, he was a philosopher, and because the reading of the Platonic dialogues formed the center of his teaching, he taught how to philosophize by reenacting the dramas of Plato with his students. During the Leipzig years, when courses were first disrupted by regular bombing raids and then took place under a Communist regime, he also turned to interpreting the great German poets, Goethe, Hölderlin, and Rilke.[38] After succeeding Karl Jaspers at Heidelberg, Gadamer began the ten years he spent composing *Wahrheit und Methode*. In that work he wanted to reflect on and to "give an account of" his own performance as a student and teacher and philosopher who had dedicated most of his time to preparing and teaching his lecture courses and seminars, and to working in intensive personal contact with his graduate students.

The *Wahrheit* of the book's title is neither propositional truth, nor the abstractly formulated correlations verifiable in sensible data appropriate to the natural sciences. Instead it is the truth of existence as accessible in experiences of art and of history in contrast to the prevalent superficialities of the aesthetic and historical consciousness that had

---

38 See Hans-Georg Gadamer, *Ästhetik und Poetik I. Kunst als Aussage*, Gesammelte Werke 8 (Tübingen: Mohr Siebeck 1999); *Ästhetik und Poetik II. Hermeneutik im Vollzug*, Gesammelte Werke 9 (Tübingen: Mohr Siebeck,1999).

emerged in the nineteenth century. According to Gadamer, the superficiality of aesthetic consciousness and historical consciousness is due to their having been imprisoned in subjectivity; both aesthetic and historical consciousness are outgrowths of the Enlightenment prejudice that functions within the horizon of *Vorhandenheit*, so they share the nominalist presupposition, which is itself based on an exorbitant and false notion of truth as correspondence. Aesthetic consciousness and historical consciousness foment relativist skepticism about the truth. In contrast, *Wahrheit und Methode*'s phenomenological account of hermeneutic experience exposed the illusory assumptions grounding these forms of consciousness by responding to *de facto* rather than *de jure* questions: What are we doing when we are experiencing the work of art? What are we doing when we are interpreting texts, or doing historical research? The phenomenological response to these questions in *Wahrheit und Methode* is grounded upon actual experiences of encountering a work of art or making sense of a text.

One of the consequences of Gadamer's analysis was a critique of scientism and of the specious distinctions between facts and values so dominant in modern institutions of learning. Penetrating the intelligibility of the relationship between truth as "dependent upon the temporal-historical movement proper to *Dasein*" and reason as "the self-empowered capacity to perceive truth and make it binding,"[39] Gadamer realized that people as human exist conversationally in relation to everything that is.[40] He found that reason is "made possible by what it is not."[41] Unlike Marx, Freud, and Nietzsche (purveyors of the hermeneutics of suspicion), he did not infer from such experience that both reason and truth are so dependent or conditioned that they become just "tools in the service of a higher, unconscious, and irresponsible power ..."[42] On

---

39 See Hans-Georg Gadamer, "Über die Ursprünglichkeit der Philosophie: 1. Die Bedeutung der Philosophie für die neue Erziehung, 2. Das Verhältnis der Philosophie zu Kunst und Wissenschaft," *Kleine Schriften I. Hermeneutik* (Tübingen: Mohr Siebeck, 1967), 11–38 at 17.

40 See Hans-Georg Gadamer, "Analyse des wirkungsgeschichtlichen Bewußtseins," *Wahrheit und Methode. Gründzüge einer philosophischen Hermeneutik* (Tübingen: Mohr Siebeck, 1965), 324–60; English translation: "Analysis of Historically Effected Consciousness," *Truth and Method*, 2nd revised edition, trans. Joel Weinsheimer and Donald G. Marshall (New York: Crossroad, 1991), 358–79.

41 Gadamer, "Über die Ursprünglichkeit der Philosophie," 19.

42 Gadamer, "Über die Ursprünglichkeit der Philosophie," 18.

the contrary, "it is the essence of our reason and our spirit to be capable of thinking against what is to our own advantage, to be able to detach ourselves from our needs and interests and to bind ourselves to the law of reality."[43] By reason we can come to terms with reality even against our own self-interest: "To be taught, even against our own subjectively certain convictions – that is the way of mediation of authentically historical truth."[44]

Indeed, the truth of existence is at issue in the experiences of creating, performing, and appreciating works of art, and of interpreting and translating meaningful documents, artifacts, and texts. Gadamer often spoke about the truth of existence in terms of the "Doric harmony between *logos* and *ergon*" – the philosophically indispensable correspondence between what one thinks and what one is.[45] In explaining the task of reading the Platonic dialogues mimetically, Gadamer wrote:

> It consists in relating the conceptual statements one encounters in conversation to the dialogical reality from which they grew. There is a Doric harmony between deed and speech, *Ergon* and *Logos*, about which in Plato there is not just talk in words. Instead it is the genuine law of the life of the Socratic dialogues. They are literally "speeches that lead one on" [*hinführende Reden*]. Only from this vantage is there to be inferred what the often Sophistic effect and actually often worst confusion-causing that the Socratic art of refutation intends. Yes, if only human wisdom were only such that it could go over from one to another like water can be guided over from one jar to another by a wool string … (*Symp.* 175 d). But human wisdom is not like that. It is knowledge of ignorance. By it the other, with whom Socrates is leading a conversation, is guided over his own ignorance –, and that means: it has to do with something about himself and his own life in its pretensions. Or, to state this with the acute phrasing of Plato's Seventh Letter: Not just one's thesis, but one's soul is refuted.[46]

The evocation of *anamnesis* already connoted the truth of existence at the heart of human individual and social identity inasmuch as one's

---

43 Gadamer, "Über die Ursprünglichkeit der Philosophie," 20.
44 Gadamer, "Über die Ursprünglichkeit der Philosophie," 21.
45 See Hans-Georg Gadamer, "*Logos* and *Ergon* in Plato's *Lysis*," *Dialogue and Dialectic: Eight Hermeneutical Studies on Plato*, trans. P. Christopher Smith (New Haven: Yale University Press, 1980), 19–20.
46 See Hans-Georg Gadamer, "Selbstdarstellung Hans-Georg Gadamer," *Hermeneutik II*, 501.

existential identity is at stake in the act of remembering. Think, for example, of the Jewish *Shema Yisroel*, or of Jesus's words in the Christian celebration of the Eucharist, "Do this in memory of me." As Voegelin said at a 1984 Boston College conference, "It is quite possible that the formulation of the Eucharist as 'in my remembrance' (which is *anamnesis*) of which Paul speaks always evokes the double-meaning of the remembering of recollection and of remembering in the sense of establishing what the reality is to be."[47]

Heidegger's vision of philosophy's great *Verfallsgeschichte* into the forgetfulness of being from Plato to Hegel and Nietzsche aided Gadamer in radicalizing R.G. Collingwood's "logic of question and answer"[48] so that contemporary philosophy's challenge to remember being "is never merely a remembering of something known before and brought to mind again, but a remembering of something called into question before; it is remembering a lost question."[49] One genuinely remembers a question that has been asked before only when one actually asks it oneself.

Thus, the most fundamental feature of hermeneutic experience[50] is the occurrence of a question. The specific openness proper to questions for understanding or questions for reflection is not something one can decide about or achieve for oneself; to have a question arise, one has to undergo it, or in Voegelin's phrase, be attuned to and participate in it. This happens when we become stuck or get lost in our efforts to understand. No wonder that Aeschylus's expression *pathei mathos* symbolizes the meaning of hermeneutic experience for Gadamer. As he learned from Plato's portrayal of Socratic dialectic, there is a "hermeneutic priority of questions,"[51] because they also constitute the heart of genuine conversation *tout court*. In *Order and History IV: The Ecumenic Age* Voegelin speaks of the symbolism of the question "as a structure in experience" that "is part of, and pertains to, the In-Between stratum of

---

47 See Voegelin, "Responses at the Panel Discussion of 'The Beginning of the Beginning,'" *The Beginning and the Beyond: Papers from the Gadamer and Voegelin Conferences*, 107.

48 Gadamer, "Logik der Frage und Antwort," *Wahrheit und Methode*, 352–60; *Truth and Method*, 369–79.

49 Gadamer, "Selbstdarstellung Hans-Georg Gadamer," *Hermeneutik II*, 501.

50 Gadamer, "Der Begriff der Erfahrung und das Wesen der hermeneutischen Erfahrung," *Wahrheit und Methode*, 330–44; "The Concept of Experience (*Erfahrung*) and the Essence of the Hermeneutic Experience," *Truth and Method*, 346–62.

51 Gadamer, *Wahrheit und Methode*, 344–52; *Truth and Method*, 362–69.

reality, the Metaxy. There is no answer to the Question other than the Mystery as it becomes luminous in the acts of questioning."[52]

Insight into the priority of the question implies that the most crucial occurrences in consciousness's life of interaction with the world are not under human control: understanding (like sensation and perception) is something one suffers, a *pati*. Moreover, for Gadamer the emergence of the inner word because of understanding or because of grasping the sufficiency of the evidence in the data is paradigmatic for finite being's *Darstellung* or occurrence, and a key to the linguisticality of being, because the emergence within consciousness of a conscious act from a conscious act is due to the intrinsic exigencies of human reason, and is not an instance of technical production.[53] People can block, obfuscate, or ignore this type of emergence within themselves, but they cannot cause it by acts of their will.

Gadamer's central analogy for the human being's subordination to and attunement to its finite ontology is his phenomenology of *Spiel* – play, or game, or game-play.[54] This is how human beings participate in being. Gadamer wrote in *Wahrheit and Methode*: "It made sense to bring the game-play of language into closer connection with the game-play of art in which I had contemplated the parade example of the hermeneutical. Now to consider the universal linguistic constitution of our experience of the world in terms of the model of game-play certainly does suggest itself."[55] People first learn to speak not so much in a learning process as in a "game of imitation and exchange." Thus, Gadamer tells

---

52 See Eric Voegelin, "Question and Mystery," *Order and History IV: The Ecumenic Age* (Baton Rouge: Louisiana State University, 1974), 316–30, cited at 330. This section is part of the section titled, "Universal Humanity," and is followed by "The Process of History and the Process of the Whole," 330–35, at the end of the book.

53 The third part of *Wahrheit und Methode/Truth and Method*, devoted to the presentation of Gadamer's ontology of language, is comprised of three parts: 1. "Language as the Medium of Hermeneutic Experience," 2. "The Fashioning of the Concept of 'Language' in the History of Western Thought," 3. "Language as the Horizon of Hermeneutical Ontology." The second section of part 2 is entitled "Language and Verbum," which is about the idea of the intelligible procession or emanation in the human mind of concepts or formulations from the act of understanding according to the human analogy as the basis for the trinitarian theology of Augustine and Thomas Aquinas (*Wahrheit und Methode* 396–404; *Truth and Method* 418–28).

54 See Gadamer, "Spiel als Leitfaden der ontologischen Explikation," *Wahrheit und Methode*, 97–127; "Play as the Clue to Ontological Explanation," *Truth and Method*, 101–34.

55 See Gadamer, "Zwischen Phänomenologie und Dialektik," *Hermeneutik II*, 5.

us, "In the receptive child's drive to imitate the forming of sounds, the enjoyment in such forming of sounds is paired with the illumination of meaning. No one can really answer reasonably the question when their first understanding of meaning occurred." This idea is both confirmed and amplified by the Russian thinker, Mikhail Bakhtin:

> All that touches me comes to my consciousness – beginning with my name – from the outside world, passing through the mouths of others (from the mother, etc.), with their intonation, their affective tonality, and their values. At first I am conscious of myself only through others: they give me the words, the forms, and the tonality that constitute my first image of myself.[56]

Bakhtin expands the theme of the conversational language game to the totality of history:

> There is neither a first word nor a last word. The contexts of dialogue are without limit. They extend into the deepest past and the most distant future. Even meanings born in dialogues of the remotest past will never be finally grasped once and for all, for they will always be renewed in later dialogue. At any present moment of the dialogue there are great masses of forgotten meanings, but these will be recalled again in the dialogue's later course when it will be given new life. For nothing is absolutely dead: every meaning will someday have its homecoming festival.[57]

Thus, rather than just a set of tools consisting of vocabulary, grammar, syntax, etc., language for Gadamer is always language-in-use, i.e., in

---

56 Tzvetan Todorov, *Mikhail Bakhtin: The Dialogical Principle*, trans. Wlad Godzich (Minneapolis: University of Minnesota Press, 1984), with reference to Bakhtin's *Estetika slovesnogo torchestva* [The aesthetics of verbal translation] (Moscow: S.G. Bocharov, 1979), 308. English Translation: "Toward a Reworking of the Dostoevsky Book," ed. and trans. Caryl Emerson, in Mikhail Bakhtin, *Problems of Dostoevsky's Poetics* (Minneapolis: University of Minnesota Press, 1984).

57 Bakhtin, *Estetika*, 373, cited by Michael Holquist, *Dialogism: Bakhtin and His World* (London: Routledge, 1990), 39. Bernard Lonergan made a similar point in *A Second Collection*, as regards the synthesis of George Herbert Mead's pragmatic and Alfred Schutz's phenomenological account of the social mediation of both self and meaning in *Elements for a New Social Ethic*: "You find out what you mean by your gesture or your words from the other person's reaction to it. So that meaning has a common origin, a social origin." See Bernard Lonergan, *A Second Collection*, ed. W. Ryan and B. Tyrrell (London: Darton, Longman & Todd, 1974), 216; and Katerina Clark and Michael Holquist, *Mikhail Bakhtin* (Cambridge, MA: Harvard University Press, 1984).

conversation; and if conversation has a *Spiel*-structure, language occurs concretely as language games. Wittgenstein in *Philosophical Investigations* also hit on the idea of "language games,"[58] but to my knowledge he did not delve as deeply into the notion of *Spiel*. As regards the centrality of *Spiel* in Gadamer's analysis of art, language, and conversation, the memoir of his early days has a photo of him sawing a log with Heidegger at the famous hut at Todtnauberg.[59] Noting how this activity, so emblematic of *Spiel* as "an elementary function of human life," presages the role of game-play in his mature philosophy, he points out that the sawing happens only if those at either end of the saw subordinate themselves to the repetitive "to-and-fro" movement that seems not only to have a "life of its own" but also to lack any purposiveness (i.e., of producing a supply of firewood). The game-play structure of conversation displays its characteristic "lightness, freedom, and the luck of success – of being fulfilling, and of fulfilling those who are playing."[60] And yet the seriousness proper both to the play of young dogs and cats and children and to genuine conversation's back and forth of statement and reply attests to the truth of Gadamer's claim that, in general, game-play really starts only when participants do not regard themselves as "just playing" or not being serious.[61] So Gadamer says, "The life of language consists ... in the constant further playing out of the game we started when we learned to speak ... It is this continuously played game in which the mutual life together of people is played out."[62]

C. *Common Opposition to Reflexionsphilosophie*

Against derailments commonly besetting the notion of reflection, Gadamer prefers the metaphor of a conversation that is in principle without end, and while Voegelin certainly privileges this metaphor,

---

58 On Gadamer's agreement with Wittgenstein on "language games," see "Die phänomenologische Bewegung," *Neuere Philosophie I. Hegel, Husserl, Heidegger*, Gesammelte Werke 3 (Tübingen: Mohr Siebeck, 1987) 150–89, esp. 185–9; "The Phenomenological Movement (1963), *Philosophical Hermeneutics*, trans. David Lingis (Berkeley: University of California, 1976), 42–146 and 173–7.

59 Gadamer, *Philosophische Lehrjahre*, 33.

60 Gadamer, "Mensch und Sprache," *Hermeneutik II*, 152; English translation: "Man and Language," *Philosophical Hermeneutics*, 66.

61 Hans-Georg Gadamer, "Mensch und Sprache," *Hermeneutik II*, 152; "Man and Language," *Philosophical Hermeneutics*, 66.

62 Gadamer, "Mensch und Sprache," *Hermeneutik II*, 152; "Man and Language," *Philosophical Hermeneutics*, 66.

too, he also emphasizes the metaphor of an ongoing existential drama. Both of them did philosophy on the model of Platonic-Socratic dialectic. Meditative exegesis and hermeneutic philosophy can be said to be conversational in the mode of heightened awareness that enables what Voegelin calls the "reflective distance,"[63] which makes it possible for the philosopher to identify and name the structures within experience and language-symbols in which and by which the human being participates in reality or being. Both Voegelin and Gadamer hold that

> man, when he experiences himself as existent, discovers his specific humanity as that of a questioner for the wherefrom and the whereto, for the ground and sense of his existence. Though this questioning is inherent to man's experience of himself at all times, an adequate articulation and symbolization of the questioning consciousness as the constituent of humanity is ... the epochal feat of the philosophers.[64]

The reflexivity immanent in human consciousness is before and much more significant than reflection wrongly understood exclusively in terms of objectification within the horizon of *Vorhandenheit*. It enables the human person to have insights into the reality of conscious participation that cannot be adequately conceived or imagined in terms of the intentional object of sense awareness. The expression "heightened awareness" means that "reflection is not an external act of cognition directed toward the process as its object, but part of a process that internally has cognitive structure." By reflection rightly understood, human reality is "engaged in becoming cognitively luminous" to itself.[65]

For both Voegelin and Gadamer the mistaken idea of reflection is epitomized in modernity by the Enlightenment project of constructing "systems" that would extirpate all prejudice and superstition (as in Descartes), or by the unfolding of Hegel's *Logik* or *Phänomenologie* in which philosophy's absolute knowledge of *Begriff* decisively supersedes the forms of *Vorstellung* in religion and art, or by any form of ideology. It

---

63 Voegelin, "The Meditative Origin of the Philosophical Knowledge of Order," *The Drama of Humanity and Other Miscellaneous Papers 1939–1985*, 393–5.

64 See Voegelin, "Reason: The Classic Experience," *Published Essays 1966–1985*, 269–70.

65 See Eric Voegelin, "The Beginning and the Beyond: A Meditation on Truth," in *What Is History? And Other Late Unpublished Writings*, Collected Works of Eric Voegelin 28, ed. Thomas A. Hollweck and Paul Caringella (Baton Rouge: Louisiana State University, 1990), 189.

is embodied in premodern (and modern) times by dogmatism or scholasticism, or by doctrinalization.[66] These are examples of attempting to control or smother or rule out as irrelevant experience as performative and participatory by mistakenly identifying "reflection" with complete objectification, thus creating the illusion of rigor and proof, and so deforming the spontaneous human desire for understanding into a quest for certitude. In this way there arises the pretense of attaining answers so "objectively true" that they are supposed to get along without the corresponding experiences of questioning and understanding. This is the "magic" of the final word, of the rigidified symbolism in detachment from any engendering experience, of "positions" that are closed, thereby putting an end to further conversation.

IV. Gadamer and Voegelin on Consciousness

Gadamer's approach to consciousness was to follow Plato and Aristotle in de-emphasizing both consciousness and subjectivity to counteract modernity's "turn to the subject" in Descartes, Kant, Husserl, and in Sartre's brand of existentialism. In this, of course, he was taking seriously the clues offered by Heidegger's turn in *Sein und Zeit* from Husserl's phenomenology of perception to hermeneutic phenomenology, which was radicalized by the complete rejection of the transcendental approach to philosophy after the *Kehre*. But, like Voegelin, he was unwilling to simply discard the language of consciousness instead of using the term correctly. Thus, he appeals to the early Heidegger's use of the scholastic distinction between *actus exercitus* and *actus signatus* to speak about the reflexivity inherent in human awareness as distinct either from explicit or thematic consciousness or from the supposition that consciousness is to be conceived in terms of inner perception of something on the model of some object of sense perception. For the early Heidegger this meaning of consciousness is legitimate, but he abandoned it along with the incorrect meanings after the *Kehre*, perhaps thinking that the mistaken meaning dominates common and even technical modern usages of the term. Gadamer prefers to hold onto the correct meaning.

In correspondence with Alfred Schütz, a friend from Austrian student days and a follower of Husserl who applied Husserl's foundations to

---

66 Voegelin, *The Ecumenic Age*, 36–8.

the sphere of intersubjectivity and society,[67] and in an essay on the theory of consciousness,[68] Voegelin essentially reproduced Heidegger's critique of Husserl (but without depending upon Heidegger). He thereby agreed with Gadamer about the fundamental features of consciousness conceived as presence-to-self as present-to-the-world. Therefore, he underlined aspects of consciousness left out of Husserl's account of intentional consciousness, which is basically conceived in terms of perceptual awareness of a circumscribed object accessible to the senses. For Voegelin, intentionality constitutes the subject-object split in its awareness of circumscribed objects in space and time, which is the source of the human knowledge of things or "thing-reality." Concomitantly with intentionality, consciousness also possesses an aspect Voegelin calls "luminosity," which is an awareness of what, following Karl Kraus and Nietzsche, Voegelin calls the "It-reality." This aspect of consciousness is never adequately reducible to thing-reality or to an adequate object of intentional consciousness. "It is neither the subject nor the object reality in its thing-ness but a reality that encompasses both, a comprehensive reality." As Voegelin goes on to explain:

> This It-reality is an "It" for, within it, such a thing as consciousness occurs in the same sense in which such things as the genesis of atoms and molecules, species, races, and so forth occur. That is to say that this It-reality, when it is now brought into relationship with consciousness becomes luminous … We are thus dealing with two structures in consciousness, an intentionality, of which we can say that the human being is the subject, and a luminosity, of which we must say that "It" is the subject and that consciousness is the predicate.[69]

Together these two aspects of consciousness constitute the "reflective distance" that enables the philosopher to reflect on, identify, and name

---

67 See Voegelin, "Brief an Alfred Schütz über Edumund Husserl," *Anamnesis. Zur Theorie der Geschichte und Politik,* 21–36; Eric Voegelin, "Two Replies to Alfred Schütz: On Christianity" and "On Gnosticism," in *The Philosophy of Order: Essays on History, Consciousness and Politics,* ed. Peter J. Opitz and Gregor Sebba (Stuttgart: Klett-Cotta, 1981), 449–57, 458–65.

68 See Voegelin, "Zur Theorie des Bewusstseins," *Anamnesis. Zur Theorie der Geschichte und Politik,* 37–60.

69 Voegelin, "The Meditative Origin of the Philosophical Knowledge of Order," *The Drama of Humanity and Other Miscellaneous Papers 1939–1985,* 392.

the structures of consciousness, resulting in the analysis of consciousness just summarized, as well as the philosopher's reenactment of the ordered series of engendering experiences and symbolic expressions that form the subject matter of Voegelin's philosophy of order.

For both Gadamer and Voegelin, then, consciousness is the site of the awareness by which human beings participate in existence or being. Gadamer was influenced, as Voegelin was not, by Heidegger's critique of Husserl in terms of *Dasein* (which is the human being's presence-to-self as present-to-the-world); and so he was less concerned to do the kind of analysis of consciousness that Voegelin considered necessary for his overall project. Within his own project of hermeneutic philosophy, however, what Gadamer strove to emphasize about consciousness was its historically constituted character as expressed in the term *wirkungsgeschichtliches Bewußtsein*. The problematic of effective-historical consciousness is analogous to what Voegelin says about the "It-reality." Negatively speaking, it is what in *Glauben und Wissen* Hegel criticized in the "reflective philosophy of subjectivity" of Jacobi, Kant, and Fichte, yet what he himself overlooked in the assumption that his system had attained a full comprehension of history in its full transparency by means of absolute knowledge. The positivist and historicist (and widespread) misunderstandings of historical consciousness share the distorted notion of what reflection can accomplish discussed above. Gadamer employed the notion of the "hermeneutical situation" to contrast this truncated understanding of historical consciousness with historical consciousness thought out adequately:

> When our historical consciousness transposes itself into historical horizons, this does not entail passing into alien worlds unconnected in any way with our own; instead, they together constitute the one great horizon that moves from within and that, beyond the frontiers of the present, embraces the historical depths of our self-consciousness. Everything contained in historical consciousness is in fact embraced by a single historical horizon. Our own past and that other past toward which our historical consciousness is directed help to shape this moving horizon out of which human life always lives and which determines it as heritage and tradition.[70]

---

70 Gadamer, "Das Prinzip der Wirkungsgeschichte," *Wahrheit und Methode*, 288; "The Principle of History of Effect," *Truth and Method*, 304.

Just as the "It-reality" cannot be properly or exhaustively objecti-fied, so also the historical method's pretense of transposing itself into another closed horizon in the past is an illusion, because "in relying on its critical method, historical objectivism conceals the fact that historical consciousness is itself situated in the web of historical effects." There is no longer a question of self and other.

> Consciousness of being affected by history is primarily consciousness of the hermeneutical situation. To acquire an awareness of a situation is, however, always a task of peculiar difficulty. The very idea of a situation means that we are not standing outside it and hence are unable to have any objective knowledge of it. We always find ourselves within a situa-tion, and throwing light on it is a task that is never entirely finished.[71]

Hence, Gadamer's notion of consciousness is inseparable from his rehabilitation of prejudice in the sense of belief or prejudgment: "The self-awareness of the individual is only a flickering in the closed cir-cuits of historical life. *That is why the prejudices of the individual, far more than his judgments, constitute the historical reality of his being.*"[72] This also explains why the chief enactment of human consciousness – *Verstehen*, which means both understanding and interpretation – "*is to be thought of less as an act of subjectivity, than as participating in an event of tradition*, a process of transmission in which past and present are constantly medi-ated. That is what must be validated by hermeneutic theory, which is far too dominated by the idea of a procedure, a method."[73]

Thus, the nub of hermeneutic philosophy is Gadamer's elaboration of Heidegger's original insight that reveals the isomorphism between the structures of human understanding/interpretation and those of Aristotle's *phronesis* in Book VI of the *Nicomachean Ethics*.[74] Gadamer

---

71 Gadamer, "Das Prinzip der Wirkungsgeschichte," *Wahrheit und Methode*, 285; "The Principle of History of Effect," *Truth and Method*, 301.
72 Gadamer, *Wahrheit und Methode*, 260; *Truth and Method*, 276–7 (the emphasis is Gadamer's own).
73 Gadamer, *Wahrheit und Methode*, 274–5; *Truth and Method*, 290.
74 See Gadamer, "Die hermeneutische Aktualität des Aristoteles," *Wahrheit und Meth-ode*, 295–307; "The Hermeneutic Relevance of Aristotle," *Truth and Method*, 312–24. The analysis agrees in all salient points with Voegelin "Das Rechte von Natur," *Anamnesis. Zur Theorie der Geschichte und Politik*, 117–33.

explained that both are enacted as effective-historical consciousness, which implies that neither the active nor the passive but the middle voice expresses the interrelationship between knower and known, between historical agent and historical situation.

To summarize, therefore, Voegelin and Gadamer go beyond Husserlian phenomenology and every form of Cartesianism – the *bête noire* of postmodern philosophers – each insisting on not reducing consciousness to the intentional side of awareness, as occurs in the act of perceiving a sensible object. Intentionality refers to awareness as awareness of some direct object of awareness. Perhaps Voegelin's luminosity-structure of consciousness is what Gadamer refers to as consciousness's non-objective reflectivity, as illuminated by the old scholastic distinction between *actus exercitus* (implicit, tacit, non-objective, background, performative awareness) and *actus signatus* (explicit, focal, objective, foreground, thematized awareness). Both were apparently content to reproduce the ambiguities of Aristotle's notion of *prohairesis* (preferential choice), and not to analyze clearly the interplay of intelligence and will, of knowledge and choice. Still, both stress the importance of intelligence or reason in coming to terms with reality; in their respective accounts of consciousness neither is interested in the *quaestio juris*, and both concentrate on the *quaestio facti*: what are we doing when we are being authentically human?

V. Key Contrast: On Differentiation

The main difference between the two thinkers' accounts of consciousness is surely Voegelin's emphasis on differentiations of consciousness that enable corresponding differentiations in human experiences and symbolizations. Thus, in his essays, "The Beginning and the Beyond" (1975–8, unfinished, posthumously published), "Immortality: Experience and Symbol" (1967), "Equivalence of Experience and Symbolization in History" (1970), "The Gospel and Culture" (1971), "On Hegel: A Study in Sorcery" (1971), "Reason: The Classic Experience" (1974), "The Remembrance of Things Past" (1978), "Wisdom and the Magic of the Extreme: A Meditation" (1981), and "Quod Deus Dicitur" (1986) and *The Ecumenic Age*,[75] Voegelin distinguished regularly between the

---

75 For the line-up of this bibliographical information, see, Voegelin, "Introduction [by Ellis Sandoz]," *Order and History V: In Search of Order*, 1–12.

"*noetic* differentiation" and the "*pneumatic* differentiation" of consciousness. The noetic differention is proper to philosophers (but possible for all human beings) in terms of the Aristotelian account of the desire to know (*orexis*) that gives rise to the realization of one's ignorance (or more properly, nescience or *docta ignorantia*), which, in turn, blossoms forth spontaneously into questions that are inexhaustible.[76] The "*pneumatic* differentiation*" proper to what was known traditionally as the charism of prophecy is epitomized for Voegelin by the Pauline Vision of the Resurrected.[77] Voegelin considers both kinds of differentiations to be rooted ultimately in mystical experience (he had long since spoken of the "Greek mystic philosophers") related to the divine ground of being. The differential is that the experience of human questing is uppermost for the noetic differentiation, while for the pneumatic differentiation, the experience of being drawn by the divine is dominant.[78]

Gadamer did not work out a theory of the movement from global and compact to differentiated experience and symbolization. His 1947 *Antrittsvorlesung* at the University of Leipzig, "The Primordiality of Science," and an essay, "The Praise of Theory,"[79] from late in his life, make it clear that he consistently held the Aristotelian distinction between the theoretical way of life and the practical way of life, and that he esteemed the life of theory highly, where theory is to be understood very much in the sense of Voegelin when he called for a re-theoretization of social and political science in *The New Science of Politics*.[80]

Both Gadamer and Voegelin dedicated their careers to combating the dangers of what Jürgen Habermas called "science as a background

---

76 See Voegelin, "Reason: The Classic Experience," *Published Essays 1966–1985*, 268–73.

77 See Voegelin, "The Pauline Vision of the Resurrected," *The Ecumenic Age*, 239–71.

78 Voegelin, "The Meditative Origin of the Philosophical Knowledge of Order," *What Is History? And Other Late Unpublished Writings*, 389, where he wrote: "Therewith, the problem of meditation moves into the center of our consideration. From the one side, namely, from the human, the search can be accentuated. I would call that the noetic posture. From the other side, the revelatory side, one can emphasize the motivational factor. I would call that the pneumatic position. Both are present in the problem of meditation. The tension exists between being moved from the godly side and the search from the human side. Thus the godly and the human sides are assumed in a process of seeking and being moved [to seek]."

79 See Gadamer, "Über die Ursprünglichkeit der Wissenschaft (1947)," *Hermeneutik im Rückblick*, 287–94; and "Lob der Theorie (1980)," *Neuere Philosophie II. Probleme, Gestalten*, 37–51.

80 Voegelin, "Introduction," *The New Science of Politics*, 1–13, 22–6.

ideology," especially in their opposition to positivism, objectivism, rationalism, and scientism. Voegelin as a political philosopher (who wished to "pursue a theoretical problem to the point where the principles of politics meet with the principles of a philosophy of history"[81]) was determined to take seriously all the differentiations and symbolizations that history had developed, as well as the major forms of derailment in human history. Gadamer's concerns as a philosopher were less architectonic and more restricted, and yet they, too, were startlingly comprehensive. By developing valid insights of Plato and Aristotle he wanted to restore balance to post-Enlightenment philosophy; and, on that basis, he wanted to redress counterpositions affecting modernity's philosophy of art, its *Geisteswissenschaften* or human sciences, its humanities, and its *belles lettres*. He argued that Hegel's philosophy of history was a failure insofar as it culminated in the absolute spirit; nevertheless, Gadamer thought Hegel provided unparalleled insights into the dimension of "what is moving in and through" the successive perspectives of individuals and particular cultures and societies. Unlike Voegelin he did not work on the "principles of a philosophy of history" on such a grand scale.

VI. The Religious Dimension in Voegelin and Gadamer

Voegelin's explicit resistance to the disorder in society led him to attend much more to the various kinds of disorder in human beings' souls – and to his language of derailment, alienation, and the magic of the extreme. He also acknowledged explicitly the human need for conversion, whether noetic or pneumatic. From the time of his early book on *The Political Religions* (published in 1938), Voegelin was sensitive to the significance of the religious dimension for human individual or collective constitutive meaning; in his most mature works Voegelin clarified the absolute transcendence of the divine ground of being that he symbolized as "the Beyond."[82] In his famous Toronto exchange with Voegelin, Gadamer voiced his hesitations about construing Plato's *epekeina* (the beyond) in terms of the god beyond the intracosmic gods.[83] We have

---

81 Voegelin, "Introduction," *The New Science of Politics*, 1.

82 See Voegelin, "The Beginning and the Beyond: A Meditation on Truth," *What Is History? And Other Late Unpublished Writings*, 173–232.

83 See Voegelin, "Structures of Consciousness," especially the Question Period, in *What Is History? And Other Late Unpublished Writings*, 371–8.

mentioned Voegelin's speaking relatively early of the Greek mystic philosophers. And while Gadamer seemed to have taken it for granted that human excellence requires a *periagoge* or reversal not vouchsafed by human exertion alone, Voegelin raised up this life-changing event in the *Republic*'s parable of the cave, and noted how like the *t'shuva* (return) or *metanoia* (turn-around) of Jews and Christians it is.[84] Moreover, in *The New Science of Politics* Voegelin had classified the major overarching symbolisms of Western culture as cosmological (as in ancient Near Eastern texts), anthropological (as in classic Greek philosophy), and soteriological (as in the Hebrew and Christian scriptures). In *The Ecumenic Age* the cosmological truth became a foil for the parallel noetic (philosophic) and pneumatic (revelational) differentiations of consciousness; and in the very latest writings, including "Wisdom and the Magic of the Extreme" and *In Search of Order*, the similarity-in-difference between philosophical and religious experiences is polemically flattened out in reaction to the severe defects stemming from hypostatizations of the supernatural sphere (as a function of doctrinalization), so that he minimized the differences between the Socratic reversal and religious conversion vis-à-vis what they share in common. Even so, in the final third of his career, Voegelin insisted that philosophy is always a matter of *fides quaerens intellectum* (using Anselm of Canterbury's formulation of the nature of theology).[85]

There can be little doubt that Voegelin was more forthright about discussing the divine ground of human and finite beings, and more at ease talking about the divine pole of the tension characteristic of authentic human existence in the Metaxy between the divine and human poles; he also seemed much more comfortable discussing the Hebrew scriptures

---

84 See Voegelin, "The Gospel and Culture," *Published Essays 1966–1985*, 184, where Voegelin writes of the parable of the cave: "There Plato lets the man who is fettered with his face to the wall be dragged (*helkein*) by force to the light (Rep. 515E). The accent lies on the violence suffered by the man in the Cave, on his passivity and even resistance to being turned round (*periagoge*), so that the ascent to the light is less an action of seeking than a fate inflicted." In this essay Voegelin parallels Plato's account of this experience with Luke's account of Paul's conversion in Acts, and with passages in the gospels of Matthew and John.

85 See Voegelin, "Response to Professor Altizer's 'A New History and a New but Ancient God,'" *Published Essays 1966–1985*, 292–303; but more fundamentally, "The Beginning and the Beyond: A Meditation on Truth," *What Is History? And Other Late Unpublished Writings*, 173–232.

and the New Testament than Gadamer. The issue of the divine was more explicitly central to Voegelin's overall project than it was to Gadamer's.

In contrast: Gadamer quoted from a letter Rilke wrote to Ilse on 22 February 1923 about his relationship to God: "Es ist eine unbeschreibliche Diskretion zwischen uns."[86] Perhaps this expresses Gadamer's stance rather well. Gadamer's ontology of finitude focused on the openness of language as horizon, and suggested that ultimately it refers to *das Wort* as a *singularetantum*,[87] as human questioning and questing heads toward the infinity that as finite beings we are always on the way to expressing.

That Gadamer rehabilitated prejudices or beliefs, in the sense of truths to which people assent without personally verifying them, has already been mentioned. No less than Voegelin's "faith seeking understanding" (St Anselm of Canterbury), this argument amounts to a deconstruction of the prejudice against prejudice and it dissociates philosophy decisively from rationalism, basing it on experience rather than on logic. For Gadamer, then, philosophy is always enacted as believing to understand: *crede ut intelligas* (to use St Augustine's older formulation). The history of hermeneutics out of which Gadamer's hermeneutic philosophy grew is utterly interwoven with theology, and theological themes and issues. Gadamer knew that Spinoza's *Theologico-Political Treatise* was geared toward refuting Augustine's *De doctrina christiana*; in recovering an integral hermeneutics from the wasteland left by the one-sided hermeneutics of suspicion, he retrieved the significant hermeneutic reflections of Chladenius and of Pietists from Oetinger to Schleiermacher; the significance of Hegel's early theological writings was not lost on him, and he had a firsthand familiarity with the roles played in the modern hermeneutical revolution by the towering figures of twentieth-century Protestant theology, Karl Barth and Rudolf Bultmann.

Gadamer's contribution to the same Bultmann *Festschrift* to which Voegelin contributed the seminal essay "Ewiges Sein in der Zeit"[88] is

---

86 See Gadamer, "Verstummen die Dichter?" *Ästhetik und Poetik II. Hermeneutik im Vollzug*, 363.

87 For this, see Gadamer's article "Témoinage et Affirmation," *Archivio di filosofia*, ed. Enrico Castelli (Rome: Istituto di Studi Filosofici, n.d.), 161–4; but this also follows from Gadamer's commentary on the Augustinian and Thomist *verbum cordis* referred to above at note 53.

88 Republished in *Anamnesis. Zur Theorie der Geschichte und Politik*, 254–80.

perhaps paradigmatic for the relationship between faith and theology in Gadamer's work. Originally entitled "Martin Heidegger und die Marburger Theologie,"[89] the essay departs from the relationship between Heidegger and theology, and between Heidegger and Rudolf Bultmann, who had used an existentialist reading of Heidegger's critique of classical metaphysics to clarify how grace bestows authenticity on human beings. With tact and courtesy, Gadamer points out that his hermeneutic philosophy takes Heidegger's later perspective as beyond transcendental philosophy more seriously than did Bultmann's appropriation of Heidegger. Hence, his philosophy is more relevant to exegesis and theology, because it eliminates both Kantian limitations left over from Bultmann's teacher, Wilhelm Hermann, and traces of existentialist decisionism and subjectivism, which are as alien to Heidegger's thought as they are foreign to the New Testament *kerygma*.

Gadamer points out there the theological origins of the notion of "self-understanding":

> For if there is anything unassailable about the idea of revelation, then it is precisely this, that the human being is incapable of attaining an understanding of himself from his own resources alone. It is an age-old motif proper to the experience of faith, which already runs through Augustine's look back upon his life, that all human beings' attempts to understand themselves out of themselves and in terms of the world as under human control must break down. In fact, the word and concept, "self-understanding," is apparently indebted for its first imprint to a Christian experience.[90]

Ironically, in the usage of Idealist philosophy, the notion of self-understanding is channeled into a trajectory heading toward "absolute knowledge." On the contrary, hermeneutic philosophy's demonstration of the insufficiency of subjectivist aesthetics in relation to the experience of art, and the parallel deficiency of the *simpliste* interpretation of the *mens auctoris* as the standard to be met in the historical critical retrieval of texts from the past is much more in harmony with the theological point concerning the ultimate inadequacy of human subjective self-understanding.

---

89 See Gadamer, "Die Marburger Theologie," *Neuere Philosophie I*, 197–208.
90 Gadamer, "Die Marburger Theologie," *Neuere Philosophie I*, 203.

Gadamer was critical of Bultmann's overemphasis on the historical-critical mediation of New Testament texts. He once half-jokingly told me, "Bultmann forgets that the books of the New Testament are not *books* in the ordinary sense of the term." He was agreeing with Franz Overbeck and his friend Helmut Kuhn that these texts belong to the genre of *Urliteratur*. This implies that "if we understand under the meaning of the text the *mens auctoris*, i.e., the 'verifiable' horizon of understanding of any given Christian writer, then we accord the authors of the New Testament a false honor. Their proper honor ought to lie in the fact that they announce the tidings about something that surpasses the horizon of their own understanding – even if they happen to be named John or Paul."[91]

In the essay "Language and Understanding," Gadamer elucidated how language works by appealing to the concrete experience of "hearing the Word":

> When I say "word" [*das Wort*], I do not mean the word whose plural are the words [*die Wörter*] as they stand in the dictionary. Nor do I mean the word whose plural is the words [*die Worte*], which with other words go to make up the context of a statement. Rather I mean the word that is a *singularetantum*. That means the word that strikes one, the word one allows to be said to oneself, the word that enters into a determinate and unique life-situation; and it is good to be reminded that behind this *singularetantum* stands ultimately the linguistic usage of the New Testament.[92]

The contrast between the word as corresponding to human reason's "thirst for existence" and the twentieth-century historical-critical retrieval of scripture (for which Bultmann was so well known) suggests that Gadamer's hermeneutic philosophy supports the function of scripture described by the great comparative religion scholar, Wilfred Cantwell Smith:

---

91 See Gadamer, "Die Marburger Theologie," *Neuere Philosophie I*, 207; English translation: "Martin Heidegger and Marburg Theology (1964)," *Philosophical Hermeneutics*, 198–212 at 210. On the issue of "self-understanding," see also Gadamer, "Hermeneutik und Historismus," *Hermeneutik II*, 403–12; and "Zur Problematik des Selbstverständnisses: Ein hermeneutischer Beitrag zur Frage der 'Entmythologisierung,'" *Hermeneutik II*, 121–32.

92 Gadamer, "Sprache und Verstehen," *Hermeneutik II*, 192. See also ch. 2, 47–8.

[Traditional reading of scripture] aimed at proffering not, in the fashion of modern exegesis, "the meaning of the text," but the meaning of the universe, of world history, of human life, of the reader's own lives as they read, or as they set forth about their affairs after reading. They aspired to that meaning considered in the light of the words here proffered. Considered in the light of "the text," one might say, except that on reflection it becomes clear that this too will not do; we shall be arguing that the idea of a text, as an object to be understood, is modern and impersonal and subordinating, characterizing present-day culture's objectivizing orientation to the world. Their intent was rather to discern that meaning in the light of what God had to say to them.[93]

I suggest that this is the way Voegelin read scripture in *Israel and Revelation*, in *The Ecumenic Age*, and in essays such as "The Gospel and Culture."

VII. Conclusion

Eric Voegelin and Hans-Georg Gadamer surely are not the first names that come to mind when people think of continental philosophy, which usually refers to the traditions of philosophy emanating from Edmund Husserl and Martin Heidegger – the two great sources of the phenomenological movement in France, Germany, Italy, England, and North America. Voegelin's chief claim to fame until now is mainly as a political scientist, and because of the inevitable snobbery connected with such conventional headings, this has tended to eliminate him from the field – and almost from the ranks of philosophy *tout court*. In Gadamer's case, it is not that he is not an epigone of Heidegger but that hermeneutic philosophy has simply gone out of fashion.

Voegelin was hoping to introduce students into the *zetesis* or quest for the truth in history about human beings in society under God by convincing them of the utmost importance of understanding the history of order and the order in history. By undertaking a wide range of anamnetic experiments, he attempted to work out a set of basic terms and relations and a basic orientation for the philosophic and scientific study

---

93 See Wilfred Cantwell Smith, *What Is Scripture? A Comparative Approach* (Minneapolis: Fortress Press, 1993), 34–5, cited by L. William Countryman, *The Poetic Imagination: An Anglican Spiritual Tradition* (Maryknoll, NY: Orbis Books, 2000), 29.

of humankind in history. Although Voegelin's thought tends to have more of a doctrinal content than Gadamer's does, it too constitutes a grand conversation in which one has to be edified by how much Voegelin is constantly learning. Serious people in search of direction within the crisis of the West will find his work both accessible and attractive.

The center of Gadamer's teaching regards "the conversation we are" (Hölderlin's phrase). Quite serious about Plato's teaching in the Seventh Letter about the conceptual inexpressibility of the *logos* at the heart of philosophy, Gadamer's philosophical hermeneutics raises up the conversational character of human being. Like Platonic dialectic, his work invites us to align our performance of living with what we are by nature through heightening our awareness of the demands of genuine human conversation.

Both Voegelin and Gadamer acknowledge the relativity and contingency that exists at the intersection of *logos* and *ethos*; and this includes the fragile, prepredicative dimension of insight, of grasping the virtually unconditioned, and of discovering what is right by nature as we come to terms with reality. They both were sensitive to "doctrinalization," dogmatism, and ideology. They realized that the formulation of the deepest truths makes them vulnerable to their inauthentic appropriation, deformation, and devaluation by people who are spiritually unprepared to receive them. In relation to this danger, Voegelin risked almost systematic articulation of his terms of analysis, while Gadamer constantly tried to show the conversational character of philosophy by hermeneutic reflections on writings worth reading, and works of art and literature worth experiencing. Thus, in hopes of being received by persons either open to conversion or already converted, Voegelin risked casting his pearls before dogs; and Gadamer, by devoting his life to interpreting recondite texts and works of art, ran the risk of attracting only those willing to read such difficult, yet perennially worthwhile, texts.

The present comparison and contrast of the thought of these two philosophers has attempted to suggest how worthwhile the study of their thought can be. In their similarities and differences, their achievements (available in complete sets of their collected works) are as estimable as any to be found now. To anyone trying to meet the deepest issues of contemporary disorientation and bewilderment they each offer fundamental versions of wisdom that are all the more worthy of attention because their *opera omnia* represent genuine transpositions of the classic wisdom of Plato and Aristotle into the world of today.

6 "Transcendence from Within": Benedict XVI and Jürgen Habermas on the Dialogue between Secular Reason and Religious Faith[1]

... [A] time of confusion ... calls beliefs into question and, because they are just beliefs, because they are not personally generated knowledge, answers are hard to come by. So to confusion there are easily added disorientation, disillusionment, crisis, surrender, unbelief. But ... from the present situation Catholics are suffering more keenly than others, not indeed because their plight is worse, but because up to Vatican II they were sheltered against the modern world and since Vatican II they have been exposed more and more to the chill winds of modernity.

Bernard Lonergan, "Belief: Today's Issue," 93–4[2]

I. Benedict XVI's Regensburg Account of the Narrowing of Reason in the West

In his open letter to the *Neue Zürcher Zeitung* (10 February 2007),[3] Jürgen Habermas comments on Benedict XVI's speech at Regensburg, saying that the pope's notion of rationality presupposes a "metaphysical"

---

1 This title phrase is taken from the following: Jürgen Habermas, "Transcendence from Within, Transcendence in this World," in *Habermas, Modernity, and Public Theology*, ed. Don S. Browning and Francis Schüssler Fiorenza (New York: Crossroad, 1992), 226–50; reprinted in Jürgen Habermas, *Religion and Rationality: Essays on Reason, God, and Modernity*, ed. Eduardo Mendieta (Cambridge, MA: MIT Press, 2002), 67–94.

2 Bernard Lonergan, "Belief: Today's Issue," *A Second Collection*, ed. W.J. Ryan and B.J. Tyrrell (London: Darton, Longman & Todd, 1974), 93–4.

3 Jürgen Habermas, "Ein Bewusstsein von dem, was fehlt," *Neue Zürcher Zeitung*, 10 February 2007.

synthesis between reason and faith that held sway from Augustine
to Thomas Aquinas. This is partially true. Benedict has consistently
emphasized the gravamen of one of the clearest patristic statements
by Tertullian recalling the Platonic Socrates: "Christ called himself the
Truth, not opinion."[4] Benedict has long stressed that the Septuagint's
translation of the Tetragammaton in Exodus 3:13 as "I Am" providentially
initiated "a profound encounter between faith and reason"; and that the
Johannine phrase, "In the beginning was the *logos*" is evidence that
"the encounter between the Biblical message and Greek thought did
not happen by chance." The Johannine passage, like Paul's Areopagus
speech, was emblematic of an encounter between "genuine enlightenment and religion" and generated a "synthesis between the Greek spirit
and the Christian spirit." Indeed, in 1983 then Cardinal Ratzinger stated,
"Christianity is … the synthesis mediated in Jesus Christ between the
faith of Israel and the Greek spirit."[5]

Yet Benedict has never been a devotee of scholastic metaphysics, however much he was sympathetic to its main goals.[6] This ambivalence was
reflected in the Regensburg speech when Benedict described the synthesis between faith and reason in terms, not of the metaphysics, but of the
"so-called intellectualism of Augustine and Thomas." Benedict uses the
expression "so-called" because he does not wish to suggest any rationalist subordination of faith to reason; and the term "intellectualism" is
drawn from medieval philosophical faculty psychology's convention of
contrasting intellect (*intellectus*) and will (*voluntas*). Hence, the intellectualism of Augustine and Thomas Aquinas is opposed to the voluntarism
of Duns Scotus. According to Benedict, Scotus initiated a tradition radicalized by William of Ockham in which "God's transcendence and otherness are so exalted that our reason, our sense of the true and the good,
are no longer an authentic mirror of God, whose deepest possibilities
remain eternally unattainable and hidden behind his decisions."

4 Cited from *De virginibus velandis*, I, 1 in Joseph Ratzinger, *Einführung in das Christentum. Vorlesungen über das Apostolische Glaubensbekenntnis* (Munich: Deutscher Taschenbuch Verlag, 1971 [1st ed. 1968]), 93.
5 See Kardinal Joseph Ratzinger, "Europa – verpflichetendes Erbe für Christen," in
   Europa. Horizonte der Hoffnung, ed. Franz König and Karl Rahner (Graz: Styria, 1983),
   61–71 at 68.
6 See Joseph Ratzinger, *Milestones 1927–1977* (San Francisco, CA: Ignatius Press, 1998)
   on his trials and tribulations with Thomistic theologians, especially when writing his
   Habilitationsschrift.

Bernard Lonergan's reading of Thomas Aquinas clarifies another nuance of the term intellectualism, although not in connection with the contrast between human intellect and human will. In Aquinas's gnoseology one may contrast *within* the exercise of intelligence itself the act of understanding (*intelligere*) and the inner word (*verbum intus prolatum*). The inner word may be either the concept proceeding from a direct insight into a phantasm or the judgment proceeding from the indirect or reflective act of understanding that grasps the sufficiency of the evidence for the truth of an affirmation.

In a January 1935 letter Lonergan noted "that Augustine talked a lot about *intelligere* and that Thomas didn't talk about universals – though knowledge of universals was supposed [by then dominant Thomistic interpreters] to be the be-all and end-all of science."[7] In *Verbum: Word and Idea in Aquinas* Lonergan later retrieved Aquinas's understanding of understanding and broke with both the closed and static conceptualism and the mistaken notion of judgment as a rubber-stamping synthesis upon which the pejorative and rationalist sense of the term "intellectualism" is based.[8] The belief (1) that concepts precede acts of understanding as impoverished replicas of what is presented by the senses and the imagination, and (2) that we know the existence or occurrence of things not by rational judgment but through sense perception prevailed within scholasticism from Henry of Ghent and Duns Scotus through Francisco Suarez to the post-*Aeterni Patris* Thomistic schools. Lonergan's close study of Thomas on the relationship between understanding and formulation/judgment in relation to the natural analogy for trinitarian theology uncovered the factual psychological basis in experience for the metaphysical account of understanding and judgment in Thomas's writings: "Aquinas attributed the key role in cognitional theory not to inner words, concepts, but to acts of understanding."[9]

Benedict's expression "the rationality of faith" parses theology's task of *fides quaerens intellectum*. According to Lonergan, Aquinas's

---

7 Cited from Lonergan's January 1935 letter to Henry Keane in Frederick E. Crowe, SJ, *Lonergan*, Outstanding Christian Thinkers Series, ed. Brian Davies, OP (Collegeville, MN: The Liturgical Press, 1992), 22, my brackets.

8 See Bernard Lonergan, *Verbum: Word and Idea in Aquinas*, Collected Works of Bernard Lonergan 2, ed. Frederick E. Crowe and Robert M. Doran (Toronto: University of Toronto Press, 1997).

9 See Bernard Lonergan, "*Insight* Revisited," *A Second Collection*, ed. W.J. Ryan and B.J. Tyrrell (London: Darton, Longman & Todd, 1974), 263–78 at 267.

understanding of the phrase means not faith seeking certainty or proof according to the requirements of Aristotle's *Posterior Analytics*, as was the case in the thesis format of the post-Reformation manuals, but faith seeking understanding in the sense of working out analogies from nature, which Aquinas acknowledged as *rationes convenientiae* (i.e., what today we would call "possibly relevant hypotheses," rather than demonstrations or proofs).[10] Ironically, the notorious voluntarists, Scotus and Ockham, applied the Aristotelian *akribeia*, or unalloyed logical rigor and coherence to theology in a way that Aristotle himself would have regarded as inappropriate. This bias toward an exclusively logical control of meaning was cultivated in scholastic *Konklusionstheologie* (or *Denziger-theologie*) until the Second Vatican Council. It fit the needs of ahistorical orthodoxy, which did not acknowledge that "terms are … defined, but definitions are not unique: on the contrary, for each term there is a historical sequence of different definitions; there is a learned explanation for each change of definition."[11] This assumption was integral to the replacement of "the inquiry of the *quaestio* by the pedagogy of the thesis." Bishop and inquisitor Melchior Cano adapted the *loci* of Agricola's forensic rhetoric in the "thesis method" of pre-Vatican II seminary theology. The thesis stated church doctrines as propositions; after briefly listing the opinions of those who rejected them, it adduced proofs from scripture, the Fathers, the councils and authoritative documents, the theologians, and finally from nature to establish how close they came to being *de fide definita*. This method presupposed "meanings fixed by definitions, with presuppositions and implications fixed by laws of logic," resulting in "what used to be called eternal verities but today are known as static abstractions."[12] It was a pedagogy that inculcated both a preoccupation with the certitudes of the faith, and with the teaching authority and sanctions of the church.[13]

The most intelligent of those suspected of "modernism" thought in all probity that faith cannot be proven. Some turned to religious experience as the starting point for both theology and apologetics, and rejected dogmas and abstract propositional truths in favor of myths, symbols,

---

10 See Bernard Lonergan, "Theology and Understanding," *Collection: Papers by Bernard Lonergan*, Collected Works of Bernard Lonergan 4, ed. Frederick E. Crowe and Robert M. Doran (Toronto: University of Toronto Press, 1988), 114–32.

11 See Bernard Lonergan, "Dimensions of Meaning," *Collection*, 232–45 at 243.

12 See Bernard Lonergan, "The Future of Thomism," *A Second Collection*, 47.

13 See Bernard Lonergan, "Theology in its New Context," *A Second Collection*, 55–67.

metaphors, and rituals as expressions of religious experience. To be sure, the legitimate motivation for the old-style scholastic apologists, and for their opposition to starting with religious experience, was their Catholic conviction that Christian beliefs are to be believed because they are true, not because they happen to appeal to someone's subjective emotions or feelings. The so-called modernists opposed the post-Reformation and post-Enlightenment preoccupation with the *praeambula fidei* and with the old fundamental theology operating under the guise of science as *certa cognitio rerum per causas* for which the core of science is understood to be logical demonstration: arguments for the existence of God, arguments for the ethical obligation to worship and adore God, arguments from prophecies and miracles to establish the divine origin of the Christian religion, and arguments for the church as the true religion. The rationale for this was always a dead-end undertaking. One in the position of "understanding seeking faith" tries to reach conclusions containing divinely revealed truths on the basis of premises that are simply rational or proportionate to "unaided reason." Such a procedure cannot justify a reasonable assent to divinely revealed truth. (The only consolation is that the reason of "the fool who says in his heart there is no God" cannot in this manner demonstrate the impossibility of such truths, either.)

While the ecclesiastical anti-modernists worried about the certainty of the *praeambula* in terms of the logical control of meaning, Maurice Blondel in *L'Action* and John Henry Newman in the *Essay in Aid of a Grammar of Assent* debunked the stock-in-trade of old-style theology and apologetics – the putatively infallible intuitions, self-evident premises, and necessary conclusions – as the subjective constructions that they were. They opened the door to the widespread *ressourcement* that paved the way for Vatican II.

The stages of dehellenization to which Benedict ascribed the atrophy and shrinkage of reason in his Regensburg speech were virtually synthesized in what the church called Modernism. First, the Reformation reacted to the putative subordination of faith and scriptural revelation to reason in late medieval scholasticism; and Kant radicalized the hermeneutic principles – *sola scriptura, sola fide*, and *sola gratia* – by his project of delimiting the scope of reason in order "to make room for faith." Reason as theoretical or speculative was confined to Kant's *simulacrum* of Newtonian science, which involved the mathematization of observable phenomena; reason as practical and aesthetic took over the traditional primacy from theoretical reason. Second, the historical critical school of New Testament studies from Reimarus to Schweitzer went hand-in-hand with what Karl Barth called the *Kulturprotestantismus* that he ascribed to liberal Protestants such as Friedrich Schleiermacher, Adolf von Harnack, Albrecht Ritschl, and Wilhelm Hermann. As far as historical knowledge of Jesus is concerned, the *religionsgeschichtliche Schule*[14] and post-Bultmannian biblical studies oscillated between Wilhelm Wrede's "thoroughgoing skepticism" and Albert Schweitzer's "thoroughgoing eschatology."[15]

While liberal Protestantism (perhaps like liberal Catholicism after Vatican II) tended to replace worship with morality more or less in the Kantian mode, out-and-out scientism has come to dominate the third stage of dehellenization sketched by Benedict. Thus, current advocates of atheism such as Richard Dawkins dogmatically assert that genuine knowledge does not extend beyond the limits of algorithmic formulation and empiricist observation; even the human sciences must be trimmed to meet these limits. Any questions about the justification of scientific knowledge itself – not to mention questions regarding the overall meaning of human existence – are interdicted because they go beyond these limits, which are arbitrarily posited as exclusively valid.

II. The Ambiguities of "Hellenization"

A. Nicene Case

Unfortunately, "dehellenization" is a misleading characterization of the processes at work in the truncation, immanentization, and alienation of reason that is destructive both to faith itself but also to the human condition *tout court*. It was used by Protestants of the historical school to argue that Jesus's own first-century Palestinian mentality was distorted by Hellenism. Again, Hellenization does not simply refer to inculturation into Gentile culture. The councils at Nicea and after were not simply rephrasing beliefs in the language of a different culture. Indeed, Benedict's remarking the contrast between truth and opinion implies a movement

---

14 The school was born in Göttingen in the 1890s, and included A. Eichorn, H. Gunkel, W. Bousset, J. Weiss, and W. Wrede.

15 See N.T. Wright, "The 'Quests' and Their Usefulness," *The Contemporary Quest for Jesus* (Minneapolis: Fortress Press, 2002), 1–22; see, too, Stephen Neill and Tom Wright, *The Interpretation of the New Testament 1861–1986*, 2nd ed. (Oxford: Oxford University Press, 1988), especially the updated chapter added to this edition by Tom Wright, "History and Theology," 360–449.

among Christians from what is first-for-us to what-is-first-in-itself. This shift characterized the trinitarian and Christological debates punctuated by the first six ecumenical councils when Church Fathers reflected on the global and compact expressions in the ordinary or commonsense language of *mythos* and adopted the techniques of logical control to refine questions and to respond with definitions using technical terms.

The Council of Nicea's use of the term *homoousios* to define the relationship between the Father and the Son did not involve a rationalist subordination of Christian belief to Greek philosophy. Athanasius explained that the term defends the biblical meaning by logically ordering statements. "Therefore, because they are one, and because the divinity itself is also one, what is said (in the Scriptures) of the Father is also said of the Son, except the name, Father."[16] Arius, the rationalist, held that if the Son is *ek tou patros* logically he would have to be a creature instead of Pantocrator. Neither Athanasius nor the assembled bishops at Nicea would have anything of such extreme Hellenization. Athanasius's balanced Hellenization only applied the second-order reflective resources made possible by the tradition of Greek philosophy to a serious controversy; he did not borrow from any extant author or school. When, commenting on the Nicene decrees, Athanasius said that the Fathers "were again compelled to gather up the mind [*dianoian*] of the Scriptures and to state and write again more clearly what they had said before, that the Son is consubstantial [*homoousion*] with the Father, in order that they might make clear that the Son is not merely like, but is from the Father as the same in likeness [*touton tê homoiôsei*]."[17] To say the Son is "from the substance of the Father" [*ek tês ousias tou Patros*] differentiates the Son's generation from any creature's generation or production, while both synthesizing the biblical teaching about Son and restating the mind of the Fathers at Nicea.[18] Alois Grillmeier has succinctly summarized the issue of Hellenization at Nicea:

---

16 Athanasius, *Orat. 3 contra Arianos*, 4, cited in Bernard Lonergan, *The Way to Nicea: The Dialectical Development of Trinitarian Theology*, trans. Conn O'Donovan (Philadelphia: Westminster Press, 1976), 101.

17 Athanasius, *Orat. 3 contra Arianos*, 4.

18 See Alois Grillmeier, "Hellenisierung – Judaisierung des Christentums als Deuteprinzipien der Geschichte des kirchlichen Dogmas," *Mit ihm und in ihm. Christologische Forschungen und Perspektiven* (Freiburg im Breisgau: Herder, 1975) 423–88; see also Bernard Lonergan, "The Structure of the Ante-Nicene Movement," *The Way to Nicea*, 105–37; and Brian E. Daley, SJ, "'One Thing and Another': The Persons in God and the Person of Christ in Patristic Theology," *Pro Ecclesia* 16, no. 1 (2007): 17–46.

If we want to use a label like "the Hellenization of the Christian faith,"
we can see from this dispute where it really applies. It does not apply to
the bishops of the council of Nicea (325) who rejected Arius' teaching. The
fathers of the council used a term which fits very well into Greek philosophy, *homoousios*, identical in substance, consubstantial. But far from implying acceptance of Greek philosophy, their use of this term was a direct
attack on it. They used it to stress the very point which no Greek philosopher would ever have conceived of, the true divinity of the Son and his
begetting – not creation – by the Father. The council of Nicea chose the
difficilior lectio of the Christian message. It resisted the temptation to adopt
Arius' theory, although it was philosophically more plausible.[19]

The term "Hellenization" is appropriate to the extent that the council
Fathers realized that they had to move from the first-for-us perspective
of the Bible to the first-in-itself perspective of theory, which Greek philosophy initiated. Lonergan clarified the theological task of reason performed by Athanasius and the council Fathers in the definition of the
divinity of the Son: "(1) avoiding metaphors and anthropomorphisms,
(2) selecting appropriate aspects of created things from which, by analogy, one can ascend to some conception of God, and (3) attending to and
applying the words of sacred scripture, through which alone the mystery of the Trinity is made known to us."[20] In this process, the Christian
faith does not change, but there occurs a growth in understanding that
had not previously been attained.

B. Chalcedon

This positive sense of Hellenization becomes characteristic of the reasonableness of Christian dogma as a rule of belief. Athanasius gave a
second-order interpretation of the *homoousios*: "Whatever is said about
the Father ... whatever is said about the Son ..." After the Council of
Nicea, Severus of Antioch and the Monophysite tradition, wishing in all
good will to adhere to the teachings of the council and of Athanasius,
did not want to admit more than one nature in Christ, and so resisted

---

19 See Alois Grillmeier, "God's Divinity and Humanity," in *The Common Catechism*,
    ed. Johannes Feiner and Lukas Vischer (New York: The Seabury Press, 1975),
    232–61 at 241.
20 Lonergan, *The Way to Nicea*, 103.

the further questions, raised by Apollinaris on the one hand, and by Nestorius on the other. On the way to the teaching of the Council of Chalcedon (451) about two natures united in "one and the same" Jesus Christ, Diodore of Tarsus, Theodore of Mopsuestia, Pope Leo the Great, and Cyril of Alexandria articulated the questions and attempted to respond to them. Here the challenge was actually methodological: to answer new and further questions by moving beyond the first-for-us perspective of the faithful (*both* in terms of the scriptures *and* in terms of the preceding Fathers and councils) to the first-in-itself perspective of theology and systematic thinking.[21] Once again, according to Grillmeier, the technique of reflection on scriptural propositions was used to reach the orthodox response:

> The council of Chalcedon canonized no metaphysical "theory of Christ." Still less did it leave any room for mythological ideas. The whole "formalistic" style of the fathers' definitions, far from making the mystery manageable, emphasizes its difficulty. The council doesn't give us an answer to the question, "Who is Jesus Christ?" It gives us instructions about how to think and talk. Whether we go into further metaphysical questions or not, we are required to resist over-simplifications and always to describe the man Jesus in such a way that God is clearly visible in his humanity, and always to describe the eternal Son of God in such a way that he has the features of the man Jesus of Nazareth.[22]

C. A Medieval Case

In 1277, the bishop of Paris, Étienne Tempier, under pressure from Peter of Spain and Pope John XXI, condemned 219 propositions associated with Latin Averroism, some of which some were ostensibly those of Thomas Aquinas as one who made use of the philosophy of Aristotle.[23] The Stagirite's comprehensive philosophy of nature, not influenced by

---

21 See Bernard Lonergan, *De Deo Trino, II. Pars systematica* (Rome: Gregorian University Press, 1964), 47–53; English translation: *The Triune God: Systematics*, Collected Works of Bernard Lonergan 12, trans. Michael G. Shields; ed. Robert M. Doran and H. Daniel Monsour (Toronto: University of Toronto Press, 2007), 93–100.

22 Grillmeier, "God's Divinity and Humanity," 258.

23 See Fernand van Steenberghen, *Thomas Aquinas and Radical Aristotelianism* (Washington, DC: Catholic University of America Press, 1980); *Aristotle in the West: The Origins of Latin Aristotelianism* (Brussels: E. Nauwelaerts, 1955).

theologoumena, did not completely accord with Christian biblical doctrine. According to Ernest Fortin, the condemnations were in all likelihood aimed not at the then recently deceased "Angelic Doctor" but at exponents of what became pejoratively known in later scholarship as Latin Averroism – Siger of Brabant and Boethius of Dacia. Fortin points out that Siger, who was so exalted by Dante in *The Divine Comedy*,[24] tethered his mind neither to the authoritative teachings of the Bible nor to church tradition. Should any doctrines not pass muster before the tribunal of reason (in Aristotelian terms), he insisted on saying what he thought was true, even if doing so would be costly. In Fortin's view, Siger's determination to follow Aristotle wherever his thought might lead was a conscious commitment to be open to the breadth and depth of Aristotle's thought as opposed to its putatively "constricted"[25] version in orthodox theology. This was a rationalist Hellenization against which the Dominican Richard Kilwardby and many Franciscans such as John Peckham reacted. J.-P. Torrell calls Peckham "the type … of the conservative Augustinian tendency that opposed the new Aristotelian ideas." Thomas Aquinas was not a rationalist.[26]

Perhaps the underlying motive for this reaction was a failure to acknowledge the need in the medieval context for a *Wendung zur Idee* or an articulation of theology as a science to answer questions raised by the gradual entry of Aristotle's works into the Latin West. As Yves Congar put the matter:

> For Albert the Great and St Thomas the sciences represent a genuine knowledge of the world and of the nature of things. For things have their own consistence and intelligibility and this knowledge is valid even in the Christian economy. Therefore, the sciences in their order have a verifiable autonomy of object and method, just as in their order they convey their own truth. In this perspective the expression "handmaid of theology," which St Thomas also uses, has a very different meaning from the primitive

---

24 Ernest L. Fortin, *Dissent and Philosophy in the Middle Ages: Dante and His Precursors*, trans. Marc A. LePain (Lanham, MD: Lexington Books, 2002); English translation of: *Dissidence et philosophie au moyen-âge* (Montreal: Fides, 1984), 50.

25 Fortin, *Dissent and Philosophy in the Middle Ages*, 44.

26 See Jean-Pierre Torrell, OP, *Saint Thomas Aquinas, vol 1: The Person and His Work*, trans. Robert Royal (Washington, DC: Catholic University of America Press, 1996), 183–7 on Peckham, and 303–16 on Peckham, Kilwardby, and the controversy over the condemnation of Thomas.

Augustinian sense, for "the better to assure the services of their slave, theology begins by freeing her."

Now we understand better why Albert and St Thomas followed the thought of Aristotle. They were looking not only for a master of reasoning but a master in the knowledge of the nature of things, of the world, and of man himself. Certainly St Thomas was not ignorant any more than St Bonaventure that all things must be referred to God. But alongside that reference to God in the order of use or exercise, he recognized an unconditioned bounty to the speculative intellect in the nature or specification of things, which was a work of God's wisdom. There was question of speculatively reconstructing the order of forms, of *rationes*, put into things and into the very mysteries of salvation by the wisdom of God. Such a program could be realized only by a knowledge of forms and natures in themselves. This is why St Thomas' Aristotelianism is not external to his theological wisdom or to the very conception he has fashioned of it.[27]

In Lonergan's analysis, the medieval context required more than the logical coherence of the doctrines that were problematized by Peter Abelard's *Sic et Non* in 158 propositions "pro" and "con." What was needed was a sapiential ordering of *quaestiones* that was capable of dealing with the fundamental issues from which other connected issues followed. Such an ordering was not available in the order of discovery (*via analytica/inventionis*) as evident in Peter Lombard's *Sentences*. Such a wisdom needed what Aquinas called the *disputatio magistralis* that instructed listeners to lead them to an understanding of the truth already believed by them, involving an investigation going to the root of the truth by presenting its reasons or grounds and by making students know why what is said is true.[28] The theologian has to pass from what is first in scripture and what is first in the patristic authorities to what is first-in-itself, thus making the transition from the *ordo inventionis* to the *ordo doctrinae*. We can note how Thomas goes back and forth between both orders in the fourth book of his *Summa contra Gentiles*, where chapters alternate between arguments ascertaining facts of Christian belief by appeals to authorities, and magisterial disputations in which reason is used to acquire further understanding

---

27 See Yves Congar, OP, *A History of Theology*, trans. and ed. Hunter Guthrie, SJ (Garden City, NY: Doubleday, 1968), 107–8; based on Congar's article "Théologie," which first appeared in *Dictionnaire de Théologie Catholique* 15 (Paris: Editions Letouzy & Ané, 1946).
28 See Thomas Aquinas, *Quodlibetum* IV, a. 18.

of the truths believed.[29] This is an achievement of theology as a science, or of theology as systematic in a more contemporary sense.

D. Modern Dehellenization

For Lonergan, modern dehellenization has two principal causes, the rise of modern science and the emergence of historical consciousness. Lonergan did not stress the *Wirkungsgeschichte* of the Reformation as Benedict did in Regensburg, because he agreed with Herbert Butterfield's position that the origin of modern science "outshines everything since the rise of Christianity and reduces the Renaissance and the Reformation to the rank of mere episodes, mere internal displacements, within the system of medieval Christendom."[30]

Modern science has in common with the Aristotelian notion of science only one feature: the movement from the first-for-us of the commonsense cognitional perspective expressed in ordinary language to the first-in-themselves of a theoretical cognitional perspective expressed in technical terms and relations. As Lonergan explains, commonsense understanding is descriptive in the sense that it understands things-in-relation-to-our-senses. Thus, operating in terms of common sense, we speak of the sun rising and setting, and of the sun as revolving around the earth. In contrast, the perspective of theoretical understanding characteristic of science is explanatory in the sense that it understands things-in-relation-to-each-other. So the scientist puts the sun at the center of the solar system, and knows that the earth spins on its axis every 24 hours at the same time as it revolves around the sun. In general, ancient science passed from common sense to theory by using logic and dialectic to replace opinions with *episteme*, with definitions *omni et soli*. But modern science moves from the raw experience of sense perception to its version of classical science (which grasps possibly relevant correlations) by measurement, and then maps the results on a number field; this evokes hypothesis formation (1), the drawing of implications from the hypothesis (2), and empirical testing of the implications (3), for the sake of a more or less probable, indirect verification of the hypothesis

---

29 See Lonergan, *De Deo Trino, II*, 8–9, and 49–53; *The Triune God: Systematics*, 9–11 and 93–100.

30 See Lonergan, "Theology in its New Context," *A Second Collection*, 55–67, citing Herbert Butterfield, *The Origins of Modern Science, 1300–1800*, 2nd ed. (New York: Collier Books, 1966), 7.

(4). This procedure is commonly simplified by saying that the modern sciences are based on *observation* (in contrast to the verbalisms of premodern science) and the *mathematization* of nature (so that valid knowledge admits only what is susceptible of algorithmic formulation). When either the more complicated or simplified conceptions of scientific procedure enter into modern rationalist ideologies, then anything that goes beyond the limits of world-immanent existence comes to be regarded as the realm of unreality expressible in metaphor, symbol, and myth (taken in the pejorative sense of the terms). This is connected inextricably with the so-called end of metaphysics.

The second factor in modern dehellenization is the rise of historical consciousness and of the procedures of critical history in the nineteenth century. Lonergan cited the Anglican theologian, Alan Richardson:

> One should never forget that it was one and the same movement of critical enquiry which first culminated in the seventeenth-century scientific achievement and later in the emergence of the fully developed historical critical method of the nineteenth. The critical faculty, once awakened, could not rest satisfied with the successful exploration of the realm of nature; it was bound to go from there to the critical investigation of the more intractable realm of human nature, and when the idea of development was fully understood, to seek to understand scientifically how, in fact, man and his institutions have come to be what they are. Since the nineteenth century it has been an axiom of Western thinking that men and their institutions cannot be understood apart from their history ... The historical revolution in human thinking, which was accomplished in the nineteenth century, is just as important as the scientific revolution of two centuries earlier. But they are not two different revolutions; they are aspects of the one great transitional movement from the mediaeval to the modern way of looking at things.[31]

Augustine's *De doctrina christiana*, which presided over the theological reading of the Bible until early modern times, set forth a hermeneutics of belief or of love. Briefly, it was considered a matter of course to read the Bible in light of the Christian creeds that emerged from the formulations of the early baptismal formulae. Although he did not champion the

---

31 See Alan Richardson, *History, Sacred and Profane* (London: SCM Press, 1964), 32–3, quoted by Lonergan in "Questionnaire on Philosophy: Response," *Philosophical and Theological Papers 1965–1980*, Collected Works of Bernard Lonergan 17 (Toronto: University of Toronto, 2004), 352–83 at 354.

sensus literalis of scripture above all, there was something hermeneutically correct about his account of the way Christian belief and worship and the practice of love influence a faithful reading of the biblical texts. In general, Hans-Georg Gadamer's account of the shortcomings of the "prejudice against prejudice" allows us to recover the real strengths in Augustine's teachings again.[32] But to do so fully requires one to overcome the specific cognitional theoretic and rationalist biases that since Baruch Spinoza's *Theologico-Political Treatise* have been regularly taken for granted by those practicing the critical historical reading of the scriptures.

During Benedict's professorial career the prime instance of this unbalanced type of historical scholarship was Rudolf Bultmann.[33] This brilliant sometime collaborator of Karl Barth and colleague of the Martin Heidegger of the *Sein und Zeit* period at Marburg, united the Kantianism he received from his teacher Wilhelm Hermann with an historicist basis for the modern split between the Christ of faith and the Jesus of history; these presuppositions have not been completely abandoned by everyone in New Testament studies. I believe Ben F. Meyer has well formulated the underlying issue:

> The key issue was the claims of reason. To practically all participants in the quest, much of what Luther and Melanchthon considered essential to Christianity ran counter to reason; i.e., it violated the conception of reality as an impermeable system of finite causes. Bultmann is the spokesman of a two-hundred-year tradition when he says that "for modern man" the conceptions of spirits and miracles, redeemer and redemption, are "over and done with." To hold the contrary would involve a *sacrificium intellectus* "in order to accept what we cannot sincerely consider true." Spoken in the tradition of Goethe and Schiller, of Kant, Schelling, and Hegel, of the post-Enlightenment mainstream. Here Christian and agnostic, rationalist and idealist, liberal and existentialist find common ground.[34]

This "conception of reality as an impermeable system of finite causes" lies at the heart of Spinoza's "hermeneutics of suspicion" as we see in the

---

32 See the second part of Hans-Georg Gadamer, *Wahrheit und Methode. Grundzüge einer philosophischen Hermeneutik* (Tübingen: Mohr, 1963).

33 See Joseph Ratzinger, "Das Dilemma der neuzeitlichen Theologie: Jesus oder Christus?" *Einführung in das Christentum*, 138–42.

34 See Ben F. Meyer, "A Review of the Quest," *The Aims of Jesus* (London: SCM Press, 1979), 25–59 at 57.

Theologico-Political Treatise's chapter, "Of Miracles," upon which all the great Germans listed in Meyer's statement ultimately depended. But as Meyer notes, Christians themselves shared the blame for this rationalist conception of nature, because they espoused it in their apologetics. Meyer quotes Butterfield on this: "If earlier in the [seventeenth] century religious men had hankered after a mathematically interlocking universe to justify the rationality and self-consistency of God, before the end of the century their successors were beginning to be nervous because they saw the mechanism becoming possibly too self-complete."[35] Quoting Butterfield further, Meyer then says, "Unwittingly, they had opened the way for 'a colossal secularization of thought in every possible realm of ideas at the same time.' This is what Paul Hazard called 'the crisis of the European mind,' and Peter Gay, 'the rise of modern paganism.'"[36] As Meyer reports, "Avant-garde Protestant theology allied itself with the spirit of the time. In eighteenth-century Germany, orthodoxy in the Wolffian mode gave way to rationalism or its opposite, Pietism." Meanwhile Catholic theology "retired to its dogmatic corner"[37] (continuing to do so in its anti-modernist stance), because as Lonergan phrased the matter, the church "acknowledged the transformation of our knowledge of nature and of our knowledge of man, not as a single momentous development in philosophy, but as a series of regrettable aberrations that unfortunately were widely accepted."[38]

III. Lonergan's Alternative Approach to the Problem of Dehellenization

Besides addressing the kinds of problems Roman Catholic theology encountered in connection with dehellenization,[39] Bernard Lonergan spent his life trying to respond to the modernist crisis. As is evident

---

35 Butterfield, *The Origins of Modern Science*, 85, cited by Meyer, *The Aims of Jesus*, 57.

36 Meyer, *The Aims of Jesus*, 57, citing Butterfield, *The Origins of Modern Science*, 137; and Paul Hazard, *La crise de la conscience européene* (Paris: Boivin, 1935); and Peter Gay, *The Enlightenment 1: The Rise of Modern Paganism* (New York: Knopf, 1966).

37 Lonergan, "Theology in its New Context," *A Second Collection*, 58.

38 Lonergan, "Questionnaire on Philosophy," *Philosophical and Theological Papers 1965–1980*, 353–4.

39 See for instance, Bernard Lonergan, "The Dehellenization of Dogma," *A Second Collection*, 11–32, which was originally a review of Leslie Dewart, *The Future of Belief: Theism in a World Come of Age* that appeared in *Theological Studies* 28 (1967): 336–51. It is a very significant piece for understanding Lonergan, because many of Dewart's opinions incorporate specifically modern counterpositions.

from what has already been said, he gave careful consideration to these issues in his theological work. But the overall crisis in Catholic philosophy and theology brought about by the rise of modern science and of modern historical studies compelled him to push beyond theology proper into what he conceived of as philosophy's contemporary role, namely, foundational methodology. Lonergan's analysis of the crisis highlights the great transition in Western culture from the classicist perspective that had permeated ecclesiastical and theological consciousness:

Always in the past it had been the Catholic tradition to penetrate and Christianize the social fabric and the culture of the age. So it entered into the Hellenistic world of the patristic period. So it was one of the principal architects of medieval society and medieval thought. So too it was almost scandalously involved in the Renaissance. But only belatedly has it come to acknowledge that the world of the classicist no longer exists and that the only world in which it can function is the modern world.

To a great extent this failure is to be explained by the fact that modern developments were covered over with a larger amount of wickedness. Since the beginning of the eighteenth century Christianity has been under attack. Agnostic and atheistic philosophies have been developed and propagated. The development of the natural and of the human sciences was such that they appeared and often were said to support such movements. The emergence of the modern languages with their new literary forms was not easily acclaimed when they contributed so little to devotion and so much, it seemed, to worldliness and irreligion. The new industry spawned slums, the new politics revolutions, the new discoveries unbelief. One may lament it but one can hardly be surprised that at the beginning of this century, when churchmen were greeted with a heresy that logically entailed all possible heresies, they named the new monster modernism.

If their opposition to wickedness made churchmen unsympathetic to modern ways, their classicism blocked their vision. They were unaware that modern science involved a quite different notion of science from that entertained by Aristotle. When they praised science and affirmed the Church's support for science, what they meant to support was true and certain knowledge of things through their causes.

But modern science is not true and certain; it is just probable. It is not fully knowledge; it is hypothesis, theory, system, the best available opinion. It regards not things but data, phenomena. While it still speaks of causes, what it means is not end, agent, matter, form, but correlation.[40]

The problems raised by the shift from the Aristotelian to the modern conception of science were exacerbated by the added problems due to historical consciousness. As Lonergan remarks, classicist churchmen worried that "the historical sciences were the locus of continuous attacks on traditional views of the church in its origins and throughout its development." And so, as classicists they "believed that [they] could escape history, that [they] could encapsulate culture in the universal, the normative, the ideal, the immutable, that, while times would change, still the changes necessarily would be minor, accidental, of no serious significance."[41]

Hence, Lonergan was convinced that, "In brief, the contemporary issue is, not a new religion, not a new faith, but a belated social and cultural transition," namely, "the transition from classicist to modern culture." The task was that of "disengagement from classicist thought-forms and viewpoints, and simultaneously, of a new involvement in modern culture." It is important to insist here that Lonergan "did not think things wrong because they were classicist; on the contrary, [he] found a number of things [he] thought wrong, and, on putting them together, [he] found what he named classicism. Again, [he did] not think things are right because they are modern, but [he] did find a number of things [he] thought right and they are modern at least in the sense that they were overlooked in the nineteenth-century Catholic theological tradition." And so, as he went on to point out, "If we are not just to throw out what is good in classicism and replace it with contemporary trash, then we have to take the trouble, and it is enormous, to grasp the strength and the weakness, the power and the limitations, the good points and the shortcomings of both classicism and modernity."[42]

This is an enormous challenge for Catholic philosophers and theologians, one for which knowledge is not enough.

One has to be creative. Modernity lacks roots. Its values lack balance and depth. Much of its science is destructive of man. Catholics in the twentieth

---

40 See Lonergan, "Belief: Today's Issue," *A Second Collection*, 93–4.
41 See Bernard Lonergan, "The Absence of God in Modern Culture," *A Second Collection*, 112.
42 Lonergan, "Belief: Today's Issue," *A Second Collection*, 93–4.

century are faced with a problem similar to that met by Aquinas in the thirteenth century. Then Greek and Arabic culture were pouring into Western Europe and, if it was not to destroy Christendom, it had to be known, assimilated, transformed. Today modern culture, in many ways more stupendous than any that ever existed, is surging round us. It too has to be known, assimilated, transformed. That is the contemporary issue.[43]

IV. Habermas, Benedict, Lonergan, and Postmetaphysical Thinking

Jürgen Habermas's *Neue Zürcher Zeitung* open letter comments on Benedict XVI's Regensburg speech, noting that the pope's brief account of the gradual decline of reason includes a brief historical genealogy of postmetaphysical thinking:

The progress from Duns Scotus to nominalism leads nonetheless not only to the voluntarist God of the Protestants, but also levels the path to modern science. Kant's critical turn leads not only to a critique of the proofs for the existence of God, but also to the notion of autonomy, which has first made our modern understanding of law and democracy possible. And historicism leads forcibly not only to a relativistic self-denial of reason. As a child of the Enlightenment, [historicism] makes us sensitive to cultural differences and protects us from the overgeneralization of context-dependent judgments.[44]

Habermas holds that modern natural sciences and history challenge philosophy not only to become self-critical but to bid farewell "to metaphysical constructions of the whole of nature and history," because "nature and history pertain to the empirical sciences, while little more is left to philosophy than the competences of knowing, speaking, and acting subjects."[45] Habermas, Ratzinger, and Lonergan agree in the main about the historical stages in the development of philosophical and theological knowledge starting with the "axial period" defined earlier by Karl Jaspers.[46] All three reject the Enlightenment rationalist accounts

---

43 Lonergan, "Belief: Today's Issue," *A Second Collection*, 99.
44 Habermas, "Ein Bewusstsein von dem, was fehlt."
45 Habermas, "Ein Bewusstsein von dem, was fehlt."
46 See Karl Jaspers, *Vom Ursprung und Ziel der Geschichte* (Frankfurt am Main and Hamburg: Fischer Bücherei, 1955).

of d'Alembert or Comte, which deny cognitive status to anything but modern empirical science.

Benedict has always affirmed that human beings can know both reality as factual and good and evil objectively even when the subject matter is not reducible to what can be observed by the senses. Jürgen Habermas believes Benedict's assertion is grounded in premodern metaphysics whereas postmetaphysical thinking signals the decline of an "emphatic concept of theory, which was supposed to render not only the human world but nature, too, intelligible in their internal structures."[47] Moreover, having undertaken the linguistic turn, postmetaphysical thinking replaces consciousness as a starting point for philosophy. It rejects transcendental approaches and reflects on the fact that "the rules (according to which signs are linked, sentences are formed, and utterances are brought forth) can be read off from linguistic formations *as if from something lying before one*."[48] Again, postmetaphysical thinking eschews thought as abstract, disembodied, and detached to consider thought only within social space and historical, cultural time, and it affirms the primacy of practice over theory.

What can be made of Habermas's proposal to adopt a postmetaphysical standpoint in the cultural conversation between secular reason and religious reason? Vittorio Possenti has rejected Habermas's proposal out of hand, arguing that unless one has a metaphysical basis, it is impossible to discriminate between either truth and falsehood or good and evil.[49] I propose instead Lonergan's foundational methodology as an account of postmetaphysical thinking to which Benedict (whose position may well be close to that propounded by Possenti) and Habermas may each be able to subscribe. In its philosophical dimension, foundational methodology displaces metaphysics from its traditional primacy within scholasticism. As Lonergan stated in a review of E. Coreth's *Metaphysik*:

I should not equate metaphysics with the total and basic horizon, the *Grund- und Gesamtwissenschaft*. Metaphysics as about being, equates with

---

47 See Jürgen Habermas, *Postmetaphysical Thinking: Philosophical Essays,* trans. William Mark Hohengarten (Cambridge, MA: MIT Press, 1992), 6.

48 Habermas, *Postmetaphysical Thinking*, 7.

49 See Vittorio Possenti, "Metafisica o postmetafisica? A proposito del dialogo tra ragione secolare e ragione religiosa. Note a commento dello scritto di Jürgen Habermas sulla 'Neue Zürcher Zeitung' del 10 febbraio 2007," reported by Sandro Magister at http://chiesa.espresso.repubblica.it/articolo/125562, March 10, 2007.

the objective pole of that horizon; but metaphysics, as science, does not equate with the subjective pole. In my opinion, [the metaphysical] subjective pole is under a measure of abstraction that is quite legitimate when one is mediating the immediacy of latent metaphysics, but is to be removed when one is concerned with the total and basic horizon. In the concrete, the subjective pole is indeed the inquirer, but incarnate, liable to mythic consciousness, in need of a critique that reveals where the counter-positions come from. The incarnate inquirer develops in a development that is social and historical, that stamps the stages of scientific and philosophic progress with dates, that is open to a theology that Karl Rahner has described as an *Aufhebung der Philosophie*.[50]

Lonergan agrees with Habermas that the methods of modern science ought to make a difference for philosophy. Just as modern science seeks to understand all the phenomena provided by the data of the senses, now philosophy must expressly adopt an empirical method. Philosophy today, Lonergan argues, must start from a *generalized* empirical method that encompasses the data of consciousness as well as the data of the senses. The phenomenologies of Heidegger, Merleau-Ponty, Gadamer, and Ricoeur have moved in this direction insofar as they radicalized the pioneering work of Edmund Husserl. A perhaps even more relevant precedent for Lonergan's approach is Jean Piaget's completely independent genetic epistemology, an organized account of empirical studies of developing human operations, including not merely biological, but also psychic and intellectual operations.[51] By starting with generalized empirical method, foundational method develops an empirically based cognitional theory to answer the question: What are we doing when we think we know? The key here is asking a factual question about what we are doing when we are learning what something is and whether it is so, instead of first asking whether we know. By scrutinizing experiences of understanding in mathematics, in the classical and statistical investigations of the natural sciences, and in the self-correcting learning processes of common sense, one attends not so much to the contents of knowing as to its compound of cognitional operations precisely as verifiable in

---

50 See Bernard Lonergan's review of Austrian philosopher Emerich Coreth's *Metaphysik. Eine methodisch-systematische Grundlegung* in "Metaphysics as Horizon," *Collection*, 188–204 at 204.

51 See, for example, Jean Piaget, *Introduction à l'épistémologique*, 3 vols. (Paris: Presses Universitaires de France, 1950).

experience. This provides a factual entrée to a methodically controlled justification for the validity of knowledge (epistemology), on the one hand; and on the other, to an explanatory heuristic structure of what we can know when we deploy this basic group of operations in theoretical or scientific experiencing, understanding, and judging (metaphysics).[52]

Lonergan's *Insight* is understood to be a transposition of Thomas Aquinas's gnoseology, which he recovered in *Verbum: Word and Idea in Aquinas*, already mentioned above. He claims that "from the structural and dynamic features of scientific knowing" he can "cast into a single perspective such apparently diverse elements as (1) Plato's point in asking how the inquirer recognizes truth when he reaches what, as an inquirer, he did not know, (2) the intellectualist (though not conceptualist) meaning of the abstraction of form from material conditions, (3) the psychological manifestation of Aquinas's natural desire to know God by his essence, (4) what Descartes was struggling to convey in his incomplete *Regulae ad directionem ingenii*, (5) what Kant conceived as a priori synthesis, and (6) what is named the finality of intellect in J. Maréchal's vast labor on *Le point de depart de la métaphysique*."[53] The point of the study is all-important, because it establishes an empirically verifiable meaning for the term "reason" as a common ground upon which all people of intelligence – secular or religious – may meet. As Lonergan wrote:

> Unless one breaks the duality in one's knowing one doubts that understanding correctly is knowing. Under the pressure of that doubt, either one will sink into the bog of a knowing that is without understanding, or else one will cling to understanding but sacrifice knowing on the altar of an immanentism, an idealism, a relativism. From the horns of that dilemma one escapes only through the discovery – and one has not made it yet if one has no memory of its startling strangeness – that there are two quite different realisms, that there is an incoherent realism, half animal and half human, that poses as a halfway house between materialism and idealism, and on the other hand that there is an intelligent and reasonable realism between which and materialism the halfway house is idealism.[54]

---

52 See Bernard Lonergan, *Insight: A Study in Human Understanding*, Collected Works of Bernard Lonergan 3, ed. Frederick E. Crowe and Robert M. Doran (Toronto: University of Toronto Press, 1992).

53 Lonergan, *Insight*, 16.

54 Lonergan, *Insight*, 22.

Four things should be noted here. First, while it is true that the starting point for such self-appropriation of oneself as a knower for Lonergan is consciousness, it is consciousness as accessible to reflection upon
our experiences of experiencing, understanding, and judging, which
we perform again and again all the time.

Second, Lonergan conceives of understanding as grasping intelligibility in the concreteness of images and of formulation as the constructive
activity of expressing descriptively in symbol or metaphor or narrative,
or explanatorily in technical terms and relations (concepts, definitions,
functional correlations, algorithms), the intelligibility one has grasped.
Further, he accepts Piaget's conception of "the real world as something
that is constructed," because construction only implies idealism or subjectivism for one who thinks that "knowing is taking a good look at
what is already out there now," an assumption that Lonergan identifies
with the "incoherent realism" noted above, which is naive.[55]

Third, for Lonergan establishing the correctness of one's knowing is
not achieved through an essentialism, which is the legitimate target of
post-Kantian critiques of metaphysics, but through the grasp of a virtually unconditioned, i.e., of a conditioned grasp of intelligibility whose
conditions have in fact been fulfilled:

> Thus the question, Does it exist? presents the prospective judgment as a con-
> ditioned. Reflective understanding grasps the conditions and their fulfill-
> ment. From that grasp there proceeds rationally the judgment, It does exist.[56]

Thus, in confining judgment to matters of fact and excluding everything that putatively "could not be otherwise," Lonergan eliminates all
the exorbitant claims about the knowledge of the truth against which
so-called fallibilists rightly object.

And fourth, Lonergan's starting point does not prejudice but acknowledges the linguistic turn, because the horizon of conscious intentionality is concretely conditioned by the horizon of language. Thus, we use
language when, to respond to a question about data, we dispose the
images in relation to which insights arise; we use language to express

---

55 See Bernard Lonergan, "Piaget and the Idea of a General Education," *Topics in Education: The Cincinnati Lectures of 1959 on the Philosophy of Education*, Collected Works of
Bernard Lonergan 10, ed. Robert M. Doran and Frederick E. Crowe (Toronto: University of Toronto Press, 1993), 193–207 at 204.
56 See Bernard Lonergan, "*Insight*: Preface to a Discussion," *Collection*, 142–52 at 150.

the contents of our acts of understanding in symbols and metaphors or technical terms; we normally verify (i.e., check the warrants for and judge the truth or falsity of) guesses or hypotheses formulated in language. Prior to all these operations, moreover, we have difficulty even perceiving what we cannot name in language. Hence, the horizons of language and of consciousness are mutually entwined with each other, and it is a mistake to isolate either horizon. One can prescind from either horizon, where "prescind" means to treat one at a time while realizing that the two can and should be brought back into relation to each other.

Because generalized empirical method basically takes seriously the empirical character, the constructive character, the contingency, and the linguistic character so emphasized by postmetaphysical communicative, genealogical, and deconstructive "anti-foundationalism," it can ground an entirely non-reductionistic account of the methods of science, scholarship, philosophy, and theology.

Insight transposes Aquinas's gnoseology into a cognitional theory[57] "sufficiently refined to do justice to the problems caused by symbolic logic, by mathematics,[58] by the probable principles employed in the natural sciences,[59] and by the ontological argument for God's existence."[60] As he turned his attention to other dimensions of foundational methodology, he made explicit the isomorphism between Aquinas on understanding and judging and the basic procedures of modern empirical science.[61] Then he was able to use Piaget's conception of the stages of human cognitive development (in terms of differentiating operations and grouping operations) through an analogy with group theory[62] to replace the notion

---

57 For the following citation, see Lonergan, "*Insight*: Preface to a Discussion," *Collection*, 149–50.

58 See Bernard Lonergan, *Phenomenology and Logic: The Boston College Lectures in Mathematical Logic and Existentialism*, Collected Works of Bernard Lonergan 18, ed. Philip McShane (Toronto: University of Toronto Press, 2001), especially 3–166 on the foundations of mathematics.

59 Lonergan, *Insight*, 304–15.

60 Lonergan, *Insight*, 360–71.

61 See Bernard Lonergan, "Isomorphism of Thomist and Scientific Thought," *Collection*, 133–41.

62 "The principal characteristic of the group of operations is that every operation in the group is matched by an opposite operation and every combination of operations is matched by an opposite combination. Hence, inasmuch as operations are grouped, the operator can always return to his starting point and, when he can do so unhesitatingly, he has reached mastery at some level of development." See Bernard Lonergan, *Method in Theology* (New York: Herder & Herder, 1972), 27–8.

of *habitus* (e.g., Aristotle's conception of moral and dianoetic habits [*hexeis*]), which was not directly accessible to internal experience, but only metaphysically deduced. In its place he used the empirically verifiable notion of differentiations of consciousness. Thus, the general characterization of development as moving from global and compact expressions of worldviews or commonsense knowing to more differentiated and specialized accounts can be specified more exactly. The key differentiations Lonergan works out are commonsense, theoretical or systematic (as in the exact sciences of nature), scholarly (as in history or the humanities), interiority (as in intentionality analysis or generalized empirical method), and religiously or transcendently differentiated awareness. Lonergan did this to resolve apparently irreconcilable "chasms" among different universes of discourse (e.g., between symbolic and mythic realms and theoretical, explanatory language) that have troubled theology in different ways throughout its development.[63] Lonergan used the notion of differentiated consciousness to analyze the control of meaning,[64] and the stages of meaning,[65] which are relevant for understanding cultural or doctrinal pluralism.[66] He also found a methodological resolution for many of theology's contemporary problems caused by varieties of undifferentiated, or combinations of multiply differentiated, consciousness by recourse to his notion of the unity of differentiated consciousness.

From the perspective of Lonergan's own development between the completion of the writing of *Insight* in 1952 and the publication of *Method in Theology* in 1972, we see how much more difficult was the transposition of Lonergan's retrieval of Aquinas on *Grace and Freedom*[67]

---

63 These issues were traced and explicitly named in Lonergan's seminar courses at Rome's Gregorian University before the publication of *Method in Theology* in 1972: *De intellectu et methodo*, 1958–9, documented in typed notes of Francesco Rossi de Gasperis and P. Joseph Cahill and in some of Lonergan's own notes; *De systemate et historia*, 1959–60, documented in the handwritten notes of Francesco Rossi de Gasperis and in some of Lonergan's own notes; and *De methodo theologiae*, 1961–2, in which Piaget's ideas are applied for the first time.

64 "For if social and cultural changes are, at root, changes in the meanings that are grasped and accepted, changes in the control of meaning make up the great epochs in human history." Lonergan, "Dimensions of Meaning," *Collection*, 235.

65 See Lonergan, *Method in Theology*, 85–99.

66 See for example, Bernard Lonergan, *Doctrinal Pluralism* (Milwaukee, WI: Marquette University Press, 1971), and the chapters "Doctrines" and "Systematics" in *Method in Theology*, 295–333 and 335–53.

67 See Bernard Lonergan, *Grace and Freedom: Operative Grace in the Thought of St Thomas Aquinas*, Collected Works of Bernard Lonergan 1, ed. Frederick E. Crowe and Robert M. Doran (Toronto: University of Toronto Press, 2000).

than had been the task of transposing Aquinas's obnubilated gnose-ology in *Verbum*. Emblematic of the further complicatedness involved in this transposition is the completely new appropriation in himself of what he calls the transcendental notion of value, of the massive role of feelings as intentional responses to values, of the reversal of the scho-lastic dictum *nil amatum nisi prius cognitum*, and of the expansion of his understanding of the good:

> In *Insight* the good was the intelligent and the reasonable. In *Method* the good is a distinct notion. It is intended in questions for deliberation: Is this worthwhile? Is it truly or only apparently good? It is aspired to in the intentional response of feeling to values. It is known in judgments of value made by a virtuous or authentic person with a good conscience. It is brought about by deciding and living up to one's decisions. Just as intelligence sublates sense, just as reasonableness sublates intelligence, so deliberation sublates and thereby unifies knowing and feeling.[68]

The full impact of these changes from *Insight* can be seen in *Method*'s chapter on the Human Good,[69] in which the structure of the human good discussed in the former work is transformed by later break-throughs connected with the fourth level of conscious intentionality.

On the way to *Method*, Lonergan also combined the notion of medi-ation adapted from Henri Niel's discussion of Hegelian dialectic[70] together with insights from Piaget to distinguish the world of imme-diacy, in which objects are immediately present to our operations from the world mediated by meaning, in which we operate "in a compound manner; immediately with respect to image, word, symbol; mediately with respect to what is represented or signified in this fashion."[71] Once we learn our mother tongue, we operate for the most part in the world mediated by meaning and guided by value, which is constructed by our operations of understanding, judging, and evaluating. As Lonergan put it in an early formulation of his breakthrough to a notion of meaning far

---

68 See Lonergan, "*Insight* Revisited," *A Second Collection*, 263–78 at 277.

69 Lonergan, *Method in Theology*, 27–55.

70 See Henri Niel, *De la médiation dans la philosophie de Hegel* (Paris: Aubier, 1945); see, too, Lonergan's exposition of the notion of mediation in "The Mediation of Christ in Prayer," in *Philosophical and Theological Papers 1958–1964*, Collected Works of Bernard Lonergan 6, ed. Robert C. Croken, Frederick E. Crowe, and Robert M. Doran (Toronto: University of Toronto Press, 1996), 160–82, especially 160–76.

71 Lonergan, *Method in Theology*, 28.

more comprehensive than the simple relationship between a sign and that which it signifies:

> I have been meeting the objection that meaning is a merely secondary affair, that what counts is the reality that is meant and not the mere meaning that refers to it. My answer has been that the functions of meaning are larger than the objection envisages. I would not dispute that, for the child learning to talk, his little world of immediacy comes first, and that the words he uses are only an added grace. But as the child develops into a man, the world of immediacy shrinks into an inconspicuous and not too important corner of the real world, which is a world we know only through the mediation of meaning. Further, there is man's transformation of his environment, a transformation that is effected through the intentional acts that envisage ends, select means, secure collaborators, direct operations. Finally, besides the transformations of nature, there is man's transformation of man himself; and in this transformation the role of meaning is not merely directive but also constitutive.[72]

This notion of the constitutive function of meaning becomes absolutely central for Lonergan:

> For it is in the field where meaning is constitutive that man's freedom reaches its highest point. There too his responsibility is greatest. There there occurs the emergence of the existential subject, finding out for himself that he has to decide for himself what he is to make of himself. It is there that individuals become alienated from community, that communities split into factions, that cultures flower and decline, that historical causality exerts its sway.[73]

V. Lonergan, Benedict, and Habermas on the Secular/Religious Dialogue

For Benedict, faith without reason leads to fundamentalism, fanaticism, and terrorist violence, but faith that insists on reason is only strengthened thereby; Christian faith historically has also been a great supporter

---

72 Lonergan, "Dimensions of Meaning," *Collection*, 232–45 at 234–5; but for the
    expanded view see the chapter on meaning in *Method in Theology*, 57–99.
73 Lonergan, "Dimensions of Meaning," 235.

of reasonableness. Hence, his claim regarding Europe's apostasy is not just a plea for a return to Christian beliefs and praxis, but a warning about Europe's loss of traditional identity: "This is, in fact, an historical, cultural, and moral identity before being geographical, economic, or political; an identity constituted by a collection of universal values that Christianity has contributed to forging, thereby acquiring a role that is not only historical, but also foundational in relation to Europe."[74] Thus, Benedict, in accord with his universal values, had reflected on salutary and humane social, economic, and political perspectives for Europe and the West in his dialogue with Habermas on January 19, 2003.[75]

Habermas, in moving beyond his earlier Weberian stance on the role of religion in society,[76] demands in the secular/religious dialogue a hermeneutical self-reflection from the side of religious faith. He insists on the following stipulation: "Under the conditions of postmetaphysical thinking, whoever puts forth a truth claim must, nevertheless, translate experiences that have their home in religious discourse into the language of a scientific expert culture – and from this language, translate them back into praxis."[77]

---

74 According to Sandro Magister at his website, http://chiesa.espresso.repubblica.it/, "The pope formulated this diagnosis while receiving in the Vatican's Sala Clementina on March 24 [2007] the cardinals, bishops, and politicians who were taking part in a conference organized in Rome by the Commission of the Bishops' Conferences of the European Community, COMECE, dedicated to the theme of 'Values and perspectives for the Europe of tomorrow.'" The citation comes from Benedict XVI's address, "That the Church May Again Be 'Leaven for the World,'" quoted in English translation by Sandro Magister, "An 'Apostate' from Itself: The Lost Europe of Pope Benedict," http://chiesa.espresso.repubblica.it/articolo/129525?eng=y, March 28, 2007.

75 Jürgen Habermas and Joseph Kardinal Ratzinger, *Dialektik der Säkularisierung: Über Vernunft und Religion* (Freiburg: Herder, 2005)<; English translation: *The Dialectics of Secularization: On Reason and Religion*, trans. Brian McNeill (San Francisco: Ignatius Press, 2007).

76 See Habermas, "Transcendence from Within, Transcendence in this World," 226–50 at 237; *Religion and Rationality*, 79: "I would also submit that I subsumed rather too hastily the development of religion in modernity with Max Weber under the 'privatization of the powers of faith' and suggested too quickly an affirmative answer to the question as to 'whether then from religious truths, after the religious worldviews have collapsed, nothing more and nothing other than the secular principles of a universalist ethics of responsibility can be salvaged, and this means: can be accepted for good reasons on the basis of insight.'"

77 Habermas, "Transcendence from Within, Transcendence in this World," 234; *Religion and Rationality*, 76.

Now if existentialists helped Lonergan to understand the world not only mediated but also constituted by human acts of meaning, phenomenologists helped him to discover the fundamental notion of horizon, which enabled him to transpose the traditional theological idea of conversion into the terms of intentionality analysis. Conversion is not a change within a given horizon, but a change from one horizon to another horizon. Great obstacles to genuine dialogue are caused by differences in horizon. One of the great Catholic conversation partners with secular reason of the pre-Vatican II era was the learned American Jesuit, John Courtney Murray, an early architect of Vatican II's Decree on Religious Freedom.[78] He once explained rather humorously to one of his putative secular interlocutors, "Not only are our minds not meeting, they are not even clashing." More often than not, this is the situation of the dialogue between secular and religious reason today. In Lonergan's analysis the postmetaphysical terms of horizon and conversion are at the center of questions of dialectic and dialogue. These terms are clearly also indispensable for an adequate hermeneutical philosophy of dialectic and dialogue, and they raise issues less clearly expressed in terms of Habermas's stipulations for translating truth claims placed upon persons of faith. Here, perhaps, Lonergan offers a bridge between the approach of Benedict and that of Habermas.

Lonergan highlights these issues surrounding horizon and conversion in *Method*'s treatment of the theological functional specialty of dialectic, which handles the concrete, the dynamic, and the contradictory within human movements. His definition of dialectic in theology is relevant to the secular/religious dialogue: "a generalized apologetic, conducted in an ecumenical spirit, aiming ultimately at a comprehensive viewpoint, and proceeding toward that goal by acknowledging differences, seeking their grounds real and apparent, and eliminating superfluous oppositions."[79] Conflicts and oppositions are rooted in horizonal differences that may be complementary and genetic, or dialectical if the oppositions are contradictory.[80] Finally, dialectical contradictions ultimately depend on the presence or absence of three distinct kinds of conversion: intellectual, moral, and religious.

---

78 See John Courtney Murray, *We Hold These Truths: Reflections on the American Proposition* (New York: Sheed & Ward, 1960); *Religious Liberty: Catholic Struggles with Pluralism*, ed. J. Leon Hooper, SJ (Louisville, KY: Westminster/John Knox Press, 1993); *Bridging the Sacred and the Secular: Selected Writings by John Courtney Murray, SJ*, ed. J. Leon Hooper, SJ (Washington, DC: Georgetown University Press, 1994).

79 Lonergan, *Method in Theology*, 130.

80 Lonergan, *Method in Theology*, 236–7.

For Lonergan conversion is a "transformation of the subject and his world"; it is "existential, intensely personal, utterly intimate." As lived, conversion "affects all of a man's conscious and intentional operations. It directs his gaze, pervades his imagination, releases the symbols that penetrate to the depths of his psyche. It enriches his understanding, guides his judgments, reinforces his decisions."[81] Intellectual conversion adds to the personal appropriation of rational self-consciousness the decision to live in accord with all the implications of discovering that knowing is irreducible to "taking a look," of rejecting "objectivity" conceived as the perceptual overcoming of the putative subject-object split, and of denying that reality is identical with the "already-out-there-now." Intellectual conversion brings the realization that knowing is an enactment of the compound comprised by experience, understanding, and judgment, that objectivity is the achievement of authentically self-transcendent subjectivity, and that reality (or being) is the objective correlative of human acts of understanding and true judgment. Moral conversion shifts the criterion of one's decisions from satisfactions as interpreted via a reductive psychology of motivations to the criterion of true values implicitly interpreted through a philosophy of orientation. Religious conversion, finally, brings about a shift from oneself as the center of the universe to the real center, which Christians understand and affirm as the transcendent mystery of love and awe. True, religious, and perhaps moral conversions may be correlated with people's changing the stories in the light of which they live, and yet there is a dimension to both human horizon and all the kinds of conversion that is irreducible to its linguisticality. In any case, for Lonergan, religious conversion is not confined to Christians.[82]

Habermas has spoken of the limit situation that the praxis of autonomy must inevitably encounter:

Of course, effective socializing or pedagogical praxis, which under the aegis of an anticipated autonomy [*Mündigkeit*] seeks to provoke freedom in the other, must take into account the appearance of circumstances and spontaneous forces that it cannot at the same time control. And, with an orientation toward unconditional moral expectations, the subject increases the degree of his or her vulnerability. This then makes the subject especially dependent upon a considerate moral treatment from other persons. Yet, the risk of failure, indeed, of the annihilation of freedom precisely in

---

81 Lonergan, *Method in Theology*, 131.
82 Lonergan, *Method in Theology*, 241–3.

the processes that should promote and realize freedom, only attests to the constitution of our finite existence. I refer to the necessity, which Peirce emphasized again and again, of a self-relinquishing, transcending anticipation of an unlimited community of communication. This anticipation is simultaneously conceded to us and demanded of us.[83]

Isn't Habermas here translating into his own postmetaphysical terms what in Christian religious terms is, at least partially a question of salvation? However, to maintain his postmetaphysical standpoint, Habermas observes the ground-rules set by Kant's *Kritik der reinen Vernunft*:

> But, in the passage through the discursive universes of science and philosophy, not even the Peircean hope in a fallible theory of the development of being as a whole, including that of the *summum bonum*, will be able to be realized. Kant already had answered the question, "What may we hope for?" with a *postulate* of practical reason, not with a premodern certainty that could inspire us with *confidence*.[84]

And so he must offer this conviction: "I believe to have shown that in communicative action we have no choice but to presuppose the idea of an undistorted intersubjectivity ... as the formal characterization of the necessary anticipation for the forms, not able to be anticipated, of a worthwhile life."[85] This Peircean reformulation of Kantian practical reason vouchsafes a kind of heuristic hope:

> In communicative action, we orient ourselves toward validity claims that, practically, we can raise only in the context of *our* languages and of our forms of life, even if the convertibility [*Einlösbarkeit*] that we implicitly co-posit *points beyond* the provinciality of our respective historical standpoints. We are exposed to the movement of a transcendence from within, which is just as little at our disposal as the actuality of the spoken word turns us into masters of the structure of our language (or of the *Logos*).[86]

---

83 Habermas, "Transcendence from Within, Transcendence in this World," 237; *Religion and Rationality*, 79–80.

84 Habermas, "Transcendence from Within, Transcendence in this World," 239–40; *Religion and Rationality*, 82.

85 Habermas, "Transcendence from Within, Transcendence in this World," 240; *Religion and Rationality*, 82.

86 Habermas, "Transcendence from Within, Transcendence in this World," 237–8; *Religion and Rationality*, 80.

Kant's definition of the Enlightenment as the human race's attainment of *Mündigkeit* as a praxis "under the aegis of an anticipated autonomy" requires that human beings become responsible for themselves instead of obeying external authorities. Yet we can reinterpret *Mündigkeit* in terms of Lonergan's explication of the difference between human psychological operations that are merely conscious and spontaneous (including any actuation of a spiritual capacity, such as raising a question, or getting insights, or performing habitual acts) from those that are conscious and autonomous.[87] Then autonomy – etymologically: giving oneself the law – is grounded in the specifically spiritual causality of what Aquinas called intelligible emanation[88] that explains the movement (1) from insight to formulation of possibly relevant intelligibility whenever it is due to one's understanding (e.g., the contrast between a memorized answer and one uttered on the basis of understanding),

---

87 See Lonergan, *The Triune God: Systematics*, 179–81.

88 See Lonergan, *Verbum*, 46–7: "All causation is intelligible, but there are three differences between natural process and the processions of an inner word. The intelligibility of natural process is passive and potential: it is what can be understood; it is not an understanding; it is a potential object of intellect, but it is not the very stuff of intellect. Again, the intelligibility of natural process is the intelligibility of some specific natural law, say, the law of inverse squares, but never the intelligibility of the very idea of intelligible law. Thirdly, the intelligibility of natural process is imposed from without: natures act intelligibly, not because they are intelligent, for they are not, but because they are concretions of divine ideas and a divine plan. On the other hand, the intelligibility of an inner word is not passive and potential; it is active and actual; it is intelligibility because it is the activity of intelligence in act; it is intelligible, not as the possible object of understanding is intelligible, but as understanding itself and the activity of understanding is intelligible. Again, its intelligibility defies formulation in any specific law; inner words proceed according to the principles of identity, noncontradiction, excluded middle, and sufficient reason; but these principles are not specific laws but the essential conditions of there being objects to be related by laws and relations to relate them. Thus the procession of an inner word is the pure case of intelligible law: one may say that such procession is a case of 'omne agens agit sibi simile'; but one has only to recall that this agent may be similar to anything, that it is 'potens omnia fieri,' to see that really one has here not a particular case but the resume of all particular cases. Thirdly, it is native and natural for the procession of inner word to be intelligible, actively intelligible, and the genus of all intelligible process; … intelligible procession [is native and natural] to intelligence in act; for intelligence in act does not follow laws imposed from without, but rather it is the ground of the intelligibility in act of law, it is constitutive and, as it were, creative of law; and the laws of intelligible procession of an inner word are not any particular laws but the general constituents of any law, precisely because of this naturalness of intelligibility to intelligence, precisely because intelligence is to any conceived law as cause to effect."

(2) from the mind's grasp of the sufficiency of evidence to judgment (affirmation or denial that some possibly relevant intelligibility is actually relevant) because of one's understanding of the virtually unconditioned (i.e., what is absent in a rash or precipitous or silly judgment), and (3) from authentic apprehension of values to value judgments occurring with an easy conscience (that is absent when the person has an "uneasy" or guilty conscience). Intelligible emanations also ground the movement from judgments of true values to authentic decisions in the desire to make our actions consistent with our knowledge of values. This reinterpretation of *Mündigkeit* not only specifies the meaning of autonomy more precisely than did Kant's, but it also brings Lonergan's account of reason and of the role of reason in deciding and acting into accord with Benedict's as worked out in his essay on "Conscience and Truth."[89] Lonergan's account of autonomy is advanced in his account of genuineness in *Insight*.[90] From a philosophical viewpoint, Lonergan (unlike Benedict) carefully distinguishes what can be affirmed in terms of proportionate being as intrinsically or extrinsically conditioned by space and time from issues that can only be coherently raised and solved once one takes care of the question of the general transcendence proper to an infinite act of understanding or God. Still, the thrust of *Insight*'s project is the unfolding of the pure, unrestricted, and disinterested desire to know as an immanent source of transcendence, which we experience and do not simply posit or presuppose, as in fact both Kant and Habermas do. Furthermore, it seems that they confine themselves to the realm of immanence at the cost of obscurantism. Benedict reaches roughly the same conclusion as Lonergan in his theological discussion of the anamnetic and judicial aspects of conscience's ability to know good and evil, due to an inbuilt light rather than a law imposed from without, relying on the authority of St Basil of Cappadocia.

This agreement between Lonergan and Benedict is, of course, based on a shared Christian horizon and on their shared Christian religious conversion. Perhaps this is why they are less sanguine than Habermas that human beings can overcome by human means alone the disabling

---

89 See Joseph Cardinal Ratzinger, "Conscience and Truth," presented at the Tenth Workshop for Bishops, February 1991 in Dallas, TX (Sponsored by the Pope John XXIII Medical-Moral Research and Education Center and through the generosity of the Knights of Columbus), 13 pp.
90 Lonergan, *Insight*, 499–503, 646, 647.

of freedom by sin and evil. It is important to note that because of his interpretation of the universalist Catholic doctrine that "God wills that all humankind be saved," so that the gift of God's love is offered to everyone on account of Jesus Christ, Lonergan does not restrict religious conversion to Christians. We can wonder then whether the presence of such an incognito gift might explain Hans Jonas's insight that, once one takes into account Kant's teaching on basic evil in *Die Religion innerhalb der Grenzen der bloßen Vernunft* together with his notion of the will's autonomy, one realizes that human freedom is dialectically equiprimordial with moral renunciation and insufficiency.[91] As far as I know, Habermas does not seem to have meditated on this aspect of Kant very clearly. Even so, I think that something akin to this sensitivity has motivated Habermas's *Philosophical Discourse of Modernity*, where he argues vigorously against radical transformations of Kant's ideas of morality and dignity in the wake of Nietzsche, who first deconstructed the enlightenment project of emancipation to come to terms with his disappointment with the historical failure of modernity evident in *Zarathustra*'s "last man."[92]

If we can describe the goal of political good of order as institutions that enable "peaceful activity in accord with the dignity of man,"[93] instead of organized collective selfishness or the institutional protection of the manipulation, suppression, and exploitation of each by all, it seems that one would have to go beyond Habermas's admission of "the weakness of the motivational power of good reasons" along with the attestation "that rational motivation by reason is more than nothing" (*auch nicht nichts ist*) or that "moral convictions do not allow themselves

---

91 See Hans Jonas, "The Abyss of the Will: Philosophical Meditation on the Seventh Chapter of Paul's Epistle to the Romans," *Philosophical Essays: From Ancient Creed to Technological Man* (Chicago: University of Chicago, Midway Reprint, 1974) on I. Kant, *Religion Within the Limits of Reason*, trans. and ed. Allen Wood with George di Giovanni (Cambridge: University of Cambridge Press, 1998), where "radical evil" is characterized as being rooted in the freedom of moral choice. See 54: "a propensity to evil can only attach itself to the moral faculty of choice [*Willkur*]"; 53–4: "the propensity for evil affects the use of freedom, the capacity for acting out duty – in short, the capacity for actually being autonomous."

92 Jürgen Habermas, *The Philosophical Discourse of Modernity: Twelve Lectures*, trans. Frederick G. Lawrence (Cambridge, MA: MIT Press, 1987).

93 This phrase is Leo Strauss's from *Natural Right and History* (Chicago: University of Chicago, 1952), 147.

to be overridden without resistance."[94] For both Benedict and Lonergan, this political order can only be realized if the individual choosers are habitually willing to align particular goods and concrete goods of order with the good of the universe; and they are more likely to do this if they believe that the goods of order within which they live participate in a transcendent order, a transcendent good. As Lonergan loved to quote Aquinas, "the purpose of the universe is a good existing in it, namely, the order of the universe itself";[95] and "the universe as a whole is a more perfect participation in and reflection of the divine goodness than any individual creature."[96]

94 Habermas, "Transcendence from Within, Transcendence in this World," 239; *Religion and Rationality*, 81.
95 Thomas Aquinas, *Summa theologiae*, I, q. 47, art. 3, *corpus*.
96 Thomas Aquinas, *Summa theologiae*, I, q. 103, art. 2, *ad* 3.

PART TWO

Theology and the Human Good

7 The Fragility of Consciousness: Lonergan and the Postmodern Concern for the Other

1. Introduction: What Is Postmodernism?

The term "postmodernist" was first coined in the 1930s to describe minor reactions to modernism in the arts. Its use expanded in the 1950s and 1960s to cover ever wider phenomena in the arts, especially certain types of eclecticism in architecture. Eventually it became a cover-all for artistic trends that tended to break down the boundaries between art and everyday life, between high and low or popular cultures; to promote a certain promiscuity in styles and codes, mixing parody, pastiche, irony, and playfulness and insisting on the absence of depth and the paradoxical importance of superficiality. This is the *reductio ad absurdum* of Romantic expressivism that ends by debunking the putative originality and genius of the artistic producer, suggesting that ultimately art may be no more than repetition.

In philosophy and theology, postmodernism embraces a wide range of "second thoughts" about Enlightenment and Romantic versions of modernity in the guise of the classic forms of hermeneutics of suspicion. Marx used political economy to debunk the bourgeois subject, and Freud used psychology. But the central figure of postmodernism is Nietzsche, who used philology to radically critique the Enlightenments in fourth-century Athens and in 17th- and 18th-century Europe as culminating in the "Last Man" of the late 19th and 20th century. In calling into question not just Enlightenment rationalism but the Romantic reaction to that rationalism ushered in by Rousseau, postmodern hermeneutics of suspicion eschews both the Enlightenment myth of progress and any form of Romantic nostalgia for a pristine past beyond restoration in present or future as well.

In Western culture this double-barreled reaction is overwhelmingly evident in the arts. It plays a role in the music of Wagner, Stravinsky, Schoenberg, and Berg; in the paintings of the Impressionists, the Post-Impressionists, the Fauvists, the Cubists, the Futurists, the Dadaists, the Surrealists, and so on; in the poetics of Mallarme, Rimbaud, and Baudelaire in France; of Kafka, Kraus, Musil, and Mann in Central Europe; of Chekhov and Dostoyevsky in Russia; and of Pound, Eliot, Joyce, Stein, Woolf, and Faulkner in literature in English.

Quite naturally, then, since Christian theology mediates between Christian communities of witness and worship and the cultures in which they exist, it has to come to terms with postmodernism precisely in the measure that postmodernism has been affecting our culture. And theologians have in fact been doing so, whether intentionally or not. In the Roman Catholic context, it is perhaps not too far-fetched to say that what the church feared in its great and fierce polemic against "modernism" was just postmodernism in its relativistic and nihilistic manifestations. This quite understandable fear continues to dominate today's skirmishes against postmodernism where it is written off as merely relativistic and nihilistic. The dangers of these trends are rampantly evident and unquestionable. Yet the understandable reaction of wholesale rejection may itself be unwise, because it is too undialectical. If postmodernists are simply wrong in their relativist and nihilist conclusions, this does not mean that they are not raising real questions about issues that need to be engaged – issues that are not engaged by the strategy of wholesale rejection of postmodernist conclusions.

But doesn't postmodernism need to be taken seriously by Christian theologians? Don't we have to grasp what is correct about the things it dismisses and what are the aspects of reality it attempts to embrace, even if mistakenly? Don't we have to find a basis upon which postmodern concerns can be addressed without adopting postmodernism's destructive conclusions? This article gives an affirmative answer to these questions. Rather unexpectedly perhaps, it offers features of Bernard Lonergan's thought as a way of doing so. I have found him to be a Christian and Catholic thinker who actually shares many of the deepest concerns of postmodernism; but he does so in a way that takes relativity seriously without being relativistic – and that takes the absurdity and apparently random and chaotic dimensions of our world experience fully seriously without capitulating to nihilism in any form.

Since this essay of necessity is exceedingly long, readers deserve an overview of its parts. In Part 2, I examine the context and chief features of postmodernism in philosophy and theology, to see whether Lonergan's approach really does meet postmodernist concerns without yielding to postmodernist mistakes. In Part 3, I survey the postmodernist critique of the modern turn to the subject, with sections on (3.1) postmodernism in the philosophy of Nietzsche and Heidegger, (3.2) hermeneutic phenomenology's postmodern correction of modern counterpositions, which includes discussions of (3.21) the critique of sheer immediacy and (3.22) human experience as mediated, and (3.3) historicity of human experience.

Part 4 treats Lonergan's postmodern thematization of consciousness as experience, with sections on (4.1) the being of consciousness, (4.2) Lonergan on the passionateness of being and human consciousness, which includes discussions of (4.21) decentering of the subject within vertical finality and (4.22) consciousness as conditioned by the passionateness of being. Part 5 delineates deconstructive/genealogical postmodernism's concern for otherness in sections about (5.1) Derrida and (5.2) Foucault, followed by (5.3) a summary of Part 5.

Part 6 looks at Lonergan and contingency through a series of sections dealing with (6.1) contingency and the virtually unconditioned, (6.2) contingency and the non-systematic, (6.3) contingency and understanding, (6.4) contingency and language, (6.5) contingency and interpretation, (6.6) contingent predication, and (6.7) contingency and liberty. Part 7 considers Lonergan and the postmodernist sublime, with sections examining (7.1) the sublime and the ambiguity of the surd, (7.2) Lyotard and the sublime, and (7.3) moving from the sublime to worship. Part 8, then, is the conclusion.

2. From Premodern to Modern Philosophy

Philosophy originated with the question about the right way to live. But to answer this question satisfactorily philosophers broke into the world of theory to discover a standard that was not just a matter of convention or *nomos*. Socratic or Platonic philosophy's heuristic name for this transconventional and hence transcultural standard was nature or *physis*. But to know any part of nature led eventually to wondering whether the whole of reality is ultimately intelligible, and so in the premodern West the question about the whole came to be traditionally asked and answered in the form of a philosophy of being.

The moral and scientific reorientation that occurred in the West in the wake of Machiavelli, Galileo, and Newton during the 16th and 17th centuries spelled the end of the philosophy of being (or of the ontology of metaphysics as it had come to be called) as the first task of philosophy.

When philosophy existed under Islamic, Jewish, and Christian auspices the question about the right way to live had been more or less taken for granted and rather isolated from the question about being as pursued in the Schools. Due to the Machiavellian revolution, that eminently practical question began to be asked and answered in a new way, in that all the premodern answers of the Great Tradition were considered to fall outside the scope of "effectual truth," and so both they and the questions that gave rise to them were relegated to the strictly private sphere of existence.

Due to the scientific revolution, the question about being as the first issue in philosophy had to yield to the question about knowing, the epistemological question. Modern physics in the style of Galileo and Newton not only did not depend for its intelligibility upon one's first understanding and agreeing about prior metaphysical terms and relations; but such physics also generated a consensus in the university faculties of natural philosophy that stood out in stark and scandalous contrast to the array of disputed questions that dominated the diverse schools of philosophy of being. The endlessly disputed questions in metaphysics with no commonly agreed upon basis for their eventual resolution naturally raised the question about the cognitive status of the scholastic theses about being *qua* being; and this in turn raised the criteriological question of how we know we know being at all.

But the writers of the great early modern philosophic propagandists for the illuminating and progressive promise of the new science – Bacon, Descartes, Hobbes, Locke, Hume, the philosophes, and Kant – were Machiavellians. In their opposition to religion or Christianity as what Hobbes called "the kingdom of darkness," they associated, or better perhaps, coopted the scientific revolution not only into the project of opposing both the *idola* (Bacon) and the "vain imaginings" (Hobbes) of religious dogmas and the verbalisms of scholastic philosophy; but they also manufactured positivist, empiricist, and rationalist cover stories for the normative achievements of the new science. By means of these cover stories, a scientific myth of rigor and proof was subordinated to purposes of technical prediction and control, so that modern science was recruited into the modern project: science "in the relief of man's estate" (Bacon) and science as the instrument for making human beings "the masters and possessors of nature" (Descartes). Henceforth, technical, productive ends were to supersede the properly theoretic goal of contemplating the truth for its own sake.

2.1 Two Phases in the Modern Turn to the Subject as Object

2.11 Early Modern Enlightenment's Truncation of the Subject

2.111 The Primacy of the Epistemological Question

Already in the late scholastic period the scientific goal of true or even convenient (in the technical sense of Aquinas's *rationes convenientiae*) understanding had been replaced within a conceptualist or nominalist horizon by a concern for certainty both in theology and in philosophy. Such an overweening concern for certitude coupled with neglect of understanding led inevitably to skepticism. But when such skepticism got joined to an orientation that screens out all but what a Machiavelli would admit as effectual truth, we have the ingredients for a quest in which the search for certitude could be generalized into a search for "sure and firm foundations" in the manner of Descartes. This then is the context for the modern "turn to the subject." In the Cartesian preoccupation with certainty, however, this turn actually attained only the subject as object. But why?

To understand the modern turn to the subject, we must grasp what is most crucially distinctive about modern in contrast to premodern reflection on human being. It is not that premodern philosophers had not distinguished clearly the human from all other species of being, for they were admirable in the way they specified the qualities proper to vegetative, animal, and human substances. When, for instance, Aristotle in *On the Soul* discriminates the human soul from that of other animals, the clear and precise determination is made in terms of examples related to the specific kinds of efficient causality undergone by the different kinds of souls and to the various sorts of final causality energizing them. But in making the relevant distinctions plain in terms of efficient and final causality, Aristotle does not speak about consciousness in its dynamisms and structures explicitly. Why not? Because premodern psychology is a subset of a philosophy of being, and in that framework it was sufficient for different ranges of objects to be correlated through their respective acts with types of potencies and souls. The different types of correlative qualities are accidents inhering in corresponding kinds of substances.

In contrast, the modern turn to the subject reflects upon human being from the standpoint not of substance, but of consciousness. When John Locke inveighs against the Aristotelian doctrine of faculties or "powers," he is making the point that we do not have direct experience of faculties; and it is true that the ancients were content to deduce the presence of the faculty from observations made about the relationships between objects and the intentional acts by which they are "known" sensitively or intellectually. If we prescind from Locke's nominalism, it becomes clear that Locke is interested not in the metaphysical paraphernalia of substantial forms or souls with their relevant faculties or accidents, but in consciousness and what we can be conscious of.

Now it is one thing to require advertence to consciousness and its objects; but it is quite another to understand and conceive of them correctly. In what follows, I argue that modern thinkers tended to misconceive consciousness, which is the range of awareness, with a type of operation that, while it is conscious, is not synonymous with consciousness as a whole, but only a part of its structure and operation: perception. By perception, I mean the act of explicit awareness, or of express advertence to ... whatever it may be. Consciousness, however, as an internal self-presence (or awareness) has to itself not only a dimension of explicit, foreground awareness, but a tacit or background dimension – namely, the most radical presence of ourselves to ourselves – that can never be made explicit exhaustively.

2.112 Consciousness as Perception

As exemplified by the *cogito*, the Cartesian variant of the modern turn to the subject conceived of consciousness itself as a perception. And this usage became fateful for modern parlance inasmuch as we are liable to say today that we are conscious of something if we perceive it expressly. Accordingly, when someone says they did something – say, started to exceed the speed limit while driving – "unconsciously," they do not mean that they were mysteriously knocked out cold as they were driving down the highway, but that they did not explicitly perceive or advert to the fact that they were driving above the speed limit. So Descartes doubles back upon himself and perceives that he is doubting/ thinking so as to be able to infer that he must exist if he is doubting/ thinking; but this doubling back is thought to be an inner perception on the part of the *res cogitans*. Just as through our external senses we perceive external objects, so too through inward perception we become aware of the subject as the primary object of our egos. By definition, consciousness as perception objectifies what it is aware of.

For Descartes, therefore, inner perception is conceived by analogy with taking a look with our eyes at something outside ourselves, and so consciousness is held – quite inconsistently, however – to be a faculty of inward perception. This Cartesian model of consciousness is pretty much shared by Hobbes, Locke, Hume, and modernity in general.

But while Kant shares it too, he does not completely agree with it. He wishes to use the perception-model much more strictly and consistently than his predecessors. According to Kant, in order for anything to be an object of knowledge at all, it must first be an object of sense perception. Since there can be no sense perception of consciousness and its acts, they cannot be known in the strict sense of objective knowledge, but only deduced, or better, postulated as conditions of the possibility of the cognitional activity. So it is odd that Kant ultimately also maintains the model of consciousness as perception even though he denies that we are vouchsafed any objective knowledge of it.

2.113 From Soul to Truncated Self

In the context of the modern project, the premodern notion of the soul as the form of the living body, endowing it with natural and inevitable inclinations that point beyond the person toward a hierarchy of ends or goods, is simply eliminated. In its place is installed the subject as object, which is imagined to be a unitary ego capable of deploying disengaged reason's rigor and proof as a means of carrying out the project of mastery and control of human and subhuman nature.

This truncated model of the self is dominated by the crucial and highly questionable idea of consciousness conceived of as an internal, reflexive perception that leads ineluctably to the modern image of the subject as primary object, whether in the form of Descartes' disengaged reason, or of Locke's punctual individual subject. In any case, reason becomes simply a calculating faculty in the service of the passions, but especially of the lower desires for self-preservation and material prosperity. Thus, if the modern subject is not the scared subject operating in fear of violent death, as in Hobbes, it is the Lockean bourgeois subject, laboring to turn nature into his or her property to be exchanged and accumulated to the greatest degree possible. The modern self on this model is nothing if not commercial and so is dedicated to utilitarian individualism, to use a term brought into vogue by the authors of *The Habits of the Heart*.[1]

This modern bourgeois subject is also truncated in still further senses: First, it is an individual, an atomic entity, related to nothing and no one

---

1 See R.N. Bellah, R. Madsen, W. Sullivan, A. Swidler, and S.Tipton, *Habits of the Heart: Individualism and Commitment in American Life* (Berkeley, CA: University of California Press, 1985).

except by voluntary choice or contract. Second, the bourgeois subject is sealed off from the sphere of the supernatural, which characteristically comes to be called "supranatural," suggesting the image of some superfluously juxtaposed upper storey of creation. Thus the bourgeois subject becomes the self-made man or woman who worships his or her maker.

2.12 Modern Romanticism's Immanentization of the Subject

2.121 Romantic Critique of the Bourgeois Subject

The life of the bourgeois individual is incredibly flat. The moderation Montesquieu believed to go hand-in-hand with the spirit of commerce does quell fanaticism and channel enthusiasm, but at the cost of the spirit's deepest longings. This was the message of Rousseau's great critique of the bourgeois, the first great assessment of the damaged existence of people socialized into believing in Hobbes's tenet that a person's worth is identical with his or her price. People in bourgeois society have lost their healthy, spontaneous self-love, which is gentle and compassionate, and exchanged it for self-esteem, which is a feeling derived from others, and so a dependent, reactive emotion. As a result we are radically alienated from ourselves, in that what would have been our own spontaneous and natural feelings now are never innocent but instead always spoiled, having been generated by a competitive and jealous regard for the opinion of others.

2.122 Consciousness as Perception-Feeling

Rousseau therefore replaces the truncated subject whose consciousness is conceived as inward, reflexive perception on the model of sense perception with the immanentist subject, whose consciousness is also perception-like, except that the privileged model now is not the look but the feeling, in contrast to the operations of disengaged observation or reasoning. The Cartesian subject perceives itself as an already-in-here-object that perceives objects already-out-there-now. But the Rousseauian and Romantic subject not only feels, but feels its feelings, which is what is meant by "sentiment." For Rousseau and the Romantics, the truncated bourgeois subject is busy about objects all the time and so is shallow, distracted from his or her own depths. The Romantic subject is deep, because it likes to feel its own feelings, which are inexhaustibly deep. These feelings are the voice of conscience, the *élan* of nature as surfacing within the self and perhaps holding the key to external nature, whose secrets are withheld from the prying gaze of the manipulative bourgeois subjects living supposedly "full and productive lives."

2.123 Romantic Expressivism

The inner feelings of the Romantic subject are so deep that they can only be discovered by expressing them through *imagination*. If for the likes of Descartes, Hobbes, and Spinoza imagination always has a negative valence, the valence is altogether reversed in the context of the Romantic expressivist's need to formulate feelings in symbols, myths, works of art, and religious rituals. Imaginative expression has the twofold function of articulating the depths of feeling and of shaping those depths: Through the imagination, we endlessly explore the depths of feeling at the same time as we constitute the quality of the feelings we encounter in those depths.

From this perspective, the difference between morality and aesthetics dissolves in favor of the latter. The view of art as mimesis is eclipsed, too. *Creativity and originality* become the passwords. Both art and morality are seen to be a matter of sheer self-expression in which the key is to see if each one can express originally the unique depths of his or her own particular self, as is evident in Schiller's *Letters on the Aesthetic Education of Man*. The expressivist idea of self-formation in an aesthetics of production gets transmitted further by the Romantics, Schelling, Hegel, and Marx. Again, the moments of creativity and originality become central to the ideal of the well-rounded self-realizing individual in the philosophies of Herder, von Humboldt, and John Stuart Mill that have exercised such a great influence upon German, English, and American educational systems.

In contrast to the bourgeois ideal of the autonomous, self-determining individual who realizes him- or herself ideally as a bourgeois entrepreneur, producer, and consumer, Romantic subjectivism idealizes the untrammelled self of the Romantic subject who realizes him- or herself by *The Habits of the Heart*'s expressive individualism.

3. Postmodern Critique of the Modern Turn to the Subject

3.1 Postmodernism in Philosophy: Nietzsche and Heidegger

In philosophy – and more belatedly in theology – the central figure is now acknowledged to be Nietzsche because of his audacious and provocative sounding of what Voegelin has analyzed as "the magic of the extreme."[2] He thus became paradigmatic for the crisis of modernity

---

2 See E. Voegelin, *Published Essays: 1966–1985*, The Collected Works of Eric Voegelin 12, ed. E. Sandoz (Baton Rouge: Louisiana State University Press, 1990), 315–75.

in the sense of making manifest and partially generating a peculiarly postmodern maelstrom of thought and feeling, thus initiating the third wave of modernity (to adopt Leo Strauss's phrase).[3]

Nietzsche first became well known as a thinker not because he was thought to be a great philosopher, but because he was in some fashion an inspirer of Hitler's National Socialism. Respect for Nietzsche as a philosopher grew once Heidegger confronted Nietzsche's thought for a 10-year period during the 1930s and early 1940s, at a time when the most grotesque regime of world history was mounting its technologically based bid for world dominion. Heidegger interpreted Nietzsche's attempt artistically or artificially to overcome nihilism and *ressentiment* in terms of the unified conception of the will to power and the eternal return of the same as the end of metaphysics.[4] In his (to Heidegger's mind) failed attempts to overcome the specifically modern results of Platonism, Nietzsche was still a model for his own quest to get over the forgetfulness of being. Heidegger learned from Nietzsche that the kinds of phenomenology, hermeneutics, and transcendental philosophy still ingredient in such a work as *Being and Time* (1927/1962) were still too deeply infected by modern assumptions of Cartesian and Kantian "subjective objectivism."[5] And so Heidegger underwent the *Kehre* or "turning."

We might say then that although Nietzsche is the turning point into postmodernism in philosophy, Heidegger has been the catalyst of the transition to postmodernity in the 20th century. Heidegger not only exerted enormous influence, but the gradual working out of his philosophy also involved negotiating several crucial issues at stake in postmodernity. On the one hand, he came out of a Christian, Roman Catholic milieu, so that even if he eventually became a non-believer and an atheist, he never stopped being religious and was constantly preoccupied with mystery. On the other hand, his task was to overcome three quite significant forms of modern philosophy in which he had been trained: conceptualist-Suarezian Scholasticism, neo-Kantianism in both its Marburg and Southwest German versions, and

---

3 Leo Strauss, *Political Philosophy: Six Essays by Leo Strauss*, ed. H. Gildin (Indianapolis, IN: Bobbs-Merrill, 1975), 81–98.

4 See Martin Heidegger, *Nietzsche*, 4 vols., trans. D.F. Krell, J. Stambaugh, and F.A. Capuzzi (New York: Harper & Row, 1987).

5 Martin Heidegger, *Being and Time*, trans. J. Macquarrie and E. Robinson (New York: Harper & Row, 1962).

Husserlian phenomenology of perception with its Cartesian and Kantian assumptions.

Before his 10-year long encounter with Nietzsche, Kierkegaard's existentialism influenced Heidegger as much as Nietzsche, alongside the interaction between Husserl's transcendental phenomenology and Dilthey's attempts to uncover the epistemological grounding for the historical and hermeneutical sciences. In spite of his portrait of Nietzsche as the "last metaphysician," Heidegger seems to have learned from him in the late 1930s and early 1940s the utter futility of grounding human horizons in any way that is not rooted in freedom as arbitrary. By this insight, Heidegger paved the way for later postmodern interpreters of Nietzsche – notably Derrida and Foucault – to discern in a way not thematized by Heidegger himself how dominant already were the respective "moves" of deconstructivism and genealogy in the fragmentary and aphoristic styles of Nietzsche's philosophizing.

The effective history of Heidegger's thought marks a divide within postmodern thought: The reception of Heidegger by Gadamer's hermeneutic phenomenology occurs under the sign of Dilthey and Kierkegaard; and the deconstructive-genealogical alternative to this reception on the part of Derrida, Foucault, Lyotard, Deleuze, and the like operates much more under the sign of Nietzsche.[6]

In reacting to the truncated, immanentist, and alienated opinions, institutions, and personalities that dominate the culture of our advanced-industrial bourgeois age, both the deconstructive-genealogical approach and the universal hermeneutic approach share the common trait of working with texts in ways that tend to favor a hermeneutics of suspicion, on the one hand, and a hermeneutics of retrieval, on the other.

3.2 Hermeneutic Phenomenology's Postmodern Correction of Modern Counterpositions

3.21 Critique of Sheer Immediacy

The truncation and immanentism of the modern problematic of the subject (as centered on the model of pure sense perception or of perception as feeling) involve several assumptions about the human subject that

---

6 See D.P. Michelfelder and R.E. Palmer, ed., *Dialogue and Deconstruction: The Gadamer-Derrida Encounter* (Albany: SUNY Press, 1989).

all the postmodern philosophers found to be untenable in the light of experience as it is concretely accessible to us.

First, the following Enlightenment (i.e., Cartesian or Kantian) presuppositions were called into question: (1) the primacy of the so-called subject/object split; (2) the putative objectivity to be attained through bridging this split by means of pure perception alone; (3) the very fact of pure perception as isolated from any mediations whatsoever; (4) the object as "already-out-there-now"; (5) the subject as the privileged "already-in-here-now" object; (6) the primacy of time as a raceway of instants (i.e., of physical or perhaps Laplacean time as opposed to psychological time) and a correlative image of the present as a punctual, isolatable, yet spatialized instant. For example, Heidegger – a veritable fountainhead of postmodern thought – called into question all these assumptions in terms of the horizon of *Vorhandenheit*. Or again, together they pretty much encapsulate what Derrida has critically labeled phono-/logo-/phallo-centrism. These assumptions and their ramifications in the construction of our world are to be dismantled or deconstructed in the interests of a certain ethical integrity.

As is clear from Husserl's famous exploration of the *Lebenswelt*, Scheler's phenomenological research, the gestalt psychologists Koehler, Strauss, Wertheimer, et al., and American pragmatists like Royce and Peirce, pure perception by the senses is a limit-phenomenon almost never verifiable in human experience once the human subject learns its mother tongue. In the same vein, Heidegger's thematization of the fact that the human phenomenon of perception – even sense perception – is mediated by language, brought about the transition from the phenomenology of perception to hermeneutic phenomenology.

As a language-animal, the human being exists only rarely in the world of immediacy. Instead, human beings inhabit worlds mediated by meaning and value. That is, concretely, we experience our world as worded: Our world is always foregrounded for us through interpretations. As a result, in almost all human lived experience, our self-understanding is mediated by the self-understandings of others. In this manner we participate in something moving in and through us that, however conscious of it we may be, can never be adequately explicitated, thematized, and explained. Hence, from the standpoint of linguistic (or hermeneutic) philosophy, to bè human is to share in a conversation that constitutes the human race as a whole. This conversation that we are (Hölderlin's *das Gespräch wir sind*) is irreducible to the perspective or the explicit knowledge of any single human person.

3.22 Human Experience as Mediated

In *Truth and Method* Gadamer speaks strangely of "an experience that ...[is] being."[7] The remote context of this expression is Kierkegaard's critique of the aesthetic stage of existence and Husserl's critique of any form of psychologism. Both of these play a role in Gadamer's own critique of the central concept of Dilthey's Romantic hermeneutics – *Erlebnis*. (Note that English uses the one term "experience" to render the two German words *Erlebnis* and *Erfahrung*.) Aesthetic existence for Kierkegaard, psychologism, and the theories of *Erlebnis* are rooted in what I have been calling Romantic expressionism: a model of existence in pure immediacy epitomized by the idea of pure perception, but enacted as a feeling supposedly removed from what Gadamer calls "the hermeneutic continuity of human existence," "that continuity of self-understanding that alone can support human existence."[8]

Consequently, Gadamer's phrase "experience as being" does not mean the subjectivization of being. Gadamer uses the German word *Erfahrung* to distinguish it from the Romantic term *Erlebnis*, which always implies a punctual discontinuity of experiences. In contrast, "experience (*Erfahrung*) as being" refers to "an encounter with an unfinished event and is itself a part of this event."[9] It has to do with self-understanding as "occur[ring] through understanding something other than the self, and includ[ing] the unity and integrity of the other."[10] "Experience as being" happens whenever we understand ourselves in and through something other than ourselves, and in doing so we "sublate the discontinuity and atomism of isolated experiences in the continuity of our own existence."[11]

For Gadamer then, "experience as being" occurs as mediation – of past and present, of self and other, of whole and part. It is enacted as *Verstehen*, as interpretation, as question and answer, as decision and self-correction. In all its compactness and undifferentiatedness, it is never merely a matter of the pure perception or feeling of internal immediacy (the "already-in-here-now" of the self) or of external immediacy (the "already-out-there-now" of objects).

7　Hans-Georg Gadamer, *Truth and Method*, 2nd ed., trans. J. Weinsheimer and D.G. Marshall (New York: Crossroad, 1990), 100.

8　Gadamer, *Truth and Method*, 96.

9　Gadamer, *Truth and Method*, 99.

10　Gadamer, *Truth and Method*, 97.

11　Gadamer, *Truth and Method*, 97.

3.3 Historicity of Human Experience

When Gadamer elaborates the structure of experience, he appeals critically to Bacon to bring out that human experience in general does have an internal reference to the negative: It wants to be confirmed and is, unless it encounters a contradictory instance. But essential to experience as human is precisely this openness for the negative, the new, the surprising.

Gadamer goes on to explicate human experience by setting it in the context of Aristotle's account of inference (*epagoge*), with its marvelous metaphor of the stand by an army in rout. Here he wants to stress a universality of experience in contrast to the universality of science or *logos*, an insight into what is common among diverse experiences but one that, while it becomes the basis of scientific generalization, is itself not yet capable of such reflexive control of meaning.

Then Gadamer invokes Hegel's dialectical account of human experience to bring out that, as a mediation of self-understanding with what is other, experience involves a reversal: In the moment of having one's anticipation of meaning or intelligibility corrected by a new experience, one finds that the elimination of past misunderstanding is actually a deepening or validation of what one thought one had already appreciated before. Yet for Gadamer, Hegel, thinking that "conscious experience should lead to a self knowledge that no longer has anything other than or alien to itself," failed to follow through on his own insight.[12] He opted for the epitome of Cartesianly disengaged reason – absolute self-consciousness – rather than for what Gadamer names the hermeneutic consciousness that is actually available to us. Hermeneutic consciousness acknowledges that "the dialectic of experience has its proper fulfillment not in definitive knowledge, but in openness to experience that is made possible by experience itself." As coming to terms with human finitude, hermeneutic consciousness realizes that "the truth of experience always implies an orientation toward new experience," because "the nature of experience is conceived in terms of something that surpasses it."

Gadamer then turns to Aeschylus. The great tragedian's adoption of the famous formula *pathei mathos* (learning through suffering) does not

---

12 Gadamer, *Truth and Method*, 355.

just teach the truism that "we become wise through suffering and that our knowledge of things must first be corrected through deception and undeception,"[13] but also, says Gadamer, expresses "insight into the limitations of humanity, into the absoluteness of the barrier that separates man from the divine."[14]

For Gadamer, the correct understanding that "real experience is that whereby human beings become aware of their finiteness" is epitomized by what he calls the hermeneutical experience of the Thou.[15]

Anyone who listens is fundamentally open. Without such openness to one another, there is no genuine human bond. When two people understand each other, this does not mean that one person "understands" the other. Similarly, "to hear and obey someone" (*auf jemanden hören*) does not mean simply that we do blindly what the other desires. We call such a person slavish (*hörig*). Openness to the other, then, involves recognizing that I myself must accept some things that are against me, even though no one else forces me to do so.[16]

The key moment of experience of the Thou is the capacity not to overlook her claim but to let her really say something to us.

If this attitude of properly hermeneutical consciousness is generalized to include the totality of human historical existence, we have what Gadamer calls *wirkungsgeschichtliches Bewusstsein*, historically effected and effective consciousness. To clarify what such a generalization of the hermeneutic experience of the Thou involves, Gadamer presents an analysis of Platonic dialectic and a correction of Collingwood's "logic of question and answer" to thematize the hallmark of realized experience or experience as being: the hermeneutic priority of the question.[17]

Gadamer has often spoken candidly about the vagueness and modesty of his philosophical hermeneutics. For instance, when Heidegger, after his decade-long confrontation with Nietzsche, eschewed completely the vestiges of transcendental philosophy in his own approach to the question about Being, he seems to have implied that transcendental phenomenology cannot be extricated from the Cartesian and Kantian presuppositions discussed and criticized above. Now while Gadamer thinks of himself

13 Gadamer, *Truth and Method*, 356.
14 Gadamer, *Truth and Method*, 357.
15 Gadamer, *Truth and Method*, 357.
16 Gadamer, *Truth and Method*, 361.
17 Gadamer, *Truth and Method*, 362–79.

as faithful to the most radical insights of Heidegger, he still associates himself with the transcendental phenomenological approach of *Being and Time*, even going so far as to coin the Kantian-sounding technical term "historically effective consciousness." While he concedes that Heidegger himself objected to this, Gadamer has remained convinced of the correctness of his position, and yet he has never satisfactorily explained how one could hold on to Heidegger's most radical insights and simultaneously continue to adopt the transcendental viewpoint and to use the language of consciousness. In light of the contrast to the deconstructive and genealogical postmodernists' complete acceptance of Marx's, Freud's, and Nietzsche's critique of consciousness, one cannot but wonder whether Gadamer may not simply have been content to be incoherent.

But as we shall see below, Gadamer was incapable of thematizing with full accuracy the idea of consciousness as experience over against the mistaken idea of consciousness as perception. In the context of the latter thematization, transcendental reflection does not have to imply an illusory escape from human finitude by departing from the realm of the phenomenologically ostensible or the empirically verifiable. This becomes clear in Lonergan's understanding of transcendental philosophy as a generalized empirical method that verifies its discoveries in the data of consciousness made available by performance. Indeed, Lonergan makes good the postmodern decentering of the subject from its modern status as the lord and master of the universe, and he redeems the implications of this decentering in a philosophy and theology of radical human displacement into a divine conversation. In comparing Lonergan's explication with Gadamer's hermeneutical correction of modern counterpositions we get a different appreciation of Abby Warburg's famous saying: "The love of God lies in the details!"

4. Lonergan's Postmodern Thematization of Consciousness as Experience

4.1 The Being of Consciousness

The comprehensiveness of Gadamer's adumbration of hermeneutic experience recalls what Lonergan says in the context of reviewing Coreth's *Metaphysik*:

> We should learn that questioning not only is about being but is being, being in its *Gelichtetheit* (luminousness), being in its openness to being,

being that is realizing itself through inquiry to knowing that, through knowing, it may come to loving.[18]

No wonder that Gadamer's notion of experience as being corresponds remarkably to Lonergan's description of "being oneself as being" since for him, too, being is not abstract but concrete.[19] As he often said:

> It is not the universal concept "not nothing" of Scotus and Hegel, but the concrete goal intended in all inquiry and reflection. It is substance and subject: our opaque being that rises to consciousness and our conscious being …[20]

In elaborating on the aspect of being oneself as conscious being Lonergan explains that it

> is not an object, not part of the spectacle we contemplate, but the presence to himself of the spectator, the contemplator. It is not an object of introspection, but the prior presence that makes introspection possible.[21]

Hence, Lonergan disagrees with the Cartesian notion of the subject or *res cogitans* as the primary object.

You will recall that for Descartes consciousness as a power of inner, reflexive perception can be known by means of a doubling back of inward, reflexive perception upon itself; and that Kant links the objectivity of knowledge indissolubly to external perception that cannot reach an internal power. Instead, for Lonergan, "[conscious being] is conscious, but that does not mean that properly it is known; it will be known only if we introspect, understand, reflect, and judge."[22] At a stroke Lonergan thereby rejects, on the one hand, the Cartesian notion of consciousness either as identical with or as knowable only by an inner, reflexive perception; while, on the other, he disagrees with Kant's position that consciousness cannot be objectively known.

---

18 Bernard Lonergan, "Metaphysics as Horizon," *Collection*, 2nd ed., Collected Works of Bernard Lonergan 4, ed. Frederick E. Crowe and Robert M. Doran (Toronto: University of Toronto Press, 1988), 192.

19 Lonergan, "*Existenz* and *Aggiornamento*," *Collection*, 229.

20 Lonergan, "*Existenz* and *Aggiornamento*," 229.

21 Lonergan, "*Existenz* and *Aggiornamento*," 229.

22 Lonergan, "*Existenz* and *Aggiornamento*," 229.

Lonergan discovered that conscious being can be known by a heightening of consciousness comparable to that which occurs in "high" therapies in which people come to experience, identify, and name their emotions and feelings:

> It is one thing to feel blue and another to advert to the fact that you are feeling blue. It is one thing to be in love and another to discover that what has happened to you is that you have fallen in love. Being oneself is prior to knowing oneself. St Ignatius said that love shows itself more in deeds than in words; but being in love is neither deeds nor words; it is the prior conscious reality that words and, more securely, deeds reveal.[23]

First, note that feeling, the "prior conscious reality," about which Lonergan is speaking here, is pure experience in the sense that as an internal experience it is a mode of consciousness as distinct from self-knowledge. In other words, consciousness itself is before and distinct from any later process in which we heighten our awareness through inquiring about and understanding, through checking out and judging what we undergo in experiencing feelings.

We can grasp the significance of this distinction in the following passage about passing from feelings as conscious experience to feelings as integrated into self-knowledge:

> Feelings simply as felt pertain to an infrastructure. But as merely felt, so far from being integrated into an equable flow of consciousness, they may become a source of disturbance, upset, inner turmoil. Then a cure or part of a cure would seem to be had from the client-centered therapist who provides the patient with an ambiance in which he is at ease, can permit feelings to emerge without being engulfed by them, come to distinguish them from other inner events, differentiate among them, add recognition, bestow names, gradually manage to encapsulate within a superstructure of knowledge and language, of assurance and confidence, what had been an occasion for disorientation, dismay, disorganization.[24]

---

23 Lonergan, "*Existenz* and *Aggiornamento*," 229.

24 Bernard Lonergan, "Prolegomena to the Study of the Emerging Religious Consciousness of Our Time," *A Third Collection*, ed. Frederick E. Crowe (New York: Paulist Press, 1985), 58.

Second, however, we can be correct in calling the "feelings as felt" knowledge in an improper sense precisely because they are conscious before being focused upon, explicated, and thematized. But it is important to specify this as performative knowledge or, as I have said, knowledge in an improper sense of the word. Nevertheless, it is knowledge of the subject as subject, not as object – a kind of knowledge to which neither Descartes nor Kant could do justice, because in one way or another, they each identified consciousness with perception. This performative or improper sort of knowing is knowledge under the formal aspect of "the experienced," as Lonergan phrased it, and not under the formal aspect of being, of intelligible form, or of the true. The latter – knowledge in the proper sense of the term – would require our adding a superstructure through introspection, through inquiry and understanding and articulation, as well as through reflection and judgment.[25]

If, in contrast to this account one conceives of consciousness exclusively on the model of perception, then one will be unable adequately to come to terms either with consciousness as external experience in sensation (as distinct from perception),[26] or with consciousness as internal experience in consciousness's own modes and operations.[27] From the postmodern as opposed to the modern perspective, consciousness means "an internal experience in the strict sense of the self and its acts."[28]

Let me stress two more points about this postmodern understanding of consciousness. First, consciousness defined as internal experience is more primitive and more originative than standard modern conceptions of consciousness would have it, rooted as they are in Cartesian or Kantian epistemologies of the subject. It is empirically accessible or phenomenologically ostensible. And yet because it is so primitive, our original access to it is not what Habermas has called "the objectifying attitude in which the knowing subject regards itself as it would entities

---

25 Lonergan, "Christ as Subject: A Reply," *Collection*, 166–8.
26 Sensation is the same as Aristotle's *aisthesis* or actuation of the sense potencies: of sight by visible objects, of hearing by sound, of touch by something felt, of taste by something flavored, and of smell by something that has an odor. Note that in contrast to perception, sensation can be utterly tacit or background for our focal awareness, like peripheral vision, for instance.
27 Note that this internal experience is that tacit, implicit, or background presence of ourselves to ourselves concomitant with any conscious acts that is the radical meaning of "consciousness" and "conscious."
28 Lonergan, "Christ as Subject: A Reply," 172.

in the external world."[29] As Lonergan insists, "one must begin from the performance if one is to have the experience necessary for understanding what the performance is."[30] Thus, one begins from "a performative attitude," in Habermas's phrase.

The second point is that properly to know consciousness as internal experience is to know something that is contingently constitutive of the being of the subject, on the one hand. But inasmuch as it involves using our ordinary language to inquire, grasp, and formulate and then to check out and judge whether articulations of possibly relevant relationships are contingently verifiable in the experiences themselves, such self-knowledge has the quality of what Habermas, borrowing from Piaget, calls reconstruction. That is to say, in the postmodern understanding of consciousness as experience, "reconstructive and empirical assumptions can be brought together in one and the same theory."[31]

4.2 Lonergan on the Passionateness of Being and Human Consciousness

4.21 Decentering of the Subject within Vertical Finality

We can overhear many overtones of Gadamer's idea of experience in Lonergan's further elaboration of "being oneself as being":

> That prior opaque and luminous being is not static, fixed, determinate, once-for-all; it is precarious; and its being precarious is the possibility not only of a fall, but also of fuller development. That development is open; the dynamism constitutive of our consciousness may be expressed in the imperatives: Be Intelligent, Be Reasonable, Be Responsible; and the imperatives are unrestricted – they regard every inquiry, every judgment, every decision and choice.[32]

If Lonergan does not go to the postmodern extreme and, with Foucault, proclaim the "death of the subject," still his postmodern conception of the conscious subject does entail a radical dismantling of the modern subject conceived in Cartesian or Kantian terms and a radical

---

29 Jürgen Habermas, *The Philosophical Discourse of Modernity: Twelve Lectures*, trans. Frederick G. Lawrence (Cambridge, MA: MIT Press, 1987), 296.
30 Lonergan, "Christ as Subject: A Reply," 174.
31 Habermas, *The Philosophical Discourse of Modernity*, 298.
32 Lonergan, "*Existenz* and *Aggiornmaneto*," 229–30.

decentering of the conscious subject correctly conceived. For if the dynamism constitutive of consciousness is actuated in fulfilling those imperatives – Be Attentive, Be Intelligent, Be Reasonable, Be Responsible – then our consciousnesses realize themselves in self-transcendence. For Lonergan, self-transcendence means just what it says. Moreover, the framework of self-transcendence in this universe gives an even more radically decentering or eccentric twist to the conscious subject, because the concrete evolution of "that prior opaque and luminous being" is swept up, in Lonergan's account, into a vertical finality that is at once possible, multivalent, obscure, and indeed mysterious:[33]

> Such vertical finality is another name for self-transcendence. By experience, we attend to the other; by understanding, we gradually construct our world; by judgment, we discern its independence of ourselves; by deliberate and responsible freedom, we move beyond merely self-regarding norms and make ourselves moral beings.
>
> The disinterestedness of morality is fully compatible with the passionateness of being. For that passionateness has a dimension of its own: It underpins and accompanies and reaches beyond the subject as experientially, intelligently, rationally, morally conscious.[34]

So we can see that the crucial upshot of a correct analysis of consciousness as experience leads us to the realization that there is nothing in our consciousnesses that has not been, in a precise sense, given to us, including consciousness itself.

4.22 Consciousness as Conditioned by the Passionateness of Being

Human consciousness is conditioned overwhelmingly from below and from above by the gift of the passionateness of being that underpins, accompanies, and reaches beyond the conscious subject. For philosophy and theology rightly to acknowledge this passionateness of being and its gift character is to carry out the delicate and complicated passage from the enlightened self-interest inscribed into the heart of the

---

33 On vertical finality, see Lonergan, "Finality, Love, Marriage," *Collection*, 19–23; and "Mission and the Spirit," *A Third Collection*, 23–34, esp. 24.
34 Lonergan, "Mission and the Spirit," 29.

modern project to the disinterestedness of morality upon which the survival of a humanly livable ecology will depend.

In the passage quoted above, Lonergan goes on to speak of the passionateness of being as underpinning conscious being:

> Its underpinning is the quasi-operator that presides over the transition from the neural to the psychic. It ushers into consciousness not only the demands of unconscious vitality, but also the exigencies of vertical finality. It obtrudes deficiency needs. In the self-actualizing subject, it shapes the images that release insight; it recalls evidence that is being overlooked; it may embarrass wakefulness, as it disturbs sleep, with the spectre, the shock, the shame of misdeeds. As it channels into consciousness the feedback of our aberrations and our unfulfilled strivings, so for the Jungians it manifests its archetypes through symbols to preside over the genesis of the ego and to guide the individuation process from the ego to the self.[35]

Then he goes on to describe how the passionateness of being accompanies the subject's conscious and intentional operations:

> There it is the mass and momentum of our lives, the color and tone and power of feeling, that fleshes out and gives substance to what otherwise would be no more than a Shakespearian "pale cast of thought."[36]

Finally, he speaks of the passionateness of being as overarching the conscious performance:

> There it is the topmost quasi-operator that by intersubjectivity prepares, by solidarity entices, by falling in love establishes us as members of community. Within each individual, vertical finality heads for self-transcendence. In an aggregate of self-transcending individuals, there is the significant coincidental manifold in which can emerge a new creation. Possibility yields to fact, and fact bears witness to its originality and power in the fidelity that makes families, in the loyalty that makes peoples, in the faith that makes religions.[37]

---

35 Lonergan, "Mission and the Spirit," 29–30.
36 Lonergan, "Mission and the Spirit," 30.
37 Lonergan, "Mission and the Spirit," 30.

5. Deconstructive / Genealogical Postmodernism's Concern for Otherness

5.1 Derrida

Under the heading of "logocentrism," Derrida began with criticizing conceptualist and perceptualist counterpositions in Husserl's theory of signs,[38] and went on from there to criticize the entire history of sign theory in the West down to Saussure as both "phonocentric" and wedded to "the determination of the Being of beings as presence."[39] This has to do with two rather closely associated matters, which we can only mention here.

First, if I may oversimplify, because of conceptualist and perceptualist accounts of Aristotle's statement that "spoken words (*ta en te phone*) are the symbols of mental experience (*pathemata tes psyches*) and written words are the symbols of spoken words,"[40] Derrida rejects the possibility of any truthful and positional construal of Aristotle's statement. As long as one is confined, as Husserlian and, it would seem, Heideggerian transcendental phenomenology are, to thinking of consciousness as perception, then it is impossible to verify an empirical meaning of Aristotle's statement that would serve as a way of controlling the seemingly limitless conventionality and metaphoricity of human language. What, then, makes more sense: to submit without reason to the imposed limits of a conceptualist or nominalist univocity of signifiers, or to let oneself in for the more wide-open plurivocity of human metaphors?

Second, Derrida opposes the metaphysics of presence he regards as explicit in Heidegger and implicit in the entire tradition of Western philosophy since Plato. He objects to Heidegger's reliance on "an entire metaphorics of proximity, of simple and immediate presence, a metaphorics associating the proximity of Being with the values of neighboring, shelter, house, service, guard, voice, and listening."[41] Anyone who

---

38 See Jacques Derrida, *Speech and Phenomena*, trans. D.B. Allison (Evanston, IL: Northwestern University Press, 1973).

39 Derrida, *Speech and Phenomena*, 11–12; also see Jacques Derrida, *Writing and Difference*, trans. A. Bass (Chicago: University of Chicago Press, 1978).

40 Cited in Jacques Derrida, *Of Grammatology*, trans. G.C. Spivak (Baltimore, MD: Johns Hopkins University Press, 1976), 11.

41 Jacques Derrida, *Margins of Philosophy*, trans. A. Bass (Chicago: University of Chicago Press, 1982), 130.

like Derrida rejects the normativity of the naive realist's "already-out-there-now" *and* the idealist's "already-in-here-now" without finding out what the position on normativity is will naturally be decentered and disoriented. If one is intelligent enough to realize that extrinsic norms, if extrinsic is all they are, are ultimately fictional and arbitrary, what is one to do? Instead of submitting to the traditional extrinsic norms, why not just make fictiveness and arbitrariness into a virtue, so that decenteredness and disorientedness are no longer signs of being lost, but rather the marks of true authenticity?

For as Derrida argues in *Of Grammatology*, Nietzsche revolutionized "the concepts of *interpretation, perspective, evaluation, difference,*"[42] by rigorously excluding the "primary" or "fundamental" or "transcendental," "whether understood in the Scholastic, Kantian, or Husserlian sense," or understood as a Heideggerian primordial homeland or absolute proximity.[43] In any of those senses, differences are derivative and secondary in relation to identities, because the other is subordinated to the same. Similarly, contingency is always governed by necessity. But when the decadent Scholastic, Kantian, Husserlian, and Heideggerian premises are eliminated, one enters the regime of *differance* in which the reverse is true: Identities are contingent upon the adventitious play of differences; and necessities are displaced by contingencies.

This is of course most evident to Derrida in the case of language, where in accord with its ineradicable conventionality, what is constitutive is not the relation of a word as signifier to its referent as signified, but the positive determination of signs by reason of the differences available in any given system of signs. Pure significance is totally unrelated to anything but the internal system of differences in traces or markings.

As with language, so too with structure in its purity. Under the tutelage of the foundational or the transcendental, structures are centered in terms of some imagined center, origin, or presence outside the structure itself. According to Derrida, this "concept of a centered structure" is "the concept of a play based on a fundamental ground, a play constituted on the basis of a fundamental immobility and a reassuring certitude, which itself is beyond the reach of play."[44] The certainty of a center "beyond the reach of play" fends off anxiety, "for anxiety is invariably

---

42 Derrida, *Of Grammatology*, 19.
43 Derrida, *Of Grammatology*, 22–3.
44 Derrida, *Writing and Difference*, 279.

the result of a certain mode of being caught by the game, of being as it were at stake in the game from the outset." The key is playfulness and the play of differences. Finally, as for the subject, he or she is simply "an effect of *differance*, an effect inscribed within the system of *differance*."[45]

Derrida makes the *differance* or the lack of origin and end or foundation or ground basic because it destabilizes any attempts to close down directions of thought or to homogenize dimensions of specificity or particularity or uniqueness in reality. It melts down distinctions between abnormal and normal, literal and figurative, serious and fictive, since they are all rooted in the contingency of arbitrary will that are forgotten either willfully or not. And so the strategy of deconstruction is one of displacement, intervention, impertinence, explosive laughter, which it shares quite comfortably with the genealogical approach of Foucault.

5.2 Foucault

Foucault's essay "Nietzsche, Freud, Marx" (1967) points to a narcissistic revolution in hermeneutics wrought by *Genealogy of Morals, Interpretation of Dreams*, and *Capital*.[46] According to Foucault each of these works demonstrates that interpretation has no foundation and points to nothing beyond itself but further signs, which are themselves sedimented interpretations. In these works the crucial signs – money for Marx, symptoms for Freud, good and evil for Nietzsche – also have a distantiating, threatening, defamiliarizing role to play. They indicate the subterranean role of dissonance in our lives, whatever the surface sweetness and light.

In a later essay, "Nietzsche, Genealogy, History" (1984),[47] Foucault calls into question all history insofar as it looks to an end point or operates teleologically, thereby obliterating the contingency of events, the discontinuity involved in emergence and decline or extinction, the conflictual singularity of events:[48]

Genealogy does not resemble the evolution of a species and does not map the destiny of a people. On the contrary, to follow the complex course of descent is to maintain passing events in their proper dispersion; it is to

---

45 Jacques Derrida, *Positions*, trans. A. Bass (Chicago: University of Chicago Press, 1981), 28.

46 Michel Foucault, "Nietzsche, Freud, Marx," *Cahiers de Royaumont* 6 (1967): 183–92.

47 Michel Foucault, "Nietzsche, Genealogy, and History," in *The Foucault Reader*, ed. P. Rabinow (New York: Pantheon, 1984), 76–100.

48 Foucault, "Nietzsche, Genealogy, and History," 76.

identify the accidents, the minute deviations – or conversely, the complete reversals – the errors, the false appraisals, and the faulty calculations that gave birth to those things that continue to exist and have value for us; it is to discover that truth or being does not lie at the root of what we know and what we are, but the exteriority of accidents.[49]

Nietzsche's affirmation that "whatever exists, having somehow come into being, is again and again reinterpreted to new ends, taken over, transformed, and redirected by some power superior to it"[50] does not mean, Foucault suggests, that in all such revisionist interpretations a "will to power has become master of something less powerful and imposed upon it the character of a function."[51] More significantly, according to Foucault, Nietzsche is teaching us to regard "the entire history of 'a thing,' an organ, a custom" as a "continuous sign-chain of ever new interpretations and adaptations whose causes do not even have to be related to one another but, on the contrary, in some cases succeed and alternate with one another in a purely chance fashion."[52] The general teaching then is that "all concepts in which an entire process is semiotically concentrated elude definition; only that which has no history is definable."[53] But this is closely related to other of Nietzsche's radical assertions, for instance, in *The Gay Science*:

The total character of the world, however, is in all eternity chaos – in the sense not of a lack of necessity, but of a lack of order, arrangement, form, beauty, wisdom, and whatever other names there are for our aesthetic anthropomorphisms.[54]

And then his famous answer to the query, What is truth? in his 1873 essay, "On Truth and Lie in the Extra-Moral Sense":

A moving army of metaphors, metonymies, and anthropomorphisms, in short a summa of human relationships that are being poetically and

---

49 Foucault, "Nietzsche, Genealogy, and History," 81.
50 Friedrich Nietzsche, *On the Genealogy of Morals* and *Ecce Homo*, ed. W. Kaufmann (New York: Random House, 1967), 77.
51 Foucault, "Nietzsche, Genealogy, and History," 77.
52 Foucault, "Nietzsche, Genealogy, and History," 77.
53 Foucault, "Nietzsche, Genealogy, and History," 80.
54 Friedrich Nietzsche, *The Gay Science*, trans. W. Kaufmann (New York: Random House, 1974), 168.

rhetorically sublimated, transposed, and beautified until, after a long and repeated use, a people considers them solid, canonical, and unavoidable. Truths are illusions whose illusionary nature has been forgotten, metaphors that have been used up and lost their imprint and that now operate as mere metal, no longer as coins.[55]

Nevertheless, for Foucault, the emergence, survival, and decline of any discourse is always inextricably joined to one mode of power or another. In his far-reaching research, he sought to show empirically how distinctions in discourse are imposed pragmatically by social institutions. Ruling metaphors or modes of discourse are constantly reconstituted in radically different ways at different times in history. His genealogical method seeks to trace these correlative changes via quite unusual stints of archival work.[56] Thus, the thrust of Foucault's practice of genealogy was to "incite the experience of discord or discrepancy between the social construction of self, truth, and rationality and that which does not fit neatly within these folds."[57]

5.3 Summary of Part 5

The program of deconstruction and genealogical strategies is one of distantiation and defamiliarization as a way of enacting a responsibility for otherness. This postmodern program thus entails championing plurality, difference, changeableness, instability, and lack of hierarchy. All this is based on the Nietzsche-instilled recognition of how much social (technological, economic, and political) and cultural set-ups are ultimately conventional, and so fallible, precarious, and always revisable. The net effect of all this, of course, can be an extreme relativism and an actual fostering of nihilist tendencies. I have chosen not to emphasize this, however, because leading interpreters like Christopher Norris on

---

55 Friedrich Nietzsche, *Kritische Studienausgabe*, ed. G. Colli and M. Montinari (Berlin: de Gruyter, 1984), 880–1; cited in Ernst Behler, *Confrontations: Derrida/Heidegger/ Nietzsche*, trans. S. Taubeneck (Stanford, CA: Stanford University Press, 1991), 84. Ernst Behler is one of the most clear and reliable interpreters of deconstructive and genealogical postmodernism in light of Nietzsche and Heidegger.

56 Compare Michel Foucault, *Discipline and Punish: The Birth of the Prison*, trans. A. Sheridan (New York: Random House, 1977); also Michel Foucault, *The History of Sexuality I: An Introduction*, trans. R. Hurley (New York: Random House, 1978).

57 William E. Connolly, "Taylor, Foucault, and Otherness," *Political Theory* 12 (1984): 368.

Derrida and James W. Bernauer on Foucault insist that these philosophers' final intent is ethical.[58] Perhaps we need to place the efforts of deconstructivist-genealogical postmodernism in the context of Lonergan's suggestion in his lectures on the philosophy of education[59] that Marx and Nietzsche expressed a more profound and effectual appreciation of the sinfulness of modern social and cultural structures than their Christian contemporaries had done.

But what is the point of this overriding ethical intent? The brief answer is: concern for the other. But we must understand by this not just – or even mainly – in the sense of other people, but in the more abstract sense of what is otherwise. Thus the heart of the postmodern protest on the part of deconstruction and genealogy is the relationship of contingency to an ultimately unlimited plurality of meanings and values, and therefore to many possible concrete solutions to the problem of human living.

6. Lonergan and Contingency

Among Christian theologians, one of the greatest tests for modern theology has been that of coming adequately to terms with what the rationalist German and Jewish philosopher Gotthold Lessing formulated as the "ghastly abyss" between necessity and contingency, especially the accidental character of history both sacred and profane. Perhaps the typical Protestant temptation in reaching a solution has been to lean in the direction of a historicism whose rejection of dogma includes the rejection of the intelligibility of the Word of God as true. In reaction, the typical Catholic temptation has been an ahistorical orthodoxy that cannot take the relativities of history seriously. Neither side is capable of handling contingency in a way that does justice to the actual historicity of Christian meanings and values. As a result, the contemporary climate of opinion in theology is dominated by what Anglican theologian Lesslie Newbegin has called "agnostic pluralism" and "fundamentalist sectarianism."[60]

---

58 See Christopher Norris, *Deconstruction: Theory and Practice* (London: Methuen, 1982); and James W. Bernauer, *Michel Foucault's Force of Flight: Toward an Ethics for Thought* (Atlantic Highlands, NJ: Humanities Press International, 1990).

59 In the summer of 1959 Lonergan directed an Institute on the Philosophy of Education at Xavier University in Cincinnati, Ohio. The transcripts of these lectures are published as *Topics in Education*, Collected Works of Bernard Lonergan 10, ed. Robert M. Doran and Frederick E. Crowe (Toronto: University of Toronto Press, 1993).

60 See Lesslie Newbegin, *Truth to Tell: The Gospel as Public Truth* (Grand Rapids, MI: Eerdmans, 1991).

This is the place not to expound Lonergan's thought on contingency, but to mention several contexts relevant to deconstructivist and genealogical postmodernism's concerns. In the measure that those concerns are legitimate, how can they be taken seriously without requiring theologians to leap headlong into Lessing's "ghastly abyss" by adopting the so-called New Historicism?

6.1 Contingency and the Virtually Unconditioned

We might begin by saying that the deconstructivist and genealogical postmodernism rejects wholesale Aristotle's conception of knowledge in accord with the logical ideal of apodictic truth. For Aristotle, science or *episteme* in the most proper sense is knowledge of things through their necessary causes. "Necessity" here entails a note of absoluteness untainted by any possibility of being otherwise. Accordingly, if the relationships among terms in a strictly scientific definition were to meet the purest requirements of the Aristotelian ideal of *apodeixis*, they would express intelligible connections among things that simply had to be such-and-such a way and couldn't be otherwise. Where the deconstructivist or genealogical postmodernist revels almost to the point of vertigo in the aleatory possibilities of being otherwise, most of the philosophical and theological tradition has identified the fulfillment of (or at least approximation to) Aristotle's logical ideal of knowledge as the only rational alternative to relativism and nihilism.

But as Lonergan has insisted, that logical ideal of knowledge is so exorbitant that it excludes the possibility of empirical science. Indeed, Aristotle's recognition that all of terrestrial reality is penetrated by contingency led him to deny the possibility of a science of earthly causes or history, since for him science properly so called regards only necessities.

In contrast, Lonergan from his earliest theological publications pointed out how Thomas Aquinas's breakthrough to divine transcendence brought with it a recognition that divine action through infinite understanding was beyond both necessity and contingency.[61] Moreover,

---

61 We are speaking of the so-called *Gratia Operans* articles, a recasting of Lonergan's doctoral dissertation for the Gregorian University published originally in *Theological Studies* during 1941 and 1942 ("St Thomas' Thought on *Gratia Operans*," *Theological Studies* 2 (1941): 289–324; 3 (1942): 69–88, 375–402, 533–578) and republished as *Grace and Freedom: Operative Grace in the Thought of St Thomas Aquinas*, Collected Works of Bernard Lonergan 1, ed. Frederick E. Crowe and Robert M. Doran (Toronto: University of Toronto Press, 2000).

because divine revelation is integrally concerned with a concrete world process that is made up of realities that occur contingently and that therefore not only might not have happened but also might have been otherwise, Aquinas proposed as a legitimate goal of theological science the attainment of *rationes convenientiae* that would explain the matter-of-fact intelligibility of merely accidental or contingent matters such as creation, fall, redemption, and revelation. These aspects of Thomist teaching tended, however, to be disregarded by decadent Scholasticism's overweening preoccupation with the certainties and necessities of *Konklusionstheologie*. Can we reject such a theology and its illegitimate preoccupations without falling into relativism?

For Lonergan, the intelligible connections between the scientific terms that express explanations of accidental or contingent realities have a necessity about them that is not absolute but only hypothetical: If A, then B; but A, therefore B. The intelligible, if-then link between terms A and B is conditioned: If the conditions for A obtain, then B exists or occurs. For modern empirical science, according to Lonergan, such hypothetical necessity is the goal of classical scientific method. Thus, classical method reveals as many instances of "If A, then B" as it can, while statistical method discloses how often those instances actually happen.[62] Whenever such classical or statistical intelligibilities are verified, Lonergan calls them *virtually* unconditioned.[63] This is to distinguish the kind of intelligible reality proper to created nature (which both as a whole and in its detailed particulars not only did not have to be as it is, and so could have been otherwise, but also did not have to be at all) from the only intelligible reality that is absolutely necessary and hence beyond the contingency and necessity of created nature – God, who is formally unconditioned.

Lonergan's highlighting the centrality of contingency for human judgment in terms of the distinction between the formally and the virtually unconditioned does take postmodern concerns seriously. In terms of this distinction, every event, with the exception of the infinite and unconditional act of understanding love that is God, is

---

62 See Bernard Lonergan, *Insight: A Study of Human Understanding*, Collected Works of Bernard Lonergan 3, ed. Frederick E. Crowe and Robert M. Doran (Toronto: University of Toronto Press, 1992), 60–76 on classical heuristic structures; 76–85 on statistical heuristic structures; 102–7 on classical and statistical laws; and 130–62 on the complementarity of classical and statistical investigations.

63 Lonergan, *Insight*, 305–6, 685–6.

conditional and conditioned.[64] Only the formally unconditioned has no conditions whatsoever; the virtually unconditioned has conditions that happen to be fulfilled, but their fulfillment may or may not happen. Correspondingly, every human judgment itself is an instance of the virtually unconditioned. So our human judgments possess that odd combination of normativity, fallibility, and possible revisability that distinguishes Lonergan's idea of the absoluteness proper to acts of judgment from both fallibilists' and the dogmatic naive realists' ideas.[65]

In contrast, deconstructivists and genealogists use their awareness of the contingency besetting the remote and the proximate contexts or grounds for judgment to deny judgment any absoluteness whatsoever. Their different versions of conventionalism lead them to advocate what amounts to agnostic pluralism. They enjoy carrying the day against fundamentalist sectarians, whose style of being concerned for the truth habitually excludes alternative approaches, overlooks the possible need for any correction and revision of their judgments, and practically rejects the possibility of honest disagreement. But in the posture of sensitivity to otherness and difference that goes together with agnostic pluralism, radical postmodernists fail to come to terms with the way in which it takes correct judgments adequately (if never exhaustively) to come to terms with the other as other. As Lonergan so eloquently put it:

> Condemnation of objectivity induces, not a merely incidental blindness in one's vision, but a radical undermining of authentic human existence … It is quite true that the subject communicates not by saying what he knows but by showing what he is, and it is no less true that subjects are confronted with themselves more effectively by being confronted with others than by solitary introspection. But such facts by themselves only ground a technique for managing people; and managing people is not treating them as persons. To treat them as persons, one must know and one must invite them to know. A real exclusion of objective knowing, so far from promoting, only destroys personalist values.[66]

---

64 Lonergan, *Insight*, 682, 692–3.
65 See Lonergan, *Insight*, "The Notion of Judgment," 296–303; "Reflective Understanding," 304–40; and "The Notion of Objectivity," 399–409.
66 Lonergan, "Cognitional Structure," *Collection*, 220–1.

6.2 Contingency and the Non-Systematic

In relation to the contingency of both knowing and the known, what the deconstructive and genealogical approaches have a keen sense of is the limitations of any claims concerning regularity (or classical intelligibility). They subversively suggest that the closure such classical formulations entail (i.e., defining *omni et soli*) is based in the final analysis not on any correspondence between intelligence and reality, but on an arbitrary decision to privilege one metaphorical expression over others. But they also possess an affinity for Aristotle's insight that (as Lonergan once put it) "events happened contingently because there was no cause to which they could be reduced except prime matter, and prime matter was not a determinate cause."[67] Indeed, Derrida's *differance* seems to function like Aristotle's *hyle* or perhaps Lonergan's "empirical residue,"[68] although its function stands outside the context of overall intelligibility.

Admittedly, it is salutary to have a feel for what Lonergan has called "the non-systematic character of material multiplicity, continuity, and frequency."[69] But if this instinct for the non-systematic becomes a basis for overlooking statistical, genetic, and dialectical methods, as well as for just debunking all classical intelligibility, it is not really taking contingency seriously. It is just glorifying the aleatory. Then the other can only be perceived as other in its punctual evanescence. This sort of acknowledgment can be exquisitely witty or filled with pathos, but isn't it also a rejection of intelligence, reasonableness, and responsibility in one's life and a failure to be faithful to the other?

The brilliant sensitivity for disjunctions, slippages, and the discontinuous in general can also be used as an excuse for not properly acknowledging higher discontinuities and leaps in being that are not explicable in terms of the logical expansion of the lower viewpoints.[70] In contrast, Lonergan explains how diverse classical higher viewpoints are related intelligibly, but not logically; and how statistical methods are complementary to classical, as we gradually come to understand concrete

---

67 Lonergan, *Grace and Freedom*, 81.

68 Lonergan, *Insight*, 50–6.

69 Lonergan, *Insight*, 641.

70 See Lonergan, *Insight*, 38–9, where arithmetic and algebra are compared as lower and higher viewpoints; for other instances, chemistry's basic terms and relations are not just a subset of the basic terms and relations of physics, nor are biology's deducible from those of chemistry, and so on.

states, trends, groups, and populations of beings. If the other happens to be an instance of "systems on the move," it does no service to reduce the intelligibility proper to genetic method into simply another case of classical intelligibility, thereby obviating intelligible accounts of the continuity-in-discontinuity involved in dynamics of development.[71] Similarly, extraordinary alertness to the aspects of dissonance, discord, and discrepancy in our moral lives cannot substitute for a dialectical analysis in Lonergan's sense that would confront the abyss of the absurd in the universe and yet still be open to being surprised by joy.[72]

6.3 Contingency and Understanding

Even before judgment, the act of direct understanding is fraught with contingency.[73] In the movement from potency into act, intelligence is marked by multiple dependencies. Most obviously, intelligence depends upon (i.e., is conditioned by and conditions) sense perception. How attentive are we? This is not something that can be taken for granted. Aside from the biases causing selective inattention to different areas of possible inquiry, there is the sheer historicity of the lower manifolds of the sensing subject. Some people just see or hear less well than others. But there is also the conditioning of the psyche, with its feelings and images. Since insight is into, or occurs in, data represented through feeling-laden images, it can rightly be spoken of as "bubbling up" in a person's psyche. But understanding is also dependent upon the asking of questions. What kinds of questions a person is liable to ask depends on all sorts of internal and external conditions. Above all, it is important to acknowledge that all the acts of consciousness except decision are not human *actions* in the ordinary sense, but operations. They occur *to* one in a way that is irreducible to one's own doing.

Therefore, the direct act of understanding or insight, the reflective act of understanding that checks the evidence, and the responsible act of understanding that follows on questions for deliberation are similarly fraught with contingency, if not more so.[74] And so the Faustian image

---

71 Lonergan, *Insight*, 486, 484–507 on genetic method.
72 See Lonergan, *Insight*, 508–11, 707–8 on dialectical method; 630 on dialectic as method in ethics; 654–6 on the dialectical manifold as requiring a higher integration.
73 See Lonergan, *Insight*, 27–56 on the direct act of understanding or insight.
74 See Lonergan, *Insight*, 632–3 on practical insight and reflection.

of Enlightenment reason as masterfully disposing of an instrument is demolished. But we cannot go into this now.

6.4 Contingency and Language

As we have seen, the deconstructivist and genealogical postmodernists delight in the possibilities of intervention, interruption, and explosive laughter provided by the conventionality of language. Their brilliance in exploiting what Husserl called *sedimentation* – namely, the possibility of detaching expressions from acts of meaning or from referentiality; and in making capital on Nietzsche's insights into the metaphoricity of linguistic conventions is spellbinding. But it is one thing to exploit these aspects of language by playing with the seemingly endless polyvalence of conventional signs as disclosive of worlds of meaning, and by thinking through the many implications of what Wittgenstein in *Philosophical Investigations* called language games.[75] It is quite another to take the position that Lyotard speaks of as "Just Gaming."[76] This involves two things: (1) debunking any link between immanent acts of meaning in direct, reflective, and responsible acts of understanding and their respective terms of expression;[77] and (2) rejecting any possible relevance of reference.[78]

Here it is important to recall that Lonergan's analysis of inner word does not deny the role played by language in perception and in imagination leading up to insight.[79] Nor does he deny the role of available and to-be-invented language when it comes to using one's own understanding of some matter to guide one in articulating and formulating just what it was that one had come to understand, prescinding from all that is irrelevant or adventitious.[80] Nor, again, does he fail to note how, when the realization that our understanding of something is only

---

75 See Ludwig Wittgenstein, *Philosophical Investigations*, trans. G.E.M. Anscombe (New York: Macmillan, 1958).

76 See Jean-François Lyotard and Jean-Loup Thebaud, *Just Gaming*, trans. V. Godzich (Minneapolis: University of Minnesota Press, 1985).

77 See Lonergan, *Insight*, 592–5.

78 See Lonergan, *Insight*, 592–5.

79 See Lonergan, *Verbum: Word and Idea in Aquinas*, Collected Works of Bernard Lonergan 2, ed. Frederick E. Crowe and Robert M. Doran (Toronto: University of Toronto Press, 1997), 1–11, 151–3, 155; and *Method in Theology* (New York: Herder & Herder, 1972), 70–3 on linguistic meaning; 92 on linguistic process; 88, 97 on linguistic feedback.

80 See Lonergan, *Method in Theology*, 88, 97.

possibly relevant prompts us to check that hunch or guess or hypothesis out, we set out to verify not simply insights, but insights formulated in language or symbolic formulae of some kind.

Nevertheless, Lonergan refuses to use this full-blown acknowledgment of the role of language in our understanding, verifying, and deliberating to deny the fact that we understand and make limited judgments of fact and value that are achievements of intentional and cognitive and real self-transcendence.[81] He insists that as intelligent, reasonable, and responsible, we finite human beings use language to get beyond ourselves in knowing reality and in transforming it. This in no way occludes all the ways in which it is also true to say that language uses us perhaps even more than we use it. But by being more attuned to the way the structure and dynamisms of consciousness mutually "horizon" language, we may be more responsible and care-full in our utterances and actions.

6.5 Contingency and Interpretation

The deconstructivist-genealogical view, on which we are used by language so that we chiefly become its instrument in the production of endless texts as interpretations and commentaries as texts, leads thinkers like Derrida and Foucault to install mirrors in between all signifiers, signs, and signifieds in the construction of an anti-hermeneutical theory of interpretation. Any attempts to talk about realities are regarded as mistakes at best, or as masks for just talk about talk, or as power moves disguised as persuasion. In other words, the contingencies besetting language usage by way of background cultural conventions and social practices render any subject's putative interpretation the effect of an inscription by some force or forces outside his or her control. Once again, this can give rise to an incredible indeterminacy in the deciphering of codes. The fertility of deconstructive-genealogical postmoderns in coming up with alternative interpretations and alternative plausible contextualizations for what to the less sophisticated scholar might appear a more straightforward matter is truly astonishing. They are maestros of the possibly productive misunderstanding.

---

81 See Bernard Lonergan, "The Response of the Jesuit as Priest and Apostle in the Modern World," *A Second Collection*, ed. William F.J. Ryan and Bernard J. Tyrrell, (London: Darton, Longman & Todd, 1974), 166–70 on self-transcendence as intentional, cognitive, and real.

With such anti-hermeneutical theories of interpretation, Lonergan would agree, interpretation is not a simple, no-nonsense, intuitive affair.[82] Rather, as he wrote in the context of a controversy with typical scholastic methods of interpretation:

> Logically, the interpretation of a writer is a matter of formulating an hypothesis, working out its presuppositions and its implications, and verifying in the text the hypothesis itself, and the implications. Deductions of what a writer must have meant are just so much fancy; in reality they are deductions from the hypothesis assumed by the interpreter; and whether that hypothesis is correct can be *determined only with probability*, a probability that increases only with the extent and variety of the verification.[83]

If, in the process of interpretation, the only grounds for certainty about any but the most obvious negative conclusions would be the ability to show that one had considered every possible alternative interpretation and had demonstrated that all but one alternative was incorrect, a great opening would be left, through which the person with a deconstructivist or genealogical bent can march with an often uncanny capacity to conceive of any number of possibly relevant alternative interpretations of a given text. Such creativity and imaginativeness can be productive. If, as Lonergan too would insist, the "principle of the empty head" is sterile in interpreting, it does follow that interpretation will be enriched by the exploration of many alternatives. But a law of diminishing returns would also seem to go into effect at the point where the probabilities of verifying possibly relevant proposals start to diminish apace; or when such further interpretations really start to become trivial or frivolous. Doesn't the art of interpretation begin at that point to turn into a glass bead game for effete intellectuals?

6.6 Contingent Predication

The deconstructivist-genealogical complaint about having an origin and end or a center of the universe is based in part on the obviousness of a contingency about terrestrial events that flies in the face of claims

---

82 For Lonergan on interpretation the basic texts are *Insight*, ch. 17.3, "The Truth of Interpretation," 585–617; and *Method in Theology*, ch. 7, "Interpretation," 153–73; ch. 8, "History," 175–96; and ch. 9, "History and Historians," 197–234.

83 Lonergan, "On God and Secondary Causes," *Collection*, 60; emphasis added.

to certainty based upon necessary causes. Since they are incompatible with contingency, such strong necessity and certitude claims would also exclude freedom and the need to risk and dare. Then, too, illusionary necessities and certitudes are employed to frame the so-called master- or meta-narratives used to legitimate people and forces who would impose disciplines upon us, depriving us of the liberty to be ourselves, to be different, to include others, and so forth.[84]

Lonergan's idea of contingent predication is based on the fact that whenever we make assertions about any matter of fact, all that is required for the truthfulness of the predication is that the conditions for the existence or occurrence of its referent be fulfilled, even though they might not have been fulfilled, and even though things might have been otherwise. By analogy, contingent predications are also made about God, whether on the basis of immanently generated judgments or on the basis of judgments based on the assent of faith.[85]

According to the analogy of contingent predication,[86] the glorious thing about the created order of this universe is the fact that it does not have to exist at all, and does not have to be as it is. That is to say, once we make the breakthrough to an explanatory conception of divine transcendence as utterly beyond necessity and contingency and completely unconditioned by space and time, it is proper to analogically understand and affirm that the infinitely loving, creative power is a mystery of freedom who in knowing, willing, and bringing about the universe that exists is completely free. Note that this statement or predication about God is not necessary but utterly contingent. All that has to have occurred in order for this contingent predication to be true is the fulfillment of the conditions for the existence of any finite order of beings, conditioned either intrinsically or extrinsically by space and time.

What we do in the analogy of contingent predication, then, is to let God be a transcendent mystery. This means that God cannot function as a presence strictly comparable to any other presence in space and

---

84 See Jean-François Lyotard, *The Postmodern Condition: A Report on Knowledge*, trans. G. Bennington and B. Massumi (Minneapolis: University of Minnesota Press, 1984).

85 See Lonergan, *Insight*, 725–39 on the distinction between knowledge as immanently generated and knowledge as belief; and *Method in Theology*, 118–19, and 123–4 on the distinction of religious belief from faith.

86 Lonergan, *Insight*, 684–91; *The Triune God: Systematics*, Collected Works of Bernard Lonergan 12, trans. Michael G. Shields, ed. Robert M. Doran and H. Daniel Monsour (Toronto: University of Toronto Press, 2007), 439ff.

time, and that God cannot function as a center or fulcrum for managing the lives of people and things, as in what seems to be the poststructuralist reading of Christian narratives. Furthermore, according to the analogy of contingent predication, there is an absolute compatibility between free creation by a divinely transcendent creator and emergent probability as the shape of the concrete, created world order.[87] Moreover, because this creation and this emergently probable (not necessary) world order is constituted by such long times and great numbers of things, no surprise or miracle can be apodictically ruled out a priori.

Such an explanatory conception of creator and creation is in complete harmony with the best and noblest instincts of the deconstructive-genealogical postmodernist, especially in its admission that "there is in this universe a merely empirical residue that is unexplained."[88] Indeed, it grounds precisely the magnificent diversity, strangeness, wonder, and surprise so deeply yet ambiguously appreciated by postmodernity's art and philosophy. In Lonergan's words:

> The empirical residue grounds the manifold of the potential good and, inasmuch as it stands under world order, it possesses the value that accrues to the contingent through the reasonableness of the freedom of a completely wise and good being.[89]

6.7 Contingency and Liberty

The freedom about which deconstructivist and genealogical postmoderns are concerned seems to be separate from any finality whatsoever. This notion of freedom is suspiciously like Sir Isaiah Berlin's idea of negative freedom. Negative freedom is "freedom *from*" as opposed to "freedom *to*": "Some portion of human existence must remain independent of social control"; "there ought to exist a certain minimum of personal freedom that must on no account be violated."[90] This judgment on these postmodernists seems to be born out in Stephen K. White's interpretation of Derrida, Foucault, and Lyotard as saying there are two options for human practical engagement: on the one hand,

---

87 Lonergan, *Insight*, 688.
88 Lonergan, *Insight*, 686.
89 Lonergan, *Insight*, 686.
90 Isaiah Berlin, *Two Concepts of Liberty* (Oxford: Oxford University Press, 1958), 46.

rationalization or total subordination to singularity-squashing master narratives purveyed by rationally purposive, bureaucratic regimes; on the other, countermodes with no rationale or goal except to unmask meta-narratives and rationalization processes.[91]

Where Lonergan agrees with deconstructivist and genealogical postmodernists' ideas about freedom is in understanding freedom as a case of contingency. But for Lonergan it is a "special kind":

> It is contingence that arises, not from the empirical residue that grounds materiality and the non-systematic, but is in the order of the spirit, of intelligent grasp, rational reflection, and morally guided will. It has the twofold basis that its object is merely possibility and that its agent is contingent not only in his existence, but also in the extension of his rational consciousness into rational self-consciousness. For it is one and the same act of willing that both decides in favor of the object or against it and that constitutes the subject as deciding reasonably or unreasonably, as succeeding or failing in the extension of rational consciousness into an effectively rational self-consciousness.[92]

For the deconstructivist-genealogical approach, the only models for rational consciousness or rational self-consciousness are either the abstract self-reflection in the mode of Kantian or (via Kohlberg) Habermasian complete internalization and complete universalization of rules; or the modern bourgeois or Romantic model of the self as subjecting itself to a dominant practice or what Lyotard calls a "phrase regime." Both of these models are dominated by the image of the unitary and controlling consciousness of the utilitarian or the expressive individualist discussed in Part 2 above. But they also fail to account for the more concrete and usual dimension of moral practice that long after *Insight* Lonergan spoke of as development from above downwards.[93] While this dimension is perfectly compatible with the model of development from below upwards in which the order is that of experience,

---

91 Stephen K. White, *Political Theory and Postmodernism* (Cambridge: Cambridge University Press, 1991), esp. 1–30, 55–94.

92 Lonergan, *Insight*, 642.

93 See, for instance, "Healing and Creating in History," *A Third Collection*, 106 on "two quite different kinds" of development: "from below upwards" and "from above downwards." This distinction becomes almost a commonplace for Lonergan in the post-*Method* essays published in *A Third Collection*.

understanding, judgment of value, decision, and action, its order is different because it takes into account the role love plays in socialization, acculturation, and education, and hence in the genesis of the person's rational self-consciousness. And it shows how practice, even before it involves extending one's intelligence and rationality into the further phase of moral and existential consciousness, ordinarily has already involved being-in-love within some communal context. Our relationships of love have already been transforming our feelings as intentional responses and thus bringing about all sorts of affective and cognitive effects in us through examples, images, symbols, stories, and beliefs that spell out for us in a performative fashion the meanings and values that enframe our moral deliberations.

It can, of course, be the case that the stories dominated by utilitarian or expressive individualism specify our horizon of deliberation and discernment as a matter of fact; but those stories as accounts of human practice contradict the way moral action actually unfolds by way of our loves and as mediated by the narratives handed over to us as paradigmatic for living out our loves. This is true even in cases of alienated dependency and disoriented loving. Even for the disordered self-love of modern individualists, the surd is socially and culturally mediated.

Now the postmodernists want to replace the homogeneous and unified ego with a decentered, detotalized, heterogeneous self, capable of unmasking and resisting controlling narratives that would smother or extinguish the self's capacity ever to be otherwise. This is why, by demonstrating the conventionality and revisability of social and cultural schemes of recurrence, postmodernists are out to deconstruct the oppositions between normal and abnormal that serve to close down certain directions of thought and action in our deliberating upon proposals for action. But in this, as White agrees, they do not even get as far as "a radicalization of John Stuart Mill's *On Liberty*."[94] Never-ending oscillation between debunking conventionally accepted and enforced social practices and the disclosure of ever new and other fictions by which to live is not enough. "The postmodern theorist who models his or her self-understanding exclusively on the role of ceaselessly exposing otherness slides all too easily into the position of the ring master of otherness."[95] To put the issue in rather Aristotelian terms, such theorizing

---

94 White, *Political Theory and Postmodernism*, 29.
95 White, *Political Theory and Postmodernism*, 32.

as unrelenting hermeneutics of suspicion regarding the imputations of ideals that support our practical judgments does not yet furnish criteria for figuring out the difference between disordered self-love and right-ordered self-love.

Instead of dwelling further on the possible defects and lack of seriousness of the postmodernists, with all the relativist and nihilist implications of their thought, I would like to propose a completely different framework in which to think about the free practice through the direction opened up by them. Let us note to begin with that this direction of postmodernist thought is in remarkable consonance with Aquinas's insight into the liberating character of prudential judgment in the context of the contingency of particular and concrete situations.[96] Because in most practical situations "there are many ways to skin a cat"; the more ways that occur to us of accomplishing some good in some situation that is inherently complicated or fraught with conflicts between quite choiceworthy courses of action, the more likely are we to hit upon the suitable course of action. By the same token, when we do at last hit the nail on the head, we feel a great weight lifted from our shoulders, and it is a glad relief.

Next, this direction of thought is also rather in the spirit of Lonergan's reflections regarding the practicality of the people on the spot for whom the insights into the concrete situations relevant to needed decisions can occur in a way that is not possible for others not so situated.[97]

Furthermore, the postmodernists typically play off the rationalization of action in the mode of what Weber formulated as the ethics of consequences (*Verantwortungsethik*) against the distantiating, defamiliarizing strategies that render agents more sensitive to plurality, differences, instability, the dissolution of arbitrary hierarchies, and so forth, to heighten our responsiveness to the other. This motif is not just akin to Weber's delimitation of the ethics of conviction (*Gesinnungsethik*); it can also remind us of Lonergan's contrast between a horizontal and a vertical exercise of liberty.[98] By the former, we operate within an already established orientation

---

96 For a more complete delineation of themes in this paragraph see Frederick E. Crowe, "Universal Norms and the Concrete 'Operabile' in St Thomas Aquinas," *Sciences Ecclésiastiques* 13 (1955): 114–49, 257–91.

97 See Lonergan, *Insight*, 259–60 for the classic statement; also, "Prologomena to the Study of Religious Consciousness of Our Time," esp. 60–3.

98 Lonergan, *Method in Theology*, 40, 122, 237–8, 240, 269.

to choose courses of action within some already understood and agreed upon horizon of meanings and values specified by some master narrative; by the latter, we undergo a radical change in the overall orientation and in which a different, incommensurate, or disproportionate horizon of meaning and value is specified by a new master narrative.[99]

If we recontextualize the postmodernists' moral and aesthetic sense of responsiveness to otherness within Lonergan's framework, then the decentering, detotalizing, and becoming heterogeneous of the self can be reinterpreted as the basic and radical displacement of the subject that occurs most paradigmatically in religious conversion. Then the epitome of responsibility for the other is achieved when we fall in love with the "mystery of love and awe." The resultant religious differentiation of consciousness, Lonergan tells us,

> begins with asceticism and culminates in mysticism. Both asceticism and mysticism, when genuine, have a common ground that was described by St Paul when he exclaimed: " ... God's love has flooded our inmost hearts through the Holy Spirit he has given us" (Rom. 5:5). That ground can bear fruit in a consciousness that lives in a world mediated by meaning. But it can also set up a different type of consciousness by withdrawing one from the world mediated by meaning into a cloud of unknowing. Then one is for God, belongs to him, gives oneself to him, not by using words, images, concepts, but in a silent, joyous, peaceful surrender to his initiative.[100]

Hence, all the postmodernist highlighting of the inexhaustibly open-textured character of language – and of what White calls the world-disclosing power of innovative linguistic expression – can be re-understood as the role played by beliefs in the light of faith as the "eyes of being-in-love."[101]

Like the deconstructivist and genealogical postmodernists, Lonergan too is concerned with the dismantling of the truncated utilitarian, the

---

99 Compare Lonergan's references to Karl Rahner's interpretation of "consolation without a cause" in the latter's commentary on St Ignatius Loyola's *Spiritual Exercises*, in Karl Rahner, *The Dynamic Element in the Church*, trans. W.J. O'Hara (New York: Herder & Herder, 1964), esp. ch. 3, "The Logic of Concrete Individual Knowledge in Ignatius Loyola," 84–170, for example; in *Method in Theology*, 106; and in *A Third Collection*, 201, nn. 47 and 48; and 249, n. 2.

100 Lonergan, *A Third Collection*, 242.

101 Lonergan, *Method in Theology*, 115–19; and White, *Political Theory and Postmodernism*, 21.

immanentist Romantic-expressivist, and the exploited and alienated subject. But for him, this dismantling only happens adequately only when by receiving the gift of God's love we enter into a horizon that corresponds with what is ultimately a friendly universe.[102] The term "friendly" here, and the stories of faith that communicate its meaning concretely, have nothing to do with Lyotard's "regimes of truth" that are just legitimating masks for powers who know what is good for us and wish to "force us to be free." Instead, I am hinting at a context of God's glory by which the postmodernist taste for excess, extravagance, and intensity is made good in the light of God's astonishing desire for the flourishing of each and every person and thing in creation in all their specificity and particularity.[103]

7. Lonergan and the Postmodern Sublime

7.1 The Sublime and the Ambiguity of the Surd

A major postmodernist theme not addressed above regards confronting the objective surd of individual and structural evil. According to White and Thomas L. Pangle,[104] the heading under which postmodern thinkers like Lyotard and Derrida treat the human response to pain, danger, and terror involves a transformation of the traditional idea of the sublime. Lonergan, of course, approaches this issue from the standpoint of the mystery of love and awe with its specifically Christian historical intelligibility of the law of the cross, again, in a way that takes the postmodern sublime seriously without just euphemizing them.

We have seen that the postmodernist disciples of Nietzsche specialize in going beneath surface, conventional normalcy to disclose the abnormal and discordant and bizarre. In doing this, they do not simply pick at the seams and slippages of the non-systematic and the contingent. Paradoxically, they are also preoccupied with evil, but from an artificial position "beyond good and evil," since for them the opposition between good and evil is just another fiction foisted on Western culture by Platonism and

---

102 Lonergan, *Method in Theology*, 117, 290.
103 Lonergan, *Method in Theology*, 116–17.
104 See White, *Political Theory and Postmodernism*; and Thomas L. Pangle, *The Ennobling of Democracy: The Challenge of the Postmodern Era* (Baltimore, MD: Johns Hopkins University Press, 1992), 23–9.

Christianity. They therefore tend to revel in ambiguity, seeming to conflate the gesture toward the incommensurability of the non-systematic or random, on the one hand, and the knowing wink toward the surd of sin's arbitrariness and lack of intelligibility, on the other.

Deconstructivist and genealogical postmodernists are nonetheless out to upset both the flatness of bourgeois commercialism and the pathos of Romantic expressivism, through working out a characteristically postmodern sensibility. To this end, they have fashioned a specifically postmodern sense of the sublime.

The classic meaning of the sublime as articulated in Longinus's treatise *On the Sublime* has to do with an exaltation or elevation of the mind beyond its normal state, inspiring a noble pride and a willingness to think critically for oneself in a way that transcends one's ordinary range of motivations and rationales. Rousseau's *Émile* gives a psychological twist to this term by elaborating a process by which erotic passions get sublimated into an internalized willingness to submit to the disciplines of parenthood and citizenship. By the time we reach the 18th-century discussions of aesthetics referring judgments of beauty to the senses, Edmund Burke's *A Philosophical Enquiry into the Origin on the Ideas of the Sublime and the Beautiful* defines the sublime in terms of our responses to pain, the dangerous, and the terrible;[105] and Kant's reflections on the sublime depart from Burke's ideas. By this time, the ancient connotations of elevation, of what people look up to, of the noble, have been all but eliminated. Henceforth, the focus will be upon what cannot be adequately expressed because it is not strictly imaginable or representable. No wonder, then, that the cataphatic philosophy of postmodernism finds the notion of the sublime congenial.

7.2 Lyotard on the Sublime

Derrida and Lyotard, according to White, are absorbed not just by "a concern with otherness expressed by undermining the false self-confidence of foundations"; they are also concerned with

> moods ... traditionally associated with the experience of the sublime (as distinct from the beautiful). A sense of the sublime is elicited when one is

---

105 See Edmund Burke, *On the Sublime and the Beautiful* and *Reflections on the Revolution in France* (New York: P.F. Collier and Son, 1909).

faced with the abyss, the gigantic, the monstrous. Moods typically associated with such experiences are awe, anxiety, and an exalted desperation.[106]

White claims that Derrida does not exploit the notion of the sublime much beyond deconstruction's typical "impulse to intervention."[107] It is Lyotard instead who "has been consistently fascinated with developing a way of thinking about the sublime as the core of postmodern sensibility that can resist the homogenizing, normalizing forces of societal rationalization."[108]

Building upon Burke's meditations on the sublime, Kant noted how our feelings of pain and agitation in the face of the monstrous do have some delight associated with them, as soon as by distantiating ourselves we realize that the terror of privation or of the threat of impending death is not presently inevitable. For Kant, a further pleasure to be associated with an experience of the sublime also stems from the mind's realization that while it cannot adequately understand the object confronting it, it can still "conceive of something like the infinite."[109] And so at this point postmodernism buys into Kant's teaching on the putative limits of *Verstand* or human intelligence, according to which we cannot reach objective truth in regard to our most important questions and human experiences but must remain content with merely conceivable or imaginable *Vorstellungen* or representations such as metaphors, allegories, and symbols.

Lyotard locates the sublime's ambivalent and contradictory feelings of pain and distress mixed with pleasure at the heart of the postmodernist penchant for "impertinently intervening in everyday life in ways that jolt normal sensibility."[110] For Lyotard, the sublime plays itself out in modern avant-garde art and, more dangerously, in certain forms of political enthusiasm. Instead of resigning ourselves to lifelessness in the face of infinite emptiness and universal hopelessness, why don't we strive for the artificial intensification of feeling that is the postmodern sublime?

---

106 White, *Political Theory and Postmodernism*, 83.

107 White, *Political Theory and Postmodernism*, 84.

108 White, *Political Theory and Postmodernism*, 85; also see 85–90.

109 Jean-François Lyotard, "The Sublime and the Avant-Garde," in *Lyotard Reader*, ed. Andrew Benjamin (Malden, MA: Blackwell, 1989), 199; cited by White, *Political Theory and Postmodernism*, 85.

110 White, *Political Theory and Postmodernism*, 84.

7.3 From the Sublime to Worship

Lonergan spent his life facing the concrete results of the longer cycle of decline in Western culture. In confronting the contemporary objective surd, he was anti-technocratic, and he was not a historicist. But he also had precious little sympathy for the *simpliste* anti-technocratic disparaging of the normative achievement of modern natural science so common in continental philosophy and theology; and he had just as little patience with dogmatic refusals to accept the correct implications of the rise of historical mindedness. In principle and in practice, he was a champion of both modern science and modern scholarship. And yet reflecting on what he called the third historical plateau or stage of meaning, he was utterly convinced of the intractability of the human condition by human resources alone. For Lonergan, our damaged total human environment requires a healing that far transcends human creativity and originality. In a strictly technical sense, the evils in this universe constitute a mystery of iniquity since they are disproportionate to our human powers to solve them sufficiently.

But Lonergan was also a person struck to his core by an even greater disproportion or incommensurability: that God so loved the world that he gave his only-begotten Son ... (Jn. 3:6). He could not repeat often enough St Paul's statement about God's love having been poured into our hearts through the Holy Spirit that has been given to us (Rom. 5:5).

Now because of his faith in God's redemption of the universe through Christ Jesus and in the Holy Spirit, Lonergan was not content to dance sublimely at the edge of the abyss. But neither would he be surprised that precisely the imperfection of human embodiments of the absolutely supernatural solution to human evil would eventually evoke both the humanist revolts of Enlightenment and the Romantic reaction, but even an anti-humanist rebellion in the manner of Nietzschean postmodernism as well. The postmodern taste for the sublime may be a pseudo-religious yearning for the intensification of experience, even if artificially or violently. In an age awash in *ressentiment* over the loss of genuine meaning and value, the feeling of the sublime can appear to be quite an attractive alternative. This seems to be a more exotic version of Heidegger's negative eschatology that, under the pretense that "only a god can save us," assumes a meditative attitude of waiting, even if it be for nothing. Compared to the posturings of certain representatives of conventional religious institutions, the cultivation of the sublime can seem rather refreshing. Hence, the surveys telling us of the huge numbers of people who believe in religious experience yet do not believe in God are not so astonishing.

But isn't this anti-humanist attitude of responsiveness to otherness a parody of that displacement away from human concerns characteristic of authentically supernatural hope? I would say it is.

It remains that in Lonergan's framework of the decentered, self-transcendent, conscious subject, responsiveness to the other is fulfilled when human consciousness falls in love and is in love in the love of intimacy (especially in families), in our self-sacrificial loyalty to our communities, and in otherworldly love.

For Lonergan, falling and being in love with God is absolutely transcendent, which means it is disproportionate to strictly human potentiality. Thus, our receiving of the gift of God's love actually achieves the supreme degree of displacement away from ourselves as the center of the universe at the same time as it constitutes the only adequate fulfillment of the unrestricted desire built into our human consciousnesses. We traditionally call the enactment of this radical displacement that both empowers us and commands us religious conversion.

If the deepest or highest longing of the human consciousness is the desire for communion with God and the universe through which God addresses us, then the universe really and not just metaphorically has a conversational structure. At its best, human consciousness responds to the cosmic Word through mind and heart in conversation; or in what Habermas and some neo-pragmatists call communicative action; or in what Gadamer calls hermeneutic experience.

8. Conclusion

My claim has been not just that the postmodern concern for the other, but even that the radical decentering of the modern subject carried out in various ways by the hermeneutic, deconstructivist, and genealogical orientations in contemporary philosophy has to be taken utterly seriously by Christian theology. The importance of this postmodern concern is underlined by the most radical movement in contemporary theology – liberation and political theology. Indeed, the evangelical call to concern for the victims is today being enlarged to embrace not only human, but also subhuman nature: Justice and love for the neighbor, we realize today, cannot be separated from care for the natural ecology proper to genuine human thriving. Neither utilitarian individualism nor expressive individualism – the regimes in which the modern subject holds the primacy – are adequate to the contemporary demands for justice and love. Hence, the relevance for Christian theology of the hermeneutic, deconstructivist, and genealogical strategies for overcoming modern subjectivism for the sake of respecting and loving the other of nature, of fellow human beings, and of God.

Nevertheless, my argument has been that the hermeneutical strategy of Gadamer is too undifferentiated, while the deconstructivist and genealogical strategies are too dialectically flawed, to offer the theoretical and systematic basis for making good the requirements of contemporary liberation and political theology. As Jürgen Habermas from the left and Leo Strauss from the right have both argued, Gadamer's hermeneutic philosophy is so general that it can all too easily devolve into an insufficiently critical traditionalism. And as we have suggested above, the deconstructivist and genealogical strategies as they stand easily justify agnostic pluralism, a posture also not critical enough for contemporary theology's needs. The alternative for those longing to recover the pristine radicality of the Christian gospel to everyday practice, of course, cannot be any form of restoration theology or of ahistorical orthodoxy that fosters fundamentalist sectarianism. But finding an adequate alternative is quite difficult, especially for us theologians who ourselves are often infected with the many different versions of Enlightenment rationalism or Romantic expressivism that dominate the cultural climate today.

This article has tried to show how Lonergan's thought takes seriously most of the major concerns of hermeneutic, deconstructivist, and genealogical postmodernism. When Lonergan thematized his breakthrough to the human subject as subject and to consciousness as experience in terms of the self-appropriation of our rational self-consciousnesses (to use the language of *Insight*) and of intellectual conversion (to use the language of *Method in Theology*); and when he explicated the radical displacement from ourselves as the center of the universe entailed by the intellectualist apprehension and affirmation of an utterly transcendent God beyond necessity and contingency, oddly enough he was carrying forward a postmodern program. All the themes of displacement of the subject as the primary object, of the fragility of consciousness and the contingency of the universe, of the constitutive role of freedom, of the radical historicality of meaning and value receive systematic treatment in terms of the structure and dynamism of finite human consciousness as gift and as precarious achievement.

But Lonergan's explication of postmodernist themes can avoid both agnostic pluralism and fundamentalist sectarianism. I say *"can avoid"* advisedly, since those claiming to have appropriated Lonergan's thought are not immune to utilitarian and expressivist individualism, either. How many of us know students of Lonergan who use Lonergan's panoply of terms and relations to serve the power goals either of individuals or of groups? How many of us have experiences of so-called Lonergan people who assume the Romantic pose of having worked so much harder, or suffered so much more, or become so much deeper than everyone else? Perhaps postmodernism under hermeneutic, deconstructivist, and genealogical auspices can offer an astringent for Lonergan scholars who may have missed the radically postmodern challenge posed by Lonergan's thought.

Conversely, my guess is that precisely because it shares postmodern concerns so profoundly, only Lonergan's thought as grounded in the fragility of consciousness offers an immanent critique of the postmodernist strategies discussed in this article. The reader will naturally judge for him- or herself whether my argument and the suggested lines of immanent critique have been successful.

8 The Recovery of Theology in a Political Mode: The Example of Ernest L. Fortin, AA

Beyond Neoscholasticism: At Home in the Old and the New

Ernest Leonard Fortin was educated in the Catholic school and seminary systems of the pre-Vatican II era during a period when these institutions enjoyed perhaps their greatest vitality, largely owing to the human capital supplied by religious congregations of women and men. Because of the Augustinian Assumptionist congregation's deep roots in French culture, Ernie became extraordinarily fluent as a reader, a speaker, and an author in both English/American and French language and literature, not to mention his ability to grapple with all the Romance languages and with Latin and Greek texts.

Ernie's education at Assumption College, at Laval University in Quebec, and at Rome's Angelicum ensured that he was schooled in neoscholastic philosophy. The familial, educational, and ecclesial recurrence schemes in which he was brought up were arranged and motivated in large part by Catholic Christian responses – many would say, reactions – to modernity. At Laval, though, he had the good fortune to be introduced to Thomas Aquinas's own thought by the extraordinary Charles de Koninck, who taught him serious philosophy in the manner that only one who was a teacher of philosophy and a philosopher in his own right could have done.[1] So at an early stage of his education,

---

1 Fortin paid tribute to Charles de Koninck in "Why I am not a Thomist," *Ever Ancient, Ever New: Ruminations on the City, the Soul, and the Church*, Collected Essays 4, ed. Michael P. Foley (Lanham, MD: Rowman & Littlefield, 2007), 175–82 at 176–7; in "Epilogue: An Intellectual Biography," *ibid.*, 319–28 at 321; and in Michael P. Foley, "An Interview with Ernest L. Fortin, AA, and Photographs of His Life," in *Gladly to Teach and Gladly to Learn: Essays on Religion and Political Philosophy in Honor of Ernest L. Fortin, AA*, ed. Michael P. Foley and Douglas Kries (Lanham, MD: Lexington Books, 2002), 279–302 at 286–7.

Ernie discerned the difference between the products of a great thinker's school and the works of genius that originated the school. In other words, there are readers, scholars, and teachers capable of taking what Ernie called a "fresh" approach to the great books – which means those who came to texts with questions on the level of the answers provided by the authors – and then there are those who read and repeat, often slavishly, the teachings of those texts with little or no clue about the questions to which the authors provide possibly relevant answers.

Great books and good readers became the hallmark of Ernie's scholarly and academic life, and they are central to what I believe he has to offer the church of the future. As you know, the post-Vatican II era of the American Catholic Church has been marked by a fairly wholesale abandonment of philosophical training not only in seminary programs but also in graduate theology/religious studies programs at Catholic colleges and universities.[2] During the mid to late 1960s before Ernie began teaching here in 1971, Boston College had revised its core curriculum, which had been dominated by the sort of scholastic philosophy and theology produced in the late 19th and the early 20th centuries by the ecclesiastical reform under the aegis of Leo XIII's *Aeterni Patris* in 1879. Like many other of its Catholic peer institutions, Boston College replaced that core with a menu of distribution requirements to be administered and taught by people, of whom not all would have been liberally educated themselves. Still, as Ernie's own experience of clarification-by-contrast in the case of Charles de Koninck indicated, the reaction against the sterility of the neoscholastic edifice was not altogether unfounded.

The overwhelming disrepute into which neoscholasticism had fallen in Catholic colleges, universities, and seminaries – Ernie spoke of "the pseudomorphic collapse of Neo-Thomism in the wake of Vatican II"[3] – was precipitated in no small part by the long period of *ressourcement* or "return to the sources" that preceded the Second Vatican Council (1962–5). Ernie's dissertation[4] reveals one trained as a scholar of the

---

2 For his own assessment of the contemporary situation of the Catholic university or college, see Fortin, "The New Catholic College," *Ever Ancient, Ever New*, 189–97.

3 See Ernest L. Fortin, "The Trouble with Catholic Social Thought," *Human Rights, Virtue, and the Common Good*, Collected Essays 3, ed. J. Brian Benestad (Lanham, MD: Rowman & Littlefield, 1996), 303–13 at 311.

4 See Ernest L. Fortin, *Christianisme et culture philosophique au cinquième siècle: la querelle de l'âme humaine en occident* (Paris: Études Augustiniennes, 1959), translated by James G. Colbert as *Christianity and Philosophical Culture in the Fifth Century: The Controversy About the Human Soul in the West* (South Bend, IN: St Augustine's Press, 2015).

Church Fathers of late antiquity and one sensitive both to ancient literary genres and the significance of myth and symbol in religious discourse, on the one hand, and one who had absorbed the complex relationship between the deliverances based on revelation and the residues of Greek philosophy in the Christian authors of late antiquity, on the other. He had been captivated by both Jerusalem and Athens. His dissertation on the soul in late antiquity and his studies in Augustine and Thomas Aquinas (among a host of others) made Ernie a real participant in the build-up of historical scholarship that gradually undermined the ahistorical orthodoxy and rigid traditionalism of the Romanized control of meaning that enabled neoscholasticism's more or less Suarezian "Aristotelico-Thomistic" reading of Thomas Aquinas and caused that reading to be enshrined in the curricula and the multitude of textbooks or manuals used in seminaries and Catholic colleges and universities. Like scholars such as Marie-Dominique Chenu, Yves-Marie Congar, Henri de Lubac, Étienne Gilson, David Knowles, Richard W. Southern, Bernard Lonergan, and Charles de Koninck, Ernie Fortin realized that the neoscholastic reading of Thomas had little to do with the actual achievement of St Thomas Aquinas.[5] Under the pressure of apologetic and polemical motives, the post-Cartesian *Schulphilosophie* of Christian Wolff and Alexander Baumgarten, who were German epigones of Descartes, Spinoza, and Leibniz (and who also induced Kant's "metaphysical slumbers"), influenced that interpretation. After Bishop Melchior Cano's (1509–30) *De locis theologicis* introduced the legal rhetoric of the thesis and the *loci communes* for "proving" the certitude of the dogmas into the manual tradition, such Enlightenment rationalism was considered a godsend in making possible the shift away from the quest for understanding cultivated by the discipline of the *quaestio* to the quest for certitude.

It is no wonder then that the most creative minds in Europe from Kant and Hegel to Dilthey, Nietzsche, Husserl, Heidegger and the postmodern deconstructionists and genealogists have been hell-bent on overcoming "Enlightenment rationalism" by which neoscholasticism

---

5　For Fortin's own account of the disreputable character of Thomism from the 1940s to the present, see "Why I am not a Thomist," 175–82, in which he wrote that at "the end of Vatican II (1965), … a funny thing happened to Neo-Thomism: it disappeared. Suffering a pseudo-mythic collapse, it was unable to defend itself from the assault mounted against it. There is only one explanation for this: something must have been lacking in Neo-Thomism" (179).

had become infected. Nor is it particularly surprising that the liveliest minds of the post-World War II generation entering the ranks to teach philosophy and theology at graduate programs in Catholic universities either learned Continental phenomenology and/or were trained in the historical study of the Bible and of philosophy and theology. Many of them played leading roles in dismantling the carapace of neoscholasticism within Catholic institutions.

With the "old school" neoscholastic dogmatic and systematic theology virtually routed from Catholic institutions in the United States, two changes occurred in the scholarship of theology or religious studies departments. The first is the prevalence of the historical-critical method that ranges from learned sensitivity to genres so well exemplified in the familiar forms of Biblical criticism – *scil.*, source criticism, *Formgeschichte*, redactional, and now rhetorical and literary analysis, and *Tendenzkritik*. Liberationist or Feminist versions of *Tendenzkritik* examine any historical document, artifact, or *objet d'art* in respect of how it legitimates or provides a cover story for some oppressive authority. Thus, in one way or another, departments of philosophy and theology in Catholic colleges and universities place a great deal of emphasis on intellectual history or the history of ideas – and do so for the most part without the benefit of philosophical foundations that would avoid the "relative perspectivism" characteristic of historicism.[6]

The second change in scholarship is the dominance of ethical concern. This concern is manifest in the overriding desire of Catholic theology or

---

6 This relative perspectivism embraces R.G. Collingwood's "absolute presuppositions" referred to by Ernest L. Fortin in his chapter on "The Decline of Political Philosophy," *Dissent and Philosophy in the Middle Ages: Dante and His Precursors*, trans. Marc A. LePain (Lanham, MD: Rowman & Littlefield, 2002), 151–5, at 152 and endnote 8, where Fortin cites Collingwood at length: "It became clear to me that metaphysics ... is no futile attempt at knowing what lies beyond the limits of experience, but is primarily at any given time an attempt to discover what the people at that time believe about the world's general nature; such beliefs being the presuppositions of all their 'physics,' that is, their inquiries into detail. Secondarily, it is the attempt to discover the corresponding presuppositions of other peoples and times, and to follow the historical process by which one set of presuppositions has turned into another ... The beliefs which a metaphysician tries to study and codify are presuppositions of the questions asked by natural scientists, but are not answers at all. This might be expressed by calling them 'absolute presuppositions'" (R.G. Collingwood, *An Autobiography* (Oxford: Clarendon Press, 1939), 65.

religious studies departments to promote the social justice called for by the papal social encyclicals.[7] Within either a liberal or Marxist horizon, its research tends to combine historical and sociological investigations in the vein of the social sciences founded by Karl Marx or Max Weber, or of the Marx/Weber synthesis originally worked out by the Frankfurt School. In philosophy departments ethical concern functions under the influence of thinkers out to "redo" Marx and/or Nietzsche. Sustained by thinkers like Jürgen Habermas, the early Derrida, Michel Foucault, Nancy Fraser, Martha Nussbaum, Judith Butler, Gilles Deleuze, Felix Guattari, and the French female theorists, Julia Kristeva, Hélène Cixous, and Luce Irigaray, the more radical forms of *Ideologiekritik* expose complicity with classism, racism, and gender bias. In the measure that any of these trends depend on assumptions drawn from the hermeneutics of suspicion that themselves frequently entail "relative perspectivism," they also tend to dissolve true meanings and the distinction between good and evil into the *fluxus quo.* To be sure, Paul Ricoeur, Emmanuel Lévinas, Charles Taylor, Alasdair MacIntyre, or the later Jacques Derrida, along with such French Christian phenomenologists as Michel de Certeau, Jean-Luc Marion, Michel Henry, Jean Greisch, Jean-Louis Chrétien, et al., have inspired more moderate and hence more valuable reflections.

Although Ernie Fortin was an adamant opponent of relativism, as he possessed too complicated an understanding of the past to be able to brook the neoscholastic approach to philosophy and theology, so he also rejected its implicit or explicit *fixisme.* As an intelligent and learned defender of the tenets of Christian faith, in him a philosophic or theoretical orientation combined with a determination to conserve what is great, good, and true in the Catholic tradition. So Ernie became a "sign of contradiction," a *vox clamans in deserto* in the world of contemporary Catholic philosophical and theological thought.

---

7 For his own assessment of the evolution of the "new moral theology" from the "old moral theology" that preceded the emergence of contemporary Christian Social Ethics, see Ernest L. Fortin, "The New Moral Theology: Genesis and Present State," *Ever Ancient, Ever New*, 113–29. When he discussed the preoccupations of today's Christian Social Ethics, he did so in light of Tocqueville's perspective, which he certainly preferred. See "A Tocquevillian Perspective on Religion and the American Regime," *ibid.*, 147–62.

Liberal Education: Integrating Athens and Jerusalem

We have to ask why the anti-philosophical and relativist climate of opinion didn't engulf Ernie, too? A first clue to the answer, I believe, is Ernie's marvelous gift for something that (I suggest) for most people is indispensable to the serious learning, liberal education, and authentic philosophy and theology he stood for: his capacity for admiration and for friendship. Ernie was exemplary in "looking up to" actual or potential greatness, especially (but not only) in the realm of intelligence. Ernie did not hesitate to look up to Allan Bloom and especially to Leo Strauss; and he admired others (from afar perhaps) – people such as Alexander Kojéve, Gershom Scholem, and Louis Massignon in the world of ideas; or people like Winston Churchill in the world of politics. He genuinely esteemed such fellow Straussians of rather different stripes as Harry Jaffa, Ralph Lerner, Muhsin Mahdi, Walter Berns, Richard Kennington, Seth Benardete, Harvey Mansfield, and Werner Dannhauser (not to mention our own David Lowenthal, Robert Faulkner, Christopher Bruell, Susan Shell, Christopher Kelly, and Nasser Behnegar), along with other scholars trained by Strauss or by his students, and, not least, those upon whom he himself exercised a formative influence. He would not only admire these people but befriend them, and often be loved by them in turn.

I hardly need to remind this group that Ernie's penchant for friendship and "looking up to" is closely connected with Strauss's approach to political philosophy, where politics is about people's concrete answer to the question, "What do people look up to?" – or, in more technical language, the theological-political problem. Ernie could genuinely echo Strauss in claiming of himself that he felt impelled by the coeval questions concerning God and politics.

The second clue to the underlying reason for Ernie's keeping his balance during the "explosion" in the church after Vatican II was the great turning-point in his life as a scholar and teacher that occurred while Ernie was doing his doctoral studies at the Sorbonne in Paris when he encountered his life-long "friend and teacher" (as he called him in his tribute to him after his death),[8] Allan Bloom, perhaps the most controversial and surely the most flamboyant follower of Leo Strauss.

---

8 See Fortin, "Friend and Teacher: Allan Bloom's Obsession with the Mystery of the Human Soul," *Human Rights, Virtue, and the Common Good*, 315–20.

Ernie was already at home in the horizon of Jerusalem because he was brought up as a Catholic Christian, trained and ordained as a priest, threw in his lot with his Assumptionist brothers, and devoted his life to the service of Catholic educational institutions. Although de Koninck had first embodied serious philosophy for him, Ernie had not learned from that genial Thomist how he could put the riches of his learning about late antiquity and the history of Western art in the service of "a new way of reading old books."[9] By introducing him to the thought of Leo Strauss, Bloom opened for him the horizon of Athens in its radicalness. Strauss said he learned from Martin Heidegger two things about the art of reading old books, both of which were of supreme importance to Ernie: first, docility, or the willingness not only to learn something true from these great old authors but also to encounter something of vital importance for one's concrete solution to the problem of human living together – in short, pointers to "the one thing needful." Second, he learned the attentiveness and care required to read authors in such a way as to notice insights that conventional readings for one reason or another systematically overlook or cover over, especially insofar as their dogmatic interests in the authors tend to overwhelm, the inclination "to accord what [the authors themselves] had to say the full importance [they] attached to it."[10]

Yet Strauss's appreciation for Heidegger's project of re-originating "first philosophy" deviated from the path of his mentor's phenomenological or linguistic or hermeneutic ontology. Strauss turned instead to what he thought philosophy had been for the Socrates of Plato and Xenophon – namely, *political* philosophy. Strauss's politics-oriented follow-through on Heidegger's "reading revolution" heightened rather than blurred the tension between Athens and Jerusalem in virtue of what for Ernie Fortin is the key to Strauss's version of the "reading revolution": the rediscovery of the significance of esoteric writing for political philosophy.[11] Ernie twice remarked to me (and later told Michael Foley in an interview) that he had been prepared to receive Strauss's discovery of esotericism by John Henry Newman's work on the pedagogy of the early Church Fathers as regards the *disciplina arcani* or secret

---

9 See Fortin, "Why I Am Not a Thomist," 175–202.

10 See Fortin, *Dissent and Philosophy*, 153.

11 See Fortin, "Islam and the Rediscovery of Political Philosophy," *Dissent and Philosophy*, 23–37.

teachings.[12] Strauss confirmed Ernie in his opinion that the standard Catholic reception of Newman had overlooked the significance of his tough-minded appreciation for esotericism.[13] Ernie saw how the legacy of Plato's *Seventh Letter*[14] is not only important for political philosophy but also relevant to the issues of the need for a prior and gradual preparation of the souls of searching persons, and of reverently communicating the mysterious core of Christian revelation.

Political Horizon

Ernie sometimes briefly characterized his own intellectual biography as shifting from the pursuit of philosophical and theological studies in terms of what might be called a "cultural" perspective to philosophizing and theologizing from a specifically "political" horizon. Ernie regarded "culture" as a vague abstraction invented by Rousseau, Kant, and Hegel. He credited Bloom with having prodded him to grasp that such abstractions are a way of "avoiding reality, which is naturally political." As Bloom explained, "the political is the comprehensive order in which human aspirations for the good and the noble are actualized. It is the practical decisions of acting men which are most interesting and most revealing of human nature." Because the political viewpoint regards "what is in the power of men to do and what they look to in doing it,"[15] it offers the point of departure for philosophy as an ascent to wisdom that begins with a concrete analysis of the human soul in action. This

---

12 For a clear summary of the issues, and of Fortin's position not only on the Fathers but also on Newman, see Fortin, "The Church Fathers and the Transmission of the Christian Message," *Ever Ancient, Ever New*, 13–29; and "The 'Rhetoric' of the Church Fathers," *Ever Ancient, Ever New*, 47–58; for a brief summary of Clement of Alexandra's approach, see also Fortin, "The Nature of the Christian Message," *Ever Ancient, Ever New*, 39. Compare John Henry Cardinal Newman, "The Position of My Mind Since 1845," *Apologia Pro Sua Vita being A History of His Religious Opinions* (London: Longmans, Green and Co., 1908), 269–71, where (on 269) in discussing "the charge of reserve and the economy," he refers the reader to "Note F, *The Economy*" (343–7); see also "Appendix: Answer in Detail to Mr. Kingsley's Accusations, 7. The Economy," *Apologia Pro Sua Vita* (New York: E.P. Dutton, 1930), 292–7.
13 See Foley, "An Interview with Ernest L. Fortin, AA, and Photographs of His Life," *Gladly to Teach and Gladly to Learn*, 279–302 at 297.
14 See Fortin, *Dissent and Philosophy*, 142.
15 See Allan Bloom, *Giants and Dwarfs: Essays 1960–1990* (New York: Simon and Schuster, 1990), 259.

transformative insight determined Ernie Fortin's wisdom and made his achievement something that those called to the intellectual apostolate in the Catholic Church ignore at their own peril.

Perhaps we can briefly suggest Ernie's relevance to the situation of the church today in relation to the so-called "culture wars." You are probably more than familiar with the Christian responses to these conflicts by the putative "progressive" or "liberal" types and by the presumptively "conservative" types, with both sides constantly compelled to act and react to the other, while often using "political" means of doing battle. Ernie learned from Bloom and Strauss about political philosophy as "first philosophy," but I believe his idea of "theology in a political mode" came from Augustine.[16] Theology in a political mode offered a viewpoint from which he could understand the practical and theoretical significance of the fact that the tension between Athens and Jerusalem actually heightens the polarities already familiar to the ancient philosophers, namely, between philosophy and the city or state, and between philosophy and poetry. Ernie realized that both the culture wars and the superficial Christian political partisanships in response to them are repercussions from the far more serious intellectual crisis of Western thought in our time. Ernie's work on Clement of Alexandria,[17] Basil the Great,[18] Augustine,[19] and Dante[20] (to name but a very few) not only demonstrated the nature of theology in a political mode but also

---

16 Fortin's most passionate, comprehensive, and brilliant exposition of this, I believe, appears in Ernest L. Fortin, "Political Idealism and Christianity in the Thought of St Augustine," *Classical Christianity and the Political Order: Reflections on the Theologico-Political Problem*, Collected Essays 2, ed. J. Brian Benestad (Lanham, MD: Rowman & Littlefield, 1996), 31–63.

17 See Ernest L. Fortin, "Clement of Alexandria and the Esoteric Tradition," *The Birth of Philosophic Christianity: Studies in Early Christian and Medieval Thought*, Collected Essays 1, ed. J. Brian Benestad (Lanham, MD: Rowman & Littlefield, 1996), 123–36.

18 See Fortin, "Christianity and Hellenism in Basil the Great's Address *ad adulescentes*," and "Basil the Great and the Choice of Hercules: A Note on the Christianization of a Pagan Myth," *The Birth of Philosophic Christianity*, 137–51, 152–68.

19 See especially Fortin, "Political Idealism and Christianity in the Thought of St Augustine" and all the essays on Augustine in the section "Augustine and Aquinas on Christianity and Politics," in *Classical Christianity and the Political Order*, 31–63, and 1–150; and the essays collected in the section "Augustine and the Refounding of Christianity," *The Birth of Philosophic Christianity*, 1–122.

20 See Fortin, *Dissent and Philosophy*, a version of whose parts were also collected under identical titles in the section "Dante and the Politics of Christendom," *The Birth of Philosophic Christianity*, 251–304.

made it possible for him to understand the complications with which serious and thoughtful Christians are confronted by the contemporary crisis of culture.

To begin with, Ernie's interest in the political made him highly sensitive to the *apolitical* character of Christian faith as expressed in the gospels and in Augustine. Yet however aware he (like Augustine) was that Christians and their leaders cannot avoid involvement in politics in various ways, he was concerned about the danger of practical and theoretical approaches to the political sphere becoming oblivious of the transpolitical, transcendent reality to which they should be oriented and in light of which they are to judge, direct, and guide human action in the temporal order. Indeed, Fortin took seriously the warning in Karl Rahner's famous essay published before the Second Vatican Council[21] about the implications of the fact that Christians today exist in a "diaspora situation," resulting from the cultural and political innovations wrought by modernity's rejection of the Great Tradition and by the general cultural decline in which the church has been all too complicit. Ernie was able to take the measure of the crisis of culture or civilization at the root of the disturbances with which Christians are now faced.

To be sure, anyone from Nietzsche and Spengler to Bob Dylan and Joan Baez can talk or sing about a culture or civilization in crisis, but it is not so easy to get beyond the level of the clichés or truths that have been unabsorbed or inadequately understood. On its face, culture is not something appealed to but something lived. J.R.R. Tolkien replied to a query about the works that made him famous by characterizing culture as "the leaf-mould of the mind." Like Rousseau, Charles Taylor regards culture as essentially a matter of imagination: "the deeper normative notions and images that underlie ... expectations ... shared by large groups of people ... that makes possible common practices and a widely shared sense of legitimacy."[22]

---

21 See Karl Rahner, "The Present Situation of Christians: A Theological Interpretation of the Position of Christians in the Modern World," *The Christian Commitment: Essays in Pastoral Theology*, trans. Cecily Hastings (New York: Sheed and Ward, 1963), 3–37, especially: "My thesis is this: In so far as our outlook is really based on today and looking towards tomorrow, the present situation of Christians can be considered as that of a diaspora; and this signifies, in terms of the history of salvation, a 'must,' from which we may and must draw conclusions about our behavior as Christians" (14).

22 See Charles Taylor, *Modern Social Imaginaries* (Durham, NC: Duke University Press, 2004), 23.

If we may concede that in principle a culture might provide a normative moment for discerning the good for human beings, Ernie agreed with Plato that culture almost inevitably turns out to be more like the "cave" in the *Republic*. Even so, his familiarity with the history of the Western culture convinced him that our present crisis of culture is unprecedented:

> Westerners were unable to defend the superiority of their civilization for the simple reason that they had renounced the standards by which that superiority could be established. They were at a loss to demonstrate that truth should prevail over error because they had finally concluded that the distinction between them was unclear. Nothing was true or false, everything was relative.[23]

Ernie agreed with Leo Strauss's judgment that "only the history of philosophy makes possible the ascent from the second, "unnatural" cave, into which we have fallen less because of the tradition itself than because of the tradition of polemics against tradition, into that first, "natural" cave which Plato's image depicts, to emerge from which into the light is the original meaning of philosophizing."[24] Ernie eschewed the church's anti-modernist strategy of ahistorical orthodoxy for overcoming the corrosive relative perspectivism of historicism. He read with the greatest care the old books of the Great Tradition of philosophy and theology outside the auspices of the tradition of philosophy and theology as "kept" in that subculture of manuals in philosophy and theology that had been so prominent in Catholic seminaries and colleges, and which epitomized Saul Bellow's line about "turning the works of genius into the canned goods of the intellectuals." Ernie taught us that one can challenge relativist or Whig or historicist history by doing even better history and in this way one can attain an "absolute perspectivism" that acknowledges relativities and complications without sacrificing the truth or the truly good.

But this alone does not exhaust the original meaning of philosophy's need for intellectual ascent and even conversion. Theology in a political

---

23 See Fortin, "A Note on Dawson and St Augustine," *The Birth of Philosophic Christianity*, 116.

24 Leo Strauss, *Philosophy and Law: Contributions to the Understanding of Maimonides and His Predecessors*, trans. with an introduction by Eve Adler (Albany: State University of New York Press, 1995), 136.

mode incorporates philosophy more in the manner of Alfarabi[25] than that of Aquinas (the *ad mentem Aquinatis* advocated by the Leonine educational reform). Ernie took seriously Alfarabi's admonition that "both (Plato and Aristotle) have given us an account of philosophy, but not without giving us also an account of the ways to it, and of ways to reestablish it when it became confused or extinct."[26] Theology in a political mode, as Ernie conceived it therefore, shares the "Socratic turn" to philosophy in the classic sense where the friendly conversation known as dialectic made the question of truth integral to answering the question about the good. In seeking to replace opinions about the whole by true knowledge of the whole, one must move beyond conventions to uncover the "nature" of the most important realities. I believe the distinction Ernie adopted from Augustine[27] and Aquinas[28] between primary and secondary precepts of the natural law[29] as the standard of the quest for the human good is what Aristotle meant by the subtle notion of *physei dikaion*, or what is right by nature. This non-doctrinaire standard for excellence is not quite congruent with either neoscholastic natural law or early modern natural right. The "right by nature" is more heuristic than propositional, more a matter of inquiry than of dogmatic assertion; it has more to do with the perennial set of problems and questions constitutive of philosophy, and in this way provides the standard by which any culture can take its bearings.

Only in the light of that more complicated view of history undertaken from the perspective of the "Socratic turn" and assessed in light of what

---

25 In his "Foreword" to his translation of Alfarabi's *The Philosophy of Plato and Aristotle*, the late Muhsin Mahdi, perhaps the world's foremost authority on Islamic philosophy, wrote: "Until the rediscovery of the authentic teachings and arguments of Alfarabi by Leo Strauss, all knowledge of Alfarabi's radically alien and provocatively challenging conception of Platonic-Aristotelian political philosophy as the key to the final truth about the human condition had been lost" (vii). See Leo Strauss, "How Farabi Read Plato's *Laws*," and "Maimonides's Statement on Political Philosophy," *What Is Political Philosophy* (Chicago: University of Chicago Press, 1988; originally published 1959), 95–169.

26 Alfarabi, *The Philosophy of Plato and Aristotle*, revised edition, trans. with an introduction by Muhsin Mahdi (Ithaca, NY: Cornell University Press, 1969), 49–50.

27 See Fortin, "Political Idealism and Christianity in the Thought of St Augustine," *Classical Christianity and the Political Order*, 46.

28 See Ernest L. Fortin, "St Thomas Aquinas, 1225–1274," in *History of Political Philosophy*, ed. Leo Strauss and Joseph Cropsey, 3rd ed. (Chicago: University of Chicago Press, 1987), 248–75.

29 See Fortin, "Natural Law," *Human Rights, Virtue, and the Common Good*, 159–64 at 161.

is "right by nature" was Ernie able to grasp that "practically all the foundational doctrines of modern thought," – according to his comprehensive listing, "social contractualism and the denial of the naturalness of civil society; the repudiation of natural teleology and its replacement by scientific mechanism; freedom as self-determination or autonomy versus heteronomy; popular sovereignty as a requirement of justice; the theory and not just the practice of religious pluralism; the idea of progress; and more recently, the extrusion of ethics from the realm of politics; value neutrality, and the radical historicity of human thought" – "have their roots in or otherwise reflect [Machiavellian] realism and are motivated by the ... desire to enhance the effectiveness of human activity by consciously lowering its standards."[30] This did not mean that Ernie necessarily opposed all these teachings; rather, he called for theologians and churchmen to moderate their support for them by acknowledging their historical limitations as well as by making this support wiser because of more philosophically and theologically adequate reasons.

Perspectives

I naturally turned to Ernie as a mentor and friend when I also began teaching at Boston College in 1971 and he was already a seasoned teacher and scholar who had just come from Assumption in Worcester. In the early 1970s, the Chair of Philosophy, Fr Joseph Flanagan, took to heart the following statement by Bernard Lonergan:

> Modernity lacks roots. Its values lack balance and depth. Much of its science is destructive of man. Catholics in the twentieth century are faced with a problem similar to that met by Aquinas in the thirteenth century ... [when] Greek and Arabic culture were pouring into Western Europe ... To grasp the contemporary issue and to meet its challenge calls ... for a collective effort. It is not the individual but the group that transforms the culture. The group does so by its concern for excellence, by its ability to wait and let issues mature, by its persevering efforts to understand, by its discernment for what is at once simple and profound, by its demand for the first-rate and its horror of mere destructiveness.[31]

---

30 See Fortin, "Augustine and the Problem of Modernity," *Classical Christianity and the Political Order*, 137–50 at140.

31 See Bernard Lonergan, "Belief: Today's Issue," *A Second Collection*, ed. William J. Ryan and Bernard J. Tyrrell (London: Darton, Longman & Todd, 1974), 87–99 at 99.

In this spirit, the late Fr Flanagan and the late Fr Thomas O'Malley, then Chair of Theology (who had invited Ernie to come to Boston College), decided to start an interdisciplinary alternative to the core intended to liberate students' minds from the managed public opinion of our day and taught by members of both the Philosophy and the Theology departments. With the indispensable aid of Prof. Thomas Owens, Fr Flanagan applied for and obtained a series of National Endowment for the Arts grants that gave the Perspectives Program campus-wide legitimacy. Ernie became the key designer of the first year of Perspectives in Western Culture.

The procedure of Perspectives is *dialectical*: as conversational, the dialectical experiment of history offers a genuine propaedeutic to philosophy today. In this dialectic, if students let themselves in for understanding the positions of the great philosophers and theologians in history *on their own terms*, giving them every benefit of the doubt, their careful reading soon brings to light radical disagreements about the most basic issues among the great thinkers. Great authors are great because they tell us *why* they hold what they do. Read together, they give rise to *quaestiones* in the classic sense of the term. As Lonergan had written in *Insight*, "The plain fact is that the world lies in pieces and pleads to be put together again, to be put together not as it stood before on the careless foundation of assumptions that happened to be unquestioned but on the strong ground of the possibility of questioning and with full awareness of the range of possible answers."[32] The genuinely dialectical spirit is driven by real questions; and real questions are concerned with the *subjects at issue* in the center of the discussion, not ourselves. Only in the last resort are ultimate arguments *ad hominem*, because the intellectual positions we hold on the big issues finally do correlate with our concrete solutions to the problem of human living. But while the quest for such a solution is underway, the beginning of a critical love of truth is attentiveness to others.[33] Ernie demonstrated this with students in his classes and seminars in relation to the authors he studied year in and year out.

For Ernie the renewal of liberal education for university undergraduates consisted in training students to read books worth reading

---

32 See Bernard Lonergan, *Insight: A Study of Human Understanding* (New York: Philosophical Library, 1970), 528.
33 See Strauss, *Philosophy and Law*, 137–8, endnote 13.

and setting conditions in which they can form friendships based on understanding and loving special books together. He had reoriented our Perspectives Program in the early stages of its formation from concentrating on epistemological issues to focusing on how the practical and political question about the right way to live shaped the course of Western philosophy and theology. As we made our way through the series of great texts in our Perspectives curriculum, I would ask him how he would handle texts of, say, Descartes or Pascal, or about the difference between Plato's and Hobbes's approaches to symbols. I believe the fact that Perspectives teachers eventually came to approximate the classic definition of the university as a *community* of scholars and learners within our multiversity was in large part due to Ernie's role in the formation of its first couple of generations of teachers. I once asked him what he thought was the characteristic of a specifically *Catholic* university. Typically, he replied with a question: "Wouldn't it be charity, with a special emphasis on community?"

In relation to Boston College's graduate programs in Theology and Political Science, once again his educational project centered on training students to read the Great Books, on enabling them to become capable of entering the Great Conversation that constitutes the vital center of the Great Tradition, and on showing what that means by his own example and by that of esteemed colleagues. He invited persons who embody that conversation to speak in the Bradley Lectures, and (as he used to joke) he "bribed" students with lovely dinners and drink to attend those lectures and discussions.

Whether he was coaching or playing tennis or participating in the rough and tumble of academic discussion, Ernie was an uncommonly spirited person. He was not about to let exponents of contemporary social ethics get away with passing off as genuinely Thomist or Christian teachings rooted in either Locke or Rousseau;[34] people who did not understand him made him pay for that. A prime example of his entry into the lion's den was his paper about how *Rerum Novarum* depended more prominently on the thought of John Locke and Adam

---

34 See Fortin, "The Trouble with Catholic Social Thought," 303–13, along with all the essays (with the exception of the one in honor of Allan Bloom mentioned above) in the section entitled, "The American Catholic Church and Politics," *Human Rights, Virtue, and the Common Good*, 253–313.

Smith than on that of the Angelic Doctor.[35] He never let poor Luigi Taparelli d'Azeglio, who first replaced legal justice with social justice, off the hook. In my opinion, anyone who has not followed his work with care will not realize how he met the hermeneutic exigencies of Leo's program *vetera novis perficere et augere* in a manner that few were equipped to do, especially those liable to the reactionary neoscholastic polemical penchant for quoting texts out of context and then arguing. Ernie was conscientious about discovering what the *vetera* really were, but he also showed his students and readers how those authors can free one from the tyranny of modern opinion, so long as one is intent on trying to understand them in relation to *their* questions. Ernie taught his graduate students to do this for an astonishingly wide range of authors – ancient and modern, pagan and Christian. He never suggested that the premodern authors had all the answers to today's questions. Instead the thrust of his pedagogy was to cultivate real rather than nominal openness. He knew that it was a "pearl of great price" not easily attained.

Because Ernie did not read Hans-Georg Gadamer and Bernard Lonergan with his usual care,[36] in my opinion he misunderstood both in key ways. Yet as he did theology in a political mode he *performed* or *embodied* just what they taught regarding the matters about which he was critical of them. In Gadamer's case,[37] Ernie's combination of prowess and modesty as an investigator enacted what Gadamer meant by his (perhaps misleading) phrases, "fusion of horizons" and "understanding an author *differently* than the author understood himself." *Horizontverschmelzung* means understanding authors, in the sense of at least reaching a shared grasp *of the realities* about which they write, enough to be able to enter into conversation with them. Gadamer would never have denied that appreciating any differences between the understanding of

---

35 See Fortin, "Sacred and Inviolable: *Rerum Novarum* and Natural Rights," *Human Rights, Virtue, and the Common Good*, 191–222.

36 As regards Lonergan, this becomes most obvious in his favorable review essay on Robert Sokolowski's *The God of Faith and Reason: The Foundations of Christian Theology*, in which he asserts that Lonergan "take(s) the createdness of the world for granted," thus ignoring Lonergan's strategy in *Insight* of the "moving viewpoint" as well as the entire argument of Chapter 19, on divine transcendence. See Fortin, "Faith and Reason in Contemporary Perspective: *Apropos* of a Recent Book," *Classical Christianity and the Political Order*, 297–316 at 301.

37 See Fortin, "Gadamer on Strauss: An Interview," *Human Rights, Virtue, and the Common Good*, 175–89.

the interpreter and that of the author presupposes understanding of the authors in some measure as they understood themselves.

Similarly, early in our relationship, Ernie told me that he thought Leslie Dewart's interpretation of Aquinas on knowing was more correct than Lonergan's.[38] To oversimplify the question at stake, Dewart contended that for Aquinas truth is determined by "taking a look and seeing what's out there, and not seeing what's not out there," whereas Lonergan held that we know the truth by making judgments based on carefully checking whether there is evidence sufficient either to affirm a possibly relevant understanding of something, to deny that it is actually relevant, or to assert that it is only probably or perhaps even only possibly relevant. When one reads Ernie's detailed reviews in *The Birth of Philosophic Christianity* of works on Augustine, his essays on Basil the Great, or his intricate reflection on Arnobius and the *viri novi*,[39] or examines his *tour de force* treatment of Dante in *Dissent and Philosophy in the Middle Ages*, one cannot but be impressed by the care with which Ernie assessed the evidence adduced in support of their views by authors with whose interpretations he disagreed; and by the way he both raised further questions overlooked by the interpreters under discussion and marshaled evidence they failed to take into account before making his own limited prospective judgments. In the case of Dante the marshaling of evidence included bringing to bear cryptography, numerology, chronology, and the exact counting of verses in establishing the correctness of his unorthodox interpretation. In fact, Ernie's account of how one approximates moral certitude in his interpretation of Dante virtually mirrors both Newman's appeal to converging probabilities and Lonergan's account of objective judgment based on the disappearance of "further relevant questions."

Ernie had a quite radical solution to any apparent contradiction between his roles of teacher and priest. He refused to be just "academic" (always a pejorative term in his usage) in his manner of concentrating

---

38 See Leslie Dewart, "On Transcendental Thomism," *Continuum* 6, no. 3 (Autumn, 1968): 389–401. Lonergan had written a critical review in *Theological Studies* (1967) of Dewart's *The Future of Belief: Theism in a World Come of Age* (New York: Herder & Herder, 1966): see Lonergan, "The Dehellenization of Dogma," *A Second Collection*, 11–32, which may have added a certain understandable animus to Dewart's comments on Lonergan.

39 See Fortin, "The *Viri novi* of Arnobius and the Conflict Between Faith and Reason in the Early Christian Centuries," *The Birth of Philosophic Christianity*, 169–97.

on the questions and problems raised by the greatest authors. Always radical, he thought of theology in a political mode not as dogmatic but as ever open to further questions, so his work had a subversive quality. Typically, he had the greatest admiration for Alfarabi and Dante as masters of esoteric communication; they were the proximate models for him of what it meant to recover philosophy and theology in a political mode. Like Strauss, Ernie was extremely wary of putative syntheses between philosophy and theology, because the evisceration of one or the other kind of inquiry would be the inevitable outcome. If he never ignored Averroes's advice in the *Decisive Treatise*[40] to use reason when considering revealed teachings, he also did not allow his faith to wane, or slip away, or be regarded with a jaundiced eye. As a teacher, he did not parade, but neither did he hide, the fact that he was a priest. He once explained to me that his aim was to teach the books in the curriculum with accuracy and integrity so that his students might just wonder and take time to think about why he was and remained a priest. He believed this Christian testimony was appropriate to the diaspora situation in which we live.[41]

Ernie made no bones about the fact that leaders in contemporary Catholic *sacerdotium* and *studium* – the church and the university – would have much to learn from Dante about the church's corruption and betrayal of its own message, and so too about the past and possible future glories of the church. His integral view of educating the person as a human being, as a citizen, and as a Christian was unmatched. The manner in which he implemented that vision was all the more extraordinary, because Ernie Fortin fulfilled what we today recognize as *the* criterion for greatness in theology: the Doric harmony between *logos* and *ergon*, between his teaching and scholarship and the way he lived his life.[42] We all can learn from that.

---

40 See Averroës, *Decisive Treatise and Epistle Dedicatory*, trans. Charles E. Butterworth (Chicago: distributed by the University of Chicago Press for Brigham Young University Press-Islamic Translation Series, 2002); also "The Decisive Treatise. Determining What the Connection Is between Religion and Philosophy," trans. George F. Hourani, in *Medieval Political Philosophy*, ed. Ralph Lerner and Muhsin Mahdi (Ithaca, NY: Cornell University Press, 1963), 163–85.

41 Fortin himself uses the expression "regime of diaspora" in "The Nature of the Christian Message," 31.

42 Fortin refers to the usually ironic use of this contrasting pair by Plato in "The Nature of the Christian Message," at 45, endnote 12.

9 The Economic Good of Order and Culture in Relation to Solidarity, Subsidiarity, and Responsibility

Each human being is the best judge of what is most conducive to his or her own self-preservation, whether this be considered strictly as security of mere life, or as comfortable self-preservation, or as the pursuit of happiness. Liberty is just a means to this end, but a means so necessary, so pervasive, so paramount, that it most resembles an end in itself. The ambiguity of modern liberty – this oscillation between end and means – may be a theoretical liability or weakness, but it largely accounts for its prodigious dynamism.

Pierre Manent, *Modern Liberty and Its Discontents*, 220[1]

Freedom and Goods of Order as Social, Political, and Economic

For Bernard Lonergan liberty or freedom is the originating principle of the human good. To exclude freedom is to eliminate authentic human existence. In agreement with Pope John XXIII's affirmation that "freedom is constitutive of human nature,"[2] he wrote in *Insight*, "there is such a thing as progress, and its principle is freedom."[3] So the importance of

---

1 Pierre Manent, "Liberalism and Conservatism: The Transatlantic Misunderstanding," *Modern Liberty and Its Discontents*, trans. and ed. by Daniel J. Mahony and Paul Seaton (Lanham, MD: Rowman and Littlefield, 1998), 220.

2 See Bernard Lonergan, "*Existenz* and *Aggiornamento*," *Collection*, Collected Works of Bernard Lonergan 4, ed. Frederick E. Crowe and Robert M. Doran (Toronto: University of Toronto Press, 1988), 226.

3 See Bernard Lonergan, *Insight: A Study in Human Understanding*, Collected Works of Bernard Lonergan 3, ed. Frederick E. Crowe and Robert M. Doran (Toronto: University of Toronto Press, 1992), 259.

freedom is not in question. In our present culture what *is* in question is the orientation of our freedom. Similarly, far from calling the free enterprise economic system into question, Lonergan argues in favor of it. It's the orientation of our so-called free market that he finds problematic, precisely because in fact the market is not a mechanism that works automatically, but depends on the genuine freedom of intelligently and critically informed human beings in the given society.

Thomas Aquinas, Lonergan discovered, specified four conditions to be fulfilled for human action to be free: (1) alternative courses of action have to exist in the world; (2) agents have to be aware of some of these alternatives; (3) they must also not be so habituated or addicted to any alternative courses of action that may be criticized insofar as they are finite, because such an habituation would eliminate the freedom of those agents; (4) there must be an awareness of what Aristotle called the "that-for-the-sake-of-which," or end, which possesses no limitations and so allows human beings to will or choose everything else freely.[4] If any of these conditions are not met, a person's decisions, commitments, or actions are not really a result of free human choice.

This formulation of conditions, however, should not mislead us into thinking that the identity of the human person is correctly understood in terms of modern individualism. That is an ideological conception based on the denial that people are social and political beings by nature. But modern individualism also happens to be a presupposition of the modern principle of liberty, which has detached freedom from the normativity of human intelligence, reasonableness, and responsibility governed by the pure, detached, disinterested, and unrestricted desire to know. The false self-image of modern individualism – whether possessive or expressive – has resulted in disoriented freedom. According to French political philosopher Pierre Manent, modern people by and large tend paradoxically to regard freedom as "a means so necessary, so pervasive, so paramount that it most resembles an end in itself"; yet at the same time they treat it as a means to any end that a person happens to judge as "most conducive to his or her own self-preservation, whether this be considered strictly as security of mere life, or as comfortable self-preservation, or as the pursuit

---

4 See Bernard Lonergan, *Grace and Freedom: Operative Grace in the Thought of St Thomas Aquinas*, Collected Works of Bernard Lonergan 1, ed. Frederick E. Crowe and Robert M. Doran (Toronto: University of Toronto Press, 2000), 96–7.

of happiness."[5] This oscillation between means and ends characteristic of the modern notion of freedom is deeply ambiguous. Does freedom exist for its own sake? Or does it involve self-transcendence?

The Ecology of Collective Human Living

To think of the individual with Hobbes and Locke as an isolated atom or with Rousseau as free and equal autonomy removes the human being artificially from the political, economic, and social relationships in which it is embedded. It is to start from the wrongheaded "assumption or fiction," in the words of Cambridge University's Nicholas Boyle, "that social relationships are something that individuals choose (or once upon a time chose) to enter into, out of a calculation of their own advantage."[6] Drawing upon the "deepest implications" of Hegel's thought, Boyle wrote:

> That individuality is a social category, in the sense that it is a category of collective human life: What it means for us to be individuals is determined by the society that gives us names and a language in which to say 'I' (and in many cases the various due gradations of 'you,' 'we' and 'they'), by the economy in which we gradually construct ourselves through our productive work for each other, and by the state that safeguards our physical integrity, prohibits our being sold as chattels, protects our lives and limbs and maintains the institutions within which we can have duties and expectations and freedoms.[7]

It is foolhardy, therefore, to think of the "market as a place where pre-existing individuals make rational choices about their own interests, free from external 'intervention.'"[8] Such is the error in proposing a paradigm for macroeconomic theory that conceives of government "as an irrational constraint on choice, as parasitic on the market and as an enemy of freedom."[9]

---

5 Manent, "Liberalism and Conservatism," *Modern Liberty and Its Discontents*, 220.

6 Nicholas Boyle, *2014: How to Survive the Next World Crisis* (New York: Continuum Books, 2010), 119–20.

7 Boyle, *2014*, 119.

8 Boyle, *2014*, 118.

9 See the most recent version published in Bernard Lonergan, *Macroeconomic Dynamics: An Essay in Circulation Analysis*, Collected Works of Bernard Lonergan 15, ed. Frederick G. Lawrence, Patrick H. Byrne, and Charles C. Hefling, Jr. (Toronto: University of Toronto Press, 1999).

Somewhat differently than Boyle, Lonergan situates the processes of economics – the aggregate of activities proceeding from the potentialities of nature and terminating in a standard of living – within an ecological framework:

An ecology is an interrelated and interconnected set of schemes of recurrence. Ecologies too have their probabilities of emergence and survival. A series of ecologies can form chains of sequential dependence, with prior ecologies grounding the probability of the emergence of the next.[10]

Today an ecological approach is perhaps what is needed to concretize the principles of Catholic social doctrine encapsulated in the terms "solidarity," "subsidiarity," and "responsibility." So let's turn to Boyle's account[11] of the distinct processes within the ecology of collective human life. These distinct processes determine social interaction in the modern world. According to Boyle, because human beings individually and collectively are "objects of force, the locus of needs and satisfactions, and agents of the reproduction of distinctively human life,"[12] they live simultaneously in the following spheres, which often are not carefully differentiated from one another:

1 *Politics* mobilizes collective power to impose the threat or fear of death by means of the state for the sake of public order.
2 The *market economy* meets the need for food, clothing, shelter, and other sources of heat that go to make up the standard of living.
3 Through affective and interpersonal relationships, *social systems* construct systems of care and support that ensure reproduction and thus a collective future.

In Boyle's description of the relationships between *modern* politics and the market economy, politics commands instruments of force inasmuch as people use political mechanisms to "decide what laws shall constrain other members of the state."[13] As such, the state "guarantees the integrity of the economic transactions" by defining and preventing fraud as

---

10 Lonergan, *Macroeconomic Dynamics*, 3.
11 Boyle, *2014*, 106ff.
12 Boyle, *2014*, 112.
13 Boyle, *2014*, 107.

well as by defining and defending our liberties, so that it "maintains the peace, order, and trust which are the prerequisites for the functioning of the market."[14] Since the market economy meets the needs of all parties by means of the free exchange of the products of labor, it "depends on the absence from its operations of the threat of force." For example, when the state "suppresses rackets and imposes minimal conditions for the survival of its members," it "ensures that *only* the relative needs of all parties – not the intimidation of one party by the threat of violence – determine the exchange of goods and labor and the ... price at which the exchange occurs."

Society is distinct from the political sphere that is responsible for publicly authorized power, and from the economic sphere's priced exchanges. For Boyle society encompasses the desire for reproduction that founds families and extends beyond kinship structures to "relationships with other personalities through which our own personalities have been formed" – "relationships understood as binding the human race together through all the variations of the erotic drive: heterosexual and homosexual, parental and infantile, loving and aggressive, sublimated, moral and altruistic."[15] The virtual image for society is the extended family, and Boyle notes that this image "is not an adequate image of the complexity of human relationships, rooted though it is in the original sociability of our species."[16] Why? First, because the need to make a living by producing and distributing the material basis for life shifts the emphasis from society in this narrow sense to economy as what Hegel called "the system of needs and their satisfactions"; and second, the need to protect both society and the market economy calls for power relations imposed by the state in the form of what Hegel called "the system of command."

The mutuality among the economic and political functions puts us in relation to those in society we will never know; and this aspect of mutuality is heightened by the invention of money. If the value of money comes from the economy, its acceptance as a wage for work and as payment for goods derives from the state's protection by means of laws and enforceable sanctions. "Caesar makes it possible to trade promises through an impersonal and enduring medium of exchange – a currency."[17]

---

14 Boyle, *2014*, 108.
15 Boyle, *2014*, 109–10.
16 Boyle, *2014*, 111.
17 Boyle, *2014*, 113.

As money passes through many hands, Boyle tells us, "it exchanges one promise for another," and the state "is the guarantee that those promises will be carried out."[18] Thus, as we have seen so often since the 2007–2008 crisis, when banks have pledged the same money too many times, their failure to make good on their promises means the state has to salvage its credit by persuading taxpayers to cover bankrupts' obligations – "for example, … by a round of quantitative easing."[19] Again, the money circulating in an exchange economy is also the source of taxes paid to the state. As Boyle explains, "[Taxes] may be imposed – whether as disincentives or as revenue raisers – for any collective purpose: political (such as the maintenance of the armed forces or of the administrators of the law), economic (such as the provision of transport and communications or other infrastructure which develops the market or makes it more efficient), or social (such as furthering cohesion and continuity by caring for the sick or by educating the next generation)." As Boyle goes on to say, "Tax is one of the means by which my activity in the market becomes an activity of the state that makes the market possible."[20]

The founder of L'Arche and Faith and Light, Jean Vanier, has said that French psychoanalyst and social philosopher Julia Kristeva "has often told me that she is ill at ease with the inconsistence of some Christians: their ideas put them on the political left, but their hands pull the financial reins firmly to the right."[21] But these considerations of the ecological relationships among society, economy, and politics make it clear that the vaunted opposition between the market and social solidarity is based on a serious misunderstanding.

The Human Good: A Framework for an Ethical Approach to Economics

Bernard Lonergan handles the ecological dimensions of collective human life in terms of the heuristic structure of the human good, which he defines as the concrete historical outcome of human acts of knowing,

---

18 Boyle, *2014*, 113.

19 Boyle, *2014*, 113–14.

20 Boyle, *2014*, 114.

21 Jean Vanier, *Signs of the Times: Seven Paths of Hope for a Troubled World*, trans. Ann Shearer (London: Darton, Longman & Todd, 2013), 23.

deciding, and acting. Lonergan's articulation of the complex facets of the human good in the structure of the human good was based on Thomas Aquinas's amplification of Aristotle's definition of the good as the object of appetite, *id quod omnia appetunt*.[22] In respect of the good as specifically human, the generality of Aristotle's definition refers to all that human beings might desire, want, or need, as well as to their operations and cooperations toward the attainment of *particular goods*. Building upon Aquinas's elaboration of the contribution to the good by intelligence, Lonergan worked out a further level corresponding to the ingenuity of human intelligence in the development of roles and skills within institutional contexts that result in different types of what he named the "good of order"[23] – namely,

> the objective arrangement of institutions that ensures for a group of people the regular recurrence of particular goods. As appetite wants breakfast, so an economic system is to ensure breakfast every morning. As appetite wants knowledge, so an educational system answers the imparting of knowledge to each successive generation.[24]

Let's move now beyond Boyle's portrayal of collective human life to highlight the influence upon Lonergan of historical sociologist Christopher Dawson regarding the centrality of "culture" for human social and historical life.[25] This led Lonergan to affirm the overarching role of culture and cultural institutions in the ecology of collective human life. For Lonergan culture is what human beings do with their liberty in the social, technological, economic, and political recurrent schemes that compose human ecology precisely insofar as human living is constituted by meaning and value.

---

22 Bernard Lonergan, "The Subject," *A Second Collection*, ed. William F.J. Ryan and Bernard J. Tyrrell, (London: Darton, Longman & Todd, 1974), 84.

23 As Aquinas said, "finis quidem universi est aliquod bonum in ipso existens, scilicet ordo ipsius universi" (*Summa theologiae* I, q. 103, a. 2 ad 3m.). See John Wright, SJ, *The Order of the Universe in the Theology of St Thomas Aquinas* (Rome: Gregorian University Press, 1957).

24 Wright, *The Order of the Universe*, 81–2.

25 See Christopher Dawson, *The Age of the Gods: A Study in the Origins of Culture in Pre-historic Europe and the Ancient East* (London and New York: Sheed & Ward, 1933; first published, London: John Murray, 1928).

As the emergently probable terrestrial schemes within the order of the universe unfolded, the world's organic and psychic manifolds gradually evolved to provide the conditions for the emergence of intelligent, reasonable, and responsible consciousness.[26] Human culture arises (along with its material conditions) as a superstructure from the gradual build-up of its infrastructure of society, technology, capital formation, economy, and state.[27] As Lonergan wrote, "over and above mere living and operating, men have to find a meaning and value in their living and operating," and that "it is the function of culture to discover, express, validate, criticize, correct, develop, improve such meaning and value."[28] Culture, then, is the human capacity "to ask, to reflect, to reach an answer (to the question of what the human drama, what being human is about) that at once satisfies our intelligence and speaks to our heart."[29] Thus, human liberty concretely functions within a cultural matrix that profoundly conditions, even if it does not determine, the measure in which a person either exists authentically, or collapses into inauthenticity, or perhaps authentically realizes inauthenticity.[30]

For Lonergan this way of thinking about culture is grounded in Thomas Aquinas's account of the will and of decisions in the *Summa theologiae*. From this perspective one deliberates to reach judgments about means appropriate to ends; but deliberation follows both previous judgments regarding the ends of action and the acts of wishing the affirmed ends (*velle*) that proceed from those judgments; and those ends are hierarchically ordered in relation to a highest end. The third and final level in Lonergan's heuristic structure of the human good is therefore the good of value that stands beyond particular goods and goods of order. The possible terminal values are correlative to (1) individual or group orientations (and the radical changes in orientation called "conversions") and (2) interpersonal relationships or friendships that are determined in accord with the normative scale of vital, social, cultural, personal, and religious values.

---

26 Lonergan, *Insight*, 484–507.
27 Lonergan, *Insight*, 232–69.
28 Bernard Lonergan, *Method in Theology* (New York: Herder & Herder, 1972), 31–2.
29 Lonergan, *Insight*, 261.
30 Lonergan, "*Existenz* and *Aggiornamento*," 226–7.

Culture, the Economic Good of Order, and Solidarity

We have suggested above that the rhythms of production and monetary circulation supply the material conditions for the emergence of human culture. In an early version of his economic analysis Lonergan discussed the genesis and the role of what he called "cultural overhead."[31] What is cultural overhead? Recall that the rhythms, in which human beings have perennially labored to produce the material conditions of human living, to a greater or lesser degree, have always involved both the *primary* production of the standard of living at any given time, and the *secondary* production of the means that accelerate that primary production, inasmuch as human inventiveness has always come up with new ideas, which both transform and in the long run exploit modes of changing the potentialities of nature into an improved standard of living.[32]

History, however, shows that "man does not live by bread alone." In certain societies the twofold rhythmic interaction characteristic of surplus and basic production is so successful that its surplus is not completely expended on the continuous provision of the *ordinary* final goods of "food, clothing, shelter, convenience, utilities, amusements." Then its accelerating surplus may be widened to produce the "material fabric of culture, the instruments of learning and the professions." Such cultural *overhead*, then, "is the medieval emergence of monasteries, churches, cathedrals, schools, universities, guild halls ... [and] the Renaissance patronage of the arts."[33]

In *For a New Political Economy* – that early elaboration of his new paradigm for economic theory – Lonergan explained three, inter-related pure and dynamic phases of economic development. Both the first *capitalist* phase of surplus production and the second *materialist* phase of basic production each "redistribute labor to make more widening possible." The third *cultural* phase "liberate[s] men from the economic to the cultural field, increasing the ministers of religion, the schools of the philosophers, the numbers of artists, scientists, professors, students,

---

31 See Bernard Lonergan, *For a New Political Economy*, Collected Works of Bernard Lonergan 21, ed. Philip J. McShane (Toronto: University of Toronto Press, 1998), 17: "Overhead final products pertain to the cultural superstructure of society: they are the flow of books, schools, hospitals, courts, prisons, armaments, public buildings, noncommercial roads and bridges, churches, and the like."

32 Lonergan, *For a New Political Economy*, 16.

33 Lonergan, *For a New Political Economy*, 24.

soldiers, sailors, airmen, and so forth according to the current conceptions of the needs of the cultural field."[34]

In Lonergan's analysis, concrete relationships of presupposition and complementarity play a significant part in constituting the intelligibility of the dynamically developing ecology of collective human living. From one standpoint, then, culture *emerges from* the complex ecology of technology, of surplus and basic economic cycles, and of polity, which it presupposes; yet concretely, culture is the superstructural complement that, because it provides the lived grounds for judgment, massively conditions the direction and guidance of the technology, of the surplus and basic economic evolution, and of the polity of any civilization.

The complex and often misunderstood finality of the pure phases of economic development within any given ecology of collective human life unfolds in "a *capitalist* phase … [that] transforms means of production" and "a *materialist* phase [that] exploits new ideas to raise the standard of living," while the *cultural* phase's "improvement of the … fabric of the culture" makes possible the "cultural development that prepares the way for another transformation of dynamic structure." In Lonergan's general theory of successive developmental phases, therefore, cultural development ultimately grounds the capitalist phase of what liberal capitalists and Marxists call "capital formation," which is "the period of radical transformation," and hence, also of the acceleration of the materialist phase of production that exploits the transformative new ideas for the sake of greater social prosperity.

Commerce, Exchange Economy, and Culture

The Emergence of Commerce

Although for Lonergan the rhythms of basic and surplus production are transcultural invariants, economies evolve through the ages as people devise different ways of doing things to survive and flourish under the conditions prevalent at any given time. For example, property as "a method of coordinating a particular person with a particular thing"[35] originally did not exist. Similarly, there was the transition from agrarian economy largely based on barter to commercial economy based on

---

34 Lonergan, *For a New Political Economy*, 23–6 at 25.
35 Lonergan, *For a New Political Economy*, 29.

money. As a result, 18th-century England, Scotland, and France witnessed the emergence of "commerce," described by Pierre Manent as "not just a human activity among a number of other human activities, but a new regime of human action itself whose development provides the axis of human progress."[36]

The Modern Exchange Economy

The emergence of commerce in this sense coincided with the beginnings of a momentous sea change in culture represented by all the great social and especially political transformations associated with modernity. In premodern societies, people "put in common their actions and their reason"[37] by establishing community in the sense of a shared way of life for which common goals and aspirations are essential. In contrast, as Montesquieu's *The Spirit of the Laws* (Books 20, 21) explained about modern commercial society, the exchange economy "links people through what they severally do, without necessarily sharing a common way of life."[38] Indeed, the rise of commercial society inspired Hegel's idea of civil society's "system of needs and satisfactions."

If the exchange economy motivated Adam Smith in *The Wealth of Nations* to call commercial society a "natural system of liberty,"[39] in Smith's parlance the term "natural" is roughly synonymous with Lonergan's description of "organistic spontaneity," that is, "the mutual adaptation and automatic correlation of the activities of many individuals as though they were parts of a larger organic unit," – e.g., an anthill or a beehive.[40] This understanding makes unnecessary two of the conditions needed for free decision – i.e., (1) awareness of objectively possible alternative courses of action and (2) uncoerced, free choice of one or other alternative – provided that the individual pursues her or his own interest or advantage in "the race for wealth and honors."[41]

---

36 Manent, "Liberalism and Conservatism," 222.

37 Aristotle, *Nicomachean Ethics*, book 4, chapter 3 (1126b11–12).

38 Manent, "Liberalism and Conservatism," 222–3.

39 See Adam Smith, *An Inquiry into the Nature and Causes of the Wealth of Nations* (New York: Modern Library, 1937), I.X.99.

40 See Bernard Lonergan, "Finality, Love, Marriage," *Collection*, 39.

41 Adam Smith, *The Theory of Moral Sentiments* (1759): "In the race for wealth, and honors, and preferments, [one] may run as hard as he can, and strain every nerve and every muscle, in order to outstrip all his competitors."

For Lonergan, the exchange economy is "an attempt to give a continuously satisfactory answer to the continuously shifting question, *Who*, among millions of persons, is to perform *which*, among millions of tasks, in return for *what*, among millions of possible rewards?" He says these questions are solved by "a dynamic equilibrium resting on the equilibrium of the markets"[42] in which

> every product of the exchange economy must mate through exchange with some other product, and the ratio in which the two mate is the exchange value. The generality of this equilibrium makes it indifferent to endless complexity and endless change; for it stands on a level above all particular products and all particular modes of production.[43]

Because individual traders "are out to do business, and *other things being equal*, no trader and no market will do much business unless its terms are as fair as the terms offered by the next trader or the next market," markets in general "tend to make uniform the ratios in which different categories exchange at every instant," "and to adjust those ratios to variations in supply and demand."[44]

In principle (or ideally), a free enterprise economy continuously answers the questions *who*, *which* task, and for *what* reward independently of any "system of command" based on power. Lonergan was always opposed to bureaucracies and criticized Weber's category of bureaucratic legitimacy, because bureaucracies tend to gravitate against the intrinsic component of authority, which is not power but human authenticity as grounded in human attentiveness, intelligence, reasonableness, and responsibility. Bureaucracies reduce the probabilities for the principle of subsidiarity to be realized because in a bureaucratic set-up, as Lonergan wrote,

> it is not enough just to have a new idea, even if the idea is just what is wanted. The idea has to combine with power, with wealth, with popular notions, before it can be realized. It cannot simply emerge from the man on the spot, diffuse, give rise to new potentialities in a chain reaction. Developments become lopsided, curtailed. Completion of the development is demanded by disaffection, but it cannot emerge in the normal fashion of

---

42 Lonergan, *For a New Political Economy*, 34.
43 Lonergan, *For a New Political Economy*, 35.
44 Lonergan, *For a New Political Economy*, 32.

the spread of an idea. It has to come by management, from above down-ward, not from below upward. Management always needs more power. Without a constant increase in power management cannot control all the outside factors that might interfere with its plans ... And so there occur the rise and growth of a bureaucratic hierarchy.

In spontaneous developments, the new ideas come where they may to the man on the spot who is intelligent, sees the possibilities, and goes ahead at his own risk. But in the bureaucracy the intelligent man ceases to be the initiator. He does not have the power, the connections, the influence, to put his ideas into practice.[45]

To promote the principle of subsidiarity, Lonergan was convinced that to begin the transformation of what *de facto* happens in so-called free market economies, he needed "to formulate the laws of an economic mechanism more remote and, in a sense, more fundamental than the pricing system ... laws which men themselves administrate in the personal conduct of their lives."[46] In a free enterprise economy, entrepreneurs, bankers, and workers need both to be aware of the objectively possible alternative courses of economic action, and to choose the course of activity that accords with ends that can be rationally assessed. According to Lonergan, discovering what the objectively possible courses of action are lies at the heart of economic process, and doing this requires an understanding of the process of production and monetary circulation to be able to judge what ought to be done, and to decide to do it freely.[47] The alternative to the exchange economy operating

---

45 See Bernard Lonergan, *Topics in Education: The Cincinnati Lectures of 1959 on the Philosophy of Education*, Collected Works of Bernard Lonergan 10, ed. Robert M. Doran and Frederick E. Crowe [revising and augmenting the unpublished text prepared by James Quinn and John Quinn] (Toronto: University of Toronto Press, 1993), 60–1.

46 See Bernard Lonergan, "An Outline of Circulation Analysis," Lonergan Archives, Toronto, Batch II, Folder 58, of unnumbered pages; now published in *For a New Political Economy*, 109–10.

47 See Bernard Lonergan, "The Transition from a Classicist World-View to Historical-Mindedness," *A Second Collection*, 1–9 at 8: "The flight from understanding blocks the insights that concrete situations demand. There follow unintelligent policies and inept courses of action. The situation deteriorates to demand still further insights and, as they are blocked, policies become more unintelligent and action more inept. What is worse, the deteriorating situation seems to provide the uncritical, biased mind with factual evidence in which the bias is claimed to be verified. So in ever increasing measure intelligence comes to be regarded as irrelevant to practical living. Human activity settles down to a decadent routine, and initiative becomes the privilege of violence."

on the basis of informed judgment and free choice has tended to be the influence of a political disposition of power – either in the form of bureaucratic authority or "the pressure of terrorism to oil the wheels of enterprise."[48]

However, as Nicholas Kaldor observed, the needed "formulation of an economic mechanism" required a shift from attending exclusively to the *allocative* functions of markets to understanding "their *creative* functions – as an instrument for transmitting impulses to economic change."[49] What was required, according to Lonergan, is a systematic or analytic framework that can explain, instead of merely recording or describing the aggregate phenomena of macroeconomics. To be able to explain the booms, slumps, and crashes of the trade or business cycles, such an analysis had to be as dynamic as the subject matter under investigation, something that only could be achieved by understanding what the significant variables are in the light of which price changes could be interpreted.

Money and Credit: The Crux of Responsibility

Not only did Adam Smith call the support furnished by the exchange economy to the earlier forms of commerce a "natural system of liberty," but the original exchange economy also gave substance to bourgeois notions of civil equality as the right to what anyone could get through their own efforts. However, crucial to the rise of modern commerce was the invention of money, which was initiated by lending at interest, by providing credit, and the use of letters (or bills) of exchange. In a comment on Montesquieu (chapter 20, Book 21) Manent wrote:

> The invention of the letter of exchange frees commerce from the limitations that circumscribed it ... Thanks to the revolution produced by the letter

---

48 Lonergan, *For a New Political Economy*, 35. Back when he wrote this about terrorism, Lonergan probably had in mind the Soviet command economy and the Gulag Archipelago that enveloped all of the Soviet Union and its satellite states. But isn't there a subtle yet effective terrorism exercised by banks "too big to fail"? And how about what MIT economist and former IMF chief economist Simon Johnson regards as the oligarchy that runs those financial institutions and supports the campaigns of presidents and legislators? See Simon Johnson, "The Quiet Coup," *Atlantic*, May 2009.

49 Nicholas Kaldor, "The Irrelevance of Equilibrium Economics," *The Economic Journal* 82 (1972): 1237–55 at 1241.

of exchange, commerce can be universalized and it does indeed become more and more universal. Over against the ordinary political world with its boundaries, sovereigns, and armies, commerce constitutes "another world" that is invisible, without a head, without territory, or rather whose territory is the universe, with no coercive physical force at its disposal but always imposing in some measure its law on political sovereigns.[50]

Money as a Relative Value vis-à-vis Absolute Value

According to the conditions of liberty set forth above, in the measure that the exchange value so crucial for economics has ultimately to be understood in the context of an (at least symbolic) apprehension of a good irreducible to economic goods, value has nothing to do with the relativism common in conventional thinking about value. Conceived in this way, "the general idea of value coincides with the idea of the good, of excellence." As Lonergan said,

> Excellence may pertain to an object itself, rise from it in isolation from all other things, and remain despite utter uselessness. Such is the absolute value of truth, of noble and heroic deeds, of the flower in the crannied wall.[51]

Only in the light of absolute value can one correctly discern the *relative value* by which "excellence may belong to an object in its relativity, its utility, its aptitude to excel in serving ulterior purposes ... only some of them relative to man." *Economic value*, therefore, is the relative value that regards abundance or scarcity. It is specified by both the proportion of a product in relation to the effort of producing it, and by the *exchange value* that results from any decision to strive for an object, *even when the decision is independent of either the striving or the effort involved in producing it.*

Adam Smith and all the proponents of the "labor" theory of value (Locke, Ricardo, Marx, Sraffa) could never adequately clarify the relationship between exchange value and "toil and trouble" in measuring

---

50 See Pierre Manent, *The City of Man*, trans. Marc A. LePain (Princeton: Princeton University Press, 1998), 43.

51 Lonergan, *For a New Political Economy*, 30–1.

the value of a commodity, and so they tended to oscillate between value as the amount of toil and trouble expended on the production of commodities and value as value-in-exchange. Lonergan clarified this by applying Aristotle's differentiation between two viewpoints from which to consider any given reality: the perspective of "what is first-for-us" (*proton pros hemas*) – for instance, the rising and setting of the sun – and the viewpoint of "things-in-relation-to-each-other," or what is "first according to nature" (*proton kata physin*) – say, the sun in relation to the planets in the solar system. Thus, Lonergan said that "an economic value [that] relates an object to human effort" is a tool for bookkeeping, and "an exchange value [that] relates objects among themselves"[52] is pertinent for measuring the phases of growth in a modern industrial and commercial society.

The growth of an exchange economy involving divided exchanges required the shift from barter as a means of exchange to money. So money, like property, is a technique or a technological advance. As Lonergan explained, "the divided exchange, selling here and buying there ... postulates a dummy that will bridge the intervals, short or long, between contributing to the process and sharing in its products."[53] Money, then, is that dummy. The exchange economy "directs the aggregate of goods, services, and property that are for others" in the expectation "of a proportionate return, to a pyramid of local, regional, national markets of various kinds"; it "leaves it to the markets to control contributions and to apportion rewards."[54] Hence, money plays (1) a functional, "time-bridging" and instrumental role within the exchange economy, and it (2) functions fairly and adequately as an instrument of accountancy – the "money of account"[55] – only if it fulfills these conditions: (a) divisibility or the capacity to be broken up into measurable units so that ratios of exchange can be correlated with quantities of money, (b) homogeneity, ensuring that equal quantities are equally acceptable, (c) constancy in exchange, so as to be neither inflationary nor deflationary, and (d) universal acceptability.[56]

---

52 Lonergan, *For a New Political Economy*, 31.
53 Lonergan, *For a New Political Economy*, 37.
54 Lonergan, *For a New Political Economy*, 34.
55 Lonergan, *Macroeconomic Dynamics*, 101.
56 Lonergan, *For a New Political Economy*, 37–8.

When we understand money as an instrument of account, we imply that *it serves the economic process of the production of goods and services and the circulation of monetary flows*. When the market *serves the overall well-being of the society*, the economic process *serves social solidarity*. For these reasons, "money has to conform to the objective exigencies of the economic process, and not vice-versa." Seen in light of a correct understanding of the demands of the economic process – not as an inevitable movement toward a Walrasian general equilibrium, but as an intelligibly ordered transition back and forth between basic and surplus circuit equilibria and disequilibria – money (or credit) functions to enable the smoothest possible shifts in monetary flows as the economy's production and circulation move from one phase in the cycling of the economic dynamism to another. That is why, for Lonergan, there is no valid reason to support the notion either that money should be integrally attached to a gold-standard,[57] or that the sheer accumulation of more and more money is the *raison d'etre* of the exchange economy. Either of these blunders wreaks havoc with the concretization of the principles of solidarity, subsidiarity, and responsibility.

*Money and Responsibility: Money's Function in
Relation to the Times of Production*

A correct understanding of the function of money is absolutely central to Lonergan's analysis of the pure cycle of economic production and monetary circulation. However much Lonergan agreed with Keynes about the need for a macro-analysis, he did not think that the so-called Keynesian revolution succeeded in working out an adequate macroeconomics because Keynes was still operating in terms of the equilibrium economics of David Ricardo's 1810 theories that were already unable to do justice to dynamic, changing, and growing economies. Lonergan wondered why business or trade cycles tend toward exaggerating their phase of major surplus (producer-goods) expansion and "systematic profits" into a boom and toward reducing what should become a basic (consumer-goods) expansion (with a higher standard of living for workers without either unemployment or inflation) into a crash that relegates a "notable proportion of the population" to "the reserve army of the unemployed."[58]

---

57 Lonergan, *For a New Political Economy*, 40–1.
58 Lonergan, *Macroeconomic Dynamics*, 115, note 38.

Although Lonergan, like Schumpeter and Kaleçky, knew that he had to take business cycles seriously, he disagreed with the doctrine of Juglar and Schumpeter that booms are the causes of slumps. Instead he suggested that money understood and used correctly could help to avoid slumps, recessions, and depressions, provided that the quantity of money flows needed both for accelerating either the surplus or the basic circuits of production at the right times during the distinct cycling phases in the unfolding expansion of the correctly understood cycles of capital and consumer goods, and (as expansions level off, as they inevitably must) for maintaining the newly attained levels of production and circulation during the static phase between expansions, is supplied.

Lonergan emphasized how destructive the misunderstanding of money as no more than a place-holder for gold is because it "effectively places money before men." It is claimed that labor simply becomes the instrument of capital in accord with the demands of capital formation and profit maximization. But, according to Lonergan, a correct understanding of economic dynamics shows the foolhardiness of the gold-standard approach to the control of money, which subordinates the entire economic process to the demand for gold/money by systematically misinterpreting the necessity of increases in the flows of money in accord with the long-term needs of:

1 the capitalist *surplus* expansion, with its anti-egalitarian concomitants, which is to be followed by
2 the materialist and egalitarian *basic* expansion that compensates consumers of the current standard of living for the sacrifices made during the surplus expansion, when it then culminates in
3 the static phase of an economic process that continues at the highest level of those previous expansions rather than entering a slump.[59]

The gold-standard principle for controlling money cannot meet the requirements of long-term economic expansion; nor can it cope with either international movements of capital or financial crises with their attendant crises of confidence in the banks and runs on the banks in crashes. The lasting illusion of considering money on the gold-standard

---

59 Lonergan, *Macroeconomic Dynamics*, 103–4.

normative is one reason why banks have traditionally had such a bad name.

Clearly, the concrete premise of money as the means of public accountancy is *credit*. If people spontaneously both desire and consider "real" only things imagined as "already-out-there-now-real" (*ad instar* gold bars stored in some fort), not only will credit be considered something that lacks palpable reality, but also it will be misinterpreted (by analogy with the gold-standard) as a commodity or *as if* it were just another commodity. This amounts to a denial that credit/money as an instrument of account actually possesses an intelligible relationship to economic process.

Now if the gold-standard (or ideas analogous to it) has no validity, it needs to be set aside, Lonergan tells us, in favor of "a frank avowal that money is simply a system of public bookkeeping," along with "a coherent and thorough transformation of all monetary practice with the fundamental fact."[60] Otherwise, "the whole economy comes to be regulated not by the social good, not by the objective exigencies of the economy itself."[61] "The money invented to serve the objective process and the social good"[62] becomes a servant of a disordered law of financial possibility "when economic cycles, guided by the likes of economists like Milton Friedman, have been intentionally manipulated to accelerate the excess wealth of huge multinational corporations and their directors at the expense of literally billions of people around the world."[63] In other words, when the intelligibility of the exchange process is subordinated to the law of money as a commodity, "the exchanges [called for by the normative demands of the pure cycle of production and circulation] cannot take place no matter how useful, how desirable, how necessary."[64]

Alternatively, for Lonergan, when the objective exigencies of the economic process govern money in its rightful role as an instrument of account, the demands of the "pure cycle" of production and distribution

---

60 Lonergan, *For a New Political Economy*, 104.
61 Lonergan, *For a New Political Economy*, 105.
62 Lonergan, *For a New Political Economy*, 105.
63 Richard Renshaw, "Reconstructing Economics," Holy Cross International Justice Office, http://www.holycrossjustice.org/resources/HCIJO%20Document%20 Library/BookReviews/2012Renshaw_EcoEcon.pdf . This is a book review of *Sacred Economics: Money, Gifts and Society in the Age of Transition* by Charles Eisenstein and *For a New Political Economy* by Bernard Lonergan.
64 Lonergan, *For a New Political Economy*, 105.

are heeded. Lonergan concedes that the rule of the law of money as a commodity may be effective "in the capitalist phase and the earlier part of the materialist phase" of an expansion.[65] But when financial possibility dominates real possibility during the later materialist and static phases of the pure cycle, it transforms the pure cycle into the secular trade or business cycle: then, as "net surplus drops, the volume of credit contracts; as credit contracts, the volume of economic activity contracts; the expansion ends by reverting to a pre-expansion position or something worse."[66] However, says Lonergan, to bring financial possibility into harmony with the needs of the pure cycle "means thinking out afresh our ideas of markets, prices, international trade, investment, return on capital." Above all "it means thinking out afresh our ideas on economic directives and controls" but not on "the facile model of the totalitarian or socialist regimes which simply seek to abolish the problems and with them human liberty."[67]

We recall (and are presently reminded by Islamic *sharia* law) that both Aristotle under the conditions of a chiefly agrarian economy and the medieval Schoolmen in a feudal economy tended to consider lending at interest as usury, and hence as an unnatural way of making a living. Aristotle had such an unfavorable view of money in the *Politics* by reasoning that when people barter to establish the value of any object, they are more likely to keep in mind the "use-value" of what is bartered, because – as Aristotle and his medieval followers assumed – this usefulness has a chance of being discerned in the light of an internal, culturally mediated, and shared sense of a hierarchy of ends oriented toward a highest good.

Nevertheless, Aristotle (like Smith, Locke, Ricardo, and Marx) did not adequately understand money in terms of exchange value as relating objects among other objects in accord with the concomitance or lack of concomitance between "the real flow of property, goods, and services and the [money] flow being given and taken in exchange for the real flow."[68] Still less did any of these thinkers grasp that in an advanced industrial society, the aggregate real flow and the aggregate money flow *are channeled within two separate circuits of production and circulation*

<hr>

65 Lonergan, *For a New Political Economy*, 105.
66 Lonergan, *For a New Political Economy*, 105.
67 Lonergan, *For a New Political Economy*, 105.
68 Lonergan, *For a New Political Economy*, 40.

functionally distinguished into producer goods and consumer goods, and operate in real time in accord with distinct phases of expansion. In short, *by not understanding "money of account," they failed to grasp the relationship of money to time – i.e., the timing of the normative cycles of an expansion.*

Therefore – and this is most significant – it seems that our culture does not adequately understand that "money of account" as based on credit is intentionally related to the future, namely, to what is implied in the Latin root of the word credit, *credo, credere*, to believe, to trust in. For Lonergan, a major aspect of the intelligibility of money is that it represents promise. That money represents the promise of future satisfaction or the promise of a future exchange with an unknown third party is fairly obvious. Lonergan challenges us to expand our notion of money as promise, to envisage money as the promise of a future expansion of surplus or capitalist production, *for the sake of* the future expansion of basic or consumer production, *for the sake of* the future expansion of the material basis of culture. To think and operate in view of the long run, though, a person would have to be moral – i.e., to live for the sake of true values, and not merely for satisfactions in a calculus of pleasure and pain.

In relation to today's economy, we can acknowledge that Aristotle's suspicion of money was not so wrongheaded insofar as, more often than not, money becomes transformed from an instrument into an *end* – whether it is regarded as a commodity (as something to be accumulated without end), or whether money (even if regarded as a bookkeeping tool based on credit and money management) is tied to schemes of recurrence (modeled on gold-standard ideas) that are completely unrelated to both the intrinsic intelligibility of the economic good of order and the normative scale of vital, social, cultural, personal, and religious values.

Another way that the money of account becomes separated from the production and distribution of the best possible standard of living regards the credit-related notion of *interest*. J.M. Keynes's praised the scholastic doctrine of usury as "directed towards the elucidation of a formula which should allow the schedule of the marginal efficiency of capital to be high, while using rule and custom and the moral law to keep down the rate of interest."[69] He said that the Schoolmen had made "an honest intellectual effort" to distinguish with respect to interest what

---

69 Frederick G. Lawrence, "Editors' Introduction," *Macroeconimic Dynamics*, lxvii.

"the classical theory has inextricably confused together."[70] The issue, as Lonergan saw it, regards discriminating between entrepreneurial lending for using liquid funds actively in production and commerce from sterile lending for the sake of sterile, nonproductive reception of interest. The reality and significance of the credit basis of money becomes corrupted whenever it becomes impossible to make the basic distinction between the productive entrepreneur and the functionless *rentier*, which seems to be the current implication of automatically denouncing such concerns as Pope Francis's for social solidarity in *Evangelii Gaudium* as socialist or communist.

A case in point would be the transformation of banking from its basic role of redistributing savings and investment to surplus (or producer-goods) and basic (or consumer-goods) circuits of production into a *commercial* enterprise which markets "financial products" that involve the transfer of assets such as outstanding loans or credit card receivables into financial securities issued on the capital market through the process of "securitization." Inasmuch as such money-making techniques are detached from the production and distribution of goods and services in the ordinarily understood sense by taking the money of account out of its rightful context in relation to the surplus and basic cycles of production, they take on a decidedly *rentier* function, notwithstanding the fact that Goldman Sachs's Lloyd Blankfein could tell a congressional committee that his firm "is doing God's work"!

Subsidiarity and the Cultural Effects of Money in the Exchange Economy

Subsidiarity as the diffusion of competences and powers from below upwards has to be understood in relation to the modern ecology of civil society, economy, politics, and culture in which the neuralgic point regards the relationship among technology, economy, and polity. Money for Lonergan is the instrument of economic process, and economic process is the instrument of society. For this actually to be the case, politics (classically understood) has to judge, direct, and guide the economy, and economic order has to judge, direct, and guide technology. However, modern culture makes the accumulation of money in the form of

---

70 Lawrence, "Editors' Introduction," lxvii.

profits into the goal of the economy. As a result, economy subordinates politics to itself, which inverts the normative order of civil society.

This process of inversion is based on massive misunderstandings: Not only is money misunderstood when it is transformed from a means into an end, but economics is misunderstood, too. As we have noted above, understanding the instrumental function of money is a key to Lonergan's analysis of macroeconomic dynamics. However, the political order's role in judging, directing, and guiding the economic order does not imply that polity can operate arbitrarily upon the economic good of order, which is often taken to be the meaning of government intervention into the economy. Once again, a correct understanding of the economic process ought to govern the control of the money supply, interest rates, and taxation by the government. According to Lonergan, arbitrary government actions damage free enterprise rightly understood, and because the bureaucratic form of state authority tends to ride roughshod over subsidiarity, where the prudence of persons at lower levels should prevail, it makes this kind damage an ongoing affair.

Hence, the correct understanding of the economic process has a two-fold effect upon politics. First, it restores the true role of politics in the ecology of human living together. When the economic good of order is not understood correctly, politics becomes mixed up with economics in a way that is disastrous for both polity and economy. Then politics fails in its role of debating questions and issues that are unanswerable by the market's adjustment of supply and demand, and of making decisions irreducible to decisions of consumers and producers.

If the economic process is understood correctly, politics is freed to be the mediator between the civil community's highest cultural values and its concrete solution to the problem of living together. For example, it would judge, direct, and guide the economic process in the service of ends, such as the arts, liberal education, and religion, which are concerned with the truths by which humanity may flourish, which transcend the economy.

Second, a correct understanding of the economic process would reveal that it would be irresponsible for the political order to legislate and impose economic policies that enforce prolonged and one-sided capital formation at the cost of basic and cultural expansions, and to encourage the *rentier*-like use of the creditor-debtor relationship in the financial sector. There seems to be a growing consensus that the current income disparity demonstrates that both labor and the middle class are exploited as instruments of unremitting profitability and/or capital formation. This is symptomatic of the oligarchical or corporate control both of those elected and those appointed to political office and of those who manipulate the public media of opinion, so that the mass of citizens are rendered passive, without either a say or a hearing in the corridors of power.

Lonergan objected to the ways that liberal democratic and socialist ideologies smother politics as based on "reflection and choice" instead of "accident and force," to use the terms of *Federalist*, #1. He held that in the measure that the concretely functioning economy provides the material conditions for human living, politics ought to pursue what Thomas Aquinas (and John Courtney Murray following him) called a *civilis conversatio* whose gravamen is "an ethos that at once subtly and flexibly provides concrete premises for practical decisions,"[71] and which would work as premises attuned to the normative scale of vital, social, cultural, personal and religious values.[72] The role of politics is to mediate between culture and the economic and technological dimensions of society. For example, if the economy should need enormous money flows to bring about the expansion of wealth at any given time either in the surplus (producer-goods) phase or in the basic (consumer-goods) phase, government has to exercise practical wisdom to relieve the stresses and strains that would inevitably accompany the transitions from phase to phase in accord with the intelligibility of the pure cycle of the economy. That would mean that those holding government positions would need to understand that intelligibility adequately, which is something neither "supply-side" nor "demand-side" orientations in economic theory have been able to provide. But that would require a kind of "cultural revolution" when it comes to education and the funding of education across the board, which would require in turn an understanding of the role of "the cultural overhead" in the unfolding of the economic good of order.

In a culture where, because of the massive misunderstanding of the money of account, the normative order among technology, economy, and politics has been inverted, the depredations of both the economy and the state (as Nicholas Boyle has elaborated in *Who Are We Now?*) have led to a monetization of civil society as all human relationships – not to mention vocations – become increasingly defined in monetary

---

71 Lonergan, *Insight*, 248.
72 See Lonergan, *Method in Theology*, 31–2, 99.

terms.[73] If people are educated to imagine their natural freedom and equality on the analogy of free and equal units of coinage, it seems that only in circumstances as have been occurring in the wake of the economic crisis of 2007–2008 does it become clear how completely people are also suddenly turned into insignificant units of account as, for instance, when thousands of skilled and conscientious workers are rewarded either with unemployment (in part, because their jobs have been exported) or with grave reductions in pensions and health care benefits. Now the claim of *The Communist Manifesto* seems prescient: "The bourgeoisie – i.e., the capitalist class – has left no bond standing between one human being and another but naked interest, unfeeling 'cash payment'… It has transformed the doctor, the lawyer, the cleric, the poet, the man of science into paid laborers."[74] Who hasn't become a proletarian in the Marxian sense of "selling one's labor for pay"? Isn't this confirmed when "the brains" graduating from Princeton and Harvard head straight for careers in financial services?

Lonergan brought out the limitations of the money-based exchange economy, by remarking the tendency to brush aside all contributions made to the common good for little or no pecuniary return: This "make[s] the exchange system an exclusive club for businessmen" and women.[75] Any human activity not done for pay is regarded as having little or no value. Hobbes put it with characteristic bluntness when he wrote, "A man's dignity is [her or] his price." Detaching money from the economic process that determines its intelligibility distorts the numerous goods that ought to result from the universal accountability proper to money. Then the "social imaginary" effectively deems economic value as separate from the culturally mediated framework of normative values in light of which alone its true meaning can be judged.

Two further points in Lonergan's exposé of the effects of misunderstanding economic process need to be underlined. The first is to do with the notion of *profit* as a motive for economic activity.[76] Lonergan calls "constant and normal" the commonsense understanding of profit as

---

73 Nicholas Boyle, *Who Are We Now?* (Notre Dame: University of Notre Dame Press, 1998), 104–5, 41, 77.

74 See Karl Marx, *Die Früschriften*, ed. S. Landshut (Stuttgart, 1971), 528, cited by Boyle in *Who Are We Now?* 65

75 Lonergan, *For a New Political Economy*, 35.

76 Lonergan, *Macroeconomic Dynamics*, 133–44, 144–56.

the excess of receipts over bills payable needed by CEOs and CFOs to keep their firms solvent and to maintain a standard of living proportionate to their contribution to the overall commonweal.[77] This meaning of profit is certainly a legitimate motive for doing business. The liberal capitalist bias toward an exclusively "bottom-line" concern transforms this motive into an absolute criterion for economic activity. This mistake rests on the incorrect understanding of money as an instrument of account, and misses the true function of both money and profit in a healthy economy.

There is nothing wrong with "constant and normal" notion of profit if only it were able to operate in the context of a correct understanding of the pure cycle of economic development with its normative phases of surplus and basic expansions. However, that explanatory context is indispensable for making the all-important distinction between profit in that ordinary sense and profit as a "social dividend." The "social dividend" denotes a group interest in the profits made possible by entrepreneurs, labor, and the infrastructure furnished by society and politics; and it is based on the idea Lonergan names "pure surplus profit." This means a profit that expands and contracts in accord with the timing of the transition from the phase of capital formation to that of the basic expansion. Absent a grasp of "pure surplus profit" as specified by the intelligible exigencies built into the unfolding phases in the pure cycle of production and monetary circulation, the agents of production entertain mistaken expectations, so that the intelligibility of the "systematic profit"[78] that arises with the movement from the stationary state of an economy to a major expansion requiring the production of a significant quantity of new plants and equipment will appear to be "counter-intuitive" in the measure that, as soon as profits and production begin to level off, one reduces the "social dividend" to the mistaken notion of profit in the conventional sense.[79] This points to the need for economic consultants, entrepreneurs, and labor leaders to acknowledge that although profit is a valid motive for action, it does not suffice as a replacement for the differentiated criteria necessary if people are to react intelligently to the various disequilibria and equilibria marking the phases of an expansion. It's the lack of perspicuous criteria that leads to slumps and crises. In its

---

77 Lonergan, *Macroeconomic Dynamics*, 81–2.
78 Lonergan, *Macroeconomic Dynamics*, 153.
79 Lonergan, *Macroeconomic Dynamics*, 133–44, 144–56.

constant focus on short-term profits and short-term financial statements (e.g., the occasional displeasure when the number of the unemployed falls), Wall Street as we know it promotes the notion that profit is a criterion for economic effectiveness as well as a motive for doing business. Need one mention the name Enron?

Lonergan criticized liberal capitalist misconceptions of the cultural effects of misunderstanding the proper functioning of the exchange economy, money, and politics based on the liberal capitalist anthropology of human fulfillment and success that exacerbates modern liberty's "oscillation … between ends and means" due to the so-called rational calculation of individual advantage. Our culture turns money into the goal of economic activity at the same time as it turns the economy into the *raison d'etre* of politics. And so Manent writes,

> If the end is a means and the means is an end, there is no motive ever to stop, no place to rest … It is not so much that money becomes all-powerful … Rather money becomes the most socially explicit thing: it proves that you have done things; it registers your doings. The abstraction of money nicely fits in with the abstraction of 'doing things.'[80]

It is significant that the transition from traditional or feudal society into modern society has resulted in the subsumption of what most people call "civil society" by the market. For Lonergan, civil society is comprised by the general institutional good of order within the framework of the human good.[81] If Lonergan wanted his work in economics to articulate the intelligibility of the economic good of order, the implication of this analysis was that the well-ordered organization of the institutions of society may not be reduced to either economic processes and institutions or to those of the government or state.

Nicholas Boyle has described civil society as the complex of intermediate social organizations that are autonomous or semi-autonomous, and so they form part of a network of constitutional checks and balances (in Montesquieu's sense of the distinction and separation of powers).[82] Because it provides a focus for loyalty and a place for engagement

---

80 Manent, "Liberalism and Conservatism," 221.

81 See Bernard Lonergan, "The Role of the Catholic University in the Modern World," *Collection*, 109.

82 Boyle, *Who Are We Now?* 18–22.

with other citizens, which are *not simply an extension of the market-place*, civil society gives shape and substance and continuity to our lives. As Tocqueville has taught us as regards mediating institutions, civil society also protects individual citizens from direct and potentially arbitrary interference by central government. The places for engagement with fellow citizens furnished by institutions of civil society include institutions such as family life, schools, trade unions, the media (when journalism is a honorable profession), and other professions such as brokers, lawyers, doctors, and teachers. Each of these operates by standards and opinions *independent of market considerations*. They provide not so much a service as a source of identity that is neither quantifiable nor marketable, and this is done not only for its members, but also for the entire civil society insofar as the identity of society members is based *not* on *what it sells*, but on *what it* is. In this sense, these organizations give society its depth and complexity.

Confirming Lonergan's statement above, Boyle claims that when civil society is subsumed into the market, service or work performed in return for payment at the market rate replaces service rendered for the common good. The true rationale for giving teachers tenure was that teaching was considered not just a job but a vocation.[83] If all institutional roles and tasks are turned into employed or unemployed work, then those institutional matrices of family life, professional morality, or corporate loyalty are dissolved into the "market."

When the market so dominates social institutions, you have countless anomalies such as churches starting to reduce evangelization to "market research," and universities and colleges being turned into playgrounds where those capable of paying the ever steeper tuitions can neither be disciplined nor given poor grades, because "the customer is always right" (Sam Walton). Moreover, assigning cash value to traditionally defined services, benefits, and injuries in the fields of healthcare and medicine has tended to destroy all pre-monetary forms of social control invested in institutional loyalty, professional self-regulation (as both non-accountable and not liable to lawsuits), deference, and *noblesse oblige*.

What then becomes the socially dominant vision of the human being in our culture? The corporate "masters of the universe" have a

---

83 Boyle, *Who Are We Now?* 28–9.

great interest in persons understanding themselves as consumers or anonymous, identity-less generators of a never-ending series of new wishes demanding instantaneous satisfaction.[84] In Alasdair MacIntyre's formulation:

> The rising standard of material prosperity in capitalist economies is itself closely related to another aspect of their failure in respect of justice. It is not only that individuals are educated or rather mis-educated to believe that what they should aim at and hope for is not what they deserve, but whatever they may happen to want. The attempt is to get them to regard themselves primarily as consumers whose practical activities are no more than a means to consumption. What constitutes success in life becomes a matter of successful acquisition of consumer goods, and thereby that acquisitiveness which is so often a character trait necessary for success in capital accumulation is further sanctioned. Unsurprisingly *pleonexia*, the drive to have more and more, becomes treated as a central virtue.[85]

The drive to have more and more stresses consumption more than production, and shunts lending at interest for productive purposes, and which, as John Maynard Keynes admitted, those hidebound scholastics deemed permissible and not usurious into the perverse "capital formation" that has come to sight in today's world of borrowing and lending of packaged debts and derivatives.[86]

---

84 Boyle, *Who Are We Now?* 155–9.

85 Alasdair MacIntyre, "Three Perspectives on Marxism," *Ethics and Politics,* Selected Essays 2 (Cambridge: Cambridge University Press, 2006), 149.

86 Rowan Williams (then Archbishop of Canterbury) in an article written for *The Spectator* (27 September 2008) provided a hair-raising description of what happens when acquisitiveness as the *beau ideal* of success combines with the notion of profit as a criterion for all economic activity:

> A lender takes a calculated risk in offering the use of their money to someone else, and rates of interest express the recognition of this – and the rewards that may be secured for taking such a risk. But it is not too difficult to see how the notional gain involved here can be used as security against a further risk. And so the transaction moves further and further from the original transaction with its realistic assessment of levels of risk within the context of measurable standards of credit-worthiness. Any face-to-face element, any direct calculation of what and who is reasonably worth trusting (which assumes some common frame of reference), fades away. Like Trollope's hapless young clerics and feckless young landowners, individuals find that their own personal financial decisions and

I hope that this paper has suggested clearly enough that Lonergan's economics provides the framework for asking and answering questions about these issues that both accords with Catholic social teaching on solidarity, subsidiarity, and responsibility, and that may also lead to both the reinvigoration of American and even global culture and the renewal of civil society, so that citizens can increasingly begin to distinguish more surely between what they individually and collectively sell and buy and what they individually and collectively *are*.

---

calculations have nothing to do with what is happening to their resources, in a process for which a debt is simply someone else's wholly disposable asset.

It is a sort of one-syllable nursery parable of what the last couple of weeks have illustrated in the world of global finance and, of course, a reminder that what we have been witnessing is not just the product of a couple of irresponsible decades.

Trading the debts of others without accountability has been the motor of astronomical financial gain for many in recent years. Primitively, a loan transaction is something which enables someone to do what they might not otherwise be able to do – start a business, buy a house. Lenders identify what would count as reasonable security in the present and the future (present assets, future income) and decide accordingly.

But inevitably in complex and large-scale transactions, one person's debt becomes part of the security which the lender can offer to another potential customer. And a particularly significant line is crossed when the borrowing and lending are no longer to do with any kind of equipping someone to do something specific, but exclusively about enabling profit – sometimes, as with the now banned practice of short-selling, by effectively betting on the failure of a partner in the transaction.

This crisis exposes the element of basic unreality in the situation – the truth that almost unimaginable wealth has been generated by equally unimaginable levels of fiction, paper transactions with no concrete outcome beyond profit for traders. But while we are getting used to this sudden vision of the Emperor's New Clothes, there are one or two questions that, in government as in society at large, we at last have a chance to ask. Some of these are elementary and practical. Given that the risk to social stability overall in these processes has been shown to be so enormous, it is no use pretending that the financial world can maintain indefinitely the degree of exemption from scrutiny and regulation that it has got used to.

10 The Human Good and Christian Conversation

1. Introduction

For the past six or seven years, I have been tantalized by a passage from Lonergan's economics manuscript; and I have been trying to come to grips with it directly and indirectly in my work as a teacher and theologian for the same period. I have had an overwhelming sense that it points to the transformation in society and culture at stake in contemporary political theology and locates the arena in which the most basic questions for political theology lie. The passage goes as follows:

> Now to change one's standard of living in any notable fashion is to live in a different fashion. It presupposes a grasp of new ideas. If the ideas are to be above the level of currently successful advertising, serious education must be undertaken. Finally, coming to grasp what serious education realizes, and, nonetheless, coming to accept that challenge constitute the greatest challenge to the modern economy.[1]

The change in living, in ideas, in education indicated here has to do with the issues of revolution and conversion associated with the achievement of a new identity. In this paper, I want to discuss issues connected with meeting the challenge and understanding what Lonergan is talking about in terms of the metaphor of learning a new language, which

---

1 Bernard Lonergan, *Macroeconomic Dynamics: An Essay in Circulation Analysis*, ed. Frederick G. Lawrence, Patrick H. Byrne, and Charles C. Hefling, Jr, Collected Works of Bernard Lonergan 15 (Toronto: University of Toronto Press, 1999), 119.

I take up in the next section (1.1). Then I look at the structure of the human good outlined by Lonergan in *Method in Theology*. Next, in Part 2, I survey the alternative answers of antiquity and modernity concerning the human good, with sections on each (2.1 and 2.2). The section on modernity covers "the three waves" of modernity identified by Leo Strauss. Part 3 considers what is involved in learning foundational language, with sections on (3.1) conflicts of meanings and values and (3.2) Christian conversion as conversational. The latter section is developed in five subtopics. Part 4, then, provides some tentative conclusions about the human good and the Christian conversation.

1.1 Learning a New Language

This metaphor, of course, is not just a metaphor, because language as I am using the term here is a component integral to the processes of communal and personal self-constitution. If human self-becoming is chiefly a matter of asking and answering questions for understanding, reflection, and deliberation and then living by the answers, it is clear just how important language is to us. Besides the verifiable correlation between aphasia and apraxia, we need language to pose questions to the situations we encounter in life. Language leads us along both preconceptually and imaginally as well as within the spontaneously ordered operations of intelligent, reasonable, and responsible consciousness. With Rosemary Haughton and Stephen Crites, indeed, we could articulate the meaning and value of the major transformations in our lives by studying the changes in language usages that are correlative with the different conversions.

But aside from its intrinsically methodical appropriateness, the metaphor of learning a language presents itself to us with a more special urgency at the present time. In a time that is felt to be a period of almost unprecedented crisis, we Christians speak languages stemming from traditions whose meanings and values are at odds both with Christian faith and with Lonergan's foundational language. Thus, the problem of the watering down or distortion of one's tradition that Lonergan has written so eloquently about enters our lives with a vengeance. These alien and alienating languages may be generating, within the Christian traditions, not merely lives of unauthentic authenticity, but lives of unconverted unauthenticity almost as a rule. And when Christianity gets co-opted into supplying a legitimating veneer for meanings and values that are un-Christian, then probabilities mount that even well-intentioned speakers and doers of what they think is the Word will not only not be doing so, but they will be unaware of the existential contradictions in which they are involved. The urgency becomes all the more pressing when we realize that "they" are we ourselves.

I have found that expressing in word and deed the horizon to which one has been moved by Christian conversion is almost as much a matter of unlearning the languages that have possessed us hitherto as of learning to speak a new language. But this general problem of learning and unlearning is particularly delicate when one tries to operate in the specialty of foundations, especially if one tries to speak with Lonergan's general and special categories. To show more exactly what I mean, I have decided to use Lonergan's structure of the human good to convey a notion of the hindrances to speaking his language authentically, especially as they arise from other competing languages by which we are already liable to be dominated.

1.2 The Structure of the Human Good as Language

Let us recall first of all the structure of the human good developed by Lonergan in the second chapter of *Method in Theology*:[2]

Individual Potentiality	Actuation	Social	Ends
capacity, need plasticity, perfectibility liberty	operation development, skill orientation, conversion	cooperation institution, role, task personal relations	particular good good of order terminal value

This structure is a component in a technical language – what I shall be calling Lonergan's foundational language. As a language in the most serious sense, it is heuristic, and so it will be learned or mastered accordingly as we are able to use it in asking our own real questions about the human situation. Its overwhelming suitableness for political theology becomes obvious, for instance, as soon as we grasp that it names at the outset what it is we are looking for when we ask the very questions from which philosophy as practical and political first originated:

---

2 Bernard Lonergan, *Method in Theology* (New York: Herder & Herder, 1972), 48.

"What's the right way to live?" "What's the best, the most choiceworthy, way of life?" I want to illustrate what I mean by learning a new language and unlearning old languages by setting the structure of the human good in the contexts of ancient and modern political philosophies and comparing the range of meaning intended by their languages with that intended by Lonergan.

2. The Human Good and the Alternative Ancient and Modern Answers

2.1 The Context of Ancient Political Philosophy

The premodern breakthrough in posing the practical-political question was crystallized in the Greek and Christian apprehension of it as a question about the good of order. Plato's *Republic* and Aristotle's *Politics* ask, "What's the best regime?" The key to the question is the clear and consistent discrimination between mere life as physical, vital, and sensitive spontaneity and the good life.[3] The latter is coordinate with "rational appetite, [and] with the specialized object of the reasonable good."[4] The following rather lengthy quotation from a 1943 article by Lonergan may provide a summary of the salients uncovered by the classical response to the question about the best regime:

> Throughout, nature is characterized by repetitiveness: Over and over again it achieves mere reproductions of what has been achieved already; and any escape from such cyclic recurrence is *per accidens* and *in minori parte* or, in modern language, due to chance variation. But in contrast with this repetitiveness of nature is the progressiveness of reason. For if it is characteristic of all intellect to grasp immutable truth, it is the special property of the potential intellect of man to advance in knowledge of truth. Nor is it merely the individual that advances, as though knowledge were classically static, a fund whence schoolboys receive a dole. On the contrary, to the historian of science or philosophy and still more to the anthropologist, the individual of genius appears no more than the instrument of human

---

3 Bernard Lonergan, "Finality, Love, Marriage," *Collection*, ed. Frederick E. Crowe and Robert M. Doran, Collected Works of Bernard Lonergan 4 (Toronto: University of Toronto Press, 1988), 38.
4 Lonergan, "Finality, Love, Marriage," 24.

solidarity; through such individuals humanity advances, and the function of tradition and education is to maintain the continuity of a development that runs from the days of primitive fruit gatherers through our own of mechanical power on into an unknown future. But not only are nature and reason contrasted as repetitive and progressive. There is also a contrast between the organistic spontaneity of nature and the deliberate friendships of reason. By "organistic" spontaneity I would denote the mutual adaptation and automatic correlation of the activities of many individuals as though they were parts of a larger organic unit: This phenomenon may be illustrated by the ant heap or beehive; but its more general appearance lies in the unity of the family, a unity which nature as spontaneously and as imperiously attains in the accidental order as in the substantial it effects the unity of the organism. Now it is not by organistic spontaneity but by mutual esteem and mutual good will that reason sets up its comparable union of friendship; and in accordance with our eternal viewpoint, we may note that human friendship is to be found not only in the urbanity and collaboration of contemporaries but much more in the great republic of culture, in contemporaries' esteem for the great men of the past, on whose shoulders they stand, and in their devotion for the men of the future, for whom they set the stage of history for better or for worse. A third contrast between nature and reason is in point of efficiency. While nature with the ease of a superautomaton pursues with statistical infallibility and regularly attains through organistic harmonies its repetitive ends, the reason and rational appetite of fallen man limp in the disequilibrium of high aspiration and poor performance to make progress of reason a dialectic of decline as well as of advance, and the rational community of men a divided unity of hatred and war as well as the indivisible unity of fraternity and peace.[5]

From this summary we need to notice several points. First, treating the question about the right way to live in terms of the second level of the structure, that of the good of order, brings with it a tendency to subordinate elements located on the third level of that structure to the second level. In St Thomas Aquinas's *Of Princely Government*, for example, needs on the level of particular goods motivate and call for a civil or political society (Book 1, chapter 1), and friendships (personal relations) are acknowledged to be the aim or goal of political rule (chapter 10); but the intelligible content of civil society is handled most profusely

---

5 Lonergan, "Finality, Love, Marriage," 38–9.

in terms of virtues and types of regime, etc. Although almost all third level components are present and treated in the ancient accounts, they do tend to get subordinated to the second level.

Second, the ancients conceive the practical and political question about the right way to live not merely empirically (i.e., as an account of possible ways of life as verified), but ethically or morally. Thus, Aristotle's *Nicomachean Ethics* is integral to his *Politics*, with the former being devoted to habits and skills (the moral and dianoetic virtues) and the latter to the institutional set-up with its appropriate roles and tasks. This same unity of the political and moral is also evident in Plato's famous parallel between the order of the polis and the order of the soul, with its tripartite division into desire (for sensible or material pleasure), spiritedness (anger, the root of the warlike virtues), and reason (the faculty for seeking the true, the good, the beautiful). As Gadamer, Arendt, and a host of others in our day have discovered, by treating the question of the good of order as a question of morality and ethics, the ancients kept questions for practical intelligence distinct from questions for technical expertise; by never reducing the former to the latter, they did not make sheer feasibility in a technical sense into a criterion for practical judgment, but normally judged against advances in technology when it was thought to jeopardize the common good.

However, this approach to practical issues also went hand-in-hand with what Lonergan calls a normative notion of culture, or what he spoke of as "the great republic of culture" in the passage cited above. This was an ambiguous achievement. To begin with, there is the normative function of culture delineated by Lonergan in the following fashion:

Corresponding to judgments of value, there is cultural community. It transcends the frontiers of states and epochs of history. It is Cosmopolis not as an unrealized political ideal, but as a longstanding, nonpolitical, cultural fact. It is the field of communication and influence of artists, scientists, and philosophers. It is the bar of enlightened public opinion to which naked power can be driven to submit. It is the tribunal of history that may expose successful charlatans and may restore to honor the prophets stoned by their contemporaries.[6]

---

6 Lonergan, "The Role of a Catholic University in the Modern World," *Collection*, 109.

Within the structure of the human good, Lonergan has brought out the differentiation of culture as the domain in which society reflects upon and appraises its way of life in distinguishing between the second and third levels. The second level regards the *social* dimension of the human good, the concretely verifiable way of life as embodied in laws, technology, economy, polity, family life; the third level comprises the *cultural* domain in the light of which the social is (to be) judged and evaluated. By this distinction, both the "social" and the "cultural" have an utterly empirical meaning, but "culture" retains the connotation of a normative function without being classicist in Lonergan's pejorative sense.

In the best of the ancients, culture and the political order are identical only in the ideal and highly improbable case where the philosopher becomes the ruler; otherwise and (we can suppose almost always) in fact, culture is only the forum before which the political order is judged, and within which justice is realized not in deed, but in speech alone. This sense of balance got lost as the "Greek mediation of meaning" was transformed into classical culture with its science of man. As Lonergan came to discover, classical culture performed the abovementioned normative function of culture by means of "a somewhat arbitrary standardization of man."[7] Classical or classicist culture transformed the Greek breakthrough – "a necessary stage in the development of the human mind"[8] – into a timeless criterion in which the content of the classically oriented science of man "easily obscures man's nature, constricts his spontaneity, saps his vitality, limits his freedom"[9] because it "concentrated on the essential to ignore the accidental, on the universal to ignore the particular, on the necessary to ignore the contingent."[10] Since it omitted so much of the data on human being, its explanations could not help but be provisional in some respects, which is understandable. The overwhelming problem with classicist culture is its inability to acknowledge these limits and its apparent unwillingness to keep learning.

---

7 Lonergan, "Dimensions of Meaning," *Collection*, 241.
8 Lonergan, "Dimensions of Meaning," 241.
9 Lonergan, "Dimensions of Meaning," 241.
10 Lonergan, "Dimensions of Meaning," 240.

2.2 The Context of Modern Political Philosophy

2.21 The First Wave of Modernity[11]

The ancient answers to the question about the right way to live focused on the common good understood as a complex good of order; and they were preoccupied with virtue. What happened in the first phase of the shift to modernity has been suggestively encapsulated in the following passage by Allan Bloom:

> The ancients talked only about virtue and not about wellbeing. That in itself is perhaps harmless, but the moderns contended that the concentration on virtue contradicts the concern for wellbeing. Aristotle admitted that "equipment" as well as virtue is needed for happiness, but said nothing about how that equipment is acquired. A careful examination of the acquisition of equipment reveals that virtue impedes that acquisition ... Equipment is surely necessary, so why not experiment with doing without virtue.[12]

In other words, thinkers like Bacon, Hobbes, Descartes, Spinoza, and Locke judged that in the light of humanity's "disequilibrium of high aspiration and poor performance," taking care of equipment not only means doing without virtue if need be, but displacing the desire to know elevated to normative status by the ancients with the desire for self-preservation.[13]

When the *summum bonum* gets replaced in modernity by the fear of death as *summum malum*, the psychology of orientation gets replaced

---

11 The hypothesis of the "three waves of modernity" comes from Leo Strauss, *An Introduction to Political Philosophy: Ten Essays by Leo Strauss*, ed. Hilail Gilden (Detroit: Wayne State University Press, 1989) 81–98. In my eight years of teaching (1) Perspectives in Western Culture and (2) New Horizons of the Social Sciences, year-long courses that cover the key texts in political science, law, economics, and sociology of the period under question (16th to 20th centuries), I have come across no evidence whatsoever that would make Strauss's interpretation controversial. See Frederick G. Lawrence, "Political Theology and 'the Longer Cycle of Decline,'" *The Lonergan Workshop* 2 (1978): 223–55 and "The Horizon of Political Theology," *The Trinification of the World: A Festschrift in Honor of Frederick E. Crowe*, ed. T.A. Dunne and J.-M. Laporte (Toronto: Regis College, 1978), 46–71.

12 Allan Bloom, "Commerce and 'Culture,'" *Giants and Dwarfs: Essays, 1960–1990* (New York: Simon & Schuster), 282–3.

13 Lonergan, "Finality, Love, Marriage," 39.

by a psychology of motivations. Motivated by the anxiety about death, only the accumulation of power and property seems a choiceworthy good; and so comfortable self-preservation becomes the primary end of human beings.

In tandem with modern science's myth of productivity, modern political philosophy undertook the vast "humanitarian" project of taking care of equipment by parleying private vices into public welfare. But this was to subordinate the second and third levels of the structure of the human good to that of needs, desires, and particular goods. It follows that the common good no longer refers to the good of order as normative, but to particular goods as satisfying needs and desires as correlative with life in contradistinction to the good life. As a mere collectivity of private goods, the common good is "common" only in the sense of an accidental genus or species instead of as the objective of rational choice correlative with the human capacity for intellectual development. Furthermore, in relation to the normative order of vital, social, cultural, personal, and religious values, the preference for mere life over the good life means the supremacy of vital values. The dominant practical question becomes not merely, "What's in it for me or my group?" but "What's the value of being good if you're not well off?"

The purpose of civil society and government on the early modern account is to protect pre-existent rights to life and the pursuit of property. Its key means will not be morality or religion, but the spirit of acquisitiveness at the root of property. Hence, governments are legitimate to the extent that they, as *The Federalist* put it, protect different and unequal faculties of acquiring wealth. This implies that the motive for political society according to the ancients becomes transformed into its criterion; even as action for the private good (conceived of as enlightened self-interest) is elevated into the standard for assessing rightness or wrongness overall.

Concerns for the third level are acknowledged by the early moderns under the rubric of natural right. Friendships are relevant as long as they are based on utility or pleasure. Liberty means either the freedom to design institutions that will provide mutual security and rules that guarantee the public good by enabling each individual to pursue private goods without obstruction from others, or at least the freedom to consent to such a design. It is clear, then, that the notion of natural right, inalienable, underivable from any authority, is an eminently selfish idea. As the product of an attempt to define human equality independently of any religion or metaphysics, it also meant to leave open the answer to the question of the right way to live, at least in principle; but in fact, that openness was a void the early moderns were content to see filled by commerce. Taking care of equipment is realized as taking care of business.

2.22 The Second Wave of Modern Political Philosophy
In his First and Second Discourses, Rousseau laid bare the opposition between nature – now identified with the satisfaction of needs on the level of organistic spontaneity – and culture or civilization. He thus set the stage for the modern use of the term culture. As Bloom has written:

> According to Kant, Rousseau in his later works, *Emile, Social Contract, Nouvelle Heloise*, proposed a possible unity that harmonized the low natural demands with the high responsibilities of morality and art. This unity Kant called "culture."[14]

Rousseau, therefore, unleashed the first cultural critique of the mercenary morality of liberalism.

From the point of view of the structure of the human good, we can say that Rousseau's scathing attack was actually an ambiguous breakthrough to the second (social) and third (cultural) levels in reaction to the early modern reduction of all elements to the first level. Both the breakthrough and its ambiguity are signaled by the notorious modern dichotomies between nature and freedom, nature and history, and nature and art, which were exploited till our own day by the movements of idealism, historicism, and Romanticism. No less than Hobbes and Locke, however, Rousseau conceived of liberty without any reference to divine transcendence. Though he did not confine freedom to the limits of scientific calculation and technical control and debunked early liberalism's utilitarianism and instrumentalism, freedom for him was coordinate with the perfectibility of the amiable but brutish human being he uncovered in the state of nature, and its matrix was that animal's "simple feeling of existence," its "conscience" as "the science of simple souls."

Out of the framework built with these ideas, Rousseau eventually developed the idea of the "general will." On the one hand, the general will was to be understood in terms of national custom, national

---

14 Bloom, "Commerce and 'Culture,'" 278.

"philosophy," or the "mystique of the nation." We have become familiar with these ideas under the guise of such terms as Hegel's *Zeitgeist* or Whitehead's "climate of opinion." On the other hand, Kant drew out the more idealist implications of the general will, for example, in his moralistic grounding of human rights. Earlier liberalism's "natural" rights to life, liberty, and the pursuit of happiness were founded not so much in the state of nature theory as on factual evidence on the dominance within human beings of the natural inclinations toward security and comfort. But Kant uses the ability (shown by Rousseau to be human and rational, but not natural) humans possess of universalizing their desire to subordinate the older liberalism's self-interest in safety and prosperity to rights conceived of as universal principles that serve to define human beings as free and independent.

One can appreciate the high moral tone of this transformation of so-called natural rights into human rights. It does seem to give primacy to the moral demands proper to the second and third levels. However, the apriorism, abstractness, and formalism of Kant's thought not only divorce his grounding from any concrete practical relevance; but his intelligible ego with its good will is so isolated from the empirically verifiable process of communication within which subjects grow to maturity that we are forced to concede that it is quite utopian (not to say unreal) as well. Kant had no way of tethering his "normative" realm of freedom to empirically verifiable fact; and so he buttressed it with postulates about God, freedom, and immortality, on the one hand; and with a speculative philosophy of history, on the other. Even on Kantian grounds, the former threesome may be argued not to exist; and Kant's philosophy of history finally settles for a distinction between morality and mere legality that represents a compromise of rational faith with *Realpolitik.*

As a result of the two waves of modernity, there are two chief forms or languages of Western liberalism. They both depart from the modern assumption that the chief concern or issue of modern politics is power. First, *commercial democracy* is based on consent to governmental power as guarantor of public safety and comfort and on the doctrine of classical political economy that if there are no restrictions to free economic activity other than enlightened self-interest, social harmony and well-being will necessarily prevail. Second, *socialist politics of compassion* grounds the legitimacy of governmental power upon the extent to which it bolsters equality not merely of opportunity (i.e., the political right to endeavor to acquire and dispose of one's property within the limits of the law and the civil right to freedom of expression and to self-government), but of the satisfaction of aggregate societal needs (under the heading of economic, social, and cultural rights to such things as health, housing, education, employment, sanitation, etc.) by attempting to reconcile older liberalism's means with socialist or collectivist ends in what has been since called welfare economics. Both versions of liberalism are staunchly convinced of the efficacy of scientific prediction and control and of institutionally contrived solutions to political problems. In general, and by way of oversimplification, advocates of commercial democracy believe that enlightened self-interest in private good is the operator of *commonweal*, and they preach the ideal of as much freedom as possible for the individual and the equality of opportunity. In the United States we tend to label this stance conservative. Secularist proponents of the socialist politics of compassion depend upon "culture" to supply the link between the self-regarding individual and disinterested respect of the law or the rights of others by generating a secular kind of compassion that educes gentle and beneficent concern for others from natural selfishness. They advocate a greater equality of conditions or results in life and preach equality of influence and power for all. In the United States we tend to reserve the name liberal for people who are considered politically progressive in this sense.

The most noteworthy proponent of the socialist politics of compassion is Karl Marx. The industrial revolution, especially after its "take-off," made plain to him that the liberal capitalist belief in a pre-established harmony between private interest and public welfare was an ideology. As he argued in *The Jewish Question*, the natural rights enshrined in such revolutionary documents as the *Declaration of Independence* (1776) and the *Declaration of the Rights of Man and Citizen* (1789) are really only bourgeois rights; they hold good for the capitalist class, but not for the proletariat. Commercial democracy in its intention to supply the equipment for freedom turns out in the final analysis to be a struggle between capitalists and workers. Marx tried to analyze that struggle by re-introducing social (second level) and, at least in his youthful writings, ethical (third level) concerns into political economy in opposition to the "possessive individualism" of liberal capitalism. However, this important attempt to redress the biases of liberal democratic political economy unfortunately got derailed by Marx's uneasy blend of idealism and materialism. That idealism trivialized the underlying problem of evil just as Rousseau and Kant had done. The materialism kept him from breaking cleanly from the utilitarianism and instrumentalism of his early liberal predecessors. He failed altogether to appreciate Rousseau's insight that to achieve freedom in equality requires small communities with religious foundations. And however much the Romantic model of artistic creation was his privileged model for the making of history by human subjects, his revolutionary idea was ultimately just a project of technical mastery, which not even a classless and stateless society would be capable of redeeming.

2.23 The Third Wave of Modern Political Philosophy

2.23 (a) Nietzsche

As the inaugurator of the third wave of modernity, Nietzsche realized that the outcome of both liberal democracy's dedication to preservation and comfort and social democracy's well-fed, well-clothed, well-sheltered human beings with their up-to-date educations, entertainment, and psychiatry would be the abolition of all ideals and aspirations. To the degree that liberalisms of both left and right choose mere life over the good life, they produce the "last man" – healthy, but without heart or convictions.

Nietzsche, therefore, has the overwhelming importance of trying to reestablish the importance of the level of liberty and terminal values. He stands just at the threshold of the religiously mediated insight so neatly formulated in the title of the book by Dorothee Sölle: *Death by Bread Alone*. He sets the stage for the rescuing consciousness of the unorthodox Jew, Walter Benjamin, and for the Christian theologian, Johann Baptist Metz. The latter's short definition for religion is interruption of the modern project of subjugating human and subhuman nature. But for Nietzsche, Christianity is just Platonism for the masses and all the supports for ultimate values in nature, God, or reason are gone. The only option left open in the face of the abyss is a creative transvaluation of all previous values on the part of solitary individuals creative enough to respond to the implications of the "will to power," especially, that human beings are originating values in the absolute sense of being able to posit values arbitrarily. In Nietzsche, the most radical breakthrough to the third level of terminal values also presents us with the epitome of human disorientation, rebellion, and disorder.

2.23 (b) Weber: Between Kant and Nietzsche

Nietzsche's perhaps most influential disciple, Max Weber, domesticated his master's concept of value for the academy by marrying it to Kant's synthesis of culture performed in his three *Critiques*. Weber thus spawned the fact/value distinction as it is commonly and erroneously understood. The realm of nature investigated by science and exploited by technology becomes the value-free domain of fact, whereas both the realm of freedom and responsibility and that of art and religion become the domain of value. As a result of this fateful distinction, the normative moment of culture intended by Lonergan's notion of terminal value gets sunk into the quagmire of the arbitrariness and caprice of values as the creation of the Nietzschean "will to power."

The devastation wrought thereby for apprehending the third level is exacerbated by the common understanding on the part of the contemporary social sciences of the way the Weberian distinction between facts and values is to govern the relationship between social science and social policy. Social science is confined to facts: It describes, and its descriptions are expected to yield information on the basis of which social policy can predict and control. Any normative judgment – either as classical intelligibility or as true judgments of fact and value – gets systematically excluded. The individual, group, or general bias of those in power leads them to repudiate true terminal values (beyond the desires and needs of organistic spontaneity) and to reject any intelligibility yielded by science that does not afford means of prediction and control. The point is to increase managerial efficiency even at the cost of human liberty or social, cultural, personal, or religious values.

Again, within the perspective of Weber's fact/value distinction, a Nietzschean slant can hold sway in personal and communal thinking and action. For it is difficult to avoid the either benevolently or malevolently nihilist conclusion that *all* standards of meaning and substantive order are relative in the last analysis. Nihilism simply eliminates the insight that

> though the things seen are at different times in their internal temporal relationships, still it is possible and proper for the human intellect to imitate the divine and by abstraction stand outside the temporal flow in which really, though not of necessity intentionally, it is involved.[15]

The nihilist operates instead on the assumption that judgments of fact or value are no more than the historically conditioned illusions – the

---

15 Lonergan, "Finality, Love, Marriage," 38.

humanly posited horizons – without which the human animal cannot live. For the benevolent nihilist, this becomes the premise for a "soft tyranny" of cultural manipulation of the many by the few – for profit. For the malevolent nihilist, this becomes the premise for the "big lie" enforced by terror.

Fortunately, however, the response to Nietzsche's call to the best of a generation to become true selves and form a new aristocracy has often been based less on nihilism than on the Kantian rational belief (so congenial to secularized Protestantism) that in principle if not in fact a human person ought never to be used as a means to any aim or purpose not freely chosen by himself or herself; no one can ever be an object of manipulative control by another. For Kantians, of course, this conviction has the cognitive status not of objective truth, but of a postulate, so that the value of the person may never be affirmed as ontic, as it is in Christian faith or in a critically realist philosophy such as Lonergan's. The Kantian conclusion follows from the inchoate acknowledgment of the human person as an originating imperative, rather than from the concrete goodness meant by terminal values, goods of order, and particular goods in Lonergan's sense.

Unfortunately, the salutary Kantian doctrine of the unconditionality of the human person gets relegated to pragmatic irrelevance by Weber's separation of "the ethics of conviction" from the "ethics of responsibility." The ethics of conviction regards ultimate ends, while the ethics of responsibility regards only the pragmatic consequences of means in relation to ends established irrationally and arbitrarily. Doesn't this make Kant's idealistic faith just a matter of conviction? Moreover, this separation would have the effect of sealing off the third level of the human good from the second level.

The ongoing mutual impenetrability of second and third levels becomes all the more disastrous when it comes to Weber's reconstruction of the reasons why people historically have obeyed authority. On the one hand, his construct of the charismatic form of legitimation is one of the few 19th century instances of evaluating religiously based existence positively, since for Weber charismatic authority is the privileged force or agency for social change. On the other hand, his hypothesis about modernity as a process of rationalization, combined with his analysis of bureaucratic control, spells out in a way that is verifiable the meaning of Nietzsche's critique of liberal democracy and socialism on the level of the good of order. Because, for all the preoccupation of liberal and socialist democracy with being emancipated from religious, feudal, monarchical, or aristocratic control; for all their preoccupation with the use of scientific prediction and manipulation "for the relief of man's estate," and of either consent and bargaining (liberal reformism) or violence (socialist revolution) to bring about an order of freedom in equality, it all seems only to have paved the way for bureaucracy and centralization: Weber's "iron cage."

3. Learning Foundational Language

3.1 Conflicts of Meanings and Values

The different political philosophies of antiquity and modernity have all shaped implicit or explicit answers to the question about the right way to live; and the latter have engendered languages that pervade our schools, homes, media, and cultural channels today. These languages often contain verbal equivalents to the language used by Lonergan to define implicitly the structure of the human good. As a result, when we speak about the human good, we are liable either to be intending meanings proper to these languages rather than Lonergan's, or at least to be mistaken by others in this way.

Take, for example, the word "liberty" in the structure of the human good. Liberty was acknowledged by the Greeks, but it was not a theme for them. They had a commonsense apprehension of the difference between slave or free. Theoretically, Aristotle was explicitly clear about the contingency of terrestrial events, which implies the contingency of all human agency. But he did not distinguish clearly between the specification and exercise of free will. And in spite of having a theory of habit, a notion that intellectual virtues liberate human beings more than even the moral virtues do, a recognition that most men know what is good yet choose what is to their own advantage, he had no theory of moral impotence. In short, we have no reason to suppose that the ancient Greek meaning of liberty coincides with Lonergan's in a more than partial way.

On the other hand, liberty has been a theme for the moderns. Indeed, some modern thinkers might agree with Lonergan that liberty is not just indeterminacy but self-determination and even perhaps that "we experience our liberty as the active thrust of the subject terminating the process of deliberation."[16] But none of the modern thinkers I have

---

16 Lonergan, *Method in Theology*, 50.

mentioned would agree with him either that "implicit in human choice of values is the absolute good that is God";[17] or, correlatively, that freedom of choice is grounded in our ability to criticize any finite course of group or individual action.[18] And similarly, despite their realization that *the* god must be a being beyond the intracosmic gods, the Greeks did not affirm an explanatory notion of divine transcendence, any more than the moderns do.

In the course of my whirlwind survey of ancient and modern philosophical approaches to issues cognate with Lonergan's structure of the human good, I adverted repeatedly to ways the range of meaning made available in Lonergan's structure suffer major reductions when shifted into the perspective of any of the various languages discussed. From my brief critical comments, it may be plain how the many different interpretations of elements and levels within the structure have the effect of reducing one's ability to ask significant questions about our concrete situation. These contrasting languages express a reduction of Lonergan's horizon of meaning and value. Since the horizons of our speech and living have been constituted by *those* languages, we must ask ourselves how we can learn the foundational language Lonergan uses so that we can mean what he meant.

When we take seriously language as operative within the matrix of conscious intentionality and as a component in human self-constitution, the issue that comes to the surface when appropriating Lonergan's foundational language is the fourth aspect of understanding any text listed by Lonergan in *Method in Theology's* chapter on "Interpretation": "One arrives at such understanding through a process of learning and even at times as a result of conversion."[19] It is the issue Lonergan put so starkly in the chapter on "History and Historians":

> For any notable change of horizon is done not on the basis of that horizon, but by envisaging a quite different and, at first sight, incomprehensible alternative and then undergoing a conversion.[20]

Although I could multiply citations at some length, this issue even gripped Lonergan in 1926, when at age 22 he had to preach to 250 students

---

17 Lonergan, "*Existenz* and *Aggiornamento*," *Collection*, 230.
18 Lonergan, *Method in Theology*, 50.
19 Lonergan, *Method in Theology*, 155.
20 Lonergan, *Method in Theology*, 224.

in the Heythrop College dining room and selected for his text: "You will indeed listen, but never understand, and you will indeed look, but never perceive" (Acts 28:26 NRSV).[21] The issue Lonergan had to face is one we may have to face, too. It is the issue of conversion and repentance.

My own sense is that conversion and repentance are crucial to the process of learning Lonergan's foundational language precisely because the languages of liberalism or nihilism are so dominant in our culture. They do not just exist "out there" or "in them." If my own experience is not unique, these languages have invaded us. They affect our day-to-day life choices and our overall way of life both in the manner in which we individually and collectively interpret our desires and needs and in the ordering of the values incorporated in the already understood and agreed upon solutions to the problem of living together that make up our institutions. These languages are *the* symptom of our implicatedness in what today is commonly called "structural sin." And so the heart of relinquishing the languages and the start of the process of learning a new foundational language – which, as I have tried to show, does not necessarily mean using different words or inventing neologisms – is metanoia, conversion, and repentance.

3.2 Christian Conversion as Conversational

3.21 The Christian Situation of Conversion

Frederick E. Crowe has written with theological intelligence about the situation in which one appropriates Christian conversion:

> At one end of the spectrum, we have ourselves ... with our religious interiority to be pondered and understood. At the other end, we have Jesus with his human consciousness and the religious interiority of God's Son in human form. In between, we have the apostles, prophets, evangelists, etc.; as well as the mystics of all ages, but especially from those times when they began to describe more helpfully their experience ... there would be the inner word of Jesus finding expression in his spoken words and deeds,

---

21 This is neither to deny nor to underplay the importance of doing with Lonergan what Lonergan did with St Thomas Aquinas, or indeed of doing with any other authors what he did. I am simply underscoring what I now feel may be a *sine qua non* (as well perhaps *the* ass's bridge) for doing this with Lonergan.

in his silence and his suffering. This expression, an outer word in the broad sense, is received, assimilated interiorly, and re-expressed by the ... intermediaries between Jesus and the people of God. It becomes then an outer word for us, to be received in faith but given new expression in virtue of our own inner word, the gift of the Spirit, on the foundations, that is, of our interiority.[22]

In being converted, in repentance, we enter a conversation within what might be called a redemptive tension as we experience the interplay between inner word (gift of the Spirit) and outer word (Jesus, who lived, suffered, died, and rose again) in the process of ongoing conversion, since conversion as Christian involves a two-sided response to God's outgoing love: a response to the operative grace of conversion that bestows a universal antecedent willingness through the gift of the Spirit; and a (not necessarily separate) response to the outer word of the Risen Lord.

3.22 Conversation with the Outer Word: Its Redemptive Function[23] I want to underline Lonergan's statement:

Without the visible mission of the Word, the gift of the Spirit is a being-in-love without a proper object; it remains simply an orientation to mystery that awaits its interpretation.[24]

Perhaps for most of us, Christian conversion involves encountering the Christ, the Son of God, whose story is to be read in the gospels and the significance of that story in the Old Testament and the New Testament, in the light of God's gift of love. As with the original disciples, it is the Risen Lord who first reveals to us our own very real implicatedness in personal and structural sin; who reveals us to be the

---

22 Frederick E. Crowe, "Lonergan's Early Use of Analogy," *Method: Journal of Lonergan Studies* 1 (1983): 41.

23 In spelling out J.B. Metz's ideas about the narrative appropriation of the dangerous memory of Jesus Christ, who suffered, died, rose again, I have been greatly helped by the work of Rowan Williams, *Resurrection: Interpreting the Easter Gospel* (London: Darton, Longman & Todd, 1982). This strikes me as a pastoral articulation of the point of Lonergan's systematic theses on the redemption in *De Verbo Incarnato* (1964).

24 Bernard Lonergan, "Mission and the Spirit," *A Third Collection: Papers by Bernard J.F. Lonergan, SJ* (New York: Paulist, 1985), 32.

co-causes of his suffering; he who shows us the extent of suffering our sin cost him, and who communicates to us the judgment of his Father on the sheer horribility of that personal and structural sin. Confronted by our responsibility for our part in sin, we want to repent, to change; but we cannot change ourselves. And so the Risen Lord forgives us for our involvement in personal and structural sin; he thereby gives us the strength at once to take responsibility for our sin and to claim a new identity by uniting us with his redemptive suffering. He enables us to accept consciously, knowingly, responsibly the *de facto* intelligibility of this concrete universe: the law of the cross as the movement through death to life eternal.

3.23 Conversation with the Outer Word:
Its Constitutive Function

When we put in terms of language the issue of conversion as a radical change in our horizon or orientation, then we need to speak of story in the sense intended by Lonergan when he wrote that "we have hunches we cannot formulate ... so we tell a story."[25] Let me cite at greater length his way of handling the category of story:

> ... being human is being-in-the-world (*in der Welt sein*), ... one can rise to full stature only through full knowledge of the world, ... one does not possess that full knowledge and thus makes use of the *élan vital* that, as it guides biological growth and evolution, so too it takes the lead in human development and expresses its intimations through the stories it inspires. Symbols, finally, are a more elementary type of story: They are inner or outer events, or a combination of both, that intimate to us at once the kind of being that we are to be and the kind of world in which we become our true selves.[26]

In terms of language, then, being converted means radically changing the story by *which* one lives. Thus, J.B. Metz has identified the emancipatory stories implicit in the liberal languages in which we have been educated, socialized, acculturated. As success stories they cover over

---

25 Bernard Lonergan, "Reality, Myth, Symbol," *Philosophical and Theological Papers 1965–1980*, ed. Robert C. Croken and Robert M. Doran, Collected Works of Bernard Lonergan 17 (Toronto: University of Toronto Press, 2004), 386.
26 Lonergan, "Reality, Myth, Symbol," 387.

the lives human beings really lead by making us oblivious to the full scope of human suffering throughout history. Metz has contrasted these success stories with the redemptive story of Jesus who suffered, died, and rose again.

Response to the linguistic and incarnate meaning of the outer word of the Risen One meets head on our need to be conversationally opened up and made sensitive to the depth of our involvement in the sinfulness of the situation brought about by the stories that have grown out of the waves of modernity in our culture; our need to absorb in detail how much we have constituted ourselves individually and collectively in these stories to the detriment of others, even Jesus. Contact – however mediated it may be – with the Risen Judge who has been victimized by our sin can open up this conversation for us. But, on the other hand, we also need to be forgiven and empowered by his spirit to gradually displace the "hunches" about our future cultivated in us by the dominant liberal languages in favor of the story of the one who suffers and dies for us, the one who rises and forgives us in befriending us. Thus, we need both his Spirit and meditative exegesis of his story to make his orientation toward the suffering and loss in the world our own. When we have been forgiven, loved, and illumined in faith by his story, a shift in probabilities takes place, and we have much more of a chance to become like the man Jesus whose overall approach to the world is portrayed by Mark's transfiguration story where Jesus moves from being utterly absorbed in conversational immediacy with the Father, Elijah, and Moses, to inquire with simple, direct, and genuine concern about the epileptic child: "How long has he been like this?"

And so the question has been urging itself upon me with increasing force whether a concrete entry into the conversation with the outer word may not be a prerequisite as a matter of fact for speaking Lonergan's foundational language, somewhat in the way he affirms that religious conversion is required not *de jure* but *de facto* for a correct conception and affirmation of the existence of God.

3.24 Conversation and Community

I have been speaking of the communication of Spirit and Word in terms of its redemptive and constitutive functions. Let us return to the two sides of Crowe's spectrum to recall the conversational situation of Christian conversion. On the one side, there is the outer word originally generated by the consciously elicited acts of meaning and value of the mind and heart of Jesus as he sought to discover how to share with us the meaning and value of being in love with his very dear Father. On the other side, there are our Spirit-enlightened questions for intelligence, reflection, and deliberation, as we enter into communication with the outer word. In either case, Jesus's and ours, we are constituting ourselves humanly by acts of meaning and value that are conversational. The conversation begins, as Lonergan once put it, in

> the experience of a transformation one did not bring about but rather underwent, as divine providence let evil take its course and vertical finality be heightened, as it let one's circumstances shift, one's dispositions change, new encounters occur, and – so gently and quietly – one's heart be touched. It is the experience of a new community ...[27]

We find in our experience that one's gift of the Spirit surges or rises up gradually to the forefront of consciousness as one falls in love with someone who lives a life of self-transcendence. One feels oneself invited or challenged to live up to a new standard, because the one or ones with whom one has fallen in love speak a language with their lives that embodies a different orientation and different judgments of value than one was used to. The eyes of being in love bring one to appreciate the implicit or explicit meanings and values that make the beloved "tick." If it is explicitly Christian, the life of the new community will have the shape, as Richard Holloway has so beautifully expressed it, of being taken, blessed, broken, and given away; if it is not explicitly Christian, similar life patterns will be in evidence together with the vital sense of living out of a gratuity to which one cannot simply lay claim. At any rate, when one is drawn by love into such a relationship, one wants to become identified with the new community, and one begins to accept the pattern or shape of its life and its story not as theories or explanations, but as a framework of beliefs. As time passes, one finds oneself assenting not only notionally, but also really to the meanings, facts, and values that are constitutive of the group's identity – not because one has grasped their underlying intelligibility or the sufficiency of the evidence, but because of what can only be described as the beauty of the lives inspired by them. "In thy light we see light." As believed and lived, such meanings and values become constitutive of oneself, "for

---

27 Lonergan, "Mission and the Spirit," 33.

they crystallize the inner gift of the love of God into overt Christian fellowship."[28]

3.25 Christian Identity and Its Cognitive Function

Besides being redemptive and constitutive, the communication of the Son and Spirit is also cognitive. The constitutive Christian story gives an existential answer to the question about the right way to live; but this answer gives rise to questions for intelligence, reasonableness, and responsibility as the Christian community tries to live out the answer it believes in the different circumstances, stages of meaning, and cultural milieux in which it exists. Hence, to keep its identity clear and to mediate its redemptive and constitutive power to every culture and every domain of human life, the Christian community focuses on its meaning and value as cognitive within the diverse stages of meaning.

Because, as St Augustine made so clear in *The City of God*, there is a strict correspondence between what we individually and communally love and the identity of the selves and communities we are becoming, the cognitive function of meaning that clarifies the objective of our faith and love has a great practical importance. This practical and existential correlation between the identity of self and community, on the one hand, and the identity of the God of the self and the community, on the other, was in the forefront of the Christian community's concern "on the way to Nicea" and in the course of the patristic and conciliar debates of the first seven or eight Christian centuries, when it made the transition from a commonsense control of its basic meanings to second-order theoretical control. If the Arian question whether Jesus was the highest creature or God's Son in the strictest sense reached its cognitive resolution on the explanatory level of logical operations on predicative statements, the need for such a resolution was practical, constitutive, soteriological: If Jesus was not God, are we really saved? Moreover, Erik Petersen, Matthew Lamb, and others have stressed the demolition of Eusebian civil theology consequent upon the Athanasian orthodoxy. These are examples of the way the cognitive function of meaning contributes to the foundational purification of the stories by which the Christian community expresses its terminal values and constitutes its identity.

---

28 Lonergan, "Mission and the Spirit," 32.

An even more telling example of the foundational significance of Christianity's cognitive function in the second stage of meaning regards the speculative theology of the Trinity based on the church doctrines worked out in those early ecumenical councils. I am referring, of course, to Augustine's breakthrough to the first non-material analogy for the immanent processions of the Son and the Spirit. His discovery of the most adequate created *imago Dei* in the human mind and heart was a great watershed of Christian and human speculation on the divine nature. It came into its own only in the mature trinitarian theology of Thomas Aquinas; yet this hypothesis of the *emanatio intelligibilis* was buried by Scotist, Ockhamist, and even Thomistic conceptualism promptly after his death. His explanation of the intrinsically conversational nature of the godhead, of its immanent processions, of its economic missions, however, is not something that could have been demonstrated outside the ambit of the stream of tradition generated by the outer word, Jesus Christ. But its virtualities both for the self-understanding of the Christian community and for the focusing of its God-given orientation to the suffering world have, I am sorry to have to say, lain almost dormant, as far as Christian theology has been concerned.

At the present time, the Christian community in its cognitive function is making the tortuous passage from the second into the third stage of meaning. Perhaps the most unsettling manifestations of the breakdown of the theoretical, logically oriented, classical control of meaning have been connected with the widespread, wholesale jettisoning of specifically Christian meanings and values in favor of one or another "progressive" product of modernity. In its preaching and its liturgies, in its counseling and its conduct, in its theology and its catechesis, Western Christianity has been in the process, as one of my colleagues at Boston College has well put it, of diluting the Good News into "nice" news. Or in another suggestion articulated by Joann Wolski Conn and Walter Conn, the oscillations in Christian self-understanding between the attitudes of self-sacrifice and self-realization have tended to cover over the attitude of genuine self-transcendence demanded by the Christian gospel.

What is at stake in the Christian community's changeover from second to third stage control of meaning is evident in Karl Rahner's foundational concentration in the 1930s (in *Geist im Welt)* on the seventh article of Question 84 of the first part of the *Summa theologiae,* which used phenomenological means to comment on Thomas Aquinas's cognitional metaphysics. It is even more apparent in Lonergan's *Verbum* articles of the early 1940s and signaled again by the epigraph to *Insight* taken from Aristotle's *De anima.* The pivotal issue in all these works was the pre-predicative, pre-propositional, phenomenologically ostensible act of direct insight into imaginatively elaborated symbolisms that grounds intelligent articulation in either other symbols or concepts, and of reflective insight into the sufficiency or insufficiency of evidence to ground true judgments. Lonergan, indeed, explicated the genuinely conversational basis of Thomas's trinitarian hypothesis within the realm of human interiority to uncover the most full-bodied and differentiated expression to date of the foundations of Christian theology in the third stage of meaning. By explicitly appropriating the way the authentic asking and answering of the eminently conversational questions – "What are we doing whenever we really understand? What are we doing whenever we are really speaking? What are we doing whenever we are really listening to or really dedicating ourselves to someone or something?"[29] – Lonergan discovered the concrete basis for theology as an integrally conversational discipline that mediates between past and future by passing from indirect discourse (research, interpretation, history, dialectic) to direct discourse (foundations, doctrines, systematics, communications). When Lonergan got clear about the last of the conversational questions, "What are we doing when we are loving?" his findings meshed with his own remarkable retrieval of Aquinas's intricate and second-stage theories on grace and freedom. That is to say, the clear differentiation of the further levels of consciousness engaged in deliberating and loving coalesced with the transposition into a third-stage framework of Thomas's doctrine on operative grace, and consequently, he was able to thematize the foundational reality for theology within the converted subject-in-love-with-God. This astounding transposition by Lonergan of Aquinas's fidelity both to church doctrines and to the systematic exigence of meaning lays the groundwork for general and special categories and a renewal of theology in a new key with implications that are immediately practical and political.

The third-stage-of-meaning systematics already inaugurated by Lonergan allows us to put the theology of God, Trinity, Christology, Pneumatology, and Eschatology into explicitly conversational terms. In this framework, the interplay between the conversational self-meaning

---

29 See Philip McShane, *Music That Is Soundless: An Introduction to God for the Graduate* (Washington, DC: University Press of America, 1977), 1–2.

essential to God and the conversational self-meaning by which we are personally and communally constituted can be integrated into a complete revision of foundational theology. Here I would like to give an example of what I mean by sketching out how the structure of the human good can be transposed into the context of the communication of the Son and the Spirit as redemptive and constitutive meaning.

4. The Human Good and the Christian Conversation

God's self-communication in grace involves not merely an entry into a new entitative, supernatural order of being, but the catching up of our human being as conversationally stunted or deformed self-meaning into the self-meaning constitutive of the Trinity. The gift of God's love liberates human *liberty* when we fall in love with God. But the *conversion* by which we fall in love with God is also an entry into a new set of *interpersonal relations* with Father, Son, and Spirit.

As sharing in the relationship of the Spirit to the Word and the Father, we are

- oriented (with the Son) toward the Father in the beatific vision in the afterlife, and in the present life, given the faith, hope, and love by which our conscious intentionalities can respond here on earth to God's outgoing love in a life of self-transcendent listening, devotion, and self-dedication;
- made ever more receptive to the goodness, truth, and intelligibility of the linguistic and incarnate meaning of the Word; and
- introduced into a dynamism of discernment by which we gradually become more pure and disinterested toward the expression of God's will in the concrete world order comprised of ranges of *goods of order, particular goods*, and natural schemes of recurrence.

As sharing in the Son's relationship to the Father (filiation), we actively desire the strictly supernatural fulfillment of the beatific vision as a *particular good* that relativizes all other *needs* and *desires*.

As sharers in the mission of the Word, listening to the Word expressed in history by Jesus under the Spirit's tutelage is just the beginning; we have also to

- use our *capacity for intellectual development* to enter into solidarity with the poor and the victims of injustice by envisaging and helping to bring about the concrete realization of God's rule on earth by understanding correctly and making wise judgments about the complex interlocking of familial, legal, technological, economic, and political *goods of order*; and by acquiring the needed *skills* and *habits* for playing the requisite *roles* and *tasks*; and

• use our faith-enlightened intelligence, reasonableness, and responsibility to transform our conversation on earth, especially the meta-institution of language, and to transvalue all vital, social, cultural, personal, and religious *values*, about us, by moving toward institutions and *personal relations* in which people can be more intelligent, reasonable, responsible, free, and friendly.

These are no more than just hints and guesses – paltry intimations – of the way the Christian community can appropriate for its foundations the intrinsically conversational character of its God and itself in the third stage of meaning.

11 Grace and Friendship: Postmodern Political Theology and God as Conversational

Introduction

I want to examine certain motifs from Lonergan's earlier theological writings for this study of grace and friendship. Expanding on Lonergan's trinitarian systematic theology from his years at the Gregorian University, Robert Doran, SJ, and Daniel Monsour have explained and helped us better to understand the meaning and the implications of the fourfold hypothesis, in which Lonergan explicated the analogy of contingent predications in terms of what Frederick Crowe called "the trinification of the world." The finality of the created universe involves a set of created participations in the fourfold relations among the persons of the Holy Trinity: the secondary act of existence that enables the hypostatic union of the Word Incarnate to occur is a created share in the relation of the Father to the Son, paternity; sanctifying grace by which we are healed and elevated to the supernatural order is a created share in the relation of the Father and the Son to the Holy Spirit, active spiration; the gift of charity is a created share in the reciprocal relation of the Holy Spirit to the Father and the Son, passive spiration; and the beatific vision is a created share in the reciprocal relation of the Son to the Father, filiation.[1]

Let us examine the aspect of grace called the gift of charity by recalling Thomas Aquinas's explanation of it as *amicitia Dei*.[2] What an audacious

---

1 See Bernard Lonergan, *The Triune God: Systematics*, Collected Works of Bernard Lonergan 12, trans. Michael G. Shields, ed. Robert M. Doran and H. Daniel Monsour (Toronto: University of Toronto Press, 2007), 437ff.
2　See Thomas Aquinas, *Summa theologiae*, 2a–2ae, qq. 23–46.

move was Aquinas's explanatory definition, which uses the analogy of friendship drawn from Books 8 and 9 of Aristotle's *Nicomachean Ethics*. No one before him had attempted this because of Aristotle's insistence that true friendship can only occur between equals; even those who celebrated the divinization of humankind were hesitant to say that graced human beings were on a plane of equality with God. Eberhard Schockenhoff concedes Bernard of Clairvaux, who considered the idea, did not follow through on it, because Christian charity entails love of one's enemies. He thought it would be too contradictory to think of an enemy as a friend.[3]

In his domestic exhortation of the 1950s[4] and his meditation on "The Mediation of Christ in Prayer,"[5] Lonergan stressed that by the gift of God's grace we are made adopted children of the Father, brothers and sisters of Jesus Christ, and temples of the Holy Spirit. In "Finality, Love, Marriage"[6] we find that the key term of "friendship" leads Lonergan to set central theorems of Aristotle's treatise on friendship in the context of revelation's ontology of creation, thereby relating Thomas Aquinas's theology of the eternal Good and its absolutely objective lovableness to his earliest treatment of sublation in terms of vertical finality. I hope to show that the contemporary malaise surrounding long-term personal relations makes these ideas relevant to certain issues of political theology.

The Drama of Human Existence

We begin with a focus – human beings as persons who spontaneously and inevitably are aware of the universe of nature and history because they are present to themselves as present to the totality of what is. This

---

3 See Eberhard Schockenhoff, "The Theological Virtue of Charity," trans. G. Kaplan and F. Lawrence, *The Ethics of Aquinas*, ed. Stephen J. Pope (Washington, DC: Georgetown University Press, 2002), 207–58; on Bernard of Clairvaux, 221–2.

4 Bernard Lonergan, Domestic Exhortation "On the Mystical Body of Christ," Typescript, Lonergan Archives. This is now published as Bernard Lonergan, "The Mystical Body of Christ," *Shorter Papers*, Collected Works of Bernard Lonergan 20, ed. Robert C. Croken, Robert M. Doran, and H. Daniel Monsour (Toronto: University of Toronto Press, 2007), 106–11.

5 Bernard Lonergan, "The Mediation of Christ in Prayer," *Philosophical and Theological Papers 1958–1964*, Collected Works of Bernard Lonergan 6, ed. Robert C. Croken, Frederick E. Crowe and Robert M. Doran (Toronto: University of Toronto, 1996), 160–82; the editors date this paper 1963.

6 See Bernard Lonergan, "Finality, Love, Marriage," *Collection*, Collected Works of Bernard Lonergan 4, ed. Frederick E. Crowe and Robert M. Doran (Toronto: University of Toronto Press, 1993 [first published in 1943]), 17–52.

self-presence as presence to everything is immediate, for if the conditions on the levels of physics, chemistry, botany, and zoology are fulfilled, human beings just are conscious. They do not have to think anything, or decide anything, or worry about anything, or do anything. Unless there is something gravely wrong with their organisms, people are present; and they are present not just *in* space and time, but also *to* space and time, and beyond. Both in their actuality and in their potential range, therefore, human beings as centers of awareness in and beyond space and time are wonderfully mysterious – *homo abyssus*.

However, for a person to be a center of awareness is not to be a transparently conscious one. Consciousness itself has an elusiveness and lack of definition that belie the spontaneous images usually evoked in us by the word "presence." Primitive self-presence is not a fact that can be mastered by any reflection or heightening of awareness, because even if we were to make consciousness explicit, we could not do so exhaustively or comprehensively. The subject as subject always outruns objectification. Then, too, as any spiritual director knows, even what we do succeed in knowing objectively of ourselves is often misunderstood or all too frequently falsely asserted, because we are so often subjects of illusion, not to say delusion. There are still further complications to self-knowledge, because, although it is a center of awareness in and beyond space and time, human consciousness is embedded in language, history, society, culture, and more or less imperfect political orders.

Once we put ourselves as mysterious centers of awareness through the ringer of modernity and postmodernity, we still need to confront our experience of "the contradiction between a plenitude of feelings in which we suffer random dispersal and a longed-for identity."[7] The "facticity, thrownness, and ceaseless internal change" of human existence central to Heidegger's *Daseinsanalytik* suggest that the subject as subject is ever conscious of an ongoing non-coincidence with itself as it negotiates the complex networks of social, cultural, and political influences insinuated most pervasively into our lives by language. The subject's performance is massively conditioned by education, socialization, and acculturation. These networks constrain us almost always to handle the non-coincidence of ourselves with ourselves by faking roles that do not really mean what we feel and think internally. It is perhaps

---

7 See Walter A. Davis, *Inwardness and Existence: Subjectivity in/and Hegel, Heidegger, Marx and Freud* (Madison, WI: University of Wisconsin Press, 1989), 99.

only rarely that such subjects reach what Lonergan calls "the critical point," when subjects realize that their existence is at stake.[8] Thus, our struggle to give integrity to our character is "an inner drama with no easy or quick solutions." This drama is made all the more complex by ongoing anxiety and bad faith as we experience the influence upon us of social, cultural, and political forces.[9] Let us briefly examine how this occurs in the West.

Enlightenment Counter-positions

The distortion, dysfunction, and disorientation built into Western historical networks of society, culture, and politics are inscribed in the dominant languages of modernity.[10] Hobbes, Locke, Bacon, and Descartes, the great inaugurators of the modern "project," invented the first language of modernity. Their humanitarian project engaged the failure of the Christian churches in the bloody wars of religion and in the oppressive alliance of altar and throne. If finite and flawed religious institutions could identify themselves with the transcendent power that ought ultimately to govern our lives, why not relinquish supernatural aspirations altogether, not to mention the natural honor and nobility of the Greeks and Romans, to establish more humane social, cultural, and political foundations on the "low but solid basis" (Winston Churchill) of "the truncated subject" (Lonergan)? Thus was forged a foundational language that represents the human being as an atomistic individual who receives sense stimuli, calculates with conceptual and propositional tools, and is motivated by self-regarding feelings centered on the needs of "organistic spontaneity"[11] or the "vital values"[12] of life, liberty,

---

8 See Bernard Lonergan, "*Existenz* and *Aggiornamento*," *Collection*, 222–31 at 223–4.

9 Davis, *Inwardness and Existence*, 102.

10 The idea of "languages" of modernity is a transposition of Leo Strauss's insight into "waves of modernity." See Leo Strauss, "The Three Waves of Modernity," *An Introduction to Political Philosophy: Ten Essays by Leo Strauss*, ed. Hilail Gilden (Detroit: Wayne State University Press, 1989) 81–98, with a bibliography of Strauss's writings, 347–55.

11 Lonergan, "Finality, Love, Marriage," 26, 30–3. Organistic spontaneity refers to desire on the level of the lower manifolds (physical, chemical, botanical, zoological, i.e., biological) of human beings insofar as they are organisms, thus prescinding from their selves as intelligent, reasonable, and responsible.

12 See Bernard Lonergan, *Method in Theology* (New York: Herder & Herder, 1972), 31, 39.

and property. Insatiable human desires require reason as a calculating faculty; knowledge is power, dominative power. The early modern accounts of the state of nature (that replace *both* the biblical account of human origins and fall *and* Plato's educational state or Aristotle's ethics) use calculating reason to present theoretical foundations for the liberal democratic regime of political hedonism. As Leo Strauss argued, Lockean liberals are truncated subjects caught up in "the joyless quest for joy."[13] Theirs is the language of "possessive individualism"[14] and of rights as self-centered claims, in contrast to duties that oblige us to transcend ourselves for the common good.

In the seventeenth and eighteenth centuries, this language overwhelmed the *civilis conversatio* that for the ancients is constitutive of political community.[15] According to the educational vision of Plato's *Republic* and Aristotle's *Politics*, of Isocrates and Cicero, an aristocratic education (that became the legacy of liberal education in more recent times) was the *sine qua non* of such a civil conversation. Machiavelli ridiculed the centrality of moral and spiritual culture as utopian and his liberal followers eliminated soulcraft from statecraft. The educational task of acquiring a language for thinking about the character of society in its fullest and loftiest dimensions has been lost in the measure that Western education interdicts any issue that does not fall under the purview of Machiavelli's "effectual truth" (*verità effettuale*).[16] With the demise of liberal education, liberal constitutionalism's justifiable removal of religious opinion from political power by the judicial separation of church and state opens the way to the highly suspect nationalization of religious loyalties, the privatization of religion in the name of religious toleration, and the secularization of educational ideas and practices.[17] Opportunities for citizens to learn the traditions that would

---

13 See the section on John Locke in Leo Strauss, *Natural Right and History* (Chicago: University of Chicago Press, 1953) 202–51; the phrase comes from 251.

14 See C.B. Macpherson, *The Political Theory of Possessive Individualism: Hobbes to Locke* (Oxford: Oxford University, 1962).

15 See Thomas Gilby, OP, *Between Community and Society* (Longmans, Green & Co., 1953), 93.

16 See Niccolò Machiavelli, *The Prince*, trans. Harvey C. Mansfield (Chicago: University of Chicago, 1998, 2nd ed.), 61: "But since my intent is to write something useful to whoever understands it, it has appeared to me more fitting to go to the effectual truth of the thing than to the imagination of it."

17 See Carnes Lord, "Education and Culture," *The Modern Prince: What Leaders Need to Know Now* (New Haven: Yale University Press, 2003), 134–40 at 136.

enable them to gain critical distance from their social, cultural, and political situation begin to disappear. As citizens or as church members, we picture ourselves as truncated subjects with, in the words of Rowan Williams, blank wills "looking out at a bundle of options like goods on a supermarket shelf."[18] Conditioned by the pushes and pulls of our desires and fears, each individual wants above all to be a success, to be a winner, because individuals, like the society at large, are imbued with what Johann Baptist Metz[19] and Peter Selby[20] call the ideology of winners, the alibi of victory and defeat.

The second great language of modernity was invented by Rousseau's reaction against the bourgeois life as "consumed by consumerism." He refigured the state of nature and of civil society in terms of the language of "expressive individualism" and a politics of compassion.[21] Liberal capitalism's relentlessly competitive commercial society had touted the calculating contract as the dominant model for human relationships. As we used to say when Rousseau was revived by the New Left in the

---

18 See Rowan Williams, *Lost Icons: Reflections on Cultural Bereavement* (Edinburgh: T&T Clark, Ltd., 2000), 39.

19 Johann Baptist Metz's "Erlösung und Emanzipation," *Stimmen der Zeit* 191 (1973): 171–84, set the tone for his last major work, *Glaube in Geschichte und Gesellschaft. Studien zu einer praktischen Fundamentaltheologie* (Mainz: Grünewald 1977); see also *Zeit der Orden? Zur Mystik und Politik der Nachfolge* (Freiburg: Herder 1971). Metz's earlier, less dialectical stance towards the Enlightenment is apparent in his books *Christliche Anthropozentrik* (Munich: Kösel, 1962) and *Zur Theologie der Welt* (Mainz: Grünewald, 1968).

20 The relevant quotation from Peter Selby appears in Rowan Williams's *On Christian Theology* (London: Blackwell, 2000):

> Christianity has to start with confronting the notion of our self-understanding that is produced by an ideology of victory and defeat; and to confront that, of course, means to re-evaluate all our defeats … Your self-understanding and mine, corrupted as they are by our involvement in the processes and the ideologies of victory and defeat, have to be turned around so that we come to see them alongside the defeat of Jesus as the world's ultimate friend, so that the world is befriended by its defeat, and not by victory achieved at the expense of other people's defeat (274).
>
> See Peter Selby, *Grace and Mortgage: The Language of Faith and the Debt of the World* (London: Darton, Longman and Todd, 1997).

21 See Jean-Jacques Rousseau, "Discourse on the Origin and Foundation of Inequality among Men," *The First and Second Discourses*, ed. Roger D. Masters (New York: St Martin, 1964).

1960s, "You can't trust anyone under 30, you can't trust anyone over 30, and you can't trust anyone 30." Rousseau saw that liberal society promotes *amour propre* or vanity, which causes compassion to atrophy, because the liberal notion of goodness means no more than "not getting caught" (and certainly not having to say you're sorry if you are caught!). There could never be enough police or whistle-blowers to execute surveillance over the many who will calculate that it is in their interest to break the law. To counter this slavishness of liberal capitalist society, Rousseau saw the need for citizens to cultivate reason as the capacity for generalization to become capable of universalizing their own particular wills or desires to attain the general will.[22]

Rousseau knew that bourgeois society needed a new kind of education to ensure the salutary transition from the human being to the citizen. Casting a jaundiced eye on the denaturing of the human being required by submission to the general will, he contended that citizens' submission to the general will could only be free and passionate if the marriage bond as rooted in the sublimation of organistic spontaneity were to be the real basis of the social contract. Hence, in *Emile, or On Education* Rousseau devised an elaborate and highly artificial education to turn the originally self-centered animal into a citizen passionately dedicated to the laws of the city.[23]

Shifting from the horizon of the "truncated subject" to that of the "immanentist subject,"[24] Rousseau sought to combine reason's abstract capacity to find the universal, whether concept or law, with more or less sublimated natural emotions. He invented a language of expressive individualism that embraces a complex range of sentiments, from those of the patriot's fellow-spiritedness to those of the Bohemian who heeds "the beat of a different drum" and drops out of society to enjoy the "solitary sense of his or her existence" (see *The Reveries of the Solitary Walker*). But the *Nouvelle Héloise* portrayed Rousseau's realization that people cannot avoid the "familiar opposition between the idealism of

---

22 See J.-J. Rousseau, *On the Social Contract*, trans. Judith R. Martin (New York: St Martin, 1978).

23 See the translation of and introduction to this work by Allan Bloom (New York: Basic Books, 1979).

24 The terms "truncated" and "immanentist subject" are Lonergan's, in his lecture entitled "The Subject," in *A Second Collection*, ed. William Ryan and Bernard Tyrrell (London: Darton, Longman and Todd, 1974), 69–86.

human aspiration and the sorry facts of human performance."[25] Rousseau's language of expressive individualism is diffused in a variety of approaches to the social surd ranging from (1) the radical remedy of revolution, in which a suffocating moralism sets up a regime of social totalitarianism – whether in the form of Robespierre's reign of terror transposed into the current predominance of "political correctness" with teeth, or of ineffectual, profound melancholy – to (2) the idealism of his great disciple, Immanuel Kant.

In his doctrine of human dignity Kant solidified Rousseau's teachings in what is probably the most consistent account of the immanentist subject.[26] Kant's famous teaching on the morally autonomous subject as the ground of human dignity demands respect for others precisely insofar as they are capable of giving themselves the law.[27] Conscientious thinkers such as Kant himself and, more recently, Hans Jonas became concerned about the possibility of a person's freely choosing evil that is equiprimordial with autonomy itself;[28] and Pierre Manent has pointed out that the prevailing language of expressive individualism has transformed the notion of human dignity[29] to imply respect for *any* decisions a person happens to make, or for *any* moral contents or "life-style" to which people happen to commit themselves.

Robert Bellah found in *Habits of the Heart*[30] that most North Americans (and probably most Westerners) speak now one, now the other of these two modern languages. We alternate between lives dominated by either possessive individualism or expressive individualism. These languages are our true mother tongues. They lead us to entertain virtual

---

25 The phrase is Lonergan's ("Finality, Love, Marriage," 39); the path from the idealism of marriage in Rousseau's *Emile* to the relative degradation of his novel, *Nouvelle Hèloise*, is traced in Allan Bloom's chapter on Rousseau in *Love and Friendship* (New York: Simon & Schuster, 1993), 39–157.

26 See Immanuel Kant, *Foundations of the Metaphysics of Morals*, trans. Lewis Beck (Indianapolis: Bobbs-Merrill, 1959).

27 See Paul Ricoeur's helpful comments on Kant's teaching in Paul Ricoeur, *Oneself as Another*, trans. Kathleen Blamey (Chicago: University of Chicago, 1992), 203–39.

28 See Hans Jonas, "The Abyss of the Will: Philosophical Meditation on the Seventh Chapter of Paul's Epistle to the Romans," *Philosophical Essays: From Ancient Creed to Modern Technology* (Chicago: University of Chicago/Midway Books, 1974), 335–48.

29 See Pierre Manent, "L'empire de la morale," *Commentaire* 95 (Autumn, 2001): 501–10.

30 Robert Bellah, R. Madsen, W. Sullivan, A. Swidler, and S. Tipton, *Habits of the Heart: Individualism and Commitment in American Life* (Berkeley and Los Angeles: University of California Press, 1985).

images of ourselves either as truncated subjects exercising reason as a calculating faculty in the service of satisfactions (i.e., Charles Taylor's "punctual" subject or Michael Sandel's "unencumbered" subject; or as immanentist subjects, torn between universalizing and disinterested reason and raw feelings – *citoyens* or romantic loners). All these cases effectively validate the post-Enlightenment self-construction of the modern abstract autonomous individual, who figures it's more humane and sensible to affirm the primacy of what Aquinas called concupiscible or self-regarding desires, distrusting higher aspirations. "Man's greatness even in his concupiscence," as Pascal put it, is that "he has managed to produce such a remarkable system from it and make it the image of true charity."[31]

Postmodern Reaction

In *After Virtue* Alasdair MacIntyre depicted a world where managers and therapists symbolize the socially dominant subjects as truncated or as immanentist.[32] Kierkegaard, Nietzsche, and Heidegger (with his many German, French, English, and American epigones) have unleashed a quest for more integral human living in the postmodern resistance to the modern Enlightenment constitution of humanity through its two languages. The late British Jewish philosopher Gillian Rose says that Nietzsche and Heidegger initiated "a pilgrimage to an imagined Jerusalem, in search of difference or otherness, love or community, and hoping to escape the *imperium* of reason, truth, or freedom."[33] Enlightenment reason is calculating or universalizing; romantic feeling is sentimental. Such reason and sentiment are dominative, imperialistic, totalizing; they subordinate others to their power or to the gratification of their desires and needs. The languages operate exclusively, silencing or suppressing woman, body as materiality or sexuality, as well as dialogue, love, and revelation. Postmodern thought reasserts the significance of woman/body/love and demonizes reason and sentiments as exclusive, oppositional, and closed.

---

31 Blaise Pascal, *Pensées*, trans. A.J. Krailsheimer (London: Penguin Books, 1966) #118, 60.

32 See Alasdair MacIntyre, *After Virtue: A Study in Moral Theory* (Notre Dame: University of Notre Dame Press, 1981).

33 See Gillian Rose, "Introduction," *Judaism and Modernity: Philosophical Essays* (London: Blackwell, 1993), 1–10 at 1.

There is a point to the postmodern complaint insofar as it targets both calculating, universalizing reason and the disoriented feelings of modernity. Emmanuel Lévinas argues that reason itself is always possessive and even violent, so that putative sovereign individuals cannot help being violent toward themselves, their God, and their others. In contrast, for Lévinas the Torah's command, "Thou shalt not kill," means heeding "the cry of other human beings as alternative to the justified demands of human rights," and substituting "cry and response for the contention of the claim."[34] He opts for what Rose calls a "gestural" ethics,[35] which is non-representational, non-institutional, and non-intentional (where "intentional" is understood in Husserlian-Cartesian terms). Such an ethics subverts both principled autonomy (Kant's categorical imperative) and heteronomy (external authorities). If we have the vision of the face, we move out of ourselves to overcome "the recoil of the enhanced sensation of the self," which is the hallmark of romantic sentimentality's penchant for feeling one's own feelings.[36] Knowledge can play no role in such self-transcendence, because it always involves sovereign seizure, possession, and violence.

Gillian Rose is rightly critical of the postmodernists' unequivocal Other, conceived and imaged as sheer alterity. She notes that this artificial construction of the Other renders the human being innocent of the interference of intermediary institutions, while at the same time showing the contradictoriness and danger of portraying human consciousness and reason as inevitably possessive. Before her untimely death, she was forging a dialogical, non-caricatured account of human consciousness and reason.[37] After all, she remarks, consciousness and reason are precisely the capacity for learning to understand the other and ourselves not just in our boundedness by external authority, institutions, and laws, but in our vulnerability to violence and injustice. Getting

---

34 See Gillian Rose, "Angry Angels – Simone Weil and Emmanuel Levinas," *Judaism and Modernity*, 211–23 at 215.

35 Rose, "Introduction," 6.

36 Rose, "Angry Angels – Simone Weil and Emmanuel Levinas," 215.

37 Besides *Judaism and Modernity*, which Rose called her *apologia pro vita mea*, see: *The Broken Middle: Out of Our Ancient Society* (London: Blackwell, 1992); "Diremption of the Spirit," in *Shadow of Spirit: Postmodernism and Religion*, ed. Philippa Berry and Andrew Wernick (London & New York: Routledge, 1992), 45–56; and *Mourning Becomes the Law: Philosophy and Representation* (Cambridge: Cambridge University Press, 1996).

beyond what she calls the intolerant postmodern subject that "gestures to an unidentified plurality of others,"[38] Rose affirms that "to present experience, with its unwelcome and welcome surprises and with its structure, is the work of reason itself as dynamic."[39] Beyond the naive insistence on the immediate experience of others, we need reason, she says, "to understand the unknown but effective actuality which forms a large part of ourselves," and "to understand our mistakes by recovering the interference of meaning" due to the ambiguous role of social, cultural, and political mediations in our lives. In a way reminiscent of Lonergan, Rose regards Fascism and Communism as "temptations arising from the failures of human rights and from the prevalence of bureaucratic rationality and domination."[40] Rose's resistance to the violence at either extreme takes a page from Lévinas and Simone Weil in initiating a political theology that takes seriously "the relation of man to man, the love of the neighbor, where love *passes* through God's love for men," so that "men … 'see that men are preserved from harm.'"[41] This seems to me a salutary far cry from attempts by many contemporary Christian and Catholic social ethicists to combine bourgeois individualism with progressive egalitarianism along the lines of the late John Rawls's social philosophy.[42]

Gillian Rose's attempt to reconcile postmodern concerns with philosophy moves into what I call theology as political. In this context I think it is important to continue on with systematic theology in a political vein by retrieving Aquinas's teaching on charity as the friendship of God, where the genitive is both subjective and objective. If we consider

---

38 Rose, "Introduction," 8.

39 Rose, "Introduction," 5.

40 Rose, "Angry Angels – Simone Weil and Emmanuel Levinas," 212.

41 Rose, "Angry Angels – Simone Weil and Emmanuel Levinas," 214: the internal citation is from Simone Weil. See also Gillian Rose, "Franz Rosenzweig – from Hegel to Yom Kippur," *Judaism and Modernity*, 127–54, esp. 142–44; "Nietzsche's *Judaica*," 89–110, esp. 104–8.

42 See, for example, George Grant, "Justice and the Right to Life: *English-Speaking Justice* (1974)," *The George Grant Reader*, ed. William Christian and Sheila Grant (Toronto: University of Toronto Press, 1998), 107–22. Briefly, on John Rawls see also Frederick G. Lawrence, "Paul Ricoeur's Practical Wisdom: Reflections on the Social Philosophy of *Oneself as Another*," in *Between Suspicion and Sympathy: Paul Ricoeur's Unstable Equilibrium*, ed. Andrzej Wiercinski (Toronto: The Hermeneutic Press, 2003), 502–17.

the first book of Aristotle's *Politics*, the *Nicomachean Ethics*, we note that while Aristotle devotes one and a half books to moral virtue and a book apiece to justice and the dianoetic virtues, he spends two full books discussing friendship. Thus, as Eric Voegelin saw, Aristotle founded justice on *philia*, and he founded *philia* on the actualization of the full self in community.[43]

Thomas Gilby says that for Thomas Aquinas, "Political health depends on friendship, *bonum civitatis in amicitia consistit*, and this is no mere bonhomie, the urbanity described in the *Ethics*, but a reaching out to nothing less than the friendship of divine charity … The conditions of pure society can be studied, though they are achieved only transitorily in this present life, when persons are playing together and, gentle and aware, are both released and neither render nor expect a service."[44] Gilby expressed the crucial role played by friendship in Aristotle and Aquinas as follows:

> Perfect friendship may be rare, … but nothing less should be the exemplar whenever human beings dwell together. It sets the tone of the true humanist condition, to which people belong who are considerate and plucky. The leaven in a civilized group – "an invincible army," reflects Mr E M Forster, "but not a victorious one." Means should be measured by ends, not ends by means.[45]

The centrality of friendship for the kind of politics intrinsic to Thomas Aquinas's adaptation of Aristotle on friendship stands in stark contrast to the modern Enlightenment's marginalization of friendship in society and politics: in Hobbes and Locke, you cannot trust that anyone is your friend, because once you accept the state-of-nature account of humanity, sin is regarded as natural, and people cannot be expected ever to transcend their concupiscent desires. Note, too, that the exemplary character of friendship also contrasts with the artificial and abstract postmodern use of the term, Other.[46] As Paul Ricoeur put it, "[Aristotle's] idea of mutuality [in friendship] indeed has its own requirements

---

43 See Eric Voegelin, *Plato and Aristotle: Order and History* 2 (Baton Rouge: Louisiana State University Press, 1957) 357, 339; see also 320–1.

44 See Gilby, *Between Community and Society*, 168–9.

45 Gilby, *Between Community and Society*, 65.

46 Rose expresses this superbly in "Introduction," 4.

which are not eclipsed by either a genesis based on the Same, as in Husserl, or a genesis based on the Other, as in Lévinas."[47]

Let us first examine briefly Thomas Aquinas's theory of the gift of charity as friendship, and then, second, consider Lonergan's account of love and friendship in his early writings.

Aquinas on Charity as Divine Friendship

As mentioned before, Aquinas explains how the divine life functions as *koinonia* or fellowship by using the analogy of Aristotle's account of lasting friendship between equals, who are alike in dignity and excellence or virtue.[48] Aristotle held that this could not take place between gods and human beings, because gods only love what is most like themselves in human beings, instead of loving them for their own sakes. For Aristotle gods do not overcome differences and distances in rank, because *philia* is love of like for like and exchange among equal partners.[49] Thomas knows on the basis of revelation, however, that the God of our Lord Jesus Christ "wills all men to be saved" (1 Tim. 2:4); and that "God is faithful, by whom you were called into the fellowship [*koinonia*] of his Son, Jesus Christ our Lord" (1 Cor. 1:9). In Aquinas's overarching vision, God out of unbounded love for his Triune nature, and in a movement in response to this original event of love, draws all creatures in accord with their own dignity back to himself as end.[50] In creation, election, incarnation the Triune God enters into intimate companionship and communication with human beings: *societas, convivere, conversatio.*[51]

The center of the mystery occurs in the incarnation when Jesus becomes human and equal to human beings; in loving them, Jesus mediates to us his own and the Father's love and shares with them the

---

47 Ricoeur, *Oneself as Another*, 183.

48 Paul J. Wadell, CP, *Friendship and the Moral Life* (Notre Dame: University of Notre Dame, 1989) exposes Aristotle's way of situating moral life overall within the context of friendship, and then treats Thomas Aquinas's transposition of Aristotle on friendship into his theology of charity.

49 Aristotle, *Nicomachean Ethics* 8, 7, 1157b 37–1158b 1.

50 Thomas Aquinas, *Summa theologiae*, 2–2, q. 23, art 1: "… cum … sit aliqua communicatio hominis ad Deum secundum quod nobis suam beatitudinem communicat … "; Schockenhoff, "The Theological Virtue of Charity," 246–8.

51 See the very insightful article by Joseph Bobik, "Aquinas on *Communicatio*, the Foundation of Friendship and *Caritas*," *The Modern Schoolman* 64 (November 1986): 1–18.

eternal Good of the beatific vision, thereby rendering human beings worthy, in virtue of their new supernatural dignity and character, of the love and friendship of God.

Aquinas disagreed with Peter Lombard who held that our charity is just the Holy Spirit operating immediately in us, coming from the Holy Spirit unmediated by any habit created in the soul.[52] Peter Lombard thought he was following Augustine's interpretation of Romans 5:5. In the *Summa theologiae,* 2–2, q. 23, art 2, Aquinas says the Holy Spirit does not operate alone in us so that we are only passive instruments or channels of the Spirit, without any cooperation of our own wills. No, "the will must be so moved by the Holy Spirit to the act of love that it must itself also produce it." To eliminate the finite structure and act of the human being would be to eliminate charity itself. Yet charity is beyond the power of the human will alone, unless God endows us individually with forms that incline us to these acts, rendering them delightful. Charity only arises when human love for God is elicited from an inner principle infused into the created structure of its soul, as the human being's free act in response to the antecedent love of God. Because love in its proper sense demands the free response of the human being, the Aristotelian condition that friendship be reciprocal is fulfilled in Aquinas's interpretation. The human being, through the faculty antecedently disposed to the relevant acts by the permanent gift of charity, produces acts of charity; and this is verified in our internal experience by the fact that our acts of charity are characterized by spontaneous joy in the good. "Now we are said to be good with the goodness which is God, and wise with the wisdom which is God, because the very qualities which make us formally so are participations [*participatio quaedam*] in the divine goodness and wisdom. So, too, the charity by which we formally love our neighbor is a sharing [*quaedam participatio*] in the divine charity" (ad 1).

When Aquinas presents charity as friendship, he makes clear that it is the culmination of a development of love or affection, which in its natural genesis, passes through the three stages of desire, well-wishing, and friendship.[53] If we love another simply for the sake of the effect it brings about in us as lovers, this is just desire as a certain concupiscence. This does not mean that it is bad; according to both Aristotle and Aquinas,

---

52 For the disagreement, see Schockenhoff, "The Theological Virtue of Charity," 248–50.
53 Gilby, *Between Community and Society,* 191–2.

it is how we all manifest the natural desire of parts to be integrated in the whole; or, in our desire for self-preservation, it is how we want to have our needs secured by living in community (i.e., the legitimate aspect of liberal democracy's passage from the state of nature to civil society). However, our initial attraction toward something or someone can be just predatory, although our passions comprise the whole set of primitive natural motions which ought never be neglected in a flourishing human life. This all happens on the level of (in Lonergan's phrase) organistic spontaneity that Aquinas calls concupiscent desire.

Following Aristotle, Aquinas insists that friendship requires a further stage of affection called *benevolentia*: that well-wishing by which we love another for his or her own sake. We wish them well, and rejoice in their good. In contrast, Allan Bloom writes of Rousseau:

> Rousseau is extremely hardheaded about what human nature permits. Man's selfishness does not allow him to sacrifice his own interest to that of another. The happy other who has all the things one would like for oneself is the object of resentment and envy. A suffering man is no threat. Rousseau asserts, with characteristic boldness and harshness, that nobody can share the happiness of even his best friend without envy. He won the lottery and got all the money. I congratulate him, but actually I would prefer to have the money myself. Aristotle would say that the true friend, although very rare, is possible, that he could rejoice in the friend's good luck, whereas Rousseau insists that this is simply impossible. It is only the friend's neediness, which one can succor, that brings out the generous, as opposed to the corrosive sentiments. Rousseau goes so far as to say that a truly self-sufficient man would have no concern for others and that his happiness would be a kind of solitary monstrosity.[54]

For Aquinas, *benevolentia* lays no claim on another, and manifests no greed to possess the other. It is the affective counterpart to disinterested inquiry into the truth for its own sake, and so is a kind of desire that is unaffected by concupiscence. Recall that Aristotle's insistence on self-love as the indispensable condition for friendship also stresses that to be rightly ordered, one's love of self has to be a love for what is best in oneself, namely, the *nous*. That is why such well-wishing can break out

---

54 Bloom, *Love and Friendship*, 68.

of the circle of oneself (egoistic bias) and of one's group (group bias)[55] through real self-transcendence.[56] In terms of theology as political, this is what enables the *conversatio civilis*, allowing the true sense of "the political" to emerge: only then can issues become the object of detached judgments that engage one in accord with objective justice, even to the point of deciding against one's immediate self-interest to the point of self-sacrifice.[57]

Aquinas then goes on to say that benevolence alone does not suffice for friendship, because a certain *mutua amatio* (*Summa theologiae*, 2–2, q. 23, art 1) is needed as well. In friendship, loving is reciprocal; there is a loving-back based on a union between lover and beloved, a *communicatio*. As Schockenhoff says, "The reciprocal good will between God and the person in whom it is manifested itself requires a sustaining ground upon which alone the exchange of life in common can be actuated, ... 'a certain communication of the person with God' (*aliqua communicatio hominis ad Deum*)."[58] This sharing and commonality consists in that the Triune God shares God's own beatitude with everyone and calls people to participate in God's own life. According to Schockenhoff, besides its active, dynamic aspect, this *koinonia* of 1 Corinthians 1:9 has an intransitive, ontological dimension, "which, on account of its substantive character, is gladly understood as a possession of a common essential form," which constitutes "the participation of the faithful in Christ and the vital union of all Christians with the Son."[59] In Aristotle, this type of *philia* corresponds to the kind of *koinonia* shared, and so in God's communication, the infinite God in the fullness of his Triune life is opened up to human beings when, in the temporal missions of Son and Spirit, the Father calls them to friendship with himself. In Gilby's words, "the fellowship of men with God is a conversation which surpasses bodily and sensitive nature, but already begins in the present life."[60] It is a spiritual intercourse because we are called to share in God's own beatitude; it happens *secundum mentem*, both in heaven and as we head toward

---

55 On individual and group bias, see Bernard Lonergan, *Insight: A Study of Human Understanding*, Collected Works of Bernard Lonergan 3, ed. Frederick E. Crowe and Robert M. Doran (Toronto: University of Toronto Press, 1992), 218–25.
56 Lonergan, *Method in Theology*, 35, 41, 51, 104, 111.
57 Gilby, *Between Community and Society*, 192.
58 Schockenhoff, "The Theological Virtue of Charity," 246.
59 Schockenhoff, "The Theological Virtue of Charity," 247.
60 Gilby, *Between Community and Society*, 192.

that end. God's communication transforms human persons inwardly by the new quality of a permanently given form. If there is such a communication, then mutual loving follows, and so there is a friendship. By the gift of charity God acts in us, and by our natural capacities we act in relation to our neighbor and the world.

Early Lonergan on God's Love

The next piece of this development of charity as friendship depends on Lonergan's explanation of the Mystical Body as a "concrete union of the divine Persons with one another and with man, and, again, of men's union with one another and with the divine Persons."[61] This explanation unfolds the following five relationships of love:

1 The love of the Eternal Father for his Eternal Son as God, which "is God, God the Holy Spirit, who is the infinite love proceeding from the infinite lovableness of God."[62]

2 The love of the Eternal Father for his Son as man, and because "the Son is the same Person in both his divine and human natures, … the Father has but a single love, the Holy Ghost, for the Son whether as God or as Man."[63] Lonergan goes on to say, "Because God became man, the love of God for God became the love of God for man, when the Word was made flesh, the divine love broke the confines of divinity to love a created humanity in the manner that God the Father loves God the Son."[64] The sanctifying grace of Christ, "the loveliness conferred upon a creature beloved by God, … though finite as an entity, is infinite as a grace."[65]

3 The love of Christ as man for man. This is so important for our thesis on charity as friendship we must cite Lonergan at length here:

It is the love of the Sacred Heart of Jesus, the love of a human will, motivated by a human mind, operating through human senses, resonating through human emotions and feelings and sentiments, implemented by a human body with its structures of bones and muscles, flesh, its

---

61 Lonergan, "The Mystical Body of Christ," 106.
62 Lonergan, "The Mystical Body of Christ," 107.
63 Lonergan, "The Mystical Body of Christ," 107.
64 Lonergan, "The Mystical Body of Christ," 107.
65 Lonergan, "The Mystical Body of Christ," 107.

mobile features, its terrible capacities for pleasure and pain, for joy and sorrow, for rapture and agony. It is the love of the Good Shepherd, knowing its own, known by its own, and ready to lose his life for them: Greater love than this no man hath, than to lay down his life for his friend. It is the love of a man with a mission in the world, the high mission of teaching truth: For this I was born and for this I came into the world, that I might bear witness to the truth. It is the love of a man with an incomprehensible, an incommunicable secret. How can a man announce that he is God? Yet Christ was God. To shout that secret from the housetops was to make himself a fool. To confide it to his friends was to mystify them. To affirm it before the court of the Sanhedrin was to earn himself the penalty of an atrocious death for blasphemy.[66]

4   The love of the Eternal Father for us. Because our Lord prayed to his heavenly Father for all who were to believe in him that the Father love them as he has loved himself, that love is the Holy Ghost: the sanctifying grace that belongs to Christ is communicated to us, the divine loveliness making the humanity of Christ beloved of the Father also is bestowed on us, to make us adoptive children. "By that adoptive sonship, by the uncreated gift of the Holy Spirit by his infusion of sanctifying grace into our souls, we are born again. Our sins are forgiven, we are made just in the sight of God, we become his friends, his children, and the heirs of the kingdom of heaven. There is implanted within us a new principle of a higher life and from it there flow the infused gifts and virtues of the Holy Ghost."[67] Again, "As the Spirit of Christ is given to us, so we are given to Christ."[68] More fully:

> It means that the life of grace within does not come to us by nature, that it is the free gift of God, that properly it belongs to Christ, the natural Son of God, the immediate beloved of the Father. Again, it means that though we live that life, still we live it by renouncing ourselves and dying to ourselves to live to Christ and with him and in him and by him. It means that the perfection of that life is being perfect as the heavenly Father is perfect, that it surpasses our comprehension and our wisdom, that we cannot live it on our own but only in light and

---

66 Lonergan, "The Mystical Body of Christ," 107–8.
67 Lonergan, "The Mystical Body of Christ," 109.
68 Lonergan, "The Mystical Body of Christ," 109.

through the direction and inspiration of the Holy Spirit who is sent, who is given to us by the Father and by the Son and who dwells within us. It means that the goal and final end of that life is the beatific vision, a vision that was Christ's by right from the first moment of his conception, a vision that will be ours inasmuch as suffering with Christ we shall be glorified with him.[69]

5   The charity of God diffused in our hearts by the Holy Ghost, who is given to us. Lonergan expands:

It is the supernatural virtues infused into the will by the omnipotent power of God both on the reception of baptism and in forgiveness of mortal sin in confession. It is a virtue that has been given you in an abundant measure and it has enabled you to persevere in that calling. But also it is an exception among the virtues, for other virtues stand on the golden mean; anyone can be excessive in prudence or justice, in fortitude or temperance; but charity cannot be excessive, for it regards not the means but the final end. Hence the great commandment is to love God with all one's heart and all one's soul, with all one's mind and all one's strength. And the second is like unto the first, to love one's neighbor as oneself, to love one another as Christ has loved us, toward the fulfillment of Christ's prayer at the Last Supper: "I in them, and Thou in me, that they may be made completely one in us, that the world may believe that Thou has sent me and that Thou has loved them as Thou has loved me."[70]

If we relate these five love-relationships to Lonergan's hypothesis of contingent predications regarding the fourfold participation in the trinitarian relationships, we see that the pure instance of grace, which is a participation in the relation of the Father to the Son as paternity may be correlated with making possible the role of the Son as man lovingly mediating the trinitarian love to the rest of humanity. The relationship of active spiration by which Father and Son are related to the Holy Spirit is considered first, as explicitly from the Father to the Son as God and from the Father to the Son as man in the infinite gift of sanctifying grace to the Son. Second, it is considered as extending to us in the economy of salvation through the mediation of the Son's human love for us

---

69 Lonergan, "The Mystical Body of Christ," 110.
70 Lonergan, "The Mystical Body of Christ," 111.

and through Jesus's prayer to the Father for us as our gift of absolutely supernatural sanctifying grace. The relationship of passive spiration by which the Holy Spirit is related back to the Father and the Son is the gift of charity. The relationship of filiation by which the Son is related back to the Father seems to be discussed as a corollary of sanctifying grace when Lonergan says that "the goal and final end of that life is the beatific vision, a vision that was Christ's by right from the first moment of his conception, a vision that will be ours inasmuch as suffering with Christ we shall be glorified with him."[71]

The role of friendship in Lonergan's exposition of the Mystical Body of Christ is underlined in the central role he assigns to Jesus's human love for us. It is crucial for the Christian understanding of the economy of salvation. The mission of the Word incarnate is similarly central for Aquinas, for whom *Christus maxime sapiens et amicus* (*Summa theologiae*, 1–2, q. 108, art. 4) mediates the New Law as a law of freedom rather than of harsh obedience in both the precepts and the evangelical counsels. In elaborating his thesis on "the just and mysterious Law of the Cross," Lonergan says that "now there is supremely to be grasped in the Law of the Cross accepted by Christ a *convenientia caritatis*" based on the relationship between friends, in which, according to Aristotle, "a friend is apprehended by a friend as 'another self' (*alter ipse*)."[72] He cites Thomas Aquinas's *Summa contra Gentiles* III, chapter 58 to clarify the process of historical causality, by which goodness overcomes evil in Jesus's crucifixion: the man Jesus so loved us in the charity of the Holy Spirit that he has become *dimidium animae meae* for us. Because of our love of friendship for him, our reaction to the sufferings of Jesus causes us to repent and to reject sin.[73]

---

71 Lonergan, "The Mystical Body of Christ," 110.

72 See Bernard Lonergan, *De Verbo Incarnato* (thesis XVII), (Rome: Pontificia Universitas Gregoriana, 1964 [*tertia editio ad usum auditorum*]), 552–93 at 580. The reference to Aristotle's idea of a friend as another self is at *Nicomachean Ethics* 9, 4, 1166a 31, 1169b 6. For a brief reprise of the "Law of the Cross" in English, see Maury Schepers, OP, "An Integral Spirituality of the Paschal Mystery, *New Blackfriars* 82, no. 964 (June, 2001): 283–90.

73 Bernard Lonergan, "The Redemption," *Bernard Lonergan: 3 Lectures*, Thomas More Institute Papers 75, ed. R. Eric O'Connor (Montreal: Thomas More Institute for Education, 1975), 1–28 at 8. Aristotle spells out the dynamic even more explicitly in his *Rhetoric* 1380b 35–1381a 6:

> We may describe friendly feeling towards anyone as wishing for him what you believe to be good things, not for your own sake but for his, and being inclined,

Just as Lonergan stresses that friendship occurs on the plane of reason beyond organistic spontaneity, Gilby speaks about Christ, who as our friend is also "the victor who has broken the endless cycle of coming to be and dying away by the sacrifice of his life. From the closed system of the community he has opened the way to *newness of life. Now if we be dead with Christ, we believe we shall live also together with Christ: knowing that Christ, rising again from the dead, dieth now no more: death shall no more have dominion over him* (Rom 6.4–10)."[74]

Lonergan on Friendship and Education

In "Finality, Love, Marriage" Lonergan contextualizes the ends of Christian marriage within an evolutionary worldview characterized by vertical finality,[75] in which "human development is a personal function of an objective movement in the space-time solidarity of men."[76] His discussion distinguishes the complex meshing of three concrete dimensions of appetite in the created universe: (1) subrational, organistic spontaneity, (2) "the antecedent spontaneity of reason to truth and goodness through which God governs the self-government of man,"[77] and (3) grace as "a heightening or elevating of the rational level's antecedent spontaneity, so that the truth through which God rules man's autonomy is the truth God reveals beyond reason's reach, and [the] good which is motive is the divine goodness that is motive of infused charity."[78] Lonergan treats

---

so far as you can, to bring these things about. A friend is one who feels thus and excites these feelings in return: those who think they feel thus towards each other think themselves friends. This being assumed, it follows that your friend is the sort of man who shares your pleasure in what is good and your pain in what is unpleasant, for your sake and for no other return.

74 Gilby, *Between Community and Society*, 332.

75 See Lonergan, "Finality, Love, Marriage," 22: "Still, though accidental to the isolated object or the abstract essence, vertical finality is of the very idea of our hierarchic universe, of the ordination of things devised and exploited by the divine Artisan. For the cosmos is not an aggregate of isolated objects hierarchically arranged on isolated levels, but a dynamic whole in which instrumentally, dispositively, materially, obedientially, one level of being or activity subserves another. The interconnections are endless and manifest."

76 Lonergan, "Finality, Love, Marriage," 27.

77 Lonergan, "Finality, Love, Marriage," 30.

78 Lonergan, "Finality, Love, Marriage," 30.

the personalist and procreative aspects of marriage in terms of the roles of friendship and of education in Aristotle and Aquinas.

Lonergan gives us an early version of his later doctrine of sublation,[79] in which lower orders are suffused and perfected by higher, and nature is perfected by supernatural grace. Throughout his career Lonergan always considered the low in the light of the high. This contrasts with modern approaches that, considering the high from the viewpoint of the low, tend toward reductionism – not only of the supernatural to the natural, but also of the natural to sin. Lonergan, like his master Aquinas, always makes the best of the natural in light of the supernatural. The theorem of the supernatural not only allows the natural to reach its full and proper stature, but it also invites the use of nature for the imperfect, analogical understanding of the revealed mysteries.[80]

Lonergan helps us understand how Aquinas improves Aristotle in the light of revealed truth. He makes explicit what really is "the logical and the ontological first in his [Aristotle's] ethical theory" by explaining that

> it is only in a tendency to an absolute that one can transcend both egoism and altruism; and such transcendence is implicit in the Aristotelian notion of true friendship with its basis not in pleasure nor in advantage but in the objective lovableness of the virtuous man (VIII, 3–7; esp 1156b 7ff). For objective lovableness involves an absolute good, so what is implicit in Aristotle became explicit in Aquinas when he affirmed that man and, as well, all creatures according to their mode naturally love God above all things.[81]

By thematizing the absolute goodness and the finality of all things to God, which Aristotle left implicit in his treatment, Lonergan gives the context for an account of friendship in terms of a temporal, historical ascent that is part of the sweep of vertical finality.

Lonergan takes pains to bring out something not yet treated in this summary of Aquinas on charity, namely, that for Aristotle friendship in

---

79 On "sublation," see Lonergan, *Method in Theology*, 241.
80 On the theorem of the supernatural, see Bernard Lonergan, *Grace and Freedom: Operative Grace in the Thought of St Thomas Aquinas*, Collected Works of Bernard Lonergan 1, ed. Frederick E. Crowe and Robert M. Doran (Toronto: University of Toronto Press, 2000), 17, 20, 158, 165.
81 Lonergan, "Finality, Love, Marriage," 25.

the true sense is based on the excellence or virtue (*areté*) of the partners.[82] In his writings Lonergan speaks repeatedly of excellence, for instance, of "the excellence of a person, of a state of affairs such as peace, happy family, or a thing,"[83] of God as "the ground of all excellence," of the ascent through participated excellence to the absolute excellence of God, of the enduring basis of friendship in the excellence of a good person.[84] Such excellence is also a component in the Greek expression for a noble person, *kalosk'agathos*, since the noble (*kalos*) is the intrinsic cause of what Lonergan calls "objective lovableness."

In an essay on "Friendship and Self-Knowledge," Hans-Georg Gadamer points out that as we mature, and before we have fully acquired the excellence of a good person, choosing a friend always involves the selection of a model, of someone who affords a proximate example of the excellence or virtue we think we ought to attain.[85] Similarly, Lonergan places the genesis of married friendship in a process of human ascent, in which a person's beauty shifts the lover's "spontaneity out of self when eros leaps in through delighted eyes," creating the "imperious" demand for company. Then, with time there emerges the appreciation of the deeper qualities of mind and heart and character when the objective lovableness of the person becomes the enduring basis of a friendship that, beyond the organistic spontaneities of nature, is rational.[86] It is a question whether Lonergan conceives of married love as the model for true friendship, or vice-versa. Whatever is the case, the steps in this ascent clearly hold true for friendship generally.

---

82 Aristotle, *Nicomachean Ethics* 8, 3, 1156b 6–11: "Perfect friendship is the friendship of men who are good, and alike in virtue; for these wish well alike to each other *qua* good, and they are good in themselves. Now those who wish well to their friends for their sake are most truly friends, for they do this by reason of their own nature and not incidentally; therefore their friendship lasts as long as they are good – and goodness is an enduring thing."

83 Lonergan, "Finality, Love, Marriage," 31.

84 Lonergan, "Finality, Love, Marriage," 32.

85 See Hans-Georg Gadamer, "Friendship and Self-Knowledge: Reflections on the Role of Friendship in Greek Ethics," *Hermeneutics, Religion, and Ethics*, trans. Joel Weinsheimer (New Haven: Yale University Press, 1999), 119–41. Gadamer stresses that friendship based on virtue or excellence is essential to friendship of every kind, even those based on utility or pleasure.

86 Lonergan, "Finality, Love, Marriage," 31–2, 36.

This has to be grasped in relation to the original nature of classical Greek philosophy as ascent or as spiritual exercise.[87] Plato and Aristotle understood politics as basically an educational project. For them the question of education is intrinsic to the theologico-political problem. The question of God and the question of the right way to live are coeval; and education for the city is above all an inculcation of virtue or excellence.[88] Earlier I said that, together with philosophy as ascent, this educational ideal has been undermined by modernity and has still not been recovered by postmodernity. A suggestion of the loss is evident in the nineteenth-century letter of James Tate II, headmaster of Rugby, to the mother of Charles Dodgson, better known as Lewis Carroll, about her precocious young son:

> You must not entrust your son with a full knowledge of his superiority over other boys. Let him discover this as he proceeds. The love of excellence is far beyond the love of excelling; and if he should once be bewitched into a mere ambition to surpass others I need not urge that the very quality of his knowledge would be materially injured, and that his character would receive a stain of a more serious description still.[89]

Mr. Tate's advice must have been efficacious, because one of the Oxford students whom Charles Dodgson tutored, Miss E.M. Rowell, had this to say about him later on:

> But while he was urging me to exercise my critical faculties, Mr. Dodgson at the same time bestowed on me another gift of aspect more gracious. He gave me a sense of my own personal dignity. He was so punctilious, so courteous, so considerate, so scrupulous not to embarrass or offend, that he made me feel I counted – counted not as much as anyone else, and certainly not more than anyone else, but just in and of myself. There was nothing competitive or precarious in this counting, and thus my own keen

---

87 See Pierre Hadot, "Part II: Spiritual Exercises," *Philosophy as a Way of Life*, ed. with an introduction by Arnold I. Davidson (Malden, MA: Blackwell, 1995), 81–144.

88 See Hans-Georg Gadamer, "Plato's Educational State," *Dialogue and Dialectic: Eight Hermeneutical Studies on Plato*, trans. P. Christopher Smith (New Haven: Yale University Press, 1980), 73–92.

89 Anne Clark, *Lewis Carroll: A Biography* (New York: Schocken; London: J.M. Dent, 1979) 36–43, cited as "[School]" in Lewis Carroll, *Alice in Wonderland/Norton Reader*, ed. Donald J. Gray (New York: Norton, 1992, 2nd ed.) 242–6 at 244.

awareness of awkwardness, ignorance, and inadequacy could not inhibit this sense of the freedom of selfhood.[90]

Consistently with adopting Aristotle's theory of friendship, Lonergan evidently still advocated this kind of education of the moral and spiritual character of the person. It is implicit in his description in *Method* of feelings as intentional responses to values, "whether the ontic value of persons or the qualitative value of beauty, understanding, truth, virtuous acts, noble deeds."[91] It appears in his University of Chicago talk on Thomas Aquinas: "Where [Aquinas] discoursed at length on the virtues as operative habits, we can think with the Greeks of *areté* as excellence and develop the moral feelings that promote it."[92] As we see in Lonergan's paraphrase of Aristotle's principle that "as a man is to himself, so he is to his friend,"[93] the themes and realities of friendship and education are inextricably entwined with each other:

> Now a man is to himself in consciousness of his being, and he is conscious of his being through activity; hence to be to his friend as he is to himself, the common consciousness of mutual other selves has to find a common activity; and since activity results from response to motive, this common activity presupposes a coincidence of views, profound or superficial, on the meaning of life, on what makes life worthwhile and sets a goal to human striving ... Now this expansion of a common consciousness cannot but be, ... also an expansion of a common conscience. For one's ideas on life, one's moral conscience, one's deeds, the expressed ideas of others near one, and their deeds, are all linked together in a field of mutual influence and adaptation for better or worse.

Because "grace inserts into charity the love that nature gives and reason approves,"[94] Lonergan emphasizes the need for an integral development of both sub-rational and rational dimensions that are stabilized

---

90 E.M. Rowell, in *Harpers* 186 (1943), 319–23, in Carroll, *Alice in Wonderland/Norton Reader*, 307–9 at 308.

91 Lonergan, *Method in Theology*, 31.

92 Bernard Lonergan, "Aquinas Today: Tradition and Innovation," *A Third Collection: Papers by Bernard J.F. Lonergan, SJ*, ed. Frederick E. Crowe (New York/Mahwah: Paulist Press, 1985), 35–54 at 52.

93 Lonergan, "Finality, Love, Marriage," 35–6.

94 Lonergan, "Finality, Love, Marriage," 32.

and integrated on the higher level of supernatural life. At this time he treated these matters in terms of an ascent from below upwards. Thus,

> It is not by organistic spontaneity but by mutual esteem and mutual good will that reason sets up its ... union of friendship; and in accordance with our eternal viewpoint we may note that human friendship is to be found not only in the urbanity and collaboration of contemporaries but much more in the great republic of culture, in contemporaries' esteem for the great men of the past on whose shoulders they stand, and in their devotion to the men of the future for whom they set the stage of history for better or worse.[95]

Here it is clear that Lonergan both esteemed and espoused the reality of liberal education to which his beloved Newman dedicated his life, and which was enshrined in the Jesuit *ratio studiorum*: the ideal of friendship with the authors of the great books and of friendships based on a common reading of those books. It is also clear that for Lonergan the expansion of a common consciousness and conscience is a function of an objective educative process, which was how he habitually thought about history from the time of those earliest Roman essays of the 1930s.[96] He could certainly wax eloquent on it:

> But if, as it should be, at some time people begin to cooperate with the scheme of things, then their hearts turn and settle on the real meaning of life; their goal will be not just fun but, here below, the humanistic goal of the Aristotelian good life, and supernaturally the beatific vision. Then their mutual actuation of a common consciousness and conscience will be a rejection of the world's dialectical rationalizations, a focal point in the stream of history for the fostering of growth in the mind and heart of Christ, a pursuit of the highest human and eternal ends. ... Hence, a mutual influence, a sustained effort of common improvement, tending to the very summit of Christian perfection. Any insertion of spontaneous union or human friendship into charity, which is *friendship in Christ*, has

---

95 Lonergan, "Finality, Love, Marriage," 39.
96 See Frederick E. Crowe's section on "File 713 – History" in "The Remote Context: Home, Studies, Formation," *Lonergan*, Outstanding Christian Thinkers Series, Brian Davies, OP, series editor (Collegeville: The Liturgical Press/A Michael Glazier Book, 1992), 1–38 at 24–7.

not the ground of supernatural excellence achieved but the end of such excellence to be achieved.[97]

The Primacy of "the Way Down" in the Drama of History: "Finality, Love, Marriage"

The ascent of love in "Finality, Love, Marriage" has a finality on the level of Christian charity and perfection. The focus is on the will as a rational appetite and hence on the capacity of rational reflection and freedom to "examine and select motives, deliberately will its own immanent perfection, and freely effect further goods ... in a field of natural spontaneity and infused virtue."[98] When Lonergan speaks of the role of grace, he highlights the fact that the "truth through which God rules man's autonomy is the truth God reveals beyond reason's reach, and the good which is motive is the divine goodness that is motive of infused charity." The strict dependence on the terminology of faculty psychology Lonergan inherited from Aquinas leads to a certain ambiguity as regards the priority of "the way up" from knowing to loving vis-à-vis "the way down" from loving to knowing. Does Aquinas espouse the priority of an intellectual apprehension of the beatific vision as the *summum bonum*? Is this what is happening in Aquinas's ordering of the theological virtues, in which intellectual apprehension almost seems to need completion on the level of the will, "for by means of his will man, as it were, rests in what he has apprehended by intellect" (*Summa contra Gentiles*, chap. 116)?

Lonergan of course does not think simply in terms of natural spontaneity reinforcing reason, and of reason reinforcing grace. From the time of those early Roman essays on the philosophy of history Lonergan had understood the priority of "man's objective unity in a common humanity with its historical solidarity" in terms of the passivity of our possible intellect.[99] In his essay on the dogma of the Assumption he had reformulated Paul's insight into the unfolding of history in terms of two solidarities – in Adam through sin to death, and in Christ Jesus through

---

97 Lonergan, "Finality, Love, Marriage," 37.
98 Lonergan, "Finality, Love, Marriage," 30.
99 See Bernard Lonergan, *"Pantôn Anakephalaiôsis," Method: Journal of Lonergan Studies* 9, no. 2 (October, 1991): 139–72.

death to eternal life.[100] For Lonergan these dialectically related solidarities remain a constant fixture through chapter 20 of *Insight*. "Finality, Love, Marriage" already explains the full sweep of God's gracious solution to the problem of evil in theological terms:

> The process of divine grace … is the gratuitous action of God. It is the trans-rational spontaneity of revelation and faith and intuition, the trans-organistic efficacy of the mystical body of Christ, the uniqueness of eternal achievement: God with us in the hypostatic union, God holding us by the theological virtues, God and ourselves, face to face, in the beatific vision.[101]

The theme of the redemptive priority of "the objective unity of Mystical Body" to "the appetitive component of love"[102] is depicted in terms of the interaction of the two solidarities:

> Just as there is a human solidarity in sin with a dialectical descent deforming knowledge and perverting will, so also there is a divine solidarity in grace which is the mystical body of Christ; as evil performance confirms us in evil, so good edifies us in our building unto eternal life; and as private rationalization finds support in fact, in common teaching, in public approval, so also the ascent of the soul towards God is not a merely private affair but rather a personal function of an objective common movement in that body of Christ which takes over, transforms, and elevates every aspect of human life.[103]

The Priority of the Way Down in the Later Lonergan

On the way to *Method in Theology* Lonergan transposed the faculty psychology characteristic of his thought through *Insight* into an intentionality analysis expanded to the fourth level of human conscious intentionality.[104] He then transposed Aquinas's theory of conversion into the idea of falling in love with God in the vertical exercise of freedom

---

100 Bernard Lonergan, "The Assumption and Theology," *Collection*, 66–80 at 71.
101 Lonergan, "Finality, Love, Marriage," 39.
102 Lonergan, "Finality, Love, Marriage," 32.
103 Lonergan, "Finality, Love, Marriage," 27.
104 On intentionality analysis, see Lonergan, *Method in Theology*, 96, 212, 289, 340–3. The fourth level of consciousness seems to emerge first in the Marquette lecture on "The Subject" already mentioned at note 24 above.

that reorients one and gives one a new horizon for living.[105] Vertical finality is explicated as a multivalent possibility and as obscurely open to divine transcendence.[106] The tender, even fragile, dynamism of conscious intentionality toward self-transcendence has a serious ally in the passionateness of being, no longer conceived simply in terms of the lower manifolds of organistic spontaneity, but as underpinning, accompanying, and reaching beyond "the subject as experientially, intelligently, rationally, morally conscious." These developments enable him to reformulate the structural dynamics of history in even more starkly conversational terms. The components of grace are formulated as "a threefold personal self-communication of divinity to humanity, first, when in Christ the Word becomes flesh, secondly, when through Christ men become temples of the Holy Spirit and adoptive sons of the Father, thirdly, when in a final consummation the blessed know the Father as they are known by him."[107] Again,

> The divine secret, kept in silence for long ages but now disclosed (Rom. 16:25), has been conceived as the self-communication of divinity in love. It resides in the sending of the Son, in the gift of the Spirit, in the hope of being united with the Father. Our question has been how to apprehend this economy of grace and salvation in an evolutionary perspective, how it precisely enters into the consciousness of man.[108]

From this perspective, Lonergan reverses the familiar ordering of the theological virtues: "But when redemption comes, it comes as the charity that dissolves the hostility and divisions of past injustice and present hatred; it comes as the hope that withstands psychological, economic, political, social, cultural determinisms; it comes with the faith that can liberate reason from the rationalizations that blinded it."[109] Note the priority of charity as *amicitia Dei*.

Lonergan describes the visible mission of the Son as the sacrament of man's encounter with God received by our *fides ex auditu*, and the

---

105 On conversion, see the Index of Lonergan's *Method in Theology*, under "Conversion," 375–6; on the "vertical exercise of liberty," see *Method in Theology*, 40, 122, 237–8, 240, 269.

106 Bernard Lonergan, "Mission and the Spirit," *A Third Collection*, 23–34.

107 Lonergan, "Mission and the Spirit," 26.

108 Lonergan, "Mission and the Spirit," 31.

109 Lonergan, "Mission and the Spirit," 31–2.

invisible mission of the Spirit who gives us the *fides ex infusione*, without which the Word enters unto his own, but his own receive him not.[110] Similarly, "Without the visible mission of the Word, the gift of the Spirit is a being-in-love without a proper object; it remains simply an orientation to mystery that awaits its interpretation."[111] These conversational formulations culminate in a description of the experience of grace as:

> Experience of a transformation one did not bring about but rather underwent, as divine providence let evil take its course and vertical finality be heightened, as it let circumstances shift, one's dispositions change, new encounters occur, and – so gently and quietly – one's heart be touched. It is the experience of a new community, in which faith hope and charity dissolve rationalizations, break determinisms, and reconcile the estranged and the alienated, and there is reaped the harvest of the Spirit that is " … love, joy, peace, patience, kindness, goodness, fidelity, gentleness, and self-control" (Gal. 5.22).[112]

Now I do not think I have to argue the significance of friendship in the change of dispositions, the new encounters, the gentle, quiet touching of the heart. This community is the *koinonia* of 1 Corinthians 1:9.

Conclusion

I want to conclude by suggesting that once the centrality of friendship in the fullest sense of friendship based on excellence is recovered,[113] we can follow Frederick Crowe's lead in transposing it into the more adequate systematic theology grounded in the analogy of conversation centered on the intelligible emanations in ourselves and in God. Thus, we can better understand how the conversational God's communication of trinitarian Self-meaning becomes constitutive of our own personal and communal self-meaning; how this occurs in a process of mutual self-mediation by which "the conversation that we are" (Hölderlin) as

---

110 Lonergan, "Mission and the Spirit," 32.
111 Lonergan, "Mission and the Spirit," 32.
112 Lonergan, "Mission and the Spirit, 32–3.
113 David B. Burrell, CSC, has been leading the way to such a recovery in the context of the Christian-Jewish-Muslim trialogue. See *Friendship and the Ways to Truth* (Notre Dame: University of Notre Dame Press, 2000).

human beings gets caught up into the Divine Conversation that constitutes the Godhead according to the Christian self-understanding. Our self-meaning becomes a function not just of the objective communal movement of the mystical body of Christ, but of the Self-meanings of Father, Son, and Holy Spirit.

Only in a context of friendship lived and correctly understood, affirmed, and valued, perhaps, can we appropriate Christian experience itself, and understand all that makes it possible. At the heart of the process are the displacements in human self-awareness we call conversions. Conversion is a revolution in our overall outlook. Christian religious conversion is by the Holy Spirit and to the historical Word of God. This engagement in a new set of friendships, in turn, invites us to and raises the probabilities of moral conversion from operating in terms of satisfactions to operating in terms of true values. And as human culture becomes increasingly differentiated, many of us may be called to an intellectual conversion from the naive realism of spontaneously extroverted consciousness into which we are born, and which a deviant culture wishes we would never "grow up" and "out" of, into an appropriation of focal meaning and value that would make us capable of the intellectual transcendence which is prophetic in a sensate culture. This kind of conversion has become thematic in the history of Christian thought precisely because, as Lonergan has helped us to retrieve, some approximation to each of these conversions has been the concrete condition in grasping the analogy from nature for the core Christian mystery of the Holy Trinity.

12 Growing in Faith as the Eyes of Being-in-Love with God

Spirituality ... derives its identity from the Christian belief that as human beings we are capable of entering into a relationship with God who is both transcendent and, at the same time, indwelling the heart of all created things ... a relationship ... lived out ... in a community of believers that is brought into being by commitment to Christ and sustained by the active presence of the Spirit of God in each and in the community as a whole.

Philip Sheldrake, *Spirituality and History*, 53[1]

Introduction

Throughout his life Bernard Lonergan (1904–1984) tried to meet the complexities of the crisis of culture, which still challenges Christians today. Lonergan devoted his long career to understanding the concrete conditions of the divine plan of creation and redemption for humankind to grow in faith, understood not just as belief but as the eyes of being-in-love with God. He considered a discipline he named "foundational methodology" the most important task to which God had called him. As *methodology*, it describes and explains "normative pattern(s) of recurrent and related operations yielding cumulative and progressive results."[2] This includes a pattern so comprehensive that it is called "transcendental," because it pertains to every sphere of

---

1 Philip Sheldrake, *Spirituality and History: Questions of Interpretation and Method* (Maryknoll, NY: Orbis Books, revised edition 1995), 53.
2 Bernard Lonergan, *Method in Theology* (New York: Herder & Herder, 1972), 4.

human questioning and questing. As *foundational*, it is aimed at giving human beings a deeper access to the spiritual bases of their lives, because the dynamism of the human spirit's conscious intentionality constitutes the heart of method not only in theology but also in every human endeavor.

This account of Lonergan's contributions in aid of human growth in faith as the eyes of being-in-love with God begins by summarizing the great transition in his thought that also reflects the axial development the church as Christian and Catholic has been undergoing during the build up to and the aftermath of Vatican II. It then sketches how Lonergan understood that spirituality/mysticism is the very basis for theology and for Christian life. After noting Lonergan's recovery of Thomas Aquinas's teaching that conscious human activities are the spiritual basis for understanding the trinitarian missions of God the Son and God the Holy Spirit, it explores how the life, passion, death, and resurrection of Jesus Christ manifests the fullness of God's love.

The Great Transition in Lonergan's Thought: Being Oneself

Lonergan gave "a domestic exhortation" entitled *"Existenz* and *Aggiornamento"* for his Jesuit community in September 1964 not long before he underwent an operation to remove a cancerous lung.[3] Its original title, "On Being Oneself [*Christliche Existenz heute*],"[4] indicates his conviction that Pope John XXIII's hopes for the *aggiornamento* or "updating" to be achieved by Vatican Council II could only be fruitful if Christians were to be themselves.[5] Reflecting on this theme, he said, involves "a becoming aware, a growth in self-consciousness, a heightening of [their] self-appropriation, that is possible because our separate, unrevealed, hidden cores have a common circle of reference, the human community, and an ultimate point of reference, which is God, who is all in all, *ta pânta en pâsin theos.*"[6]

---

3 See Bernard Lonergan, *"Existenz* and *Aggiornamento," Collection,* Collected Works of Bernard Lonergan 4, ed. Frederick E. Crowe and Robert M. Doran (Toronto: University of Toronto Press, 1988), 222–31.

4 As explained in Frederick Crowe's editorial note, *Collection,* 304.

5 Lonergan, *"Existenz* and *Aggiornamento,"* 229: "In brief, we have to ask ourselves what it is for a Catholic, a religious, a priest, to be himself today. There is the modern secularist world with all its riches and all its potentialities. There is the possibility of despoiling the Egyptians. But that possibility will not be realized unless Catholics, religious, priests, exist, and exist not as drifters, but creatively and authentically."

6 The reference is to 1 Corinthians 15:28, in Lonergan, *"Existenz* and *Aggiornamento,"* 222.

Scholastic philosophy and theology had insisted that if we were to avoid subjectivism, any reflection on being oneself should regard the human being solely under the category of *substance*, which avoids taking personal internal experience into account. "Of the human substance," Lonergan said,

> it is true that human nature is always the same; a man is a man whether he is awake or asleep, young or old, sane or crazy, sober or drunk, a genius or a moron, a saint or a sinner. From the viewpoint of substance, those differences are merely accidental. But they are not accidental to the subject, for the subject is not an abstraction: he is a concrete reality, all of him, a being in the luminousness of being. Substance prescinds from the difference between the opaque being that is merely substance and the luminous being that is conscious. Subject denotes the luminous being.[7]

What does reflection on being oneself as *subject* involve? The subject has its being in becoming. If not afflicted with pathologies, subjects have more and more to do with their own becoming, and must pass through a critical point in their increasing personal autonomy: subjects can't escape the decision either to drift or to be themselves. We never get beyond this critical point, because, as Lonergan put it,

> It is one thing to decide what one is to make oneself: … It is another to execute the decision. Today's decisions do not predetermine the free choice of tomorrow, of next week or next year, of ten years from now. What has been achieved is always precarious: it can slip, fall, shatter. What is to be achieved can be ever expanding, deepening. To meet one challenge is to effect a development that reveals a further and graver challenge.[8]

So being oneself "is substance and subject: our opaque being that rises to consciousness [the self as substance] and our conscious being by which we save or damn our souls [the self as subject]."[9] There is no risk involved in being oneself as substance: no matter what one thinks or affirms or decides or does, one always remains the same substance.

---

7 Lonergan, "*Existenz* and *Aggiornamento*," 223.

8 Lonergan, "*Existenz* and *Aggiornamento*," 224.

9 Lonergan emphasizes that the subject "is conscious, but that does not mean that properly it is known. It will be known only if we introspect, understand, reflect, and judge" ("*Existenz* and *Aggiornamento*," 229).

About being oneself as subject Walter Davis says the "self is not a substance one unearths by peeling away layers until one gets to the core, but an integrity one struggles to bring into existence."[10] According to Lonergan, the "prior, opaque and luminous being" of the subject evolves into "true, proper, authentic and genuine human being" by integrating physical, chemical, botanical, and biological laws in a higher synthesis that is achieved only to the degree that human subjects perform acts that are attentive, intelligent, reasonable, and responsible in their living. So this higher integration of lower-level regularities does not happen automatically; it requires that persons exercise reason and personal freedom.

> That prior, opaque and luminous being is not static, fixed, determinate, once-for-all; it is precarious; and its being precarious is the possibility not only of a fall but also of fuller development. That development is open; the dynamism constitutive of our consciousness may be expressed in the imperatives: [be attentive,] be intelligent, be reasonable, be responsible; and the imperatives are unrestricted – they regard every inquiry, every judgment, every decision and choice. Nor is the relevance of the imperatives restricted to the world of human experience, to the *mundus aspectibilis*; we are open to God.[11]

Since being oneself in this life is a risk-filled, ever precarious struggle to bring our personal identity into existence, Lonergan named what Davis called "integrity" genuineness or authenticity.

"The self," as Rowan Williams said, "at any given moment is a *made* self: it is not a solid, independent machine for deciding and acting efficiently or rationally in response to stimuli, but is itself a process, fluid and elusive, whose present range of possible responses is part of a developing story."[12] The part of the developing story with which subjects have to deal, however, is liable to be affected by an admixture of people's lack of authenticity. Because "the unauthenticity of individuals generates the unauthenticity of traditions … if the subject takes the tradition as it exists for his (or her) standard, he (or she) can do no more

---

10 See Walter A. Davis, *Inwardness and Existence: Subjectivity in/and Hegel, Heidegger, Marx and Freud* (Madison, WI: University of Wisconsin Press, 1989), 105.

11 Lonergan, "*Existenz* and *Aggiornamento*," 229–30.

12 See Rowan Williams, *Resurrection* (London: Darton, Longman & Todd, 1982), 29.

than authentically realize unauthenticity."[13] But, rather than confronting that fact, it's quite common to confront the unauthentic tradition by reacting against its lack of authenticity by authentically or unauthentically assimilating counter-traditions that are themselves unauthentic. Perhaps this is why Lonergan regarded the higher integration of the self as problematic: it does *not* have to happen, even if it *ought* to happen.[14] That the subject is an "autonomy disposing of itself" or is always capable of "open-eyed, deliberate self-control" can never be taken for granted, because human autonomy is concretely conditioned – not determined – by both finitude and sin. Without God's grace our effective freedom never matches our God-given natural liberty. As Lonergan wrote:

> We do not know ourselves very well; we cannot chart the future; we cannot control our environment completely or the influences that work on us; we cannot explore our unconscious and preconscious mechanisms. Our course is in the night; our control is only rough and approximate; we have to believe and trust, to risk and dare.[15]

We are unable by ourselves to close the existential gap between what we are and what we authentically should be, so "the critical point" continues for as long as human subjects are becoming themselves.

From "the Substance in Christ Jesus" to
"the Subject in Christ Jesus"

Understanding the distinction between being oneself as substance and being oneself as subject may help our comprehension of the Christian experience of "being in Christ Jesus." Lonergan contrasted "the substance in Christ Jesus" and "the subject in Christ Jesus" with great feeling and without caricature. It is a way of characterizing the vast change that has occurred in the landscape of the Christian spirit.

---

13 Lonergan, "*Existenz* and *Aggiornamento*," 228.
14 See Bernard Lonergan, *The Ontological and Psychological Constitution of Christ*, Collected Works of Bernard Lonergan 7, translated from the fourth edition of *De constitutione Christi ontologica et psychologica* by Michael G. Shields (Toronto: University of Toronto Press, 2002), 21.
15 Lonergan, "*Existenz* and *Aggiornamento*," 224.

Here is how Lonergan writes about being in Christ as the being of substance:

> It is known only through faith [in the sense of belief], through affirming true propositions, meditating on them, concluding from them, making resolutions on the basis of them, winning over our psyches, our sensitive souls, to carrying out the resolutions through the cultivation of pious imagination and pious affects, and multiplying individual effort and strength through liturgical union. Inasmuch as it is just the being of substance, it is being in love with God without awareness of being in love. Without any experience of just how and why, one is in the state of grace or one recovers it, one leaves all things to follow Christ, ... one gets through one's daily heavy dose of prayer ... Quietly, imperceptibly there goes forward the transformation operated by the *Kurios*, but the delicacy, the gentleness, the deftness of his continual operation in us hides the operation from us.[16]

In Lonergan's portrayal, "being in Christ Jesus as substance" is known by believing: trusting those who hand on the tradition, Christians assent to the truth expressed in creedal and theological statements. Having affirmed the truths about life in Christ, those in Christ Jesus as substance can meditate on them, using devotional readings from scripture and other books, or sermons, or sacramentals such as statues, places of pilgrimage, rosaries, holy pictures, special devotions to saints, and so forth. Drawing inferences from the mysteries contemplated, they may apply them to their lives, and make resolutions for action – as for example, when the Jesuit poet Gerard Manley Hopkins counseled those having a hard time believing to give alms; they may stir up suitable emotions in their hearts; together they may make novenas, pray the rosary, participate in eucharistic adoration, go to Confession frequently, and attend Mass daily. As they strive to perfect their lives by "offering up" their prayers and efforts, their patience in times of trial, and their performance of spiritual and corporal works of mercy, they trust that they are growing in grace, even if often unawares, and they hope that they are coming closer to Christ, in however hidden a way. You may yourselves be or know people who became truly holy by living out this being in Christ Jesus as substance.

---

16 Lonergan, "*Existenz* and *Aggiornamento*," 230–1.

Since at least the late 1960s, Karl Rahner and other contemporary interpreters of Ignatius Loyola have told us that the spiritual practice known as the "examination of conscience" means examination of our consciousness. Lonergan's depiction of being in Christ Jesus that is the being of subject grows out of the perspective of the Ignatian practices of "spiritual exercises" and "discernment of spirits":

> Inasmuch as being in Christ Jesus is the being of the subject, the hand of the Lord ceases to be hidden. In ways you all have experienced, in ways some have experienced more frequently or more intensely than others, in ways you still have to experience, in ways none of us in this life will ever experience, the substance in Christ Jesus becomes the subject in Christ Jesus. For the love of God, being in love with God, can be as full and as dominant, as overwhelming and as lasting, an experience as human love.[17]

The Theological Significance of the Shift from Substance to Subject

The shift from substance to subject parallels the shift in dogmatic or systematic theology (or indeed "theology" in general) that has taken place, roughly since Vatican II. As Philip Sheldrake characterized the situation before Vatican II, in *Spirituality and History*:

> The approach of the manuals of ascetical and mystical theology was to seek to reduce the study of the Catholic life to manageable categories, precise distinctions and reliable definitions. This accorded with the static approach to theology in general which applied during the period up to the Second Vatican Council. The method used was primarily deductive because divine revelation and rational knowledge were assumed to be its principal sources. Unless universal principles governed the study of the spiritual life it could not claim to be scientific, within a scientific theology.[18]

In a recent lecture my Jesuit colleague John Baldovin stated, "In my opinion a theology which begins with metaphysical principles has no credibility. It is only when we appreciate the process of how one comes

---

17 Lonergan, "*Existenz* and *Aggiornamento*," 231.
18 See Sheldrake, *Spirituality and History*, 53.

to faith, how one experiences discipleship, that we have a theology that can speak to our contemporaries."[19] For Lonergan this meant shifting theology from the perspective of being in Christ Jesus as substance to that of being in Christ Jesus as subject; it involved working out theological foundations accessible to conscious human experience. Such foundations would be based on the "self-appropriation of the subject, … coming to know at first hand," as he said, "oneself and one's own operations both as a believer and as a theologian."[20]

Let's consider a passage where Lonergan explained being conscious:

> Conscious being is not an object, not part of the spectacle that we contemplate, but the presence to himself [or herself] of the spectator, the contemplator. It is not an object of introspection, but the prior presence that makes introspection possible. It is conscious, but that does not mean that properly it is known; it will be known only if we introspect, understand, reflect, and judge. It is one thing to feel blue and another to advert to the fact that you are feeling blue.

So human consciousness is a preliminary, unstructured, and concomitant awareness that renders us present to ourselves, to our acts, and to the world. It is not the same as either sense perception or introspection, because properly to know consciousness and its various acts is something quite different. As we see in the following quote, there is first the conscious reality of ourselves as subjects:

> It is one thing to be in love and another to discover that what has happened to you is that you have fallen in love. Being oneself is prior to knowing oneself. St Ignatius said that love shows itself more in deeds than in words; but being in love is neither deeds nor words; it is the prior conscious reality that words, and more securely, deeds reveal.[21]

Second, Lonergan challenges us to undertake Augustine's procedure in *The Confessions* and *On the Trinity*: "recall, scrutiny, penetration, judgment,

---

19 See John F. Baldovin, SJ, "Idols and Icons: Reflections on the Current State of Liturgical Reform," *Worship* 84, no. 5 (September, 2010): 386–402 at 399.

20 See Bernard Lonergan, "The Future of Thomism," *A Second Collection*, ed. William J. Ryan and Bernard J. Tyrrell (London: Darton, Longman & Todd, 1974), 43–53 at 51.

21 Lonergan, "*Existenz* and *Aggiornamento*," 229.

evaluation, decision."[22] To introspect, then, is to heighten our awareness by experiencing our internal experiencing in such a way that we can understand its patterns; and then by reflecting on our understanding of the patterns of internal experience, we check whether our actual experience confirms our understanding. By attending to our conscious selves we can learn enough about these operations to explicitly identify them and relate them to each other, and to affirm them; finally, we have to commit ourselves to the real demands proper to these different conscious acts.

To summarize this section of my talk, I believe Lonergan experienced being-in-love with God, and that he appropriated himself as being in Christ Jesus as subject by thematizing that "prior conscious reality" through acts of attending, understanding, judging, and deciding. What I want you to keep in mind for what follows is how *self-appropriation* and *being-in-love with God* played central roles in Lonergan's theology, and enabled him to clarify how the process of growing in faith is integral to doing theology.

The Primacy of Love and Conversion

In the late 1940s and early 1950s Lonergan completed the set of articles that were eventually published in book form as *Verbum: Word and Idea in Aquinas*. His intent was to recover Thomas Aquinas's achievement in working out an adequate explanatory analogy for the Christian

---

22 See Lonergan, "The Dehellenization of Dogma," *A Second Collection*, 29. See also *The Triune God: Systematics*, Collected Works of Bernard Lonergan 12, trans. Michael G. Shields, ed. Robert M. Doran and H. Daniel Monsour (Toronto: University of Toronto Press, 2007), 215–17: "It is one thing to be conscious, but it is quite another to know, through knowledge in the proper sense, that one is conscious. To be conscious belongs to everyone, for consciousness is simply presence of mind to itself. This self-presence is effected by the very fact that our sensitive and intellectual nature is actuated by both apprehending and desiring. It does not matter what object is apprehended or desired, since we as conscious subjects consciously apprehend and desire different things. Nor do we become conscious by adverting to ourselves, since consciousness is on the side of the adverting subject and not on the side of the object adverted to. But when this adverting to ourselves is done, we begin the second step, namely, knowing that we are conscious. For one who is conscious places oneself on the side of the object inasmuch as one understands and conceives consciousness and truly affirms that one is conscious. But unless we define what consciousness is, and unless we truly affirm that we are conscious in the sense of the definition, we do not attain knowledge, properly speaking, of our own consciousness."

doctrine of one God in Three Persons. Aquinas had chosen the analogue elaborated by St Augustine in (Books IX, XIV, and XV of) *De trinitate*: the human being as an *imago Dei*. Lonergan found that although Aquinas used the language of the metaphysics of the soul to speak about the procession of the *verbum* or Word from the divine self-understanding, Aquinas's metaphysical language was based on having performed what he was unable to express: a "phenomenology of the subject."[23] Soon Lonergan thought he should transpose the implications of his *Verbum* discoveries into the 20th century, and so in 1957 he finished writing *Insight: A Study of Human Understanding* – "an essay in aid of the self-appropriation of one's own rational self-consciousness."

Although Lonergan shifted from substance to subject in this work, when he came fully to terms with the truth of Augustine's statement, "My weight is my love, and wherever I am carried, it is this weight that carries me,"[24] he recognized that love, not knowledge, plays the determinative role in people's personal orientation and authenticity, and so in their lives. So he left behind the scholastic axiom that "nothing is loved unless it has first been known" (*Nihil amatum nisi prius cognitum*),[25] and stopped describing coming to believe in terms of a decision to assent to Christian beliefs based on prior judgments of credentity and credibility;[26] he began to speak instead of religious conversion as "God's gift of his love poured into our hearts by the Holy Spirit that is in us" (Rom 5:5) and to describe its effect as "falling in love with God."[27] The following statement became typical of his writing: "[T]he

---

23 See Lonergan's updated introductory essay to the publication of his "*Verbum* articles" from the 1940s in book form: "Introduction: Subject and Soul," *Verbum: Word and Idea in Aquinas*, Collected Works of Bernard Lonergan 2, ed. Frederick E. Crowe and Robert M. Doran (Toronto: University of Toronto Press, 1997), 3–11.

24 The Latin reads: *pondus meum amor meus, eo feror quocumque feror*. See Augustine, *Confessions* XIII.9.10; *De civitate Dei* XIV.xxviii.

25 Lonergan, *Method in Theology*, 33, 36, 105–6, 122, 240, on the revolution caused by falling in love.

26 Thus, for instance, he would relate that the chief problem for Christian missionaries in Japan was to teach possible converts the principle of non-contradiction; or again, in relation to an earlier version of functional specialties, the third functional specialty, called history, established the Yes's and No's of the councils; and the fourth, conversion, was a matter of willing to believe in accord with the councils.

27 Lonergan, *Method in Theology*, 105; see too, "Bernard Lonergan Responds," *Foundations of Theology: Papers from the International Lonergan Congress 1970*, ed. Philip McShane (South Bend, IN: University of Notre Dame, 1972), 223–34 at 225–7.

fulfillment that is the love of God is not the fulfillment of any appetite or desire or wish or dream impulse, but the fulfillment of getting beyond one's appetites and desires and wishes and impulses, the fulfillment of self-transcendence, the fulfillment of human authenticity, the fulfillment that overflows into a love of one's neighbor as oneself."[28]

This recognition of the primacy of love in human living led Lonergan to acknowledge how fundamental *conversion* is for human and religious living. "Conversion," he tells us,

> is not merely a change or even a development; rather, it is a radical transformation on which follows, on all levels of living, an interlocked series of changes and developments. What hitherto was unnoticed becomes vivid and present. What had been of no concern becomes a matter of high import. So great a change in one's apprehensions and one's values accompanies no less a change in oneself, in one's relations to other persons, and one's relations to God.[29]

One consequence of realizing the significance of conversion was that the real goal of *Insight*'s project of self-appropriation was to be reached not just in judging that we are knowers (as he wrote in *Insight*), but in deciding to commit ourselves to live by the demands for self-transcendence built into human consciousness, so that fully self-appropriating our rational self-consciousness, then, is a matter of undergoing an *intellectual* conversion *ex umbris et imaginibus ad veritatem* (from shadows and images to the truth).[30] However, it also meant that such intellectual conversion is unlikely to happen without a prior *moral* conversion from mere satisfactions to the truly good, and – what's more – that to be *morally* converted people ordinarily need to be *religiously* converted.

For Lonergan, moreover, *belief* had meant assenting to truths on the basis of someone else's communicating them to us without our having marshaled and weighed the evidence to be able to affirm them personally. Due to the fallout from his recognition of the pivotal roles of love and (especially of religious) conversion he realized[31] that *faith* is distinct

---

28 See Lonergan, "Theology and Man's Future," *A Second Collection*, 147.
29 See Lonergan, "Theology in Its New Context," *A Second Collection*, 69.
30 See Lonergan, "Cognitional Structure," *Collection*, 219.
31 Lonergan, *Method in Theology*, 115–18 on faith; 118–24 on religious belief.

(though not necessarily separate) from *belief*. Faith, which precedes belief's assent (at least in the religious sphere), is "the eyes of being in love with God" or "the transvaluation of values as a result of the gift of God's love."[32] Lonergan could at last give a positive account of Pascal's saying that "the heart has reasons that reason does not know." Finally, Lonergan affirmed in *Method in Theology* that religious being-in-love with God constitutes the foundation for theology.[33]

A further benefit of his new clarity about the primacy of the dynamic state of being-in-love with God was Lonergan's reformulation of the analogy for speaking of three distinct and conscious subjects of divine consciousness:

> Now in God the origin is the Father, … who is identified with *agapê* (I John 4:8, 16). Such love expresses itself in its Word, its Logos, its *verbum spirans amorem* (word breathing forth love), which is a judgment of value. The judgment of value is sincere, and so it grounds the Proceeding Love that is identified with the Holy Spirit.[34]

Realizing the primacy of love revealed that "the dynamic synthesis of being in love …" yields "judgments of value based on evidence perceived by a lover, and the acts of loving grounded on judgments of value."[35]

To conclude this section, the role of the dynamic state of being-in-love compelled Lonergan ultimately to distinguish two distinct vectors of human development:[36] *the way of heritage* from above downwards, which operates through love's influence upon one's decisions, judgments, understandings, and experiential perceptions; and *the way of achievement*, which works from below upwards, from experience through insight and formulation, critical understanding and judgment,

---

32 See Bernard Lonergan, "Faith and Beliefs," *Philosophical and Theological Papers 1965–1980*, Collected Works of Bernard Lonergan 17, ed. Robert C. Croken and Robert M. Doran (Toronto: University of Toronto Press, 2004), 30–48 at 43.

33 Lonergan, "Foundations," *Method in Theology*, 267–93.

34 See Bernard Lonergan, "Christology Today: Methodological Reflections," *A Third Collection*, ed. Frederick E. Crowe (Mahwah, NJ: Paulist Press, 1985), 93.

35 Lonergan, "Christology Today," 93.

36 I think this formulation also articulates the ontological structure of the hermeneutic circle.

to evaluation, decision, commitment, and love.[37] Now I want to suggest briefly what these developments meant for Lonergan's theology, especially his Christology.

Breakthroughs in Christology

When he taught *De Verbo Incarnato/On the Incarnate Word* at Rome's Gregorian University in the 1950s and early 1960s, Lonergan's new foundations based on self-appropriation transformed and transposed Aquinas's Christology. Using a metaphysics whose terms and relations were grounded empirically in *Insight*'s parallel between the set of conscious acts of knowing and the basic structure of the realities known, he clarified Chalcedon's definition of the hypostatic union of the fully divine nature and the fully human nature in the second Person of the Trinity. He also began to relocate the (dogmatically enshrined) ontological constitution of Christ in the context of the history of the dialectical development of Christological thought made possible by the indispensable historical-critical *ressourcement* that had been going forward for a century and a half, but which had been neglected by scholastic theology.

But the chief advance, I believe, was to work out what it means to affirm one Person in two natures in terms of Christ *as subject*. Lonergan discerned, "however imperfectly, the possibility of a single divine identity being at once subject of divine consciousness and also subject of a human consciousness."[38] His earlier work in trinitarian theology had explicated the meaning of three distinct and conscious subjects of one divine consciousness, namely, that each divine subject, in its own manner, is the "subject of the infinite act that God is, the Father as originating love, the Son as judgment of value expressing that love, and the Spirit as originated loving." This understood then, it becomes plausible (rather than implausible because unimaginable) that in the incarnation of Jesus, a single divine identity or Person became at once the subject of a divine consciousness and the subject of a human consciousness.

---

37 Frederick E. Crowe, "An Expansion of Lonergan's Notion of Value," *Appropriating the Lonergan Idea*, ed. Michael Vertin (Washington, DC: Catholic University of America Press, 1989), 344–99 is the breakthrough reflection on this development in Lonergan's thought.

38 Lonergan, "Christology Today," 94.

Jesus's Grace and Knowledge[39]

To quote "*Existenz* and *Aggiornamento*" again:

> As Christ in his humanity did not will means to reach an end, but possessed the end, the vision of God, and overflowed in love to loving us, so too those in Christ participate in the charity of Christ: they love God *super omnia* and so can love their neighbors as themselves; they participate in that charity because they are temples of Christ's Spirit, members of his body, adopted children of the Father whom Christ could name *Abba*; the risen Lord, the *Kurios* of things invisible and visible, has bought them at a great price; he possesses them; *qui Spiritu Dei aguntur, ii sunt filii Dei* (those who live by the Spirit of God are the children of God).[40]

God's loving self-communication to any and every human being is utterly gratuitous and absolutely exceeds the limits of our created nature, and so it is completely disproportionate to human nature, human performance, or human deserving. This is no less true for the human nature assumed by the second Person of the Trinity, who is the subject of that human nature. Our Christian belief that the Father sent Jesus to mediate saving and elevating grace to all human beings means that Jesus as human was also given divine grace.

However, the human being Jesus, as the Word of the Father and the second Person of the Trinity (with both a fully divine and a fully human

---

39 The following sections on Lonergan's Theology of Christ depends on Thesis 11, On Christ's Grace; Thesis 12, On Christ's Knowledge; Thesis 14, On Christ's Liberty, Thesis 15, On the Redemption; Thesis 17, On the Law of the Cross, in Bernard Lonergan, *De Verbo Incarnato* (Rome: Gregorian University, 1964 [ad usum auditorum, editio tertia]), 313–416, 423–43, 445–85, 552–95. Theses 12 and 14 are available in Bernard Lonergan, *The Incarnate Word*, Collected Works of Bernard Lonergan 8, trans. Charles C. Hefling, Jr, ed. Robert M. Doran and Jeremy D. Wilkins (Toronto: University of Toronto Press, 2016). Besides the article by Frederick Crowe (See note 41), I owe a great deal of my understanding on the knowledge of Christ to Charles C. Hefling, "Revelation and/as Insight," *The Importance of Insight: Essays in Honor of Michael Vertin*," ed. John J. Liptay, Jr and David S. Liptay (Toronto: University of Toronto Press, 2007), 97–115; and Jeremy D. Wilkins, "Love and Knowledge of God in the Human Life of Christ," *Pro Ecclesia* 21, no. 1 (2012): 77–99.

40 Lonergan, "*Existenz* and *Aggiornamento*," 230.

nature), has both a divine consciousness and a distinct human consciousness by which he is present to himself, to his acts, and to the world. As in the case with every other finite human being, the supernatural gifts of grace and glory given to the man Jesus's human consciousness are utterly disproportionate to the human capacity to know or will. But because Jesus possessed the fullness of grace God intends to give us, "Christ in his humanity did not will means to reach an end, but possessed the end, the vision of God, and overflowed in love to loving us." Lonergan is alluding here to the teaching that the human consciousness of the divine Person Jesus was given both "grace" – the dynamic state of being-loved by and being-in-love with God – and he was given "glory" – the beatific knowledge of God that is only bestowed on finite human beings after death. Jesus knew what it means to be unconditionally in love with God because he possessed the end: he knew God face-to-face. What Lonergan could emphasize in a way that the medieval theologians could not, however, is that Jesus's beatific knowledge did *not* give him knowledge of this in human, this-worldly terms. He had to discover that during his earthly life.

Because by grace Jesus had the dynamic state of being unconditionally loved by God (that human beings share either by baptism or by implicit faith) and of complete being-in-love with God, Lonergan called Jesus a *viator* or one who is a pilgrim. Jesus "overflows in love to loving us" during his earthly life by sharing our journey. And in this way Jesus had to "will means to reach an end," even though he had an immediate beatific knowledge that was *ineffable* (infinitely unutterable or inexpressible). This knowledge was unlike the mediated knowledge human beings are equipped to acquire. Mediated knowledge depends for its existence on human acts of sensing, imagining, inquiring, understanding, expressing, reflecting, checking, judging, deciding, and acting in relation to persons and things conditioned by space and time. In contrast, Jesus's beatific knowledge is a comprehensive insight that in no way depends on sensation or imagination. It cannot be likened to a long movie about history in its entirety or to a narrative account of the coming to be and passing away of all things or to a complete map or blueprint of creation in which at any moment he could read out what was, is, and will be.[41] Movies, narratives, or maps would all be instances of

---

41 See Crowe, "Eschaton and Worldly Mission in the Mind and Heart of Jesus," *Appropriating the Lonergan Idea*, 193–234 at 203.

effable knowledge that can be immediately uttered or directly expressed in human terms with words, symbols, gestures, and all that pertains to incarnate meaning.

As human beings we have a kind of ineffable knowledge in our experience of the "heart that," Augustine said, "can know no peace until it rests in thee." This has traditionally been called "the light of reason" – our unrestricted, and at times detached and disinterested, desire to know and love everything about everything that is good. This eros of our minds and hearts enables questions to occur to us – our questions for understanding, our questions about truth, and our questions about the good or value. By it we experience a limitless desire to know and also an unending desire to love all that is – Seamus Heaney's "listening to the music of what happens"; and we can discern whether or not we have attained answers to all our questions and can criticize every finite good – the capacity which grounds our freedom of choice. This desire to know and love is ineffable in us, inasmuch as we can never adequately express what it intends. Yet our life-long mediating activity of asking and answering questions and deciding and acting in accord with our judgments gradually makes this desire effable, expressible, utterable to a greater or less extent in our lifetimes.

To communicate to us what he wishes us to know and love in the creation and salvation of the universe, God sent the Word Incarnate, Jesus of Nazareth, to live a human and historical life. As I mentioned above, Jesus knows God face to face along with everything that ever actually occurs in the created world order in the past, present, or future by the light of glory, but before actually living his human life he does not know it, nor can he express it, in human terms. To convey God's meanings and values to us in terms that are humanly understandable, Jesus had to move dialectically from not knowing how to communicate what he already apprehended by his beatific knowledge to gradually finding out how to express and communicate it to us.

How then is the human ineffable desire that the tradition calls the light of reason or Augustine's "restless heart" related to the ineffable beatific knowledge or light of glory possessed by Jesus? Lonergan hypothesized that Jesus's ineffable beatific knowledge actuated in him by the light of glory worked in his human consciousness the way the light of reason as a sheer desire to know and love works in us.[42] The Father wanted Jesus to engage us in sharing the eternal loving relationships that belong to the Second Person of the Trinity. So Jesus in living the divine life humanly and historically had to learn how to express the meaning of the truth of God's unconditional love by eliciting acts, as we do, one at a time: asking and answering questions, making decisions, and performing actions in the human world mediated by meaning. By his incomparable artistry Jesus used the socially and culturally available meanings and values garnered over time from his conversations in first-century Palestine to shape a new language of loving action and relation.

This communication was (and still is) complicated by the fact that all the people (save, in part, his mother, Mary) to whom the Father sends Jesus to communicate God's friendship live under the regime or reign of sin, which Lonergan interprets as the probability of sin that surrounds and invades human beings individually and collectively. Moral impotence (or the incapacity to avoid sin for long by our human powers alone) results in the probability that we will fail to respond consistently to the inner pressure of unconditional claims to love built into our conversational interactions with ourselves, with our fellow human beings, and with God. By individual bias or personal sin our selfish needs and interests deflect us from following the demands of our intelligence, reason, and responsibility, so that our consciousnesses serve only egoistic purposes, as we become engrossed with our own comfort and prestige; in group bias or social sin, collective selfishness and alienation place the needs and interests of the group ahead of the good of the larger society; and the general bias of so-called common sense subverts social and cultural critique by manipulating public opinion to a massive extent,

---

42 The comparison of the ineffable knowledge of Jesus's beatific knowledge with the ineffable knowledge of the human light of reason is an analogy to help us understand the general transition from ineffable to effable knowledge. The analogy can in no way be understood to exclude the light of reason from Jesus's human consciousness. As already fulfilled by the gift of glory, the light of Jesus's human reason still enables him to wonder about how to make his ineffable beatific knowledge expressible and intelligible in human terms. It makes Jesus's human learning possible, and (I would hold) is even open to what Lonergan called "the self-correcting process of knowing" with which we are all familiar. It differs from our light of reason in that, to speak the language of the tradition, it is not conditioned by the darkening of intellect and weakening of the will due to original sin, and so is not subject to the deformation to which the human need to live before knowing how to live leaves the rest of humankind prey.

thus fostering either resignation to the status quo or activist *Realpolitik*. As Herbert McCabe wrote about the resultant objective falsity or surd ingredient in the recurring patterns within which we live out our lives,

> We build a world unfit for humans. The only way to get by in it is to restrict your humanity rather carefully, otherwise you will get hurt. The world is not totally unfit for human habitation, but it can take just so much of it. You have to ration your love, keep a wary eye out for enemies if you want to survive … We live in a world that cannot afford too much humanity, too much love. Love is permissible on the surface down to a certain relatively shallow level. But beneath that, what keeps chaos at bay, what keeps our world fairly stable, is not love but domination and fear (Hobbes gives a perfectly accurate account of all this).[43]

The personal upshot of this sinful human situation is, as James Bernauer learned from Michel Foucault, that "the Christian experience of subjectivity declares itself most clearly in the sounds of a rupture with oneself, of an admission that 'I am not who I am.'"[44]

So Jesus was sent by his Father to share divine friendship with human persons in a state of alienation – from God, from fellow human beings, and from themselves. In eliciting historical, contingent, and free acts of knowing and willing, he had to will means to achieve the end of communicating to us God's unconditional, saving love. The Easter Triduum gives Christians a retrospective awareness that because Jesus was sent to share the divine friendship in a sinful world, he had to learn how to overcome human enmity due to human transgressions; and because he had to show what it means to live human life simply for love, he had to learn how to overcome evil with good. In Lonergan's theology of redemption, Jesus "first loved us while we were still sinners" by discovering that his life, teaching, deeds, passion, death, and resurrection needed to incarnate "the law of the cross." Only in this way could he "come to terms" with the complex and dialectical intelligibility of the

---

43 See Herbert McCabe, OP, "He was Crucified, Suffered Death, and was Buried," *God Still Matters*, ed. with introduction by Brian Davies, OP; foreword by Alasdair MacIntyre (London & New York: Continuum, 2002), 97.

44 See James Bernauer, "Confessions of the Soul: Foucault and Theological Culture," *Philosophy & Social Criticism* 31 (2005): 557–72 at 561.

historical pattern of redemption and reconciliation articulated in the scriptural narrative of fall and redemption:

> There are two solidarities: a first in Adam through sin to death; a second in Christ through death to resurrection. Adam sinned, and through his sin death entered into the world. The death was threefold: there was the spiritual death of the loss of sanctifying grace in the soul; there was the metaphorical death, the curse of Adam, so vivid to us today in the host of the moral and physical evils of the world; finally, there was the material death of the grave where dust returns to dust. Now Christ, the Son of God, knew not sin; still he died, but only to rise again; and as he died for the remission of sin, so he rose again to give us grace (Romans 4:25).[45]

Jesus's Loving Obedience to the Law of the Cross and Our Life in "the Darkness and Obscurity of Faith"

As subjects in Christ Jesus we are on a journey just as Jesus was. By the dynamic state of being-in-love with God we participate in the way "from above downwards" that in many ways resembles Jesus's overflowing in love to loving us. However, our journey is one of faith as the eyes of being-love-with God. Even as graced we do not yet have the knowledge of God granted to the blessed in heaven. Paul's first letter to the Corinthians (13:12) tells us, "now we see in a mirror dimly ... and now [we] know in part." In a letter to Matthew Lamb, Lonergan spoke of the "darkness and obscurity of faith" – a phrase that calls to mind John of the Cross's "dark night of the soul." It is also redolent of Eric Voegelin's reflection on "the tenuous bond of faith in the sense of Heb. 11: 1, as the substance of things hoped for and the proof of things unseen":

> Ontologically, the substance of things hoped for is nowhere to be found but in faith itself; and, epistemologically, there is no proof for things unseen but again this very faith. The bond is tenuous, indeed, and it may snap easily. The life of the soul in its openness toward God, the waiting, the periods of aridity and dullness, guilt and despondency, contrition and repentance, forsakenness and hope against hope, the silent stirrings of love and grace, trembling on the verge of a certainty which if gained is

---

45 See Lonergan, "The Assumption and Theology," *Collection*, 71.

loss – the very lightness of this fabric may prove too heavy a burden for men who lust for massively possessive experience.[46]

Drawing out the implications for our situation of grace, Rowan Williams says that "faith in Christ is not straightforwardly a recognition of the satisfaction of my needs; the form of Christ is always a revelation of our untruth (and thus unreality and unloveliness) and also a demand to follow Christ into the abyss of Holy Saturday, into *silence*, before the Holy Spirit is capable of bringing forth a new language in Easter and Pentecost, the Word restored to the Father's throne, yet simultaneously given to the community of believers as their heart and their life."[47] As John Henry Newman said in one of his early sermons, "We attempt great things with the certainty of failing, and yet the necessity of attempting; and so while we attempt, need continual forgiveness for the failure of the attempt."[48]

Still, Jesus already possessed the beatific knowledge promised to us when Paul wrote to the Corinthians, "Then I shall understand fully even as I have been fully understood" (1 Cor 13:12). Hence, can we honestly claim of Jesus, even though he already possessed the goal of our pilgrimage, what Lonergan said of *our* journey of faith: that his course was in the night, that his control was only rough and approximate, that he had to trust, to risk, and to dare?

Lonergan's answer is, Yes. As Christians we believe that Jesus was "like us in all things except sin." Jesus as *comprehender* of the vision of God was sent as a human being living in human history to be a *viator* or pilgrim to communicate the ineffable friendship of God in human terms. If the effect of Jesus's beatific knowledge is more like that of our desire to know and love everything good than like a clear picture of the historical past, present, and future, and, if Jesus needed to grow in wisdom and truth, surely the gospels tell us, when he asked his Father

---

46 Eric Voegelin, *The New Science of Politics: An Introduction* (Chicago: University of Chicago Press, 1952), 122.

47 See Rowan Williams, "Balthasar, Rahner, and the Apprehension of Being," *Wrestling with Angels: Conversations in Modern Theology*, ed. Mike Higton (Grand Rapids, MI: Eerdmans Publishing, 2007), 99.

48 This was printed on the ordination card of friend and theologian David W. Tracy. Dorothy Cummings kindly found the reference for me: John Henry Newman, "Sermon 7: Sins of Ignorance and Weakness," *Parochial and Plain Sermons* (San Francisco: Ignatius Press, 1987), 57–64 at 62.

to "let this cup pass" in the Garden of Gethsemane, or when he cried to his Father asking why he was forsaken on the cross, he suffered the pain of unjust condemnation, persecution, and of having to pass through death's dark door (just as we must). He had to obey the Father's will in trust that his self-sacrificial love would be redemptive; we have to believe in hope that ultimately self-sacrificial love is humanly fulfilling.[49]

By Jesus's passion, death, and resurrection we know we are his beloved. Lonergan suggests this realization may be understood by the analogy of perfect contrition as grounded in the reality of charity as friendship, when the crucifixion reveals the gravity of our selfish lack of love. Because Jesus died and rose to forgive us and befriend us, we regret our transgressions and are sorry for them not so much because of what they have done to us but because of the death-dealing pain suffered by Jesus as by one who, in Aristotle's phrase, has become "half our soul" due to the gift of the Holy Spirit poured out in our hearts. In forgiving us, as in the story of Jesus's first post-resurrection appearance to his disciples (Jn 20:19–23), Jesus breathes the Father's Spirit into us; and without the Spirit we could not hope to live our lives in a Christlike manner. In Lonergan's extraordinary words: "In Christ Jesus we are not only referred to God as to some omega point, but we are on our way to God. The fount of our living is not *erôs* but *agapê*, not desire of an end that uses means but love of an end that overflows."[50] As the church catches us up into the liturgical and eucharistic rhythm of repentance and thanksgiving, we become more able to absorb the meaning of the fact that, again in Lonergan's words,

> being in Christ Jesus is not tied down to place or time, culture or epoch. It is catholic with the catholicity of the Spirit of the Lord. Neither is it an abstraction that dwells apart from every place and time, every culture and epoch. It is identical with personal living, and personal living is always here and now, in a contemporary world mediated by immediacy, a contemporary world mediated by meaning, a contemporary world not only mediated but also constituted by meaning.[51]

---

49 See Randall S. Rosenberg, "Christ's Human Knowledge: A Conversation with Lonergan and Balthasar," *Theological Studies* 71, no. 4 (December, 2010): 817–45.

50 Lonergan, "*Existenz* and *Aggiornamento*," 230.

51 Lonergan, "*Existenz* and *Aggiornamento*," 231.

Selected Writings of Frederick G. Lawrence

1 "Self-knowledge in History in Gadamer and Lonergan." In *Language, Truth and Meaning*, ed. Philip McShane. Dublin: Gill & Macmillan, 1973, 167– 217, 332–8.

2 "Dialectic and Hermeneutic: Foundational Perspectives on the Relationship between Human Studies and the Project of Human Self-Constitution." In *Stony Brook Studies in Philosophy 1: Philosophy and Social Theory* (1974): 37–59.

3 "Discussion." In *Stony Brook Studies in Philosophy 1: Philosophy and Social Theory* (1974): 60–73.

4 "Response to Lecture by Hans-Georg Gadamer." *Cultural Hermeneutics* 2 (1975): 321–5.

5 "A Response to Gerald McCool." *CSTA Proceedings* 32 (1975): 90–6.

6 "Editor's Note." In *Lonergan Workshop* 1, ed. Frederick G. Lawrence. Missoula: Scholars Press, 1978, v.

7 "Political Theology and the 'Longer Cycle of Decline.'" In *Lonergan Workshop* 1, ed. Frederick G. Lawrence. Missoula: Scholars Press, 1978, 223–55.

8 "The Horizon of Political Theology." In *Trinification of the World, Festschrift for F.E. Crowe, SJ*, ed. Thomas A. Dunne and Jean-Marc Laporte. Toronto: Regis College, 1978, 46–70.

9 "Questioning the Culture: Liberal Education?" In *Dialogue in Celebration*, ed. Cathleen Going. Montreal: Thomas More Institute, 1980, 185–209.

10 "Gadamer and Lonergan: A Dialectical Comparison." *International Philosophical Quarterly* 20, no. 1 (1980): 25–47.

11 "Editor's Note." In *Lonergan Workshop* 2, ed. Frederick G. Lawrence. Chico: Scholars Press, 1981, v.

12 "'The Modern Philosophic Differentiation of Consciousness' or What is the Enlightenment?" In *Lonergan Workshop* 2, ed. Frederick G. Lawrence. Chico: Scholars Press, 1981, 231–79.

13 "Transcendence as Interruption: Theology in a Political Mode." In *Transcendence and the Sacred,* ed. Alan Olson and Lee Rouner. Notre Dame: Notre Dame, 1981, 208–55.

14 "Method in Theology as Hermeneutical." In *Creativity and Method: Essays in Honor of Bernard Lonergan,* ed. Matthew Lamb. Milwaukee: Marquette University, 1981, 79–104.

15 "Translator's Introduction." Hans-Georg Gadamer, *Reason in the Age of Science.* Cambridge: MIT Press, 1981, vii–xxxiii.

16 "Editor's Note." In *Lonergan Workshop* 3, ed. Frederick G. Lawrence. Chico: Scholars Press, 1982, v–vi.

17 "Editor's Notes." In *Lonergan Workshop* 4, ed. Frederick G. Lawrence. Chico: Scholars Press, 1983, iii–iv.

18 "Translator's Introduction." Jürgen Habermas, *Philosophical-Political Profiles.* Cambridge: MIT, 1984, vii–xxv.

19 "Voegelin and Theology as Hermeneutical and Political." In *Voegelin and the Theologian: Ten Studies in Interpretation,* ed. John C. Kirby and William Thompson-Uberuaga. New York: Edwin Mellen Press, 1984, 314–55.

20 "The Human Good and Christian Conversation." In *Searching for Cultural Foundations,* ed. Philip McShane. Lanham: University Press of America, 1984, 86–112, 185–6. (See also no. 41 below.)

21 "Editor's Note." In *The Beginning and the Beyond: Papers from the Gadamer and Voegelin Conferences,* Supplementary Issue of *Lonergan Workshop* Journal 4, ed. Frederick G. Lawrence. Chico: Scholars Press, 1984, v–vi.

22 "On 'The Meditative Origin of the Philosophical Knowledge of Order.'" In *The Beginning and the Beyond: Papers from the Gadamer and Voegelin Conferences,* Supplementary Issue of *Lonergan Workshop* Journal 4, ed. Frederick G. Lawrence. Chico: Scholars Press, 1984, 53–67.

23 "Editor's Notes." In *Lonergan Workshop* 5, ed. Frederick G. Lawrence. Chico: Scholars Press, 1985, iv–v.

24 "Basic Christian Community: An Issue of the 'Mind and Mystery of Christ.'" In *Lonergan Workshop* 5, ed. Frederick G. Lawrence. Chico: Scholars Press, 1985, 263–88.

25 "Editor's Notes." In *Lonergan Workshop* 6, ed. Frederick G. Lawrence. Atlanta: Scholars Press, 1986, iii–iv.

26 "Elements of Basic Communication." In *Lonergan Workshop* 6, ed. Frederick G. Lawrence. Atlanta: Scholars Press, 1986, 127–42.

27 "Editor's Note." In *Communicating A Dangerous Memory: Soundings in Political Theology,* Supplementary Issue of *Lonergan Workshop* Journal 6, ed. Frederick G. Lawrence. Atlanta: Scholars Press, 1986, v–vii.

28 "Dangerous Memory and the Pedagogy of the Oppressed." In *Communicating A Dangerous Memory: Soundings in Political Theology*, Supplementary Issue of *Lonergan Workshop* Journal 6, ed. Frederick G. Lawrence. Atlanta: Scholars Press, 1986, 17–35.

29 "Political Theology." In *The Encyclopedia of Religion* 11, ed. Mircea Eliade. New York: Macmillan, 1987, 404–8.

30 "Orthopraxis." In *The New Dictionary of Theology*, ed. Joseph A. Komonchak, Mary Collins, and Dermot A. Lane. Wilmington: Michael Glazier, 1987, 733–6.

31 "Lonergan as Political Theologian." In *Religion in Context: Recent Studies in Lonergan*, ed. Timothy P. Fallon and Philip Boo Riley. New York: University Press, 1988, 1–21.

32 "Human Voice and Democratic Political Culture: The Crisis of True Professionalism." *Texas Law Review* 66, no. 3 (1988): 601–5.

33 "Editor's Note." In *Lonergan Workshop* 7, ed. Frederick G. Lawrence. Atlanta: Scholars Press, 1988, iii–v.

34 "Editor's Introduction." In *Ethics in Making a Living: The Jane Jacobs Conference*, Supplementary Issue of the *Lonergan Workshop* Journal 7, ed. Frederick G. Lawrence. Atlanta: Scholars Press, 1989, iii–vii.

35 "Systems of Economic Ethics: A Response." In *Ethics in Making a Living: The Jane Jacobs Conference*, ed. Frederick G. Lawrence. Atlanta: Scholars Press, 1989, 191–201.

36 "On the Relationship between Transcendental and Hermeneutical Approaches to Theology." *Horizons: The Journal of the College Theology Society* 16, no. 2 (1989): 342–5.

37 "Bernard Lonergan." In *New Catholic Encyclopedia* 18. Washington, DC: The Catholic University of America, 1989, 263.

38 "Baur's 'Conversation with Hans-Georg Gadamer' and 'Contribution to the Gadamer-Lonergan Discussion.'" *Method: Journal of Lonergan Studies* 8, no. 2 (1990): 135–51.

39 "Editor's Note." In *Lonergan Workshop* 8, ed. Frederick G. Lawrence. Atlanta: Scholars Press, 1990, iii–v.

40 "The Fragility of Consciousness: Lonergan and the Postmodern Concern for the Other." *Theological Studies* 54, no. 1 (1993): 55–94.

41 "The Human Good and Christian Conversation." In *Communication and Lonergan: Common Ground for Forging the New Age*, ed. Thomas J. Farrell and Paul A. Soukup. Kansas City: Sheed & Ward, 1993, 248–68. (See also no. 20 above.)

42 "Editorial Note." In *Lonergan Workshop* 9, ed. Frederick G. Lawrence. Atlanta: Scholars Press, 1993, iii–iv.

43   "Lonergan's Foundations for Constitutive Communication." In *Lonergan Workshop* 10, ed. Frederick G. Lawrence. Atlanta: Scholars Press, 1994, 229–77.

44   "Editorial Note." In *Lonergan Workshop* 10, ed. Frederick G. Lawrence. Atlanta: Scholars Press, 1994, iii–vi.

45   With Glenn Hughes, "The Challenge of Eric Voegelin." *The Political Science Reviewer* 24 (1995): 399–452.

46   "Editorial Note." In *Lonergan Workshop* 11: *Language of the Heart: Lonergan, Images and Feelings*, ed. Frederick G. Lawrence. Atlanta: Scholars Press, 1995, iii–ix.

47   "Aiming High: Reflections on Buckley's Theorem on Higher Education." *Finding God in All Things: Essays in Honor of Michael J. Buckley, SJ*, ed. Stephen J. Pope. New York: The Crossroad Publishing Company, 1996, 318–39.

48   "La fragilidad de la conciencia: Lonergan y la preocupación postmoderna por lo otro." *Theologica Xavieriana* 45 (1995): 223–75.

49   "Editorial Note." In Joseph Komonchak, *Foundations in Ecclesiology*, Supplementary Issue of the *Lonergan Workshop* Journal 11, ed. Frederick G. Lawrence. Boston: Boston College, 1995, iii–ix.

50   "Editorial Note." In *Lonergan Workshop* 12: *In Tune with the Divine Ground: Cultural and Social Conditions for Political Order*, ed. Frederick G. Lawrence. Boston: Boston College, 1996, v–vii.

51   "John Courtney Murray and the Ambiguities of Liberalism." In *John Courtney Murray and the Growth of Tradition*, ed. J. Leon Hooper and Todd David Whitmore. Kansas City: Sheed & Ward, 1996, 41–59.

52   "Leo Strauss and the Fourth Wave of Modernity." In *Leo Strauss and Judaism: Jerusalem and Athens Critically Revisited*, ed. David Novak. Lanham: Rowman & Littlefield, 1996, 131–54.

53   "The Seriousness of Play: Gadamer's Hermeneutics as a Resource for Christian Mission." In *From One Medium to Another: Communicating the Bible through Multimedia*, ed. Robert Hodgson and Paul Soukup. Kansas City: Sheed & Ward, 1997, 109–31.

54   "The Problem of Eric Voegelin, Mystic Philosopher and Scientist." In *International and Interdisciplinary Perspectives on Eric Voegelin*, ed. Stephen A. McKnight and Geoffrey L. Price. Columbia: University of Missouri Press, 1997, 35–58.

55   "Editorial Note." In *Lonergan Workshop* 13: *The Structure and Rhythms of Love: In Honor of Frederick Crowe, SJ*, ed. Frederick G. Lawrence. Boston: Boston College, 1997, iii–vi.

56 "Editorial Note." In *Lonergan Workshop* 14: *Redeeming the Time: In Honor of Sebastian Moore, OSB*, ed. Frederick G. Lawrence. Boston: Boston College, 1998, iii–vi.

57 "The Church and American Culture." Paper requested by Cardinal Law via Mary Ann Glendon for an inquiry conducted by the Vatican office then led by Cardinal Poupard. Unpublished. 8 pp. 1998.

58 "Response to Marilyn McCord Adams." For Boston College's Medieval Bradley Lecture. Unpublished. 4 pp. 1998.

59 "Response to Richard Tuck on Hobbes." For Boston College Bradley Lecture. Unpublished. 6 pp. 1998.

60 "*Fides et Ratio* in the University." For Boston College panel on Papal Encyclical, April. Unpublished. 9 pp. 1999.

61 "Editor's Introduction." In *Lonergan Workshop* 15: *Letting Ourselves Dream: Anticipating the Future in the Light of the Past: In Honor of Joseph Flanagan, SJ*, ed. Frederick G. Lawrence. Boston: Boston College, 1999, iii–v.

62 "Editors' Introduction." In Bernard Lonergan, *Macroeconomic Dynamics: An Essay in Circulation Analysis*, Collected Works of Bernard Lonergan 15, ed. Patrick H. Byrne, Charles C. Hefling, and Frederick G. Lawrence. Toronto: University of Toronto Press, xxv–lxxii.

63 "Athens and Jerusalem: The Contemporary Problematic of Faith and Reason." *Gregorianum* 80, no. 2 (1999): 223–44. The Joseph Gregory McCarthy Lecture, delivered in the Faculty of Philosophy at the Gregorian University, May 5, 1997.

64 "A Comparison of Lonergan and Voegelin." Paper for panel at Eric Voegelin Society Session of Annual Meeting of American Political Science Association. Unpublished. 44 pp. 1999.

65 "Jesus as Divine." Paper for parish education on the Feast of the Epiphany. Unpublished. 8 pp. 1999.

66 "Editorial Note." In Frederick E. Crowe, *Three Thomist Studies*, Supplementary Issue to *Lonergan Workshop* Journal 16, ed. Michael Vertin. Boston: Lonergan Institute, 2000, xiii–xv.

67 "Editor's Introduction." In *Lonergan Workshop* 16: *Lonergan and the Human Sciences: In Thanksgiving for the Gifts of the Past 1000 Years*, ed. Frederick G. Lawrence. Boston: Boston College, 2000, iii–vi.

68 "Lonergan, the Integral Postmodern?" *Method: Journal of Lonergan Studies* 18, no. 2 (2000): 389–420.

69 "Hermeneutics and the Problematic of Experience," *QUID Revista de Filosofia: Sobre a experiência* 1 (2000): 371–89.

70 "Ontology *of* and *as* Horizon: Gadamer's Rehabilitation of the Metaphysics of Light," *Revista Portuguesa de Filosofia* 56, nos. 3–4 (2000): 389–420.

71 "Reply to James F. Ross on Believing for Profit." Paper for Medieval Institute at Boston College. Unpublished. 8 pp. 2000.

72 "Core Humanity and God as Conversational." Paper for Anthropological Section, Catholic Theological Society of America. Unpublished. 16 pp. 2001.

73 "Baptism and Grace." Paper for parish education. Unpublished. 8 pp. 2001.

74 "Editor's Note." In *Lonergan Workshop* 17: *Looking Ahead: Lonergan for the 21st Century*, ed. Frederick G. Lawrence. Boston: Boston College, 2002, iii–vi.

75 "On Being Catholic?" Paper for a Boston College lecture organized by Prof. Stephen J. Pope. Unpublished. 12 pp. 2002.

76 "Gadamer, the Hermeneutic Revolution, and Theology." In *The Cambridge Companion to Gadamer*, ed. Robert J. Dostal. Cambridge: Cambridge University Press, 2002, 167–200.

77 "Lonergan and Aquinas: The Postmodern Problematic of Theology and Ethics." In *The Ethics of Aquinas*, ed. Stephen J. Pope. Washington, DC: Georgetown University Press, 2002, 347–455.

78 "'There's a Wideness in God's Mercy.'" In *Sic et Non: Encountering Dominus Iesus*, ed. Stephen J. Pope and Charles Hefling. Maryknoll: Orbis Books, 2002, 89–95.

79 "The Hermeneutic Revolution and the Future of Theology." In *Between the Human and the Divine: Philosophical and Theological Hermeneutics*, International Congress on Hermeneutics, ed. Andrzej Wiercinski. Toronto: The Hermeneutic Press, 2002, 326–54.

80 "Narrative and Conversion: Voegelin and Jonas on Freedom in Augustine." Paper for a panel at the Eric Voegelin Society Session of the Annual Meeting of American Political Science Association. Unpublished. 13 pp. 2002.

81 "Paul Ricoeur's Practical Wisdom: Reflections on the Social Philosophy of *Oneself as Another*." In *Between Suspicion and Sympathy: Paul Ricoeur's Unstable Equilibrium*, ed. Andrzej Wiercinski. Toronto: The Hermeneutic Press, 2003, 502–17.

82 "Voegelin and Gadamer: A Brief Comparison." Paper for a panel at the Eric Voegelin Society Session of the Annual Meeting of American Political Science Association. Unpublished. 8 pp. 2003.

83 "Lonergan's Postmodern Subject: Neither Neoscholastic Substance nor Cartesian Ego." In *Deference to the Other: Lonergan and Contemporary Continental Thought*, ed. Jim Kanaris and Mark J. Doorley. Albany: State University of New York Press, 2004, 107–20.

84 "Expanding Challenge to Authenticity in *Insight*: Lonergan's Hermeneutics of Facticity." *Divyadaan: Journal of Philosophy and Education* 15, no. 3 (2004): 427–56.

85 "Grace and Friendship: Postmodern Political Theology and God as Conversational." *Gregorianum* 85, no. 4 (2004): 795–820. (See also no. 90 below.)

86 "Heidegger and Voegelin on Augustine." Paper for a panel at the Eric Voegelin Society Session of the Annual Meeting of American Political Science Association. Unpublished. 14 pp. 2004

87 "Editor's Note." In *Lonergan Workshop* 18: *Lonergan's Openness: Polymorphism, Postmodernism, and Religion*, ed. Frederick G. Lawrence. Boston: Boston College, 2005, iii–v.

88 "Person and Society: A Trinitarian Perspective from the Work of Bernard Lonergan." Paper for an International Philosophical Conference on "Person and Society" held in November at the Catholic University of Portugal, Braga. 24 pp. 2005.

89 "Two Tough-minded Thinkers: Lonergan & Strauss on *the* What-Question." Paper for a Boston College Bradley Lecture. Unpublished. 22 pp. 2005.

90 "Grace and Friendship: Postmodern Political Theology and God as Conversational." In *Il Teologo e la Storia: Lonergan's Centenary (1904–2004)*, ed. Paul Gilbert and Natalino Spaccapelo. Rome: Editrice Pontificia Università Gregoriana 2006, 249–64. (See also no. 85 above.)

91 "The Dialectic Tradition/Innovation and the Possibility of a Theological Method." In *Il Teologo e la Storia: Lonergan's Centenary (1904–2004)*, eds. Paul Gilbert and Natalino Spaccapelo. Rome: Editrice Pontificia Università Gregoriana, 2006, 249–64.

92 "Editor's Introduction." In *Lonergan Workshop* 19: *Celebrating the 450th Jesuit Jubilee*, ed. Frederick G. Lawrence. Boston: Boston College, 2006, iii–vii.

93 "How God Loves Us." Paper for talk at the Jesuit Campion Center, Weston, MA. Unpublished. 8 pp. 2006.

94 "Lonergan on Transcendence." Paper for a conference on Karl Rahner, John Courtney Murray, and Bernard Lonergan, held to commemorate their 100th Anniversary of Birth in Mainz, March, 2006. Unpublished. 21 pp. 2006.

95 "Is the Distinction between Reason and Revelation/Faith Obsolete?" Paper for a panel at the Eric Voegelin Society Session of the Annual Meeting of American Political Science Association. Unpublished. 7 pp. 2006.

96 "On Conversion." Paper for a panel discussion sponsored by the Boston College Center for Jewish/Christian Studies on the theme Should

412   Writings of Frederick G. Lawrence

Catholics Convert Jews (If Jews are in True Covenant with God)? Unpublished. 6 pp. 2006.

97   "Between Capitalism and Marxism: Introducing Lonergan's Economics." *Revista de Filosofía* 63, no. 4 (2007): 941–59.

98   "The Ethics of Authenticity and the Human Good, in Honor of Michael Vertin, an Authentic Colleague." In *The Meaning and Importance of* Insight: *Essays in Honor of Michael Vertin*, ed. John J. Liptay and David S. Liptay. Toronto: University of Toronto Press, 2007, 127–50.

99   "Philosophy, History, and Apocalypse in Voegelin, Strauss, and Girard." In *Politics and Apocalypse*, ed. Robert Hamerton-Kelly. East Lansing: Michigan State University Press, 2007, 95–137.

100   "Response to Russell Hittenger's 'Two Thomisms, Two Modernities.'" For Boston College's Bradley Lecture. Unpublished. 8 pp. 2007.

101   "Faith Seeking Understanding? A Response to Stefan Rossbach." Paper for a panel of the Eric Voegelin Society at the Annual Meeting of the American Political Science Association. Unpublished. 19 pp. 2007.

102   "Editor's Introduction." In *Lonergan Workshop* 20: *The 'Not Numerous Center': For* Insight's *50th Anniversary and* Method in Theology's *35th Anniversary*, ed. Frederick G. Lawrence. Boston: Boston College, 2008, iii–v.

103   "Heidegger and the Hermeneutic Revolution." *Divyadaan: Journal of Philosophy and Education* 19, nos. 1–2 (2008): 7–30.

104   "Hans-Georg Gadamer and the Hermeneutic Revolution." *Divyadaan: Journal of Philosophy and Education* 19, nos. 1–2 (2008): 31–54.

105   "The Hermeneutic Revolution and Bernard Lonergan: Gadamer and Lonergan on Augustine's *Verbum Cordis* – the Heart of Postmodern Hermeneutics." *Divyadaan: Journal of Philosophy and Education* 19, nos. 1–2 (2008): 55–86.

106   "The Unknown 20th Century Hermeneutic Revolution: Jerusalem and Athens in Lonergan's Integral Hermeneutics." *Divyadaan: Journal of Philosophy and Education* 19, nos. 1–2 (2008): 87–118.

107   "Jerusalem and Athens: Contrasting Tendencies in the Hermeneutic Revolution of the 20th Century." Unpublished. 45 pp. 2008.

108   "Introduzzione al pensiero economico di B.J.F. Lonergan." In *Il Teologo e l'Economia. L'orizzinte economico di B. Lonergan*, ed. Frederick G. Lawrence, Natalino A. Spaccapelo, and Michele Tomasi. Rome: Armando Editore, 2009, 89–136.

109   "Lonergan's Retrieval of Thomas Aquinas's Conception of the *Imago Dei*: The Trinitarian Analogy of Intelligible Emanations in God." *American Catholic Philosophical Quarterly* 83, no. 3 (2009): 363–88.

110   "The Problematic of Christian Self-Understanding and Theology: Today's
      Challenge to the Theological Community." In *Meaning and History in
      Systematic Theology: Essays in Honor of Robert M. Doran, SJ*, ed. John D.
      Dadosky. Milwaukee: Marquette University Press, 2009, 253–310.

111   "Editor's Introduction." In *Lonergan Workshop* 21: *"... and God's Own Glory,
      in Part, Is You": What Aspect of the Lonergan Legacy Needs to be Stressed Right
      Now?*, ed. Frederick G. Lawrence. Boston: Boston College, 2009, iii–xii.

112   "Hope and Friendship: Response to Buckley and Doyle on the New
      Humanism." Paper for a conference / seminar (organized by and
      featuring his former students) in honor of Michael J. Buckley, SJ, 23–4
      October. Unpublished. 6 pp. 2009.

113   "Hans-Georg Gadamer: Philosopher of Practical Wisdom." *Theoforum* 40
      (2009): 257–90.

114   "Money, Institutions, and the Human Good." *The Lonergan Review* 2, no. 1
      (2010): 175–97.

115   "The Implementation of Lonergan's Economics." *The Lonergan Review* 2,
      no.1 (2010): 370–3.

116   "The Implementation of Lonergan's Economics: Panel Discussion." With
      Gregory Barron and Philip McShane. *The Lonergan Review* 2, no. 1 (2010):
      366–76.

117   "The Recovery of Theology in a Political Mode: The Example of Ernest
      L. Fortin, AA, Mentor and Friend." Bradley Lecture, Boston College.
      Unpublished. 17 pp. 2010.

118   "Growing in Faith as the Eyes of Being-in-Love with God." C21 Lecture,
      Boston College. Unpublished. 23 pp. 2010.

119   "The Question of the Complete Intelligibility of the Universe: Two
      Approaches." Unpublished talk for Thomas More Society, Boston
      College. 10 pp. 2010.

120   "The Notion of Experience in the Historical Trajectory of Philosophy/
      Theology." Unpublished paper for Lonergan on the Edge Conference,
      Marquette University. 15 pp. 2010.

121   "Editor's Prefatory Note." In *Lonergan Workshop* 22: *Lonergan and Loyola:
      "I Will Be Propitious to You in Rome,"* ed. Frederick Lawrence. Boston:
      Boston College, 2011, iv–xviii.

122   "Voegelin and Gadamer: Continental Philosophers Inspired by Plato
      and Aristotle." In *Eric Voegelin and the Continental Tradition: Explorations
      in Modern Thought*, ed. Lee Trepanier and Steven F. McGuire. Columbia:
      University of Missouri Press, 2011, 192–218.

123   "Gadamer's Hermeneutics and Aristotle's Practical Philosophy." In
      Hermeneutic Rationality. La rationalité herméneutique, ed. Maria Luísa

Portocarrero, Luis António Umbelino, and Andrzej Wiercinski. Münster: LIT Verlag, 2011, 199–218.

124   "Heidegger and Voegelin on Augustine." In *Hermeneutic Rationality. La rationalité herméneutique*, ed. Maria Luísa Portocarrero, Luis António Umbelino, and Andrzej Wiercinski. Münster: LIT Verlag, 2011, 297–312.

125   "Editor's Introduction." *Lonergan Workshop* 23: *Ongoing Collaboration in the Year of St Paul*, ed. Frederick G. Lawrence. Boston: Boston College, 2012, iii–xii.

126   "Finnis on Lonergan: A Reflection." *Villanova Law Review* 57, no. 5 (2012): 849–72.

127   "Lonergan's Sublation of Integral Hermeneutics." In *Going Beyond Essentialism: Bernard J.F. Lonergan an Atypical Neo-Scholastic*, ed. Cloe Taddei-Ferretti. Napoli: Nella Sede Dell'Istituto, 2012, 39–55.

128   "'Transcendence from Within': Benedict XVI and Jürgen Habermas on the Dialogue between Secular Reason and Religious Faith." In *Christianity and Secular Reason: Classical Themes and Modern Developments*, ed. Jeffrey Bloechl. Notre Dame: University of Notre Dame Press, 2012, 239–75.

129   "Editor's Introduction." *Lonergan Workshop* 24: *Reversing Social and Cultural Decline "In a Friendly Universe,"* ed. Frederick G. Lawrence. Boston: Boston College, 2013, iii–viii.

130   "A Jewish and a Christian Approach to the Problematic of Jerusalem and Athens: Leo Strauss and Bernard Lonergan." *Divyadaan: Journal of Philosophy and Education* 26, nos. 1–2 (2015): 217–318.

131   "Lonergan's Search for a Hermeneutics of Authenticity: Re-originating Augustine's Hermeneutics of Love." In *Lonergan's Anthropology: The Next Fifty Years of Vatican II*, ed. Gerard Whelan, SJ. Rome: Gregorian & Biblical Press, 2015, 19–56.

132   "Lonergan's Hermeneutics." In *The Routledge Companion to Hermeneutics*, ed. Jeff Malpas and Hans-Helmuth Gander. New York: Routledge, 2015, 160–75.

133   "*Cor ad cor loquitur*: Augustine's Influence on Heidegger and Lonergan." In *Augustine Our Contemporary: Essays on Augustine and the Self*, ed. Susan Schreiner and Willemien Otten. Contribution to a living Festschrift in honor of David W. Tracy. Notre Dame: University of Notre Dame Press, forthcoming 2017.

Index

Aeschylus, 175, 242

aesthetic consciousness, 32, 43–4, 172–3, 197, 241, 254, 270

aesthetic experience, 189, 237, 272

Aeterni Patris, 125, 195, 279

agnosticism, 206–8

agnostic pluralism, 256–9, 276–7

Alfarabi, 78 n18, 81–3, 95, 107, 110, 151–2, 289, 295

Already-out-there-now reality, 24–5, 59, 147, 214, 221, 236, 240–1, 314. *See also* realism: naive

analogy, viii, 47–9, 140, 171, 176 n53, 195, 200, 344, 349, 354, 382–3, 392, 400 n42; of contingent predication, 140, 264–6, 353, 371

Anselm of Canterbury, 187–9

apprehension, 49, 57, 138, 150, 224, 276, 329, 379, 394

appropriation, 61–2, 65, 129, 134, 142, 157, 192, 214, 276, 343, 385, 391–6

Aquinas. *See* Thomas Aquinas

areté, 375, 377

Aristotle, xii, 9–10, 18–20, 24–9, 53–7, 63, 68–70, 77–8, 81–3, 87–93, 95, 99–100, 103, 107–12, 125–7, 131, 141–2, 146, 151, 155, 162, 164–9, 180, 183–6, 192, 196, 201–4, 208–9, 216, 233, 242, 247, 251, 257, 260, 268, 280, 289, 297, 302, 311, 315–16, 329, 331–3, 341, 350, 354, 357, 364–8, 372–8, 404

atheism, 20, 26, 82–3, 115, 158, 198, 208, 238

Augustine, Saint, ix, xxiii, 5–6, 9, 15–22, 44–9, 56–7, 65, 67, 69–70, 118, 124–5, 144, 148, 164, 176, 188–9, 194–5, 202–6, 278–80, 286–90, 294, 348–9, 366, 391–3, 399

authenticity, 20, 60–1, 64–7, 147, 157, 189, 252, 303, 327, 387–8, 393–4

autonomy, 54, 79, 168, 202, 210, 221–5, 290, 298, 360–2, 373, 379, 386–8

Averroës, 78 n18, 81–3, 96, 110, 295

Avicenna, 81–3, 92, 95, 107

Bacon, Francis, xxiii, 88, 112, 152, 232, 242, 333, 356

Bakhtin, Mikhail, 177

Balthasar, Hans Urs von, ix–xi, 124 n118

Barth, Karl, vii–viii, x–xi, 7–8, 11, 32, 74–5, 80, 82, 188, 198, 206

Basil the Great, Saint, 224, 286, 294
Baumgarten, Alexander, 280
Baur, Michael, 9
being (Being), ix, xii, 24–33, 58–64,
    81, 122, 136–50, 170–1, 182, 221–2,
    231–3, 241–57, 345, 351, 389–92,
    404; forgetfulness of, 25, 29, 60,
    122, 175, 238; notion of, 62, 70, 143,
    148; as proportionate, 122 n111,
    136–41, 149, 224. See also *Dasein*;
    existence
being in love, xii, xxii, xxvii, 67, 246,
    268, 270, 275, 344, 347, 382, 384–5,
    389–92, 395, 398, 402, 413
Bellah, R.N., 235 n1, 360
Benedict XVI, Pope, xxii, 99, 193–9,
    204, 206, 210–11, 218–20, 224, 226.
    See also Ratzinger, Joseph
Benjamin, Walter, xi, 338
Berlin, Isaiah, 25, 266
Bernauer, James W., 256, 401
Betti, Emilio, 28
bias: in hermeneutics, 13, 32;
    liberalism and, 321, 337; Lonergan
    on, 117–19, 147, 159, 261, 339, 368,
    400; neoscholasticism and, 196;
    postmodernism and, 282
Bible: as authority, 6, 86, 196, 199–202,
    205, 389; and hermeneutic
    consciousness, 40–2, 155, 187–90;
    historical-critical study of,
    96–103, 116–17, 281; as revelation,
    8, 200
Blondel, Maurice, 197
Bloom, Allan, xiv, 283–6, 292 n34,
    333, 335, 359 n23, 360 n25, 367
Bonhoeffer, Dietrich, 38–9
Boyle, Nicholas, 298–302, 319–24
Brague, Rémi, 95–6
Bruell, Christopher, xiv, 114 n86, 283

Bultmann, Rudolf, x, 7, 40, 44, 165–6,
    188–90, 198, 206
Burke, Edmund, 272–3
Burrell, David B., 382 n113
Butler, Judith, 282
Butterfield, Herbert, 204, 207. *See also*
    scientific revolution
Byrne, Patrick H., xvi, xxviii, 77 n14,
    77 n16

Calvin, John, xi, 115–16
Carroll, Lewis, 376–7
Cassirer, Ernst, 28, 106, 167–9
Cassuto, Umberto, 97
Catholic social teaching, 325. *See also*
    justice
Certeau, Michel de, 282
certitude, 59, 109, 180, 196, 233,
    252, 280; and judgment, 61, 128,
    265, 294
Chalcedon, 200–1, 396
charity, 69, 152–3, 156, 292, 353–4,
    361, 363–82, 397, 404. *See also*
    friendship; gift of God's love;
    Holy Spirit
Chekhov, Anton, 230
Chenu, Marie-Dominique, 280
Chrétien, Jean-Louis, 282
Christology, xiii, 198–201, 348–50,
    395–7
church (Church), viii, ix, xxii; and
    modernism, 196–7, 208, 236;
    and modernity, xix, 10, 80, 207;
    and political power, 88 n35;
    and *praeambula fidei*, 197; and
    subordinationism, 48
Cixous, Hélène, 282
cognition, xi, 57–62
cognitional structure, 137–8,
    148–9, 179

cognitional theory, 121–6, 130, 136, 158, 195, 204, 206, 212, 215, 235, 349

Collingwood, R.G., 36, 175, 243, 281 n6

concept, xii, 32, 36, 84–5, 120, 124, 137, 189, 214, 270, 350; and inner word, 52, 56, 125, 128, 195; and preconceptual awareness, 17–18, 46, 70, 327

conceptualism, xxii, 125, 133–5, 154–5, 195, 349

Congar, Yves, 202–3, 280

consciousness, xv, 13–14, 45, 62, 67, 76, 127, 130, 146–7, 169–73, 211–18, 229–77, 350, 355, 377, 386–92, 394–6; as experience, 244–50, 276–77; hermeneutical, 13–14, 45–7, 57, 66–9, 97–8, 180–5, 242–4; historical, 32, 172–3, 204–5; as perception, 234–9; rational self-, 32, 39, 65, 127–9, 133–4, 146–8, 157, 169–70, 267–71, 385, 393–4

conversation, vii, xx–xxii, 33–8, 65, 172–80, 192, 240, 275, 291–3, 326–52, 368, 381–3; the conversation that we are, xxi, 192, 240, 382. *See also* language; Trinity

conversion, 15, 21, 61–4, 99, 171, 186–7, 220–5, 303, 326–8, 342–6, 380–3, 392–6; intellectual, moral, and religious, 65–71, 136–7, 149–50, 157–9, 270, 276

creation, 200, 236, 354, 399; doctrine of, 93, 99–103, 266, 365, 384

crisis: of culture, xx, xxiii–xxiv, 10, 64, 129, 161, 192, 286–8, 327, 384; financial, 301, 320; of modernity, 96–104, 161, 207–8, 237

Crowe, Frederick, 125 n124, 343–4, 346, 353, 378 n96, 382

culture: classical or normative notion of, 331–3; classicist and modern, xxiv–xxv, 10, 73, 79, 91, 118, 130, 157, 162–3, 191, 208–10, 218–19, 285; empirical notion of, 132–6, 302–5; and longer cycle of decline, 274

Dante Alighieri, 78 n18, 83, 202, 281, 286, 294–5

Dasein, 9, 13, 25–9, 31–4, 173, 182, 355

Dawson, Christopher, ix, 288 n23, 302

decision, xxiv, 54, 61–2, 66, 71, 103, 127, 131, 149, 217, 221, 224, 241, 248, 261, 268, 297, 303, 306, 310, 318, 360, 386, 395–6, 400

decisionism, 14, 27–9, 189

Deleuze, Gilles, 239, 282

Derrida, Jacques, xxiii, 16, 23, 47, 70, 231, 239–40, 251–3, 255–6, 260, 263, 266, 271–3, 282

development: as economic, 120, 304–6, 321; human, 199, 205, 248, 267, 302–4, 330, 345, 351, 366, 373, 386–7, 394–6

dialectic, 30–2, 36–8, 65, 67, 71, 76–7, 110, 165, 168–9, 175, 179, 192, 204, 217, 220, 225, 242–3, 289, 291, 330, 350

Dilthey, Wilhelm, 9, 165, 239, 241, 280

divine attributes, 154, 157

Doran, Robert M., xiii, 126, 353

Dostoevsky, Fyodor, 8, 177, 230

dynamism, xxv, 127, 134, 139, 142, 233, 248–9, 263, 276, 296, 312, 351, 381, 385, 387

Ebeling, Gerhard, x
education, 6, 63, 79, 81, 95, 101, 110,
    237, 256, 268, 283–4, 289, 291–2,
    302, 318–19, 326, 330, 337–8,
    355–9, 373–8
effectual history, 97 n53; as
    Wirkungsgeschichte, 57, 118,
    182–3, 204
Eliot, T.S., 230
empirical residue, 260, 266–7
Enlightenment rationalism, 72,
    79–81, 83, 86, 151, 173, 179, 194,
    207, 210, 223, 225, 229, 233, 240,
    262, 276, 280, 356, 361, 364
epistemology, ix, 6, 29, 69, 125,
    130, 158, 212–13; as distinct from
    cognitional theory, 121
eschatology, 65, 198, 274, 350
evil, 19, 75, 95, 100–4, 124, 144 n169,
    150–6, 211, 224–5, 253, 271, 274,
    282, 337, 347, 360, 372, 380, 382,
    401–2
evidence, 59–60, 110–21, 176, 195,
    224, 261, 294, 347, 394–5
existence, 45, 49, 56, 110, 136, 142–6,
    167, 187, 198, 241, 296, 354–6, 387;
    act of, 57–8, 353; truth of, 9, 14–23,
    69–70, 167–74

faculty psychology, 66, 107, 194,
    379–80
faith, 39–40, 64–5, 72, 79, 130–1,
    153, 155, 193, 209, 218, 265, 270–1,
    348, 351, 384–8, 394–5, 402–4; and
    reason, x, xxii–xxiii, 7, 44, 72–80,
    193–8, 218–26, 293–4; as seeking
    understanding, 77, 130, 187–8,
    195–6; understanding as seeking,
    130, 159, 197
Fascism, 363

Faulkner, Robert, xiv, 230, 283
Fichte, Johann Gottlieb, 13, 139, 182
fideism, xxiii, 116, 156
Flanagan, Joseph, xiii–xvi, 290–1
Fortin, Ernest L., vii, xiv, 80, 83,
    202, 278–95
Foucault, Michel, xxiii, 23, 231, 239,
    248, 253–5, 263, 282, 401
foundations: of modern science, 86;
    of philosophical inquiry, 80–2,
    124, 168, 233, 272, 281, 344; in
    theological method, 328, 350,
    391, 396
Francis, Pope, 317–18
Frankfurt School, xi, 282
Fraser, Nancy, 282
freedom, 11, 18–19, 27, 42, 64, 147,
    218, 221–5, 249, 265–7, 290, 296–8,
    335–42, 380, 399. *See also* liberty
Freud, Sigmund, 6, 173, 229, 244, 253
Friedman, Milton, 314
friendship: charity and divine,
    365–9, 400–4; as philosophical and
    theological theme, 64–9, 71, 283,
    303, 330, 353–83
fundamental alternative, 150–4
fundamentalism, 96, 218
fundamental theology, 197

Gadamer, Hans-Georg, vii–xv,
    xviii–xxvi, 8–13, 24–45, 45–71, 80,
    82, 97, 111, 124, 160–92, 206, 212,
    239–48, 276, 293, 331, 375–6
Galileo Galilei, 84–5, 231–2
Geiger, Max, x–xi
generalized empirical method, viii,
    121, 212, 215–16, 244
gift of God's love, 65–7, 150, 159,
    225, 271, 275–6, 344–7, 351–4,
    365–76, 381–2, 393–5, 398, 404

Gilson, Étienne, 124 n118, 280
Girard, René, vii, xviii
God: as absolute good, 127, 342,
    374; acting in history, 73–9,
    99–103, 108, 155–8; and causality,
    51, 145, 223; as infinite act of
    understanding, 145, 155, 224, 258;
    knowledge of, 89, 92, 141–50, 197,
    203, 210, 265, 346, 350–1, 397–8,
    402; love of, 65–8, 152–3, 244,
    274–6, 344, 351, 368–71, 379–82.
    See also gift of God's love; Trinity;
    unconditioned, the
good(s): economic of order,
    xxiv–xxvi, 296–325; finite, 17;
    highest, 17, 22, 315; human,
    xxi–xxvi, 30, 217, 289, 296, 301–5,
    326–53; Idea of the, 24–31, 310; of
    order, 225, 328–34, 340
grace, 39, 69–70, 353–83, 397–403;
    and nature, 88 n35, 93, 189;
    operative, ix, 123, 129, 155 n195,
    197, 344, 350; sanctifying, 353,
    369–72, 402; and sin, 18–23. *See also*
    gift of God's love
Greisch, Jean, 13, 47, 282
Guattari, Felix, 282

Harnack, Adolf von, 7, 198
Hazard, Paul, 72–3, 80, 86, 207
Hefling, Charles C., xvi, 298 n9, 326
    n1, 397 n39
Hegel, G.W.F., xi, 175, 179, 182,
    186–8, 206, 217, 237, 242, 245, 285,
    298, 306, 336
Heidegger, Martin, ix–xv, 5–23,
    24–37, 44–7, 53, 57, 60–71, 72–82,
    88, 93, 112, 121–4, 132, 161–9,
    175–83, 191, 212, 231, 237–40, 244,
    251, 274, 284, 355, 361

Hellenism, 198
Henry, Michel, 47, 282
Herder, J.G., 237
hermeneutic circle, xi–xii, 80,
    395 n36
hermeneutic revolution, xi, 5–23,
    24–44, 57, 80
hermeneutics: integral, 27–32, 71,
    188; of love, 6, 67, 73; of suspicion,
    6, 73, 173, 188, 206, 229, 269, 282.
    See also consciousness; crisis: of
    culture
historicism, 7, 26, 81, 105, 132–7, 166,
    210, 256–7, 281, 288, 335
historicity, 11, 28, 70, 80, 135, 147,
    231, 242–8, 256, 261, 290
history: of dogma, 7, 96, 99 n55,
    396; of effects, 97 n53; as field of
    study, x–xi, 5, 14–16, 65, 79, 162–5,
    205, 210, 253, 257, 393; human,
    14, 43, 73–5, 86 n30, 120, 132, 153,
    166, 170, 177, 182, 191–2, 257,
    288, 291, 330–1, 346, 351, 379–83;
    of philosophy, 25, 47, 161, 186,
    288. *See also* effectual history;
    historicity
Hobbes, Thomas, 20, 79 n19, 81–94,
    107–10, 147, 232–7, 292, 298, 320,
    333, 356, 364, 401
Hölderlin, Friedrich, 64, 163, 172,
    192, 240, 382
Holy Spirit, xxi, 67–9, 75, 270, 274,
    344–54, 366–71, 281–5, 393–5,
    403–4
horizon, xi–xxiii, 13–17, 26, 33,
    38–41, 58–62, 70, 112, 130, 149,
    157, 173, 182–8, 211–15, 220–4, 263,
    270–71, 293, 328, 342, 359, 381
human good. *See* good
Humanism, 72, 152–9

human nature, 18–20, 134, 205, 235,
285, 296, 338, 367, 386, 396–7. *See
also* authenticity; culture; history
Hume, David, xxiii, 79, 139, 232, 234
Husserl, Edmund, 12–13, 32, 47, 64,
163–5, 180–4, 191, 212, 239–41,
251–2, 262, 280, 362–5

idealism, 213–14, 335–7, 359–60
Ignatius of Loyola, Saint, 246, 270
n99, 390–1
illative sense, 56–7, 69
imagination, 7, 83, 107, 195, 221, 237,
262, 287, 357, 389, 398
individualism, 235–7, 275, 297, 363;
expressive, 237, 268, 275, 358–60;
possessive, 337, 357, 360
insight, viii, xiv, 36, 50–64, 109, 129,
135 n143, 176, 192, 214, 223,
250, 350
intellect: agent, 19, 50, 83, 125, 126
n129, 142; possible, 50, 329, 379.
See also cognition
intellectualism, 29, 66, 154, 194–5,
213, 276
intelligibility, 29–31, 87–90, 104–12,
131–58, 202, 214, 223–4, 242, 260–1,
305, 322, 339, 345, 351, 401
intentionality, 13, 130–54, 181–4, 214,
217, 380; analysis, 15, 66, 216,
220, 380
interdependence, 128
interiority, xi–xii, 16, 39, 69–70,
148–9, 216, 343–4, 350
Irigaray, Luce, 282
Islam, 73, 82, 91–6, 151, 232, 284,
295, 315

Jacobi, Friedrich H., 81, 106, 182
Jaspers, Karl, x, 161, 172, 210

John XXIII, Pope, 296
John Paul II, Pope, xxii n15, xxiii,
xxiv n21, 73 n4
Jonas, Hans, 80, 225, 360
Joyce, James, 230
judgment, xii, 25, 31, 53–71, 105,
109–10, 121–41, 147–8, 183, 195,
210, 224, 248–9, 258–9, 294, 303,
339, 350, 391; practical, 31, 269,
331; of value, 137 n151, 217, 221,
224, 265, 268–9, 331, 339, 347, 352,
368, 395–6. See also *phronesis*;
unconditioned, the
justice, 275–82, 290–3, 324, 332, 351,
362–71, 381

Kafka, Franz, 230
Kant, Immanuel, xi, 7–8, 13–14, 29,
53, 70–1, 79, 109–10, 121–2, 133–4,
165–8, 180–2, 197, 206, 210, 222–5,
235–48, 272, 285, 335–40, 360–2
Keane, Henry, 124 n120, 126 n126,
195 n7
Keynes, John Maynard, 312, 316, 324
Kierkegaard, Søren, xiv, 8, 113–16,
144, 239–41, 361
Klein, Jacob, 84–6, 123, 164
knowing, 15, 33, 60, 77, 108, 120–30,
137–41, 210–15, 232, 355, 379, 396,
400 n42; and loving, 244–5, 379; as
means of control, 15, 92, 112, 180,
235, 266–8; practical, 54–9; and the
real, 135–6, 259, 263
known unknown, 136, 143
n168, 171
Kojève, Alexandre, 94, 283
Komonchak, Joseph, ix, xiii
Kristeva, Julia, 282, 301
Krüger, Gerhard, xiv, 80, 164
Kulturprotestantismus, 7, 82, 198

Lamb, Matthew, ix, xi, xvi, 348, 402
Lampert, Lawrence, 151–2
language, 12, 32–53, 169, 176–80,
    214–19, 251–2, 262–3, 327–9, 341–7;
    and linguistic turn, 211, 214
law of the cross, 271, 345, 372, 401–4
Leibniz, Gottfried Wilhelm, 145, 280
Lessing, Gotthold E., 6, 79, 103,
    256–7
Levenson, Jon D., 97–104
Lévinas, Emmanuel, 70, 282, 360–5
liberty, 19, 149, 167, 266–9, 296–8,
    303, 306–10, 322, 328, 334–41, 351,
    388. *See also* freedom
Locke, John, xxiii, 7, 20, 79 n19, 139,
    232–5, 292, 298, 310, 315, 333, 335,
    356, 357 n13, 364
Lonergan, Bernard J.: *Grace and
    Freedom*, 11, 123, 149, 216; *Insight*,
    viii–xv, 10, 66, 117, 120, 129–30,
    142, 148–59, 213–19, 276, 291–6,
    380, 393–6; *Method in Theology*, vii,
    xii, xv, 11, 136, 157, 216, 276, 327–8,
    342, 380, 395; *Verbum*, viii, 46–51,
    65–6, 123–9, 146, 195, 213, 349, 392
Lowenthal, David, xiv, 283
Löwith, Karl, xiv, 27–8, 80, 113–14,
    144, 164
Lubac, Henri de, 124 n118, 280
Luther, Martin, 42, 115–16, 164, 206
Lyotard, Jean-François, 239, 262,
    266–7, 271–3

MacIntyre, Alasdair, 282, 324, 361
Mahdi, Muhsin, 151, 283, 289 n25,
    295
Maimonides, Moses, 81–6, 91–5, 100,
    107–10, 288–9
Manent, Pierre, 88 n35, 296–7, 306,
    309, 322, 360

Marion, Jean-Luc, 47, 282
market economy, 297–301, 307–12,
    317–18, 323
Marx, Karl, xi, 6, 14, 118, 178, 229,
    237, 244, 253, 256, 282, 305, 310,
    315, 337
Massignon, Louis, 283
materialism, 88, 143, 213, 337
meaning: acts of, 220, 262, 346–7;
    constitutive, 18, 186, 351;
    incarnate, xxi, 346, 351, 399;
    performative, 17, 167; world
    mediated by, 13, 167, 217, 240,
    270, 400, 404
Meier, Heinrich, 113–16
Mendelsohn, Moses, 81, 106
metaphysics, ix, 17–18, 33, 57, 69, 99,
    106, 113, 121–3, 130, 149, 158, 189,
    199, 211–14, 232, 251, 334, 396; as
    integral heuristic structure, 122,
    150, 213, 258 n62, 301–3
Metz, Johann Baptist, vii, xi, xii, xiii,
    xv, xix, 338, 344 n23, 345–6, 358
Mill, John Stuart, 237, 268
modernism, 196–7, 208
modernity, xix, 10, 46, 73, 162,
    179–80, 209, 225, 229, 290, 306, 327,
    356, 376; three waves of, 119, 151,
    238, 333–41, 346
money, 300–1, 306, 309–22, 367
Montesquieu, 236, 306, 309, 332
Murray, John Courtney, 220, 319

National Socialism, 147, 160, 238
Natorp, Paul, 9, 164
neoscholasticism, viii, xii, 278–82
Newbigin, Lesslie, 256
Newman, John Henry, ix, 56–9, 65–6,
    69, 125, 150, 197, 284–5, 294,
    378, 403

Newton, Isaac, 197, 231–2
Nicea, 197–200, 348
Nietzsche, Friedrich, xiv, 6, 15, 22–3,
    70, 80, 91, 121–2, 131, 134, 151–2,
    173, 237–9, 243–4, 252–6, 282,
    338–41, 361
nihilism, 23, 64, 132, 230, 238, 255,
    269, 339–43
nominalism, 58, 89, 91, 107, 110, 147,
    210, 233–4, 251
Norris, Christopher, 255–6
Nussbaum, Martha, 282

objectivity, 12, 130–41, 221, 240, 259;
    and authentic subjectivity, 158
ontotheology, ix, 22, 122
Ott, Heinrich, x

Pascal, Blaise, 44, 292, 361, 395
Peirce, Charles Sanders, 222, 240
perception, 12–13, 36, 47, 107–11,
    137, 147, 176, 180, 204, 234–47, 251,
    261, 391
Peter Lombard, 203, 366
phenomenology, 9–15, 45–7, 69,
    130, 180–4, 231, 238–43,
    281, 393
phronesis, 10, 24–31, 53–61, 67–71,
    169, 183; and Newman's illative
    sense, 56–7, 69
Piaget, Jean, 212–17, 248
Pines, Shlomo, 91
Plato, 24–6, 29–32, 76, 82–6, 90–4,
    132, 151, 160–92, 251, 285, 329, 338,
    357, 376; and Socratic dialectic, xx,
    10, 65, 90, 243
pneumatology, 350. *See also* Holy
    Spirit
political theology, xi–xii, 275–6, 328,
    353–83

postmodernism, 22, 81, 229–77
pragmatism, 166

question(s): of God, 113–17, 137,
    157–8, 376; logic of and answer,
    33, 36–8, 175, 241–3; for reflection,
    59–60, 109, 125, 137–8, 175; for
    understanding, 60, 109, 125–6,
    137–8, 173, 327, 399
questioner, human being as, 19,
    143, 179

Rahner, Karl, ix, xi, xviii n4, 194 n5,
    212, 270 n99, 287, 349, 390, 403
    n47, 411 n94
Ratzinger, Joseph, 99 n55, 194, 206,
    210, 219 n75, 224 n89. *See also*
    Benedict XVI, Pope
realism, 290; critical, 213–14; naive,
    139 n155, 214, 383
Reimarus, J.A.H., 79 n19, 197
Rerum Novarum, 292
responsibility: and the existential
    subject, 218; and Habermas
    on universal ethics, 219; and
    judgment, 147; and money, 309,
    312; and otherness, 255, 270; and
    sin, 101–3, 345, 352; and solidarity
    and subsidiarity, 296, 299; and
    third wave of philosophy, 339–40;
    and transcendental precepts, 260,
    297, 307, 400
revelation, 79, 85–8, 92–3, 102–4,
    113–17, 119, 151, 189, 258, 280,
    354, 365, 380, 403. *See also*
    supernatural, the
Ricardo, David, 310, 312, 315
Ricoeur, Paul, xviii, 6, 12, 70, 73, 212,
    282, 360 n27, 363 n42, 364, 365 n47,
    410 n81

Romanticism, 133, 236, 335
Rose, Gillian, 361–4
Rosenberg, Randall, 404 n49
Rosenzweig, Franz, 82, 363 n41
Rousseau, Jean-Jacques, xxiii, 20,
    116, 229, 236, 272, 285, 287, 292,
    298, 335–8, 358–60, 367

Schelling, F.W.J., 139, 165, 206, 237
Schiller, Friedrich, 206, 237
Schleiermacher, Friedrich D.E., xi,
    165, 188, 198
Schmitt, Carl, 116 n96. *See also*
    decisionism
Scholem, Gershom, 283
Schumpeter, Joseph, 313
scientific rationality, 72, 85, 89 n38,
    144–5, 192, 198, 205, 213, 219,
    231–3, 257–8, 290, 335, 341, 390
scientific revolution, 205, 232
Scotus, John Duns, 125, 194–6,
    210, 245
Second Vatican Council, 193, 196–8,
    219–20, 278–9, 287, 385, 390
secularism, 9, 207, 211–13, 218–26,
    337, 357, 385 n5
self, 14–21, 27–44, 51–9, 69, 182,
    189–90, 235–51, 267–72, 327, 348,
    355–64, 375–7, 387, 391–8. *See also*
    subject
sensation, 57 n46, 107, 137–41, 176,
    247, 362, 398
sin: basic, 144 n169; and conversion,
    70, 118; Heidegger on, 9, 18–23;
    naturalization of, 364; probability
    of, 400; and redemption, 224–5,
    345–6, 371–2, 380, 400; Strauss on,
    102–3, 155; structural, 343–4
Smith, Adam, 306
Socrates, 76

solidarity, 69, 250, 296, 299, 301, 304,
    312, 317, 325, 330, 351, 373, 379–80
Sölle, Dorothee, 338
Spinoza, Baruch, 6–7, 77, 79 n19, 81,
    83, 94, 96 n49, 106–7, 114–15, 131,
    156 n196, 188, 206, 237, 280, 333
Sraffa, Piero, 310
Strauss, David Friedrich, 7
Strauss, Leo, xiv, 30, 72–159, 161–6,
    238, 283–95, 327, 356 n10, 357
subject, 7, 20, 39–40, 46, 59, 127,
    136–48, 157–8, 180–3, 210–14,
    221–2, 231–50, 261–3, 275–6, 336,
    341, 355–61, 381, 386–93, 396–7,
    402. *See also* self
sublation, 354, 374. *See also* vertical
    finality
subsidiarity, 296, 299, 307–8, 312,
    317–18, 325
supernatural, the, 18, 79, 95, 153–9,
    236, 274–5, 351–6, 366, 371–9, 398;
    and supranatural, 236; theorem
    of, 153, 155 n195, 187, 236, 370
    n80, 374
surd, 119, 149 n169, 153–5, 231, 268,
    271–2, 360, 401. *See also* sin

Taubes, Jacob, 74
Taylor, Charles, 282, 287
Tertullian, 78 n18, 116, 194
theory, 29–30, 47, 108, 120–3, 183,
    185, 201, 208, 211, 231. *See also*
    cognitional theory; supernatural,
    the: theorem of
Thomas Aquinas, viii, ix, xi–xii, xxiii,
    10–11, 18–19, 46–51, 54, 56–8, 65,
    69–71, 78, 83, 92–3, 109, 122–30,
    140–8, 155–6, 176, 194–6, 201–3,
    210–16, 223, 226, 233, 257–8, 262,
    269, 278–80, 289–90, 294, 297,

424   Index

302–3, 319, 330, 343, 349–50, 353–4,
      361–80, 385, 392–3, 396
Torah, 96
Tracy, David, ix, x, xiii n5, xv, 403 n48
Trinity: and conversation, xxii,
      350–1; course on, xiii; Gadamer
      and, 49; and human nature of
      Christ, 397; mystery of, 49, 200,
      350, 383; participation in, 353;
      psychological analogy of, 200,
      349, 391–2

unconditioned, the: and God, 127;
      virtually, viii, 58–62, 70, 110,
      126 n27, 127, 134, 141 n114, 192,
      203, 214, 224, 257–9, 265
understanding: direct, xii, 125,
      261; faith seeking, 77, 130, 187–8,
      195–6; reflective, viii, 57–9, 69, 214;
      understanding of, 124–30

Vanier, Jean, 301
vertical finality, 248–9, 250, 347, 354,
      373–4, 381–2. *See also* sublation

Voegelin, Eric, xii–xiii, 70, 78, 124
      n118, 160–92, 237, 364, 402
Voltaire, 79 n19
voluntarism, 66, 116, 194–6, 210

Weber, Max, 10, 132–4, 162, 219, 282,
      307, 338–41
Weil, Simone, 363
White, Stephen K., 266–73
Whitehead, Alfred North, 336
William of Ockham, 58, 194, 196, 349
Wilkins, Jeremy D., 397 n39
Williams, Rowan, 324–5 n86, 358,
      387, 403
Wirkungsgeschichte, xii, 46, 57, 97 n53,
      118, 182, 204, 243. *See also* effectual
      history
Wittgenstein, Ludwig, 35 n39, 38,
      178, 262
Wolff, Christian, 207, 280
wonder, 112, 126 n127, 137–9, 266
word: of God, 74, 256, 383; inner,
      49–53, 70, 125, 176, 195, 223 n88,
      262, 343–4; outer, xxi, 52, 343–9